(Old) Ninety-Six & Abbeville District SOUTH CAROLINA

Wills *and* Bonds

(Volume #2)

D1595394

By:

Larry E. Pursley

Please direct all correspondence and orders to:

www.southernhistoricalpress.com
or
SOUTHERN HISTORICAL PRESS, Inc.
PO BOX 1267
375 West Broad Street
Greenville, SC   29601
southernhistoricalpress@gmail.com

ISBN #0-89308-348-8

Printed in the United States of America

DEDICATION

In Recognition of the Legacy left to us by

Willie Pauline Young

INTRODUCTION

In 1950 Southern Historical Press published *Abstracts of Old Ninety-Six and Abbeville District Wills and Bonds* by Willie Pauline Young. The book truly ranks among the most monumental and influential southern genealogical books. Untold numbers of genealogical researchers and individuals have been aided in their search for their ancestors through this book and the efforts of the small, unmarried and only modestly educated textile worker who abstracted and compiled the book. She literally spent countless hours, days and months pouring through and abstracting the old probate records housed in the Abbeville Court House, all the while working full time at the local textile mill.

The present volume follows in Pauline Young's footsteps by taking up where she left off and continuing the process of abstracting the records for ease of use and availability. The probate records of Abbeville District and County are still housed at the Abbeville Court House. They are arranged in individual packets housed in sliding metal boxes. This arrangement of the records was done during the depression in 1932 as a project of the WPA. Prior to this time, the records were just stacked in stacks with very little rhyme or reason. Accessing and locating the particular papers of an estate settlement was an ardurous and adventurous undertaking. The arranging of and numbering the records into the individual packs and boxes was done by a lady hired for the project. Her methodology was to take the records of each estate and place them in an as chronological order as possible. She began with the oldest estate record and numbered it as number 1 and placed it in what she numbered as Box 1. Thus she continued until all the estate records were properly sequentially numbered and placed in the metal boxes which were also consecutively numbered. This system worked very well and resulted in what we have today. The only failings of the system occurred when in the haphazard mess that she had found the records in she came across records that were chronologically earlier than what she had already cataloged and numbered. To address this, she kept the boxes sequentially numbered but it resulted in some boxes containing packs out of sequential date with the previous packs or following packs.

Pauline Young abstracted the estate records from Box 1 Pack 1 through Box 149 Pack 4227 with the abstracting seemingly covering the earliest probate records of Abbeville up through the year 1859. The exception to this is those subsequent boxes that contain estate packets earlier than the year 1859. This volume, as stated takes up at Box 150 and continues through Box 184 with

3

every estate pack being found included. Thus, this volume covers many estates from the late 1840s, even more estates of the 1850s and takes up at 1860 and goes through the 1860s into the early 1870s. Even a few records from as far back as 1816 are included. The format of the book is the same as that of the earlier book but goes into quite a bit more detail such as complete listings of the buyers at sale, persons who were indebted to the deceased etc. Also the book gives the complete listings of those persons listed on the account books of the merchants etc. at the time of their deaths. Those familiar with old estate settlements are aware that the papers contained are often scribbled on small bits of paper, often torn and battered making it very difficult to read and making out names and spellings. Everything is written in long hand, often with writing that is barely legible or not decipherable at all. Additionally, the spelling of names often varied within the same set of papers and thus, in searching for surnames any potential spelling should be examined.

Some of the estates had very little information while others had extensive amounts of information. Some estates had papers missing whiles others just abruptly ended. The same is true in these abstracts, as it will sometimes appear that there should be more when there is no more information or more that adds meaning to the abstract. This will be apparent as one goes through these abstracts. Some of the estates were extremely involved, confusing and almost impossible to follow without having a more intimate knowledge of the persons being referenced or their relationshhips. All genealogical name references and indications have been noted and included in these abstracts. Additionally, those interacting with the estates through purchasing at the estate sales, witnessing of wills, appraising property, owing money to the deceased or having accounts with the merchants are all included. Information such as taxes, costs of funerals, coffins, shrouding, digging of graves, final medical expenses payments for care taking etc are included where they were given.

Hopefully, these abstracts, will aid those researching their ancestors in the Abbeville area and add to the work begun by Pauline Young some 65 years ago.

BOX 150 PACK 4227   CHARLES DENDY   1859

Appraisal: Nov. 4, 1859 by James M. Perrin, A. J. Lythgoe, John White, N. J. Davis. Sale of Property: Nov 8 & 9, 1859. Buyers at Sale: H. T. Lyon, John T. Lyon, James A. Allen, Thomas S. Grisham, David O. Hawthorne, Dr. Taggart, Andrew L. Gillespie, Augustus Edwards, Samuel B. Cook, G. W. Brooks, J. W. W. Marshall, D. R. Sondley, J. F. Marshall, James H. Cobb, Robert Jones, Wm. Hill, John Eaton, J. T. Ashley, John McClelland, Ben. P. Hughes, Samuel Jordan, James A. Wardlaw, John D. Adams, T. Warren Allen, Thomas J. McCracken, John White, T. J. Ellis, P. Searles, Thomas Eakin, John Smith, Joseph T. Moore, Mrs. Dendy, R. H. Wardlaw, A. M. Smith, Boozer & Mounce, J. T. Creswell, J. W. Perrin, Pat O'Keefe, David J. Jordan, Wm. Hill, Wm. M. Hughey, John Knox, Thomas Hinton, Talbert Cheatham, W. McCord, Thomas J. Douglass, Harvey McCrea, George Syfan, Wm. Mooney, John A. Wier, F. P. Robertson, W. L. McCord, T. Davis, John F. Livingston, Enoch Nelson, Augustus M. Smith, James W. Means, James H. Cobb, Thomas Thomson, John McLaren, Ben. P. Hughes, J. J. Wardlaw, John H. Wilson, J. M. Wilson, Robert C. Gilliam. Owned 1381 acres. Owned 52 slaves. First Bond: Nov 8, 1859 of $36,000 by Harvey T. Lyon, John T. Lyon, James A. Allen. Second Bond: Nov 29, 1861 of $27,000 by James A. Allen, Harvey T. Lyon, Charles H. Allen. Settlement Jul 17, 1861. Amount for Distribution: $74,258. Receiving shares: 1. Children of Thomas B. Dendy (Elizabeth Ellen Dendy, James A. Dendy, Thomas McClellan Dendy) 2. Fannie E. Allen 3. Harriet B. Lyon 4. Sallie E. Dendy 5. Charles N. Dendy.

BOX 150 Pack 4228   SAMUEL C. EDMUNDS   1860

Will dated Jul 18, 1857. Witnesses: James A. Jennings, John W. Rochelle. Executors of Estate: Frederick H. Edmunds & Ellington Searles. Wife: Susan. Children: 1. Frederick H. 2. Sarah H. wife of Patrick S. Rogers 3. James A. 4. Whitfield F. 5. John F. 6. Henry H. 7. Emma Atchison wife of Chesley Walker 8. Samuel F. 9. Elizabeth S. Appraisal by Pleasant Searles, Zephaniah Harris, James C. Jennings. Owned 18 slaves. Owned 947 acres of land. Estate Sale at Mapleton Post Office Nov 21, 1859. Buyers at Sale: Samuel Walker, George W. Newby, Elias Banks, Frederick H. Edmunds, J. Cowell, Simpson Carroll, Calvin Hendricks, Samuel Carter, Green Martin, Wm. Banks, Samuel F. Edmunds, Peter Smith, M. B. Sturkey, W. Adams, P. P. Holloway, Green Callahan, Patrick H. Bradley, H. C. Edmunds, John F. Edmunds, P. A. Searles, Ben. Gibert, M. L. Cox, Wm. Tompkins, J. C. Jennings, P. S. Rogers, Wm. Minor, W. S. Headwright, Alex Sharpton, J. Alex Edmunds, James A. Corley, Wm. Willis, Wm. Cross, Mr. Hunter, Geo. W. Mitchell, W. B. Cantborn, Daniel P. Self, Aquilla Deason, Wiley Newby, Chesley Walker, T. L. Martin, John Martin, Elijah Beagles, Thomas McAllister, A. J. Harris, Mrs. Edmunds, Mr. Porcher, James Banks, C. T. Whitten, Geo. Crawford, Free Wash, Wm. Brown. Final Settlement of Estate: Sep 9, 1873.

BOX 150 PACK 4229   MARY ANN ELLISON   1860

Will dated Jun 15, 1857. Witnesse: Thomas C. Perrin, Joseph L. Wardlaw, Thompson H. Lyon. Codicil dated May 23, 1859. Witnesses: Joseph J. Wardlaw, J. T. Robertson, John T. Owen. Children names mentioned: 1. Elizabeth Chambers of Charleston 2. Margaret wife of John Adger of Fairfield 3. Harriet Harrison of Louisville, Ky. 4. Isabella W. Boggs wife of George W. Boggs of Fairfield 5. Mary wife of Alex. W. Youngue of Florida 6. Sarah Chambers, deceased (Children Were: Mary Campbell of Louisiana, William of York, Margaret wife of Luther Myers of Orangeburg, Harriet wife of Andrew Myers of Orangeburg). Great-granddaughter: Mary Harrison Hoyt. Executors of Estate: Robert B. Boyleston of Winnsboro and James M. Perrin. Legatees, not named, paid Jan 31, 1863. Final Estate transaction Jan 1, 1878, names not mentioned.

BOX 150 PACK 4230   MINORS OF THOMAS FUILTON   1860

Estate Value: $255. Bond: Jan 16, 1860 of $2198 by Sarah Ann Fulton, Thomas J. McCracken, H. A. Jones. Wife: Sarah Ann Fulton. Children: 1. Leonora B. 2. Ann Adolio, 3. Jordan Wesley, 4. Thomas Beckham.

BOX 150 PACK 4231   JOHN L. GRIFFIN   1860

Administrator: David Ephraim Andrews. Wife: Mary K. who married Robert W. Seymour prior to settlement. Children: 1. Elizabeth Estelle 2. John Ephraim 3. Thomas. Appraisal Nov 29, 1860 by Willis Smith, Joseph J. Marshall, S. S. Marshall, Thomas J. Lipscomb. Owned 800 acres of land and 17 slaves. Estate Sale: Nov 30, 1860. Buyers at sale: E. Andrews, Vincent Griffin, Nitus Malone, Allen Puckett, J. Ellis, Henry Wilkinson, Wm. G. Kennedy, C. E. Brooks, W. B. Brooks, Wm. C. Hunter, Ed Whatley, James Malone, L. Hearst, John Hutchinson, J. P. Bonds, R. F. McCaslan, Thomas Fell, Samuel B. McClinton, Wm. P. Andrews, Joel Lites, John Davis, Willis Smith, Gaines Ross, John T. Parks, James Ross, Robert Lites, J. B. McClinton, M. C. Taggart, John McKellar, B. L. Reynolds. Partial Settlement made Jan 15, 1863. Land on Hard Labor Creek in White Hall Township reappraised in Sep. 1873 by John Wilkinson, T. J. Hearst, Joseph L. Hearst, Thomas N. Talbert. Taxes for the year 1872: State $46.60, Penalty on state tax $9.82, County Tax $11.65, Hwy Tax $7.77, District School Tax $3.88, Penalty on County Tax $4.66, Treasurers Cost $4.19.

BOX 150 PACK 4232   FRANCIS HENDERSON   1859

Executors: Daniel P. Self-died in 1863 then Sterling S. Freeman. Wife: Cassandra Henderson. Children: 1. Judson 2. James L. 3. Thomas J. 4. Robert E. 5. Francis M. Bond of $2,500 by Daniel P. Self, Robert Jennings, J. H. Jennings. Appraisal Oct 10, 1859 by John F. Burress S. T. Freeman, John B. Self. Sale of Estate Oct 11, 1859. Buyers at sale: Widow, Sanders Harrison, Daniel P. Self, Wiley Jeter, J. S. Rich, J. P. Self, Henry Holloway, -- McAllister, Ransom Self, A. Price. Estate was still in process on May 23, 1882 when a Petition for Account was filed by Judson Henderson and James L. Henderson versus Sterling S. Freeman as administrator.

BOX 150 PACK 4233   JOHN HUGHES   1860

Administrator: B. P. Hughes. Bond of $1,000 on Apr. 12, 1860 by John T. Lyon, A. L. Gillespie, James A. Richey, John W. Lesly, J. R. Wilson. Settlement Jan 21, 1862.

BOX 150 PACK 4234   ELIZABETH HARRIS   1860

Will dated Aug 17, 1859. Witnesses: J. S. Griffin, John J. Seal, M. W. Coleman. Filed Jun 19, 1860. Nee: Elizabeth Lipscomb. Children: 1. William 2. Willis 3. Elizabeth Watson-deceased, Rebecca V. wife of George A. Addison, Ann J. Irwin. Grand Daughter: Lucy Watson. Executors: Willis G. Harris and George A. Addison. Appraisal Nov 27, 1860 of $45,800 by S. S. Marshall, Johnson Sale, M. C. Taggart, Willis Smith, Larkin Reynolds. Held notes due on: W. G. Harris, George A. Addison, E. S. Irvine, Gaines Ross, M. C. Taggart, Hiram Adams, John McDowell, Stanley Crews, Wm. Harris, Owned 1797 acres of land, 46 slaves, 100 hogs, 70 cows, 235 sheep, 11 mules, 6 horses. Estate Sold Nov 28, 1860 for $10, 650. Buyers were: Johnson Sale, E. S. Irvine, W. G. Harris, J. W. Hutchinson, Geo. McDuffie Watson, W. F. McNeill, J. C. White, Hugh Hollingsworth, G. R. Caldwell, Robert Sentell, Willis Ross, M. W. Coleman, L. M. Fisher, George A. Addison, Wm. T. Shadrack, Charles Hammond, W. B. Brooks, J. F. McLain, Jacob Miller, J. L. Henderson, John R. Seals, Edward Byrd, Wm. Boozer, M. D. Mead, R. F. McCaslan, John Foster, B. Dill, A. Hollingsworth, John Foster, John Chipley, C. W. Sproull, M. C. Taggart, John Calvert, Thomas Ross, Daniel Malone, Wm. Bell, James Callison. State Tax for 1860 $92.55. Confederate Tax for 1862 $45.10. Final Settlement: May 5, 1863.

BOX 150 PACK 4235   L. D. JOHNSON   1859

Administrator: Thomas J. Roberts. Wife: Mary M. Johnson returned to her father's home in North Carolina on Feb 22, 1860. Bond of $500 on Mar 9, 1860 by Thomas J. Roberts, H. G. Klugh, James H. Cobb. Appraisal Mar 26, 1860 by Henry B. Nickles, Samuel Smith, W. C. Nickles, W. G. Lomax. Estate Sale Mar 27, 1860. Buyers at sale: Col. Roberts, W. C. Klugh, Capt. Nickles, John Algers, W. C. Nickles, Samuel Guinth, L. Bigham, Henry Nickles, John McCord, Gen. Hodges, T. E. Graydon, Michael Hackett, L. Chandler, John Turner, John D. Pace, Widow, Hy Nickles, Wm. Nickles, James Smith, H. B. Nickles, T. J. Roberts, D. Lomax, L. Turner, V. M. Goodman, J. Hagen. James W. Irwin paid $10.25 for making coffin. Final Settlement Jul 24, 1862. No details.

BOX 150 PACK 4236   LEWIS LOGAN   1859

Sep 15, 1859 Wm. J. Arnold petitioned for Letters of Administration. Bond Oct 3, 1859 of $3,000 by Wm. J. Arnold, C. Augustus Cobb, Robert P. Buchanan, W. B. Roman. Appraisal Oct 3, 1859 by John G. Boozer, James Bailey, Ephraim Calhoun, Charles A. Cobb, J. W. Cobb. Confederate Tax on estate of $15.50 paid Oct 28, 1863.

BOX 150 PACK 4237   Peggy McClain   1859

Administrator: John McClain who was her husband. Bond of $1146 on Aug 16, 1859 by John McClain, James F. Donnald, Robert Martin. Children (8) but only 4 named. 1. Joseph Robinson 2. S. M. McClain 3. A. Burgess 4. S. N. Griffin. Estate received $860 from the estate of John Webb. Final Settlement Aug 16, 1859. Husband and 8 children received shares.

BOX 150 PACK 4238   ISABELLA MARSHALL

Will Apr 29, 1858. Witnesses: W. L. Appleton, R. M. Perryman, W. W. Perryman. Executor: J. Y. L. Partlow who was the husband of her daughter, Mary. Grandchildren who received shares at settlement: S. E. Partlow, M. J. Partlow, J. M. Partlow, N. A. Partlow, J. A. Partlow, E. E. H. Partlow, F. J. A. Partlow, M. R. R. Partlow, W. S. Partlow, J. H. Partlow, S. O. Partlow. Owned 23 slaves. She held notes on: J. M. Partlow, W. W. Perryman, J. Y. L. Partlow.

BOX 150 PACK 4239   TARLETON P. MOSELEY   1859

Administrator: John G. Boozer. Bond Oct 11, 1859 of $300 by John G. Boozer, Thomas Riley, W. C. Davis. Appraisal Oct 26, 1859 of $113 by J. F. H. Davis, James Bailey, D. R. Calhoun, Robert H. Mounce, Stanley Crews. Sale of Estate Oct 26, 1859 for $103.74. Buyers at sale: John Irvin, T. C. Fletcher, John G. Boozer, William Boozer. R. M. Bushart paid $32 for making coffin. Boozer & Mounce paid $13.64 for funeral expenses. Estate was insolvent with creditors receiving $18.55 against $733.33 of debt. Creditors were: McGowan & Perrin, J. Bailey, Davis & Boozer, White & Wier.

BOX 150 PACK 4240   GRACE MATTISON   1841

Will dated Sep 13, 1841. Witnesses: A. S. Liddell, John D. Christopher. Bond Mar 6, 1860 of $1,600 by G. M. Mattison, Stephen Latimer, B. M. Latimer. Children names were: 1. Harriet C. Magee 2. Theodocia Gaines 3. Mary Gaines 4. Lucretia Mitchell 5. Nancy C. Hodges 6. Gabriel Mattison who was willed nothing as he had already been advanced more than the other children. Grand Daughter: Grace A. P. Gaines. Inventory conducted by G. M. Mattison on Mar 7, 1860. Cash found in hands of deceased $814.20. Settlement of Estate: Jun 12, 1860 with 8 shares each receiving $94. 84. Heirs were: 1. (10) Children of Mrs, H. Magee 2. Theodosia Gaines 3. (5) Children of Mary Gaines 4. (8) Children of Lucretia Mitchell 5. Julia Ann Johnson 6. Child of B. D. Mattison 7. Nancy Hodges 8. G. M. Mattison.

BOX 150 PACK 4241   DDAVID McWILLIAMS   1860

Will dated Oct 2, 1853. Witnesses James C. Stevenson, Andrew Stevenson, Wm. Stevenson. Codicil to Will dated Sep 6, 1859. Witnesses: Charles Evans, Thomas S. Gordon, Jane Donnald. Executors: Wm. Gordon, Samuel Reid. Children names: 1. Esther 2. Ann 3. Mary 4. Martha who married a Duncan 5. Nancy 6. Alexander 7. Jane wife of John Crawford and now deceased 8. William Gordon. Grand Children named: 1. Esther Ameline McWilliams 2. Jane Eleanor McWilliams 3. John Watson 4. Wm. Hamilton 5. John David Duncan. Appraisal Mar 5, 1860 by J. C. Stevenson, Wm J. Stevenson, J. F. Simpson. Held notes on: Hunter Simpson, J. P. Bowie, W. G. McWilliams, Sterling Bowen, J. A. Crawford & Wm. Bell. Estate Sale Mar 9, 1860. Buyers were: Widow, J. C. Stevenson, W. G. McWilliams, G. Duncan, A. L. Hughes, Wm. Gordon, Edward Hagen, Thomas Stevenson, James Cunningham, Wm. McComb, F. E. Bowie, Ben. H. Eakin, Thomas Eakin, T. J. Ellis, W. B. Bowie, Franklin Bowie, John Cowan, John Nickles, J. D. Pace, J. F. Simpson, Wm. J. Stevenson, David O. Hawthorne, Samuel Bratcher, Mathew Cochran, E. P. Ballard, W. L. Radcliffe, R. P. Doyle. Confederate Tax for 1862 $21.38. Dr. D. S. Benson paid $5.50 for medical services. Settlement of Estate Oct 1862: 11 Legatees: 1. Alex. McWilliams 2. W. G. McWilliams, 3. Esther McWilliams, 4. Ann McWilliams, 5. Elizabeth McWilliams, 6. Nancy McWilliams, 7. Mary McWilliams, 8. J. W. Crawford grandson, 9. W. H. Crawford grandson 10. Jane E. Crawford granddaughter 11. Esther E. Crawford granddaughter.

BOX 150 PACK 4242   JANE D. POWER   1859

Will dated Sep 19, 1859. Witnesses: James N. Cochran, John C. C. Allen, F. W. Connor. Proved: Oct 1859. Executors: Samuel B. Jones, John H. Power. Had (4) children only (1) named, Mary A. R. Power. Bond Mar 5, 1860 of $4,000 by John H. Power, Ephraim F. Power, James Martin. Appraisal Nov 22, 1859 by L. A. Connor, F. W. Connor, S. E. Graydon. Owned 7 slaves, house and lot. Held notes on: S. A. McCurry, Wm. M. Griffin.

Estate Sale: Nov 24, 1859 for $8,350. Buyers at sale: S. B. Jones, J. H. Power, Ephraim F. Power, P. W. Connor, Joel W. Townsend, C. R. Hanvey, J. B. Black, J. F. McComb, W. Joel Smith, J. C. Allen, Sterling E. Graydon, B. C. Hart, J. A. Ellis, M. R. Power, B. K. Harvey, Samuel Turner, W. E. Caldwell, D. C. Moore, Samuel A. Hodges, Wm. A. Moore. Estate Settlement: Jun 25, 1861. Legatees were: 1. John H. Power 2. Ephraim F. Power 3. Wm. C. Power 4. Charlotte E. wife of Samuel B. Jones 5. W. C. Power in trust for Mary R. Buchanan.

BOX 150 PACK 4243   JAMES L. PRATT   1860

He died Sep 4, 1859. Administrator: Wm. Robertson uncle of deceased. Bond Oct 4, 1859 of $6,000 by Wm. Robertson, Wm. Moseley, Andrew C. Hawthorne. Estate was insolvent very heavily in debt. Wife Mary and (2) children, names not given. Appraisal Nov 29, 1859 by Ezekiel L. Rasor, Ben F. Moseley, Asberry M. Dodson, Benjamin Smith. Estate Sale: Nov 30, 1859 of $2822. Buyers at sale: Larkin Barmore, Wm. Maddox, Ezekiel Rasor, Wm. Allen, Moses Winestock, H. Latimer, James M. Vandiver, James Taylor, George W. Richey, Andrew Agnew, W. P. Martin, Asberry M. Dodson, J. W. Richey, W. A. J. Ware, J. E. Gaines, W. Y. Davis, James Killingsworth, W. Stone, Andrew C. Hawthorne, J. L. Brock, W. P. Kay, W. A. Bigby, Wm. Dunn, Thomas Moore, A. C. Davis, James Adams, N. C. Davis, E. B. Rasor, Wm. Robertson, Perry Gaines, N. W. Ware, B. Knight, Thomas J. Higdon, Wm. A. Pratt, J. L. Ballentine, B. Smith, A. Myers, M. C. Henderson, J. S. Magee, A. J. Patterson, Enoch M. Sharp, W. Y. Jones, Thomas Higdon, Dr. Ebeneezer Pressly, B. M. Latimer, Alex. Padgett, W. F. Monroe, James Davis, J. C. Gambrell, W. Vermillion, James Seawright, James Jones, John Donnald, J. H. Shaw, Wm. Moseley, Samuel Martin, M. B. Magee, R. Owens, Ben. F. Moseley. Paid Brock & Gantt $35.58 for funeral expenses. Settlement filed Feb 22, 1861. No details.

BOX 150 PACK 4244   JOHN SWILLING   1860

Will dated Oct 1, 1859. Witnesses: M. B. Latimer, Aaron W. Lynch, J. N. McKeown. Executors: Zachariah Hall, Wm. J. Milford. Children named were: 1. James Zachariah 2. Martha Ann who married Joseph Charles prior to 1874 3. Tobitha Clesinda 4. Mary Frances wife of a Conner 5. Harriet Lucinda wife of James D. Houston 6. Belinda A. Grandson: John Swilling. 1st Appraisal Mar 19, 1860 by M. B. Latimer, J. J. Cunningham, James W. Black, George B. Clinkscales, J. W. Power. Owned 737 acres of land, 29 slaves, 14 shares of the Greenville & Columbia Railroad. Held notes on: J. J. Cunningham, H. L. Cason, M. B. Latimer & Robert C. Harkness, John T. Owen. 2nd Appraisal Feb 11, 1871 by Elijah Tribble, John L. Martin, A. Kind. 1st Estate Sale: Mar 20, 1860. Buyers: G. B. Clinkscales, M. B. Latimer, Jacob Alewine, Frank Haddon, Alfred Gailey, J. W. Power, Pleasant Ferguson, John Brownlee, Wm. J. Robertson, Joshua Ashley, Ben. F. McAllister, F. P. Robertson, J. T. Haddon, John Alewine, A. Johnson, R. E. Gaines, Washington Cochran, Harvey Hall, Henry S. Cason, Pink Haddon, George W. Bowen, Wm. J. Milford, Wm. Gaines, J. J. Cunningham, Wesley Brooks, Monroe Bowen, Thomas J. Hill, John Smith, Ben. Adams, S. Johnson, Dr. Bell, G. Halal, Dr. Aaron W. Lynch. 2nd Estate Sale Nov 12, 1862. Buyers: J. W. Black, J. J. Lipford, F. P. Robertson, John Brownlee, W. C. Durham, Dr. Benson, S. P. Magee, Dr. Steifer, Wm. T. Phillips, W. B. Latimer, Adolphus A. Williams, Hugh M. Prince, J. W. Power, Z. Hall, A. McAllister, J. T. Owen, D. S. Jordan, M. Magee, Jeptha R. Hamlin, Wm. Wickliffe, Philip Rutledge, Dr. John F. Livingston, Henry S. Cason, Col. Haskell, Wm. M. Tate, Dr. Latimer, A. J. McCurry, G. Allen, Wm. J. Milford, John A. Calhoun, Robert S. Hardin, D. O'Neal, J. F. Saxon, J. J. Cunningham, James A. Norwood, Wm. Bell, Albert Johnson, Bartlett S. Tucker, J. T. Haddon, J. T. Moore, Hiram T. Tusten, Sterling Bowen, James Swilling, John A. Mars, James

Neighbors, W. H. Mulliken, J. E. Uldrick, Jacob Alewine, George W. Bowen, Joseph T. Moore, S. J. Carrough, Wm. Mann. Paid Confederate tax collector, M. S. McCay, $1,335 in Confederate currency on May 9, 1865. 11 returns made on estate. Final Settlement made Jan 7, 1874. All children dead except Harriet Lucinda. Martha Ann Charles had died in 1869.

BOX 150 PACK 4245   ANN SPENCE   1859

Administrator: Adam Wideman. Bond Sep 30, 1859 of $128 by Adam Wideman, Archibald Bradley, Nathaniel J. Davis. Appraisal Oct 15, 1859 by Archibald Bradley, Simpson Evans, Samuel P. Leard, E. A. Moragne. Estate Sale Oct 15, 1859 brought only $1.50. Estate insolvent and unable for distributions or payments owed.

BOX 150 PACK 4246   THOMAS W. SLOAN   1859

Administrator: S. Harris Rykard. Bond Dec 14, 1859 of $280 by Levi H. Rykard, W. C. Davis, Thomas M. Smith. Deceased was late of Mississippi. 1st Return and Settlement: Dec 14, 1859. (2) not named distributees with each receiving $61. 78.

BOX 150 PACK 42447   MARY G. SHIRLEY   1859

Minor. Administrator: Richard Shirley-father. Bond Sep 1, 1859 of $800 by Richard Shirley, James Shirley, Andrew Callaham. She was owed money in the hands of Uriah J. Mattison and Eliza Mattison from the estate of William Mattison. Settlement: Dec 16, 1863. (5) Legatees each received $66.71. Legatees: 1. Richard Shirley her father now deceased 2. Wm. M. Shirley now deceased 3. Nancy E. wife of Wm. H. Crawford 4. Catherine E. wife of G. Burriss, 5. Benjamin N. Shirley. Dr. J. F. Donnald was paid for medical services.

BOX 150 PACK 4248   LEWIS SMITH   1859

Will dated Dec 13, 1857. Witnesses: James H. Cobb, Andrew Paul, Hiram T. Tusten. Executor: John White. Wife: Mary Ann Smith. Children named were: 1. James T. 2. Lewis 3. Robert 4. Leonora. Appraisal Nov 22, 1859 by James W. Frazier, Sam. B. McClinton, J. J. Devlin, Wm. Lyon, Jonathan Jordan. Owned 479 acres of land, 11 slaves. Confederate tax for 1863 $150, State tax for 1865 $138.63. Estate Sale Nov 23, 1859. Buyers at sale: Wm. Smith, Dr. Taggart, David Atkins, Sam. Jordan, Samuel Wilson, John White, Leroy Purdy, David Wardlaw, Bartholomew Jordan, Thomas Fell, Dr. Pressly, George Bradley, J. W. W. Marshall, Gen. Bradley, Thomas O. Creswell, J. D. Adams, James Devlin, T. M. Fisher, Jeff Douglass, S. McClinton, Lewis Smith, Wilson Watkins, David Wardlaw, J. T. Fell, S. A. Wilson, Jonathan Jordan, Wm. G. Kennedy, Edward Hinton, F. P. Robertson, J. T. Moore, John Smith, Thomas J. Wilson, Nathaniel J. Davis, James Drennan, David Boozer, Dr. Devlin, Wm. Butler, Wm. Wilson, F. Edwards, D. Atkins, George Ruff, John Jordan, John Smith, Wm. Smith, Dr. Benson, Mr. Sloan, Wm. Lyon, Mary A. Smith, James Wharton, Joseph Hearst, Alex. P. Connor, James W. Frazier, Andrew J. Ferguson, Sam. Jordan, J. C. Walker, Enoch Nelson, Gene Bradley, J. D. Adams, Wm. Hill, A. L. Gray, W. M. Hughey, S. H. Smith. Final Return on estate made May 20, 1881.

BOX 150 PACK 4249   JOHN SCOTT   1860

Administrator: Vachel Hughey. Bond by Vachel Hughey, John D. Adams, Levi H. Rykard. Wife: Mary Ann Scott. Appraisal Jan 19, 1860 by Levi H. Rykard, Nidus Malone, Edmond

Anderson, Henry Riley. Owned 2 slaves. Held notes on: Wm. Motes, Wm. Scott. Estate Sale Jan 19, 1860. Buyers at sale: Widow, Wm. Scott, S. Ray, R. H. Rykard, F Logan, J. E. Hughey, R. S. Cobb, Henry Riley, J. S. Marshall, Wm E. Scott, James Watt, Levi H. Rykard, J. H. Stockman, Vachel Hughey, S. H. Smith, J. Williams, E. Anderson, James Rykard. Last return on estate: Jul 1866.

BOX 150 PACK 4250   SABRY K. TULLIS   1860

Administrator: Peter L. Guillebeau. Appraisal of $4,513 Feb 2, 1860 by W. Tennant, Andrew Guillebeau, B. E. Gibert. Estate Sale Feb 3, 1860. Buyers at sale: Henry Holsenback, Redmond Brown, H. M. Johnson, S. C. Guillebeau, B. E. Gibert, J. W. Isom, Wiley Newby, Dr. A. Gibert, John Holsenback, J. S. Bouchillon, Peter L. Guillebeau, Andrew Guillebeau, John LeRoy, J. A. Crawford, H. Lawton, Dr. W. Tennant, S. C. Lawton, Marion Sturkey, George W. Nelson, John Martin, W. Reid. Taxes for 1859 $9.00. Estate Settlement: Nov 9, 1866. Legatees: E. M. Tullis, S. C. Lawton in right of his wife, Catherine.

BOX 150 PACK 4251   THOMAS TAYLOR   1859

Will dated Jun 6, 1859. Witnesses: John Patterson, L. D. Deal, Harrison Tucker. Executor: Amaziah Rice. Wife: Elizabeth L. Names Children: 1. Mary Ann Burress, 2. Edward, 3. Sarah O'Briant, 4. Joanna S. Campbell, 5. Frances. Grand Children: Gustavia Sarah wife of William Jasper Jones. Appraisal Nov 23, 1859 by Thomas T. Cunningham, James S. H. Stark, Wm. S. Baskin. Owned 8 slaves. Notes held on: J. M. Latimer, W. M. Bell, H. J. Burton, C. G. Milford, Conrad Wakefield, Thomas Blanchett.

BOX 150 PACK 4253   FRANCES E. H. WITHERSPOON   1860

Will dated Jul 14, 1853. Witnesses: S. McGowan, T. W. Allen, J. Alex. Sale. Executors: J. J. Wardlaw, Littleton Yarborough. Grand Daughters: 1. Julia Caroline McCaw 2. Margaret Frances McCaw, Mary McGehee McCaw. Grandson: John Todd McCaw. Appraisal Apr 21, 1860 by Wm. Speer, S. S. Baskin, Andrew Giles. Owned 1037 acres of land, 35 slaves. Owned 60 shares in Planters & Mechanics Bank of S. C., 15 shares Bank of South Carolina, 14 shares Union Bank of S. C., 39 shares Bank of Augusta, Ga., 8 shares Georgia Railroad & Booking Company, 25 shares Greenville & Columbia Railroad. Held notes on: John Enright, J. W. Norris. Estate Sale Nov 27, 1860. Buyers at sale: James E. Calhoun, Hiram Cowan, G. Miller, F. DuPre, John F. Livingston, Wm. M. Bell, James Frith, Samuel Speed, Wm. J. Cheatham, J. S. Williams, James Clark, F. Cowan, S. S. Walker, J. Moseley, John M. Mann, F. Miller, Littleton Yarborough, Thomas A. Cater, Wm. H. Wilson, Joseph T. Walker, Francis A. Wilson, W. W. Belcher, Wm. H. Parker, John A. Crawford, J. W. Crawford, John M. Bell, Frank Robertson, Wm. G. Anderson, Wm. Moore, John F. Livingston, Major Jones, Mary McCane, Sidney McCurry, Wm. Cook, Samuel J. Hester, Julia McCaw, Alex. F. Wimbish, Dr. Wardlaw, J. J. Grant, C. T. Latimer, F. E. Cowan, Thomas Townsend, Franklin Miller, W. M. Burton, John T. Mabry, Samuel Hunter, James Cunningham. Confederate taxes for 1864 $450. Final return on estate made Jan 1870.

BOX 150 PACK 4254   REV. ARTHUR WILLIAMS   1860

Will dated Jun 22, 1859. Filed May 21, 1860. Witnesses: John R. Wilson, unknown, unknown. Named Children: 1. Mary, 2. Dorcas Mitchell, 3. Nimrod, 4. William, George, 5. James, 6. John H., 7. Sally Hughes, 8. Elizabeth McWhorter. Appraisal Jun 25, 1860 of $7,323 by J. R. Wilson, James F. Donald, David Moore. Owned at least 450 acres of land,

11

6 slaves. Held notes on: James Seawright, J. C. Williams, John McClain. 1st Estate Sale Jul 10, 1860 netted $3,455. Buyers at sale: Mason Kay, George Williams, J. J. Copeland, J. R. Willson, James Wilson, Hezekiah Elgin, J. M. Shirley, Larkin Mitchell, James McDill, Archibald Armstrong, Samuel Bratcher, Wm. B. Hutchins, Samuel Donald, Thomas Traynham, Robert Coleman, Mary Williams, Wm. Williams, John Moore, C. C. Armstrong, J. F. Donald, F. P. Templeton, 2nd Estate Sale Nov 1, 1860 netted $97. Buyers at sale: James Shirley, Samuel McClain, S. M. Tribble, Mary Williams, Henry Bratcher, J. C. Williams. Funeral expenses $7.75. Oct 5, 1872 Petition for Account Settlement filed by A. T. Williams and D. M. Williams of Floyd Co., Ga. versus James Williams and George Williams. They claimed that they were entitled to the amount that their deceased father, Jesse Williams would have received in 1866 partial settlement agreed to by Jesse Williams and John W. Corley in right of his wife, Jessie, (payout agreement was to have been $75 each). In 1864 agreement legatees of Sally Hughes to have received $300. In Sep 1862 Nancy A. Williams and Margaret C. Williams received $117 each. Majority of land sold Oct 8, 1881 to J. L. Williams for $500. Final estate return made Oct 13, 1881. Final Estate Settlement May 5, 1891. (8) Legatees. 1. Elizabeth McWhorter deceased 2. Sallie Hughes deceased 3. John Williams deceased 4. William Williams deceased 5. James C. Williams 6. George W. Williams 7. Jesse Williams deceased whose 7 children, no names, received their portion of the land sale of 1881 8. Nimrod Williams deceased.

BOX 150 PACK 4255   JAMES F. WATSON, JR.   1859

Administrator: Mrs. Almira Hazeltine Watson widow who became Mrs. Almira Hazeltine McNeill, wife of A. M. McNeill. Bond Oct 10, 1862 of $35,000 by Almira Hazeltine McNeill, Harriet S. Simmons, Stephen Elmore. Grand Mother: Harriet S. Simmons. Uncle: Stephen Elmore. Appraisal Dec 8, 1862 by C. E. Brooks, Wm. Core Watson, Wm. B. Brooks, John McKellar, Henry A. Anderson. Owned 17 slaves, 50 shares of Greenville & Columbia Railroad stock. Held notes on: Leonidas Malone, E. C. Brooks, George W. Tolbert, Robert R. Tolbert, Dr. Moses Taggart, Stephen Elmore, Elisha Brooks, Elizabeth Harris, Wm. S. Shadrack, Knitas Malone, Wm. Bentley, Wm. Wardlaw, George Tolbert, Miss D. F. Watson, Thomas Watson. Property in Virginia valued at over $11,000 but became greatly reduced by the war. Estate Sale Dec 11, 1860 netted $16, 987. Buyers at sale: Mrs. H. Simmons, Stephen Elmore, D. McKellar, George W. Tolbert, P. McKellar, P. M. McKellar, A. H. Watson, P. Rykard, George McDuffie Watson, W. F. Hackett, Mrs. A. H. Watson, Robert R. Tolbert, Moses C. Taggart, Wm. S. Shadrack, Robert Quarles, J. Quiley, Willis Ross, A. Stallworth, F. W. Traynham, Jonathan Sale, H. W. Wardlaw, Thomas J. Hearst, Miss E. Simmons, L. J. Ellis, C. E. Brooks, W. A. Sale, J. R. McKellar, J. S. Williams, F. Miller, J. T. Henderson, L. M. Fisher. Estate Settlement Jan 22, 1864. (2) Legatees: Mother, James F. Watson. Dec 28, 1887 James F. Watson as only heir took a note of $2,100 from J. R. Tolbert, 45 bales of cotton and a gold watch and relinquished all other rights.

BOX 150 PACK 4256   ELIHU WATSON   1859

Administrators: A. T. Watson, P. W. Watson. Bond Dec 3, 1859 of $40,000 by A. T. Watson, P. W. Watson, L. J. Johnson, J. E. Watson. Appraisal Dec 21, 1859 of $16, 883 by F. J. Connor, Wm. E. Caldwell, Ben. Z. Herndon. Owned 19 slaves. Held notes on: John L. Clark, J. F. Smith, Ben. F. Smith, James W. Wightman, John T. Waite, John Watson, A. E. Scott, Susannah Arnold, N. T. Watson, John Smith. Estate Sale Dec 21, 1859. Buyers at sale: P. W. Watson, Asbury O. Watson, Alpheus T. Watson, Paul W. Connor, Leroy J. Johnson, G. C. Allen, F. A. Connor, Rev. J. C. Williams, Thomas Mahon, J. A. Ellis, G. M. Hodges, E. W. Watson, L. N. Carter, G. A. Allen, Charles Smith, J. D. Pace,

H. B. Nickles, T. J. Ellis, Martin G. Zeigler, Wesley Robinson, John Hagan, --Blake, J. W. Cochran, Wm. McComb, A. M. Agnew. Confederate tax for 1864 $1,800. Estate Settlement Jan 28, 1865. (6) Legatees. 1. Leroy J. Johnson in right of his wife, Mary F. 2. A. F. Watson 3. E. W. Watson 4. J. E. A. Watson 5. Asbury O. Watson, W. P. Watson.

BOX 150 PACK 4257   CORNELIA E. WARE a minor   1859

Guardian: Elizabeth Ware. Bond Feb 28, 1860 of $200 by Elizabeth Ware, Abner H. Magee, Wm. T. Jones. Daughter of Nicholas Ware. She was due money from the estate of Wm. Ware. Estate Settlement May 15, 1862 of $76. 96. She had married Richard A. Griffin prior to the settlement date.

BOX 151 PACK 4258   AARON ASHLEY   1863

Administrator: Wm. Ashley. Bond Jul 27, 1860 of $300 by Wm. Ashley, Moses Ashley, J. S. Barnes. Appraisal Aug 13, 1860 by James M. Carwile, Basil Callaham, John M. Briant. Estate Sale Aug 14, 1860. Buyers at sale: Widow, Moses Ashley, Wm. Burton, S. W. Callaham, James M. Carwile. Estate Settlement Dec 28, 1860. Wm. Ashley, the administrator, had filed a claim for $250 for expenses in taking care of the deceased.

BOX 151 PACK 4259   JESSE S. ADAMS   1866

Administrator: John James Adams, son of deceased. Bond Feb 8, 1866 of $10, 000 by Thomas J. Roberts, James N. Cochran, Thomas C. Perrin. Appraisal Dec 10, 1860 by Henry B. Nickles, P. D. Klugh, Wm. J. Lomax, J. C. Ellis. Owned 20 slaves. Estate Sale Dec 12, 1860 netted $18, 466. Buyers at sale: J. T. Cromer, James Anderson, J. J. Adams, A. P. Boozer, H. B. Nickles, John Adams, J. C. Allen, George Adams, Thomas J. Roberts, B. C. Hart, Nathaniel Cobb, J. F. Marshall, David O. Hawthorne, F. F. Gary, Richmond S. Cobb, Marshall Hodges, Asa Lipford, Wm A. Moore, M. M. Mars, J. C. Allen, John D. Adams, J. C. Ellis, Thomas Robertson, John P. Cromer, J. W. McRady?, Jesse Beasley, John Mundy, George Nickles, W. C. Norwood, Wm R. Hilton, J. W. W. Marshall, Newton Sims, A. F. Cromer, W. M. Mars, Wm. J. Lomax. Jan 5, 1866 T. J. Robertson who had married Cynthia S. Adams applied for administration due to the death of John James Adams.

BOX 151 PACK 4260   ELIZABETH H. ATKINS   1860

Administrator: Robert W. Lites. Bond Aug 18, 1860 of $1,000 by Robert W. Lites, A. P. Boozer, J. C. Lites. Elizabeth H. Atkins died Jul 11, 1860 leaving two minor sons. Appraisal Sep 4, 1860 by Wm. C. Puckett, A. Wideman, A. P. Boozer E. O. Reagan, Isaac Caldwell. Held notes on: Daniel Atkins, James Evans, B. Harvely. Cash on hand $3.74. Estate Sale Sep 5, 1860 netted $50. Buyers at sale: R. W. Lites, A. P. Boozer, B. Weed, P. H. Bradley, S. Cothran. Estate was insolvent with (2) distribute sons, Razemiah and James F. receiving nothing. Apr 19, 1883 R. W. Lites appeared in court and requested release form administration as there had been little activity for years. Both Razemiah and James F. were then deceased.

BOX 151 PACK 4261   DR. ROBERT F. BELL   1860

Administrator: J. E. G. Bell. Bond Oct 19, 1860 of $3,000 by James E. G. Bell, James G. Johnson, Allen T. Bell. Never married. Appraisal Nov 3, 1860 by John M. Moseley, James T. Baskin, J. F. C. DuPre. Held notes on: N. J. Deal, J. Speer, Jr., Wm. Wilson, James Hill. Cash on hand at death $2.60. Unpaid medical accounts: Elbert Stenson, J. Swades, J. G.

Jonson, John J. Uldrick, James M. Martin, Wm. Moore, John Martin, James Beasley, A. V. Brooks, John Speer, H. H. Zeigler, Monroe Mulliken, James B. Allen, Wm. H. Bell, John Grant, J. C. Speer, John Brownlee, Jacob Martin, James M. White, P. W. Clinkscales, H. W. Cole, L. G. Johnson, Robert H. W. Hodges, John A. Martin, Daniel Carlisle, George Graves. Estate Sale Nov 3, 1860 netted $217. Buyers at sale: Jonathan Johnson, Bartley S. Tucker, Mr. Jones, Sugar Jonson, L. H. Baker, A. Sutherland, Wm. Prater, Margaret Moore, Robert Hodges, Samuel Rampey, Samuel L. Jones, Samuel Hill, W. A. Giles, James T. Allen, Mrs. M. Cowan, Wm. M. Bell, W. Sutherland, John Newby, N. J. Deale, Joseph Hill, Samuel Hunter, Jasper Grant, Daniel Hill, Edward Taylor, Nathaniel Cunningham, Ephriam F. Power, B. M. Smith, Dr. Archer, S. S. Baker, Joseph Burton, George Clinkscales, Wm. Brownlee, H. Loftis, James M. White, John J. Tucker, Thomas M. Tucker, Jesse Scott, John C. Speer, Wm. Patterson, James Clark, James Boles, Wm. Shaw, B. S. Tucker. Massilon Bell, J. E. G. Bell, George L. Bell. Ed Taylor paid $45.60 for making coffin. Estate Settlement Apr 3, 1867. No names.

BOX 151 PACK 4262   JACOB B. BRITT   1861

Will dated Jan 21, 1861. Filed Mar 11, 1861. Witnesses: S. S. Willard, Hiram Palmer, J. C. Willard. Executors: sons Thomas Johnson Britt, James Uel Britt. Wife: Permelia who had previously been married to Jesse Limbecker. (8) Children named. 1. Susan Caroline, 2. Charles Ansel, 3. Jacob Louis, 4. Thomas Johnson, 5. James Uel, 6. Miriam Louise, 7. Jane Elizabeth Jones, 8. Sarah Ann. Held notes on Benjamin McKittrick, B. F. Landrum, John Landrum, Arthur Kennedy, W. W. Hill, W. A. Millan, David Bodie, J. H. Jones, T. J. Britt. Owned 35 slaves.   Confederate tax 1862 $169.70.

BOX 151 PACK 4263   JOHN BRADLEY   1860

Administrator: W. K. Bradley. Bond May 6, 1861 of $40,000 by Patrick H. Bradley, Wm. K. Bradley, A. T. Wideman, J. W. Hearst, J. H. Williams. Appraisal Nov 4, 1862 of $14, 301 by Wm. Gibson, Larkin Reynolds, Wm. McCelvey, Charles W. Cowan. Owned 11 slaves. Held notes on: Archibald B. Kennedy, John Faulkner, James Martin, Arch Bradley, Wm. K. Bradley, Andrew J. Weed, Alex. P. Connor, Wm. G. Neel, James Clatworthy, Samuel Link, Patrick H. Bradley, Samuel Jordan, Wilson Watkins, John Baughman, A. S. McCaslan. Estate Sale Nov 5, 1867 netted $3, 846. Buyers at sale: James Cobb, Hiram Tusten, Wm. K. Bradley, Patrick H. Bradley, Alex. L. McCaslan, Wm. Gibson, A. S. McFarland, B. McKittrick, John McBride, W. H. Parker, Archibald Bradley, David McLane, James Gibson, W. W. McKinney, Alex. L. McCaslan, John H. Baughman, Thomas Creswell, Mrs. Wilson, Humphrey K. Jackson, Wm. McKelvey, Alex. Wier, John Gilchrist, Cato Bradley, Charles W. Cowan, James Devlin, A. B. Hamlin, John Sanders, Phil Rutledge, Joseph Moore, John Owen, James Creswell, David Morrah, Wm. Belcher, -- McDowell, Wm. S. Harris, Samuel Jordan, Adolphus A. Williams. Estate Settlement Jun 30, 1863. Those receiving distributions: David and L. R. Morrah, Alex. P. Connor, E. H. Connor, James McCaslan.

BOX 151 PACK 4264   TRAVIS BEARDEN   1861

Adminsitrator: A. T. Wideman. Bond Jan 22, 1861 of $1,000 by A. T. Wideman, W. K. Bradley, W. F. Link. Appraisal Jan 23, 1861 of $597 by John Wideman, A. S. McFarland, Wilson Watkins. Estate Sale Jan 23, 1861 netted $467. Buyers at sale: Mrs. Bearden, Wm. Watkins, John Wideman, Wm. Lands, C. A. Wideman, J. F. Creswell, James McLane, F. B. Robinson, Samuel O. Young. Estate was insolvent with creditors receiving 3 cents on the dollar. Estate Settlement Apr 10, 1863. John J. Shanks paid $5.43 for making

14

coffin, J. H. Wideman paid $11.182 for funeral expenses. A. W. McCaslan filed protest against the settlement.

BOX 151 PACK 4265   FRANKLIN BOWIE   1860

Will dated Nov 19, 1860. Filed Dec 21, 1860. Witnesses: Wm. Gordon, Andrew Morrison, Wm. McIlwain. Executors: Malinda Bowie, Williston W. Franklin. Appraisal Jan 8, 1861 by Wm. B. Roman, F. M. Morrison, Andrew Morrison. Owned 5 slaves. Notes held on: Wm. B. Roman, Ben H. Eakin, John Moore, James P. Bowie, Franklin Bowie. Estate Sale Jan 25, 1861 netted $1891. Buyers at sale: Malinda Bowie the widow, Wm. G. Gordon, John Nickles, Wm. Bowie, Asa Bowie, Brawner Bowie, Ben. Eakin, Thomas Botts. Estate Settlement Feb 8, 1864. Legatees: Widow, Malinda Bowie 2/3, remainder to his sister, not named, mother, not named, 5 brothers only 3 named 1. James P. 2. W. B. 3. Henry B. Jan 21, 1867 Hezekiah Bowie of Attala, Miss. appointed his son-M. E. Bowie or brother-W. B. Bowie to collect money due from his brother-Franklin's estate. Mar 18, 1867 Wilson Bowie sought to collect money due his father-Hezekiah from the estate. Jan 15, 1869 Asa Bowie, James P. Bowie, Jane Bowie, Katherine Bowie each received money owed them form the estate.

BOX 151 PACK 4266   MINORS of G. W. CROMER   1861

Guardian: George W. Cromer. Bond Mar 26, 1861 of $259 by George W. Cromer, Frances E. Cromer, Nancy E. Cromer. (7) Minors. 1. Nancy E. Cromer 2. Frances E. Cromer 3. Florence R. Cromer 4. Cornelia S. Cromer 5. George A. Cromer 6. John D. Cromer 7. James I. Cromer.

BOX 151 PACK 4267   DAVID CLARY   1860

Administrator: Mathew M. McDonald. Appraisal Nov 11, 1861 by David McLane, Wm. McCaslan, Samuel Jordan, John J. Shanks, Wm. G. Neel. Owned 17 slaves. Held notes on: Jim Greer (free person of color), Richard M. Clary, Wm. T. Shockley, S. E. Brown, Thomas Link, John H. Wilson. Estate Sale Nov 13, 1861 netted $9867. Buyers at sale: B. Tinsley, Wm. W. Belcher Jr., Samuel Jordan, S. E. Brown, James Martin, Edward Westfield, Joseph T. Moore, Robert Keoun, Thomas J. Clary, Thomas Link, F. B. Robison, Enoch Nelson, D. McLane, Widow, John S. Reid, James Shanks, Edward J. Taylor, John A. Wier, Albert B. Hamlin, F. P. Robertson, Dr. Sanders, S. F. Clary, Wm. G. Neel, Wm. T. Drennan. Paid Edward J. Taylor $11.85 for funeral expenses. Estate Settlement Apr 3, 1863. Mrs. Eliza Clary 1/3 share. Remainder to his (5) children: 1. Thomas J. 2. S. F. 3. Jane 4. John 5. Sallie. Final estate activity Apr 5, 1867.

BOX 151 PACK 4268   JOHN W. COCHRAN   1861

Administrator: James N. Cochran. Bond Jan 18, 1861 of $25,000 by James N. Cochran, Albert J. Clinkscales, Jesse C. Ellis. Appraisal Feb 9, 1861 of $4952 by S. A. Hodges, L. Harp Vance, B. Z. Herndon, F. A. Connor. Owned 6 slaves. Held notes on: Wm. W. Cochran, Allen & Martin. Estate Sale Feb 9, 1861 netted $4,455. Buyers at sale: Francis A. Connor, John K. Vance, J. N. Cochran, M. Strauss, Wm. E. Caldwell, J. C. C. Allen, S. Weber, J. C. Ellis, Franklin F. Gary, James Townsend, Wm. McNairy. Estate Settlement Jul 3, 1863. (2) Legatees. 1. Wm. McNairy in right of his wife, Mary Ann 2. J. N. Cochran.

BOX 151 PACK 4269   JOHN COTHRAN   1859

15

Will dated Oct 11, 1860. Filed Dec 12, 1860. Witnesses: Samuel Perrin, John C. Chiles, Thomas P. Quarles. Executors: Thomas C. Perrin, Samuel G. Cothran. Appraisal Jan 15, 1861 by J. W. Hearst, John H. Chiles, P. H. Bradley. 97 slaves appraised separately Jan 22, 1861 by John McClellan, P. H. Bradley, J. H. Wideman, W. P. Sullivan, John H. Chiles. Slaves were appraised again Jan 26, 1864 by Thomas W. Chiles, P. H. Bradley, John Rush, Robert W. Lites. Held notes on 75 individuals. Estate Sale Jan 17, 1861. Buyers at sale: Charles W. Sproull, E. L. Cothran, L. H. Wideman, J. H. Wideman, Robert W. Lites, Wm. S. Harris, R. L. Talbert, Wm. Kennedy, Samuel McQuerns, Thomas O. Creswell, Peter Smith, George Dais, Samuel Cothran, James Martin, Samuel G. Cothran, Thomas C. Perrin, G. W. Johnson, John B. Adamson, John S. Reid, J. F. Creswell, W. B. Kemp, W. A. Smith, Wm. Butler, Robert W. Lites, J. H. Wideman, Wade E. Cothran, John McClellan, Moses C. Taggart, H. T. Sloan, Albert Gaskins, R. R. Tolbert, R. Talbert, George Young, Wm. M. McCain, R. L. Bell, J. W. Stewart, John S. Creswell, Jane G. Cothran, J. Steifle, C. C. Montgomery, A. J. Roundtree, John Rush, Irvin Clegg. Huge estate with much financial activity, land transactions, advancements to children, etc. that cover many, many pages. Children named in advancements: 1. Samuel G. Cothran 2. Mary R. Stephens 3. Wade E. Cothran 4. Elizabeth P. Cothran 5. Samuel Cothran 6. Mary Cothran.

BOX 151 PACK 4270   JOSHUA DUBOSE   1848

1st Will Dated May 12, 1848. Witnesses J. T. Roberts, Thomas J. Hester, Wm. Norwood. 2nd Will dated Mar 9, 1857. Witnesses: Samuel J. Hester, Wm. Wilson, John C. Scott. 3rd Will dated Aug 1, 1859. Witnesses: Moses O. Talman, T. A. Rogers, John C. Scott. Filed Dec 3, 1860. Executor: James A. Norwood. Executor: James A. Norwood. Wife: Elizabeth. Nephew: Joshua Dubose. Grand Nephews: John Alex. Dubose, Benjamin Dubose who were sons of Joshua W. Dubose. Appraisal Dec 12, 1860 by Samuel J. Hester, J. E. Lyon, Thomas J. Hester. Owned 16 slaves, 550 acres of land, owned 16 slaves. Estate Sale Dec 19, 1860 netted $7, 124. Buyers at sale: John Link, Thomas J. Hester, J. B. LeRoy, J. E. Lyon, D. Wilson, John E. Calhoun, Wm. H. Taggart, James A. Norwood, J. Dubose, E. Hilburn, H. Fleming, R. Earnest, Samuel J. Hester, J. W. Child, S. S. C. McGaw, D. M. Rogers, W. A. Clay, P. Waller, Armistead Burt, Louis Covin, John B. Cofer. Nov 2, 1875 Wm. D. Mars, a creditor, petitioned to become executor following the death of James A. Norwood. Bond Nov 17, 1860 of $8,000 by Wm. D. Mars, Edwin A. Mars, A. T. Wideman.

BOX 151 PACK 4271   THOMAS M. FINLEY   1860

Administrator: John G. Baskin. Bond Jun 4, 1860 of $400 by John G. Baskin, Thomas Thomson, Robert A. Fair. The deceased was late of Tennessee with a wife and children out of state.

BOX 151 PACK 4272   J. H. FLEICHER   1860

Administrator: J. Bailey who was the largest creditor. Appraisal Sep 11, 1860 of $683 by J. F. H. Davis, R. H. Mounce. Estate Sale Sep 11, 1860 netted $780. Buyers at sale: Hiram W. Lawson, Wm. Smith, Lewis D. Merriman, John Logan, Thomas Chatham, Joseph Marshall, J. Bailey, J. Smith, L. Silks, L. L. Leonard, John R. Tarrant, E. T. Walker, Paschall D. Klugh, James Creswell, Stanmore Brooks, Rev. Jones, R. M. Bushart, J. Irwin, S. Jones, John Pitts, J. F. H. Davis, Joe Hughey, James Gilliam, John B. McLees, Major Vance, W. N. Blake, R. M. White, John Williams, Wm. Fooshe, Gideon P. O'Neall, J. D. McKellar, John Hunter, Richmond S. Cobb, W. B. Brooks, L. Bailey, L. Logan, L. Smith, C. R. Calhoun, Marion M. Tarrant, Hugh W. Wardlaw, Dr. Lyon, F. B. Logan, Samuel Turner,

John B. Sample, E. J. Walker, Stanley Crews, Felix G. Parks, M. Blake, L. M. Arnold, Sherard Smith, F. M. McClenan, F. Beasley, Allen Bell. Nov 25, 1863 paid $5.12 Confederate War Tax. Estate insolvent. Jan 1, 1864 paid creditors 50 cents on the dollar. Final estate activity Mar 2, 1868.

BOX 151 PACK 4273   THOMAS HODGE   1861

Will dated Sep 22, 1860. Filed Aug 5, 1861. Witnesses: Lewis C. Clinkscales, W. M. Campbell, John McCurry. Listed as legatees: Wife: Martha Hodge. Sons: John Hodge, Francis P Hodge., James Hodge, Thomas P Hodge., Alexander Hodge. Daughter: Eliza Hodge. Executor: Alexander Hodge. Appraisal Sep 30, 1861 by Alexander Hodge. Owned 300 acres of land. Paid W. Dickson $5 for making coffin. Settlement Jan 22, 1870 with all legatees named in settlement receiving $50. 1. J. W. Hodge 2. T. P. Hodge of Miss. share of his father, Thomas Hodge 3. James Hodge of Miss. share of his father, Thomas Hodge 4. F. P. Hodge of Miss. share of his father Thomas Hodge.

BOX 151 PACK 4274   WILLIAM HUNTER   1860

Deceased had no relatives in S. C. Administrator: Wm. B. Bowie. Bond Oct 6, 1860 of $250 by W. B. Bowie, Wm. Z. Radcliff, D. W. Agnew. Appraisal Oct 27, 1860 by Wm. A. Hagan, Andrew J. McKee, Hezekiah B. Bowie. Held note on: Andrew C. Hawthorne. Estate Sale Oct 27, 1860 netted $27.93. Buyers at sale: Wm. B. Bowie, Thomas McCombs, J. Simpson, Ben. H. Eakin, Marion Hawthrone, Z. Radcliffe, John Botts, G. Duncan, J. P. Bowie, Robert Gordon, T. Ellis, H. B. Bowie, Thomas McCord, John Mundy, J. Calvert, E. Bowie, J. Hagan, Thomas Russell. Estate Settlement Jan 22, 1861. Sep 15, 1865 D. W. Haney, Elizabeth Haney each received $29 but were each charged $3.00 for the coffin.

BOX 151 PACK 4275   GREEN W. HUCKABEE   1861

Will dated Nov 15, 1859. Field Aug 7, 1860. Witnesses: Robert H. Wardlaw, W. C. Davis, Samuel McGowan. Legatees named: 1. Wife: Caroline Amanda 2. Daughters: Anna Caroline Gamewell Huckabee, Ella Margaret Huckabee. Executors: son, James Welborn Huckabee, son-in-law, Franklin C. DuPre. Appraisal Aug 10, 1860 of $36,555 by John M. Moseley, John Brownlee, J. H. Baskin. Owned 1300 acres of land 25 slaves. Held notes on: Aaron W. Lynch, J. H. Hughes, John McCurry, S. A. and John McCurry, W. M. Bell, J. F. C. DuPre, James Grant, Mary A. Magruder, Clark & DuPre, Joseph F. Bell, George W. Bowen, Wm. L. Campbell, E. H. Bell. Blacksmith by trade and accounts owed at death: John McMahan, Leslie McMahan, Jesse Cann, T. T. Hill, Alex. Winn, John P. Campbell, John Campbell, Alex. McAllister, Ripley Morrow, Mrs. M. A. Martin, Aaron W. Lynch, R. L. Williams, James W. Black, James Hodge, Alex. Hodge, Elias Kay, John Brownlee, H. H. Scudday, E. W. Daniel, Robert C. Harkness, Elbert Johnson, John H. Power, Wm. W. Belcher. Estate Sale Feb 20, 1868. Buyers at sale: J. M. Moseley, John McMahan, Jouette W. Huckabee, J. B. Patterson, F. P. Robertson, Wm. M. Bell, Coke Mann, James T. Barnes. Confederate Tax paid in 1864 $254.

BOX 151 PACK 4276   DEWITT Y. JONES   1862

Administrator: Robert Jones. Bond May 14, 1861 of $4,000 by Robert Jones, Joseph T. Moore, Mathew McDonald. Appraisal Sep 5, 1861 of $52. Notes held on: Ben. F. Roberts, Thomas Jones, Robert Jones, Cobb Hunter, John C. Roberts. Estate Sale Sep 5, 1861 netted $37. Buyers at sale: B. T. Roberts, Jane Jones, R. Jones, Willie Ellis, Thomas Jones. Estate Settlement May 4, 1864. Legatees: Mother-died just prior to the settlement, (2) brothers, (2) sisters. Names not given. Abbeville Town tax for 1862 50 cents, Confederate tax for 1862 $3.50.

BOX 151 PACK 4277   PRISCELLA JESSUP (Woman of Color)   1861

Administrator: Wm. S. Harris. Bond Jan 28,, 1861 of $300 by Wm. S. Harris, J. H. Cobb, John McLaren. Appraisal Feb 12, 1861 by John M. Ewing, Wm. Butler, Wm. Gibson. Confederate tax for 1864 $1.25, State Tax for 1864 98 cents. Estate Sale Feb 12, 1861 netted $220. Buyers at sale: Wm. Marion, Mathew Bugg, James Marion, David Marion, John Marion, Israel Rouse, James Wharton, Joseph Marion, Wm. Quarles, D. H. Drennan, James Martin, Wm. S. Harris, Walter G. Kellar, John C. Martin, David Clary, Dr. George W. Pressly, Allen Puckett, Thomas Fell. Estate Settlement Mar 3, 1864. Only legatee mentioned was James Marion. It was noted that the deceased had children and grandchildren.

BOX 152 PACK 4278   WILLIAM KNOX   1861

Will dated Dec 17, 1860. Filed May 13, 1861. Witnesses: T. C. Seal, H. D. Russell. Wife: Rachel to get all property. Executor: Washington W. Russell, Robert Jones. Bond Jan 25, 1861 of $1,000 by Robert Jones, Hugh Wilson, G. C. Bowen. Appraisal Feb 19, 1861 by D. R. Sondley, George W. Syfan, Francis McCord. He was the proprietor of a Blacksmith Shop. Accounts due him at his death were: James Pursley, James A. Norwood, Joseph T. Moore, Moses T. Owen, D. R. Sondley, Samuel Robison, Robert A. Fair, Thomas McCord, John A. Hamilton, James Moore, James D. Chalmers, David Robison, George W. Syfan, J. T. Marshall, James Carlisle, James H. Cobb, Lewis J. Wilson, Cobb & Hunter, Greenville & Columbia Railroad, Mrs. Nancy Wilson, Pool & Rutledge, Albert B. Hamlin, Wm. M. Hughey, Rochel & Christian, Isaac Branch, David S. Benson, Connor & Anderson, Joseph T. Marshall, John Lyon, D. Y. Jones, John S. Hunter, F. W. Davis, John McLaren, H. A. Jones, Joseph Wardlaw, Ben Johnson, James A. McComb, Frederick Ives, Louis H. Russell, James Martin, Hugh Wilson, John G. Wilson, S. W. Shillito, Henry S. Kerr, D. A. Paul, John Douglass, David Robertson, Agnes McDonald, James Lomax, Jesse Carlisle, Dr. Thomas J. Mabry, James M. Perrin, Lewis Wilson, Leroy Wilson, Wm. Magill, Wm. Pace, James Purdy, Edwin Parker, Augustus Lythgoe, Alex. Wier, Wm. W. Belcher, Warren Richey, Hugh Wardlaw, J. F. Marshall, Frank Adams, David Dansby, Littleton Yarborough, J. H. McCree, Thomas McCord, Thomas C. Perrin, Rutledge & Rutledge, Luther Martin, James C. Cothran. It was noted that all the open accounts had been successfully collected. Estate Sale Feb 19, 1861 netted $69. Entire contents of Blacksmith shop sold for $20. Buyers at sale: D. R. Sondley, W. W. Russell, James Carlisle, R. Jones, Widow, Samuel Robertson, F. McCord, Jack Fulton, Henry Russell. Abbeville town tax for 1860 50 cents.

BOX 152 PACK 4279   NANCY JANE & WILLIAM HENRY KERR (Minors)   1860

Minors of John Kerr and Louisa C. Kerr. Guardian: John H. Gray. Bond Aug 2, 1860 of $5,000 by John H. Gray, B. P. Hughes, John G. Edwards. John H. Gray died and William O. Pursley became guardian Dec 20, 1861 with bond of $5,000 by William O. Pursley, John C. Pursley, Leroy J. Johnson. Value of estate due them estimated at $1,600. Dec 23, 1861 both minors received $235 their portion of their father's land value. Aug 11, 1864 they each received in total $769.51. William O. Pursley died insolvent indebted to the minors of about $700. Francis A. Wilson became their guardian and he recovered $23.49 from the estate of William O. Pursley. Wilson then sought monies from the estate of John C. Pursley who had been killed in the Civil War. Pursley estate settlement papers included in the Kerr package of papers. Apr 6, 1878 John A. Brooks was representing the legatees of Frances E. Edwards the wife of John C. Pursley who had subsequently married Nathan Augustus Edwards. The estate had (3) minor legatees: 1. John C. Pursley, Jr. 2. Nannie C. Pursley 3. Hollis E. Edwards. A fourth legatee, Harper R. Edwards had also died after his mother's death. Estate valued at less than $300.

BOX 152 PACK 4280   WILLIAM LONG   1861

Administrators: Wm. P. Martin, James R. Latimer. Bond Jul 1, 1861 of $20,000 by Wm. P. Martin, James R. Latimer, Stephen Latimer, G. M. Mattison. Appraisal Nov 19, 1861 by Stephen Latimer, B. M. Latimer, James H. Shaw, N. J. Mattison, G. M. Mattison. Owned 9 slaves. Held notes on J. R. Latimer, Thomas Moore. Merchant. Accounts due him at his death: Wm. Morrison, Sarah M. Long, John Moore, Lucretia Mitchell, Wyatt Norwood, Wesley Medlock, Jane Webster, James Moseley, R. R. Seawright, W. L. Latimer, Wm. Robertson, Thomas Moore, Isaac Seawright, W. P. Martin, James M. Vandiver, L. H. Whitlock, S. Latimer, E. Carwile, D. V. Garrison, Samuel Donald, W. A. J. Ware, Albert Mattison, H. H. Prather. Estate Settlement May 5, 1868 with $297.57 to be distributed. (10) Legatees. Names mentioned: 1. Mary A. Long-widow and her 6 children who were all minors 2. W. W. Long-deceased 3. Henry S. Long. 4. W. M. Callaham in right of his wife-Sarah F. Advancements had been made by deceased during his lifetime to: 1. W. W. Long 2. J. R. Latimer and wife 3. W. M. Callaham and wife 4. Henry S. Long.

BOX 152 PACK 4281   LAVINIA LITTLE   1860

She died intestate in 1851. She possessed some small property, chiefly 3 slaves. Administrator: Daniel Johnson of Newberry District, S. C. Bond Aug 14, 1860 of $8,000 by Daniel Johnson, John F. Golding, James E. Peterson, Henry M. Livingston. To sell slaves for heirs to gain their inheritance.

BOX 152 PACK 4282   FRED B. LOGAN   1861

He died Nov 30, 1860 possessed of considerable property. Legatees were widow Rebecca S. now Rebecca S. Cobb and (9) children. Names not given. Administrators: Richmond S. Cobb, Elizabeth Logan. Bond Dec 26, 1861 of $40,000 by Richmond S. Cobb, Elizabeth Logan, Silas Ray, Willis Smith, Vachel Hughey. Appraisal Jan 14, 1861 by L. H. Rykard, Birt Riley, James Watt, Thomas Riley, Henry Riley. Owned 22 slaves. Held notes on: W. J. Arnold, John L. Logan, J. T. Logan, Zachary Logan, Silas Ray, Frederick B. Logan, Joseph S. Marshall, Lemuel O. Shoemaker, Tyler Logan, J. G. Boozer, Albert Waller, Wm. Smith, W. Motes, W. A. Mundy, Tabus Story, Wilkinson Motes, Andrew J. Woodhurst, Nathaniel Anderson, S. R. Coppack, Isaac Logan, John McLaren, S. A. Crawford, Francis Logan, James Verrell, J. A. Ellis, Aaron Butler. Estate Sale Jan 15, 1861 netted $16, 864. Buyers at sale: Widow, J. Bailey, Wm. Blake, Silas Ray, Richmond S. Cobb, J. Watt, J. W. Lites, N. Manse, J. Anderson, C. R. Medley, J. F. Davis, A. P. Boozer, T. Smith, John Vance, R. H. Hughes, A. Ellis, W. Smith, F. Robertson, H. Mounce, John J. Tharp, Abiah M. Blake, Thomas D. Douglass, Paschall D. Klugh, W. Arnold, James Logan, T. Malone, T. C. Lites. Paid R. M. Bushart $16 for making coffin, 1860 tax for indigent families $3.90. 1862 general tax $2.10, Confederate tax $44.42. Estate Settlement Mar 27, 1865. Richmond S. Cobb now deceased. Present at settlement: 1. Elizabeth Logan 2. Willis Smith 3. Willis Smith 4. Mrs. Sarah Jane Cobb 5. Silas Ray.

BOX 152 PACK 4283   MARGARET MATHEWS   1860

Will dated Nov 30, 1857. Filed Dec 12, 1860. Witnesses: Samuel Link, Robert McCaslan, Robert Drennan. Executor: James McCaslan. Children: Mary and Lucretia. Other children but names not mentioned.

BOX 152 PACK 4284   JAMES A. McDONALD   1860

Will dated Aug 14, 1860. Filed Sep 5, 1860. Willed $100 in trust for construction of Methodist (Rehobeth) Church now under construction at a place 300 yards from R. R. Tolbert's, to brothers George M. and Patrick H., to benefit of Mrs. Lucinda Brant, to Rev> J. M. Carlisle. Witnesses: T. C. Lipscomb, T. L. Brooks, E. T. McSwain. Executor: W. L. Anderson. Estate Settlement May 10, 1866. Only legatee was Irvin Hutchison in right of his wife who was the mother of the deceased. Both brothers were deceased.

BOX 152 PACK 4285   WILLIAM & ELEANOR McCLINTON   1860

Administrator: James M. McClinton. Bond Sep 12, 1860 of $700 by James McClinton, G. A. Davis, Tyra Jay. July 1860 James McClinton of Arkansas petitioned that under will of Robert McClinton certain property given to the heirs of John McClinton, the father of the petitioner. Eleanor McClinton, mother of James and William McClinton, brother of the petitioner were both now deceased in Arkansas.

BOX 152 PACK 4286   J. H. B. MOSELEY (Minor)   1860

Guardian: John M. Moseley, father. Bond: Jun 18, 1860 of $1449 by John M. Moseley, Jonathan Johnson, James Bruce. He was due a legacy of $665.72 from the estate of P. H. Moseley. Jan 13, 1863 paid Confederate general tax $7.50, State and District tax $4.09. Estate Settlement Aug 11, 1866. Now of age received $919.57.

BOX 152 PACK 4287   REBECCA D. McKEE   1861

Administrator: A. J. McKee. Bond Jun 4, 1861 of $2,500 by Andrew J. McKee, James C. Stevenson, Benjamin H. Eakin. Sister, Eleanor, owned ½ of the estate. Decided to sell entire estate to make a proper division. Appraisal Jun 20, 1861 by Ben. H. Eakin, W. B. Bowie, James C. Stevenson. Held notes on: J. R. McKee, J. & R. J. White, Andrew C. Hawthorne, Henry M. Winn, Andrew J. McKee. Estate Sale Jun 21, 1861. Buyers at sale: Andrew J. McKee, Edward Hagen, John Hagen, B. H. Bowie, John Nickles, E. McKee, B. Eakin, J. Wright, H. B. Bowie, A. Bowie, Wm. H. McCombs, W. McCombs, W. Sharp, H. G. Gordon, M. F. Hawthorne, Ben. H. Eakin, J. D. Bowie, Quincy Radcliffe. Paid 1862 war tax $4.99. Final return Mar 25, 1868.

BOX 152 PACK 4288   MINORS of JAMES M. McCLAIN   1860

Guardian: William Clinkscales. Bond Jul 25, 1860 of $600 by William Clinkscales, J. R. Clinkscales, E. R. Clinkscales. Minors were: 1. James O. McClain 2. Hannah R. McClain 3. Andrew B. McClain. Paid district tax $1.17, 1863 Confederate tax $1.20, 1861 state tax 30 cents, 1862 state tax 18 cents. Settlement May 4, 1863 James O. McClain received $121.21. Settlement Nov 24, 1865 Hannah McClain received $141.26

BOX 152 PACK 4289   JAMES L. McCELVY   1863

Administrator: William McCelvy, brother. Bond Mar 23, 1861 of $10,000 by Wm. McCelvy, James McCaslan, M. O. McCaslan. James McCelvy died in Texas. Held notes on: W. R. Wilson, D. L. Wilson, Jenny Stark, E. Jones, Hugh Saxon, Wm. G. Darracott,

Isham Mouchett, A. W. Lathrop, W. Tennant, Alex. R. Houston, W. Tennant Jr., John C. Scott, Edwin Parker, J. Taggart, Pleasant Searles, Wm. T. Drennan, Wm. McCelvy, Nathaniel Harris & J. S. Reid, Herny Callaham (Free Man of Color), James Algood, J. P. Graves, J. Dubose, Mrs. Cofer. Jul 11, 1866 State of Texas County of Houston petition of Mary J. McCelvy, widow of deceased and Martha J. McHenry wife of Wm. P. McHenry and daughter of James L. McCelvy. 1863 Legatees 1. Mrs. M. J. McHenry and Mrs Lizzie A. Ansley each received $1,844.02 and they again split $1,312.45 on Jun 16, 1866.

BOX 152 PACK 4290   MARY JANE MATHIS   1861

Administrator: Nancy Leslie. Bond Mar 16, 1861 of $1,000 by Nancy Lesley, N. J. Davis, T. W. McMillan. Appraisal Apr 2, 1861 by Andrew Kennedy, John A. Hamilton, Nathaniel J. Davis. Estate Sale Apr 2, 1861 netted $63.46. Buyers at sale: Nancy Lesley, J. A. Hamilton, Thomas W. McMillan, Jane A. Hawthorne, Nathaniel J. Davis, A. J. Woodhurst, Thomas M. McClellan, Thomas M. Christian, Jane Kennedy, Paid Edward J. Taylor $15 for coffin. Paid 1860 taxes 60 cents.

BOX 152 PACK 4291   JOHN W. MOORE   1861

Will dated Apr 9, 1860. Witnesses: John A. Stuart, J. N. Cochran, J. K. Vance. Codicil Apr 28, 1860. Witnesses: W, M. Griffin, J. H. Vance, J. N. Cochran. He died May 1, 1861. Wife: R. Amanda (5) Children: 1. Rosalee A.2. John W. 3. James O. C. 4. Lucy J. 5. Wm. H. Administrator: Wm. A. Moore, brother. Bond $9, 950 by Wm. Henry Moore, Jared Sullivan, R. A. Moore, R. A. Sullivan. Many pages of account activity. Appraisal Nov 18, 1862 by Wm. A. Moore, Robert A. Fair. Owned 1077 acres of land. 1st Estate Sale Jan 1, 1868. Buyers at sale: Widow, Marcus A. Cason, Wm. H. Moore, T. M. Thomas, Wm. Hodges, W. A. Moore, J. T. Jonson, Lewis C. Merriman, Franklin F. Gary, Henry Wood, Wm. Riley, W. T. Jones, Greenberry Riley, B. C. Hart, T. C. Waters, Francis A. Connor, Allen Dickson, Henry Isrealite (Free Man of Color), F. Hodges, Basil Graham, Moses Norris (Free Man of Color), Wm. Butler (Free Man of Color), Simpson Waits. 2nd Estate Sale Jan 28, 1868. Buyers at sale: J. W. Daniel, Wm A. Moore, John C. Waters, M. B. McKee, Paul Connor, Leonidas D. Connor, John K. Vance, Warren Lomax, W. C. Norwood, Franklin F. Gary, Robert A. Archer, Wesley Klugh, Nathaniel Ingram. Land sold Dec 4, 1871. Legatees were: 1. William H. Moore, 2. Rosalee A. Sullivan 3. J. W. Moore 4. James C. Moore 5. Lucy J. Moore. Each received payouts on Dec 14, 1866, Jan 1, 1872, Jun 15, 1872, Dec 3, 1874. Each received an amount totaling $2,860.

BOX 152 PACK 4292   Dr. SAMUEL MARSHALL   1861

Very large estate with much ownership, financial and other activity. Great detail included in estate papers. Will dated Oct 18, 1860. Witnesses: John Gray, Wm. A. Lee, John T. Owen. Executors: J. W. W. Marshall, J. Foster Marshall, Samuel S. Marshall. Wife: Eliza C. Marshall. (8) Children named. 1. John H. 2. George W. 3. J. Foster 4. Samuel S. 5. Joseph W. 6. Eliza wife of James C. Spruell 7. Mary wife of James L. Orr 8. Kitty F. Williams. Appraisal of goods and holdings, except lands, by Joseph S. Marshall, John Foster, Samuel B. McClinton, Willis Smith, Jonathan Jordan. Appraisal of lands by L. W. White, J. T. Robertson, Jacob Miller. Owned in excess of 6,000 acres of land in Iowa, Minnesota, Missouri, South Carolina. Owned 2 brick store buildings on the square in Abbeville. A brick making operation near Abbeville covering 60 acres of land. Owned Graniteville Mill stock, Columbia & Greenville Railroad stock, Bank of Charleston stock. Held notes on more than 100 individuals and businesses. A detailed listing of property and goods given to children in 1844 and to his wife in 1860. Partial settlement on Feb

2, 1872 with average share to each child being $11, 390.23. In another settlement each received $2,217.28. Lands in Missouri and Minnesota not sold prior to these payouts.

BOX 152 PACK 4293   SIMON McCLINTON   1860

Administrator: James McClinton. Bond Sep 12, 1860 of $350 by James McClinton, Tyra Jay, George A. Davis. Aug 21, 1860 Petition of James McClinton states that brother, Simon recently died in Texas.

BOX 152 PACK 4294   ROBERT MARS   1861

Administrator: W.D. Mars. Bond Jun 7, 1861 of $30,000 by Wm D. Mars, John A. Mars, Asbury T. Wideman. Merchant. Appraisal of store contents Jun 17, 1861 of $4,638 by Moses O. Tallman, Moses O. McCaslan, Wm. H. Taggart, James McCaslan, D. M. Rogers. Open accounts of store: W. B. Anderson, Thomas M. Ard, Artillery Company, L. Anderson, Georgia Burtwhistle, Rebecca Belcher, Wm. S. Baker, W. D. Bullock, Caldwell Lodge, W. A. Drennan, Wm. T. Drennan, M. Fortescue, L. Hester, Thomas J. Brough, Jane T. Baker, Sarah Brady, Wm. H. Brough, Archibald B. Boyd, Lizzie Baker, J. L. Brown, Edward Calhoun, James L. Covin, J. R. Dubose, W. M. Dwight, John Gutrie, Thomas Hemminger, John F. Calhoun, Richard Callaham, Covin & McAllister, Eliza Calhoun, Francis A. Calhoun, F. J. Calhoun, John B. Cofer, G. W. Cox, J. W. Child, Wm. H. Davis, E. Finley, M. Galloway, Thomas Hester, Charles W. Cowan, Shepard G. Cowan, J. Callaham, James E. Calhoun Sr., Louis Covin, Sarah Covin, Guilford Cade, Philip A. Covin, Edwin Calhoun, David Dowtin, E. Fortescue, A. Gibert, Nathaniel Harris, Alex. R. Houston, John H. Hester, E. Hester, E. Hilburn, P. J. Hayes, A. W. Lathrop, Hugh G. Middleton, Moses O. McCaslan, J. C. Mouchett, James McCelvy Sr., Mary McComb, Wm. P. Noble, P. J. Price, C. D. Pennal, John Partlow, D. M. Rogers, W. M. Rogers, Rogers & Shaw, Estate of J. Ried, John C. Scott, W. Sutherland, Elijah M. Tullis, J. Taggart Jr, W. H. Taggart & Co., E. H. Walker, M. Wideman, Peter Hemminger, Thomas Horton, Samuel J. Hester, J. W. Jones, H. M. Johnson, Thomas McAllister, Peter B. Moragne, Andrew H. McAllister, John A. Mars, Hugh McCelvy, John McBride, A. A. Noble, Porcher & Mitchell, Edwin R. Perryman, Esther Pennal, J. A. Richey, Paul Rogers, A. G. Russell, Susan Ramsay, Peter Shaw, Phoebe Strother, Gilbert Tennant, P. Tennant, Dr. W. Tennant, D. A. Wilson, J. A. Wideman, T. Johnson, M. B. Kennedy, L. C. Lawton, J. L. Lesly, John O. Lindsay, J. H. Morris, Samuel C. McGaw, J. F. McCombs, Anna Moragne, J. W. McCelvy, Isabella Morrow, Alex. Pennal, Dr. Edwin Parker, J. W. Porter, Ellen Pennal, Rogers & Calhoun, L. B. Rogers, G. W. Robinson, Estate of J. O. Scott, Howard Strother, Cornelia Sloan, W. Tennant Jr., W. T. Tatom, Josiah Wells, Cate Wells, C. Zimmerman, Agnes Lane, John E. Ligon, J. N. LeRoy, A. P. LeRoy, Thomas LeRoy, Robert McCraven, Wm. D. Mars, W. S. McBryde, W. McCelvy, S. R. Morrah, Stephen McGowen, Octavious T. Porcher, Pool & Rutledge, Wm. H. Tennant, T. A. Rogers, Dewitt Rogers, J. S. Robinson, T. B. Scott, W. C. Scott, Moses O. Tallman, W. H. Taggart, George Turnispeed, Joshua Wideman, Hugh Wilson, W. B. Anderson, Carrie Baker, John H. Brady, James M. Brown, Benjamin Brascomb, Armistead Burt, James Belcher, John H. Ligon, J. C. Mouchett, J. H. Morris, George W. Nelson, George Marshall, Mary McComb, A. R. Rucker, Peasant Searles, Patrick Tennant, Thomas Frith, Clinton Belcher, James Belcher, Caldwell Lodge, Agnes Cox, George W. Cox, Joshua Dubose, L. A. DeGraffenreid, J. J. Lee & Boxx, J. B. McKittrick, Wm. G. Neel, Wm. P. Noble, Ellen Pennal, Thomas M. Sloan, Thomas B. Scott, Taggart & McCaslan, Joseph Bouchillon, Mrs. E. Vandiver, S. McGeer, Dr. A. Gibert, J. F. Holiday, Claudius McAllister, John Hayes, Jopseh B. Cofer, E. Branscomb, E. W. Fleming, J. C. Guillebeau, P. D. Guillebeau, David Dowtin, R. Earnest, Alex. R. Houston, John M. Harris, John O. Lindsay, James McLane, James A. Norwood, John C.

Pursley, George W. Robinson, George Zaner, Peter Shaw, J. S. Talbert, Dr. E. M. Roberts, Samuel Link, David Wardlaw, Richard Callaham, James Shanks, C. B. Guffin, George Graves, John A. Mars, Elijah M. Tullis, John W. Isham, S. H. Jones, James Hanvey, Jane Lee, Peter E. LeGrand, John E. Lyon, W. Land, Johnson Link, A. S. McFarland, Thomas Mabry, David Knox, John Partlow, B. Rothchild, Mattie Seals, Ninian Thomson, Riley Wilson, H. G. Middleton, Jane Foster, Mollie Foster, W. A. Clay, W. K. Bradley, Cowan & Britt, Stephen Lee, George W. Drinkard. Held notes on 50 individuals. All accounts and notes not collected were sold at a public auction Sep 25, 1871. Wm. D. Mars relieved of administrative duties in Nov 1873 as the estate had been settled in the Court of Common Pleas in 1871.

BOX 152 PACK 4295   THOMAS E. OWEN   1861

Administrators: John T. Owen, Moses T. Owen. Bond Jun 18, 1860 of $60,000 by Moses T. Owen, John T. Owen, Thomas J. McCracken, James Taggart, Wm. McMillan, Dr. J. W. W. Marshall. Appraisal Oct 31, 1860 by J. W. W. W. Marshall, John A. Wier, John A. Hamilton. Owned 30 slaves. Estate Sale Nov 1, 1860. Estate Settlement Feb 9, 1866. Widow and (13) Children. Widow's share, $5738. Children received $1,044 each. Only (5) children named 1. Bethia Roche 2. Martha McCracken 3. Mary Cason 4. Ann Bailey 5. M. T. Owen. Mars was a large merchant in Abbeville with accounts dating from 1831. Open accounts were: Wm. Williams, Hugh Armstrong, Andrew J. Weems, John Taggart, Wm. Dunn, W. W. Higgins, Samuel Goff, T. P. Moseley, Mrs. J. Mathis, Edward Bailey, Robert H. Wardlaw, Joseph Eakin, Uriah Mars, George Miller, Edward Roche, Andrew Kennedy, James Fell, Mrs, Kingsmore, Wm. Kirkpatrick, M. Boshell, Larkin Mattison, Mrs. Houston,James Craven, James Perrin, Stephen Lee, Charles Dansby, Mrs. McMillan, Joseph Edwards, Isaac Dansby, Michael Wilson, Wm. Lomax, Mrs. Ellison, H. A. Jones, Mrs. Deal, Johnson Ramey, James Shillito, Pleasant Beal, Silas Anderson, Benjamin Barksdale, John Rasor, Joshua Beal, George M. Brown, Vandal Mantz, A. W. Shillito, Robert Kay, Wm. M. Sale, B. Y. Marftin, Dr. Livingston, John Cowan, Wm. Wagoner, David Wardlaw, Mrs. Cannon, Robert M. Palmer, Thomas Jackson, John Cobb, Wm. E. Woody, Ben. V. Posey, John A. Hamilton, Henry Kingsmore, H. W. Lawson, J. B. Courtright, Edward J. Taylor, A. L. Gray, Pinckney Davis, Henry Stat, John Enright, Henry Allen, E. White, M. D. DeBruhl, Henry Jones, Mrs. E. Hill, John Taggart, Thomas C. Perrin, Robert Douglass, M. C. Owen, Lewis Wilson, Joseph Reynolds, Wm. Kennedy, Christian Barnes, Wm. Boswell, James Henson, Robert A. Fair, James Pursley, Wm. Kerr, Wm. McMillan, Nathaniel J. Davis, N. McEvoy, Mrs. Stock, R. C. Starr, Samuel McGowan, John Adams, Mrs. Hodge, John McCree, Wm. H. Parker, John H. Wilson,John Coumbe, Robert McAdams, Wm. Richey, James Barnes, David L. Wardlaw, B. Randolph, R. N. Kay, Thomas Perry, Robert A. Wilson, L. L. Mathis, John A. Wier, E. Holden, Wm. Knox, Elijah Wilson, J. F. Marshall, M. McDonald, Augustus Lomax, Allen West, James W. Child, Andrew J. Woodhurst, J. H. Abbey, A. Slager, F. M. McNear, Dr.Joseph Togno, W. Leslie, B. C. Guffin, Thomas Fulton, Wm. McAllister, Gibson Mann, Richard Fulton, Emri Vann, Abram Lites, Thomas J.McCracken, John Lomax, Dr. Aaron W. Lynch, Wm. Adams, L. Nicholson, Wm. Mathis, Jane Kay, M. Bracken, John A. Hunter, Dewiit J. Davis, John Allen, Wm. H. Wilson, Robert Martin, Israel Holt, Thomas Christian, M. Wilson, M. C. Cox, Thomas Cochran, Charles Dendy, Philip Moseley, John Douglass, Jane Lites, David Lesly, E. Nelson, Aug. Lee, Harmon Stevenson, M. T. Owen, D. W. C. Tillotson, Asbury Ramey, M. Calhoun, M. Zachary, Charles T. Haskell, M. Radcliffe, John West, A. McCord, C. C. Puckett, S. G. W. Dill, Hiram T. Tusten, Dr. J. J. Wardlaw, Mr. Deal, John McLaren, Jon Dale, John Burnett, Jabe Story. ACCOUNTS 1831-1839. John Taggart, C. Houston, Wm. Lomax, David L. Wardlaw, A. Hamilton, Benjamin Mattison, Alelx. Bowie,

23

Armistead Burt, C. Dansby, Dr. R. L. Taggart, Dr. P. H. Davis, Samuel Pennal, Mrs. Kingsmore, George N. Sims, Ed Calhoun, Robert McClain, John Patterson, Peter Warson, Dr. Wheton, John Turbin, James Patterson, Jacob Belot, Thomas Maxwell, Ed Robertson, Wm. Thomas, Thomas Ford, Madison Weems, John McGee, Nat Lomax, Ransom Fuller, Samson Celvy, Pleasant Love, John Morrow, Alex, McBryde, Joseph Weems, Dr. E. Calhoun, John McDonald, John Allen, J. T. Burnett, George Kay, Charles Dendy, M. McCurdy, H. H. Cosby, Henry Wilson, John McLaren, Major Hil, David Rabon, Thomas N. Davis, Thomas Hamilton, Joseph Love, Luke Mathis, B. McKittrick, Pat Calhoun, Wm. Thomson, James Shillito, F. M. Davis, Townsend Watkins, James Wharton, John Calvert, Keath Bowie, Moses Taggart, Robert M. Means, John Yarbaorough, John A. Burton, John McFall, Wm. Jones, Gilliam Sales, Galeland Reid, S. B. Robertson, Hugal Lawlson, J. Calhoun, Thomas parker, James Hochison, M. Guillebeau, Dr. Aaron Lynch, Thomas P. Sperien, Dr. F. Thomas, Col. Douglass, Dougal McKellar, S. W. Walker, John Tittle, Alpheus Baker, Benjamin Saxon, Joseph Wilson, Douglas Gray, Dr. John Reid, Dr. A. B. Arnold, Dr. Cochran, Thomas Morrow, Alex. McKinney, John Dannon, Lewis Davis, John Scott, M. B. Tatom, Wm. Merriman, Robert Patterson, George Bigby, John F. Calhoun, M. McKay,James Taggart, Robert Yeldell, Thomas Caldwell, S. Thomson, Oliver Taggart, Mrs. Herbert, Christian Barnes, John Norris, James Crawford, S. Shoemaker, Wm. Harris, Arabella Crawford, James Anderson, Lewis Wilson, Thomas Bigby, Robert Cummings, Mrs. Crait, Wm. Pratt, Thomas Parker, Wm. Sales, Turner Hodges, Wm. Stone, James Hamilton, Cicero McCracken, Dr. John F. Livingston, Hugh M. Wardlaw, Alex. Houston, W. C. Robinson, James Burnett, W. Meriwether, Mrs. Dale, George Dale, George Owen, Andrew Stuart, Mrs. Mary Perrin, John Williams, John Hall, Wm. Smith, Lawrence Calhoun, John Brownlee, J. Robertson, James Houston, Wm. Armstrong, Thomas Hodges, Titus Murray, John Calvert, Robert Caldwell, Andrew Hamilton, Redmond Bagwell, Thomas J. Foster, Charles Haskell, David Dain, John H. Caldwell, Henry Bentley, Wm. Bull, Alex. Hamilton, Wm. Cameron, S. McAster, Moses Vernon, Wm. Morrow, Dr. R. Atkins, Duke Good, Robert Houston, Samuel McCraven, Mrs. Haten, Patrick Calhoun, Mrs. Thomas, John Weatherall, James C. Wharton, George Bigby, Dr. Richey, Ludlow Calhoun, John Cheatham, Dr. Wardlaw, Thomas Malone, John McKellar, Walter Anderson, Shadrick Clay, J. C. Kingsmore, Thomas C. Perrin, Thomas Roberts, Wm. Livingston, John Wilson, John Frazier, Wm. Tennant, Mrs, Jones, James Shillito, Moses Taggart, John Robertson, Armistead Burt, John Pelot, Charles Smith, Milton Childs, Peter McKellar, James Cobb, Wm. A. Black, James Calvert, Wm. Calhoun, Samuel Fisher, W. Anderson.

BOX 152 PACK 4296   ELIZABETH PRATT   1860

Administrator: Thomas Crawford. Appraisal Jan 22, 1861 by J. L. Ellis, John Pratt, Robert Pratt. Estate Sale Feb 21, 1861 netted $960. Buyers were: David Duncan, John R. Willson, Nancy Pratt, John Pratt, Thomas Crawford, Mary Kay, R. H. Haddon, John Burton, J. L. Pratt, Wm. Burton, John Duncan, R. H. Winn, James Winn, Benjamin Williams, F. A. Noblet, Caleb Shaw, Thomas Crawford, John F. Simpson, Peter Henry, G. W. Duncan, John F. Clinkscales, H. M. Winn, Wm. Clinkscales, W. O. Radcliffe, Andrew Winn, Wm. Young. Chalmers paid $69.75 for gravestones. Final return made Jun 12, 1863.

BOX 152 PACK 4297   REV. EBENEEZER E. PRESSLY   1860

He died Jul 26, 1860. Administrators: Wm. R. Pressly, J. C. Boyd. Bond Sep 5, 1860 of $60,000 by Wm. L. Pressly, J. C. Boyd, Adam Wideman, W. W. McDill. Appraisal Dec 4, 1860 by G. B. Richey, John Miller, S. E. Pruitt. Library valued at $150. Held notes on:

Elizabeth Taylor, Wm. Long, Joshua Goodwin, Charlotte G. Darlington, Wm. McCaslan, J. G. E. Branyon, J. N. Seawright, John Cowan, Joseph M. Ellis, Ben. E. Ellis. Estate Sale Dec 5 & 6, 1860 netted $5406. Buyers at sale: W. W. McDill, Ben. F. Moseley, S. M. Pruitt, J. M. Pruitt, Wm. Robinson, Larkin Barmore, J. R. Wilson, Marietta Pressly, E. L. Patton, Samuel Pruitt, Alex. Drake, P. J. Bonner, Col. L. Donald, Mrs. E. A. Reid, Robert Ellis, James Stone, Isaac Richey, Wm. Agnew, Dr. H. Latimer, David O. Hawthorne, J. C. Boyd, John Hagen, J. P. Kennedy, P. J. Bowen, W. L. Pressly, J. Galloway, Josiah Ashley, J. N. Seawright, W. W. Bowie, E. N. Young, J. W. Richey, J. W. Brooks, J. J. Bonner, Wm. Robinson, Cornelius Lee, C. M. Sharp, M. J. Mattison, James Seawright, Wm. Pratt, F. V. Pruitt, Ben. Eakin, F. W. Nance, Isaac Seawright, T. J. Ellis, James McDill, Dr. R. A. Archer, E. L. Patton, W. D. Stone, J. F. Simpson, Joseph Lindsay, Andrew C. Hawthorne, Robert C. Sharp, Dr. Andrew Dunn, Wm. Austin, Dr. Robert C. Grier, J. Galloway, Samuel Bratcher, J. N. Young, R. R. Seawright, A. P. Lindsay, J. R. Ellis, A. J. McKee, J. Roland, Wm. Stone, John Mathis, Gideon Stone, W.m. B. Hemphill, George Rasor, Thomas Bayent, Albert Johnston, Ed Hagen, Z. Haddon. Estate Settlement Oct 21, 1865. Last estate activity Mar 1868. During the deceased's lifetime he was guardian of Antoinette Richey and had $1565.90 in his hands for her at the time of his death.

BOX 152 PACK 4298   JOSIAH PATTERSON   1860

Administrators: Nancy Patterson-widow, A. Bradley. Bond Oct 3, 1860 of $600 by Archibald Bradley, Nancy Patterson, Peter Smith, James Leard. Appraisal Oct 19, 1860 by F. B. Robinson, John Creswell, Wilson Watkins. Estate Sale Oct 19, 1860. Buyers at sale: Mrs. Nancy Patterson, John Creswell, Mrs. F. Robinson, D. Bowie, Mrs. W. Kennedy, Mrs. J. B. Creswell, John Patterson, Thomas O. Creswell, Dr. J. Sanders, S. Young, Thomas A. McBride.

BOX 152 PACK 4299   EZEKIEL STEPHENS   1860

Administrator: W. C. Cozby. Bond Nov 26, 1860 of $4,000 by W. C. Cozby, R. M. Davis, Henry S. Kerr. Wife and (2) minor children. Appraisal Dec 12, 1860 by John M. Moseley, W. A. Pressly, R. H. Davis. Held notes on John Hill, S. W. McAllister, A. A. Bowen G. Vanhausen. 1st Estate Sale Dec 13, 1860. Buyers at sale: Mrs. G. Stephens, James Cann, John Scott, Wm. C. Cozby, Christian V. Barnes, L. W. McAllister, Frank C. DuPre, M. Mulliken, J. E. Anderson, R. W. Carlisle, W. M. Bell, J. M. White, J. W. Carlisle, Rignul N. Groves, Thomas W. Mauldin, F. P. Robertson, Wm. V. Clinkscales, W. D. Pressly, Robert H. Harkness, N. Cunningham, R. M. Davis, E. W. South, A. Oliver, G. W. Daniel. 2nd Estate Sale Dec 28, 1861. Buyers at sale: A. Oliver, James T. Barnes, Mrs. G. Stephens, A. Brooks, W. H. Rampey, F. P. Robertson. Partial Settlement Aug. 1866. Alice Dean received $18 and Miss Lizzie Stephens received $30. Estate Settlement Sep 10, 1867. (3) Legatees. 1. E. F. Dean in right of his wife Alice $6.53 2. Elizabeth "Lizzie" Stephens $60.72 3. George Stephens received $159.53.

BOX 152 PACK 4300   JEMINA SHIRLEY   1860

Administrator: William Shirley. Bond Jan 30, 1861 of $800 by Wm. Shirley, James M. Carwile, James Clinkscales. Appraisal Feb 13, 1861by John F. Clinkscales, J. C. Wakefield, James Clinkscales, James M. Carwile. Estate Sale Feb 14, 1861 netted $444. Buyers at sale: Wm. Shirley, John W. Shirley, W. Pearman, Jonathan Weldon, James Bannister, John Hinton, B. Callaham, Joseph Alewine, Nancy Shirley, W. L. Burton, Jacob Alewine, John L. Ashley, C. Wakefield, George Shirley, W. C. Fisher, Samuel A. Shaw, B. Lowe, S.

M. Fisher, Wm. Pruitt, Thomas Elgin, Amaziah Fisher, H. Brock. Estate Settlement Sep. 12, 1862. (8) Legatees with each receiving $3.22. John W. Shirley only name given.

BOX 153 PACK 2534   WILLIAM WHITLEY   1845

Administrators: Stephen Whitley, Thomas Whitley. Bond Jan 25, 1845 of $10,000 by Stephen Whitley, Meedy Mays, Thomas Rosemond. Wife and (6) Children. Appraisal Feb 9, 1845 by John Gaulden, Wiley Marlowe, Charles B. Gaulden. Held notes on: L. Burnett, Meedy Mays, John Gaulden, James W. Child, Charles Floyd, Samuel Beard, John Christly, Joseph Beaver, Wm. Whitley, Frances Whitley, L. G. Carter, Thomas Whitley, John Marlowe, L. Mays. Estate Sale Feb 10, 1845 netted $4,800. Buyers at sale: Frances Whitley, Thomas Whitley, Larkin Carter, Larkin Mays, Charles Floyd, Samuel Beard, John Holland, Daniel Pitts, Wm. Whitley, Wiley Marlowe, Elihu Stephens, Josiah Picams, J. M. Golding, J. W. Childs, D. Holloway, J. Christie, Charles Gaulden, Meedy Mays. Estate Settlement Mar 9, 1848 with (5) legatees. 1. Sampson Whitley 2. Frances Whitley 3. Thomas Whitley 4. Wm. Whitley 5. Elizabeth Waite wife of Simeon Waite.

BOX 153 PACK 2535   HENRY, SAMUEL, CATHERINE, ANNIE WAITS   1845

Minor children of Aaron Waits who had been dead for years. Stephen Whitley had been the administrator of his estate but had died prior to closure of estate. Wife: Alice Waits. Had one additional child of age. Guardian: John Burnett. Bond Jan 7, 1845 of $100 by John Burnett, Wiley Culbreth (both were residents of Edgefield). Dec 25, 1845 Henry Waits paid $12. Nov 6, 1847 Samuel Waits paid $15.18. Dec 23, 1853 Catherine Waits paid $18. Mar 22, 1856 Ann Waits paid $20. Jun 1857 Henry Waits paid $12.02, Samuel Waits paid $15. 18, Catherine Waits paid $18, Annie Waits paid $20.04.

BOX 153 PACK 2536   JOHN WILSON   1847

Will dated May 31, 1844. Witnesses: J. F. Marshall, John McIlwain, S. W. W. Marshall. He died Jul 1844 and buried at Long Cane Cemetery. Wife: Louisa. Daughter: Eliza Stewart Wilson. Executor: Andrew Jefferson Weems. Appraisal Nov 5, 1844 by John Wier, James H. Tusten, A. L. Gillespie, John Nash, Addison F. Posey. Owned lot and house with 6 acres of land in Town of Abbeville purchased from the estate of Samuel Branch. 41 acres purchased from estate of Samuel Branch and 217 acres below town purchased from John Cunningham that had belonged to Gov. Andrew Noble. Owned 10 slaves. Held notes on Oliver Taggart, F. Henderson, T. Bird, A. English, Wm. S. Shoemaker A. Arnold, T. W. Tallman, H. F. Power, James L. Leslie, H. R. Wilson, James Kennedy, Isaac H. McCalla, A. H. Patton, R. S. Markee, J. B. Richey, A. Baker & B. L. Posey, Thomas E. Owen, Issac Branch, James H. Cobb, Jesse Berry, J. L. Branch & John E. Navy, James S. Wilson, D. D. Baker, B. L. Taggart, Edward Calhoun, B. A. Calhoun, Thomas Graves. Estate Sale Nov 6, 1844. Buyers at sale: Joseph A. Hamilton, Mrs. Wilson, H. A. Jones, John White, Robert Richey, B. Y. Martin, C. V. Barnes, T. P. Moseley, James Carson, Henry Wilson, John Wier, Dr. Isaac Branch, T. D. Williams, R. H. Canady, Johnson Ramey, Dr. Dendy, Andrew J. Weems, Thomas C. Perrin, Robert H. Canady, A. Lomax, John E. Navy, Rev. Turner, B. V. Posey, Andrew L. Gillespie, Robert H. Wardlaw, J. N. Dixon, Thomas E. Owen, Henry A. Jones, Charles Dendy, F. Robinson, Dr. Joseph Wardlaw, James H. Tusten, Joel J. Lipford, Wm. Brooks, Samuel Cochran.

BOX 153 PACK 2537   A. L. WATKINS   1832

Jan 2, 1832 Hiring of the Negroes of A. L. Watkins. Jim to A. P. Watkins for $52. Nancy to A. P. Watkins for $29. Peggy to A. P. Watkins for $5.

26

BOX 153 PACK 2538   DR. R. W. WOODS   1832

Administrator: Wm. Covington. Bond mar 18, 1831 of $500 by Wm. Covington, James H. Baskin. Estate paid in 1831: Jonathan Johnson $156.85. Estate paid in Aug 1832 for services: 1. Young Cunningham 2. J. Harper 3. J. G. Caldwell 4. Thomas Scott.

BOX 153 PACK 2539   JANE YOUNG   1836

Will dated Jul 30, 1836. Witnesses: Elizabeth B. Gibert, J. Gibert, A. Hunter. Executor: John Baskin. Niece: Ann Carlisle. Nephew: Samuel Y. Carlisle. Grand Daughters: Martha Jane Callaham, Ann Dickson, Elizabeth Dickson. Grand Sons: Berry Wilson, Samuel Wilson. Daughter –in-law: Charity Wilson. Appraisal Dec 1838 by, Sugar Johnson, Jonathan Johnson, M. Speer. Owned 5 slaves, 209 acres of land. Held notes on: Wm. F. Baker, James F. Cook, James Caldwell, Wm. Speed, Archa Scott. Estate Sale Dec 13, 1838. Buyers at sale: B. Allen, W. McCaw, Mrs. C. Wilson, T. Cunningham, F. Anderson, A. Giles, J. Gray, T. Caldwell, Wm. Bradshaw, John Baskin, A. D. Hunter, A. Scott, A. Swearingham, Littleton Yarborough, E. Baird, Robert Hutchison, Francis Y. Baskin, James Caldwell, W. Belcher, Sugar Johnson, Alex. Hunter, Mrs. T. Wilson, T. Anderson, A. Huse, W. Speed, James A. Norwood, J. D. Nixon, Thomas Graves. Estate Settlement 1838 (4) Legatees $331 each: 1. Children of Jane Callaham-Martha Jane, Charles T. 2. Child of Martha Dickson 3. Elizabeth Dickson wife of Daniel Dickson 4. Ann Dickson wife of Wm. Dickson. Estate Settlement in 1840 (6) shares of $444.94 each: 1. Martha J. Callaham 2. Thomas J. Young 3. Ann Dickson 4. Elizabeth Dickson 5. Berry Wilson 6. Samuel Wilson. Also $111.12 each to the (4) children of Marttha Jones: 1. Andrew W. Dickson 2. Julian Dickson, 3. Jane Dickson 4. Samuel J. Dickson. Oct 24, 1854 Julia A. Dickson sued the estate of John Baskin for money may be due to her from her grandmother's, Jane Young, estate. A court case involving the estate was held in Dec 1885 with witnesses: George C.Bradley, George B. McCaslan, A. W. Weed, Robert T. Creswell, James C. Tittle, Wm. Bufort, Joseph McBride, Dr. J. D. Neel, John F. Creswell, Robert A. Crawford, James H. Drennan, John W. Young, Samuel T. Young.

BOX 153 PACK 2540   VALENTINE YOUNG   1856

Will dated Jul 11, 1820. Proved Dec 12, 1838. Bond Dec 17, 1838 of $10,000 by Valentine Young, James Dodson, D. Douglass. Wife: Polly Young. Son-in-law: Alba Burton. Executor: Valentine Young. 1st Appraisal Feb 1838 by Wm. Swain, Samuel Agnew, John Rasor, James Dodson, Wm. Barmore. Owned 15 Slaves. Estate Sale Jan 2, 1839. Buyers at sale: W. J. Young, J. C. Richey, Wm. Young, S. Agnew, Nathaniel Rowlin, Marshall Sharp, W. McNary, Andrew Pruitt, Mastin Williams, E. Rasor, Issac A. Young, D. Mabry, Issac Richey, Wm. Franklin, James Graham, Samuel A. Hodges, John Weatherall, Wesley Norwood, Wm. Barmore, John Rasor, Ezekiel Rasor, W. Hughes, Thomas Hawthorne, James Dodson, Isaac Agnew, W. Swain, S. Miller, J. B. Callahan, G. W. Hodges, Wm. R. Swain, W. Richey, W. Robertson, J. L. Sims. 1st Estate Settlement Jan 1, 1841. (9) Children legatees: 1. Abram Beardon in right of his wife 2. James Graham in right of his wife 3. Wm. Franklin in right of his wife 4. Thomas Young 5. James Franklin in right of his wife 6. Isaac Young 7. Wm. Young 8. Washington J. Young 9. Valentine Young. Another appraisal in 1845 by Samuel Agnew, Isaac C. Richey, Joseph Weatherall, John Rasor, Joseph Agnew. 2nd Estate Settlement Feb 16, 1846 (7) Legatees: 1. Valentine Young 2. Wm. Young 3. Washington Young 4. Wm. Franklin in right of his wife 5. J. Franklin and wife, Margaret 6. J. Burden in right of his wife 7. James Graham and children. Apr 1846 Thomas Young of Choctaw Co., Miss received legacy. Estate Settlement Jan 18, 1847 wife, now Mary Moore, received $95.

BOX 153 PACK 2541   SAMUEL YOUNG   1817

Papers from (2) Estates and possibly (3) in the same pack. 1ST ESTATE: Executor: Elizabeth Young. Appraisal Oct 24, 1817 by Wm. Graves, James Glover, George Maddox. Estate Sale Oct 25, 1817. Buyers at sale: James Glover, Pleasant Wright, Enoch Hensley, Alex. Sample, James Mitchell, Nicholas Meriwether, Nicholas Overby, Alex. W. Adams.

2ND ESTATE: Will dated Nov 10, 1817. Filed Nov 8, 1823. Witnesses: James Carlisle Sr., Elijah Brown, Hugh Brown. Executors: Elizabeth Young, James Caldwell. Deceased died Nov 1821. Step Son: Andrew Wilson. Step grand daughter: Jane B. Wilson. 1st Appraisal Dec 29, 1821 by John Baskin, Samuel McBride, Samuel Young. 2nd Appraisal Apr 1, 1823 by John Drennan, John McComb, John McBride, Wm. Robinson. 3rd Appraisal Nov 28, 1838 by Jonathan Johnson, Sugar Johnson, M. Speed. Notes & Accounts due Sep 30, 1822: Philip Barnes, Archibald McMullin, John Morrow, Wm. H. Caldwell, Pleasant Crenshaw, Mathew Jackson, C. Daniel, Thomas Taylor, John Cameron, Francis Young Sr., Walter H. Ward, Rev. John Porter, John Baskin, Samuel Buchanan, John B. Ward, Wm. Bradshaw, Hugh Harris, John Harris, Wm. Speer, Dr. Jepsa Boshell, Robert Biggens, James Woods, Thomas Cunningham, Thomas Caldwell, Lewis Sims, Thomas L. Hall, Dubose Jones, Samuel Cowan, John Thomas, Wm Speer Jr., David Kerr, A. E. Scudday, Thomas Jones, Rev. James Gamble, Widow Johnson, Widow McCelvy, Samuel McBride, Samuel Young. Estate receipts received 1823 to 1824: George McFarland, Robert McCaslan, John McBryde Sr., John Leard, James McBryde, John Young Jr., Amos Lasseter, James Fife, Alex. Jordan, Mathew Goodwin, Joseph Creswell, Isaac Lasseter, Caleb Cain, Zach Goodwin, John Ferguson, Philip Cook, Thomas Wylie, James Watkins, John Weed, Allen Glover's estate, Mary McHenry, Sarah Findley, John Young Sr., James Puckett, Wm. Robinson Jr., Pleasant Crenshaw, James Spence Sr., John B. McBryde, Andrew McCombs, James Smith, Samuel McBryde, John Chiles, John Hearst, Dr. Samuel Pressly, John Young Sr., David Kerr, Andrew Milligan, Zach. Goodwin, Wm. Robinson Sr., John Creswell Sr., Wyatt A. Taylor, Thomas Cunningham, Joshua Dubose. Estate Sale Dec 13, 1838 (This may be a 3rd estate). Receipts received from this sale: Francis Young, Abraham Bell, Edward Moseley, Michael Speed, Joseph Baker, George W. Tinsley, Christy Wilson, Thomas Anderson, James Cobb, A. R. White, John Baskin, Wm. Speed, George Smith, Wm. Simpson, S. Y. Caldwell, James Gray, Wm. Reid, John Hall, John Gibson, Wm. Bradshaw, A. Swearingen, Elihu Bond, Henry Moseley, Bannister Allen, D. F. Bulger, James Murray, Archibald Scott, James Norwood, Wm. Magruder, Howard B. Shackleford, Wm. Smith, Washington Belcher, Littleton Yarborough. Partial Estate Settlement Jan 8, 1822 with (2) Legatees. 1. James Caldwell 2. Andrew Wilson (he died before Samuel Young leaving wife, Charity).

BOX 153 PACK 2542   WILLIAM YARBOROUGH   1837

Will dated Sep 10, 1835. Witnesses: Robert Lewis Taggart, John Barnett, Leroy Purdy. (9) Children Named: 1. Moses 2. John 3. Fannie Murray wife of James Murray 4. Littleton 5. William 6. Drusilla Taggart wife of Oliver Taggart 7. Mary Miller wife of N. MIller 8. Sarah Nelson wife of R. Nelson 9. Elizabeth "Betsy". Appraisal Oct 5, 1835 by A. Bowie, Robert Richey, Robert Lesly. Owned 23 slaves. Accounts & notes due Estate: John W. Lesly, Moses Yarborough, Margaret Mann, John & Oliver Taggart, John Findley, Leroy Purdy, John Yarborough, John Allen, Daniel Robison, John Able, Henry Brooks, Andrew Gillespie, Thomas Jackson, John Richey, Elizabeth Drinkard, James Purdy, Lewis Wardlaw, Sterling Bowen, John Gillespie, Gutridge Lucas, James English, Wmm. Brooks, James Spence, James B. Huey, Alston Scudday, Ezekiel Douglass, Michael Wilson, James Pursley, Dr. L. Taggart, David R. McAllister, Richard Hill, J. H. Baskin, White & Smith, O.

Taggart, Henry Simpson, James Huey, J. S. & L. Bowie, Moses Taggart, Henry Penney, Wm. Bowie, Thomas Efford Owen, Wm. Lesly, Littleton Yarborough, Robert Richey, Andrew Gillespie, Leroy Purdy, Morgan McMorries, Alex. Bowie, James B. Dickson, Robert Wardlaw, Samuel Lockridge, John Adams, Thomas C. Perrin, Green W. Huckabee, John H. Zimmerman, Robert H. Lesly, James Williams, Samuel Gilmer, Henry Wilson, James Boyd, Daniel Robison, John Allen, Andrew Brown. Estate Sale Dec 7, 1835 netted $15,783. Buyers at sale: Leroy Wilson, Moses Yarborough, Alex. Wilson, George A. Miller, John Boyd, James N. Dickson, Andrew Giles, Peachman Alford, Robert H. Lesly, Alston Scudday, Ezekiel Beam, Jefferson Douglass, A. McCoy, Sterling Bowen, Joseph Williams, Samuel Gilmer, Miss E. Yarborough, David Robison, Andrew Gillespie, Richard S. Davis, Robert Brady, John Robison, John L. Lockridge, Thomas Sperrien, James S. Bowie, Alex. Foster, Daniel Robison, James Huey, Olliver Taggart, Daniel A. Weed, Robert Richey Sr., John Wier, Robert Wardlaw, James Murray, James Purdy, John Allen, Ezekiel Douglass, Thomas Guffin, Thomas Jackson, James Pursley, Joel J. Lipford, Samuel Shoemaker, John Donald, Hudson Prince, George Watson, Moses Mann, Rev. Wm. H. Barr, John Outon, John A. Calhoun, Bartlett Cheatham, Franklin Cochran, John T. Herrin, Wm. H. Kyle, Derry Donaldson, Samuel Lockridge, John Adams, Thomas C. Perrin, Robert Nelson, John Campbell, Littleton Yarborough, Dr. John Livingston, Wm. Brooks, Wm. Speed, N. H. Miller, Christian B. Barnes, Samuel S. Baker, James Bell, James Spence, Thomas Graves, Harvey Wilson, Robert Davis, Wm. McClinton, Henry Brooks, Henry Lipford, Ben. J. McFarland, Wm. J. Thompson, Ezekiel Gunnin, P. L. Calhoun, Robert Richey Jr., Craven Frazier, Michael S. Mann, Joseph Lyon, G.W. Huckabee, Henry Penney, John H. Zimmerman, Henry Simpson, John S. Barnett, Nathaniel Moore, Joseph P. Jones, Arch McGowan, John Richey, Daniel A. Weed, Joseph P. Jones, Hugh Armstrong, John J. Barnett, Robert W. Cary, Mark P. Stewart, Samuel Houston, Washington Hddon, Oliver Shoemaker, Zach. Arnold, Charles M. Pelot, John S. Turnbull, Henley Lipford, Andrew Edwards, Robert F. Black, Alex. Russell, Frances Moore.

BOX 153 PACK 2543   NATHANIEL YOUNG   1784

Spartanburg District, S. C. Administrator: Patty Young. Bond 2,000 pounds by Patty Young, Richard Nally, Thomas Young. Appraisal Sep 3, 1784 by Alex. Alexander Cox, Jacob Earnest, Wm. Cleaton, Richard Chesney. Feb 28, 1787 Edward Hacker filed against the estate due to a purchase by Joel Hembrey. The parties settled.

BOX 153 PACK 2544   WILLIAM YOUNG   1820

Administrator: Benjamin Adams. Bond Nov 20, 1817 by Benjamin Adams, Robert Woolbridge, Alex. C. Harrelton. Appraisal Dec 4, 1817 by Thomas Ross, Wm. Lomax, John Downey, Edward Vann. Notes held on: David Thomas, Wm. Thomas, Samuel Wier, Wm. Robison, Mary Young, Frances Young, Peter Lomax, Edward Vann, James Conn, David H. McCluskey, Wm. Lomax. Estate Sale Dec 4, 1817. Buyers at sale: Ben. Adams, Frances Calvert, Arthur Rhodes, Wm. Lomax, David Kelley, A. Lesly, Francis Young, Robert Wilson, James Conn, George Conn, Mary Young, Edward Vann, David Keller, David Muluskie, Wm. Robertson, Wm. Thomas, David Thomas, Peter Lomax, Samuel Ware.

BOX 153 PACK 2545   ROBERT YOUNG   1811

Will dated Apr 14, 1810. Filed Dec 22, 1812. Witnesses: Samuel Young, Wm. Phillips, Basil Hallum. Wife: Rebecca. Sons: Wm., James, Samuel. Daughters: Margaret Phillips wife of Wm. Phillips, Rebecca Childs. Executors: Joseph C. Neely, Samuel Young.

Appraisal Oct 20, 1810 by Basil Hallum, Ben. Mitchell, Alex. Stuart. Owned 6 slaves. Estate Sale Nov 16, 1810. Buyers at sale: Rebecca Young, Snelling Johnston, John Shotwell, Andrew Anderson, Robert Golden, Wm. Phillips, George Madden, Charles Collins, Richard Jonott, James Jones, Samuel Young, Alex. Stuart.

BOX 153 PACK 2546   JOHN YOUNGBLOOD   1829

Administrator: David Thomas, Robert Kay. Bond Apr 10, 1826 of $500 by David Thomas, John Douglass, Timothy Hughes. Bond Sep 25, 1829 by Robert Kay, Thomas Jackson, John Hanley. Appraisal Apr 27, 1826 by John Marshall, Benjamin Johnson, John Burnett, John Thomas. Estate Sale Apr 27, 1826. Buyers at sale: Ben. Johnston, John Thomas, Timothy Hughes, T. G. Thomas, John Cochran, John Buchanan, David Thomas, John Thompson, Jesse Adams, John Youngblood, Robert Carlisle, John Marshall, Andrew McGill, Robert Turner, Henry Gray, Wm. Chastund, Owen Selby, F. G. Thomas, Harriet Youngblood.

BOX 153 PACK 2547   JOHN F. YOUNGBLOOD   1823

Administrator: Joseph Davis. Bond Jan 18, 1823 of $8,000 by Joseph Davis, John Quarles, John Cochran. Legatee: John F. Burley. Appraisal Feb 5, 1823 by Wm. Mantz, Henry Nelson, Samuel Gordon, George Penney. Owned 11 slaves. 1825 tax $1.76. Blacksmith. Accounts open and due at death: John McLaren, James Fell, Wm. Cowan, Wm. Drennan, James Davis, Samuel Jordan, Young Reagan, Mary Buskey, John C. Cowey, Robert McBride, James Gray, J. L. Cochran, Ben. Perry, John Igner, Robert North, David Rayney, John McComb, Sam. Cowey, J. M. Craven, Hewey Huffman, John Quarles, Elizabeth Dorris, Robert Omosga, James L. Morrow, Elias Gibson, David Black, Charles Creswell, Wm. Perry, Hudson M. Pitman, Susannah Briskey, Hiram Scott, John McFerrin, Elizabeth Hunter, Jos. McCreary, Josiah Patterson, Abner Perrin, Adam McDonald, Margaret McFerrin, Henry Nelson, Wm. Marsh, Wm. Cowan, Clarke Ethridge, James Dixon, James C. Watson, John Argo, Francis Pitman, John McCarter, Wm. H. Brown, James Richey, John Chiles, Wm. Frazier, Allen McWhorter, David Robertson, Josiah Drinkwater, Elizabeth Perry, Robert Brooks, James Gaften, James Clem, Dr. John C. Dansby, John Zimmerman, Joel Ethridge, Mathew McClinton, John Foster, Reuben Weoven, Sam. Bratcher, Wm. Patton, Nancy Martin, Hiram Moore, John Hughey, Est. of Wm. P. Sillivant, John L. Weed, Leon Pressly, Young Reagan, Thomas McFerrin, J. Clem & I. Atchison, Hugh Henry, Robert Houston, Wm. Morrow, Alex. Leard, Amos Chapman, George Samon, Sam. Gilmer, Jared Ellison, Sarah Finley, Thomas McLane, Sam. Hughey, James Shanks, John Fulton, Henry Dilbone, Henry Dilbone, Est. of McCuen Kay, James Able, Mathew Roady, Brothers French, Ben. Lyon, Adam Henry, Wm. A. Clem, Wm. Dorris, Joshua Hill, John McComb, Stephen Witts, West Donald, Beverly Burton, John Chiles, Phillip Cook, Wm. Ethridge, John Able, Robert McFerrin, Robert F. Cochran, Hugh Wiseman, David Mullins, Wm. Yarborough, Reuben Weed, Alex. Pressly, Ben. McGill, Est. of James McLane, Stephen Witty, Hannah Little, Larkin Davis, Andrew McGill, Nancy Gable, Mathias Igner, James Miller, John Steward, Jacob Wilson, Aaron B. & James C. Watson, Alex. Gray, Dan. Wideman, David McClelland, Peter B. Rogers, James Gray, Nancy Ruff, Allen Bass, Wm. Calhoun, Archibald Tittle, J. Dorris & W. Truitt, Hugh McBride, James Clem, Loot Etheridge, James Lissman, Henry Huffman, Alex. Legg, James Roche, David Dansby, Charles Dansby, Henry Cromer, Sam. Anderson, Sam. Cross, Sarah Houston, Rebecca Harper, David Smith, John McCartney, John McFerrin, Ben. Burton, James Hesterton, Sam. Patterson, James Leard, James Glasgow, Joel Mullins, Wm. Turner, John L. Pressly.

BOX 154 PACK 3697   MARY MOORE   1859

Administrator: Valentine Young. Bond Jun 7, 1852 of $100 by Valentine Young, M. C. Henderson. Appraisal Jun 23, 1852 by T.Z. Martin, Mason C. Henderson, Samuel Agner. Estate Sale Jun 23, 1852.

BOX 154 PACK 3698   WILLIAM MORRISON   1852

Will dated Oct 29, 1849. Witnesse: Thomas Ware, John L. Livingston, B. Martin. Wife: Nancy who died Apr 1854. Sons: James, Andrew, John who moved to Mississippi. Daughter: Caty who married Wm. Hawthorne and moved to Brown Co., Ohio. Executor: James Morrison. Bond Jun 7, 1852 of $1,000 by James Morrison, Thomas Eakin, John McIlwain. 1st Appraisal Jul 30, 1852 by Thomas Eakin, Wm. McIlwain, David Robison. 2nd Appraisal Nov 2, 1853 by W. M. McIlwain, David Robison, W. B. Roman. Owned 320 acres of land, 5 slaves. 1st Estate Sale Dec 30, 1852. Buyers at sale: Andrew Morrison, James Morrison, Thomas Eakin, David Robison, Ben. H. Eakin, Thomas Gordon, James Carlisle, Gordon Martin, Mathew McDonald, A. Moore, Nancy Morrison, D. O. Hawthorne, Wm. McIlwain, J. P. Gilmer, J. W. McCree, T. J. Ellis, Wm. Nickles, John Richardson, Asa Bowie, james A. Hamilton, B. W. Roman, Silas Ray. 2nd Estate Sale Oct 2, 1854. Buyers at sale: John L. Davis, Augustus Lomax. 1855 tax on slaves who had not been sold $2.88. Estate Settlement Jun 2, 1855 & Aug 14, 1855. Legatees: (4): 1. James Morrison 2. John Morrison 3. Andrew Morrison 4. Caty Hawthorne. All received $791.89 except Caty who received $4523.33.

BOX 154 PACK 3699   AGNES McLAREN   1851

Will dated Mar 20, 1846. Filed Jun 21, 1851. Son: John. Executor: John McLaren. Witnesses: Francis Henderson, Andrew W. Shillito, Thomas Henderson.

BOX 154 PACK 3700   J. THOMAS MOORE   1852

Will dated Jun 4, 1850. Witnesses: Enoch Carter, Wm. Graham, Thomas Rosamond. Executor: James Moore. Bond Jan 5, 1852 of $2,000 by James Moore, Enoch Carter, C. N. Graham. Appraisal Feb 14, 1852 by James Robertson, Wm. C. Graham, C. N. Graham.

BOX 154 PACK 3701   DAVID MATHEWS   1850

Will dated Aug 28, 1850. Filed Dec 12, 1850. Witnesse: E. C. martin, H. G. Middleton, James Martin. Executrix: Cinthia Mathews. Wife: Cinthia. Sons: Robert Pickens, Joseph Wiley, James Chapel, William, Thomas McPherson, David Lewis. Daughters: Esther Ann Shuttlesworth, Sarah Moore, Mary. Appraisal Sep 28, 1850 by E. C. Martin, H. G. Middlelton, Joseph Britt. Owned 242 acres of land. Notes held on: W. Hill, L. Covin, V. McCelvey, E. Cowan & Co., B. E. Gibert, Mary A. Moragne, W. H. Price, Uel Wideman, Britt & Brother, Sayers & Rogers, Ja. A. Gibert, Britt & Cowan, Drennan & Hester, J. L. Bouchillon, Edward Cowan, W. Cook, J. H. LeRoy, Thomas A. Wideman, Ann Clarke. Taxes 1852-37 cents, 1856-62 cents, 1858-83 cents, 1859-90 cents.

BOX 154 PACK 3702   HUGH MAXWELL   1850

Will dated May 11, 1837. Filed Mar 12, 1851. Witnesses: E. B. Gibert, James L. McBride, A. Hunter. Executor: Ann Maxwell-daughter. Wife: Jane. Daughters: Ann, Jane, Mary Boyd, Eliza Patterson. Appraisal Apr 1, 1851 by Joel Lockhart, Alex. Oliver, Wm. A. Pressly. Ann and Jane received $150, Mary and Eliza received $5.

BOX 154 PACK 3703   WILLIAM McDILL   1850

Administrator: A. L. Gray. Bond Dec 28, 1850of $1,400 by A. L. Gray, A. R. Ramey, Wm. Adams. Appraisal Dec 31, 1850 by John Douglass, Wm. Adams, William Riley. Held notes on: M. Hutchinson, Thomas McDill, H. A. Jones, Robert A. Martin. Estate Sale Dec 31, 1850. Buyers at sale: Widow, David M. Wardlaw, A. F. P. Douglass, Wm. Riley, A. L. Gray, John Douglass. Estate Settlement Nov 8, 1852. (6) Legatees, widow and (5) Children. 1. Cornelia F. widow received $14. 64 2. Thomas R. McDill and Robert A. McDill were only children named. All children received $35.36 each.

BOX 154 PACK 3704   RICHARD A. MARTIN   1853

Administrator: Margaret P. Martin-widow. Bond Oct 2, 1851 of $35,000 by Margaret P. Martin, J. Foster Marshall, J. F. McComb. Held notes on: John Cox, Wm. McKinney, J. C. Mathis, Sheppard Cowan, A. S. McFarland, John Finley, John Creswell, John A. Calhoun, James Cason, Edward Foster, John Watson, Sam. P. Leard, Giles Burdette, James P. Weed, Jacob Miller, John Gray, Henry Bentley, Wm. K. Bradley, Archibald Tittle, Thomas Link, E. Jones, Samuel McQuerns, John Brady, James Drennan, P. C. McCaslan, George W. Brown, Ralph Burnett, A. C. Brown, Thomas Wideman, John Wideman, James Shanks, Dr. Tatom Wideman, Dr. Mrs. Sanders, J. P. Kennedy. Estate Sale Nov 20, 1851. Buyers at sale: Widow, J. C. Martin, J. E. Foster, James Cason, M. P. Martin, P. C. McCaslan, John Creswell, J. Bradley, W. Watson, Jacob Miller, Moses Owen, Levi Hilburn, J. A. Calhoun, Sarah Kennedy, J. C. Mathews, A. L. Gray, Silas Anderson, Wm. Martin, John Watson, W. Bradley, J. W. Williams, W. J. Hammon, Eli Thornton, J. F. McComb, Robert McKinney, T. J. Douglass, S. McQuerns, S. G.Cowan, A. Murphy, A. McLane, Robert LItes, A. P. Robinson, E.D. Cherry, N. A. Edwards, W. McKinney, George Zaner, James Martin, E. F. Parker, W. Burdette, John Hayes, J. W. Wilson, David McLane, E. G. Derby, Wm. K. Bradley, J. F. Marshall, Archibald Tittle. Estate Settlement Aug 2, 1853. Legatees: Wife, Margaret and (2) Daughters. Each received $2,995. Amended settlement Mar 1, 1854 named legatees. 1. Margaret, widow had now married W. J. Hammond 2. R. Agnes Martin 3. Kitty Foster Martin.

BOX 154 PACK 3705   JOHN THOMAS MCKEE   1857

Administrator: Elizabeth Ann McKee-widow. Bond Nov 25, 1851 of $800 by Elizabeth Ann McKee, Andrew A. McKee, James A. McKee. Deceased died Sep 1851. Appraisal Dec 14, 1851 by James McKee, John Patterson, Alex. L. Gray. Estate Sale Dec 16, 1851. Buyers at sale: Elizabeth Ann McKee, James A. McKee, John Patterson, Levi Gable, E. P. Holloman, Joseph O'Brient, James H. Wiles. Estate Settlement Mar 6, 1854. Legatees: Elizabeth Ann McKee received $123 and (6) children-each received $41.07. Children not named.

BOX 154 PACK 3706   JAMES D. MURDOCK   1851

Administrator: Stephen M. Fisher. Bond Jan 29, 1851 by Stephen M. Fisher, Caleb Burton, Jacob Alewine. Deceased died May 1850. Appraisal Feb 14, 1851 by Caleb Burton, Jacob Alewine, John W. Shirley. Estate Sale Feb 14, 1851 netted $321.17. Buyers at sale: Widow, John Saylors, James M. Hopkins, John Fields, Stephen M. Fisher, Michael Taylor, Thomas Fields, Ben. Pearman, Wm. Bell, S.C. Fisher, Caleb Burton, James Bannister. Estate Settlement Jan 25, 1855. Widow received $37.22 and each of (5) Children received $14.89 each. Children not named.

BOX 154 PACK 3707   WILLIAM C. MOORE (minor)   1850

Guardian: James Moore-father. Bond Mar 13, 1850 of $2,000 by James Moore, Joseph T. Moore, Augustus Lomax. Was of age Mar 1850. Had been left a legacy of $1,000 by his late aunt, Mrs. Mary Crawford.

BOX 154 PACK 3708   OLIVER J. MOORE   1852

Administrator: John W. Moore-brother. Bond Jan 16, 1851 of $5,000 by John W. Moore, Wm. A. Moore, Augustus W. Moore. Appraisal Jan 31, 1852 by J. N. Sims, J. Carter, Wm. Smith. Owned 6 slaves. Estate Sale Feb 3, 1852. Buyers at sale: Jesse Lomax, John W. Moore, Wm. A. Moore, J. W. Cobb, James McRady, Wm. Mundy, Henry May, John Carter, David W. McCants, John Rodman, Lucy Moore, A. W. Moore, Cokesbury School, W.C. Anderson, T. R. Gary, W. W. Franklin.

BOX 154 PACK 3709   CATHERINE McCOWN   1857

Will dated Nov 6, 1851. Witnesses: John Bowie, R. P. Bowie, John Hagan. Executor: Hezekiah Bowie, son-in-law. Daughters: Sarah, Mary, Margaret Ann. Sons: Robert, Joseph. Appraisal Jan 5, 1852 by Robert C. Sharp, Samuel W. Agnew, John Hagan. Estate Sale Jan 6, 1852. Buyers at sale: Samuel W. Agnew, Wm. Hagan, Hezekiah Bowie, Henry Nickles, John Hagan, David O. Hawthorne, R. P. Doyle, S. M. Smith, John R. Sharp, J. P. Bowie, Wm. Nickles, Alex. M. Agnew, John Hawthorne, Wm. Dunn. Estate Settlement Oct 8, 1852.

BOX 154 PACK 3710   CHRISTOPHER VANDEL MANTZ   1853

Will dated Nov 15, 1851. Witnesses: John Zimmerman, Hugh Robertson, L. B. Hammond. Executor: John W. Hearst. Wife: Mary P. Brother: Andrew Mantz. Sister: Mary Steifle. Nephews: Charles J. Glover, David M. Glover. Niece: Adaline Lanham. Willed money to Wm. Leggett Walker son of Rev. David Walker, to Jonathan Augustus White and Sarah Savannah White children of A.G. & Sarah White, for the support of Rehobeth Church for enclosure of the graves of his father and brother. 1st Appraisal Feb 4, 1852 by John Cothran, John L. Harmon, Samuel Perrin, James W. Wideman, C. W. Sproull. 2nd Appraisal Feb 14, 1852 by C. W. Sproull, Hugh Robertson, John Zimmerman, Henry Rush James H. Wideman. Owned 15 slaves of which 6 were entailed from the will of Wm. Jeter. Held notes on: Mary Harrison, John Ruff, Josiah Patterson, Nicholas Henderson, Mary G. Adams & W. H. Adams, C. Weatherington, Levi Weatherington, Noah Weatherington, Thomas Price. 1st Estate Sale Feb 26, 1852. Buyers at sale: Wm. Sproull, J. W. Hearst, R. Fuller, James Hollingsworth, Wm. Hunter, Mrs. M. Eaton, L. F. Stephens, Jacob Miller, John McClellan, Williamson Briscoe, Samuel Cook, J. T. Webber, Fred Cook, Samuel Perrin, Silas Lagroon. 2nd Estate Sale Nov 6, 1856 netted $8,828. Buers at sale: Abner White, S. B. Cook, C. H. Sproull, Wm. Walker, F. W. Chambers, Peter Rampey, F. O. Wensby, Joseph Creswell, John Briskey, John Cothran, Thomas Goodwin, A. Smith, George Galpin, James Carlisle, Wm. McCain, Allen Reagan, John Cheatham, R. R. Tolbert, John B. Gardner, Wm. Harris, W. P. Goodwin, John L. Harmon, J. W. Hearst, Israel Bond, R. P. Harrison, Mrs. Quarles, A. McNeill, James Hollingsworth, John Rush, P. M. Fuller, J. Hutchinson, Gorge Briskey, W. C. Puckett, J. T. Webber, Wm. A. Flinn, John L. Griffin, A. Wideman, A. Gaskin, A. J. Roundtree, John H. Chiles, John Spearman, James Reagan, Wm. Jay, Willis Smith, Jacob Miller. 1st Estate Settlement Jun 8, 1859. (3) Legatees: 1. J. Augusts White $500 2. Sarah J. White $300 3. George F. Steifle $5 only survivor of Mary Steifle. 2nd Estate Settlement Mar 13, 1860.

BOX 154 PACK 3711   EMMA JOHN McCARTNEY (minor)   1863

Guardian: Leroy Purdy. Bond Jan 6, 1851 of $2,500 by Leroy Purdy, Bartholomew Jordan, Jonathan Jordan. Father, John McCartney had died in Dec 1849. Mother: Mary A. McCartney. Emma John and her mother resided in Georgia in 1856, Arkansas in 1859. Confederate tax for 1863 was $10.20. Final payment of estate Mar 1, 1871.

BOX 154 PACK 3712   ISAAC MORAGNE   1860

Will dated Sep 13, 1841. Filed Mar 19, 1850. Witnesses: P. F. Moragne, J. T. Allen, N. B. Moragne. Executor: W. C. Moragne. Wife: Margaret B. Moragne. Sons: Wm. C., John B. Daughter: Mary E. Appraisal Jun 20, 1850 by P. B. Moragne, Wm. Tennant, Dr. N. Harris, Dr. H. C. Middleton. Owned 35 slaves. Held notes on: A. A. Larrimore, Samuel Carter, Samuel Morrow, M. Ivey, James M. McCaslan, D. M. Rogers, W. McAllister, O. W. Wideman, Thomas Thompson, John Harmon, E. Tankersly, Wm. Glending, M> Gardner, O. T. Terry. Estate Sale Dec 25, 1852. Buyers at sale: Wm. H. Davis, Mary Moragne, M. L. Moragne, W. Atchison, Ann E. Moragne, H. H. Moragne, B. E. Gibert, P. B. Moragne, J. E. Martin, P. L. Guillebeau, W. C. Ware, E. C. Martin, D. M. Rogers, C. D. Palmer, Hugh G. Middleton, James P. Graves. 1851 taxes $56.75, 1852 taxes #38.36. Estate Settlement Dec 28, 1860. (9) Legatees received $119.69 each. No names.

BOX 154 PACK 3713   JANE McCREE   1850

Administrator: James Irwin. Bond Apr 15, 1850 of $1,600 by James Irwin, Samuel Irwin, Wm. Hill. Niece: Jane married Wm. N. Purdy. 1st Appraisal May 10, 1850 of $74.80 by David Keller, James Cunningham, Robert Goudy. 2nd Appraisal May 11, 1850 of $77.25 by Andrew Gillespie, John L. Boyd, Francis M. Brooks. Held notes on: James J. Gilmer, John McCord, Samuel Irwin. No Estate Sale made. Mar 28, 1850 Wm. N. Purdy ordered to appear at the Court of Ordinary held Apr 2, 1850 to answer why he had illegally seized the property of Jane McCree. Estate Settlement Jan 19, 1852. (2) Legatees each received $339.99. 1. James Irwin 2. Wm. N. Purdy in right of his wife Jane.

BOX 155 PACK 3365   JOHN CALVERT   1847

Long, involved estate with much litigation among sparring parties. Will dated Aug 20, 1846. Filed Jan 9, 1847. Witnesses: B. M. Stewart, W. S. Robertson. Executors: Robert A. Archer, Wm. C. Hill. Bond Jan 19, 1847 by Robert A. Archer, Wm. C. Hill, Joseph Dickson, J. S. D. Weatherall. Deceased died Jan 6, 1847. Daughters: Frances E. wife of Robert A. Archer, Lizzie D. wife of Wm. Davis, Percy Spillers, Lydia Wardlaw, Milly Patterson. Sons: James M., Mason, Jesse now deceased. Grandson: Wm. C. Hill who was born 1822 and his mother died in the same year following child birth. Appraisal Jan 25, 1847 by G. W. Hodges, Thomas E. Eakin, Joseph Dickson. Appraisal of land Aug 1857 by Aaron Lomax, Joseph Dickson, H. H. Penney. Owned 489 acres of land, 19 slaves. Estate Sale Jan 26, 1847. Buyers at sale. Silas Pace, John W. Moon, R. A. Archer, Wm. C. Hill, Thomas J. Douglass, G. W. Hodges, John Strawhorn, N. S. Cobb, Robert H. Winn, N. Simms, Joseph Dickson, John K. Vance, Wm. McNary, J. S. Adams, Joel Smith, G. W. Nickles, Wm. Smith, Nathaniel Rowland, Wm. H. Richey, T. L. Johnston, Thomas Eakin, Wm. Robertson, F. B. Logan, D. R. Caldwell, Joshua Davis. Apr 19, 1847 the following heirs ordered to appear in Ordinary Court: 1. Wm. Smith and his wife Frances 2. J. S. Anderson and his wife Caroline 3. Alex. Turner and his children 4. J. C. Elliott and his wife Dorcas 5. James Shillito and his wife 6. Wharton guardian of Mary Paul a minor 7. Wm. Purdy guardian of Eleanor Spillers a minor 8. Wm. C. Hill 9. Robert A. Archer and his wife Fannie 10. James Calvert. Again to appear in Ordinary Court: 1. J. J. Anderson and his wife 2. Mary Beasley 3. John Davis 4. Nancy Robertson 5. Silas Ray and Catherine his wife 6. Wm. Smith and his wife 7. James Shillito and his wife 8. J. C. Elliott and his wife 9. Alex Turner and his children. Sep 28, 1848 John Mason Calvert of Mississippi sold his right in estate for $5. Mason L. Calvert, the only child of Mason Calvert and Sarah who was now the wife of John Patterson also sold his right. Long case in Ordinary Court resulted.

BOX 155 PACK 3366   JOHN CALHOUN   1847

Administrator: Downs Calhoun. Bond Nov 29, 1847 of $6,000. Deceased had died 13 years previously. Widow: Agnes. Daughter: Margaret wife of Joseph B. Ware of Lincoln Co. Ga. Sons: Nathan P. age 22, Leonard age 20, Washington age 17, Thomas age 16, John age 13, Wm. P. now deceased with widow and infant son, Wm. W. Widow paid off all debts owed by the estate and completed the raising of her children. Appraisal Jan 1, 1848 by James H. Johnson, Wm. Campbell, Hazle Smith, Nathan Calhoun. Owned 12 slaves. Estate Sale Jan 4, 1848. Buyers at sale: Agnes Calhoun, Wm. Fooshe, Wade Anderson, Nathan Calhoun, James Gilliam, Hazle Smith, Thomas Pinson, Samuel Beard, Jasper Pinson, Walter Meriwether, George Anderson, John Sample, Thoomas Johnson, James Johnson, J. W. H. Johnson. Estate Settlement May 11, 1849. Widow received $1009.20. All children each received $312.67.

BOX 155 PACK 3367   JAMES CONNOR   1848

Administrator: A. P. Connor. Bond Nov 27, 1848 of $5,000 by A. P. Connor, W. W. Belcher, James Hanvey, James O. Connor. Deceased died Nov 3, 1848. Sons: A. P., Thomas, James O., Andrew J., George M. who had left S.C. 16 years earlier unmarried and not heard from since. Daughters: Elizabeth wife of A.C. Cofer, Matilda Ann wife of James A. Hanvey, Rebecca wife of M. D. Woods, Isabella Louise. Estate entered Court of Ordinary Mar 9, 1850. Appraisal Dec 9, 1848 by W. W. Belcher, Wm. McCelvey, Robert M. Craven. Estate Sale Dec 11, 1848 netted $1,627. Buyers at sale: A. P. Connor, T. P. Dowtin, N. Darracott, J. McCaslan, F. Wideman, W. M. Calhoun, C. Scott, Wm. McCelvey, J. O. Connor, S. J. Cowan, J. E. Foster, S. Zaner, O. Morrow, N. J. Middleton, T. B. Scott, Wm. N. Burdette, Wm. Cole, G. Burdette, S. S. Wilson, James Smith, W. D. Gallagher, T. Darracott, R. Thomson, J. LeRoy, James Hanvey, R. Keoun, -- Hudson, J. S. Foster, R. M. Craven, J. Y. Alexander, James Wilson, W. K. Bradley, A. L. Gibert, V. E. Nickles.

BOX 155 PACK 3368   WILLIAM P. CALHOUN   1849

Administrator: W. B. Meriwether. Bond May 11, 1849 of $300 by W. B. Meriwether, Downs Calhoun, Agnes Calhoun. At time of his death had Wife and (6) Children. Appraisal May 26, 1849 by Hugh Smith, Thomas J. Pinson, David W. Anderson. Estate Sale May 11, 1849 netted $85.43. Buyers at sale: Nancy Calhoun, Nathan Calhoun, Hugh Smith, David McCants, Samuel Johnson. Estate Settlement in 1849. Nancy Calhoun who received $138.28 and (1) child, not named.

BOX 155 PACK 3369   JOHN CARLILE   1848

Administrator: Frances Carlile-widow. Bond Nov 2, 1846 of $1,000 by Frances Carlile, Michael Kennedy, James T. Allen. Sons: James H., John P. Daughters: Ethel T., Margaret T. wife of Wm. T. Patterson. Son-in-Law: James O. Cosby. Appraisal Dec 23, 1846 by Alexander Oliver, James T. Allen, Charles Allen, James Grant. Estate Sale: Dec 23, 1846. No information on. Partial Estate Settlement Mar 7, 1848. No Information. Apr 2, 1849 Ethel T. Carlile received $15.

BOX 155 PACK 3370   ELIZABETH CARLILE & OTHERS (minors)   1855

(5) Minor Children of John Carlile deceased. Mother: Frances Carlile. Guardian: Frances Carlile. Bond Mar 12, 1848 of $1,000 by Frances Carlile, James H. Carlile, John J. P. Carlile. Minors were: 1. Elizabeth Frances 2. Wm. H. B. 3. Isaac N. 4. Daniel E. 5. Robert Wesley. Settlement Mar 11, 1848 each child to receive $31.15. Oct 27, 1851 Elizabeth Frances Carlile now wife of Wm. A. Lackey received $19. Feb 2, 1855 Wm. H. B. Carlile received $68.44.

BOX 155 PACK 3371   H. E., W. A., A. A. CHEATHAM (minors)   1852

Guardian: John Sadler who was the brother of Frances Cheatham, the mother and widow of Robert Cheatham whose estate had been settled Nov 29, 1849. 1st Bond Jan 1, 1850 of $2,500 by John Sadler, Nathaniel McCants, Simon Chaney. 2nd Bond Nov 3, 1851 of $900 by John Sadler, Simon Chaney, Alfred Cheatham. Minors were: 1. Amanda E. 2. Wm. Albert 3. Allen A. Jan 15, 1852 Allen A. received $88.74. Apr 24, 1854 Amanda E. now wife of W. W. Rotten received $92.93. Jan 13, 1859 Wm. A. received his legacy, amount not stated.

BOX 155 PACK 3372   MILTON CHEATHAM (his minors)   1847

Guardian: Mary A. Cheatham, mother. Minors: Martha Elizabeth, Mary Frances. Bond Mar 2, 1847 of $300 by Mary A. Cheatham.

BOX 155 PACK 3373   JOHN & THOMAS CALHOUN (minors)   1849

Guardian: Agnes Calhoun, mother. Minors: Thomas H. Calhoun, John W. Calhoun. 1st Bond Feb 7, 1849 of $1,500 by Agnes Calhoun, C. B. Fooshe, W. B. Meriwether, Meedy Mays. 2nd Bond Feb 7, 1849 of $1,500 by Agnes Calhoun, W. B. Meriwether, John Sadler. Settlement of Thomas H. Calhoun Feb 6, 1885 for $251.48. Settlement of John W. Calhoun Jul 12, 1859 for $330.09.

BOX 155 PACK 3374   LEONARD & GEORGE WASHINGTON CALHOUN (minors)   1850

Guardian: Downs Calhoun. Bond May 11, 1849 of $1,500 by Downs Calhoun, Wm. Carter, Pat Hefferman. Minors of John Calhoun. Each minor received on May 11, 1849 $304.86 from his father's estate. Settlement of Leonard Calhoun Jan 6, 1851. Settlement of George Washington Calhoun Jul 8, 1852. Downs Calhoun had died prior to the settlements.

BOX 155 PACK 3375   JOHN WILLIAM CALHOUN (minor)   1857

Guardian: Waller B. Meriwether. Bond May 7, 1849 of $600 by Waller B. Meriwether, C. B. Fooshe, James Owens, Newton M. Smith. Mother: Nancy Calhoun. Feb 6, 1857 John William Calhoun due $444.17. Still open Mar 2, 1863. Bond Feb 10, 1858 of $1,000 by Waller B. Meriwether, N. W. Stewart, John Wilkerson. Settlement Feb 8, 1867 in Court of Ordinary. John William Calhoun had been killed in the late war and Meedy Mays, his step-father, obtained Letters of Administration.

BOX 155 PACK 3376   JOHN CHILES   1850

Will dated Nov 22, 1843. Filed Aug 3, 1846. Witnesses: John C. Cothran, Thomas W. Chiles, Wm. O'Quinn. Executor: Thomas Chiles Perrin. Wife: Mary Elizabeth Chiles.

Son: James. Daughter: Mary wife of John W. Hearst. Step Son: Wm. P. Sullivan. Appraisal Jan 8, 1847 by John Cothran, Thomas W. Chiles, John Ruff, Samuel Perrin. Notes Held on: W. Chiles, Allen Reagan, John McBride, T. W. Talman, W. G. Keller, Jefferson Lyon, Edward Reagan, Samuel Jordan, Reed Rusell, J. M. Finley, J. B. Anderson, Thomas Law, W. White, Wm. Brown, A. Pressly. Owned 33 slaves. Accounts due the deceased: Bird Beauford, James Davis, W. White, M. Wanslow, Henry Bradley, J. M. Child, J. B Adamson, Mathew Cochran, Mary Robinson, W. P. Morris, Buck Smith, Caps Gallagher, Cato Reagan, Samuel Perrin, Tyra Jay, Mathew McClinton, James Drennan, Wm. Royal, John McCravy, W. G. Keller, Dr. H. Royall, Burkley Harris, Samuel Cook, John Reid Creswell, W. Clesky, T. W. Talman, John McClellan, A. Tittle, John Cothran, P. H. Bradley, T. W. Chiles, David Wiley, A. Bell, Craven harris, P. C. McQuinn, Andrew Weed, david Walker, Bead Harrison, W. Sullivan, W. Davis, Widow Skinner, John Jorbertson, Samuel Boggs, John McBryde, Allen Reagan, James White, Wiley Harris. Estate Settlement Jan 31, 1847. Wm. P. Sullivan was only name mentioned.

BOX 155 PACK 3377   JOHN L. CHEATHAM   1846

Oct 26, 1846 J. Bailey petitioned for a settlement of the estate as a creditor having claim for the funeral expenses. Dr. J. P. Calhoun agreed that he would see to a sale of the estate as he was soon to move out west. Personal property consisted of 1 horse, cows, hogs, corn & fodder, 2 guns and various furniture.

BOX 155 PACK 3378   JOSEPH CANTEY   1847

Administrator: S. Cantey, widow. Had Wife and (2) minor children. Personal goods sold in 1846. Owned 16 slaves that were sold in 1847 and 1848 for $5,668. Had an interest in an estate in Sumter District. Estate Settlement Jan 27, 1848 widow received $1802 as her 1/3 of estate.

BOX 155 PACK 3379   EDMOND COBB   1849

Will Dated Dec 5, 1848. Witnesses: S.G. Stewart, R. P. Stuart, Wm. M. Selby. Executors: Willis Smith, Henry Riley. Wife: Elizabeth Cobb. Son: Richmond S. Cobb. Appraisal Dec 12, 1849 by L. H. Rykard, S. G. Stewart, James Tolbert, George Weatherall. Estate Sale Dec 13, 1849 netted $3773. Buyers at sale: John Anderson, J. J. Tharp, L. H. Rykard, Widow, N. Anderson, W. Smith, E. Anderson, J. W. W. Marshall, S. G. Stewart, J. Foster, John Hughey, B. Reynolds, H. Riley, B. White, E. Davis, H. Boozer, Silas Ray, A. Vance, F. Atkins, J. Watson. Estate Settlement Dec 30, 1850. Legatees were Widow and (8) Children. Widow received $1,070 as her 1/3rd share. Children divided the remainder equally. 1. John Anderson received $326.93 the share of his (8) children: 1a. Wm. 2a. Edward 3a. Mary 4a. John 5a. James 6a. Andrew 7a. Nathaniel 8a. Margaret 2. Mary wife of Ephraim Davis 3. Edmond 4. Nathaniel 5. James 6. Not named 7. Not named 8. Not named.

BOX 155 PACK 3380   WILLIAM CHILES   1872

Will dated Nov 1, 1849. Witnesses: Thomas C. Perrin, Nathan T. Skinner, Mary R. Coleman. Executor: John Cothran, Thomas C. Chiles. Bond Feb 5, 1866 of $5,000 by T. C. Chiles, John C. Chiles, W. E. Cothran. Wife: Jane Chiles. Sons: Thomas Coleman, John William. Daughters: Julia A. wife of Samuel W. Cochran, Susan wife of – Spence, Emmaline wife of James T. Livingston, Ann, Eliza, Eunice Rebecca, Agnes wife of –White. 1st Appraisal Dec 10, 1849 by Thomas W. Chiles, John W. Hearst, W. Wideman, Samuel Perrin, Cary Patterson. 2nd Appraisal Feb 19, 1866 by W. E. Cothran, John C. Chiles, R.

H. Bradley. Thomas C. Chiles became Executor in Jan 1866. Jan 1, 1866 Jane Chiles received $946.53. Estate Sale Feb 20, 1866. Buyers at sale: Thomas C. Chiles, James Steifle, Andrew Weed, Tyra Jay, Wm. Johnson, Wade E. Cothran, R. T. Bell, James Martin, James Atkins, Samuel McQuerns, Wm. McCain, Hiram Tusten, John R. Moore, Henry Steifle, James F. Lyon, R. F. McCaslan, Lemuel O. Shoemaker, T. A. Watson, James Brannon, Wm. H. Butler, F. I. Cook, J. L. Ward, W. H. Rush, Thomas M. Jay, T. M. Stalnaker. (5) Legatees in Mar 1868: 1. Ann Steifle 2. Eunice Rebecca 3. Thomas C. 4. Agnes W. 5. John W. Jan 1, 1870 Eunice Rebecca, Agnes W., John W. each received $1,197.94. Estate Settlement Mar 2, 1870. James C. Steifle in right of his wife, Ann Eliza legacy of $353. This couple had a son, William C. Steifle.

BOX 155 PACK 3381   LUCY E. CALVERT   1847

Administrator: Wm. Smith. Bond May 18, 1847 of $2,000 by Wm. Smith, John White. She was the daughter of Jesse Calvert.

BOX 156 PACK 3661   ANN GOFF   1853

Administrator: John H. Wilson. Bond Feb 5, 1852 by John H. Wilson, Lucian H. Lomax, Wm. M. Haddon.

BOX 156 PACK 3662   DR. THOMAS R. GARY   1852

Administrator: S. M. G. Gary, Mary A. Gary. Bond May 12, 1852 of $100,000 by S. M. G. Gary, Mary A. Gary, Martin C. Gary, Hillery W. Gary. Wife: Mary A. Gary. Appraisal Jul 6, 1852 by Wm. Suber, N. Sims, W. McCants. Owned 38 slaves, 158 shares stock in Greenville & Columbia Railroad. Held and equal in the drug store of Dr. F. F. Gay. Held equal interest in the lands, property and slaves in Newberry managed by Martin C. Gary. Held notes on: P. W. Connor, T. C. Griffin, H. W. Ledbetter, Franklin F. Gary, M. Strauss, P. W. Suber, J. H. Stokes, L. D. Connor, W. C. Anderson, Elihus Watson, J. W. Suber, R. L. Mabry, Carter Rosamond. Old Notes due the firm of Gary & Gary, all of which considered to be worthless: W. H. Greene, Y. Beasley, R. P. Doyle, Stanmore Collins, Jesse C. Davenport, Jane Montague, John Chandler, Ethel Loveless, Nelson Norris, James W. Norris, Larkin Pulliam, Wm. Wilson, John Williams, James Knight, J. H. Sills, Edmund Smith, John W. Robertson, Nathaniel Haney, A. E. Scott, Wm. C. Smith, John W. McKellar, George Penney, Samuel A. Hodges. Taxes for 1853 $47.49. Estate Settlement Dec 1, 1854. Legatees were: 1. Widow, Mary A. received $12,002 2. M. Witherspoon Gary received $2.400 3. B. F. Griffin and wife, Elizabeth 4. Ann Victoria Gary & John H. Gary (minors) each received $2400 5. Wm. Gary, Allanta Gary, Luella Gary (minors) each received $7,200.

BOX 156 PACK 3663   JOSEPH GROVES   1850

Will (date missing). Filed Dec 3, 1850. Witnesses: James M. Latimer, Samuel Lindsay, C. T. Latimer. Deceased was a native of Prince George County, Maryland. He was the son of Solomon Groves and Elizabeth Nicholson. Wife: Sarah Groves. Sons: John Joseph, James Algary, Rignul Nicholson. Daughters: Elizabeth Yancey Arnold, Martha Hannah wife of Nelson Carter, Sarah Joseph wife of Wm. T. Hackett, Frances Emily wife of Thomas W. Gantt. Appraisal Dec 14, 1850 by John C. Mauldin, Alex. Oliver, Charles P. Allen, James T. Allen. Estte Sale Dec 22, 1859. Buyers at sale: James T. Barnes, Rev. L. W. Barnes, Rev. Christian V. Barnes, Wm. M. Bell, James Bruce, Dr. James T. Baskin, W. L. Brooks, J. T. Allen, J. F. C. DuPre, Rignul N. Groves, Ben. D. Kay, R. Hutchison, John M. Moseley, Wm. T. Mauldin, J. W. Power, T. M. Tucker, J. T. Groves, Wm. Kennedy, L.

L. Blackwell, W. Scoggins, R. H. Wilson, John V. Schroeder, John C. Speer, N. Cunningham, Joel Lockhart, E. Y. Arnold, Thomas Grant, John M. Middleton, T. O. McAdams, John Newby. Paid George W. Kelley $20 for coffin. Wm. T. and Sarah Joseph lived in Habersham Co., Ga. in 1859. Estate Settlement Dec 12, 1859 at Gantts in Dallas, Ga.

BOX 156 PACK 3664   MARGARET GRAHAM (minor)   1850

Daughter of John Graham. Grand Father: Wm. Graham. Guardian: Wm. Graham the grand father. Bond Oct 5, 1850 of $500 by Wm. Graham, Wm. C. Graham, W. J. Graham. Bond Jan 24, 1851 of $520 by Wm. Graham Sr., Wm. Graham Jr., Albert M. Graham. Jan 24, 1851 Grandfather petitioned that she was entitled to $260.55 from the estate of her father. Amount received the same month from Albert M. Graham, the executor of John Graham's estate. 1851 taxes 36 cents. Final return on estate took place in 1858.

BOX 156 PACK 3665   SARAH GLASGOW (minor)   1850

Guardian: Richard A. Martin. Bond Jul 10, 1850 of $1,500 by Richard A. Martin, A. Kennedy, J. McLane. She had a legacy coming from her grand mother Morrow's estate in Kentucky.

BOX 156 PACK 3666   JAMES N. GLASGOW (minor)   1850

Guardian: John Hunter, he died in early 1853 and W. W. Hunter became guardian. Bond Oct 7, 1850 of $1,000 by Richard A. Martin, J. F. McComb, A. P. Connor. Bond Mar 10, 1853 of $1,200 by John Hunter, Wm. W. Hunter, Absalom L. Gray. Settlement May 7, 1856. Minor received $37.78. Son of James Glasgow.

BOX 156 PACK 3667   BARNETT GOOLSBY   1850

Administrator: Wm. Goolsby. Bond Nov 13, 1850 of $180 by Wm. Goolsby, T. Brough, A. A. Humphries. He was entitled to a legacy from the estate of Harriet Goolsby. His father, Barnett Goolsby of Lincoln Co., Ga. was a brother of Harriet Goolsby.

BOX 156 PACK 3668   WILLIAM C. HACKETT   1851

Administrator: Martin C. Hackett. Bond Apr 7, 1851 of $8,000 by Martin Hackett, John White, T. L. Coleman. Father: Martin C. Hackett. Appraisal Apr 11, 1851 by T. L. Coleman, W. L. Templeton, Charles R. Moseley, Bennett Reynolds. Owned 5 slaves and Drug Store in Greenwood, S. C. T. G. Parks purchased the entire contents of the drug store. Estate Settlement May 13, 1853. (3) Legatees: 1. Thomas L. Coleman in right of his wife 2. M. B. Hackett, 3. Lewis Rogers of Ouchita Co., Ark. Open accounts due the drug store at time of his death: Wm. Burns, Adolphus Anderson, W. B. Buchanan, Y. Y. L. Partlow, J. W. Whitlock, Marion M. Tarrant, T. S. Bowie, Charles R. Moseley, W.W. & B. F. Wardlaw, Thomas Skinner, John Boozer, M. G. Ross, J. W. Watson, Thomas Chatham, John McKellar, L. B. Cobb, Nathan Calhoun, Miss Susan Crews, W. G. Bass, Miss Mary A. Boggs, Wm. Anderson, Peter Goodwin, Samuel Major, John West, Peter McKellar, J. O. Waller, Ben. Sales, Alex. Turner, James Ragsdale, James W. Pert, J. M. Tarbut, T.C. Crews, James M. Griffin, A. Waller, J. R. Tarrant, G. E. Leitner, Thomas Cobb, Wm. Cobb, Stanley Crews, C. A. Blake, Rev. John Boggs, Henry Boozer, Wm. Perryman, Dr. Spires, Ben. Blackaby, J. J. Tharp, M. B. Hackett, James Anderson, John Ferguson, Henry Wilkerson, Mrs. E. & W. H. Gaines, J. W. Childs, John Hefferman, R. M. White, W. Waller, Milton Osborn, Mandy Clark, C. N. Cunningham, M. A. Crews, Stanmore Brooks,

James Buchanan, J. J. Boozer, Lewis Bonds, R. M. White, M. G. Pope, James C. Ray, Nathaniel McCants, T. B. Byrd, Joel Fooshe, C. C. Hutchison, Rev. P. W. McCants, B. F. Roberts, D. Vaughn, Allen Vance, Martin Hackett, Martin Delaney, John F. Clark, James Creswell, T. C. Crews, W. C. Burns, Willis Buchanan, Mrs. E. Buchanan, Joshua Turner, David McCants, Henry Garrett, John Hill, John Johnson, A. P. Pool, Robert Leavel, W. B. Brooks, Mrs. E. Ross, John McKary, J. L. White,J. W. Richardson, Allen Dedrick, Alfred Dendy, Allen Dozier, James Douglass, William Douglass, Robert Ellis, John Ferguson, Jones Fuller, W. C. Fooshe, Joel Fooshe, James Fooshe, J. W. Fooshe, Mrs. E. Gaines, W. H. Gaines, Henry Garrett, J. M. Gage, Robert Gilliam, Sumter Gilliam, R. C. Gilliam, M. H. Green, W. C. Glover, John Goodwin, P. W. Goodwin, Gideon Hagwood, Ed Hinton, R. W. Hill, John Hill, C. C. Hutcherson, Vachel Hughey, J. M. Hughes, J. B. Johnson, J. W. Jones, Mrs. E. Jones, W. G. Kennedy, Joel Leary, Robert Leavel, Leavel & Cheatham, Dr. J. H. Logan, Anderson Logan, A. J. Logan, Andrew Logan, W. W. Logan, N. L. Lipscomb, M. Moss, Dr. J. Marshall, Mitchell Herndon, Nathaniel McCants, F. Miller, J. McNeill, Samuel Major, H. Malone, Dr. C. R. Moseley, Thomas Nichols, John Nickson, P. Y. L. Partlow, J. W. Pert, W. W. Perryman, Mathew Pool, --Pulliam, Rev. C. A. Raymond, B. Ramey, J. N. Ragsdale, J. Ray, J. N. Reeder, Andrew Riley, James Riley, D. Richardson, John Richardson, J. W. Richardson, B. Reynolds, Scott Sheldens, Miss Ann Sego, Mrs. E. Selvy, Henry Spikes, Dr. Spires, Miss A. Statom, Richmond Still, John Suber, M. M. Tarrant, Josh Turner, A. P. Roe, Mrs. N. Waller, Miss E. Waller, Pelius A. Waller, S. A. Walker, Hugh M. Wardlaw, Est. of Leroy Watson, G. Mc. Watson, S. W. Whitlock, Thomas Wier, Henry Wilkerson, Mrs. P. Wilson, Jefferson Wiss.

BOX 156 Pack 3669   LINSDSAY HARPER   1853

Will dated Nov 12, 1849. Filed Apr 22, 1850. Witnesses: Wm. H. Caldwell, Robert Hutchison, Peter S. Burton. Executor: James C. Harper. Bond Jan 18, 1851 of $13,745 by Henry H. Harper, James C. Harper. Wife: Jane Harper. Sons: Wm. H., Ezekiel W., James C., Lindsay Robert A., Henry H. B., John A. R. Daughters: Martha G. Oliver her son was Lyndsay H. Oliver, Sarah C. McGehee. Gave one acre of land to Ridge Meeting House for a grave yard. Merchant. Appraisal May 9, 1850 by Wm. Speer, Alex. Oliver, Peter S. Burton. Held notes on: Wm. H. Speer, Joseph Manning, John H. Moseley, James Marion Latimer, Thomas R. Seal, Philip Moseley, John Speer, Mrs. S. Raiford, G. W. Gantt, James Carlisle, Samuel Hill, Nelson Norris, W. P. Jones, E. Tribble, Josiah Burton, John Power, Wm. Prather, John A. Campbell, James E. Bell, M. Spearman, Robert H. Davis, H. L. Harden, James Speer, James Beasley, J. Warren, Ralph Gaines, Robert M. Davis, Dr. L. Yarborough, G.W. Kelley, A. Swearingham, Wm. Pruitt, Peter L. Burton, Alben Shackleford, Thomas O'Brient, Stephen H. Tucker, Ezekiel Tribble, John Eaton, Mathew Young, Mrs. Mary Moseley, Wm. H. Bell, Joseph Groves, E. T. Thompson, A. McCord, Thomas Hill, W. P. Jones, J. H. Cleveland, P. Crenshaw, John A. Harper, Andrew Hamilton, Nathaniel Gray, James Boles, Mrs. R. Leopard, L. McAllister, Mrs. Sarah Groves, B. Y. Martin, Wm. Gaines, Allen Shackleford, Mary Oliver. Open Accounts due to business at time of his death: J. B. Pressly, A. Swearingham, L. Yarborough, W. H. Caldwell, John Bowie, J. Manning, W. Scott, W. T. Scott, G. W. Kelley, James Bell, A. A. Moore, James M. Latimer, L. McAllister, J.A. Crawford, J. E. Caldwell, W. H. Bell, Wm. Prather, Dr. J. Barrett, B.S. Will, B. F. Williams, Amon Hall, J. E. Manning, W. C. Harper, Garland Jones, R. B. Carter, Mrs. Rosa Leopard, J. L. Boles, W. A. Speer, Thomas Tucker, J. W. Gantt, James Clark, Wm. Shaw, B. Stalnaker, Bartlett Tucker, John Tucker. Estate Sale Jan 7, 1851 netted $12,022. Estate Settlement Jun 7, 1853. Widow Jane had died Apr 24, 1853. Ezekiel W. harper had also died unmarried. Settlement was disputed and moved to Ordinary Court. Court of Ordinary Settlement Feb 18, 1856. $42738

40

distributed among the children listed earlier. Grandson: L. H. Oliver son of Martha G. Oliver and now Martha G. Caldwell received ½ of her share.

BOX 156 PACK 3670   SARAH HOGAN   1850

Administrator: A. L. Gray. Bond Nov 5, 1850 of $100 by A. L. Gray, J. W. Ramey, A. R. Ramey. Had one minor child, not named. Appraisal Dec 7, 1850 by Henry Atkins, Wm. Adams, Wm. Richey. Estate Sale Dec 8, 1850. Buyers at sale: Asbury R. Ramey, Wm. Adams, J. Wetherington, A. S. Gray, A. Stevenson, A. F. P. Douglass, B. Ramey, J. J. Hamilton, W. J. Hammond, W. Riley, Joseph Bridges, Thomas Cobb, Wm. Reynolds. Estate Settlement Jan 12, 1852.

BOX 156 PACK 3671   MARTHA HOUSTON   1849

Will dated Apr 10, 1849. Witnesses: Samuel W. Walker, Robert C. Harkness, John S. Carwile. Executor: Ezekiel L. Tribble. Bond Apr 5, 1852 by Ezekiel Tribble, Thomas J. Hill, Sterling Bowen. Grandson: Hugh D. Fleming. Appraisal Apr 23, 1852 by John Brownlee, Sterling Bowen, Robert C. Harkness, John S. Carwile. Owned 1 slave, 68 acres of land. Estate Sale Apr 23, 1852. Buyers at sale: Bailey Fleming, A. Parnell, H. D. Fleming, Wm. M. Carwile, E. H. Robertson, Wm. Mann, James H. Baskin. Estate Settlement Aug 6, 1856. (4) Legatees each receiving $64.58: 1. Bailey Fleming and wife Mary D. 2. Heirs of George Houston out of state 3. Nancy Hall or her heirs out of state 4. Mathew Houston out of state and received his payment on Feb 21, 1859.

BOX 156 PACK 3672   JOHN HARRIS   1851

Administrator: James McCaslan. Bond May 5, 1851 of $1,200 by James McCaslan, W. K. Bradley, P. M. O. McCaslan. Appraisal May 21, 1851 by M. O. McCaslan, J. E. Foster, Thomas A. Dowtin. Held notes on: James L. Lesly, F. A. Calhoun, Thomas Link, Joshua Wideman, John Faulkner, John Clem, John Faulkner.   Open Accounts due to deceased at the time of his death: Henry Cason, Pruitt & Cowan, Wm. K. Bradley, James A. McKee, John Robinson, Alex. L. McCaslan, A. T. Wideman, R. M. Stokes, Samuel Stewart. Estate Sale May 21, 1851. Buyers at sale: James McCaslan, Milly Harris, J. E. Foster, Wm. Watkins, Catherine Harris, James McLane, Columbus Wideman.   Estate Insolvent. Estate Settlement Dec 7, 1852.

BOX 156 PACK 3673   LOUISA HAYNIE   1851

Will dated Jun 26, 1851. Witnesses: W. P. Martin, B. F. Moseley, James Blain. Executor: Wm. Robertson. She was the daughter of Andrew Robertson and married Patrick C. Haynie on Dec 17, 1848. Sons: Wm. A. Pratt, James L. Pratt. Daughters: Sarah L. Pratt, Matilda Ophelia Pratt. Brothers: Andrew Robertson, Wm. Robertson. Appraisal Dec 1, 1851 by W. P. Martin, Ezekiel Rasor, Benjamin Smith. Owned 14 slaves. Held notes on: Nancy Robertson, Wm. Robertson, Wm. H. Austin. Estate Sale Dec 23, 1851. Buyers at sale: G. F. Mattison, Wm. Robertson, David Junkin, J. F. Coker, Nimrod Richey, Henson Posey, John Donald, Nancy Robertson. Paid $20 railroad assessment fee in 1853. Estate Settlement Mar 29, 1864. Only (2) Legatees mentioned. 1. Children of James L. Pratt with one the children now being dead 2. Daughter, Mrs. S. L. Tolleson $801.

BOX 156 PACK 3674   THOMAS S. HARRIS   1852

Administrator: James McCaslan. Bond Jan 5, 1852 of $2,000 by James McCaslan, M. O. McCaslan, David McLane. Wife died after his death leaving (3) children. Wade Cowan married his sister, Margaret Harris. 1st Estate Settlement Sep 5, 1852. Distributees 1. Robert W. Harris 2. Braxton Cason and wife, Elizabeth. 2nd Estate Settlement Dec 2, 1852. (8) Distributees each received $123.61.   1. Wm. H. Harris 2. M. C. Harris 3. John L. Cowan 4. Milly Harris 5. Mary Rentz 6. Catherine Harris.

BOX 156 PACK 3675   SUSAN & SAMUEL HANVEY (minors)   1852

Guardian: Wm. C. Hanvey, father. Bond Jun 2, 1852 of $50 by George M. Hanvey, James McGill, W. K. Bradley.

Box 156 PACK 3676   SAMUEL T. & MARGARET S. HANVEY (minors)   1852

Children of Wm. C. and Susan Wilson Hanvey. Grandfather was James Wilson. Guardian: Wm. C. Hanvey. Bond Dec 14, 1850 of $150 by Wm. C. Hanvey, W. K. Bradley, G. M. Hanvey. Guardian: Alexander P. Connor Dec 1853. Bond Jan 2, 1854 of $250 by Alexander P. Connor, James O. Connor, Wm. Watson. Settlement of Margaret S. Hanvey Feb 18, 1869. She received $60.58.

BOX 156 PACK 3677   JAMES THOMAS & WILLIAM H. HORTON (minors)   1852

Father: James C. Horton. Petition in 1850 of Mary Bentley shoed that she was the mother of the minors. Guardian: Wade Cowan. Bond Dec 5, 1850 of $1,200 by Wade Cowan, David McLane, James McCaslan. Guardian: James McCaslan. Bond of $1,813 by James McCaslan, David McLane, Wm. McCaslan. Settlement Nov 3, 1856 of Wm. Hollis Horton received $453.49 and Mar 16, 1866 received $126.77. Settlement Mar 10, 1863 of James Thomas Horton received $603.38. 1862 war tax $2.27 Confederate tax 1865 $26.40.

BOX 156 PACK 3678   NANCY ADELINE HINTON (minor)   1851

Guardian: Nathaniel Jeffries. Bond Dec 7, 1850 of $328 by Nathaniel Jeffries, H. A. Jones, Andrew Mantz. Bond Feb 11, 1854 of $500 by Nathaniel Jeffries, Henry A. Jones, Wm. Adams. She was due a legacy from the estate of her sister, Martha Turner. Settlement Dec 7, 1857. Nancy Adeline Hinton received $249.40.

BOX 156 PACK 3678 ½   NICHOLAS H. MILLER   1855

Settlement of Estate stretched over many years with several different executors or administrators. Sales were made several times and payouts made several times.   Will dated Aug 18, 1853. Witnesses: John Tennant, H. C. Miller, A. J. Oliver. Executors who served in order that they served: Littleton Yarborough, Thomas P. Quarles, Wm. Y. Miller. Wife: Mary died Jul 23, 1893. In 1855 owned 8 slaves and (5) separate tracts of land. Lands were sold Jan 6, 1874. Wm. Y. Miller became administrator in Aug 1893. Bond Aug 14, 1893 of $1,000 by Wm. Y. Miller, J. L. Mattison, B. T. Whitner. Appraisal Aug 1893 by Thomas P. Milford, Fraser Livingston, George C. Dusenberry. Estate Sale Nov 8, 1893. Buyers at sale: Mrs. Andrew J. Lythgoe, Aaron Harris, Richard Sondley, Pat Roche, Sanders Crawford, Mary Cowan, Phillip Martin, John Crawford, Henry Taylor, Henry Cowan, Ben. Bradley, Robert Smith, R. E. Cox, Wm. E. Lesley, Alf Aiken, J. F. Miller, Miss Mary Benson, Louis H. Russell, Henrietta Miller, Henry Bowen, Isaac Jenkins, M. M. Benson, W. P. Ferguson, H. Wilson, T. F. Ferguson, Wm. Y. Miller, James S Stark, J. R. Miller, M. Y. Ferguson, Stewart Williams, M. H. Wilson. Funeral expenses $44, tombstone $60, state taxes for 1893 $8.10. Estate Settlement Feb 12, 1894. (9) Distributees each received $36.28. All had received advancements 1876. 1. M. E.

Benson 2. Wm. Y. Miller 3. Henrietta F. Miller 4. Sallie A. McClung 5. James S. Stark 6. George W. Miller deceased 6a. W. M. Miller 6b. George A. Miller 6 c. Caroline Miller 6 d. Mary 6 e. J. Reed Miller 7. V. C. Lesley deceased 7 a. W. E. Lesley 8. Cornelia D. McClung wife of C. A. McClung deceased 8 a. Corrie Y. McClung 8 b. Mary Ferguson 8 c. C. H. McClung 9. Caroline Cozby wife of T. L. Cozby deceased 9 a. Langdon Cozby.

BOX 157 PACK 3415   SAMUEL D. GILLESPIE   1848

Oct 1848 Janet Gillespie, a minor, about 20 years old petitioned for John G. Baskin to be made her guardian to collect monies due her deceased brother, Samuel D. Gillespie for his services as a private in Co. E Palmetto Regiment in the late Mexican War. Guardian: John G. Baskin. Bond Nov 13, 1848 of $50 by John G. Baskin, Wm. Leslie Harris, -- Washington, D.W. Hawthorne. Apr 27, 1850 Land warrant, $211.62 in full distribution of mother's, not named, estate. Aug 5, 1850 Distributees were James L. H. Gillespie, Mary E. Gillespie.

BOX 157 PACK 3416   JOHN GARVIN   1848

Will dated Sep 25, 1836. Witnesses: James Caldwell, James Eaton, John Eaton. Willed Sarah C. Bowman a plantation of 160 acres in Gilmore Co., Ga. She had (5) children.

BOX 157 PACK 3417   HENRY R., JOHN M., ELIZABETH H. GOLDING (minors)   1850

Guardian: R. G. Golding. Bond Jan 1, 1850 of $650 by R. G. Golding, N. W. Stewart, Samuel Beard. Minors were children of John M. and Lucinda Golding. Money received in 1853 from the estate of N. C. Golding. Settlement in Ordinary Court Sep 25, 1855. Elizabeth $214, John M. $228, Henry R. 208. Jan 2, 1857 Washington Fooshe of Montgomery Co., Tex applied for letters of guardianship.

BOX 157 PACK 3418   MARY W. & ELIZA R. GAGE (minors)   1848

Father: J. M. Gage. Guardian: Ephraim R. Calhoun. Bond Sep 1, 1848 of $2,000 by Ephraim R. Calhoun, L. J. White, Wm. N. Blake.

BOX 157 PACK 3419   CADOR GANTT   1846

Will dated Aug 3, 1845. Proved Jan 2, 1849. Witnesses Wm. D. Hampton, George W. Nelson, John Milford. Wife to get all real estate, sale of property to Bible Society, following relatives to get $2 each: Joseph Pratt, Wm. Pratt, Josiah Burton, Tyra Gantt, Frederick Gantt, John Gantt, Giles Gantt, James Pratt, David Pratt, Jacob Lollar, Yate Perkins, Richard Alexander, Sampson Gantt. Cador Gantt Milford, son of Mary Milford $100, Gantt Wright, son of John L. Wright $100. Negro woman, Phyllis, to be made free. 1st Executor A. G. Latimer died Jan 16, 1850. 2nd Executor: Thomas Crawford. Bond Aug 12, 1849 of $1,600 by Thomas Crawford, Wm. Pratt, Andrew C. Hawthorne. 1st Appraisal jan12, 1849 by John Callaham, Wm. Duncan, Basil Callaham, John Clinkscales, Bennett McAdams. 1st Estate Sale Jan 17, 1849. Buyers at sale: Jesse Robinson, Wm. D. Hopkins, J. R. Wilson, J. Alewine, John Callaham Sr., J. F. Burton, Stephen Latimer, Wm. Armstrong, J. Bryant, Sherard G. Callaham, B. Netts, James M. Carwile, Basil Callaham, H. Robinson, B. Lowe, John Pratt, R. Ashley, W. Duncan, John M. Hopkins, Thomas Davis, J. Pearman, Col. Haney, J. L. Callaham, O. Shirley, Wm. Fisher, James Murdock, J. M. G. Branyon, George Ricketts, Thomas F. Branyon, J. R. Wilson, A. G. Latimer, John Kay, Wm. Burton, J. Pratt Sr. 2nd Estate Sale Nov 15, 1858. Buyers at sale: F. Mitchell, Caleb Burton, Peter Ricketts, George Shirley, J. Barnes, John Branyon, Ben. F. Hughes, George

Alewine, James Hopkins, J. A. Alewine, Nancy Pratt, John B. Armstrong, Jacob Alewine, James Darby, Sherard Calllaham, Bird Shaw, Wm. T. Shaw, Thomas Branyon, John Clinkscales, Samuel Callaham, H. E. Hughes, Wm. L. Burton, James Callaham, Wm. Duncan, J. W. Shirley, Thomas Crawford, T. J. Hughes, John Duncan, Jackson Shaw, David Duncan, Jackson Griffin, George Duncan, Basil Callaham, Fields Burton, James Hopkins, James Adams, Wm. Fields, James Darby, Stephen Latimer, S. M. Fisher, Joseph Alewine, S. McClelland, Wm. Armstrong, Mrs. Ashley. Taxes for 1850 $2.26, for 1853 $2.56, for 1854 $3.14. Gravestones (J. D. Chalmers) $15.68. Funeral expenses (H. Robinson) $2.20. Estate Settlement Nov 21, 1859. No names.

BOX 157 PACK 3420   HARRIET GOOLSBY   1848

Administrator: Henry A. Jones. She had no husband or lineal descendant. Appraisal Dec 16, 1848 at Mount Carmel by H. H. Townes, James McKelvey, Albert A. Humphreys, R. A. Martin. Estate Sale Dec 1848 netted $850. Estate Settlement Jan 16, 1850. (8) Distributees each received $79.81. Only (2) names mentioned: 1. Thomas Brough 2. Mary Hanvey represented by her son, Charles K. Hanvey.

BOX 157 PACK 3421   VINCENT GRIFFIN   1855

Very large estate with pages of names owing to estate, due money from the estate, buying at the Estate sale, etc. Will dated Dec 8, 1846. Witnesses: James F. Watson, John P. Barrett, John Marshall. To be buried at the grave yard at Nathan Lipscomb's old place by the side of his first wife. Tombstones to be placed over both graves. Wife: Agnes Griffin. Sons all under the age of 21: John Leonard, James Monroe, Vincent, George White, Thomas Joseph. Daughters: Frances E. Williams, Lucinda S. Crozier, Sarah Ann Edwards. Grandson: James Edwards. Appraisal Jan 22, 1847 of $28,226 by John P. Barratt, John Hearst, James F. Watson. (84) Individuals had notes or accounts due him. Estate Sale Nov 29-Dec 6, 1852. Many buyers.

BOX 157 PACK 3422   JESSE GHENT   1849

Administrator: Gabriel M. Mattison, Wm. P. Martin. Bond Oct 1, 1849 of $14,000 by Gabriel M. Mattison, Wm. P. Martin, A. H. McGehee, Wm. M. Moseley, Noah R. Reeve. The deceased died Sep 14, 1849. Appraisal Nov 19, 1849 by Noah R. Reeve, Wm. M. Moseley, Wm. Long, C. T. Latimer. Owned 19, slaves. Held notes on 81 individuals. Estate Sale Nov 20, 1849 netted $9,998. More than 80 buyers at sale. Daniel Ghent and Noah Ghent were brothers that lived in Benton Co., Alabama. Sally Ghent was a sister that lived in Benton Co., Alabama. Sarah Nash was a sister that married George Nash and died in Benton Co., Alabama Sep 10, 1849. Nov 5, 1849 Benjamin Mattison who had married Jane Ghent, a sister, protested against the possibility of Daniel Ghent being granted as administrator. Greenville & Columbia Railroad stock sold Dec 18, 1854. No later entries.

BOX 157 PACK 3423   JAMES GLASGOW   1849

Will dated Feb 12, 1847. Witnesses: James F. Mabry, James Cason, A. N. Darracott. Executor: Moses O. McCaslan. Daughters: Sarah, Mary McClellan, Jane E. Burdette wife of Giles Burdette, Nancy C. Hunter wife of William W. Hunter. Sons: James, Thomas M. Appraisal Nov 30, 1849 by James McCaslan, Thomas P. Dowtin, John Wideman. Estate Sale Nov 30, 1849 netted $232. Buyers at sale: Thomas P. Dowtin, James Cason, Wm. Hunter, W. T. Glasgow, Robert Kerr, Daniel Holder, Dr. Sanders, Elizabeth Thornton, John Wilson, Fannie Beard, S. Zaner, Giles Burdette, Ren. G. Burdette, Thomas Link,

George McKinney, Thomas Glasgow, Dr. McComb, George Zaner, Stephen Smith, James Kerr, J. E. Foster, John Creswell, John Baughman, Henry Charles, J. V. Alexander. Jan 2, 1850 Thomas M. Glasgow, Wm. W. Hunter, Giles Burdette filed petition stating dissatisfaction with the unfavorable paper field in the Ordinary Office concerning their claim of the imbecility of James Glasgow. Estate Settlement Aug 3, 1853. (2) Legatees each received $95.48. 1. James N. Glasgow 2. Sarah McKinney. The will was disputed as Mrs. Glasgow brought the will to Clear Spring Academy for the witnesses to sign. Witnesses did not see the contents nor have the will read to them prior to signing as witnesses.

BOX 157 PACK 3424   JOHN M. GOLDING   1849

He died Oct 9, 1848. Administrator: R. G. Golding. Bond Nov 4, 1848 of $1,000 by R. G. Golding, N. W. Stewart, C. B. Fooshe, A. Cheatham. Wife: Lucinda Golding. Appraisal Nov 8, 1848 by John R. Tarrant, C. B. Fooshe, John Pardue. Owned 179 acres of land. Accounts & Notes held on: R. G. Golding, James Pert, E. Hodges, N. W. Stewart, S. K. Taylor, John Pardue, E. W. Seawright, Wm. Eddins, Nathaniel McCants, J. R. Tarrant, H. Clark, James Malone, Thomas C. Lipscomb, A. Vance, R. C. Griffin, Zachariah W. Carwile, J. T. Carter, Watson & Waller, H. Y. Gilliam, James Gilliam, James Creswell, J. Turner, Dudley Bird, J. L. Cheatham, S.G. Cook, W. H. Griffin, Wm. Douglass. Estate Sale Apr 1, 1850 netted $672.48. Buyers at sale: James W. Pert, Charles W. Fooshe, John Pardue, D. W. Anderson, John R. Tarrant, W. H. Griffin, Wm. Milford, Dr. Sampson V. Caine, Reuben G. Golding, Nathaniel McCants, Wm. Thompson, W.A. Douglass, Harris Y. Gilliam, Thomas Hanvey, Charles B. Fooshe, Alfred Cheatham, Samuel Beard, Patrick Hefferman, James Malone, Thomas Farmer, N. L. Lipscomb, N. W. Stewart, James W. Johnston, Wm. L. Golding, Henry Briand, Allen Vance, Guilford Waller. Estate Settlement Apr 1, 1850. All the children of John M. Golding were deceased. Legatees: 1. Lucinda Golding $29.24 2. (3)Minor children of James M. Golding (Henry R., John M., Elizabeth Helena) each received $19.49.

BOX 157 PACK 3425   JEREMIAH GIBERT   1849

Administrator: Alexander Hunter. Brother had refused to act as administrator. Bond Oct 15, 1849 of $2,000 by Alex. Hunter, Alex. Scott, Andrew Giles. Physician. He died Sep 13, 1849. Appraisal Nov 17, 1849 by Andrew Giles, Jacob Martin, Thomas Cunningham. Owned 4 slaves. Held notes on: D. T. Saxon, Peter Gibert, Anthony Harmon. Estate Sale Nov 23, 1849. Buyers at sale: Peter Gibert, Alex. Hunter, Thomas Cunningham, Jacob J. Uldrick, Dr. A. B. Arnold, D. T. Baskin, Wm. Power, Jacob, Martin, Samuel Hester, Dr. Walker.

Box 157 PACK 3426   JOHN GRAHAM   1847

Administrator: Albert M. Graham. Bond Nov 1, 1847 of $6,000 by Albert M. Graham, Wm. Graham Sr., Wm. Graham Jr. Appraisal Nov 1, 1847 by Larkin Griffin, T. Coleman Griffin, John W. Moore, Thomas Rosemond. Estate Sale: Nov 16, 1847 netted $3,846. Buyers at sale: E. Carter, Richard Goings, C. W. Graham, Wm. Ware, E. T. Graham, G. W. Huckabee, E. Y. Graham, Alex. Agnew, Wm. C. Hill, Thomas Ivins, J. H. Vance, H. Mays, A. M. Graham, W. Graham, S. Graham, Samuel Agnew, John W. Moore, D. C. Griffin, J. T. Hill, John Shackleford, Meedy Mays, James M. Calvert, Evesley Robertson, J. R. Roderic, Newton Sims, James Rosamond, Abram Henderson, John Smsith, Larkin Griffin, R. Gaines, Isaac Richey, John Shanklin, James Moore, Miss Susan Hill, E. Campbell, Samuel Agnew, J. Strain, Neeley Robertson, John Rosamond, Thomas

Rosamond, Joseph Daniel, John Strawhorn, H. Callahan, Wm. Moore, Thomas Akins, W. Franklin, Daniel Ligon. Estate Settlement Feb 6, 1869. Daughter Sarah M. Paddon wife of James E. Paddon of Cobb Co., Ga. Earlier Distributees had been: 1. Son, James M. Graham 2. Son, Calvin Graham 3. Son, John Graham had received his share Jan 4, 1859 4. Daughter, Mary H. received her part Feb 10, 1857 5. Daughter, Eliza wife of Franklin Gaines had received $240 Feb 10, 1857 5. Son, James M. Graham received his part Nov 11, 1862 6. Daughter, Martha J. Graham received her part Jan 25, 1851 7. Wm. P. Graham 8. Daughter, Sarah M. Graham. Original Settlement had been made on Jan 9, 1850 with there being (9) Distributees. Albert M. Graham married Frances E. Hill.

BOX 158 PACK 3427   GEORGE A. ALLEN   1861

Will dated Dec 28, 1861. Witnesses: Thomas Mahon, F. A. Connor, S. E. Graydon. Wife: Sophronia Allen. Daughter: Lynn Allen. Son: George Gabriel Allen. Step Daughters: Imogen Cantey, Mary J. Cantey. Appraisal Oct 21, 1861 by J. N. Cochran, F.A. Connor, S. E. Graydon. Owned 26 slaves, owned ½ interest in power plant at Ware Shoals, owned 721 acres of land in several tracts, owned a house and lot of 6.5 acres in Cokesbury. Estate Sale Nov 11, 1862. Buyers at sale: Mrs. M. C. Wilson, M. Strauss, J. B. Black, F. F. Gary, Thomas Mahon, Ezekiel Rasor, L. D. Connor, Jesse Kennels, Dr. N. Sims, Larkin Mays, J. Killingsworth, W. Ware, W. McNary, John Vance, J. C. Allen, S. B. Jones, A. T. Watson, J. J. Smith, J. W. W. Marshall, Gabriel Hodges, S. Agnew, S. E. Graydon, D.S. Beacham, J. F. smith, L. D. Connor, P. W. Connor, J. J. Adams, J. C. Rasor, L. Bailey, M. M. Wilson, B. C. hart, Mrs. S. A. Allen. Taxes for 1861 $91.73 for 1862 $52.67.

BOX 158 PACK 3427 ½   JAMES R. TODD   1878

Will dated Sep 4, 1876. Witnesses: Andrew C. Hawthorne, H. E. Bonner, D. W. Hawthorne. Deceased die Sep 29, 1878. Executors: James E. Todd, A. Y. Thompson, H. M. Young. Wife: Jane L. Todd. Son: James E. Todd. Daughter: Eliza Frances Todd. Heirs in 1886 were: 1. May wife of A. Y. Thompson 2. John M. Todd 3. Flora wife of H. M. Young 4. James E. Todd 5. Eliza F. Todd 6. Louisa J. Todd 7. Charles E. Todd 8. Carrie L. Todd 9. Nannie W. Todd 10. Maggie M. Todd 11. Samuel J. Todd. Estate Settlement Mar 15, 1917. Widow had recently died. Previous accounting had taken place Sep 8, 1886. Amount of estate was $15, 834. Disbursements were to: 1. Mrs. Mary E. Thompson $1, 199.24 2. Estate of E. O. Todd same amount 3. Mrs. Flora Young wife of D. M. Young same amount 4. J. E. Todd same amount 5. Mrs. Eliza F. Stewart same amount 6. Mrs. Louisa J. McCain same amount 7. Mrs. Carrie L. Fleming same amount 8. Mrs. Nannie W. Barton same amount 9. Samuel J. Todd same amount. 10. Mack Lumus, Catherine Lumus, John Lumus each received $399.74 11. A. L. Eckles, Rogers Eckles, Joseph Eckles each received $399.74. Pack also contains papers relating to Complaint for relief filed in Laurens and Court of Equity in Laurens in case of James B. Higgins of which James R. Todd stood as a bond surety in Apr 1864.

BOX 158 PACK 3428   JOSHUA J. ASHLEY   1863

Administrator: Martha F. Ashley, wife. Bond Aug 1, 1862 of $300 by Martha F. Ashley, Moses L. Ashley, John Smith. Appraisal Aug 19, 1862 by Basil Callaham, Thomas Davis, S. B. Kay. Estate Sale Aug 19, 1862 netted $261. Buyers at sale: James Pressly, James Taylor, Thomas Davis, Richard Taylor, James M. Callaham, John Smith, James Davis, Moses Ashley, W. T. Phillips, James Patterson, Charlotte Moore, Martha Ashley, Nancy Pratt, Hugh Robinson, Samuel Hall, J. E. Uldrick. Estate Settlement Jan 13, 1863

BOX 158 PACK 3428 ½   WILLIAM H. PEAKE   1880

He died Nov 26, 1878. Wife: Julia F. Peake was the only heir. Administrator: James W. Peake. Bond Dec 24, 1878 of $800 by James W. Peake, J. C. Jennings, P. A. Covin. Much litigation between Julia F. Peake and James W. Peake. James W. Peake protested setting out 425 acres to Julia F. Peake on the grounds that he had promised to pay on Feb 24, 1874 $8,000 for mortgage on 1,400 acres. 425 acres excessive as mortgage was not paid. Court named E. G. Newby , Cat Corley, P. A. Covin on Jul 21, 1879 to set out land due Julia F. Peake. 260 acres set aside for her. Mar 14, 1882 mortgage declared fraudulent as James W. Peake had not paid debts. Estate held notes on: M. M. Brown, Willie Norman, Powell Pinckney, Jerry Butler, P. W. Sale M. Tanhorn. All notes worthless. Estate Sale Jan 17, 1879. Buyers at sale: J. J. Hussie, N. W. Stevenson, B. F. Bouchillon, Fred Searles, J. Peake, John Price, Andrew Guillebeau, Dr. Gibert, Wm. Harmon Julia Peake, J. C. Jennings, J. A. Deason, E. A. Searles, W. T. Jennings. Estate Insolvent.

BOX 158 PACK 3429   WILLIAM A. ALLEN   1861

He died Jun 28, 1861. Administrator: Charles H. Allen. Bond Oct 14, 1861 of $3,000 by Charles H. Allen, James A. Allen, Jane L. Allen. Owned a set of dental instruments.

BOX 158 PACK 3430   JOSIAH ASHLEY   1863

Confederate Soldier died at Warrenton, Va. Sep 11, 1862 from wounds at Manassas. Widow and an infant child. Administrator: Joshua Ashley, father. Bond Nov 24, 1862 of $3,000 by Joshua Ashley, George W. Bowen, J. P. Milford. Appraisal Dec 12, 1862 by John T. Haddon, George W. Bowen, Basil Callaham. Estate Sale Dec 12, 1862 netted $954. Buyers at sale: Nancy Patterson, Joshua Ashley, George W. Bowen, Samuel L. Davis, Rebecca M. Ashley, John T. Haddon, Sterling Bowen, John Smith, Robert A. Tucker, Wm. S. Phillips, Jacob Alewine, Jesse M. Cann, Christopher Ellis, Wm. Clinkscales, J. L. Simpson, Malinda J. Anderson, Thomas Davis, Albert Johnson, John M. Bryant, Sarah Black, Abraham F. Haddon, Basil Callaham. Confederate tax for 1863 $1.36, for 1864 $3.80. Estate Settlement May 17, 1868. Widow was now wife of D. P. Hannah. Widow $235.38, Child $470.78.

BOX 158 PACK 3430 ½   JAMES GILLIAM   1878

Will date Oct 2, 1875. Witnesses: John McLees, J. Bailey, Thomas Duckett. Executor: Robert C. Gilliam. Deceased died Jul 25, 1878. (6) Parts to the will: 1. Susan Rudds Children except Meredith who had previously received large legacy 2. Elizabeth Hill 3. Mary S. Gilliam wife of Son, Robert C. Gilliam 4. Cornelia Holland's children including the son of Carrie Law 5. Children of James M. Gilliam deceased 6. Sallie C. Anderson. Elizabeth Shile to have home place. Appraisal Oct 22, 1878 by J. Bailey, G. M. Jordan, A. M. Aiken. Estate Sale Dec 11, 1878. Buyers at sale: Sallie Anderson, S. V. Hinton, F. R. Puckett, James Bailey Sr., Robert C. Gilliam, C. A. C. Waller, Edward V. Hinton, A. M. Aiken, K. Langley, Aaron Richardson, Major Chappell, George Williams, A. Blythe, Mrs. E. A. Hill, H. F. Fuller, Wm. Scott, Jerry Evans, C. Jackson, A. McNeill, T. T. Riley, J. F. Watson, W. W. Coleman, Wm. E. Anderson, Mrs. Emma Anderson, E. P. Holland, B. Reynolds. Estate Settlement Aug 8, 1882. Legatees (6) each received $694.9: 1. Mary S. Gilliam 2. Susan Rudd's children: W. G. Rudd, G. H. Rudd, S. C. Owens 3. Sallie C. Anderson 4. Elizabeth Hill 5. Cornelia Holland's children: E. P. Holland, E. J. Anderson,

Carrie Law 6. James M. Gilliam's children: Lillie Gilliam, Anne J. Brown who lived in Arreondo, Fla.

BOX 158 PACK 3431   THOMAS J. BRITT   1862

Confederate Soldier. Killed in battle in Virginia. Pine case and box $161, transportation of body home $36.35. Partner in the store of Cowan & Britt. Administrator: James U. Britt. Bond Aug 22, 1862 of $20,000 by James U. Britt, Joseph S. Britt, James H. Britt. Appraisal Aug 30, 1862 by J. S. Britt, Benjamin Talbert, J. H. Britt. Estate Sale Sep 16, 1862. Accounts due Cowan & Britt 1861-1862: Travis Bearden, G. W. Nelson, J. C. Guillebeau, D. J. Wardlaw, J. B. Britt, J. B. McKittrick, Samuel Jordan, Jesse Jay, N. B. Petit, Henry Wideman, Phares Martin, J. L. Lesly, Mathew Goodwin, Jane B. Foster, James W. Porter, James Hanvey, Edwin R. Perryman, David Morrah, A. B. Houston, Peter B. Moragne, Jane B. Foster, M. Magrath, L. B. Wideman, Thomas Link, Ben. E. Gibert, C. W. Cowan, Wm. G. Neel, N. Ennis, M. Wideman, Henry Pinder, Joshua Wideman, L. N. Talbert, J. A. Crawford, James McLane, Enoch Breazeal, Redmond Brown, B. C. Walker, John Elkins, J. J. Palmer, A. L. Sullivan, Elizabeth Walker, W. C. Scott, Samuel Jordan, M. B. Sturkey, J. L. Bouchillon, James Hanvey, Wm. Bradley, Nicholas Cook, J. C. Cox, E. Cowan, G. & C. W. Corsaw, L. L. Wells, M. L. Cox, John Sanders, Agnes Law, B. C. Napper, Amelia Dowtin, W. N. Franklin, John Agner, Joshua Wideman, Francis Wideman, Wm. Truitt, John W. Jones, Shepard G. Cowan, W. M. Brown, Josiah Patterson, N. T. Crawford, J. H. Jones, C. A. Wideman, Peter B. Moragne, Levi Pitts, W. W. Belcher, J. C. Tull, Samuel Carter, Wm. D. Mars, C. A. Wideman, M. W. Lyles, Hiram Palmer, A. Bradley, W. Walker, Permelia Britt, Wiley Newby, Wm. Tennant, N. W. Palmer, James A. Ennis, W. A. Tucker, A. A. McKittrick, John W. Roberts, P. D. Guillebeau, J. L. Bouchillon, J. Wm. Mathis, Rogers & Calhoun, B. E. Gibert, M. O. McCaslan, B. McCraven, L. A. Link, L. J. Willard, L. T. Willard, J. S. Talbert, Robert Crawford, H. P. Brown, J. C. Henderson, R. McCraven, M. S. Talbert, P. A. Covin, J. T. Jordan, H. P. Black, Thomas Hemminger, B. E. Gibert, David W. Dowtin, M. L. Cox, George W. Cox, W. McKelvey, S. H. Jones, James Taggart, George Brown, Mrs. L. Bearden, J. P. Kennedy, Adam Wideman, Wm. McCaslan, R. A. McCaslan, Hezekiah Burnett, James H. Reagan, Isaac Kennedy, Miss M. A. Wilson, P. C. McCaslan, Wm. Bradley, John Baughman, James Banks, George Bradley, J. C. Belcher, Monroe Beauford, Miss M. A. Elmore, Miss J. B. Foster, Dr. T. T. Skinner, James Hanvey, Turnage Johnson, S. S. Wells, W. A. Tucker, Howard Strother, Est. of J. B. Britt, H. P. Black, J. C. Hayes, J. F. Edwards, James Martin, John Patterson, G. T. Barksdale, Edward O. Reagan, F. McNair, E. B. Perry, W. Ford, Sarah Wideman, Ed Wideman, N. W. Willard, H. Bonder, N. U. Palmer, M. B. Sturkey, W. H. Taggart, W. M. Rogers, G. T. Banks, Mrs. S. Searles, W. W. Hill, J. A. Crawford, John Sanders, Miss M. L. Traylor, W. O. Palmer, Miss H. P. Brown, H. T. Cox, Sarah Jordan, Miss M. C. Foster, Mrs. S. Kennedy, Joseph Creswell, J. H. Wideman, James Shanks, Wm. Postell, Wm. S. Mathis, Mrs. Agnes Lane, James Glasgow, James McLane, L. G. Patterson, Wm. Truitt, Wm. Ponder, Don Jay, Samuel Brown, James Morris, Daniel New, W. E. Link, Est of John DeLa Howe, C. B. Guggin, Josiah Patterson, J. C. Belcher, J. L. Lesly, Patrick Lindsay, Samuel Levall, Otis Dilleshaw, J. E. Foster, Thomas Link, Mrs. S. B. Jones, A. J. Harris, Mrs. H. Goodwin, James Searles, Miss M. Dowtin, J. C. Dowtin, James McLane, N. Napier, J. F. Calhoun, A. P. Connor, Mrs. E. Clary, James Creswell, J. L. Bouchillon, Wm. M. Brown, Miss S. Britt, John Young, Samuel Tucker, Wm. Barksdale, G. W. Nelson, J. E. Foster, Dr. J. A. Gibert, John McBryde, Mrs. M. Wideman, Est. of Mrs. S. Mathis, Jane Cain, Robert Keoun, A. McCaslan, Samuel Zaner.

BOX 158 PACK 3432   JAMES BENSON   1862

Administrator: James A. Ellis, son-in-law. Bond Nov 15, 1861 of $6,000 by James A. Ellis, John R. Sale, James C. Ellis. Appraisal Dec 3, 1861 by A. P. Boozer, John S. Hinton, N. M. Mars. Estate Sale Dec 3, 1861. Buyers at sale: Widow, Milton Blake, J. A. Bailey, J. W. Irwin, Ben. Roberts, Thomas Ellis, S. B. Jones, James Riley, Allen Vance. Taxes for 1861 $8.50. Confederate tax for 1862 $12.14.

BOX 158 PACK 3433   W. W. BURRISS   1862

CSA soldier who died in Virginia.   Widow, (3) brothers, (1) sister, no children. Administrator: Mary Ann Burriss, wife. Bond Sep 19, 1862 of $15,000 by Mary A. Burress, Elizabeth L. Taylor, T. B. Milford. Appraisal Oct 28, 1862 by A. Rice, Robert Stuckey, W. S. Bakin. Owned 3 slaves. Estate Sale Oct 29, 1862 netted $4,039. Buyers at sale: Thomas Gantt, J. F. C. DuPre, Wm. M. Bell, J. L. Bryant, J. A. Burriss, Ben. D. Kay, Doris Hall, J. P. Tucker, Wm. A. Lesly, W. S. Baskin, Henry Burton, J. N. Burriss, Adnrew Latham, W. J. Milford, Pleasant Ferguson, D. Whitman, J. R. Caldwell, G. McMahan, R. H. Hall, Wm. Campbell, Robert Simpson, Wdow Cann, R. H. Hall, Dr. N. J. Newell, J. W. Cann, Joshua Burriss, Oziah L. McMahan, James McKee, Thomas T. Cunningham, Frank Adams, Thomas B. Milford, W. J. Robertson, Rev. A. Rice, Wm. Boyd, Wm. White, Jesse Campbell, B. A. McAllister, F. P. Robertson, S. Bowen, Robert S. Harden, M. Simpson, Henry S. Cason. Joanna Campbell was a sister of Mary Ann Burriss who testified that her sister had held back items from the sale. The sisters were not on speaking terms. 1862 war tax $14.27. Estate Settlement Mar 28, 1864 with (5) Legatees: 1. J. C. Burriss $39.85 2. Jane C. Burriss $302.34 3. J. F. Burriss $39.85 4. Sarah Burriss $302.34 5. Joseph N. Burriss $302.34. Final Estate Settlement Oct 31, 184 with each of the above receiving $39. 85.

BOX 158 PACK 3434   SAMUEL R. BROWNLEE   1861

Will dated Dec 6, 1861. Witnesses: Andrew C. Hawthorne, Robert C. Sharp, James P. Pressly. Executors: Louisa Brownlee, wife, J. L. Miller. Wife: Louisa Brownlee. Mother: Ann Brownlee. Sons: 1. James Lawrence Brownlee who lived in Rankin Co., Miss. in 1882 2. Robert Calvin Brownlee 3. Davis Brownlee. Appraisal Oct 30, 1862 of $18,709. Owned 15 slaves, 313 acres of land with some of the land being in the Town of Due West. Held notes on: Robert Archer, Robert Brownlee, Martha McGaw. In 1882 children all agreed to take the property together and not sell it as specified in the will.

BOX 158 PACK 3435   JOHN A. BURTON   1863

Administrator: Joseph F. Burton. Appraisal Nov 17, 1862 by James M. Carwile, James B. McWhorter, M. McGee. Held notes on: Wm. Crowther, R. A.Tucker, Nancy L. Burton, Sarah Burton, Thomas M. Tucker, B. T. Gray, Wm. L. Burton, M. McGee, Samuel Shaw, James M. Hopkins, C. Wakefield, Basil Callaham. Estate Sale Nov 17, 1862. Buyers at sale: B. T. Gray, Samuel Shaw, James M. Carwile, R. A. Tucker, F. Robertson, J. M. Hopkins, P. S. Burton, H. M. Prince, R. H. Hall, Wm. Crowther, J. F. Burton, H. S. Miller, W. L. Young, Wm. Wickliffe, H. Robinson, W. J. Robertson, J. M. Bryant, Christopher Ellis, Basil Callaham, Jacob Alewine, W. B. Martin, John Pratt, F. Clinkscales, Michael McGee, Luvenia Burton, Thomas Hill, S. M. Hall. Estate Settlement Jul 31, 1863. James F. Burton had died and Wm. Crowther was now the administrator.

BOX 158 PACK 3436   THOMAS BANNISTER   1862

Administrator: Wm. Pruitt, Son-in-law. Appraisal Feb 25, 1862 by J. G. Branyon, George Shjrley, Wm. Armstrong, W. Y. Walker. Children: Ebby Bannister, Elizabeth Ricketts,

Tabitha Emmaline Bannister. Estate Sale Feb 25, 1862. Buyers at sale: Wm. Armstrong, Rolly Bannister, Widow, James Armstrong, Ben. Pearman, George Shirley, W. T. Brock, John Shirley, Elizabeth Carwile, James Darby, Jesse Robinson, R. N. Wright, W. Y. Walker, J. M. Branyon, Wm. Pruitt, John S. Carwile, Emmaline Bannister, J. T. Kerr, W.C. Armstrong. Estate Settlement Apr 16, 1864.

BOX 158 PACK 3437   JOHN BRADLEY   1862

C. S. A. Soldier killed Sep 1, 1862 at the Battle of Manassas. Administrator: Horace Drennan, Brother-in Law. Bond Nov 18, 1862 of $3,000 by Horace Drennan, Reuben Weed, John L. Adamson. Widow and (4) infant children. Appraisal Dec 8, 1862 by George W. Pressly, A. S. Weed, Adam Wideman, Robert W. Lites. Estate Sale Dec 9, 1862. Buyers at sale: James Drennan, B. B. Harveley, Thomas Creswell, E. O. Reagan, John L. Adamson, John H. Wideman, Widow, Reuben Weed, Adam Wideman, B. P. Creswell, George W. Pressly, Thomas O. Creswell, Andrew J. Weed, Robert W. Lites, J. Colwell. Confederate tax for 1863 $3.25.

BOX 158 PACK 3438   R. W. BULLOCK   1862

Administrator: Wm. Carter. Bond Sep 16, 1862 of $1,000 by Wm. Carter, J. W. Fooshe, S. A. Crawford, John Sadler. Appraisal Oct 3, 1862 of $74 by Wm. Carter. Estate Sale Oct 3, 1862. Buyers at sale: H. B. McNeill, S. A. Crawford, Wm. Carter, Fooshe & Carter. Estate was Insolvent. Estate Settlement Mar 17, 1864. Debts were prorated.

BOX 158 PACK 3439   JANE BICKETT   1862

Will dated Feb 8, 1862. Witnesses: George W. Pressly, W. P. Sullivan, F. T. White. Executor: Joseph L. Pressly. Willed to: 1. Sarah McComb wife of Andrew Brown 2. John Bickett, son, 132 acres 3. John Hamilton Young. Appraisal Apr 23, 1862 by W. P. Sullivan, J. C. Lindsay, F. T. White. No Estate Sale. Settlement Oct 13, 1896.

BOX 158 PACK 3440   JAMES WESLEY BUCHANAN   1870

Confederate Soldier killed Aug 29, 1862 at the Battle of Manassas as a member of Zeigler's Company F Holcomb Legion. Administrator: Robert P. Buchanan, Brother–in-Law. Bond Nov 10, 1862 of $10,000 by Robert P. Buchanan, Wm. Buchanan, F. A. Buchanan, Wm. J. Arnold. Wife had been dead for two and ½ years. Two minor children ages 4 & 6. Appraisal Nov 27, 1862 by Samuel Turner, Charles A. Cobb, Larkin Pulliam. Owned 6 slaves. Estate Sale Nov 27, 1862. Buyers at sale: Wm. Buchanan, R. P. Buchanan, John T. Parks, Wm. McNary, Marcus A. Crews, Dr. R. C. Moseley, James A. Bailey, Charles C. Pinckney, J. J. Smith, Charles Cunningham, John Roman, Dr. Boozer, Felix G. Parks, Capt. Delaney, W. Hilton, James Rampey, Samuel Turner, J. B. Sample, Christopher Smith, Thomas Franklin, Wm. Mundy. Estate returns still active as of May 29, 1875.

BOX 158 PACK 3441   WILLIAM S. BAKER   1862

Will dated Sep 21, 1861. Witnesses: J. O. Lindsay, Joseph J. Lee, Wm. Tennant. Executor: John T. Baker, Brother. Wife: S. P. Baker. Children: S. T. Baker, C. W. Baker. Appraisal Sep 19, 1862 by James Taggart, F. A. Calhoun, D. M. Rogers, Wm. T. Drennan. Notes held on: Jane J. Baker, Moses O. Talman, Phares Martin, S. S. Crafton, Wm. H. Taggart, M. A. Crafton, J. J. Crafton. Last estate activity Dec 10, 1866.

BOX 158 PACK 3442   THOMAS J. BEACHAM   1862

Confederate Soldier. Deceased died Aug 1, 1862. Wife: Sarah J. Beacham. (3) Infant children, no names stated. Appraisal Dec 3, 1862 by Marshall Sharp, Wm. Hodges, John Vance, T. Yancey Martin. Owned 3 slaves. Notes held on: P. W. Watson, A. T. Watson. Estate Sale Dec 4, 1862 netted $5,089. Buyers at sale: Sarah J. Beacham, James C. Cason, Samuel Agnew, T. T. Carter, R. A. Griffin, T. Y. Martin, J. R. Vance, Wm. Hodges, J. C. Waters, A. T. Watson, N. Simms, M. B. McGee, Charles C. Pinckney, Green B. Riley, Larkin Mays, J. B. Black, John Vance.

BOX 158 PACK 3443   GEORGE M. CROMER   1860

Confederate Soldier died Aug 5, 1861 at Charlottesville, Va. 1st Administrator: John P. Cromer, Brother who died prior to settlement of the estate. Bond Sep 28, 1861 of $20,000 by John P. Cromer, Andrew McIlwain, Samuel Robertson. 2nd Administrator: James F. Tolbert, died prior to settlement. Bond Jan 9, 1862 by James F. Tolbert, D. M. Cromer, James T. Barnes. 3rd Administrator: W. H. Parker. Never Married. Appraisal Dec 3, 1861 by W. C. Cozby, Samuel Houston, John McCurry, Elias Kay, J. H. Cunningham. Notes held on: John Enright, T. C. Perrin, T. J. McCracken, J. A. & D. W. McCord, J. H. Cunningham, Alex. Hunter, R. P. Cromer, James F. Tolbert & Joseph B. Black, John H. Wilson- I. Branch-J. Foster Marshall, John Enright-R. C. Fair-Thomas Savage-James T. Moore, T. J. McCracken-John T. Owen, Juette Huckabee-C. A. Huckabee-J. H. Power, J. H. Wilson-I. Branch-J. Foster Marshall, James F. Tolbert-James B. Black, Bowie &Mundy.

BOX 158 PACK 3444   DR. FRANK CLINKSCALES   1860

Administrator: Wm. Clinkscales. Bond Aug 8, 1862 of $25,000 by Wm. Clinkscales, John F. Clinkscales, Robert Ellis, James M. Carwile. Appraisal Aug 25, 1862 by Bennett McAdams, James B. McCarter, Basil Callaham. Notes held on: Wm. Duncan, Joseph M. Blackwell, Wm. Y. Walker, Mathis Alewine, Reuben Clinkscales, James Darby, John A. Sims, Joseph Alewine, W. L. Young, Thomas Elgin, Wm. F. Duncan, W. A. Black, Moses Smith, W. L. Burton, George W. Alewine, H. W. Shaw, John McDonald, J. W. Brock, Wm. Burton, J. F. Burton, Richard Taylor, John T. Kerr, John S. Alewine, John A. Sims, J. B. McWhorter, Bartholomew Darby. Estate Sale Aug 26, 1862 netted $8,174. Buyers at sale: Joshua S. Barnes, Wm. Clinkscales, Reuben Clinkscales, John W. Shirley, R. A. Archie, Dr. Wardlaw, John A. Robinson, Patsy Griffin, Christopher Ellis, Lewis C. Clinkscales, Jacob Alewine, James Clinkscales, John F. Clinkscales, Robert Hall, Hugh Robinson, J. T. Lyon, Dr. Newell, Caleb Shaw, H. Armstrong, David Duncan, Henry Clamp, John J. Bonner, John T. Owen, John R. Clinkscales, Dr. T. Brown, Dr. Cook, Wesley A. Black, James Patterson, John M. Pruitt, James Taylor, John B. Strickland, Ephraim Alewine, Wm. Dawkins, W. L. Dukes, J. F. Lyon, Dr. J. Miller, Wm. Allen, W. S. Richardson, B. F. Bryson, Peter S. Burton, F. Bell, Samuel Shaw, James B. McWhorter, Addison Clinkscales, Clinkscales Hodges, James Cowan, James Mathis, E. Rasor, Wm. L. Young. Estate Settlement Feb 23, 1864. (9) Heirs: 1. Wm. C. Clinkscales 2. John L. Clinkscales 3. Mrs. Ellis wife of Christopher Ellis 4. Lewis C. Clinkscales 5. Addison C. Clinkscales 6. James Clinkscales 7. Reuben Clinkscales 8. Children of Abner Clinkscales 9. Children of Mrs. Robinson.

BOX 158 PACK 3445   WILLIAM H. COCHRAN   1862

Administrator: Wm. Mann. Estate Sale Jul 2, 1862. Buyers at sale: Wm. Wickliffe, Thomas Tucker, Wm. Bell, P. Rutledge, A. Martin, Sterling Bowen, A. Winn, Alonzo

Harris, Wm. Hill, H. Burton, G. W. Bowen, A. Gailey, J. B. Black, Wm. Lesly, J. W. Cann, John McMahan, R. H. Wilson, W. L. Prince, F. P. Robertson, Widow, L. C. Clinkscales, James Barnes, W. D. Mann, John Moseley, E. Westfield, James Mann. Confederate tax for 1862 $2.47. Estate Settlement filed Feb 3, 1863. Widow $205.91. (4) Children, not named, $102.95 each.

BOX 158 PACK 3446   LUKE L. COYNE   1868

Deceased died Sep 21, 1861. Administrator: James Martin. Bond Oct 15, 1861 of $500 by James Martin, J. S. Reid, Wm. S. Harris. No Wife: No Children: No Known Relatives. Appraisal Nov 2, 1861 of $33.98 by W. S. Harris, John L. Devlin, Walter G. Keller. Estate Sale Nov 2, 1861 netted $39.50. Buyers at sale: James Martin, Robert Thornton, M. G. Keller, Tyra M. Jay, Wm. S. Harris. Estate Settlement Feb 7, 1868.

BOX 159 PACK 4301   JOSEPH H. CUNNINGHAM   1864

Confederate Soldier. Died at Meridan, Miss. Jun 9, 1862. Administrators: Sarah J. Cunningham-Wife, Thomas L. Cunningham-Brother. Bond Aug 29, 1862 of $25,000 by Thomas L. Cunningham, Sarah J. Cunningham, James T. Liddell, James R. Cunningham. Appraisal Dec 9, 1862 by Wm. A. Giles, James T. Liddell, James F. Tolbert, A. F. Clinkscales. Owned 6 slaves. Estate Sale Dec 10, 1862 netted $17,754. Buyers at sale: Sarah J. Cunningham, George Allen, Ben. D. Kay, B. M. Winestock, Frank Wilson, W.C. Hix, N. E. Bell, L. C. Mauldin, Eliza McCurry, W. H. Rampey, Johnson Ramey, Andrew J. Speer, Frank Miller, J. T. Liddell, Clement T. Latimer, F. P. Robertson, Charles T. Haskell, J. F. C. DuPre, J. D. Burkhead, R. M. Davis, Wm. A. Giles, Robert Jones. Estate Settlement Oct 24, 1864. Widow received $5938, (4) Children, not named, each received $2,969.

BOX 159 PACK 4302   H. B. CLARKE   1867

Administrator: John Davenport. Bond Jul 11, 1862 of $2,500 by John Davenport, Richard Harris, Hampton Finley. Wife: Frances Clarke. Appraisal Jul 11, 1864 by James B. Jones, F. F. Gary, B. Z. Herndon, L. H. Vance. Held notes on: T. D. Nickles, Joseph Cunningham, M. C. Cunningham, W. T. Finley, W. G. Rice, F. D. Coleman, Leander Brown, A. A. King, Samuel P. McCrady, Frederick Harley, J. S. Rolen, S. M. C. Bowman, Francis A. Connor, D. S. Helms, H. P. Sharp, Christopher Sharp, Andrew Cobb, John Boyle, Wm. D. Johnson, J. M. Forgy, Jesse E. Ellis. 1859 Accounts Open: Wm. T. Finley, Jane Huggins, Robert Adams, M. C. Cunningham, James C. Collins, W. H. Langston, Dr. G. C. Finley, D. L. Helms, John S. Bolt, Michael Burts, J. H. Hudgens, Dr. John Watts, Joseph Cunningham, Eliza Miller, John Boyle, Robert Cunningham, John Dvenport, John Wharton, John Anderson, A. G. Young, L. L. Young, Joel Smith, Wade Anderson, John Wait, John B. Gray, Henry Fuller. 1861 Accounts Open: J. C. C. Allen, Joseph Blackwell, George M. Griffin, G. W. Hodges, Wesley Norwood, J. N. Cochran, Wm. E. Caldwell, Martha Gary, W. W. Lawson, Miss Eliza Pelot, Marshall Sharp, A. T. Watson, C. H. Graham, D. L. Browning, Miss Emma Cantey, Franklin Gary, J. C. Mundy, George Scythe, J. K. Vance, J. H. Vance, Miss Mary Cantey, S. R. Dantzler, Charles Harvey, D. C. Moore, Anderson Smith, Allen Vance, A. H. King, J. A. Ellis, J. C. Ellis, Wm. Hilton, Wm. Moore, B. F. Flint, Martin G. Zeigler, Robert Anderson. Estate Sale Aug 9, 1862.

BOX 159 PACK 4303   EDWARD CALHOUN   1863

Administrator: Sons, John F. Calhoun, Edwin Calhoun. Bond Aug 22, 1862 of $100,000 by John F. Calhoun, Edwin Calhoun, F. A. Calhoun, H. G. Middleton, D. M. Rogers. Wife was deceased. Appraisal Dec 15, 1862 by Wm. Tennant, F. A. Calhoun, J. A. Gibert, D.

M. Rogers. Notes held on: John B. Wilhite, John F. Calhoun, Josiah Wells. Estate Sale Dec 16 & 17, 1862 netted $12,817. Buyers at sale: John F. Calhoun, M. O. Talman, B. E. Gibert, J. A. Gibert, R. E. Gibert, James A. Norwood, John Baughman, James Taggart Sr., W. G. Darracott, D. M. Rogers, Dr. Wm. Tenant, Alex. R. Houston, C. A. Alexander, Peter B. Moragne, F. M. Mitchell, J. Wells, Dr. Roberts, J. L. Lesly, A. W. Lathrop, W. H. Taggart, W.A. Crozier, N. Ennis, T. M. Ard, A. M. Johnson, R. M. Craven, R. A. McCaslan, J. R. Clark, Wm. Tennant Jr., R. C. Scott, T. M. McAllister, Francis A. Calhoun, Thomas Hemminger, J. W. Shaw, Dr. Thomas J. Hester, Wm. D. Mars, J. R. Perryman, Dr. N. Harris, W. O. Partlow, Shepard G. Cowan, J. W. Eskew, Hugh G. Middleton. Estate Settlement Jan 5, 1866 and Feb 22, 1866. Apr 4, 1874 Charles Alexander and his wife, Ida who was a daughter of deceased and Rosa Calhoun received payments due them.

BOX 159 PACK 4304   GEORGE M. CONNOR   1861

Will dated Aug 31, 1861. Witnesses: E. R. Calhoun, W. W. Leland, Wm. Blake. To Alice J. Bailey whom he loved most dearly a double cased gold ladies watch to be presented to her as a gift of remembrance. Executor: James A. Bailey. Mother: Henrietta M. Connor. Brothers: Wm. S. Connor, John H. Connor, Wesley O. Connor. Sisters: Harriet A. Wright, H. Cornelia Kincaid.

BOX 159 PACK 4305   MARY CLINKSCALES   1862

Administrator: William Clinkscales. Bond Jul 7, 1862 of $6,000 by Wm. Clinkscales, S. M. Tribble, Bennett McAdams. Appraisal Jul 31, 1862 by Bennett McAdams, S. B. McWhorter, B. Wilson. Notes held on: Wm. Clinkscales, Reuben Clinkscales, T. Clinkscales, Addison Clinkscales, Lewis C. Clinkscales. Estate Sale Jul 31, 1862. Buyers at sale: John F. Clinkscales, Addison Clinkscales, James Clinkscales, Wm. Clinkscales, Lewis C. Clinkscales, Reuben Clinkscales, Robert Hall, C. Ellis, J. W. Brooks, James Cowan, James Patterson, Robert C. Grier, James B. McWhorter, J. J. Bonner, Hugh Robinson, Samuel Martin, James Taylor. Estate Settlement Feb 15, 1864. (10) Distributees, each received $335.73: 1. Wm. Clinkscales, John Clinkscales, Lewis C. Clinkscales, Addison Clinkscales, James Clinkscales, Reuben Clinkscales, Mrs. C. Ellis, Children of Mrs. Robison, Frank C. Clinkscales. Confederate tax for 1861 $12.69.

BOX 159 PACK 4306   OBEDIAH LYNCH CANN   1862

Will dated Feb 8, 1862. Witnesses: Robert Stuckey, W. C. Ferguson, Jesse Cann. Executor: Frances A. Cann. Appraisal May 31, 1862 by P. Ferguson, Jesse W. Cann, W. C. Ferguson. Owned 120 acres of land. Notes held on: A.B. Campbell, John W. Corpin, J. W. Cann.

BOX 159 PACK 4307   WILLIAM F. DUNCAN   1862

Administrator: Wm. Duncan, Father. Bond May 6, 1862 of $1,000 by Wm. Duncan, James H. Cobb, John Enright. Wife: Mary M. Duncan. Appraisal May 21, 1862 by James Clinkscales, John R. Willson, Wm. Clinkscales. Estate Sale May 21, 1862. Buyers at sale: Ben. Pearman, Wm. Duncan, John R. Willson, Martha Griffin, John T. Miller, Bartholomew Darby, Jacob Alewine, Peter S. Burton, James M. Carwile, James M. Callaham, Michael Alewine, Wm. L. Young, James Darby, Ephraim Alewine, Bennett Lowe, Wm. Armstrong, John W. Shirley, Wm. Y. Walker, John M. G. Branyon, Wm. Clinkscales, John F. Clinkscales. Jul 31, 1883 mother received 1/3. Collected by her son, J. P. Duncan.

BOX 159 PACK 4308   NEWTON DEAL   1861

Administrator: James T. Barnes (Largest Creditor). Bond Nov 4, 1861 of $400 by James T. Barnes, Christian V. Barnes, John M. Moseley. Appraisal Nov 23, 1861 by Wm. C. Cozby, James T. Baker, John M. Moseley. Estate Sale Nov 23, 1861 netted $52.95. Buyers at sale: John M. Moseley, R. H. Wilson, E. White, J. C. Speer, J. F. DuPre, James T. Barnes, W. M. Bell, A.V. Brooks, E. W. South, Joel Smith, R.S. Hardin, Rev. Christian V. Barnes, J. A. Deal. 1862 Confederate tax $1.20.

BOX 159 PACK 4309   JOHN D. DUNCAN (minor)   1865

Guardian: J. C. Stevenson. Bond Oct 21, 1865 of $1,000 by James C. Stevenson, Alex. G. Hagen, Peter Henry. Was about 3 years old. Due a legacy from the estate of his grand father, David McWilliams.

BOX 159 PACK 4310   ROBERT M. ELLIS   1860

Administrators: Christopher Ellis, Martha A. Ellis. Bond Sep 1, 1862 of $5,000 by Christopher Ellis, Martha A. Ellis, John E. Ellis, Wm. T. Newell. Wife: Martha A. Ellis. (2) Children, not named. Appraisal Sep 23, 1862 by A. C. Hawthorne, J. C. Stevenson, J. T. Bonner, John Cowan. Estate Sale Sep 23, 1862. Buyers at sale: Martha A. Ellis, A.C. Hawthorne, John T. Bonner, James Wright, John Cowan, Thomas J. Ellis, M. M. Ellis, David O. Hawthorne, John Pratt, F.V. Bell. Estate Settlement Mar 3, 1864. Wife Martha A. Ellis received $391.82.

BOX 159 PACK 4311   JESSE C. ELLIS   1860

Administrator: Thomas J. Ellis, Brother. Bond Mar 3, 1862 of $12,000 by Thomas J. Ellis, James C. Ellis, Wm. L. McCord. Appraisal Mar 18, 1862 by W. C. Klugh, W. M. Mars, A. P. Boozer, John Seal, C. A. Cobb. Notes held on: Wm. R. Mundy, D. S. Benson, L. H. Lomax, J. E. Anderson, J. D. McKellar, Samuel Turner, T. A. Watson, Louisa C. Logan, E. T. McIlwain, Jesse A. Lomax, Thomas Benson, James Pratt, J. A. Ellis, John Robertson, James Benson, Charlie Cobb, John Mathis, James W. Irwin, J. W. Arnold, John Butler, G. M. Harrison, Moses C. Taggart, James Hanvey, Wm. Harris, John Calvert, James Anderson, W. J. L. Burrell. Estate Sale Mar 18, 1862 netted $6,304.15. J. K. Vance, Thomas Mahon, Rev. T. S. Arthur, Widow, J. A. Ellis, H. B. Nickles, James C. Ellis, A. P. Boozer, J. H. Vance, James Hughey, J. J. Adams, James H. Cobb, Peter Henry, J. H. Riley, John D. Adams, Dr. G. W. Lomax, T. J. Ellis. 1863 war tax $30. Estate Settlement May 30, 1864. Widow, now Lou Fisher, received $987.94, (2) Children each received $987.94. Estate Settlement Aug 15, 1866. Widow received $125.45, (2) Children each received $125. 45.

BOX 159 PACK 4312   JAMES A. EDWARDS   1861

Administrator: John J. Edwards. Bond Jul 6, 1861 of $700 by John J. Edwards, D. M. Wardlaw, James H. Cobb. Appraisal Jun 15, 1861 by Y. Y. Gaines, D. M. Wardlaw, Robert S. Dixon. Estate Sale Jun 15, 1861 Netted $326.07. Buyers at sale: Hiram W. Lawson, Robert Keoun, A. L. Gray, Thomas Link, David McLane, Mary Strickland, John Able, Thomas McNeill, W. G. McWilliams, John Armstrong, S. F. Edwards, James Wilson, Samuel Brown, Andrew J. Woodhurst, Samuel Burdette, S. C. Zaner, J. J. Edwards, James Edwards, David M. Wardlaw, Wm. Bradford, John Charles, Dr. McNeill Turner, John Brooks, H. S. Harmon, Augustus Edwards, Sarah Armstrong, John Brown, Robert Dixon,

F. M. McMillan, H. R. Burdette, James H. Cobb. Estate Insolvent. Estate Settlement Dec 14, 1861. Robert S. Dixon paid for coffin, Dr. Andrew Paul paid for medical services.

BOX 159 PACK 4313   JAMES T. FELL   1862

Died in Confederate Army. Administrator: Samuel B. McClinton. Appraisal Oct 16, 1862 by Jonathan Jordan, James W. Frazier, W. Fell. Estate Settlement Dec 21, 1863. Widow, Louisa J. Fell received $190.20. (2) Young children, Wm. A. Fell and Jane T. Fell, each received $190.20.

BOX 159 PACK 4314   JOHN H. GRAY   1862

Will dated May 18, 1862. Witnesses: Robert M. Palmer, Wm. H. Brooks, Thomas J. Mabry. Executor: Jane C. Gray, Wife. Son: John Gray in Confederate Army. 1st Appraisal Oct 25, 1862 by Wm. H. Brooks, Francis M. Brooks, Robert M. Palmer, Henry S. Hammond. Owned 42 slaves, 866 acres of land. 2nd Appraisal Jan 1, 1868 by J. W. Norwood, John S. Williams, F. A. Wilson. Estate Sale Jan 1, 1868 netted $379.20. Buyers at sale: Widow, Lucius B. Ramey, F. Johnson, J. J. Gray, Dr. Thomas, E. P. Gray, Wm. H. Brooks, Joe Cheatham, Charles Gray, Wm. Butler, Thomas Hutchinson, Alfred Gray, D. R. Penney. 1862 war tax $89.45. Estate Insolvent.

BOX 159 PACK 4315   J. J. GRANT   1862

Administrator: James T. Baskin. Bond Sep 1, 1862 of $100 by J. T. Baskin, W. S. Baskin, John G. Baskin. Appraisal Sep 6, 1862 of $70.35 by John A. Martin, Wm. M. Smith, John A. Crawford. Estate Settlement Jan 27, 1865. Estate Insolvent.

BOX 159 PACK 4316   POLLY HAWKINS   1860

Administrator: Wm. Clinkscales, deceased had left a small amount of money in his hands. Appraisal Jul 9, 1862 of $30 by Robert Wilson, Robert McAdams, J. J. McAdams. Notes and accounts, $13.50, held on: Joshua Ashley, James Darby, Washington Clem, Yancey Dove, Eliza Rouse.

BOX 159 PACK 4317   JAMES H. HADDON   1862

Will dated Mar 5, 1862. Witnesses: E. S. Patton, J. N. Young, Robert Ellis, J. P. Kennedy. Executors: America Haddon, Robert C. Grier. Wife: America Haddon. Son: Chalmers Haddon. Daughters: Josephine Haddon, Indiana Haddon, Mary Haddon, Martha Haddon. Appraisal Nov 20, 1862 by Robert McAdams, J. J. McAdams, Robert Ellis. Notes held on: J. J. Bonner, J. J. McAdams, Robert C. Sharp. Owned 12 slaves.

BOX 159 PACK 4318   JAMES GIDEON JOHNSON   1861

Will dated Sep 18, 1861. Witnesses: John Brownlee, James E. G. Bell, W. M. Bell. Executor: Amanda Johnson. Wife Amanda Johnson. Sons: Bazzy Johnson, John Johnson, James Gideon Johnson, Samuel Williams Johnson. Daughters: Ella Johnson, Anna Mariah Johnson, Mary Amanda Johnson. Owned 12 slaves, 400 acres of land.

BOX 159 PACK 4319   FRANCIS JENKINS   1862

Confederate Soldier died Mar 1862. Administrator: Charles B. Guffin. Bond May 6, 1862 of $100 by Charles B. Guffin, Thomas Guffin, L. L. Guffin.

BOX 159 PACK 4320   SAMUEL KNOX   1862

Administrator: David McLane. Bond Sep 9, 1862 of $1,000 by David McLane, James McCaslan, John L. Devlin. Shoemaker. Appraisal Sep 13, 1862 by Wm. McCaslan, Samuel Link, W. W. Hunter. Estate Sale Sep 13, 1862 netted $102.90. Buyers at sale: Samuel Link, J. W. Ford, Alex. P. Connor, J. Patterson, Bolivar Kennedy, J. K. Wideman, J. H. Wideman, A. McCaslan, David Knox, W. Lyon, Jordan A. Ramey, J. S. Barnes, Thomas Link, J. T. Clatworthy, Wm. W. Hunter, Henry Cason. Estate Settlement Dec 22, 1863. (6) Legatees each received $58. 95. 1. David Knox 2. John Knox 3. Joseph Knox 4.Children of Mrs. Pennal 5. Child of Nathaniel Knox 6. Robert O. Knox.

BOX 159 PACK 4321   DAVID KELLER   1871

Deceased died Oct 13, 1862. Very extensive estate with many pages of notes, accounts, financial transactions etc. Held notes on over 100 individuals. More than 100 individuals had open and due accounts with him at his death. Much money to collect with many of the debts being bad. Very contentious settlement disputes, including refusal to accept Confederate currency at the 1864 settlement. Appraisal Nov 17, 1862 by John Davis, W. B. Roman, James Irwin, George W. Cromer. Estate sale held Nov 19, 1862 brought in $30, 464. Several settlements took place. Administrator: Nancy Keller, Wife. Bond Oct 29, 1862 of $100,000 by Nancy Keller, W. Henry Wilson, Susan Keller, David Z. Keller, James F. Mabry, John T. Owen, Joseph T. Moore, James I. Gilmer. 1st Settlement took place in 1864. Several refused to accept Confederate money including Wm. A. McCord and his wife. 2nd Settlement took place Sep 28, 1866 with each of the following receiving $100: Samuel R. Lomax, T. A. Keller, D. Z. Keller, Wm. A. Lomax, J. W. Keller, James F. Mabry. Final Settlement took place Sep 18, 1873. All (13) of his children were represented in this settlement (there was still a huge amount of money not collected as only $16,000 had been collected against the debts). Widow received 1/3 and each child's share was 1/13 of the remainder. Those receiving shares were: 1. Salyy wife of James A. McCord 2. Eliza wife of John W. Lomax 3. Elvira wife of Samuel R. Lomax 4. Angeline R. wife of Wm. A. Lomax 5. J. Wesley Keller 6. Susan Keller, not married and deceased 7. David Z. Keller 8. Julia wife of James F. Mabry 9. Isaac Keller 10. Emma Keller 11. John J. Keller lving in Sabine Co., Tex. 12. Anna wife of William Henry Wilson living in Welbourne, Fla. 13. Warren Keller living in Wellbourne, Fla.

BOX 160 PACK 4322   BUFORD LAWSON   1863

Administrator: W. W. Lawson. Bond Jul 25, 1862 of $3,000 by W. W. Lawson, Frank A. Connor, W. C. Anderson. Wife: Mary Lawson. (7) Children, not named. Appraisal Aug 14, 1862 by S. Latimer, J. R. Latimer, James H. Shaw. Held notes on: James H. Shaw, B. M. Latimer. Estate Sale Aug 14, 1862. Buyers at sale: Widow, L. H. Whitlock, J. R. Latimer, J. H. Shaw, Obediah Shirley, S. Latimer, W. A. J. Ware, S. Bagwell, J. G. Gantt, Enoch Gambrell, B. M. Latimer, J. C. Gambrell, John Wilson, W. P. Kay, R. A. Griffin, Wm. Stone, J. H. Shaw, John Ross, W. C. Moseley, James Seawright, James Davis, Aaron Pitts, G. M. Mattison, L. G. Davis, Sanford Bagwell, Mason Kay, A. Austin, Henderson Bagwell, Samuel Pitts, J. J. Nicks, Haywood Davis, John W. Lawson, John Pitts, M. Erwin, David Moore, C. A. Aiken, W. W. Lawson, J. L. Davis, W. H. Whitlock. Estate Settlement Nov 26, 1863. Widow, Mary Lawson received $355.94. Each of (7) Children received $101.69. John McLaren named as a distributee.

BOX 160 PACK 4323   JOHN N. LeROY   1862

Administrator: John LeRoy. Bond Jan 27, 1862 of $4,000 by John LeRoy, E. B. LeRoy, Peter L. Guillebeau. Held notes on: A. Burt, J. A. Calhoun. D. M. Rogers, John B. LeRoy, E. Calhoun, Moses O. Talman, Andrew Guillebeau.

BOX 160 PACK 4324   JAMES YANCEY LOCKHART   1862

Will dated Apr 1, 1862. Witnesses: James T. Baskin, Wm. A. Ellis, J. F. C. DuPre. Executor: James Marion Latimer. Son: John Bunyan Lockhart. Daughters: Mary Catherine Lockhart, Sarah Margaret Lockhart. Daughter's guardian was James Marion Latimer. Sister: Ellen Latimer (she had 4 children). Appraisal Aug 26, 1862 by R. M. Davis, J. F. C. DuPre, Wm. A. Giles, W. M. Bell. Owned 13 slaves. Estate Sale Sep 15, 1862. Buyers at sale: James White, James Latimer, E. Lockhart. 1864 state tax $49.80, 1865 state tax $87.12, 1865 Confederate tax $456.

BOX 160 PACK 4325   JOHN E. LAKE   1860

Will dated Oct 16, 1861. Witnesses: John T. Henderson, W. S. Hutchison, Martha E. Sale. Wife: Josephine Lake. Sons: Felix Fletcher Lake, Joseph Lake. Daughter: Elizabeth Lake. Father-in-Law: Johnson Sale was guardian of the children. Executor Johnson Sale. Appraisal Nov 6, 1862 by Irvin Hutchinson, Nathaniel Henderson, Esma Jones. Owned 2 slaves which were sold Dec 29, 1862, Held notes on: Felix Lake, John A. Cannon, E. T. Lake, W. J. Lake, Nathaniel Henderson, J. A. Bonds, Irvin Hutchinson.

BOX 160 PACK 4326   DR. JOSEPH S. MARSHALL   1860

Administrator: Ann E. Marshall. Bond Nov 25, 1861 of $100,000 by Ann E. Marshall, Stanmore B. Brooks, M. W. Coleman. Deceased died Sep 16, 1861. Appraisal Dec 12, 1861 by Peter McKellar, J. S. Hearst, W. Smith, Wm. B. Brooks. Owned 50 slaves. Held notes on: J. D. Creswell, Allen Vance, Peter McKellar, Israel C. Bond, V. Griffin, Leroy Purdy, S. H. Smith, J. A. Bailey, J. D. McKellar, J. H. Martin, Bond & Harrison, Nathaniel McCants, S. B.Brooks, T. C. Lipscomb, James Creswell, J. P. Bond, W. L. Anderson, James M. Chiles, Thomas H. Chappell, R. M. Scurry, J. L. Hearst, Wm. G. Kennedy, Wm. Scott, John & Elizabeth Scott, Wm. W. White, Wm. Lyon, T. W. Nicholls. Wife: Ann E. Marshall. (7) Children, no names given. Estate Sale Nov 19, 1862 netted $10,011. Slaves sold separately for $32,762. Buyers at sale: Ann E. Marshall, John Hinton, S.B. B. Brooks, W. W. White, R. T. Bell, W. J. Smith, John McBryde, H. Beard, Wm. Y. Quarles, Felix G. Parks, Wm. C. Hunter, Martin Hackett, J. D. Creswell, J. S. Smith, H. A. Hollingsworth, W. P. McKellar, W. K. Tolbert, E. T. McSwain, L. A. Anderson, H. Mayo, James A. Bailey, Mrs. H. McNeill, John T. McKellar, B. Reynolds, D. W. Aiken, L. Reynolds, James Creswell, Allen Vance, W. W. Coleman, E. Hinton, D. McKellar, M. A. Crews, J. Bond, Thomas W. Aiken, Samuel B. McClinton, John Foster, Mrs. E. Walker, Peter McKellar, Thomas Creswell, James Martin, Thomas C. Lipscomb, H. L. Rykard, B. Jordan, S. B. Brooks Jr., I. Hutchinson, G. M. Jordan, W. Youngblood, Johnson Sale, Marcus A. Crews, W. P. McKellar, Walter G. Kennedy, Gideon P. O'Neal. Estate Settlement Oct 18, 1871. Ann Elizabeth Marshall received $7,934.36. Each child received $2,301.55.

BOX 160 PACK 4327   ABNER H. MAGEE   1862

Administrators: Michael B. Magee, Wm. P. Magee. Appraisal Nov 14, 1862 by E. Rasor, Benjamin Smith, G. B. Riley. Held notes on: James Pratt, Valentine Young, Moultrie Griffin, Abner H. Magee, James M. Vandiver, W. W. Higgins, Board of Trustees Cokesbury College, T. P. Moseley, Jesse W. Robertson, T. Y. Martin, Wm. Clinkscales, M. & W. Magee, J. K. Vance, John Milam, Dudley Mabry, Marshall Hodges, H. A. Jones,

Thomas W. Smith, Elizabeth Ware, Wesley Robertson, Enoch M. Sharp, Michael Magee, Dr. E. Agnew, Frost Snow, Wm. Donald, Ben. F. Jones, W. T. Jones, G. W. Jones, James Killingsworth, P. H. Nixon, Wm. Holmes, Samuel Caldwell, Wyatt L. Norwood, Catherine Williamson, Marshall Sharp, G. M. Mattison, Wm. Magee Sr., Andrew Agnew, W. L. Magee, W. W. Sharp, Mastin Bell, Edward Boney. Owned 25 slaves. Estate Sale Dec 30, 1862 netted $26,422 Buyers at sale: Louisa Magee, W. P. Magee, M. B. Magee, E. M. Sharp, Jesse L. Magee, A. C. Magee, John T. Magee, Allen Dodson, A. M. Agnew, Dudley Mabry, W. M. Griffin, Joel F. Smith, Dr. James Ware, J. T. Bonner, G. W. Hodges, Chris Smith, Charles C. Pinckney, H. N. Maddox, John B. Wilson, J. B. Riley, J. J. Smith, --Deal, A. M. Dodson. 1864 Confederate tax $1,104.90, 1865 Confederate tax $198. Estate Settlement Mar 26, 1868. (9) Legatees with Widow, Louisa Magee receiving $13,340 and the remaining legatees each receiving $3,335.22. 1. E. M. Sharp in right of wife Mary A. Sharp 2. Jesse S. Magee 3. Louisa, wife 4. Hezekiah R. Magee 5. Amaziah C. Magee 6. Abner H. Magee 7. John I. Magee 8. Wm. P. Magee 10. Michael B. Magee.

BOX 160 PACK 4328   NANCY AGNES MOORE   1862

Will dated Nov 23, 1861. Witnesses: W. Magill, J. M. Gilliam, James Patterson. Executor: A. L. Gray, who did not charge any administration fee. Coffin cost $8.00. Settlement Sep 2. 1862. Isabella Moore received $123.37.

BOX 160 PACK 4329   MARY W. McWILLIAMS   1862

Will dated Apr 3, 1860. Witnesses: Wm. Gordon, J. C. Stevenson, Wm. G. Gordon. Part owner of property with (4) sisters. Sisters: Esther McWilliams, Ann McWilliams, Nancy McWilliams, Betty McWilliams.

BOX 160 PACK 4330   CHARLOTTE McADAMS   1861

Administrator: James B. McWhorter. McWhorter had boarded and taken care of her for 8 years, the last 4 years she had been bed ridden. Appraisal Mar 20, 1861 of $17.50 by Basil Callaham, John M. Bryant, Francis Clinkscales. Held notes on James B. McWhorter, Wm. Clinkscales. Estate Sale Mar 30, 1861 Netted $22.95. Buyers at sale: James B. McWhorter, Dempsey Callaham, D. Callaham. Estate Settlement Jul 8, 1861. Heirs: 1. R. B. McAdmas-her son, he protested the settlement 2. Dempsey Calhoun and wife 3. Mary Ann McClain wife of John McClain 4. J. B. McWhorter $644. James B. McWhorter was awarded $800 at the request of neighbors, Wm. Pratt, Francis Clinkscales, James Clinkscales, J. W. Brooks, Christopher Ellis, J. Fields Burton, J. B. Kay for his care of the deceased.

BOX 160 PACK 4331   COL. J. FOSTER MARSHALL   1862

Very long and very detailed estate. Will dated Jul 17, 1861. Witnesses: R. H. Wardlaw, Andrew Simonds, F. W. Marshall. Executors: Elizabeth Ann Marshall, Joseph W. W. Marshall. Owned more than 5,000 acres of land in South Carolina and Florida. Owned the Long Cane Church tract of land. Owned 11 mules that he had named, 150 hogs, 85 sheep 50 cows. Owned at least 54 slaves. Willed $3,000 to Episcopal Church in Abbeville, $3,000 to the Episcopal Seminary in Abbeville, $5,000 to the widows and orphans of the Confederate soldiers in the 1st Regiment S. C. Rifles. Appraisal Jan 10, 1862 by G.W. Cromer, John Davis, J. A. McCord, James Irwin. Executors collected $389,290.16 for disbursement. Wife: Eliza Beth Ann Marshall. Sons: Wm. T. Marshall, Samuel F. Marshall, J. Foster Marshall, J. Quitman Marshall, Arthur M. Marshall. Daughters: Eliza D. Marshall, Mary F. Marshall.

BOX 160 PACK 4332   PATRICK C. McCASLAN   1862

Administrator: A. L. McCaslan. Bond Mar 25, 1862 of $12,000 by Rachel McCaslan, Alex. L. McCaslan, James McCaslan, M. O. McCaslan, James J. Shanks. Wife Rachel C. McCaslan. Sons: James age 18, Wm. E. age 16, Patrick H. age 14, Robert J. Daughters: Margaret Lucretia who married Johnson Link and lived in Hardeman Co. Tenn. in 1875, Mary E. McCaslan. Robert Jones was the guardian of minors James D. McCaslan, W. E. McCaslan, Patrick H. McCaslan. Appraisal Mar 26, 1862 by David McLane, Wm. K. Bradley, J. J. Shanks, Samuel Link. Owned 12 slaves, 264 acres of land on Bold Branch. Notes held on: Wm. G. Neel, Thomas Link, Samuel C. Zaner, John Patterson, Wm. McCaslan, R. H. McCaslan, Leroy J. Johnson, John Baughman. Had business account open and due on: John Baughman, Johson Link, George Zaner, Milly Harris, David McLane, Wm. Kennedy, W. M. McCaslan, Thomas Link, D. M. Rogers, B. C. Napier. Estate Sale Mar 27, 1862. Buyers at sale: R obert McCaslan, James M. McCaslan, Moses O. McCaslan, J. H. Morris, Alex. L. McCaslan, Wm. McCelvey, Wm. Rogers, Wm. H. Taggart, Wm. K. Bradley, James Cason, Joseph Burt, George Zaner, J. P. Kennedy, David Wardlaw, Ben. McKittrick, Rachel McCaslan, Charles W. Cowan, Wm. Watkins, Wilson Watkins, E. C. Cowan, James H. Morris, James Martin, James Taggart, W. M. McCaslan, James Horton, F. Lathrop, Thomas Clatworthy, Johnson Link, T. Thompson, Clark McGaw, Wm. K. Bradley, D. McNeill Turner, James Shanks. Rachel C. McCaslan died prior to the settlement and David McLane became the administrator of her estate. Petition for settlement filed Oct 23, 1873 favoring 1/3 for widow who was alive at the time and 1/7 share to each child. Estate Sale Nov 11, 1873 with each child to receive $87. Settlement postponed as all wanted the land sold prior to final settlement. Land was sold to J. H. Watson for $1550 on Jan 15, 1874. 1862 Confederate tax $33.75, 1864 tax $12.35, 1865 tax $78.

BOX 160 PACK 4333   EBENEEZER WALLACE   1862

Administrator: George Wallace who was in the Confederate Army (Larkin Barmore acted as his agent). Bond Nov 4, 1862 of $2,000 by George Wallace, Larkin Barmore, James Seawright. Appraisal Nov 17, 1862 of $56 by Benjamin Smith, Wm. Donald, John Dunn. Notes Held on: B. G. Stone, N. D. Stone, B. F. Brown, E. W. Bowie, George Wallace, Jane Wallace. Estate Sale Nov 21, 1862 netted $75. Buyers at sale: Eleanor Stone, Lee Wallace, Jane Wallace, N. Wallace, Sue Wallace, Joanna Wallace. Estate Settlement Mar 3, 1864. (10) Distributees, not named, each received $55. 1863 Confederate tax $4.34.

BOX 160 PACK 4334   ALEXANDER WINN   1862

Deceased died Oct 26, 1862. Will dated Oct 8, 1862. Witnesses: Henry S. Cason, Wm. Wickliffe, Jesse W. Cann. Wife: Drucilla Winn died prior to settlement. Executor J. H. Bell. 1st Appraisal Nov 21, 1862 by L. C. Clinkscales, Wm. L. Campbell, Pleasant Ferguson. 2nd Appraisal Apr 29, 1872 by Robert C. Harkness, Preston C. Suber, Elbridge H. Bell, Robert Stuckey. Estate Sale May 2, 1872. Buyers at sale: Roger L. Williams, Emily Tribble, George W. Daniel, George Winn, Wm. Mann Jr., Thomas Moore, Robert Stuckey, Marcus Winn, Joseph Bowen, John H. Bell, Wm. N. Hall, Obediah L. Cann, Wm. Giles, Wm. Mann Sr., Wm. A. Fleming, John McCurry, Thomas J. Hill, Wm. McMahan, Peter Hunter, J. S. Cann, Jesse Cann, Pleasant Ferguson, Preston C. Suber, Eliza Harkness, Wm. Moore. Land had to be sold to satisfy estate debts. Funeral expenses $5. Estate Settlement Feb 21, 1873. (8) Distributees each received $2.72. 1. Frances wife of G. W. Daniel 2. Marcus Winn 3. George A. Winn 4. Louisa Alice wife of N.

McAllister 5. Daniel Winn 6. Alexander Winn 7. Letha wife of Thomas Moore 8. Mary Jane Patterson.

BOX 160 PACK 4335   VINCENT WALKER   1862

Administrator: Micajah W. Lyles. Bond Feb 1, 1862 of $1,000 by Micajah W. Lyles, E. A. Searles, J. A. Edmunds. Appraisal Feb 6, 1862 by T. Harris, Berry Deason, Catlett Corley. Notes held on: Uriah Brown, Sanders Walker, Burton Walker. Estate Sale Feb 7, 1862 netted $219.144. Buyers at sale: Wm. D. Harmon, Catlett Corley, Mary J. Walker, John Deason Jr., Elizabeth Mackey, Micajah W. Lyles, W. W. McKinney.

BOX 160 PACK 4336   ELIZA THOMAS WILLIAMS   1861

Will dated Oct 21, 1857. Witnesses: S. E. Graydon, F. F. Gary, Joel W. Townsend. Executor: Chesley D. Evans-Nephew. Sisters: Jane Beverly Evans lived in Marion, S. C., Ann M. Turpin, Martha M. Giles. Nephews: Alfred B. Turpin, Chesley D. Evans. Nieces: Ann Eliza. Appraisal: Oct 25, 1861 by S.E. Graydon, J. N. Cochran, Charles Smith. Owned 11 slaves, 460 acres of land, house and lot in Cokesbury. Held notes on: H. J. Norman, W. A. Moore, W. P. McKellar. Estate Sale Dec 31, 1861. Buyers at sale: Martin G. Zeigler, Wm. A. Moore, P. W. Connor, Ben. Z. Herndon, A. Cobb, C. D. Evans, O. B. Rice, John Mundy, B. C. Hart, Dr. Franklin F. Gary, Miss C. Giles, Rev. J. F. Smith, Wm. Joel Smith, Rev. J. M. Carlisle, James Killingsworth, Francis A. Connor, John Adams, John C. Allen, Thomas Mahon, W. R. Hilton, D. S. Beacham, M. Strauss, A. T. Watson, Mrs. A. M. Turpin, Dr. Ephriam R. Calhoun, L. D. Giles, W. C. Anderson. To Jane Beverly Evans (9) slaves to Ann M. Turpin carriage and horses, to Alfred B. Turpin library.

BOX 160 PACK 4337   SANDERS WALKER   1863

Administrator: Ellington Searles. Bond Jan 21, 1862 by Ellington Searles, George W. Mitchell, Z. Harris. Appraisal Feb 6, 1862 by T. Harris, John Brown, Berry Deason, Catlett Corley, Peter Smith. Owned 10 slaves. Held notes on: H. E. Corley, Elijah Beagles, Redmond Brown, J. R. Bodie, M. McKinnney, Chesley Walker, Andrew Harris, Levi Furqueron, Elias Banks, John Elkins, Burton Walker, Wm. C. Fleming, Peter Smith, Andrew J. Harris, Wm. Finley, Wm. Minor, James Newby. Estate Sale Feb 7, 1862 netted $9,259. Buyers at sale: Redmond Brown, John Deason Jr., John Willis, Rev. A. G. Harmon, F. H. Edmunds, W. W. McKinney, J. Simpson Talbert, Ben. E. Gibert, Ellington A. Searles, Chesley Walker, John Martin, D. P. Self, Wiley Newby, George Rosenwike, W. S. Headwright, Henry Holloway, James Henderson, Wm. C. Ludrick, Wade Walker, George Whitfield Cox, S. W. Willis, Joseph Britt, Zephaniah Harris, Francis Wideman, Elizabeth Walker, Dr. Patrick H. Bradley, Wesley A. Smith, Clement Corley, Green B. Martin, Peter Smith, Landon Tucker, Miss Jane Walker, John Willis, Berry Deason, Robert Johnson, Dr. John Sanders. Taxes1860 $18.18, 1862 $10.57, 1864 $108, 1866 $2.08. Mar 19, 1876 Wm. P. Dillashaw petitioned heirs against selling land. (7) Heirs: 1. Eliza Walker-Widow 2. Hulda wife of Redmond Brown 3. Minerva Harris, children a. Louisa b. Mitchell 4. Wade died after his father with wife, Sarah and no children 5. Jane wife of Henry Brewer6. Wife of --- Willis, 7. Chesley B.

BOX 160 PACK 4338   GEORGE McDUFFIE WATSON   1863

Will dated Feb 19, 1861. Witnesses: Moses C. Taggart, N. G. Kennedy, Willis Smith. Executor: James H. Wideman. Brothers: Thomas A. Watson, James Franklin Watson deceased. Sister: Dorothy wife of George W. Tolbert. Nephew: James Franklin Watson Jr. Appraisal Oct 24, 1862 by Samuel B. McClinton, Willis Smith, M. W. Coleman,

Jonathan Jordan, Charles W. Sproull. Appraisal of slaves Jan 19, 1863 by Samuel B. McClinton, Willis Smith, Johnson Sale, John McClellan. Owned at least 31 slaves, 927 acres of land 50 shares of Greenville & Columbia Railroad. Held notes on: Charles E. Brooks, Moses O. Taggart, J. P. Bond, Andrews & McNeill, H. W. Wardlaw, Hugh B. Maxwell, Robert R. Tolbert, George W. Tolbert, Thomas A. Watson, John R. Tolbert, David Malone, Wm. C. Hunter, W. H. Watson, W. P. Andrews, J. F. Watson, Henry Moore, J. L. Hearst, George R. Caldwell, Wm. Scott. Estate Settlement Jul 1, 1863. (3) Legatees: 1. Thomas A. Watson $1095.90 2. Dorothy J. Tolbert $695.90 3. James Franklin Watson $495.90.

BOX 160 PACK 4339   JAMES A. WARDLAW   1863

Administrator: John F. Livingston. Bond Nov 24, 1862 of $6,000 by John F. Livingston, Robert H. Wardlaw, Mathew W. McDonald. Appraisal Nov 28, 1862 by John T. Owen, B. P. Hughes, J. A. Hunter. Held notes on: James Gordon, John Robinson & Wm. Gordon, J. Wardlaw Perrin, A. L. Gillespie, George Dusenberry. Estate Sale Nov 29, 1862 netted $1,148.94. Buyers at sale: Mrs. E. Wardlaw, Wm. Hill, B. H. Wardlaw, J. J. Wardlaw, J. F. Livingston, John T. Owen, Mathew McDonald, Dr. Harvey T. Lyon, Charles H. Lyon, James A. Allen, James D. Chalmers, Robert E. Hill, John W. Lesly.

BOX 160 PACK 4340   JOHN G. WILSON   1862

1st Administrator: John Rosemond Wilson. Bond Oct 27, 1862 of $2,000 by John Rosemond Wilson, Lemuel Reid, Robert Ellis. 2nd Administrator: Edwin Wilson in 1868. Wife: L. A. Wilson. Bond May 9, 1868 of $1,000 by Edwin Wilson, John H. Wilson, John A. Wier. Appraisal Nov 10, 1862 by John Enright, B. P. Hughes, Charles H. Allen. Owned 1 slave. Held notes on: J. R. Hamlin, John McLaren, Dr. T. J. Mabry, G. C. Bowers, A. W. Wilson, B. M. Blease, Andrew Small, J. Sperien, Thomas J. Price, F. P. Robertson, David Goff, T. E. Bigby, Bernard O'Connor, Charles Cox, T. D. M. Edwards, J. B. Courtright, Robert Lisenber, Wm. McGill, Samuel Fife, Nimrod McCord, Morton Dansby. Open Accounts owed and due him at his death. R. A. Fair, Thomas Blease, Charles Cox, Wm. Mooney, Wm. H. Parker, John McLaren, John Corbett, W. J. Lomax, S. H. Jones, D. T. Jones, Donald McLaughlin. Estate Sale: Mar 11, 1862. Buyers at sale: George Allen, D. J. Jordan, James H. Cobb, Talbert Cheatham, J. T. Moore, N. J. Davis, Joseph T. Moore, R. H. Wardlaw, Mathew McDonald, N. P. Davis, Lemuel Reid, J. R. Wilson, Frederick Ives, Thomas Christian, Jeptha R. Hamlin, Edward Roche, Alpheus Lesly, Mrs. McCracken, Mrs. Stacey, Thomas Thomson, Wm. Mooney, Wm. Smith, Dr. J. J. Wardlaw, Hiram W. Lawson, John White, Dr. McNeill Turner, John Enright, Robert Cheatham, John H. Wilson, Edward Westfield, Mrs. Wilson, John McLaren. 1862 tax $#6.41. Paid Edward J. Taylor $40 for making coffin.

BOX 160 PACK 4341   WILLIAM H. WHITE   1863

Confederate Soldier killed at the Battle of Manassas Aug 30, 1862 as a member of Co. K Moore's Regiment S. C. Volunteers. Never Married. Administrator: John White. Bond Nov 8, 1862 of $4,000 by John White, John A. Wier, B. P. Hughes. Appraisal Dec 13, 1862 by B. P. Hughes, J. A. Allen, Charles H. Allen. Had large library. Held notes on: Thomas J. Douglass, Wm. Wilson, Ben. P. Hughes, J. Foster Marshall, John White, Robert N. Cheatham, Est. of Charles Dendy, J. R. F. Wilson, Charles H. Allen, Robert H. Wardlaw, J. J. Wardlaw, Littleton Yarborough, John McBryde, Isaac Branch, Augustus W. Smith, Augustus Kyle, H. A. Jones. Open Accounts owed and due payment to him: James Cobb, George Graves, Charles G. Bowers, Robert Slager, John A. Calhoun, John White, Thomas

61

C. Perrin, Robert H. Wardlaw. 1863 Confederate tax $25, 1863 state tax $2.04, 1868 tax $1.50. Last return and estate activity Apr 1881.

BOX 160 PACK 4342   DR. DELANEY WILSON'S MINORS   1860

Guardian: Joseph T. Moore. Bond: Nov 3, 1860 of $6,000 by Joseph T. Moore, James Moore, Wm. C. Moore. George M. Wilson & Delaney T. Wilson. Rebecca E. Wilson due $480 in Nov 1860 being over 14 years of age.

BOX 160 PACK 4343   MARGARET WILLIAMS   1861

Administrator: John C. Williams, the deceased had lived with for 11 years. Bond Feb 16, 1861 of $5,000 by John C. Williams, Newton Sims, M. Strauss. Appraisal Mar 23, 1861 $36.01 by W. E. Caldwell, Newton Sims, M. Strauss. Held notes on: S. J. Williams, J. C. Williams, John Cunningham. Estate Settlement Sep 5, 1861. (2) Distributees with each receiving $2,332.65. 1. Estate of brother (S. J. Williams) 2. John C. Williams. J. A. Williams was a daughter of deceased but was not a distributee.

BOX 160 PACK 4344   JOHN WILLIAMS   1856

Will dated Feb 11, 1856. Witnesses: Wm. B. Gaines, John W. Moore, John C. Waters. Wife: Drusilla Williams. Daughters: Drucilla wife of Samuel Agnew, Susan wife of Elijah Watson, Tabitha wife of John Brock. Executor: John C. Waters. Bond Sep 4, 1860 of $25,000 by John C. Waters, Wesley Robertson, Marshall Sharp. Appraisal Nov 14, 1860 by John Vance, Marshall Sharp, Wm. Hodges, Green Berry Riley. Owned 12 slaves. Estate Sale Nov 15, 1860 netted $9,412. Buyers at sale: Marshall Sharp, Alex. M. Agnew, John Vance, John C. Waters, Rap Hughes, A. R. Singleton, Susan Hughes, James Jones, Larkin Mays, Green B. Riley, Wesley Robertson, Wm. Hodges, J. D. Adams, A. T. Watson, Newton Sims, John Brock, Dr. B. C. Hart, Wm. A. Moore, W. W. Higgins, Wm. A. Pratt, Ezekiel Rasor, J. C. Williams, Wm. Maddox, Dr. W. T. Jones, W. A. Richey, B. H. Aiken, J. T. Johnson, Susan Swain, James Anderson, James Wright, J. L. Rasor, John Rotherick, Robert Y. Jones, J. B. Chandler, W. M. Griffin, T. J. Beacham, Samuel Agnew, W. H. Robertson, J. A. Ellis, Andrew J. McKee, Henry Redden, A. S. Koon, Robert Anderson, John Hefferman, J. C. Allen, M. Strauss. Paid James D. Chalmers $18.50 for Tombstone. 1862 war tax $45.13. Estate Settlement Sep 2, 1863. (5) Legatees: 1. Widow 2. Elijah Williams -son 3. Susan Swain-daughter 4. John Brock and his wife 5. Children of Samuel Agnew.

BOX 160 PACK 4345   ALLEN WEEKS   1863

Administrator: Stephen B. Smith. Bond Dec 7, 1860 by Stephen B. Smith, Peter Smith, James A. Edwards. Appraisal Dec 27, 1860 by John Brown, James Newby, John Deason. Owned 1 slave. Estate Sale Dec 27, 1860 netted $1,482. Buyers at sale: Elizabeth Weeks, George W. Newby, Redmond Brown, James Brown, W. H. Smith, Samuel Walker, Dr. Patrick H. Bradley, M. W. Lites. Estate Settlement Apr 21, 1863. 1/3 to widow, Elizabeth Weeks $370.62. (8) Children, all minors, received $92.65 each.

BOX 160 PACK 4346   SARAH WEEKS (minor)   1860

Guardian: Wm. McCain. Bond Nov 21, 1860 of $500 by Wm. McCain, John G. Thornton, John Lyon. She was due money from the estate of her mother's father, Cuthbert Price that had been settled Jul 31, 1855. She was entitled to $133.05. She was the only child of her mother. She became Sarah Walker. Final return and estate activity Apr 19, 1868.

BOX 161 PACK 4347   ALEXANDER AUSTIN   1853

1st Will dated Jan 23, 1860. Witnesses: J. H. Irby, W. D. Watts, John W. Watts. 2nd Will dated Feb 23, 1864. Witnesses: Robinson Cobb, M. Erwin, G. M. Mattison. Executor named 1st will Robert C. Austin. Executor named 2nd will John Austin. Wife: Isabella Austin. Sons: John Austin, Robert Austin, Wm. Austin, Samuel Austin, Mathew J. Austin. Daughters: Susan Austin, Sarah Austin, Martha Austin. Grand Daughter: Letha Ann Ragsdale. Brother: Robert C. Austin. 1st Appraisal May 14, 1864 by Joel Kay, M. Erwin, James Gambrell, Ellihu Campbell, G. M. Mattison. 2nd Appraisal Dec 16, 1878 by James Gambrell, Joel Kay, M. Erwin. Owned 420 acres of land. Held notes on: W. M. Callaham, M. T. Davenport, W. P. Martin, H. Austin, J. F. Gambrell, David Coleman. Estate Sale Dec 17, 1878. Buyers at sale: W. F. Austin, M. J. Austin, John H. Austin, Letha Ann Bagwell, Sarah Austin, J. F. Gambrell, M. Erwin, T. J. Crawford, Harrison Latimer, W. L. Woods, Frank Eppes, Robert W. Burts, Henry Pinson, Joel Kay, R. S. Cheshire, Aaron Robinson, Reed Gambrell, Levi Shaw, Robert Raines, Enos Gambrell, Enoch Watson, John Ridge, C. Lollis Jr., Baylis Acker, George W. Gambrell, W. P. Bagwell, Thad Gambrell, C. E. Harper, Austin Magee, G. M. Mattison, B. Arnold, G. N. Ballentine, Fielding Seawright, M. B. Gaines, Enoch Watkins, Adam Bagwell, J. L. Brock, S. P. Taylor, W. L. Latimer, Jesse T. Kay, Luke Butler, R. T. Kirkpatrick, D. S. McCullough, Chilsolm Austin, Wm. Simpson, A. W. Ashley, R. M. Grier, Peter Smith, W. H. Shirley, Charles Acker, R. E. Hughes, Abe Herndon, G. M. Greer, F. M. Godbolt. Estate Settlement May 13, 1879. (7) Distributees each receiving $408.86: 1. Susan F. Gambrell 2. John H. Austin 3. Sarah Austin 4. M. J. Austin 5. W. F. Austin 6. Letha Ann Ragsdale-grand daughter 7. Sallie Gunnels-granddaughter.

BOX 161 PACK 4348   DR. ENOCH AGNEW   1878

1st Administrator: John C. Waters died before completion. 2nd Administrator: James B. Agnew who died shortly after assuming position. Bond Mar 13, 1878 of $2,200 by James B. Agnew, Eola H. Agnew, M. B. McGee. 3rd Administrator: Charles D. Smith. Bond May 1, 1878 of $4,000 by Charles D. Smith, Anna M. Smith, James Agnew. Physician. Appraisal Nov 8, 1863 by Andrew Dunn, G. B. Riley, John Vance, Wm. Hodges, Marshall Sharp. Slaves appraised Jan 11, 1864. Owned 11 slaves 6 of whom were sold Jan 12, 1864 for $16,226. Medical Accounts due at time of his death: John Higgins, A. Dodson, Mrs. S. Barmore, Samuel Graham, M. Godbolt, W. Watson, Mrs. Algary, James Gilmer, J. C. Richey, Silas Jones, Tilda Flinn, Marion Sharp, Andrew Cobb, Ross Bonham, Samuel Agnew, W. T. Jones, D. N. Sims, Rev. Valentine Young, John Algary, David Jones, A. Singleton, Frances Arnold, A. H. McGee, Wm. Pratt, H. Y. Gilliam, Wesley Robertson, W. L. McGee, T. Y. Martin, G. B. Riley, Mrs. S. Robertson, Wm. Armstrong, Dudley Mabry, Edward Roney, M. Freeman, Elizabeth McGee, W. W. Higgins, John Vance, Miss Byphenia Watson, Mrs. Cat. Moore, James Rasor, Larkin Mays, W. Boyd, Terry Shannon, Mrs. T. Prater, Abner Freeman, Michael McGee, Wm. Hodges, Wm. Gaines, Miss S.J. Barmore, Mrs. F. Higgins, J. K. Vance, Mrs. Marshall Hodges, James Brock, James J. Richey, Jackson Linton, Wm. Freeman, Wm. McGee. Estate Sale Nov 10, 1863. Buyers at sale: Samuel Agnew, John Adams, Andrew Agnew, John C. Waters, John Vance, J. D. Sullivan, Pauil Connor, M. Strauss, A. Morgan. Gabriel Hodges, Ezekiel Rasor, Cat. Cason, L. B. Jones, G. W. Rasor, F. M. Godbolt, W. T. Jones, H. R. Banks, J. Bailey, J. K. Vance, W. T. Jones, Thomas Harris, Widow, A. M. Agnew, Aaron Pitts, Dr. Andrew Dunn, J. T. McCuen, R. H. Mounce, Newton Sims, W. P. McGee, Ross Bonham, M. B. McGee, W. A. Moore, Marshall Sharp, Dr. Wm. C. Norwood, G. W. Rasor. A. M. Dodson, Mrs. Singleton, Francis A. Connor, Harris Y. Gilliam, Charles C. Pinckney, Dr. Franklin Gary, Dr. J. F. Donald, E. R. Ridgeway, Sterling E. Graydon, J. M. Williams, Joseph Webb, J. H.

Shaw, Rev. J. C. Williams, Dr. M. B. Latimer, Thomas Pearlstein. Last estate entry Aug 3, 1885.

BOX 161 PACK 4349   WILLIAM S. ASHLEY (minor)   1863

Son of Joshua J. Ashley and Martha F. Ashley. Age 3 in 1863. Guardian: Martha F. Ashley. Bond Jan 13, 1863 of $115.50 by Martha F. Ashley, John Smith, Mathew McDonald. Received $57.

BOX 161 PACK 4350   JOHN ANDERSON   1863

Confederate Soldier. Administrator: Edmund Anderson. Bond May 11, 1863 of $3,000 by Edmund Anderson, Vachel Hughey, Henry Riley. Appraisal May 30, 1863 of $179 by Vachel Hughey, Levi H. Rykard, Henry Riley. Estate Sale May 30, 1863. Buyers at sale: James Hughey, E. A. Anderson, Henry Riley, T. H. Harrison, A. C. Collins. Estate Settlement Jan 18, 1864. (7) Distributees each received $114.79. Mother and (6) brothers and sisters, not named.

BOX 161 PACK 4351   JONATHAN B. ADAMSON   1863

Administrators: M. M. Adamson, Robert W. Lites. Bond of $75,000 by Robert W. Lites, M. M. Adamson, Adam Wideman. Appraisal Dec 3, 1863 by Adam Wideman, Isaac Caldwell, W.E. Bradley, George H. Pressly, A. J. Weed. Owned 8 slaves. Held notes on: James Russell, Timothy Russell, T. W. Talman. Estate Sale Dec 4, 1863. Buyers at sale: Widow, Wm. Adamson, Issac A. Keller, Mrs. S. Walker, Miss Margaret Adamson, T. O. Creswell, Dr. H. Drennan, W. C. Robinson, Robert W. Lites, Wm. K. Bradley, James Steifle, James Creswell, D. T. Oliver, James Dowtin, Joseph Keller, Wm. Weed, Dr. A. P. Boozer, J. Gilchrist, Patrick H. Bradley, J. Gibson, R. A. McCaslan. 1865 state tax $85.53, 1865 Confederate tax $250.42, 1870 state tax $13.50. Widow and (6) children at time of death. Estate Settlement Oct 10, 1877. (5) Distributees: 1. Wm. H. Adamson 2. J. F. Adamson 3. Sarah C. Walker 4. Mary E. Keller wife of Issac Alpheus Keller 5. M. T. Adamson.

BOX 161 PACK 4352   JOSEPH F. BURTON   1864

Administrators: Hugh Robinson, James M. Carwile. Widow & (6) Children. Appraisal Jul 22, 1863 by Bennett McAdams, W. L. Young, B. Callaham, J. F. Clinkscales. Owned 3 slaves. Held notes on: Wm. Clinkscales, J. J. McAdams, David Loner, Wm. Allen, John F. Clinkscales, John A. Burton, Peter S. Burton, Michael McGee, John Gunter. Open Accounts due him at his death for 1861-1863: 1861: S. M. Tribble, Robert Ellis, John W. Brock, Peter S. Burton, Albert Johnston. 1862: J. T. McAdams, R. F. Bryson, Basil Callaham, John M. Bryant, Peter S. Burton, James B. McWhorter, Wm. Pratt, J. W. Brooks, Rev. Robert C. Grier, R. A. Tucker, Elizabeth Duncan, Wm. Crowther, Wm. L. Young, James M. Carwile, John M. Bryant, L. C. Clinkscales, Conrad Wakefield, Samuel Shaw, B. T. Gray, Thomas Pearlstein, James Hopkins. 1863: Wm. Clinkscales, Robert McAdams, Robert Ellis, Mary Kay, John F. Clinkscales, Robert Fair, Richard Taylor, James M. Calllaham, John W. McBride, Nancy Burton, Adam Clamp, Malinda Bratcher, Robert A. Archer, Wm. L. Burton. Estate Sale Jul 23, 1863. Buyers at sale: R. Pratt, David Loner, Mrs. John J. Copeland, Wm. M. Alewine, David Duncan, A. W. Branyon, Hiram T. Tusten, Ben F. Moseley, J. J. Shirley, Wm. Prewitt, Samuel Mitchell, J. W. Shirley, Ben. Pearman, Wm. Dawkins, Widow, Thomas Davis, James B. McWhorter, R. F. Bryson, John F. Clinkscales, George Allen, Robert Parker, Wm. Y. Walker, J. H. Bannister, E. Harris, John Bell, Wm. C. Armstrong, Robert E. Hill, R. Clinkscales, R. Ellis, Miss Mary A. McClain, F.

W. R. Nance, Wm. Wickliffe, J. G. E. Branyon, James Patterson, S. S. Fisher, Noble Bell, J. B. Kay. J. J. Bonner, Samuel Sims, J. M. Carwile, Martha Griffin, John Shirley, Yancey Dove, H. Robinson, W. L. Young, Jeptha R. Hamlin, E. Ashley, R. H. Hall, John M. Bryant, P. Hopkins, J. H. McRea, Nancy Pratt, Mrs. E. Duncan, Dr. A. Branyon, Mrs. L. M. Hopkins, James Darby, James Davis, Robert C. Grier, J. J. Uldrick, Albert B. Hamlin, B. C. Rutledge, J. Ashley, Joseph Ellis, Thomas Pearlstein, B. T. Gray, J. J. Cunningham, G. W. L. Mitchell, J. Galloway, Mrs. P. S. Burton, John A. Wier, John Shirley, Basil Calllaham. 1ˢᵗ Estate Settlement Feb 23, 1864. Widow received $2,851. (6) Children all minors: 1. Wm. L. Burton, 2. John W. Burton 3. Jane E. Burton 4. Mary A. Burton 5. Joseph F. Burton 6. Elizabeth S. Burton.

BOX 161 PACK 4353   REBECCA BARR   1863

Will dated Apr 16, 1861. Witnesses: Robert H. Wardlaw, Lemuel Reid, Thomas C. Perrin. Executor: Wm. Barr. Appraisal Apr 14, 1863 by John T. Lyon, Lemuel Reid, J. J. Wardlaw. Owned 2 slaves.

BOX 161 PACK 4354   JOHN BROWNLEE   1864

Administrator: Rosa Brownlee-wife, Henry H. Harper-son-in-law. Bond Aug 8, 1863 of $125,000 by Rosa Brownlee, Henry H. Harper, George B. Clinkscales, James W. Black, J. J. Cunningham. Appraisal Aug 7, 1863 by George B. Clinkscales, James W. Black, Robert C. Harkness, J. J. Cunningham. Owned 46 slaves. Notes & Accounts due the Estate: Christian Barnes, J. C. Speer, James Taylor, John A. Martin, A. D. Hunter, Aaron W. Lynch, T. M. Tucker, W. R. Morrow, Hugh M. Prince Jr., J. E. Bell, A. Johnson, J. F. C. DuPre, M. B. Latimer, W. J. Robertson, Robert C. Harkness, J. W. Black, James A. Brownlee, J. Cowan, J. F. Bell, J. J. Cunningham, R. L. Harden, B. W. Williams, C. A. Huckabee, N. & B. Winestock, J. T. Boyd, Thomas Davis, W. F. Wright, Henry H. Harper. Estate Sale Apr 8, 1863. Buyers at sale: Wm. R. Brownlee, W. Dawkins, G. W. Bowen, Wm. Brownlee, Dr. John Bell, Mrs. Aaron Lynch, W. A. Gaines, Dr. Baskin, Ed Bell, Elbridge H. Bell, W. R. Morrow, John Craft, J. W. Black, Mrs. Brownlee, Robert Pettigrew, Thomas J. Hill, James A. Brownlee, J. J. Cunningham, Henry H. Harper, L. C. Mauldin, J. B. Pruitt, Henry S. Cason, Jacob Alewine, Thomas F. Lanier, Wm. Pratt, R. F. Bell, James M. Martin, J. J. Pratt, S. J. Davis, Amanda Johnson, A. M. Pettigrew, M. Alewine, Phil Rutledge, John A. Crawford, Jonathan Johnson, D. R. Sondley, Pressly Suber, T. P. Martin, G. P. Brownlee, W. D. Mann, J. W. Lesly, J. R. Black, Lewis Clinkscales, Wm. Hicks, J. W. Martin, W. B. Latimer, F. A. F. Noblet, S. J. Davis, Edward Westfield, Francis A. Wilson, Wash Bowen, H. Parker, Wm. Alewine, J. J. Shirley, L. C. Clinkscales, F. P. Robertson, Dr. Isaac Branch, J. A. Murdock, Wm. Johnson, Monroe Bowen, Samuel Sharp, N. N. Mitchell, Samuel Robertson, J. H. Bell, Wm. Dickson. 1866 tax $16.33.

BOX 161 PACK 4355   WILLIAM C. BARMORE   1863

Administrator: J. F. Donald. Estate Settlement Sep 29, 1863. Mother and (7) brothers and sisters. Each received $249.65.

BOX 161 PACK 4356   MARTHA & MARY BUCHANAN (minors)   1864

Guardian: Wm. Buchanan. Bond Mar 15, 1864 of $5,000 by Wm. Buchanan, Robert P. Buchanan, Gabriel D. Buchanan. Settlement Sep 7, 872.

BOX 161 PACK 4357   ALANSON W. BRANYON   1864

Will dated Sep 7, 1863. Witnesses: R. N. Wright, Thomas W. Branyon, John McAdams. Wife: Manerva Catherine Branyon who married John McAdams in 1864. Sons: John Wm. Branyon, Jefferson Davis Gustave Beauregard Branyon. Executors: Manerva Catherine-wife she died in 1874, James E. G. Branyon-brother. 1st Appraisal Feb 12, 1864 by John McAdams, T. W. Branyon, S. M. Tribble. Owned 172 acres of land in 3 tracts. Held notes on: J. G. Gantt, W. L. Moseley, R. N. Wright, N. H. Armstsrong, H. Latimer, J. H. Seawright, H. Hughes, M. A. Jones, Wm. Clinkscales, A. J. Brock, Wm. Holmes. 2nd Appraisal Jun 24, 1874 by S. M. Tribble, J. S. Carwile, John Shirley, R. N. Wright. (7) Children, 4 by wife's former husband and 3 by the deceased. R. N. Wright was the guardian of the children as all were minors in 1874. Estate Sale Dec 2, 1874. Buyers at sale: Z. H. Carwile, B. G. Martin, James Adams, A. H. Stone, D. Mitchell, J. T. Ashley, James Wilson, W. Ricketts, Robert W. Burts, R. P. Calhoun, John Shirley, G. L. Mitchell, G. Pearman, A. M. Armstrong, E. W. Richey, W. Richey, Joshua Ashley, M. C. Simmons, M. S. Strickland. A. T. Armstrong, James G. Branyon, J. H. Clamp, T. M. Maddox, A. N. Cullins, G. W. Grubbs, John Bratcher, L. M. Stone, Dr. Robinson, F. J. Bell, C. Bratcher, Samuel Latimer, B. J. Martin, John Moore, G. M. Bigby, John Manson, Alice Armstrong, J. M. Ashley, James Armstrong, T. M. Branyon, Joseph Ashley, J. M. Ashley, James N. Shirley, D. Armstrong, W. Bradley, Lou Branyon, J. G. Branyon. Estate Settlement Dec 9, 1880 Dec 9, 1880. (3) Legatees each received $353.10: 1. J. W. W. Branyon 2. J. D. Branyon 3. Lou E. J. Branyon. William Ricketts was the guardian of J. D. Branyon. 1871 taxes state and county $4.80, 1879 taxes $12.12, 1880 taxes $15.60.

BOX 161 PACK 4358   J. P. BLACWELL   1863

Administrator: L. E. Blackwell-wife. Bond Nov 14, 1863 of $8,000 by L. E. Blackwell, B. B. McCreary, A. A. Williams. Estate Settlement Dec 18, 1866.

BOX 161 PACK 4359   SAMUEL BRANYON   1863

Administrator: J. E. G. Branyon. Appraisal Aug 27, 1863 by Wm. Clinkscales, Wm. Armstrong, John S. Carwile. Estate Sale Aug 27, 1863 netted $1,333. Buyers at sale: James Wilson, James E. G. Branyon, George Darby, James Adams, A. Branyon, B. McClain, A. W. Branyon, Samuel Martin, J. M. G. Branyon, John Shirley, Wm. Armstrong, J. J. Copelan, Thomas Branyon, R. H. Branyon, Stephen Strickland, A. S. Armstrong, John A. Branyon, Margaret Jones, James Darby, T. G. Branyon, Zachariah Jones, John Tribble, John S. Carwile, Henry Bratcher, John M. G. Branyon, John Moore. Estate Settlement Oct 16, 1865. (6) Distributees each received $108.62: 1. J. E. G. Branyon 2. John A. Branyon 3. Child of Alanza W. Alford 4. R. H. Branyon 5. M. A. Branyon, now Mrs. McAdams 6. Margaret A. Jones wife of Sev. Jones.

BOX 161 PACK 4360   JOHN G. BARRATT   1864

Will dated Mar 29, 1862. Witness J. I. Chipley, T. J. Chipley. Executors: Elizabeth C. Barratt, John T. Parks. Wife: Elizabeth C. Barratt. Sons: John A. Barratt, Wm. P. Barratt. Daughters: Flora Pauline Barratt, Irene C. Barratt. Appraisal Jan 11, 1864 by Allen Vance and others. Owned 44 slaves, large library, 50 shares of stock in The Greenville & Columbia Railroad. Cash on hand at death $7,180. Held notes on: C. E. Brooks, Moses C. Taggart, J. W. Brooks, Henry Wilkerson, Thomas C. Chatham, Lewis C. Parks, Wm. G. Kennedy, Esma Jones, Allen Vance, Felix G. Parks, J. Foster Marshall, M. W. Coleman, Elizabeth Harris, J. R. Seal, Lemuel Bell, John D. Creswell, W. W. Perryman, W. L. Appleton, Estate of Richard Watson, P. A. Waller, R. R. Tolbert. Estate Sale Jan 13 & 14, 1864. Buyers at sale: Elizabeth C. Barratt, J. B. Sherman, Jonathan S. Chipley, J. D.

McKellar, Col. Erwin, Irwin Hutchinson, John W. Suber, C. N. Arnold, J. Callison, Henry Watson, Dr. S. S. Marshall, John Calvert, Johnson Sale, Franklin Johnson, G. F. Anderson, Wm. C. Sproull, John T. Parks, Stephen Elmore, Allen Vance, Willis Ross, G. H. Waddell, Henry Wilkerson, E. C. Perryman, Mrs. Vaughn, Edward Hinton, A. Williams, H. H. Creswell, Wm. Hunter, Wm. Butler, H. M. Pinson, Moses C. Taggart, R. W. Seymour, A. H. Watson, J. C. Chiles, Thomas McClenon, Nathan Ingraham, Wm. McNeill, Dr. Williams, W. A. Baker, Wm. Ramsey, G. F. Anderson, N. Henderson, John McKellar, John Devlin, J. Bell, Uriah Mars, W. B. Brooks, Thomas Chatham, Thomas Lipscomb, W. C. Hunter, J. A. Myers, W. H. Watson, A. P. Boozer, Leonidas D. Connor, J. M. Roche, Jacob Miller, John T. Parks, S. D. Deal, H. H. Creswell, H. Stallworth, J. A. Bailey, J. Z. Johnson, M. S. Ingraham, Wm. Griffin, W. K. Blake, Dr. B. Manley, G. Durst, J. Matherson, S. A. Wilson, F. G. Martin, James Creswell, Samuel Wilson. Wm. A. Upton of Monroe Co., Tenn. married the widow Elizabeth C. Barratt. All of the children were minors and lived in Tenn. Upton appointed their guardian Nov 2, 1870.

BOX 161 PACK 4361   ALEXANDER C. BOWEN   1863

Administrator: Sterling Bowen. Bond Oct 19, 1863 of $6,000 by Sterling Bowen, Conrad Wakefield, Wm. Wickliffe. Appraisal Nov 5, 1863 by George B. Clinkscales, Michael McGee, L. T. Hill, David Callaham, Robert Stuckey. Estate Sale Nov 6, 1863 netted $1,999. Buyers at Sale: Elizabeth Bowen, Sterling Bowen, Thomas T. Cunningham, J. H. Bannister, Dr. Aaron W. Lynch, J. Alewine, D. Young, F. P. Robertson, J. B. Clinkscales, Conrad Wakefield, A. McAllister, R. F. Bell, Martha Burton, M. A. Douglass, A. Gailey, J. M. McGee, J. J. Smith, Dr. Wm. J. Milford. 1864 taxes $66. Estate Settlement Feb 13, 1865. (3) Legatees, widow and (2) children each received $709.76. Widow: Elizabeth Bowen. Children: 1. Amanitha Bowen 2. Mary Ann Bowen. Mother was their guardian.

BOX 161 PACK 4362   W. H. BENTLEY   1864

Administrator: Sarah Ann Bentley-wife, she received $550 on Jan 1, 1861 as an heir from the estate of P. M. Little. Miller by trade. Appraisal Nov 15, 1863 by W. S. Richardson, John Sadler, Charles W. Fooshe. Mill Accounts 1861: J. M. Hill, James Long, Wm. Abney, John Owens, Joe Wilkerson, John Malone, Tapley Anderson, S. Calhoun, Thomas Calhoun. Mill Accounts 1860: John Owens, H. M. Pinson, James Malone, Thomas Milford, John White, Frederick Nance, H. M. Pinson, W. Abney, D. Abney, C. Owens, M. Arnold, W. White, T. Anderson, Wm. Malone, James Anderson, W. Verrell, G. M. Harrison, G. M. Hill, John Jones, James Verrell, Patrick Hefferman, Maxwell Smith. Mill Accounts 1861: Thomas Calhoun, T. Sheppard, D. Whiteford, Dr. J. S. Watts, E. G. Simpson, Ransom Chaney, C. Owens, J. Stillwell, J. Pert, John Pinson, Joe Wilkerson, Wm. Pert, J. R. Puckett, H. F. Pergeson, Thomas Calhoun, J. W. Lipscomb, A. S. Holt. Mill Accounts 1862: David Whiteford, Robert Chaney, Wm. Pert, F. Crawford, Mary Wood, S. A. Holt. Held notes on: James M. Sanders, D. R. Whiteford, J. R. Profitt, T. G. Melander. Sarah Ann Bentley unable to collect on debts due to collapse of the Confederacy. Confederate tax for 1862 $9.64, for 1864 $4.50. District tax for 1863 $8.30, for 1864 $15.84.

BOX 161 PACK 4363   JAMES T. BUCHANAN   1863

Administrator: John A. Stuart. Appraisal Jun 18, 1863 by Samuel Turner, F. A. Buchanan, Wm. Verrell, Wm. Buchanan. Held notes on F.A. Buchanan, R. P. Buchanan. Estate Sale Jun 18, 1863. Buyers at sale: Widow, Wm. Buchanan, R. P. Buchanan, Lewis D.

Merriman, Milton Blake, Dr. Charles R. Moseley. Estate worth $20.15 at time of settlement. Date nor names not given.

BOX 161 PACK 4364   HUGH M. BROWNLEE   1863

Administrator: Robert Brownlee. Bond Mar 2, 1863 of $8,000 by Robert Brownlee, James F. Donald, James Seawright. Appraisal Mar 21, 1863 by Samuel Donald, R.R. Seawright, B. F. Moseley. Owned 4 slaves. Held note on Sallie Barmore. Estate Sale Oct 21, 1863 netted $4,828. Buyers at sale: Robert Brownlee, Joel F.Smith. Estate Settlement Mar 4, 1864. Widow, name not given, received $1608.59. (3) Children, names not given, each received $1072.39.

BOX 161 PACK 4365   JAMES CROWTHER   1864

Administrator: Wm. Crowther. Sons: James Crowther, Wm. Crowther. Daughters: Sarah Alewine, Mary A. Boyd, Elizabeth Bowen. Appraisal Aug 26, 1863 by Robert Boyd, Sterling Bowen, Wm. Boyd. Held notes on: John Murdock, Christian V. Barnes, Conrad Wakefield, A. C. Bowen, James Crowther Jr., Wm. Boyd. Estate sale Aug 27, 1863 netted $1776. Buyers at sale: Sarah Alewine, J. Alewine, Wm. Crowther, J. R. Black, Sterling Bowen, J. W. Cann, Nimrod Morrison, C. E. Bowen, Pleasant Ferguson, Chesley Hall, Wm. Lesly, Henry S. Cason, G. W. Bowen, C. Frasier, J. McMahan, Robert Stuckey, Gustave Bowen, J. Alewine, A. Harris, B. Anderson, Hannah Crowther, Thomas Stokes, Micahel McGee, J. Dixon, Elizabeth Bowen, E. Robertson, Keziah Campbell, J. Crowther, John C. Speer, E. Robertson, J. Hopkins, Robert Boyd, W.A. Hall, F. P. Robertson, W. J. Robertson, Lucinda Crowther, Thomas J. Hill, Lewis Hall, Mary A. Boyd, J. Young, Elizabeth Hall, W. Moore, J. W. Bowen, J. Ashley, S. M. Bowen, Mrs. Welch. Estate Settlement Jun 27, 1864 amended Jul 1, 1864. (7) Shares 1. E. Bowen-$304.14 2. Mary A. Boyd-$305.14 3. Hannah Crowther-$323.79 4. Sarah Alewine-$302.44 5. James Crowther-$246.79 6. Wm. Crowther-$259.79 7. John Crowther-$259.79.

BOX 161 PACK 4366   JOHN P. CROMER   1862

Administrator: Rosa P. Cromer. Bond Dec 22, 1862 of $12,000 by Rosa P. Cromer, James T. Barnes, Wm. H. Wilson. Appraisal Jan 7, 1863 by John Davis, J. I. Gilmer, Wm. H. Wilson. Held notes on: Wm. H. Wilson, J. H. Bell, Joseph Cunningham, J. A. Allen, J. McLaren & E. Nelson, Robert M. Palmer. Estate Sale Jan 8, 1863. Buyers at sale: Widow, Christian V. Barnes Sr., Mrs. D. A. Cromer, Nathaniel Cobb, J. T. Moore, H. T. Tusten, John McBryde, Dr. W. H. Parker, John R. Seal, Robert E. Hall, Jeptha R. Hamlin, A. B. Hamlin, David Hannah, John T. Owen, Philip S. Rutledge, A. McCord, John Davis, W. Romans, R. P. Cromer, James D. Chalmers, J. F. Keller, Nancy Keller, Isaac Keller, Dr. Isaac Branch, Dr. J. J. Wardlaw, Wm. Lomax, T. J. Ellis, B. Z. Keller, Andrew Morrison, Mathew McDonald, T. J. Kanoff, J. F. Tolbert, C. M. Sharp, Henry Hammond, Robert Jones, David Robertson, F. P. Robertson, Wm. McIlwain, Andrew McIlwain, Jesse Carlisle, B. W. Moore, J. A. Allen, W. E. Simmons, Wm. Henry Wilson, James J. Gilmer. 1862 Confederate taxes $74.20, 1862 state & district taxes $9.65. Last return and activity on estate Feb 6, 1867.

BOX 161 PACK 4367   WASHINGTON S. COCHRAN   1863

Administrator: Samuel W. Cochran. Bond Feb 6, 1863 of $10,000 by Samuel W. Cochran, Samuel Gilmer, John A. Hunter. Appraisal Feb 9, 1863 by Samuel Gilmer, James T. Liddell, Robert H. Winn. Owned 2 slaves. Held notes on: J. T. Liddell, J. P. Martin, C. H. Allen, T. J. Lipford, L. J. Johnson, R. H. Cochran, John M. Martin. 1st Estate

Sale Feb 10, 1863 netted $991. Buyers at sale: Mrs. James Miller, A. B. Cochran, A. P. Boozer, J. T. Owen, Ben. Williams, Samuel Gilmer, James Cunningham, George Nickles, A. M. Hawthorne, F. P. Robertson, H. T. Tusten, Moses Winestock, Wm. McComb, Robert Pratt, J. H. Watson, Thomas Stevenson, D. J. Gordon, R. H. Winn, J. T. Miller, Philip Rutledge. 2nd Estate Sale Nov 20, 1863 netted $9,476. Buyers at sale: Wm. McDuffie Cochran, Dr. T. J. Boyd, Edward Noble, Wm. H. Wilson, John T. Miller, Sallie J. Cochran, Dr. S. H. Beard, Moses Winestock, John T. Lyon, J. T. Liddell, Henry Clamp, J. T. Owen, T. B. McCord, Jeptha R. Hamlin, Mrs. Dendy, James Gibbs, J. E. Uldrick, R. P. Knox, Lemuel Reid, Wm. H. Sharp, R. H. Winn, Wm. M. Newell, T. B. Means, John Hagen, R. P. Doyle, James Cunningham. Paid Edward J. Taylor $57 for coffin. 1862 district tax $5.53, 1862 war tax $9.85. Estate Settlement Feb 12, 1868. (9) Shares each received &812.58. 1. Robert H. Cochran 2. Samuel H. Cochran 3. W. T. Cochran 4. J. B. Cochran 5. A. G. Cochran, minor 6. George W. Cochran, minor 7. H. M. Cochran 8. S. J. Cochran 9. Wm. McDuffie Cochran. Final Estate notice published in Press & Banner Aug 31, 1875. Petition filed by S. W. Cochran Oct 6, 1875.

BOX 161 PACK 4367 ½   ALLEN REAGAN   1877

Deceased died Jan 7, 1876. Will dated Jan 6, 1877. Witnesses: W.G. Kennedy, J. H. Kennedy, J. W. Ligon. 1st Executor: James M. Reagan died Jun 27, 1879. 2nd Executor: M. G. Zeigler. Wife: Nancy Reagan. Sons: James Reagan, Wilson Reagan, Harvey J. Reagan. Appraisal Feb 3, 1877 by W. G. Kennedy, John Wilkerson, Willis Smith. Estate Sale Feb 3, 1877 netted $9. Estate Settlement Apr 2, 1881. Final account Nov 16, 1881. No names. He had sold 50 acres to John C. Chiles in 1860 that was his wife's dowry. Much details and wrangling among parties involved included in this estate packet. John C. Chiles died Sep 9, 1879.

BOX 161 PACK 4368   RICHARD L. CHALMERS   1863

Administrator: James D. Chalmers-brother. Sisters: Cecelia wife of James W. Fowler, E. J. Leavell wife of John R. Leavell, Eliza P. wife of F. L. Boozer, Jessie Chalmers. Brothers: James Chalmers, W. S. Chalmers. Appraisal Oct 19, 1863 by H. T. Lyon, Robert Jones, B. P. Hughes. Held Notes on: J. W. Trowbridge, Wm. Welch, W. S. Chalmers, T. M. Neel, H. H. Harper, James D. Chalmers, James W. Fowler, G. F. Steifer. Estate Sale: Nov 2, 1863 netted $9,241. Buyers at sale: S. D. Deale, W. S. Chalmers, Jessie Chalmers, James D. Chalmers, John T. Owens, G. A. Visanka, J. I. Bonner, F. P. Robertson. Jan 2, 1864 paid Dr. W. A. Allen, dentist $69.54. Gold filling $2, tin filling $1, Extracting 3 teeth $2, Box of tooth powder 50 cents, amalgum $1, extracting 17 teeth $5, selou plate full upper set $45. Aug 17, 1863 paid Boyne Sproull of Newberry for monument $340, cutting 16 letters $4, 116 small letters $5.80, gilding 15 letters $1.20, base for monument $49.50. Buried at Newberry. Paid Dr. Isaac Branch for 1863 slave visits: Boy $1 plus 50 cents for medicine, boy $1 plus 25 cents for medicine, Boy $1 plus 25 cents for medicine, Boy $1 plus 25 cents for medicine, Woman $1, Woman $1, Girl $1 plus 50 cents medicine, Girl $1 plus 25 cents medicine, for visit to girl $7.50. Estate Settlement Jan 29, 1864. (8) Distributees: 1. Cecelia Fowler $1367.38 2. E. J. Leavell $823.33 3. Eliza P. Boozer $823.33 4. W. S. Chalmers $823.33 5. Thomas H. Chalmers $833 6. Martha N. W. Chalmers $833.

BOX 161 PACK 4368 ½   DR. JOHN S. REID   1877

Deceased died Jan 1, 1877. Very long and detailed estate with much petitioning and wrangling among persons participating in the estate. Will dated Jan 28, 1873.

Witnesses: Charles Evans, J. S. Gibert, Samuel Evans. Executor: John F. Livingston. Wife: Agatha Conway Reid. Adopted Daughter: Anna E. R. Martin. Niece: Rosalie H. W. Farley. Nephew: W. L. J. Reid. J. F. C. DuPre was the guardian of Caroline M. Reid and Margaret M. L. Reid. Appraisal Jan 25, 1877. Estate Sale Feb 9, 1877. Buyers at sale: W. P. Kennedy, J. T. Cheatham, H. A. Napier, John Wright, John F. Livingston, H. K. Burdette, Morris Patterson, Thomas Mann, Hiram T. Tusten, J. A. Devlin, Isaac Lee, A. Golding, Thomas C. Seal, Alllen McCanty, Robert Bell, Samuel Evans, Elbert Jackson, Thomas Thomson, J. H. Morrah, Wm. H. Taggart, Abel Savage, W. L. Phillips, Joseph Wright, James Evans, Charles Sibert, Willis Cannon, J. A. Devlin, Robert McKinney, James Evans, George A. Hanvey, Marion Beauford, W. H. Britt, Wm. K. Bradley, Charles Evans, Epaminandos Edwards, W. O. Bradley, Dr. T. J. Mabry, Samuel Burns, Wm. A. Hunter, Miss S. Livingston, Andrew J. Ferguson, J. L. Martin, J. C. Lites, Maria Smith, David Morrah, K. C. Reid, Hal Baker, W. O. Bradley, Lee Smith, John T. Lyon, Miss Clatworthy, Dr. J. W. Marshall, Mrs. E. L. Wardlaw, Dr. Wm. E. Link, W. C. Reese, James White, Aggie Thomson, John F. Livingston, Wm. D. Mars, J. E. Bradley, R. N. Pratt, H. C. Reese. Medical Accounts Open and Due from 1858: Edmund Allen, Rock Alston, Seaborn Allen, Thomas Anderson, Lacy Allen, Cage Alston, Laura Brown, Simon Belcher, J. A. Brown, Wm. Brown, Gracie Belcher, R. Blackman, John Brown, Ben. Calhoun, Adam Bowen, Henry Bishop, Alex. Bowie, Thomas Banks, Kitty Barmore, Wm. Britt, Samuel Brady, Brista Butler, L, Crawford, Mary Calhoun, James Crawford, Lewis Clay, Henry Cason, Jefferson Brown, Jack Edwards, Stephen Freeman, Ed Frazier, Henry Gary, H. Howland, Tony Jenkins, Jim Johnson, A, Jordan, Robert Keoun, Caesar Lee, Caroline Lee, Thomas Link, J. H. Ligon, Mrs. E. M. Ligon, Henry Levette, Hamp Latimer, Tom Lee, Ollah Lee, James Cason, Miss Margaret Clatworthy, N. Clatworthy, James Clatworthy, Betsy Chamlin, Jerry Butler, J. Earnest, M. Denion, Gary Giles, A. Gray, Lewis Jackson, Shala Jenkins, A. Jenkins, Ishmael Jenkins, George Kennedy, Isaac Lee, S. F. Gibert, L. McCaslan, Sarah McCaslan, James McCaslan, Charles McCaslan, Jim Marion, Susan McCelvey, Sam Morris, Lewis McCaslan, Mose Morris, Abram Mars, Isam Morris, Carrach Morrow, Harriet McCaslan, John Martin, N. Moore, Mary McComb, Clarke Link, Nails Jenkins, H. Jervey, Ben. Jenkins, L. Johnson, Samuel Houston, Annie Gibert, Samuel Donaldson, Isaac Evans, Jon Bibbs, Jim Brady, John Burnette, P. Belcher, A. Collier, Lewis Covington, Edmund Covington, Charles Evans, A. Collier, A. Bibbs, George Birch, Dan Beauford, Hulda Baskin, Scott Burton, Jim Burton, Andrew Edwards, Lewis Dendy, Ivory Gray, Henrietta Hamilton, Becky Jenkins, James Johnson, Isaac Jenkins, Adaline Jenkins, Amelia Link, Andrew McCelvey, Bill Morrow, Andrew McAllister, Hilda Mars, Jim Mars, Samuel McAllister, Pernice McCann, Bob Morris, Mrs. C. Nelson, Dick Plummer, Joe Plummer, John Perrin, Oliver Patton, Caroline Patton, John Patton, Edmund Oliver, W. D. Neal, Enoch Nelson, Mose Lee, J. J. King, Jeannet Jenkins, Thomas Jackson, C. Jackson, M. Hopkins, C. S. Gary, Eliza Davis, Harvey Edwards, Brenda Butler, Janet Butler, Nat Butler, Dick Baker, Billy Belcher, Mat brooks, Dan Collier, Alex Cason, Betty Collier, Wm. Douglass, A. Collins, Wm. Perrin, Bill Perrin, Joe Rogers, Cy Reid, Joseph Seigler, Mary Taggart, Jack Taylor, Bob Taggart, A. W. Wideman, George Williams, Nelson Willard, Lewis Wideman, Josh Gibert, John Kennedy, Lee Thomas, Ben Parker, Milton Phillips, Ben Rogers, Sam Smith, C. Sloan, George Taylor, Aggie Thomson, James Taggart, George Wardlaw, Lou Williams, Jim Wilson, Caesar Young, Phyllis Allen, Charles Kennedy, Tom Parker, Arch Perrin, Samuel Robinson, Tom Smith, C. Sprouse, Louise Thomas, Joe Thomson, Moses Taylor, Daniel Wardlaw, Tony Williams, Alfred Waller, M. O. Johnson, Green Smith, Newton Wideman, Dave Parker, Shed Rogers, Anderson Reid, Edmond Smith, Minnie Scott, Jack Thomas, Becky Thomson, G. Wideman, Bob Wardlaw, Lewis Winestock, J. A. Wilson, Mary Green, Mary Savage, Gideon Giles, Sam Parker, Amelia Parker, Sarah Rogers, Dick Rogers, Jake Reid, Cy Rogers, John Smith, Jim Smith, Robert

Scott, Alex. Sitton, Stephen Thomas, Isom Thomas, Charles Thomson, Abram Wideman, Jack Taggart, Wm. Wideman, Sally Wells, A. J. Woodhurst, Henry Wardlaw, Andrew Williams, Joseph Walker, Milton Phillips, Lewis Belcher, J. J. Belcher, Jennie Tatom, Thomas Banks, Stephen Taggart, R. Washington. Distributees: 1. Anna C. Reid wife of W. L. J. Reid 2. Anna M. O'Bryan 3. Samuel H. Reid 4. Julia L. Reid 5. Joseph W. Reid 6. Sarah C. Davidson 7. Charles W. Reid 8. David S. Reid 9. Mary B. Reid 10. Lenora T. Reid 11. John S. Reid 12. Caroline Reid, grand daughter of W. L. J. Reid 13. Margaret Reid grand daughter of W. L. J. Reid 14. Mary Reid wife of Daniel Reid 15. Mary P. Reid daughter of Daniel Reid, 16. Rosalie H. W. Farley lived Sierra Co., California. Dec 31, 1884 ruled that the legacy under will to the deceases W. L.J. Reid had lapsed and as such his descendants had no claim. Settlement, no date: Anna E. R. Martin 1/3 and Rosalie H. W. Farley 1/3.

BOX 161 PACK 4369   JOHN M. CAMPBELL   1863

Administrator: Charles Evans. Appraisal Jul 16, 1863 by J. Allen Ramey, John Crawford, Samuel Carter. Estate Sale Jul 17, 1863 Buyers at sale: Widow.

BOX 161 PACK 4370   BENJAMIN F. DANIEL   1864

Confederate Soldier. Taken prisoner Nov 1862. He died at Camp Hollingswotrth, Virginia. Administrator: John Patterson. Wife, Mary E. Daniel and (1) child. Brother: G. W. Daniel. Appraisal Feb 19, 1864 by Alex. McAllister, W. D. Baskin, J. H. Baskin. Estate Sale Mar 8, 1864 netted $3,161. Only buyer listed, Mary E. Daniel. Feb 29, 1864 Arbiters ruled that widow had to turn over to the administrator 1 horse, 4 hogs, 260 lbs. of bacon, 20 lbs of lard. Arbiters were: J. H. Baskin, W. C. Cozby, W. A. Pressly, W. S. Baskin, Robert Hutchison. Widow married O. L. Cann and they received the entire estate.

BOX 162 PACK 4371   DR. ROBERT DEVLIN   1863

Administrator: James J. Devlin. Appraisal Nov 9, 1863 by Wm. Lyon, Wm. Butler, W. S. Harris, John L. Devlin, A. P. Connor. Owned 40 slaves. Estate Sale: J. Bailey, Hiram W. Lawson, Felix P. Robertson, B. Manley, James H.. Morris, Stephen Elmore, Catlett Corley, Edward Westfield, Capt. Weldon, Thomas P. Lipscomb, J. A. Allen, J. L. Harmon, Wm. Riley, J. M. Mitchell, Wm. Jay, Dr. John Reid, Jane Wilson, D. T. Oliver, J. J. Devlin, J. A. Talmadge, J. McCombs, R. H. Mounts, Mary Drennan, Ben, P. Neel, Wm. K. Blake, J. Allen, J. T. Gilmer, R. M. Lites, J. E. Pressly, J. L. Pressly, J. A. Bailey, Wm. H. Taggart, F. S. Lawson, David McLane, J. L. Devlin, J. H. Morris, R. S. McCaslan, James Drennan, O. H. Marshall, J. J. Bonner, H. P. Helper, J. D. McKellar, John Deal, A. P. Connor, John Gilchrist, John Enright, B. A. McAllister, J. Z. Johnson, Joe Irwin, Mrs. L. Ramey, Enoch Nelson, W. Williams, J. Calvert, J. Owens, H. T. Sloan, J. T. Owen, J. J. Devlin, F. J. Bonner, J. T. Boyd, J. O. Lindsay, Wm. Butler, David Atkins, Wm S. Harris, Andrew J. Weed, Thomas Alexander, Samuel B. McClinton, A. Harrell, J. Jordan, James Gibbes, J. W. W. Marshall, James Steifle, Thomas Boyd, P. H. Bradley, Dr. Roberts, Wm. McCelvey, J. L. Harmon, F. McCombs, Wm. H. Taggart, Lewis Drennan, J. T. Cheatham, Wm. Lyon, B. S. Barnwell, John McLaren, J. N. Briscoe, J. T. Lyon. Estate Settlement Aug 15, 1864. (5) Distributees each received $21,887. 1. James Drennan for wife Peggy Ann 2. W. H. Drennan for wife Elizabeth 3. Mary Drennan, sister. Other 2 distributees not named.

BOX 162 PACK 4372   ROBERT M. DAVIS   1864

Will dated Jan 2, 1863. Witnesses: W. A. Pressly, Wm. C. Cozby, James T. Baskin, James M. Latimer. Wife: Catherine Jane Davis. Son: Bannister Andrew Davis. Daughters: Matilda Mildridge, Mary Elizabeth Davis, Susan L. Davis, Hester Ann Davis, Simon Louisa Davis. Brother: Wm. H. Davis. Executors: Wm. H. Davis, J. H. Reid. Held notes on: W. S. & A. F. Mauldin, Ben. D. Kay & B. Alonzo Harris, George Pettigrew, John M. Moseley, Wm. P. Drennan, P. B. Moragne, A. H. McMahan, G. A. Christopher & W. D. Lomax, John M. Simpson, James G. Bell, A. A. Bowie, John H. Reid, James S. Allen, James Huckabee, B. S. Hall, Ben. Adams, Thomas Deal, Edward Shaw, J. J. Uldrick, B. McClellan, John Scott, Thomas McClellan, John W. Brown, James L. Boles, Franklin Robertson, Wm. Morrow, Robert Keoun, John Nash, H. A. Jones, Joel Ashworth, H. J. Burton. 1st Estate Sale Dec 7, 1864. Buyers at sale: M. N. Boyd, J. S. Sadler, J. S. Brookhead, John M. Moseley, Thomas McGaw, Wm. O'Bryant, James Clark, James Bowen, A. M. Pettigrew, H. R. Freeman, H. R. Cooper, C. B. Latimer, Joshua Burriss, W. B. McClellan, C. S. Beaty, P. C. Suber, Jesse Cann, J. S. Cobb, James M. Martin, Jacob Alewine, C. T. Beasley, Robert Hutchison, A. V. Brooks, John M. Craft, James Barnes, John H. Reid, J. B. Allen, John A. Martin, John V. Craft, John Cook, R. H. Pettigrew, Frannklin Brown, W. T. Mauldin, Henry H. Harper, B. D. Kay, Wm. M. Kooun, H. H. Scudday, W. M. Bell,E. G. Power, Hugh Simpson, C. S. Beasley, Ehecian E. White, R. N. Boyd, John Blanchett, J. W. Prince, Wm. A. Giles, Dr. J. Speer, James H. Mills, W. D. Simpson, J. T. Baskin, J. H. Carlisle, W. S. Baskin, J. S. Allen, C. A. Latimer. 2nd Estate Sale Dec 12, 1866: Buyers at sale: L. A. Baker, B. A. Davis, Wiley Waters, J. H. Baskin, W. L. Baskin, J. C. Mauldin, Mrs. C. L. Davis, J. H. Reid, John V. Schroeder, M. C. Cozby, M. M. Craft, B. D. Kay, J. W. Brown, James B. Burroughs, C. P. Allen, W. T. Mauldin, J. M. Martin, G. P. Pettigrew, Joshua Burroughs, Robert Hutchison, S. L. Hester, J. M. Simpson, N. Cunningham, J. M. Craft, Allen V. Brooks, J. H. Reid, Wm. Burdette, L. J. Hester, L. A. Hutchison, James T. Allen, Theodore Kennedy, Jones Taylor, R. Hutchison, Joshua Burriss, W. C. Cozby, Christian V. Barnes, Mrs. Carlisle, Clement T. Latimer, Wm. A. Giles, J. T. Baskin, Wm. O'Bryant, James Bruce, B. Allen, B. D. Kay, R. E. Sadler, George W. Kelly, A. Z. Bowman, F. P. Robertson, Miss Bell, C. S. Beaty, G. F. Burdette, J. A. Gray, Miss Mary Davis. 1865 Confederate tax $84. Last estate activity Feb 7, 1881.

BOX 162 PACK 4373   AQUILLA DEASON   1864

Administrator: Berry Deason. Bond Jan 18, 1864 of $4,000 by Berry Deason, John Deason, W. W. Beasley. Never Married. Notes held on: W. & J. Dorn, D. Pressly, John Deason, Berry Deason, Peter McCain, Jeter & Searles, Vines & S. Walker, A. E. Harmon, Edmund Jeter, Daniel P. Self. Estate Settlement Feb 13, 1864. (5) Distributees each received $31.55: 1. John Deason, father 2. John Deason, brother 3. Berry Deason, brother 4. J. M. Self, step brother 5. Children (2) of Wm. Price.

BOX 162 PACK 4374   THOMAS D. DOUGLASS   1862

Administrator: Thomas J. Douglass. Bond Jun 13, 1862 of $8,000 by Thomas J. Douglass, Isaac Branch, B. P. Hughes. Wife: Nancy Douglass. Appraisal Nov 4, 1862 by Alex. Stevenson, James A. Wilson, Samuel Carter. Owned 1 slave. Held notes on: James Strawhorn, Thomas W. McMillan. Estate Sale Nov 5, 1862. Buyers at sale: Nancy Douglass, Talbert Cheatham, James Gilliam, Lewis Owen, J. S. Williams, Samuel Carter, A. McWilliams, W. Arnold, Thomas J. Douglass.

BOX 162 PACK 4375   WILLIAM C. DAVIS   1865

1st Administrator: J. F. H. Davis. Bond Dec 5, 1862 of $20,000 by J. F. H. Davis-brother who married a sister of L. H. Rykard, J. T. Parks, T. L. Coleman. 2nd Administrator: L. H. Rykard. Bond Oct 9, 1865 of $10,000 by L. H. Rykard, Henry Riley, Vachel Hughey. Appraisal Dec 23, 1862 by L. L. Coleman, J. A. Bailey, J. P. Bailey. Owned 2 slaves, 33 shares of Greenville & Columbia Railroad stock. 1st Estate Sale: Dec 23, 1862. Buyers at sale: Mrs. E. Cobb, R. H. Mounce, J. T. Parks, J. Creswell, Lewis D. Merriman, A. Vance, T. L. Coleman, W. H. Lawton, J. L. Morgan, W. T. Farrar, James Bailey, J. F. H. Davis, Martha Rykard, J. F. Davis, C. Cunningham, E. J. Walker, John Leland, Charles Pitts, Wm. Tolbert, Ben. F. Davis. 2nd Estate Sale Nov 21, 1868. Buyers at sales: Thomas F. Riley, W. K. Blake, J. W. Rykard, J. L. Morgan, A. M. Aiken, W. T. Farrar, James Smith, Joseph Hughey, L. W. Jordan, L. H. Rykard. Law Library Sale Nov 20, 1868. Buyers at Sale: Thomas Thomson, Samuel McGowan, Thomas C. Perrin, A. Lee, W. H. Parker.

BOX 162 PACK 4376   ROBERT DRENNAN   1863

Administrator: Mary Drennan-wife. Appraisal Oct 30, 1863 by J. J. Bonner, A. C. Hawthorne, R. C. Sharp. 1st Estate Sale Nov 3, 1863. Buyers at sale: J. L. Devlin, J. Jordan, J. W. Drennan, J. Z. Johnson, Wm. Butler, W. B. Purdy, Mary Drennan, Willis Smith, J. N. Briskey, A. Morton, Wm. Lyon, J. J. Devlin, S. B. McClinton, G. W. Drennan. 2nd Estate Sale. Nov 6, 1865. Buyers at sale: Mrs. M. Drennan, Miss Lou Drennan, Oscar Drennan, Miss Lucretia Drennan, M. B. Latimer, T. Pearlstine, J. I. Bowen, John Drennan, Robert Bryson, J. P. Kennedy, J. J. Bonner. Estate Settlement Feb 2, 1866. (6) Distributees each received $294.38 except widow, Mary L. Drennan who received $883.16. 1. Mary L. Drennan 2. Elizabeth L. Drennan 3. N. O. Drennan 4. Mattie Drennan 5. John Drennan 6. Rebecca J. Drennan.

BOX 162 PACK 4377   GEORGE A. DAVIS   1863

Will dated Aug 16, 1861. Witnesses: Wm. Gibson, R. D. Drennan, Wm. Butler. Executor: Jane M. Davis-wife. Appraisal Mar 10, 1863 by Wm. McCain, S. B. Cook, J. G. Thornton. Held notes on: John McCreary, Jabez Robinson, W. P. Sullivan, Ben. B. Harveley, A. L. Gray, John K. McCain. Estate Sale Mar 11, 1863. Buyers at sale: John Gilchrist, James Drennan, B. B. Harveley, James Morris, Dr. G. Pressly, Wm. Watkins, James H. Wideman, A. J. Weed, W. K. Bradley, J. Caldwell, John H. Wideman, S. B. Cook, H. T. Tusten, F. P. Robertson, Edward O. Reagan, Wm. S. Harris, Sarah J. Wideman, Wm. Butler.

BOX 162 PACK 4378   E. LEWIS DAVIS   1865

Administrator: N. J. Davis. Held notes on: John Selby, Edmond C. Selby, T. J. McCracken, J. Allen Ramey, Frances Burton, Frances Mantz, M. T. Owen, Adam Wideman, N. J. Davis, A. Wideman & A. Bradley, Joe Clark. Estate Settlement Mar 14, 1866. Ben. F. Davis only Heir.

BOX 162 PACK 4379   DAVID DUNCAN   1864

No papers found in packet.

BOX 162 PACK 4380   DAVID EDWARDS   1863

Administrator: E. O. Reagan. Bond Apr 1863 of $250 by Edward O. Reagan, Robert W. Lites, Adam Wideman. Appraisal Apr 25, 1863 by George W. Pressly, Adam Wideman, James Russell, H. K. Russell. Estate Sale Apr 25, 1863 netted $157.10. Buyers at sale: J.

O. Spence, B. B. Harveley, Thomas J. Edwards, Mary Rykard, H. K. Russell, A. Wideman, G. W. Pressly, L. J. Edwards. Last estate return Jun 4, 1866. Estate Insolvent.

BOX 162 PACK 4381   PROVIDENCE ELMORE   1863

Will dated Apr 2, 1862. Witnesses: John R. Moore, W. R. Brinkley, Stephen Elmore. Wife: Martha A. Elmore. Executrix: Martha A. Elmore. Bond Aug 17, 1863 of $4,000 by Martha A. Elmore, Stephen Elmore, J. A. Ellis.

BOX 162 PACK 4382   NIMROD FREEMAN   1863

Administrator: M. B. McGee. Appraisal Feb 5, 1863 by E. Agnew, J. Higgins, C. Rasor. Held notes on: Wm. Freeman, Milton Freeman, George Freeman, J. B. Algary, James V. Young, Nancy Roney. Estate Sale Feb 5, 1863 netted $111.96. Buyers at sale: M. B. McGee, Jesse Kernels, Ross Bonham, D. T. Jones, Elizabeth Freeman. Estate Settlement Apr 26, 1869. Estate Insolvent.

BOX 162 PACK 4383   W. C. FERGUSON   1863

Administrator: Frances J. Ferguson-wife. Appraisal May 17, 1863 by L. C. Clinkscales, Wm. T. Campbell, Sterling Bowen, Wm. A. Ashley. Estate Sale May 19, 1863. Buyers at sale: Widow, Pleasant Ferguson, H. Daniel, W. W. Lesly, J. C. Long, J. W. Bowen, Wm. Moore, Robert Stuckey, Thomas Daniel, L. C. Cl;inkscales, Jesse Cann. Children: John P. Ferguson, Thomas L. Ferguson, Wm. B. Ferguson, George A. Ferguson, Robert B. Ferguson.

BOX 162 PACK 4384   G. E. FARRINGTON   1863

Administrator: Wm. H. Parker. Tailor. Appraisal Jun 11, 1863 by John A.Wier, J. A. Allen, B. P. Hughes. Estate Sale included content of his tailor shop. Buyers at sale: J. W. Lomax, C. H. Allen, J. A. Wier, Armistead Burt, Charles Cox, D. R. Sondley, Charles Dendy, J. D. Chalmers, J. H. McCree, Dr. Pettigrew, George W. Syfan, John Owens, Harvey T. Lyon, Philip S. Rutledge, R. J. W. Hill, John T. Owen, Louis H. Russell, John Enright, Dr. Boyd, Hiram W. Lawson, Langdon C. Haskell, Ben. P. Hughes, R. W. Morris, R. Knox, John Connor, Patrick O'Keefe, Wm. Morris, Mrs. Andrew Small, Edward J. Taylor, Wm. Lipford, John McLaren. Final estate return and activity 1866.

BOX 162 PACK 4385   JOHN FREE   1860

Will dated Feb 27, 1863. Witnesses: John Wilson, John Patterson, John Neel. Executors: John E. Wilson, Mathew McDonald. Wife: Nancy Free, she married John E. Wilson. Daughters: 1. Nancy Jane Wilson, 2. Martha Caroline wife of Bird Beauford 3. Elizabeth Walton 4. Mary Ann Yarborough, given only $25 and to receive nothing more. Appraisal Mar 19, 1863 by John Patterson, Samuel Link, W. M. Clatworthy. Owned 1 slave. Held notes on: Samuel Jordan, W. G. Neel, John E. Wilson, James Clatworthy. Estate Sale Mar 20, 1863 netted $710.27. Buyers at sale: A. P. Connor, J. E. Williams, Wm. Hunter, James R. Crawford, H. T. Foster, Wm. Smith, H. Wilson, D. O. Neel, John E. Wilson, W. McCaslan, James Morris, Hiram T. Tusten, Edward Roche, W. S. Neel, Thomas Link, David Wardlaw, Thomas Jackson, David Jordan, James Clatworthy, Dr. John Sanders, J. Patterson, Wm. G. Neel, Jeptha R. Hamlin, W. C. Smith. 1863 Confederate war tax $7.55. Coffin cost $6. 1ˢᵗ Estate Settlement Nov 6, 1863. (2) Legatees each received $38.74. 1. Martha Beauford 2. Jane Wilson.

BOX 162 PACk 4386   WILLIAM ALONZO & JANE T. FELL (minors)   1863

Guardian: Louisa Jane Fell-mother. Bond Dec 21, 1863 of $400 by Louisa Jane Fell, Samuel B. McClinton, Wm. M. Wilson.

BOX 162 PACK 4387   JAMES A. FOOSHE   1863

Will dated Nov 10, 1861. Witnesses: D. L. Bozeman, L. C. Parks, W. B. Meriwether. Executor: John B. Bozeman. Wife: Martha Fooshe. Appraisal Jan 25, 1864 by Simon Chaney, John Sadler, Thomas G. Deason. Owned 3 slaves, 52 acres of land.

BOX 162 PACK 4388   JOHN FOOSHE   1864

Administrator: Charles W. Fooshe. Bond Mar 10, 1864 of $5,000 by Charles W. Fooshe, Joel Fooshe, Benjamin Fooshe. Chalres W. Foohe was the only Heir.

BOX 162 PACK 4389   THOMAS W. GAINES   1863

Confederate Soldier. Administrator: Wm. A. Gaines-brother. Bond Apr 18, 1863 of $6,000 by Wm. A. Gaines, George W. Bowen, T. J. Hill. ½ Owner of Gaines & Gassaway. Appraisal May 6, 1863 by M. B. Latimer, Michael McGee, Clayton Jones. Notes he personally held: John B. Saylors, A. J. Shaw, James Wilburn, Robert Caldwell, Wm. A. Gaines, Arthur W. Brock, Joel Arnold, James W. Black, T. J. Hill, Nicholas Bookman, Wesley A. Black, Mrs. H. C. Johnson, A. J. Hall, C. F. Holcomb, Bailey Fleming, J. A. Elgin, Wm. Gassaway. Accopunts held by the deceased and not part of the Firm of Gaines & Gassaway: Dr. G. F. Steifer, Conrad Wakefield, Wm. Wickliffe, Wickliffe & Armstrong, Acker & Stone, John Whitt, Mathias Roberts, Nancy Major, Joshua Ashley, J. W.Brooks, Ramsey Black, Fleming Bell, Daniel Ragsdale, Smith Phillips, Ben. Barnett, Cyrus Smith, Wm. Black, John Burton, Robert Bell, Chesley Hall, Jerry Smith, Robert Holiday, James Wright, Hiram Turner, Berry Kay, Eleanor Cobb, Robert Adams, Wm. Gilkerson, Ben. Rhodes, Wm. Clinkscales, John Cobb. Estate Sale May 6, 1863. Buyers at sale: J. J. Lipford, Pleasant Ferguson, J. M. Milford, Bailey Fleming, W. L. Young, Widow, A. Rice, Talbert Cheatham, George Allen, L. C. Clinkscales, T. D. Young, C. W. Daniel. Notes held own by firm of Gaines & Gassaway: W. P. Strickland, H. H. Kay, Wm. Morrison, Nicholas Callaham, M. B. Gaines, Alfred Gailey, W. T. Milford, Andrew H. Callaham, Thomas McAdams.   Accounts of the Firm of Gaines & Galloway: Joshua Ashley, Est. of John Swilling, James Sims, Jesse A. McAllister, S. W. Bowen, Dr. W. J. Milford, S.V. Milford, Wm. Pratt, James B. Saylors, R. F. Bell, George Milford, W. B. Martin, John Mann, Jefferson McIver, Jesse W. Cann, Alfred Gailey, John L. Campbell, Wm. Mann, Asa Lipford, Dr. Aaron W. Lynch, J. W. Brooks, Joshua P. Milford, Dr. John Bell, L. P. Gaines, James W. Black, F. P. Robertson, J. R. Black, Chesley Hall, Green Fleming, Wm. Stokes, Wm. Wickliffe, N. Gaines. 1863 Confederate tax for the Firm of Gaines & Gassaway $20.00. Last estate enry Dec 16, 1869, no names.

BOX 162 PACK 4390   WILLIAM GIBSON   1859

Administrators: Mary L. Gibson, James H. Morris. Bond Dec26, 1862 of $20,000 by Mary L. Gibson-wife, James H. Morris-brother—in-law, Margaret Morris, M. O. McCaslan. Appraisal Jan 13, 1863 by Wm. Butler, John T. Devlin, John McCreary, P. H. Bradley, W. S. Harris. Estate Sale Jan 14, 1863 netted 9,811. Buyers at sale: Louisa Gibson, James Steifle, W. G. Kennedy, Margaret Morris, Lewis Rich, J. H. Morris, R. H. Wardlaw, Wm. McCain, R. B. McClinton, A. L. Gray, John McLaren, John T. Owen, A. Sanders, Samuel Jordan, Wm. Butler, B. Jordan, P. H. Bradley, J. A. Chalmers, J. L. Gibert, Ben. Kennedy,

N. Keller, James Martin, J. L. Devlin, A. J. Weed, John McClellan, James Drennan, John McDowell, Abbeville Salt Co., John Gibson, Robert W. Lites, R. F. McCaslan, Robert Jones, Wm. S. Harris, J. L. Talmadge, Nathaniel J. Davis, Daniel Atkins, Josiah Gibson. Tombstone $32.64, coffin $42.98. 1863 Confederate tax $113.20. Estate Settlement Feb 19, 1864. (6) Heirs: 1. Mother $5181 2. John-brother $863.51 3. James E.-brother $863.51 4. Josiah-brother $863.51 5. Patrick-brother $863.51 6. Rebecca-sister $863.51.

BOX 163 PACK 4391   ELIZABETH COBB   1864

Will, no date. Witnesses: F. H. Sanders, John T. Coumbe, Bettie Hill. Executor: James A. Norwood. Appraisal Mar 3, 1864 by John A. Wier, Enoch Nelson, H. T. Lyon. Owned 4 slaves. Estate Sale Mar 4, 1864. Buyers at sale: Mathew M. McDonald, John A. Wier, J. T. Boyd, L. Bowie, Harvey T. Lyon, Dr. L. C. Service, W. W. Shillito, D. R. Sondley, Miss Bettie Hill, S. A. Allen, Samuel J. Hester, Samuel Bevin, Mrs. A. Dendy, Wm. H. Parker, James H. Cobb, James A. Norwood, Phil S. Rutledge, Mrs. Andrew Woodhurst, A. Baker, Mrs. Andrew Small, James Richardson, J. F. McCombs, Joseph T. Moore, Mrs. D. McNeill Turner, J. Ferguson, Mrs. Harberson, Dr. J. J. Wardlaw, R. J. Hill, J. Owen, Dr. McNeill Turner, Andrew M. Hill, Andrew Simonds, Thomas Thomson, Mary Black, David J. Jordan, Dr. Thomas Mabry, J. Hammond, Mrs. C. Golding, J. Crawford, W. W. Shillito, J. Gibbes, John Enright, Jeptha Hamlin, Mrs. Turner, Miss Mary Douglass, H. S. Beard, E. Noble, J. W. Lesly, James Taggart, J. A. Calhoun, Stephen F. Gibert, Hiram T. Tusten, David B. Smith, John Conner, John Hunter, Hiram W. Lawson. Paid John Enright for coffin $77. Last estate entry May 3, 1866, no names.

BOX 163 PACK 4392   THOMAS M. CHILES   1863

Administrator: Thomas W. Chiles. Bond Jan 19, 1863 of $1,000 by Thomas W. Chiles, P. H. Bradley, W. K. Bradley. 1ˢᵗ estrte return made Jul 15, 1864.

BOX 163 PACK 4393   JAMES B. CRAWFORD   1864

Administrator: Wm. H. Wilson. Appraisal Sep 12, 1863. Held notes on: J. W. Trowbridge, Thomas J. Price. Accounts due the Firm of Cobb & Crawford: Andrew Edwards, George Spires, James Lomax, Charles Cunningham, Rev. B. Johnson, Barney O'Connor, John Lyon, Thomas Lynch, Jasper Britt, W. W. Tatom, Edwin Parker, Dr. Harvey T. Lyon, Wm. Belcher. 1861 Judgement against Andrew Paul & R. J. White collected.

BOX 163 PACK 4394   SAMUEL W. COCHRAN   1863

Will dated Nov 13, 1863. Witnesses: W. T. Newell, Rosemond Wilson, R. T. Gordon, S. W. Cochran. Wife Frances Cochran was the daughter of John Callaham. Sons: Samuel W Cochran, Wm. Hamilton Cochran. Daughter: Jane Eleanor Crawford. Brother-in-Law: Basil Callaham. Appraisal Dec 21, 1863 by R. T. Gordon, Wm. T. Newell, Jesse Carlisle. Estate Sale Dec 30, 1863 netted $385.15. Buyers at sale: Samuel W. Cochran, Wm. Mann, Jesse Carlisle, Frances Cochran, Basil Callaham, E. Cox, James Cunningham, Mary J. Cochran, Henry Winn, J. F. Simpson, J. W. Means, Mrs. M. J. Cochran, James Carlisle, J. R. Wilson, J. E. Crawford, E. E. Pressly, S. J. Cochran, Wm. Gordon, Wm. B. Bowie, Thomas Gordon, W. B. Bowie, Thomas Stevenson. Estate Settlement Feb 5, 1864. (4) Heirs: 1. Mrs. Frances Cochran $87.11 2. Samuel W.Cochran $87.11 3. Jane Eleanor Cochran $87.11 4. Children of Wm. H. Cochran (4 chn. Each received $21.78).

BOX 163 PACK 4395   SHERARD W. CALLAHAM   1865

Administrators: Mary J. Callaham, Samuel J. Callaham. Bond Jan 1, 1864 of $50,000 by Mary J. Callaham, Stephen Latimer, Basil Callaham, Samuel L. Callaham. 1st Appraisal Jan 18, 1864 by Wm. Clinkscales, Dempsey Callaham, Robert Ellis, C. Ellis, G. M. Mattison. Notes held on: Wm. Pratt, J. F. Clinkscales, Joseph Ellis, W. M. Callaham, E. Calllaham, J. R. Wilson, M. A. Hairston, W. L. Young, H. P. Wright, James Darby, S. T. Kerr, M. J. Robinson, S. H. Stone. 1st Estate Sale Jan 19, 1864. Buyers at sale: R. F. Bryson, Basil Callaham, A. M. Hall, E. Cox, Edward Ashley, J. W. Shirley, J. J. Shirley, Martha Griffin, W. Y. Walker, M. E. Brock, S. J. Callaham, B. Darby, Wm. Armstrong, J. W. Mattison, Wm. Dawkins, W. N. Callaham, Thomas J. Hill, Nancy Callaham, Jacob Alewine, Stephen Latimer, C. Ellis, Wm. Alewine, Richard Taylor, Wm. Callaham. 2nd Appraisal Mar 22, 1867 by C. Ellis, Dempsey Callaham, Wm. Clinkscales, J. Carwile, H. Robinson. 2nd Estate Sale Mar 22, 1867. Buyers at sale: Mary J. Callaham, R. F. Bryson, Basil Callaham, Martha Griffin, S. J. Calaham, S. S. Fisher, Wm. Clinkscales, Thomas J. Hill, Stephen Latimer, Nancy Callaham, Jacob Alewine. Last estate return and activity 1868.

BOX 163 PACK 4396   MARIAH CHANDLER   1852

Appraisal Jul 17, 1863 by James Cowan, Thomas Hawthorne, C. M. Sharp, John Hagen, John M. Hawthorne. Had owned 7 slaves at one time. Estate Sale Jul 17, 1863. Buyers at sale: John Chandler, Thomas Pearlstine, James Chandler, John M. Bell, David O. Hawthorne, Miss H. Ransom, Mrs. A. B. Chandler, Wm. Spruell, John A. B. Chandler. Estate Settlement Sep 13, 1879. D. O. Hawthorne, Trustee received $410 leaving $205. Trustee had received on an annual basis money beginning in 1847. Claimed to have paid out in expenses far more than he had received. Mariah had sons, Timothy & James. She had young male slave named Rutu and expenses for his funeral $7.55. Packet filled with slave hiring out activities, including to whom hired and amounts paid, provisions, medical expenses etc.

BOX 163 PACK 4397   WILLIAM J. CHEATHAM   1863

Confederate Soldier. Will dated Mar 12, 1862. Witnesses: Edward Westfield, James W. Fowler, Robert P. Knox. Wife: Sallie C. Cheatham. Father-in-Law: Amaziah Rice. Had minor children, not named. Executors: Sallie C. Cheatham, Amaziah Rice. Appriasal Nov 3, 1863 by James Pursley, Talbert Cheatham, Francis A. Wilson. Owned 5 slaves. Held notes on: T. D. Douglass, John A. Ware, J. H. Gray, S. E. Cheatham, M. C. Thomas.

BOX 163 PACK 4398   J. WESLEY CLINKSCALES   1866

Will dated Mar 18, 1862. Filed Apr 6, 1866. Witnesses: J. Adams, J. H. Boozer, D. N. Boozer. Executors: Lewis D. Merriman, W. D. Mitchell. Sisters: Louisa Jane Merriman, Sarah Cowan deceased, Mary C. Hamilton. Brothers: John B. Clinkscales deceased, George B. Clinkscales deceased, Albert J. Clinkscales. Nieces: Rowena Elizabeth Merriman, Eleanor Brownlee. Nephew: Frank Clinkscales. Estate Sale: Dec 18, 1865. Buyers at sale: A. Vance, Lewis D. Merriman, Ephraim R. Calhoun, W. C. Sproull, Wm. Templeton. Paid $65 in 1864 for dressing preparations for funeral. Judgement of Oct 10, 1859 against Issac Logan & John B. Sample for $1,121.36 settledd Jun 1, 1868. 1869 paid heirs of John Clinkscales in Texas $1,773. 1872 paid John H. Oldham for his wife in Texas $1,173.

Box 163 PACK 4399   JAMES M. CALLAHAM   1863

Administrators: 1st Wm. Pratt. Bond Dec 24, 1863 of $3,500 by Wm. Pratt, Albert Johnson, J. B. Kay. 2nd J. M. Carwile. Bond, date unknown, of $3,000 by James M. Carwile, John F. Clilnkscales, Hugh Robinson. Appraisal Jan 8, 1863 by Wm. Clinkscales, James B. McWhorter, Hugh Robinson. Held notes on: Dempsey Callaham, Bennett McAdams, Wm. Duncan, Caleb Smith, James M. Hopkins, Yancey Dove, Ben. McClain, Richard Taylor, Moses Ashley, Wm. M. Callaham, T. C. Callaham, Wm. Pratt, Wm. Y. Walker, Wm. Ellison, John Moore, Wm. L. Burton, Peter Ricketts, Samuel Mitchell, James Darby, John S. Carwile, J. T. Kerr, S. W. Callaham, John M. O'Bryant, Wm. Clinkscales, Samuel Shaw, Samuel J. Callaham, Wm. F. Duncan, Nancy Pratt, Christian V. Barnes, John Gunter, John M. Calaham. 1860 Accounts: F. M. Kay, John B. Strickland, Stephen G. Murdock, Josiah Ashley, Wesley A. Black. 1861 Accounts: Wm. Strickland, Jesse T. Murdock, Joseph M. Blackwell, Wm. Ashley, Joseph F. Burton, Joseph Alewine, Moses Smith, James Darby, Augustus Ashley, Samuel Fields, Elizabeth H. Carwile, Freeman Smith, David Loner, Wm. L. Loner, Ezekiel B. Norris, John M. G. Branyon. 1862 Accounts: Wm. Duncan, Wm. F. Duncan, S. W. Callaham, Mrs. Franklin Black, James M. Carwile, Noble Bell, John M. Callaham, Wesley A. Black, Wm. Pratt, Conrad Wakefield, Joseph R. Black, Elizabeth Duncan, J. M. McClain. Estate Sale Jan 8, 1863 netted $997. Buyers at sale: Widow, W. L. Bannister, J. M. Bryant, W. Clinkscales, W. Y. Walker, B. McAdams, J. R. Black, J. R. Ellis, G. W. Derley, Mrs. M. Griffin, H. Robinson, B. Callaham, J. M. Carwile, Joseph Pratt, Mrs. S.W. Callaham, D. Callaham, Mrs. W. L. Burton. 1st Estate Settlement Dec 15, 1864. Widow $584.56. Child $407.64. 2nd Estate Settlement Jan 8, 1883. One child had died in 1864, no name given. Wife, Sarah G. Callaham $4.40. Son, J. W. Callaham $8.81.

BOX 163 PACK 4400   ANN GREEN   1863

Adminisstrator: Edward Noble. Bond May 19, 1863 of $2,500 by Edward Noble, Wm. P. Noble, Andrew A. Noble. Estate due $1,500 from Equity Court.

BOX 163 PACK 4401   JOHN B. GORDON   1862

Administrator: Wm. Hill. BondOct 211, 1862 of $2,000 by Wm. Hill, Peter Henry, Alexander Hagen. Appraisal Nov 21, 1862 of $220 by J. C. Stevenson, Peter Henry, A. G. Hagen. Apr 1, 1868 a note due to Jane Donnald paid in full by W. Gordon.

BOX 163 PACK 4402   GEORGE W. GRIFFIN   1863

Adminisstrator: M. L. Bullock. Bond Dec 25, 1862 of $20,000 by M. L. Bullock, John P. Watts, E. G. Simpson, Larkin Reynolds. Owned 7 slaves. Appraisal of slaves Dec 26, 1862 by John McClellan, P. H. Bradley, Moses C. Taggart. Estate Settlement Mar 12, 1863. $8,425 split into 3 equal shares of $2,804. Shares to: 1. J. M. Griffin 2. T. J. Griffin 3. Vincent Griffin.

BOX 163 PACK 4403   CHARLES NEWTON GRAHAM   1863

Will dated Jun 24, 1862. Witnesses: James M. Perrin, J. W. Calhoun, Wesley Robertson. Brothers: Samuel Graham, Albert M. Graham. Appraisal Feb 27, 1863 by Larkin Mays, James Robertson, John Adams. Owned 3 slaves, 154 acres of land.

BOX 163 PACK 4404   J. B. GRAHAM   1863

Administrator: Samuel E. Graydon. Bond Oct 19, 1863 of $300 by Samuel E. Graydon, B. C. Hart, John C. Allen.

BOX 163 PACK 4405   JAMES CRAVEN GAMBRELL   1865

Administrator: James Gambrell. Father: James Gambrell. Appraisal Jan 11, 1864 by Joel Kay, Stephen Latimer, Elihus Campbell. Held notes on: Enoch Gambrell, Wm. Gambrell. Estate Sale Jan 12, 1864 netted $5,938. Buyers at sale: Enoch Gambrell, H. Robinson, A. M. Dodson, Henderson Bagwell, Michael Burts, W. N. Mitchell, Amanda Arnold, A. P. Shirley, Rhodom Trussell, Wm. Norwood, Wm. Harper, W. B. Acker, J. W. Medlock, B. M. Latimer, Elihu Campbell, James H. Shaw, J. W. Mattison, S. V. Gambrell, R. Rodgers, Stephen Latimer, J. M. Gambrell, James Taylor, Alex. Austin, Malcom Erwin, James Gambrell, W. C. Moseley, Abner Cox, Joel King, H. L. Eaton, Mason Kay, Wm. Davis, J. T. Nabors, Larkin Mays. Estate Settlement Jan 31, 1865. 1/3 to Widow, Sintha Gambrell $2008.39. $803.35 to each of (5) children. 1. Martha J. Gambrell 2. Evelyn Gambrell 3. J. P. Gambrell 4. Not named 5. Not named. 1864 tax on animals $7.

BOX 163 PACK 4406   W.C. C. HODGES   1864

Administsrator: William Hodges. Appraisal Oct 9, 1863 by G. B. Riley, J. C. Richey, T. J. Martin. Owned 2 slaves.

BOX 163 PACK 4407   ASBURY HINTON   1863

Will dated Dec 1`6, 1862. Witnesses: J. C. Rasor, A. M. Agnew, John M. Carlisle. Borther: Nathaniel lived in Jefferson C., Ala. Willed to Methodist Church in Abbeville. Executor: John M. Carlisle. Appraisal Dec 7, 1863 by Marshall Sharp, Samuel Agnew, H. Y. Gilliam. Estate Sale Dec 28, 1863. Buyers at sale: G.B. Riley, Rev. John M. Carlisle, Marshall Sharp, M. C. Henderson, J. S. Magee, W. A. King, Mrs. Samuel Agnew, W. M. Robertson, Abner H. McGee, C. Riley, Wm. Dunn, V. Young.

BOX 163 PACK 4408   W. W. HIGGINS   1863

Administrator: Wm. Hodges. Bond Jan 12, 1863 of $10,000 by Wm. Hodges, G. B. Riley, Marshall Sharp. Appraisal Jan14, 1863 by Michael B. McGee, Samuel Agnew, A. M. Agnew. Held notes on: Thomas A. Mellon of Mississippi, W. A. Ware, Nancy Roney, H. Y. Gilliam, James M. Vandiver, Abner Freeman, Wesley Robertson, J. C. Richey, Newton Sims. Held 1/2 interest in Accounts due the firm of W. W. Higgins & W.C. C. Hodges: G. B. Riley, Dr. Larkin Agnew, Wesley Robertson, Est. of John Williams, Wade H. Robertson, Nimrod Freeman, George Freeman, H. H. Cooper, W. H. McGee, Joseph Bigham, Jefferson Buchanan, Henry Algary. Estate Sale Jan 15, 1863. Buyers at sale: Anderson Agnew, Wm. Maddox, John Waters, A. M. Agnew, T. Y. Martin, James Brooks, Ed Hodges, J. M. Wright, John Adams, Dr. E. Agnew, Newton Sims, T. J. Ellis, Larkin Barmore, J. T. Richey, Leonidas D. Connor, Ezekiel Rasor, W. T. Jones, B. A. Griffin, Samuel Agnew, Wm. Hodges, W. P. McGee, G. M. Mattison, Allen Dodson, Mrs. Yancey, Mrs. Shannon, Sarah T. Higgins, John Higgins, Wm. E. Barmore, D. T. Jones, M. C. Henderson, W. M. Griffin, T. C. C. Allen, John Millam, Ross Bonham, A. T. Watson, Thomas Maghorn, Michael B. McGee, V. Young, Charles C. Pinckney, George W. Rasor, Dr. Paul Connor, Gabriel Hodges, James Smith, M. M. Mars.

BOX 163 PACK 4409   WiLLIAM B. HARKNESS   1863

Confederate Soldier. Will dated Nov 25, 1861. Witnesses: Ben. W. Williams, John Wm. Power. Executor: Robert C. Harkness-father. Bond Dec 15, 1862 of $6,000 by Robert C. Harkness, M. B. Latimer, Joseph R. Black. Appraisal Dec 23, 1862 by M. B. Latimer, Elias Kay, John Brownlee, George B. Clinkscales. Owned 1 slave. Held notes on: David

Crawford & J. W. Black, S .S. McCurry, Hugh M. Prince. Personal property was not sold with great majority being turned over to the widow. Estate Settlement Feb 5, 1864. Widow, not named, $600.92. (3) Children, not named, each $440.61.

BOX 163 PACK 4410   ROBERT H. HARKNESS   1863

Administrator: Robert C. Harkness. Appraisal Aug 7, 1863 by M. B. Latimer, George B. Clinkscales, Elias Kay, L. C. Clinkscales, James F. Tolbert. Estate Sale Dec 5, 1866. Buyers at sale: Elias Kay, J. M. Moseley, Thomas A. Daniel John M. Martin, W. J. Robertson, James T. Barnes, J. W. Griffin, F. P. Robertson, James Martin, James H. Alewine.

BOX 163 PACK 4411   REV. W. P. HILL   1863

Will dated Sep 17, 1862. Witnesses: John T. Parks, W. P. McKellar, Stanley Crews. Executors: W. P. Andrews, John C. Hill. Buried at Mount Moriah Church. Wife: Susan Hill. Son: John Chiles Hill. Daughters: Elizabeth Lydia wife of W. P. Andrews, Sarah deceased. Appraisal Apr 9, 1863 by J. F. H. Davis, Joseph W. Harrison, Thomas M. Cater. Owned 3 slaves, house and lot of 16 acres in the town of Greenwood. Estate Sale Apr 23, 1863. Buyers at sale: S. D. Deal, Dr. C. Moseley, M. Hackett, Dr. Sims, W. G. Lomax, Mrs. Dr. Templeton, T. M. McClennan, Dr. Felix G. Parks, Mrs. Stanley Crews, Dr. Anderson, Mrs. Montgomery, Rev. McLees, Wilson Robertson, J. W. Lipscomb, Dr. J. R. Davis, W. T. Farrar, John Davis, J. T. Parks, ---McNary, R. C. Gilliam, Mrs. Mounce, Charles Cunningham, J. Sale, H. G. Hackett, Dr. McKellar, Cat. Irwin, Dr. A. P. Boozer, Dr. C. Waller, J. A. Bailey, T. H. Carey, W. Cater, Rev. McSwain, W. P. Andrews, Bennett Reynolds, A. Vance, King Vance,James Bailey, D.B. Glymph, R. H. Mounce, James Creswell, W. P. McKellar, James Silks, H. C. Venning, J. R. Tarrant, J. M. Cochran, Mrs. Buchanan, John McKellar. 1st Estate return Mar 2, 1866, also the last estate entry.

BOX 163 PACK 4412   ORANGE B. HALEY   1863

Administrator: George W. Kelly. Bond Jan 30, 1863 of $1,000 by George W. Kelly, Robert Keoun, John W. Brown. Appraisal Feb 16, 1863 by Alex. Oliver, Robert N. Boyd, G. F. Burdette. Held notes on: J. B. F. Adams & Thomas Jones, Martha & Albert Roach, J. S. Bryan & J. Smith, Matilda Haley, Willis Haley, John Haley, Robert Todd. Estate Sale Feb 17, 1863. Buyers at sale: Mrs. Haley, Jane Scott, John Morgan, Mrs. Hutchison, Wm. Burdette, B. D. Kay, Dr. Henry H. Scudday, George W. Kelly, J. W. Prince, John M. Craft, George Seigler, J. M. Moseley, Robert Keoun, Robert Boyce, Mrs. Patterson, Augustus Sutherland, Samuel Hutchison, D. Young.

BOX 163 PACK 4413   MARY HARMON   1866

Deceased died Nov 1862.Administrator: Appleton G. Harmon, son. Bond Dec 23, 1862 of $40,000 by Appleton G. Harmon, Charles M. Freeman, George Gibert. Appraisal Jan 7, 1863 by W. T. Headwright, Ellington Searles, Peter Smith. Estate Sale Jan 8, 1863 netted $15,665. Buyers at sale: C. Freeman, A. Harmon, J. W. Parks, S. W. Willis, S. G. N. Furqueron, Landon Tucker, John Willis, W. W. Banks, Lucinda Johnson, J. L. Gibert, E. R. Perryman, P. H. Bradley, John Harmon, J. C. Cox, R. E. Carroll, Redmond Brown, F. H. Edmonds, Peter Smith, James Banks, W. Newby, W. A. Smith, L. C. Coleman, W. S. Tatom, G. W. Crighton, Mrs. Brown, Z. W. Isom, Catlett Corley, J. M. Cothran, Peter Carroll, Wm. Feguson, A. Laramore, Henry Barrett, G. W. Mitchell, W. Harmon, J. C. Griffin, E. J. Lyon, Pleasant Banks, E. P. Holloway, W. S. Headwrgiht, Lee Henderson, J. W. Parks, Nicholas Cook, W. Harmon. Confederate tax 1862 $382, tax for 1864 $408. Estate Settlement Jan 1866. (11) Heirs each received $1,217.43: 1. Rev. Appleton G.

Harmon 2. J. Anthony Harmon 3. S. G. N. Furqueron and wife 4. Emmanuel Harmon, minor 5. A. L. Laramore and wife 6. John Harmon 7. Stephen W. Willis and wife 8. William Harmon 9. C. M. Freeman and wife 10. James Banks and wife 11. Children of Luke Harmon deceased 11a. W. D. Harmon 11b. Pickens Harmon 11c. Cornelia Harmon. A further samall amount was paid to heirs Dec 1872.

BOX 164 PACK 4414   ELIZA HEARST   1862

Administrator: Henry L. Murphy. Bond Mar 7, 1862 of $25,000 by Henry L. Murphy, J. L. Hearst, Wm. Lyon, Thomas J. Lipscomb. Estate Settlement Jan 11, 1864. (5) Shares each received $2,051.41. 1. J. L. Hearst 2. J. T. Hearst 3. J. N. McCain and wife 4. Henry L. Murphy and wife 5. J. A. Ansley in right of his mother.

BOX 164 PACK 4415   JAMES R. HODGES   1862

Administrator: Andrew Dunn. Bond Dec 19, 1862 of $3,000 by Andrew Dunn, Wm. Dunn, Robert Dunn.

BOX 164 PACK 4416   JOHN J., MARY FRANCES & ELLEN HARKNESS (minors)   1864

Children of Wm. B. Harkness deceased. 1st Guardian: Robert C. Harkness who became insolvent and out as guardian in 1868. Bond Mar 12, 1864 of $4,000 by Robert C. Harkness, J. W. Black, M. B. Latimer. 2nd Guardian: Eliza Harkness. Bond May 9, 1868 of $2,000 by Eliza Harkness, John H. Bell, Ebeneezer H. Bell, W. R. Morrow. All (3) minors were under 10 years of age in 1868. Settlement of Ellen Harkness, now Pettigrew, 1877. Settlement of John J. Harkness Jan 17, 1877. Settlement of Mary Frances Harkness, now Crowther, Dec 18, 1882.

BOX 164 PACK 4417   JAMES D. HALL   1863

Administrator: Wm. Wickliffe. Bond Apr 13, 1863 of $1,000 by Wm. Wickliffe, James Young, Henry S. Cason. 1st Appraisal Apr 30, 1863 by Robert Stuckey, James Young, J. W. Stokes. 2nd Appraisaal Apr 17, 1872 by D. M. Milford, James Elgin, J. T. Milford. Held notes on: A. D. Gray, R. H. Hall, Samuel C. Hall, W. H. Hall, Samuel C. Hall. Estate Sale May 1, 1863 netted $960. Buyers at sale: B. Gray, Wm. Wickliffe, Dr. Wm. Milford, Eliza Ann McAdams, W. A. Hall, Lewis Hall, Ben. Strickland, Tucker W. May, Jane Ann Hall. Estate Settlement May 16, 1872, not completed. Estate Settlement Feb 4, 1878. Widow and (2) Children: 1. Jane Hall 2. Andrew Hall.

BOX 164 PACK 4418   JAMES IRWIN   1863

Will dated Sep 25, 1863. Witnesses: Isaac Branch, John McCord, H. Cannon. Executrix: Charlotte Irwin, wife. Son: Samuel. 1st Appraisal Dec 18, 1863 by John McCord, J. J. Gilmer, Henry Cannon, G. W. Cromer. Owned 9 slaves. Held notes on: J. Robertson, W. L. McCord, H. M. Wardlaw, A. McCord, Isaac Branch & D. R. Sondley, J. P. Cromer & John Davis, J. H. Gray & John J. Gray, D. W. McCord & Thomas B. McCord, J. F. Marshall & J. W. W. Marshall, S. W. Cochran & Peter Henry, D. Sondley, John Pratt, A. Irwin, Henry Cannon, B. Dill, F. McCord, James A. Wilson, W. S. Robertson & Thomas Eakin, L. Breazeale & W. L. McCord, B. Dill & W. L. McCord. 2nd Appraisal Oct 26, 1868 by G.W. Cromer, John McCord, Wm. McIlwain. Estate Sale Oct 28, 1868. Buyers at sale: Louis H. Russell, John Davis, Levi H. Rykard, J. A. Keller, J. W. Keller, J. A. Keller, George W. Cromer, Grant T. Jackson, George A. Douglass, John McCord, John Mundy, J. L. McCord, R. S. Anderson, Wm. H. Adamson, Charles Botts. In 1864 Wm. Purdy received $300 as part of the share of his children in the estate. Widow married George W. Cromer in 1868.

BOX 164 PACK 4419   CHILDREN of JAMES IRWIN (minors)   1863

Bond Mar 6, 1863 of $300 by James Irwin, J. J. Gilmer. Minor children: 1. Samuel Irwin 2. Robert Irwin 3. James Irwin 4. John Irwin 5. William Irwin. Jul 1870 Charlotte Cromer requested that James A. McCord be appointed guardian of 1. William Irwin 2. Thomas Irwin both to the age of choice. Feb 10, 1880 Thomas Irwin received as his inheritance $8.68. Feb 7, 1881 William Irwin received as his inheritance $16.97.

BOX 164 PACK 4420   JOHN CALHOUN IRWIN   1863

Will dated Sep 2, 1861. Filed Nov 2, 1863. Witnesses: E. R. Calhoun, Wm. N. Blake, James Bailey. Mother: Mary Irwin. Father: John Irwin. Sister: Isabella Z. Irwin.

BOX 164 PACK 4421   DAVID A. JORDAN   1864

Administrator: Samuel Jordan. Oct 6, 1869 Edmund Cowan, John Lyon received their inheritance share. Oct 15, 1869 James W. Wideman, James C. Lites received their inheritance share. May 28, 1870 Wm. G. Neel received his inheritance share.

BOX 164 PACK 4422   JONATHAN L. JORDAN   1863

Appraisal Nov 21, 1863 A. P. Connor, Wm. G. Neel, John Patterson, Samuel Link. Held notes on: Wm. G. Neel, Wm. Butler, David Clary, James Belcher, E. E. Kennedy, Wm. McGill, Wm. H. McCaslan, Allen Ramey, M. Harris, Thomas Smith, S. Jordan, Eliza Clay. Estate Sale Jan 8, 1864. Buyers at sale: W. G. Neel, S. Jordan, A. Watson, James Martin, Samuel Link, Edward O. Reagan, Dr. John Sanders, W. G. Kennedy, J. G. Gilmer. Oct 6, 1869 John Lyon and Edmund Cowan received inheritance share. Oct 15, 1869 James C. Lites and James Wideman received inheritance share. May 1869 Wm. G. Nell received inheritance share.

BOX 164 PACK 4423   JANE JONES   1863

Administrator: Robert Jones. Bond Mar 7, 1863 of $4,000 by Robert Jones, J. T. Moore, J. H. Cobb. Appraisal Mar 28, 1863. Held notes on: R. Jones, Willey Ellis, B. F. Roberts. Estate Sale Mar 28, 1863 netted $344. Buyers at sale: Mary Miller, R. Jones, Thomas Jones, B. F. Roberts, Mrs. Willey Ellis, Mary Miller. Horses for funeral hears rented from Russell & Russell $4. Pid John Enright $25 for coffin. 1862 state tax $1.80, Confederate tax $3.50. Estate Settlement: no date. Heirs (6) each received $318.08. Mother, (2) Brothers, (3) Sisters.

BOX 164 PACK 4424   MISS SUSAN KELLER   1863

Administrator: David Z. Keller. Bond Jan 13, 1863 of $10,000 by David Z. Keller, Nancy Keller, James F. Mabry. Appraisal Mar 2, 1863 by Talbert Cheatham, James Irwin, John Davis. Owned 2 slaves. Estate Sale Mar 2, 1863. Buyer at sale: Newton Cochran. 1st Settlement Jan 30, 1863. Estate consisted of 1 slave woman and child. Gold watch, interest in her father's estate and a note on Sarah C. Buchanan for $5.50. Money for sale of slaves and gold watch never collected until 1875. 2nd Estate Settlement Apr 28, 1875. (8) Heirs mentioned: 1. Mother, Nancy Keller received $76.19 as did L. Emma

Keller, W. W. L. Keller, William H. Wilson and Wife Anna E. 2. Issac A. Keller 3. M. Julia Mabry 4. T. Z. Keller 5. John W. Keller. 1863 Confederate tax $4.54.

BOX 164 PACK 4425   JAMES H. KAY   1863

Administrator: George H. Kay. Bond Mar 17, 1863 of $4,000 by George H. Kay, James F. Donnad, Benjamin F. Moseley. Appraisal Apr 3, 1863 by David Moore, Wm. C. Moseley, U. J. Mattison, John W. Bigby. Held notes on: James Seawright, R.R. Seawright, James A. Lyon & J. F. Donnald. 1ˢᵗ Settlement Apr 5, 1864. (6) Heirs: 1. James H. Kay $241.52 2. Charles W. Kay $241.52 3. E. C. Mattison $2241.52 4. Child of John B. Kay and wife Savannah $241.52 5. Children of S. W. Richey wife of George W. Richey $190.40 not paid until Jan 1, 1875 6. Mother $190.40. 2ⁿᵈ Estate Settlement Jan 1, 1875. (4) Shares: Each share received $73.14 in gold except the children of John B. Kay who received $24.38 each. 1. George H. Kay 2. Mrs. E.C. Mattison 3. Children of John B. Kay 4. George W. Richey.

BOX 164 PACK 4426   ROBERT N. LYON   1863

Administrator: Wm. Lyon. Bond Feb 13, 1863 of $2,000 by Wm. Lyon, E. G. Kennedy, Wm. C. Smith. Appraisal Feb 27, 1863 by Samuel B. McClinton, Jonathan Jordan, Willis Smith. Notes held on: Lewis Rich, C. Boyd, H. Drennan, George Chiles, Larkin Reynolds, J. B. Murphy, Jane Foster, Mrs. M. Wardlaw, Wm. Gaston, Wm. Butler, James M. Purdy, Wm. G. Neel, W. B. Morrow, George McDonald.

BOX 164 PACK 4427   W. WINFIELD LINDSAY   1863

Administrators: J. O. Lindsay-brother, John I. Bonner, brother-in-law. Appraisal Feb 11, 1863 by J. N. Young, A. C. Hawthorne, J. P. Kennedy. Held notes on: D. O. Hawthorne, J. M. & Ally Priest, J. O. Lindsay, J. J. Bonner, P. A. Lindsay. Estate Sale Feb 12, 1863 netted $620.95. Buyers at sale: J. P. Kennedy, J. N. Young, Robert Pratt, J. M. Young, S. H. Fant, T. R. Pratt, E. Cox, J. O. Lindsay, J. J. Bonner, P. Bradley, James Wideman, Josiah Moffatt, James Cowan, John Pratt, A. T. Boozer, S. C. Hawthorne, Dr. G.W. Pressly, Dr. Miller, Robert C. Grier, Oliver P. Hawthorne, A. B. C. Lindsay. Estate Settlement Feb 21, 1863. (2) Distributees: 1. A. B. C. Lindsay $903.10 2. Peter Lindsay $903.10.

BOX 164 PACK 4428   A. P. LINDSAY   1863

Administrator: Lindsay & Bonner. Bond of $10,000 by J. I. Bonner, J. O. Lindsay, J. P. Kennedy, M. O. Talman. Appraisal Feb 11, 1863 by J. N. Young, Andrew C. Hawthorne, J. P. Kennedy. Owned 5 slaves, 95 acres of land and lot in Town of Due West, library of books. Held notes on: P. A. Lindsay, J. I. Bonner, J. M. Bell. Estate Sale Feb 12, 1863 netted $6,817. Buyers at sale: J. O. Lindsay, Andrew C. Hawhtorne, A. B. C. Lindsay, Robert C. Grier, Jospeh F. Lee, John N. Young, John I.. Bonner, E. L. Patton, G. M. Mattison, Dr. Latimer, F. Bradley, Mrs. P. A. Lindsay, S. H. Fant, Thomas J. Ellis, James Seawright, James Cowan, David W. Aiken, J. M. Carwile. Estate Settlement Feb 21, 1863. Distributees each received $1,743. 1. Mother, not named 2. (1) Sister, not named 3. (2) Brothers, Peter Lindsay and A. B. C. Lindsay.

BOX 164 PACK 4429   ANDREW J. LYTHGOE   1863

Confederate Soldier. Administrator: John A. Wier. Bond Mar 17, 1863 of $50,000 by John A.Wier, B. P. Hughes, J. J. Cunningham. Wife: Margaret J. Lythgoe. Brother in Law: John A. Wier. Appraisal Apr 1, 1863 by B. P. Hughes, Samuel Gilmer, W. J. Lomax.

Owned a sizeable number of corporate bonds. Held notes on: H. T. Lyon, J. J. Wardlaw, James M. Perrin, D. McNeill Turner, Mrs. A. P. Lythgoe, John Hefferman, Wm. D. Stone, D. J. Jordan, A. P. Lythgoe & Thomas R. Roberts. Owned 12 slaves. Estate Sale Apr 3, 1863 netted $11,315. Buyers at sale: Mrs. Lythgoe, J. D. Chalmers, John A. Wier, B. Winestock, J. T. Boyd, Jeptha R. Hamlin, W. J. Lomax, Thomas C. Perrin, Mrs. Paisley, D. McNeill Turner, W. H. Belcher, J. T. Owen, J. A. Allen, Ben. P. Hughes, J. F. Bonner, Wm. Tomlin, Mathew McDonald, John T. Lyon, F. P. Robertson, John Enright, Wm. H. Parker, W. H. Wilson, Philip H. Rutledge, -- Stacy, Hiram T. Tusten, Talbert Cheatham, Andrew Simonds, Wm. Hill, J. L. Lyon, John McLaren, Samuel Cochran. 1863 town council tax $5.75, state tax $26.23, Confederate tax $117.76. 1864 corporation tax $6, Confederate tax $480. Estate Settlement Apr 12, 1865. Widow received $7,560.97, (3) Children each received $2,520.32. Settlement did not include the amount to be received from the accounts due the late firm of Wier & Lythgoe. Deceased had owned 3/8 Shares of business.

BOX 164 PACK 4430   GEORGE W. LOMAX   1863

Will dated: Aug 25, 1863. Witnesses R. C. Oliver, John W. Lomax, John Robertson. Executors: John Foster, brother-in-law, Wm. A. Lomax. Brother: Samuel R. Lomax willed 600 acres of land. Niece: Sallie Foster daughter of his Sister, Savannah Foster the wife of John Foster willed 13 slaves. Barabara J. Lomax the daughter of his friend, Wm. A. Lomax willed 3 slaves. Appraisal Sep 4, 1863 by P. D. Klugh, Nathaniel Cobb, John Lomax, J. J. Adams. Owned 16 slaves. Held notes on: T. W. Smith, S. R. Lomax, John Turner, John Foster, Wm. A. Lomax, John Calvert, Wm. Robertson. Estate Settlement Nov 23, 1864. Samuel R. Lomax received all of the estate.

BOX 164 PACK 4431   B. M. LATIMER   1860

Confederate Soldier. Administrator: Joseph Ellis. Bond of $50,000 by Joseph Ellis, Robert Ellis, Wm. Ellis. Had been partner with Robert Ellis in the firm of Ellis & Latimer. Appraisal Nov 10, 1862 by John L. Ellis, John Pratt, Robert Pratt. Held notes on: F.W. R. Nance, H. W. Story, J. N. Young, J. M. Morris, W. & J. R. Clinkscales, J. B. Murphy, Stephen Latimer, H. G. G. Gilliam, James Y. Sitton, L. W. Tribble. Owned 7 scholarships to Erskine College that were sold to Joseph Ellis for $19.60. Estate Sale Nov 11, 1862. Buyers at sale: Widow, R. F. Bryson, Dr. J. L. Miller, M. Winestock, Joseph Ellis, M. M. Ellis, S. M. Tribble, Dr. H. T. Lyon, B. M. Winestock, Robert Ellis, W. R. Hemphill, John Bell, Thomas Hawthorne, John A. Wier, J. P. Pressly, Christopher Ellis, Robert C. Grier, J. R. Ellis, Andrew C. Hawthorne, F. P. Robertson, Wm. Allen, J. P. Kennedy, David Duncan, Dr. J. F. Donald, J. R. Clinkscales, Stephen Latimer, Oliver P. Hawthorne, J. Blackwell, J. N. Young, Thomas Crawford, J. C. Branyon, W. J. Phillips, T. J. Roberts, John T. Lyon, James Cowan. 1st Estate Settlement Jan 21, 1864. Widow, Hester A. M. Latimer received $5706.60. Only Child, Robert M. Latimer received $11,413.21. 2nd Estate Settlement Jan 12, 1870. Widow received $99.62, child received $49.81. 3rd Estate Settlement May 18, 1880 Widow received $99.55, child received $199.09. Indications of yearly distributions of some amounts being made from 1864 through 1880.

Box 164 PACK 4432   THOMAS LESLY   1863

Administrator: John W. Lesly. Bond Nov 22, 1862 of $20,000 by John W. Lesly, Wm. Lesly, A. E. Lesly. Appraisal Nov 27, 1862 B. P. Hughes, Samuel Gilmer, D. J. Jordan. Owned 8 slaves. Accounts Owed to deceased at his death: James Gordon, D. McLaughlin, Charles A. Allen, Miss Jane Gordon, Thomas Christian, L. H. Beard, John T.

Lyon, J. J. Wardlaw, --Buchanan, James Shillito, Edward Roche, W. C. Moore, --Cromer. Held notes on: G. G. Dawson, J. F. Marshall. Estate Sale Dec 4, 1862 netted $12,248. Buyers at sale: Talbert Cheatham, Alpheus Lesly, D. McNeill Turner, John A. Allen, J. J. Wardlaw, J. A. Richey, Nancy Keller, Ben. P. Hughes, John McLaren, John T. Owen, David J. Jordan, W. H. Wilson, J. W. Lesly, John A. Calhoun, Mrs J. A. Fraser, W. A. Lesly, Robert H. Wardlaw, Wm. Simmons, John McBryde, Thomas Gordon, James Carlisle, Wm. Hill, J. A. Fraser, John F. Livingston, George Dusenberry, John T. Lyon, Robert Thomas Gordon. Estate Settlement Feb 15, 1864. (5) Distributees each received $2,341.19. Only (2) distributees named: 1. Wm. A. Lesly 2. P. A.Dawson.

BOX 164 PACK 4433   JOSEPH F. LEE   1863

Administrator: J. J. Lee. Owned stock in the Memphis & Charleston Railroad, Spartanburg & Charleston Railroad, Charleston & Savannah Railroad. Estate greatly reduced due to heavy investment in Confederate securities. Estate Settlement Feb 15, 1867. (4) Distributees each received $940.49. 1. J. J. Lee 2. Joseph F. Lee 3. Wm. A. Lee 4. Thomas S. Lee.

Box 164 PACK 4434   MICHAEL SMITH MANN   1863

Will dated Jul 1, 1862. Witnesses: H. H. Scudday, Epaminandos Edwards, Landy O. Shoemaker. Executor: Armistead Burt. Wife: Nancy Mann. Daughters: Jane Ann Hogan, Elizabeth M. Mann. Son: John Thomas Mann. Appraisal Aug 5, 1862 by Andrew Edwards, Wm. O. Pursley, Samuel Carter, Landy O. Shoemaker, James H. Cobb. Owned 6 slaves, several hundred acres of land along Flagreed Creek. Estate paid notes due to: Wm. O. Pursley, James Pursley, John White, George B. Clinkscales, Edward Westfield, Talbert Cheatham, D. M. Rogers, Isaac Branch, James McCaslan, John A. Wier, A. B. Hamlin, Hiram T. Tusten, Charles Cox, Samuel Lockridge, Jesse Charles, Hiram W. Lawson. Estate Sale Aug 23, 1862. Buyers at sale: W. J. Smith, Dr. Thomas J. Mabry, John T. Owen, E. Mann, W. H. Taggart, F.A. Wilson, Nancy Mann, John Bass, A. B. Hamlin, W. H. Wilson, Talbert Cheatham, Jane Hogan, Samuel Carter, Thomas Cheatham, John A. Hunter, John A. Allen, John A. Wier, Landy O. Shoemaker, W. B. Kennedy, James H. Cobb, Harvey T. Lyon, Adolphus A. Williams, J. W. W. Marshall, Naathaniel J. Davis, Edward Roche, Wm. Hicks, Joseph T. Moore, James A. Norwood, J. W. Thomas, J. H. Edwards, S. C. McCaw, Nathan A. Edwards. Estate Settlement Aug 8, 1863. (4) Distributees: 1. John Thomas Mann $1,144 2. Miss Elizabeth Mann $1,194 3. Jane A. Hogan $ 1,494 4. Widow $1,494. Paied Edward J. Taylor $30 for coffin. 1862 war tax $27. 15.

BOX 164 PACK 4435   JACOB MARTIN   1863

Will dated Jul 29, 1856. Witnesses: A. Z. Bowman, Wm. C. Cobb, Thomas T. Cunnigham. Executors: James M. Martin, John J. Martin. 1st Bond Nov 24, 1863 of $8,255 by James M. Martin, John J. Martin. 2nd Bond Nov 24, 1863 of $10,476 by John J. Martin, John H. Wilson. Sons: James M. Martin, Benjamin Y. Martin, William N. Martin, John J. Martin, Charles W. Martin deceased whose children were Lyman W. Martin and Laura E. Martin, Thomas P. Martin. Daughter: Elizabeth Carloss? Appraisal Nov 10, 1863 by Albert Clinkscales, J. W. Griffin, Wm. M. Smith. Owned 4 slaves. Estate Sale Nov 11, 1863. Buyers at sale: J. J. Martin, James C. Clark, Wm. A. Sutherland, L. L. Blanchett, J. D. Burkhead, Wm. A. Giles, James M. Martin, Thomas Lanier, Henry S. Cason, Ben. Pooser, W. J. Robinson, P. P. Carloss, Mrs. Kennedy, T. C. Young, James Kennedy, R. A. Pressly, Les Baird, Dr. Boyd, James Hopkinson, G. W. Gantt, W. N. Martin, J. W. Griffin, Francis

A. Wilson, E. Pearlstein, Samuel J. Hester, R. L. Hardin, John E. Calhoun, Moses Winestock, H. Levine, Edward Noble, John E. Calhoun, W. M. Brooks, J. W. Crawford, John A. Wier, Wm. Holmes, B. A. McAllister, Mrs. J. C. Martin, D. Turner O'Neill, T. W. Syle, Phil Rutledge, Christian V. Barnes, Wm. Speer, Talbert Cheatham, Confederate Government. Coffin cost $45.

BOX 165 PACK 4437   ABNER H. McGEE JR.   1863

Will dated Jul 16, 1861. Witnesses Marhall Sharp, W. A. J. Ware, J. C. Rasor. Executor: Elizabeth McGee-wife. Wife: Elizabeth McGee. Daughters: Esther C. McGee, Mary A. McGee, Georgianna V. McGee, Sallie U. H. McGee, Lucinda R. McGee. Son: Wm. Z. McGee. Appraisal Nov 18, 1862 by John C. Waters, J. C. Rasor, Green Berry Riley. Owned 14 slaves, 450 acres of land, scholarships at Masonic Female College $40. Held notes on W. W. Sharp, W. A. J. Ware, Elizabeth Ware, J. J. Jennings. Estate Sale Nov 19, 1862. Buyers at sale: Michael B. McGee, J. T. Carter, J. C. Rasor, Marshall Sharp, R. C. Sharp, Joel F. Smith, A. Robertson, Widow, Wm. McGee, S. T. Hodges, C. M. Sharp, F. F. Gary, G. M. Mattison, James F. Smith, L. J. Rasor, J. W. Sherard, Abiah M. Agnew, Lucinda McGee, M. Strauss, M. Griffin, J. R. Smith, A. C. Hawthorne, W. S. Vandiver, Thomas Ellis, George Robertson, Wm. Wilson, Joel F. Smith, James Killingsworth, T. Y. Martin. 1862 Confederate tax $41.75.

BOX 165 PACK 4438   ROBISON B. McADAMS   1863

Administrator: Eliza Ann McAdams-wife. Bond Jan 19, 1863 of $20,000 by Eliza Ann McAdams, W. McAdams, Robert Hall, Conrad Wakefield, Amaziah Rice. Appraisal Jan 27, 1863 by John N. Harkness, John Hall, C. W. Welch, George W. Bowen, Wm. Dickson. Owned 12 slaves. 1868 tax on estate $8.68, 1870 taxes $30.92.

BOX 165 PACK 4439   MARY MOSELEY   1863

Will dated Sep 6, 1858. Witnesses: James M. Latimer, M. L. Kennedy, H. Latimer. Codicil: Pct 7, 1859. Witnesses: James M. Latimer, M. L. Kennedy, Christian V. Barnes Jr. Son: John M. Moseley to receive ½ of estate. Daughter: Charlotte Moseley to receive ½ of estate. Son: Philip H. Moseley died in 1859. Executor John M. Moseley. Coffin cost $30 paid to Bell & White. Marble stones to be placed at his grave site. 1st Estate return made May 7, 1863. Nothing else in pack.

BOX 165 PACK 4440   THOMAS H. MAULDIN   1863

Administrator: Archibald Mauldin-father who died prior to the sale of the estate. Bond Feb 10, 1862 of $2,000 by Archibald Mauldin, T. Alonzo Harris, Robert H. Pettigrew. Not Married. Father and (4) Brothers, not named. Appraisal Feb 28, 1862 by T. Alonzo Harris, James M. White, Alonzo Z. Bowman, George P. Pettigrew, Ben. D. Kay, John C. Speer. Estate Sale Jan 1, 1863 netted $267.87. Buyers at sale: T. Alonzo Harris, Robert H. Pettigrew, Allen V. Brooks, John Morgan, Alonzo Z. Bowman, W. C. Cozby, W. T. Mauldin, B. D. Kay, T. W. Gantt, W. M. Bell, Andrew J. Speer, J. M. Moseley, J. F.C. DuPre, Christian V. Barnes, W. H. Rampey, J. T. Baker, J. M. White, James T. Barnes. 1863 Confederate tax $2.50. 1863 general tax 63 cents.

BOX 165 PACK 4441   GEORGE H. MAXWELL   1862

Confederate Soldier killed in Virginia. Administrator: H. B. Maxwell-brother. Bond Mar 17, 1862 of $600 by H. B. Maxwell, Wm. P. Andrews, Johnson Sale. Appraisal Apr 4,

1862 by F. M. Spikes, Johnson Sale, Irvin Hutchison. Estate Sale Apr 4, 1862. Buyers at sale: W. Henderson, H. B. Maxwell, Johnson Sale, Thomas Maxwell. Estate Settlement May 30, 1866. Estate Insolvent. Paid debts at 35 cents on the dollar.

BOX 165 PACK 4442   SAMUEL MITCHELL   1863

Administrator: Martha Mitchell-wife. Bond Jan 15, 1863 of $5,000 by Martha Mitchell, W. James Lomax, Littleton Yarborough. Appraisal Jan 29, 1863 by James T. Barnes, James T. Baskin, W. A. Pressly. Estate Sale Jan 30, 1863 netted $893.58. Buyers at sale: Martha Mitchell, Dr. J. T. Baskin, Dr. A. Walker, John Bowen, W. A. Pressly, Thomas A. Daniel, James Clark, Alex. Oliver, Dr. Andrew J. Speer, Mrs. J. Harkness, E. White, J. Uldrick, J. Rampey, F. Boronys, Clement T. Latimer, Wm. McBryde, James T. Barnes, A. Bowman, R. Hutchison, Ben. D. Kay, Wm. A. Sutherland, Thomas A. Cater, Andrew Sutherland, W. M. Bell. 1863 Confederate tax $10. 1864 Confederate tax $150.

BOX 165 PACK 4444   JOHN McCLAIN   1863

Will dated Sep 19, 1858. Witnesses: Bennett McAdams, James H. Haddon, N. G. Hughes. Executors: J. R. Wilson, he died and Lemuel Reid the executor of his estate became the executor of this estate. Ezekiel Harris became the administrator in 1880. Bond Sep 28, 1880 of $1,500 by Ezekiel Harris, J. S. Williams, H. S. Taylor, Benjamin J. McClain, Andrew J. Shaw. Appraisal Jun 10, 1863 by Wm. Clinkscales, Bennett McAdams, Robert McAdams. Held notes on: James Hughes, N. J. Hughes, James Shirley, John Moon, Bennett, McAdams, Ben. McClain, Wm. McClain, John MClain Jr. Estate Sale Dec 25, 1880. Buyers at sale: Edna McClain, J. A. Elgin, Ben. McClain, L. Elgin, Latta McClain, Jack Kay, Wesley Joseph, Richard Saylors, Robert Galloway, W. A. Hall, J. R. Hughes, Charles Henderson, Henry Stephens, John Shirley, S. J. Davis, J. C. Clamp, Wm. Saylors, J. Smith, A. J. Hawthorne, Mary Robinson, Isaac McClain, Alex. Armstrong, J. W. Ashley, Mary Ann Grimes, W. C. Armstrong, S. P. Dunlap, Ed Cowan, F. J. Caumel, A. J. Shaw, Joshua Ashley, Robert McAdams, Wm. B. Cliinkscales, J. C. McClain, George Smith, J. A. Gilmer, B. L. Morrison, J. H. Bannister, L. A. Morris, Samuel Starke, Cater Crawford, Wm. Pruitt. Estate Settlement Apr 3, 1882. (12) Legatees: 1. Ephraim McClain deceased with one child, John R. McClain 2. James M. McClain deceased with (8) children: 2a. Mary A. Robinson 2b. Nancy J. Burgess 2c. Ophelia E. Williams 2d. James O. McClain 2e. Andrew B. McClain 2f. Theodosia Elgin 2g. John M. McClain deceased with children; J. R. McClain, Margaret M. McClain, Sallie McClain, Mary H. McClain, R. H. T. McClain, G. R. L. McClain, Samuel D. McClain 2h. Hannah McClain deceased with one child, Margaret C. Graham 2i. Samuel McClain deceased with one child, Wm. McClain 3. Benjamin McClain 4. John McClain 5. Isaac McClain 6. William McClain deceased with children all in Pope Co. Ark.   6a. James A. McClain 6b. Nancy E. wife of Green B. Hunter 6c. Mary E. wife of Joseph Headrick 6d. Candis A. wife of James A. Talley 6e. Sarah J. wife of Samuel A. Hood 6f. John R. McClain 6g. Wm. M. McClain 6h. Francis McClain 7. Elizabeth Ashley deceased with two children: Nancy L. Ashley, Mary E. P. Ashley 8. Lottie McClain 9. Jane Shaw 10. Mary A. Taylor 11. Nancy E. wife of Joseph Headrick 12. Sallie E. Sep 9, 1882 J. M. Headrick and wife Mary E. of Gordon Co., Ga. petitioned appointment of J. M. Carlisle agent to collect on grandfather's estate.

BOX 165 PACK 4445   ARCHIBLAD MAULDIN   1862

Administrator: Mary Mauldin-wife. Bond Nov 28, 1862 by Mary Mauldin, T. Alonzo Harris, Robert A. Avery. Appraisal Dec 31, 1862 by B. D. Kay, T. Alonzo Harris, J. F. C. DuPre. Estate Sale Dec 31, 1862. Buyers at sale: W. A. Giles, J. F. C. DuPre, B. D. Kay,

Joel Ashworth, J. C. Carlisle, J. W. Prince, J. T. Barnes, J. D. Mauldin, R. Hutchison, W. T. Mauldin, L. C. Mauldin, T. M. Tucker, Miss McAdams, J. N. Newby, W. A. Sutherland, F. P. Robertson, C. V. Barnes, T. A. Harris, J. M. White, S. A. Hutchison, John Morgan, Fenton Hall, T. W. Gantt, E. J. Stevenson, R. H. Pettigrew, John M. Moseley, Wm. O'Bryant, George Burdette, H. Tucker, W. M. Burton, W. H. Rampey, Mary Mauldin, G. W. Kelly.

BOX 165 PACK 4446   WILLIAM A. McCRACKEN   1863

Administrator. John Rosemond Wilson. Bond Jun 9, 1863 of $2,500 by John R. Wilson, Robert Ellis, Lemuel Reid. Estate Settlement Jun 27, 1863. S. E. McCracken (mother) was the only heir $1,363.26.

BOX 165 PACK 4447 JOHN T. McCAW   1863

Administrator: John F. Livingston. Appraisal Feb 13, 1863 by D. J. Jordan, John T. Lyon, Samuel Gilmer. Estate Sale Feb 13, 1863 netted $360. Buyers at sale: Wm. H. McCaw, John F. Livingston, T. McCaw, Mary McCaw, Samuel J. Hester, Julia McCaw. Estate Settlement Feb 21, 1863. (2) Legatees both minors each received $2,066.56. !. Mary McCaw, her guardian was J. J. Warldaw 2. Wm. H. McCaw, his guardian was Littleton Yarborough.

BOX 165 PACK 4448   EUGENE & WILLIAM L. MATHIS (minors)   1862

Guardian: Nancy Lesly who died in 1872 and guardian became Thomas W. McMillan. Bond Apr 1, 1862 of $1,000 by Nancy Lesly, Edmund G. Kennedy, Thomas W. McMillan. 1862 general tax 24 cents, 1862 Confederate tax $1.16.

BOX 165 PACK 4449   OBEDIAH McMAHAN   1863

Administrator. Keziah C. McMahan-wife. Bond Jan 2, 1863 of $5000 by Keziah C. McMahan, James McKee, Wm. L. McMahan. Appraisal Jan 19, 1863 by T. B. Milford, F. P. Robertson, James McKee. Estate Sale Jan 20, 1863. Buyers at sale: Widow, James McMahan, Steward Cann, Elizabeth McKee, T. B. Milford.

BOX 165 PACK 4450   S. S. McCURRY   1862

Administrator: Henry S. Cason. Bond Sep 19, 1862 of $500 by Henry S. Cason, F. B. Milford, Sterling Bowen Sr. Appraisal Oct 9, 1862 by Robertr Stuckey, James Campbell, James Crowther, Sterling Bowen. Estate Sale Oct 10, 1862 netted $263.70. Buyers at sale: Robert L. Harden, Wm. S. Robertson, Robert H. Hall, Felix P. Robertson, A. P. LeRoy, John L. Campbell, Wm. J. Robertson, David Murdock, Sterling Bowen, Henry S. Cason, Andrew W. Sutherland, Pleasant Ferguson, Miss A. E. McCurry, Wm. Moore, Dr. G. W. Daniel, Dr. J. J. Marshall, Miss E. Drennan, Wm. Wickliffe, T. F. Hill, Joseph F. Bell. Estate Settlement May 5, 1864, no details.

BOX 165 PACK 4451   JOHN JULIAN MILLER   1864

Guardian: Samuel L. Miller. Bond Jan 3, 1859 of $6,800 by Samuel L. Miller, John A. Wier, Samuel A. Brownlee. Appraisal by Robert C. Grier, J. P. Kennedy, F. W. R. Nance. Estate Settlement Apr 15, 1864. Half Sister, not named, only heir received $10,063.77. 1863 Confederate tax $75.99.

BOX 165 PACK 4452   E. H. McDOWELL   1862

Deceased died in 1860. Was the ward of Dr. J. S. Marshall. Administrator: Irvin Hutchison. Bond Nov 12, 1862 of $7,000 by Irvin Hucthison, Johnson Sale, Rebecca H. Ogilvie.

BOX 165 PACK 4453   ANDREW McILWAIN   1863

Confederate Soldier. Will dated Aug 18, 1862. Witnesses: Samuel H. Beard, J. M. McDonald, John T. Owen. Wife: Sallie E. McIlwain. No Children. Brother William McIlwain. Executrix: Sallie E. McIlwain-wife. Appraisal May 14, 1863 by Wm. McIlwain, W. B. Roman, James H. Cobb, Mathew McDonald, Thomas Eakin. Estate Sale Jun 3, 1863. Buyers at sale: Wm. H. Parker, James D. Chalmers, Joseph T. Moore, J. J. Gilmer, Wm. C. Adnerson, Edward Roche, Wm. Hill, Dr. Isaac Branch, James Mabry, Thomas Eakin, John A. Allen, Henry McCree, Jones & McDonald, Dr. J. F. Livingston, Hugh M. Wardlaw, John Turner, Gilmer & Wilson, J. J. Adams, John Mundy, Samuel Cochran, Robert Hagen, John Keller, Hiram T. Tusten, Robert Jones, Henry B. Nickles, J. T. Owen, J. R. Hawthorne, Hiram W. Lawson, Andrew Morrison, Lewis D. Connor, John A. Allen, Thomas Robison, J. I. Gilmer, Wm. A. Lomax, A. B. Hamlin, John Darraugh, Gabriel Hodges, Mathew M. McDonald, Wm. Spruill, S. H. Beard, Thomas Robison, J. R. Cunningham, W. B. Roman, Jesse Carlisle, Asa Bowie, Jeptha R. Hamlin, John Enright, A. Haddon, Charles Cox, Wm. McIlwain, John A. Norwood, Wesley Cromer, James McIlwain, Charles Dendy, Wm. A. Belcher, J. M. Hawthorne, John K. Vance, Wm. H. Wilson, Joseph Knoll, Harper Shillito, David R. Sondley, R. P. Doyle, Wm. Gordon, Nancy McIlwain, J. H. Cobb, J. T. Moore, R. T. Gordon, Samuel Cochran, John Hagen, B. Rutledge, Wm. E. Simmons, J. J. Adams. Dec 23, 1869 Andrew T. McIlwain, son of Wm. McIlwain, received distribution of legacy from the estate of his Uncle, Andrew McIlwain.

BOX 165 PACK 4454   JOHN McLAREN   1864

Will dated Apr 19, 1864. Witnesses: B. P. Hughes, P. S. Rutledge, John McBryde. Executors: Jeanette H. McLaren, John McBryde. Sisters: Margaret G. Williams, Agnes J. Chovin, Eliza A. Robinson, Julia Ann Baker of Virginia. Nephews: Arthur Robinson, Clarence Robinson, Adolphus A. Williams, Robert James McBryde, John M. McBrude. Postmaster of Abbeville. Appraisal May 21, 1864 $118,922. By A. P. Conner, Robert Jones, John T. Owen, Enoch Nelson. Owned extensive property in both South Carolina and Georgia. Owned 14 slaves, 25 shares of Columbia & Greenville Railroad stock. Held Notes on: W. F. Hackett, O. J. Farrington, A. P. Conner, A. A. Williams, John McBryde, M. C. Owen, J. R. Martin, John Young, J. B. Crawford, Dr. E. Parker. 1864 paid Legacy to Mrs. E. H. Robinson $2,000, Arthur Robinson $500, Clarence Robinson $500, Mrs. H. J. Chovin $2,000. 1864 Georgia land tax $355.90. Accounts Open at Abbeville Post Office as of Jun 30, 1864: Dr. Robert Archer, Warren Allen, O. H. Allen, W.W. Belcher, Wm. P. Belcher, Armistead Burt, W. K. Bradley, L. Bowie, Mrs. John A. Bowie, J. S. Baker, W. B. Bonner, Lt. Baxter, Isaac Branch, S. E. Brown, Francis M. Brooks, Dr. D. S. Benson, S. A. Beard, John G. Baskin, W. B. Buchanan, A. Bradley, Branch & Parker, J. P. Cromer, John Corbett, Henry Cannon, R. A.Crawford, Miss E. Cobb, John Conner, Dr. & Miss Campbell, Jesse Carlisle, Mrs. R. L. Chalmers, John Coumbe, Charles Cox, Wm. Cook, Mrs S. E. Cheatham, Edward Calhoun, James Carlisle, J. H. Cobb, John A. Calhoun, James S. Cothran, James D. Chalmers, John Duncan, Jeff Davis, Miss P. T. Dale, Thomas J.

Douglass, R. P. Doyle, J. D. Dailey, Andrew Edwards, J. Evins, J. J. Edwards, C. Evans, Nathan A. Edwards, John Enright, Henry Fosbrook, Mrs. J. W. Fowler, Rev. James Gibert, Andrew L. Gillespie, Wm. Gilmer, Robert T. Gordon, J. J. Gilmer, Andrew L. Gray, Samuel Gilmer, Thomas Gibbs, Miss M. E. Gray, Charles B. Guffin, J. C. Gray, Jackson Griffin, John Gray, Gray & Robertson, Andrew Houston, Daniel Holder, Wm. Hunter, Wm. J. Hammond, Abraham Haddon, James Hopkinson, C. Harberson, J. S. Horton, T. H. Horton, Charles T. Haaskell, Wm. Hill, J. A. Hamilton, Benjamin P. Hughey, W. H. Inglesby, D. F. Jones, D. J. Jordan, Leroy J. Johnson, J. N. Kennedy, T. J. Knauff, Theodore Kennedy, David Knox, Henry S. Kerr, James T. Liddell, J. W. Lesly, Alpheus E. Lesly, H. T. Lyon, Wm. L. Lesly, John T. Lyon, Lesly, Reid & Lesly, Long Cane Mail, J. J. Lesly, Wm. Lickes, John Link, Dr. Wm. E. Link, Mrs. H. Lee, W. J. Lomax, Miss I. C. Ligon, F. M. Mitchell, Mrs. Means, Miss M. Maddox, Franklin Miller, Joseph T. Moore, Rev. John Moore, Wm. C. Moore, Thomas J. Mabry, Wm. McCaslan, M. A. McCracken, Arthur McIlwain, Thomas W. McMillan, James A. McCord, D. McClain, Wm. McClinton, Wm. McCants, Rev. C. McCarthy, Wm. McIlwain, Samuel McGowan, Miss A. B. McBryde, W. G. Neel, J. A. Norwood, Enoch Nelson, Edward Noble, M. T. & J. T. Owen, James Pursley, F. A. Porcher, J. Patterson, Dr. Andrew Paul, Dr. E. Parker, Wm. H. Parker, Robert M. Palmer, Thomas Robison, Jordan A. Ramey, G. A. Robinson, Lemuel Reid, L. Robinson, Wm. Riley, W. B. Roman, Philip S. Rutledge, Russell & Russell, Louis H. Russell, Rutledge & Russell, Johnson Ramey, F. A. Stevenson, John Shillito, Rev. A. G. Stacy, Susan Sassard, Mrs. Stockher, Dr. Sanders, A. Sanders, Andrew Small, Augustus M. Smith, John Taggart, J. A. Talmadge, M. K. Timmerman, Hiram T. Tusten, James W. Thomas, Rev. D. McNeilll Turner & Miss Gibson, David M. Wardlaw, Andrew Weed, James Walker, Moses Winestock, A. Watson, Mrs. W. H. Wilson, Miss C. W. Waring, Mary Walker, Miss L. Walker, L. C. Wilson, B. M. Winestock, Hugh Wilson, Robert J. White, John White, John A. Wier, David L. Wardlaw, Wier & Lythgoe, D. J. J. Wardlaw, John H. Wilson, Dr. A. T. Williamson, J. G. Wilson, Adolphus A. Williams, Samuel A. Wilson,

BOX 165 PACK 4455   VIRGINIA McKITTRICK   1863

Bond Nov 2, 1863 of $8,000 by Benjamin McKittrick, W. K. Bradley, A. P. Connor.

BOX 165 PACK 4556   WILLIAM C. NICKLES   1864

Administrators: Sarah E. Nickles-wife, Henry B. Nickles who died in 1864. Bond Nov 4, 1861 of $8,000 by Henry B. Nickles, Sarah Nickles, Thomas Eakin, Thomas Robison. Appraisal Nov 27, 1861 by Thomas Robison, Andrew Stevenson, John R. McCord, Thomas J. Ellis. Owned 4 slaves, a gin house. Held notes on: D. O. Hawthorne, James Davis. Estate Sale Nov 28, 1864 netted $2170. Buyers at sale: Ben. H. Eakin, John Turner, Sarah Nickles, Thomas Botts, Thomas Robison, T. J. Ellis, Joshua Ashley, Sarah Richardson, Michael Hackett, Samuel A. Hodges, Lewis Dantzler, Wm. A. Richey, Josiah Ashley, John Nickles, Jacob Clamp, Franklin E. Bowie, John H. Mundy, Asa Bowie, Wm. T. Morris, Wesley Klugh, George Nickles, H. B. Nickles, Dr. G. W. Lomax, N. A. Haynes, Gabriel Hodges, Wm. Agnew, David Glymph, T. A. Ellis, Wm. McIlwain, Marshall Everett, J. D. Pace, Wm. N. Mundy, Hugh M. Wardlaw, John Hagen, Thomas B. McCord, John McCord, John Allen, Thomas J. Roberts, J. H. Ellis, W. B. Roman, Ben. White, J. W. Duncan, David Hannah, Wm. Mundy. Estate Settlement Feb 26, 1864. Widow $902.76, (5) Children each $361.10, not named.

BOX 165 PACK 4457   JANE G. NORTH   1863

Will dated Jul 31, 1860 at Badwell. Witnesses: Sarah B. Jones, Hiram Palmer, John H. Jones. Codicil to Will dated Sep 29, 1863. Witnesses to the codicil: M. L. Petigru, J. A. Gibert, C. P. Allston. Executrix: Louisa G. North. Daughters: Mary wife of Joseph Blythe Allston, Caroline wife of Charles C. Pettigrew, Louise wife of Wm. Porcher. Grandson: Charles Lewis Pettigrew willed 100 acres of land. Sister: Mary Pettigrew. Brother: James Louis Petigru deceased. Appraisal Nov 27, 1863 by J. A. Gibert, Hiram Palmer, Jamces C. Willard, J. H. Britt. Owned 40 slaves.

BOX 166 PACK 4461   MOSES T. OWEN   1863

Will dated Apr 7, 1861. Witnesses Samuel McGowan, Joseph Moore, Hiram W. Lawson. Executrix: Marrtha A. Owen-wife. Brother: John T. Owen. Sister: Berthenia wife of Morris D. Roche living in Alabama. Merchant. 1st Appraisal Sep 1, 1863 by John S. Reid, Stephen F. Gibert, Charles Evans. Owned 19 slaves. 2nd Appraisal Nov 13, 1866 by Walter G. Keller, J. L. Sibert, Henry Moselely, B. F. Brown, J. H. Wideman. Estate Sale Nov 14, 1866. Buyers at sale: Martha A. Owen, G. M. Sibert, B.F. Brown, J. H. Wideman, J. L. Sibert, Charles Dendy, L. O. Young, G. W. Mayson, G. S. Patterson, Joohn Owen, Anthony G. Harmon, Wm. Kennedy, J. W. Cook, James Finley, Wesley Deason, Thomas O. Creswell, G. B. McCaslan, Thomas Moseley, Stephen Smith, Wm. Bosdell, J. B. Palmer, A. F. Young, James Truitt, F. H. Edwards, Thomas C. McBryde, Edward O. Reagan, J. S. Ward, H. F. Corley, J. C. Griffin, Lewis Owen, John Cheatham, John Lyon, Miss Virginia Owen, Mrs. M. C. Lyon, George W. Mitchell, Mrs. M. Waller, Mrs. Harmon, John H. Jones, F. H. Russell, Redmond Brown, Wm. Dillalshaw, Walter G. Keller, J. C. Lites, Andrew J. Weed, T. J. Stuckey, John Jones, A. A. Traylor, Daniel New, W. B. Dorn, J. S. Bosdell, R. Weed, John Deason, R. T. Bell, Hugh Moseley, Dr. Virtress, Mary Cothran, G. L. Patterson, Andy Crozier, Philip H. Bradley, Daniel Holder, B. B. Harveley, A. M. Martin, Wm. Johnson, Joseph Lykens, Michael Cuddy, Ed. Cowan, J. F. Keller, Isaac Caldwell, J. F. Creswell, Wm. T. Jennings, L. W. Lyon, Dr. J. S. Sanders, James Creswell, J. F. Edmunds, Ben. Henderson, Josh Gibson, G. S. Patterson, Patrick Lindsay, James Creswell, J. B. Palmer, W. C. Ludrix. 1864 Confederate Animal Tax $22.60. Accounts open and on books dating from 1849: Jame Anderson, J. W. Appleton, W. W. Anderson, Thomas Atkins, Robert A. Archer, E. H. Atkins, Jesse Adams, Thomas Adams, J. B. Algary, John Allen, James T. Allen, James A. Allen, Wm. A. Allen, Charles H. Allen, W. P. Anderson, John Anderson, Wm. Appleton, R. H. Appleton, Jonathan Adamson, Armistead Burt, Wm. Bullock, W. S. Baskin, H. O. Baker, L. L. Blackwell, B. F. Blasingame, Wm. Butler, E. S. Bailey & Co., C. E. Brooks, W. H. Belcher, S. L. Brooks, Sterling Bowen, John G. Baskin, Thomas Barksdale, Branch & Allen, Miss M. Buchanan, Miss Sallie Baker, Miss Margaret Bass, Henry Belcher, Fleming Bell, Wm. Bentley, John Boozer, John Bullock, D. D. Brooks, G. C. Bowers, Wm. Bell, Miss Martha Brooks, David Boozer, Alex. Bass, S. B. Barnes, -- Burdette, Aiken Breazeale, Allen Brooks, Daniel Boyd, Josiah Burton, Mrs. Bentley, Jane Baker, E. S. Bailey, John B. Burton, Samuel S. Baker, G. W.A. Beardon, G. A. Christopher, R. L. Chalmers, Elizabeth Cobb, G. W. Caldwell, John Calvert, Conner & Anderson, James H. Caldwell, Cobb-Hunter & Co., B. J. Cochran, James Cochran, Edmund Cobb, Thomas P. Campbell, Hugh M. Calhoun, Enoch Cater, John Cowan, Richard Crosson, E. Campbell, Wm. Clinkscales, Thomas M. Christian, Andrew Conn, John Cunningham, Thomas B. Crews, Alex. Cochran, S. A. Crawford, James E. Calhoun, John Cothran, L. V. Cain, M.

Conner, M. C. Calhoun, John Clem, A. J. Conner, C. M. Calhoun, Wm. Clinkscales, R. N. Cheatham, Thomas R. Cochran, Charles Cox, E. L. Clark, Thomas Cheatham, James Cowan, W. Cowan, M. W. Coleman, Wm. Cook, Miss Sarah Calhoun, John Calhoun, Mrs. M. L. Cochran, W. Conner, E. Cowan, Charles M. Dansby, Isaac W. Dansby, Stephen C. DeBruhl, B. A. Davis, J. M. Davis, Shadrack Deale, Wm. Donald, James Devlin, J. R. Dukes, Thomas Dowtin, S. G. W. Dill, D. L. Dessame, Jane Dendy, J. P. Davis, M. M. Donald, J. W. Davis, Mrs. D. Douglass, Rev. W. H. Davis, F. W. Davis, David Donald, James S. Douglass, J. W. Dansby, W. Davis, H. L. Devann, Misses Davis & Boozer, George Davis, J. N. Dailey, R. M. Davis, John Evans, John Enright, Stephen Elmore, Nathan A. Edwards, Epamenandos Edwards, David Edwards, Miss Martha Elmore, John W. Franks, Misses Fooshe & Sample, J. H. Fell, Thomas Fell, James Fair, Mrs. J. A. Fraser, John J. Gilmer, Wm. Gaines, Alfred Gailey, Thomas Gordon, Wm. Giles, Dr. John Gray, J. P. Graves, Robert Gilliam, D. F. Gary, James Glasgow, John Griffin, John Gibson, Wm. Gaines, Wm. Gallagher, S. E. Graydon, Andrew Gillespie, James Gilliam, Dr. Gibert, Wm. Gray, James Hanson, Thomas A. Harris, Anthony Harmon, Susan Hilburn, Wm. J. Holt, Alex. Houston, Samuel A. Hodges, Coleman Henderson, Cornelius Houston, Israel Holt, J. Fletcher Hodges, W. M. Hughey, Edward Hilburn, B. Z. Herndon, J. F. Hodges, H. H. Holland, David O. Hawthorne, Franklin Howlet, J. P. Hunter, Andrew Hawthorne, Mrs. Sarah Hill, W. E. Haskell, Dr. J. W. Hearst, Wm. Harris, Sandy Holmes, Dr. Nathaniel Harris, Samuel Hunter, Langdon C. Haskell, John M. Harris, B. Haddon, Andrew M.. Hill, P. Hazzard, John Irwin, John Irwin, J. W. Jewin, Humphrey K. Jackson, Thomas Jackson, L. E. Jackson, Nathaniel Jeffries, John S. Jeffries, Joseph Jeffries, Thomas Jeffries, L. H. Jones, W. W. Jones, Jonathan Jordan, Samuel Jordan, Leroy Johnson, P. L. Jones, D. J. Jordan, G. M. Jordan, Rev. B. Johnson, C. H. Kingsmore, Jane A. Kary, F. Keller, David Kerr, Paschall D. Klugh, H. T. Lyon, P. H. Ligon, W. James Lomax, W. B. Lackey, J. H. Ligon, James Leslie, Dr. W. G. Lomax, Thomas Link, W. J. Lomax, P. B. Levy, L. Lockridge, Joseph Ligon, J. J. Lipford, T. J. Lyon, Dr. John H. Logan, Robert Lites, A. J. Lythgoe, J. W. Leslie, Rev. J. O. Lindsay, Mrs. L. Ligon, Samuel Link, Wm. Lyon, W. Lindsay, J. T. McNeill, W. S. McCall, A. A. McKittrick, Ben. McKittrick, Wm. McMillan, Mathew McDonald, John McLaren, J. S. McMorris, Thomas McCord, J. L. McNeill, John McBryde, John McKellar, James A. McKee, Thomas H. McCurry, Miss E. McGowan, Archibald McCord, Wm. McCaslan, Joseph McKittrick, J. T. McNeill, David McLane, Thomas McAllister, Samuel W. Mabry, James M. Martin, John M. Martin, James F. Mabry, M. W. Mabry, T. P. Martin, J. M. Martin, G. B. Morrah, John C. Martin, W. J. Morris, Henry Moseley, R. H. Mounce, E. Moseley, James Morris, John Mundy, George Marshall, Samuel Morrah, Miss Mary Means, Wm. Motes, Ed Moore, Rev. James Moore, Dr. Samuel Marshall, Robert Mars, H. W. Martin, James Means, Thomas Moseley, A. Murphy, W. G. Neel, Edward Noble, Miss E. Noble, A. A. Noble, Samuel Noble, Thomas Nichols, Thomas E. Owen, John T. Owen, Samuel H. Owen, R. L. Owen, John Patterson, W. T. Pace, Andrew Paul, Wm. T. Penney, Wm. C. Puckett, John T. Parks, Josiah Patterson, Wm. Pace, --Parnell, Misses W. W. & R. Perryman, Thomas Pettigrew, J. J. Philpot, Colonel Patterson, Wm. Penney Sr., James Peate, ---Pruitt, Wm. H. Parker, Henry Patterson, Dr. T. F. Pleasants, John Patterson, Misses Perryman & WallerC. C. Puckett, F. P. Robertson, Beckham Ramey, L. O. Russell, S. O. Russell, L. L. Russell, John Robinson, George Rasor, M. G. Ross, Misses Roberts & Adams, J. W. Richardson, Bennett Reynolds, Wm. Rogers, E. H. Robertson, Wm. Robinson, James Russell, B. G. Rollinson, Edward O. Reagan, B. L. Reynolds, Mrs. Reid, Johnson Ramey, Matilda Richey, Lemuel Reid, Franklin Ruff, J. W. Smith, Abram

Smith, W. W. Sharp, Thomas W. Smith, W. W. Sprouse, W. W. Shillito, Robert E. Smith, Wm. Smith, M. Strauss, Lewis Smith, W. C. Sproull, C. H. Selleck, Marshall Sharp, L. H. Smith, J. H. Strong, John Sample, Mrs. Stokes, Edward Selby, Issac Sibert, N. W. Stewart, John W. Suber, John Selvy, Dr. Spires, A. Slager, Andrew Small, Dr. Skillern, Henry Spikes, John Sentell, Dr. John Sanders, E. Speer, Moses O. Talman, James Taggart Jr., J. W. Trowbridge, James F. Tolbert, James Taggart Sr., Wm. H. Taggart, John Taggart, Wm. Thomas, Thomas W. Talman, J. J. Tucker, W. T. Tatom, Miss Virginia Traylor, E. Taggart, Dr. Wm. Tennent, Elijah Vinney, J. F. Verrell, James Verrell, R. Vandiver, R. J. White, S. A. Wilson, Wm. H. Wilson, D. M. Wardlaw, Wardlaw & Lyon, Andrew J. Woodhurst, Nancy Wilson, P. A. Waller, Joshua Wideman, Ben. Williams, Joshua Wilson, D. Wilson, C. H. Wilson, Wm. H. Wideman, Wm. Whitlock, Henry Wilson, W. W. Waller, James A. Wideman, Wm. Wilson, J. D. Wilder, John G. Wilson, Adolphus A. Williams, John Watson, ---Whatley, Robert Wilson, James A. Wilson, Edward Westfield, Williams & Kerr, Dr. T. A. Wideman, W. Williams, W. Willis, Hugh Wilson, E. H. Witherspoon, Dr. Willard, Patrick Wilson, Thomas White, Andrew J. Weed, J. W. Wardlaw, James T. Young, Capt Zaner, Mrs. Zimmerman.

BOX 166 PACK 4462   JOHN BELTON O'NEALL   1864

Will dated May 28, 1863 in Laurens, S.C. Witnesses: R. B. Ligon, John W. Ferguson, A. E. Carter. Executor: Gideon P. O'Neall. Sisters: Martha Day, Parvlona O'Neall. Brothers: Jesse O'Neal, Gideon P. O'Neall. Nephew: Henry Belton Babb. Appraisal Nov 21, 1864 by R. M. Anderson, Wyatt Aiken, Jones Fuller. Owned 8 slaves, 285 acres of land. Estate Settlement Aug 23, 1866. (3) Heirs: 1. Jesse O'Neall 2. Martha Day 3. Parvlona O'Neall.

BOX 166 PACK 4463   ELIZABETH A. PURDY   1863

Administrator: James Irwin. Bond Mar 26, 1863 of $3,000 by James Irwin, J. J. Gilmer, James A. McCord. Appraisal Apr 6, 1863 by Andrew Morrison, Benjamin H. Eakin, Wm. L. McCord.

BOX 166 PACK 4464   JOHN & THOMAS PRICE (minors)   1864

Father: Wm. Price deceased. Guardian John Deason. Bond Jan 4, 1864 of $10,000 by John Deason, Berry Deason, James A. Edmunds. 1864 Confederate tax $48, 1864 state tax $4.15.

BOX 166 PACK 4465   ENOCH W. PRUITT   1862

Administrator: Samuel E. Pruitt. Bond Aug 15, 1862 of $2,200 by Samuel E. Pruitt, James Cowan, Alley Reid.

BOX 166 PACK 4466   SAMUEL E. PRUITT   1864

Administrators: Elizabeth Pruitt-wife, James Seawright. Bond Feb 3, 1863 of $20,000 by James Seawright, Elizabeth Pruitt, Samuel Donald, Robert Branyon. Appraisal Feb 17, 1863 by James Cowan, Robert brownlee, J. F. Donald, John Mills. Owned 8 slaves. Estate Sale Feb 18, 1863 netted $10, 502. Buyers at sale: Elizabeth Pruitt, James Seawright, J. J. Bonner, David O. Hawthorne, A. C. Hawthorne, Dr. J. L. Miller, T.

Pearlstein, Mrs. Cohen, W. W. McDill, Ben. F. Moseley, B. M. Latimer, Robert Brownlee, J. G. Branyon, F. W. Nance, T. J. Ellis. 1863 Confederate tax $99.18. Estate Settlement Mar 29, 1864. 1/3 to Widow $3,434.20, (3) Children, not named, each $2,289.47.

BOX 166 PACK 4467   EPHRAIM D. PURSLEY   1875

Confederate Soldier. Died Nov 26, 1861. Administrator: James Pursley-father. Bond Dec 14, 1861 of $8,000 by James Pursley, John White, B. P. Hughes. Appraisal Dec 31, 1861 by Andrew Gillespie, Leroy J. Johnson, John C. Pursley, David Knox, Wm. O. Pursley. Owned 3 slaves, 255 acres of land, large number of books. Held notes on: Wm. Power, Wm. O. Pursley, J. W. Power, J. N. Cochran, Basil Callaham, John A. Wier, Henry A. Jones, John H. Wilson. Estate Sale Dec 31, 1861 netted $3,450. Buyers at sale: Widow, John T. Owens, James Pursley, David Knox, Charles Evans, Samuel Carter, Leroy J. Johnson, James Smith, David R. Penney, John C. Pursley, James A. Richey, James Chalmers, John Williams, Wm. O. Pursley, A. Blackman. 1861 taxes $7.46. Paid John Enright $37 for coffin, paid J. D.Chalmers $24.32 for tombstone. Estate Settlement Jul 16, 1864. Widow and (2) minor daughters. Widow $569.98. Remaining child received $1,139.96.   Daughters: Mary E. Pursley died two years after death of her father, Narcissa became the guardian of David R. Penney. Feb 5, 1875 Emeline, widow and Narcissa, daughter petitioned to sell the farm as they were not able to manage it nor pay the taxes. Land sold to Emeline Purlsey on Mar 2, 1875 for $5 by L. P. Guffin, Sheriff.

BOX 166, PACK 4468   ALLY PRUITT   1863

Administrators: A. C. Hawthorne, John Pratt. Bond Jan 26, 1863 of $30,000 by A. C. Hawthorne, John Pratt, J. R. Wilson, Joseph Ellis. Appraisal Jan 27, 1863 by James Cowan, Jonathan Galloway, Robert C. Sharp. Owned 14 slaves. Held notes on: James Cowan, David O. Hawthorne, James Y. Sitton, Robert A. Archer, A. J. Hawthorne. Estate Sale Jan 28, 1863 netted $16,256. Buyers at sale: Moses Winestock, F. Pearlstein, J. Ramsey Black, J. M. Bell, Allen Dodson, A. C. Hawthorne, W. A. Black, Robert Hill, Joseph F. Lee, W. R. Magee, J. W. Brooks, Thomas Bryan, Dr. J. L. Miller, J. M. Pruitt, Robert A. Archer, Robert C. Grier, D. S. Jones, D. H. Latimer, Wm. Allen, J. M. Carwile, John Webb, J. T. Owen, Wm. Barmore, C. M. Sharp, J. P. Kennedy, John Cowan, J. R. Ellis, James Cowan, James D. Chalmers, James Taylor, Peter Henry, J. N. Young, J. R. Wilson, Robert Pratt, E. L. Patton, John Watson, B. M. Winestock, James Y. Sitton, Oliver P. Hawthorne, J. T. Ransom, Dr. Thomas Lyon, Gabriel Hodges, John Hagen, J. P. Pressly, Wm. Robertson, Wm. Dunn, Gabriel M. Mattison, A. T. Watson, S. R. Pratt, Wm. G. Gordon, Wm. Sproull, Moses Smith, David O. Hawthorne, Jonathan Galloway, Joseph Blackwell, John Pratt, J. J. Bonner, George Nickles, James Seawright, R. F. Bryan, John H. Mundy, Wm. M. Griffin, J. M. Bell, J. C. Williams, Robert R. Seawright, J. F. Donald, J. D. Pace, Gideon G. Stone, J. F. Simpson, Wm. Sharp, Asberry Dodson. Estate Settlement Mar 11, 1864. (6) Children each received $2,396.12. Only (3) named Louisa Jane Pruitt, J. M. Pruitt, T. V. Pruitt.

BOX 166 PACK 4469   JAMES A. PENNAL   1863

Will dated Jun 2, 1861. Witnesses: David Knox, Wm. E. Link, Johnson J. Link. Guardian: Moses O. McCaslan. Bond Mar 10, 1863 of $5,000 by Moses O. McCaslan, James McCaslan, James H. Morris. Aunt: Esther D. Pennal entire estate willed to her. Brother

Wm. H. Pennal. 1863 war tax $24, 1864 Confederate tax $144. Final return on estate and final activity Apr 21, 1876.

BOX 166 PACK 4470   WILLIAM PRICE   1863

Administrator: John Wesley Deason. Bon Jan 18, 1864 of $5,000 by John Wesley Deason, Berry Deason, W. W. Beasley. Wdiow: Jane Deason married John Boswell and had son, George Price Boswell. (2) Children: 1. John 2. Thomas. Appraisal Feb 4, 1864 by Peter Smith, John Brown, Zephaniah Harris. Held notes on: James N. Briscoe-Josiah Langley-R. M. Hendrix, B. Henderson-P. Smith-B. McKittrick, George Rosenwike-F. M. Hendrix, Wm. Elkins-John –Elkins-M. W. Lyles, W. A. Smith-James S. Cartledge-T. E. Jennings, Ben McKittrick-P. Smith-Bennett Henderson, John Elkins-T. E. Jennings-W.A. Smith, F. M. Hendrix-Henry Slater-W. A. Smith. Estate Sale Feb 4, 1864 netted $2,795. Buyers at sale: Catlett Corley, George W. Mitchell, R. T. Lites, John Elkins, Redmond Brown, Ben. McKittrick, Widow, Bennett Henderson, Wm. Elkins, W. A. Smith, Wm. Bosdell, Henry Hester, J. N. Briskey, Berry Deason, Dr. Thomas Jennings, Marion Hendricks, J. C. Griffin. Appraisal of old notes made Feb 1, 1876 by J. F. Edmunds, Catlett L. Corley, J. A. Edmunds.

BOX 166 PACK 4471   JAMES M. PURDY   1866

Administrator: Mary R. Purdy, wife. Bond Jan 21, 1863 of $1,500 by Mary R. Purdy, Leroy Purdy, Samuel B. McClinton. Appraisal Feb 19, 1863 by Daniel Atkins, A. J. Furqueron, --- Jordan. Notes held on: J. S. & F. Williams, A. H. Martin. Estate Sale Feb 19, 1863 netted $276. Buyers at sale: Mary R. Purdy, Toliver Kennedy, Leroy Purdy, John Able, E. G. Kennedy, Daniel Atkins, M. B. Kennedy, John Furqueron, R. F. McCaslan. Estate Settlement Jul 13, 1866. Widow $108.38. (1) Child, not named, $216.77.

BOX 166 PACK 4472   RICHARD M. PUCKETT   1861

Confederate Soldier. Will dated Jun 12, 1861. Witnesses: Wm. H. Bentley, H. M. Pinson, Henry Hitt. Brother: Thomas R. Puckett. Sister: Mary A. Puckett. Nieces: Mary Louise Puckett, Eliza Caroline Puckett, Nancy Louisa later wife of ---Vance and living in Fulton Co., Ga. age 17 in 1873. Nephew: Henry Clark Puckett. Executor: Thomas R. Puckett. Appraisal Jan 1, 1862 by H. M. Pinson, W. C. Fooshe, Wm. H. Bentley. Owned 3 slaves, 50 acres of land. Held notes on: M. L. Bullock, H. M. Pinson, R. W. Hill, Thomas Stuart, Nathaniel Ingraham, J. R. Puckett, W. C. Fooshe, G. W. Long, Wm. H. Bentley, Thomas C. Chappell. Estate Sale Jan 1, 1862 netted $4,253. Buyers at sale: Thomas R. Puckett, John R. Puckett, A. Wells, J. B. Johnson, Henry Hitt, A. Dukes, Joel Fooshe, Henry Carter, David Whiteford, Mary A. Puckett. Appraisal of old notes May 8, 1875 by R. E. Chaney, Henry Brewer, F. M. Pope. (Notes on R. W. Hill, Nathan Ingraham, Wm. H. Bentley, W. L. Dukes, R. C. Starnes all deemed worthless). Estate Settlements Dec 19, 1873, Jun 14, 1874. Final Estate Settlement May 24, 1875. 1873 Settlement (5) Legatees: 1. Thomas R. Puckett 2. Mary A. Pinson 3. Mary Louisa Puckett 4. Eliza Puckett 5. Nancy Louisa Vance.

BOX 166 PACK 4473   JAMES M. PERRIN   1863

Confederate Soldier. Will dated Feb 7, 1863. Witnesses: Mathew McDonald, Wm. H. Parker, B. Johnson. Wife: Kitty Perrin. Son Joel Smith Perrin. Brother: Thomas C. Perrin. Executor: Thomas C. Perrin. Appraisal Aug 7, 1863 by David L. Wardlaw, B. P. Hughes, Mathew McDonald, John White. Very large estate with many pages of financial activities, etc. Owned 42 slaves, extensive tracts of land, owned house and lot in Town of Abbeville, owned extensive Confederarte bonds ($37.000 worth), 41 shares of stock in Greenville & Columbia Railroad. Confederate taxes for 1864 $3,194.68. Held notes on: John D. Adams, W. K. Bradley, James A. Allen, Blease & Baxter, G. A. Allen, Est. of Mrs. Ellison, W. T. Jones, John W. Lesly, W. J. Lomax, Samuel McGowan, W. E. Mauldin, Augustus Kyle, T. C. Griffin, James Carlisle, Burt & Calhoun, J. Bailey, Joseph F. Bell, Robert A. Archer, George McDuffie Miller, Wm. Calvin, Sampson V. Caine, W. C. Davis, James D. Chalmers, R. B. Holliman, Samuel A. Lomax, J. Foster Marshall, Wm. L. McCord, Joseph T. Moore, Ben. F. Moseley, Phares Martin, John Gray, John Douglass, James S. Cothran, John Cothran, T. R. Cothran, J. S. Cothran, B. C. Cuthbert, B. B. Foster, Thomas E. Eakin, Robert A. Fair, Thomas A. Hoyt, A. L. Gray, T. J. Hill, J. H. Ligon, A. H. Morton, Joel M. Lites, Samuel Perrin, Marshall Sharp, Warren Richey, Samuel A. Wilson, R. J. White, Edward Westfield, James A. Walker, Robert Thornton, Thomas Stacy, Thomas C. Perrin, L. J. Patterson,J. Wardlaw Perrin, John A. Stuart, Augustus M. Smith, Joseph Togno, E. White, Abner Perrin, Ben. Rothchild, George W. Sproull, Hiram Tilman, J. K. Vance, G. M. Pelot, James M. Perrin, W. P. Sullivan, R. C. Wilson, David J. Wardlaw. Estate Sale Dec 15, 1865. Buyers at sale: Thomas B. McCord, Robert H. Wardlaw, Thomas C. Perrin, Patrick N. Wilson, Jesse Carlisle, James A. Wilson, Ephraim Alewine, Robert E. Bowie, J. A. Alewine, Wm. J. Wilson, J. J. Wardlaw, T. Kennedy, T. J. Wilson, Thomas Bigby, Andrew J. Ferguson, J. N. Wilson, Philip S. Russell, James McCravey, John A. Wier, Kitty Perrin, John McCord, Robert Jones, A. M. McCord, A. F. McCord, John T. Lyon, G. & C. Railroad, J. A. McCord, C. S. L. Wilson, John A. Hamilton, Grant T. Jackson, C. H. Wilson, John Wilson, David McNeill Turner, Samuel H. Beard, John A. Hunter, Hiram T. Tusten.

BOX 166, PACK 4474   ALLEN PUCKETT   1864

Confederate Soldier 5th Regiment S. C. Reserves commanded by Capt. Hearst, stationed Camp Griffin, Colleton District, S. C. Will dated: Jan 1, 1863. Witnesses: J. W. Hearst, W. P. Sullivan, J. H. Wideman. Wife Elizabeth Puckett. Mother: Margaret Boggs. Executor: Joseph F. Keller. Appraisal Mar 17, 1863 by Tyra Jay, A. P. Weed, J. J. Edwards. Owned 4 slaves. Estate Sale Mar 18, 1863 netted $1,888.89. Buyers at sale: Elizabeth Puckett, Andrew J. Weed, J. Martin, Walter G. Keller, Larkin Reynolds, B. B. Harveley, Mary Boggs, R. W. Lites, Edward O. Reagan, Wm. Adams, Adam Wideman, Hiram Tusten, Oliver Richey, Wm. Butler, Samuel B. Cook. Land sold Dec 23, 1863. Estate Settlement Feb 1, 1866.

BOX 166 PACK 4475   FRANCIS R. PINKERTON   1862

Confederate Soldier. Administrator: Albert Johnson. Bond Dec 24, 1862 of $2,000 by Albert Johnson, T. A. Pinkerton, Wm. Pratt, Thomas Davis. Wife: T. A. Pinkerton. Father-in-Law: Albert Johnson.

BOX 166 PACK 4476   ANDREW BLUM PASLAY   1862

Will dated Aug 21, 1862. Witnesses: J. J. Wardlaw, Thomas J. Maabry, J. K. Cunningham. Wife: Susan Paslay. Executor: Susan Paslay. Appraisal Jan 19, 1863 by John T. Lyon, David J. Jordan, Samuel Gilmer. Owned 5 slaves.

BOX 166 PACK 4477   WILLIAM C. PUCKETT   1864

Administrator: P. H. Bradley. Bond Jun 27, 1863 of $30,000 by P. H. Bradley, E.A. Puckett, R. W. Lites, Adam Wideman. Appraisal Aug 186 by George W. Pressly, R. W. Lites, Adam Wideman, A. P. Weed. Owned 17 slaves. Held notes, accounts and judgements on: Wm. Lites, J. M. Drennan, J. M. Franklin, Wm. Caldwell, G. W. Kennedy, Robert W. Lites, Joseph Creswell, John Taggart, James McKinney, Allen Reagan, Thomas J. Edwards, James Russell, Wm. H. Davis, Wm. Bosdell, Sampson Weeks, John B. Adamson, Edward O. Reagan, Allen Puckett, Edwin Fron, Walter G. Keller, Robert Walker, L. N. Traylor, Wideman-Lites & Co., John Sanders, John L. Adamson, P. H. Bradley, Wm. Puckett, M. Eves, Thomas Dill, Wm. Corley, Aura Mundy, J. C. Cheatham, Mt. Plleasant Church, A. T. Traylor, Nancy Reagan, Henry Pinder, Wm. Posey, Thomas H. Cox, John Gibson, Stephen Willis, A. J. Harrison, Adam Wideman, Adaline Goodwin, John Cox, Jesse Jester. Estate Sale Dec 5, 1865. Buyers at sale: Mrs. Puckett, P. H. Bradley, Joseph Keller, Andrew J. Weed, Alex. L. McCaslan, A. P. Boozer, James Reagan, J. F. Atkins, B. B. Harveley, Dr. J. Sanders, J. B. Herbert, Wm. P. Kennedy, Thomas O. Creswell, J. L. Sibert, James Creswell, Reuben Weed, Edward O. Reagan, Wm. S. Harris, Thomas C. McBryde, W. C. Robinson, Samuel B. Cook, Robert W. Lites, James Martin. Paid Mathias Bugg $3 for coffin. 1864 Confederate tax $342.55. 1864 animal tax $18.40. Estate was still open and not settled in 1869.

BOX 166 PACK 4478   WILLIAM PRATT   1863

Deceased die Jan 1863. Will dated Jan 9, 1863. Witnesses: J. B. Kay, Moses Ashley, Joseph Pratt. Wife: Martha Pratt. Daughters: Martha Jane Pratt, Sarah G. M. widow of James M. Callaham. Adopted Daughter: Emily Katherine Bryant. Son: Thomas James in Confederate service. Executors: John Pratt physically unable, John R. Wilson died, Addison F. Carwile. Bond Jan 5, 1888 of $2,000 by Addison F. Carwile, Robert M. Pratt, A. E. Ellis. Appraisal Feb 25, 1863 by Robert A. Haddon, James A. Black, M. P. McCarter. Owned 6 slaves. Children in 1863: 1. Charles F. Pratt 2. Joseph A. Pratt, deceased in California leaving widow and children-names unknown 3. Elizabeth Kay 4. Sarah J. Callaham 5. Martha Carwile wife of Addison F. Carwile, she died 1880 leaving children: Frank, Ira, Emma, Annie, James 6. Emily McKeown 7. James. Estate Settlement Mar 16, 1889. (6) Legatees each received $122.44. 1. M. E. Kay 2. Sarah G. Callaham 3. E. P. McKeown 4. E. C. Bryant who became E.C. Callaham in 1889 5. T. J. Pratt 6. M. J. Carwile.

BOX 166 PACK 4479   WILLIAM A. PRATT   1863

Will dated Mar 24, 1862. Witensses: James H. Shaw, Ben. Smith, Wm. Donald. Wife: Mary Z. Pratt. Executors: Marshall Sharp who died before completion, James C. Martin. Bond Mar 23, 1875 of $1,200 by James C. Martin, Wm. Robertson, Wm. Maddox. Apprasial Nov 3, 1863 by G. M. Mattison, Ben. Smith, larkin Barmore, Ezekiel Rasor. Owned 8 slaves. Estate Sale Nov 4, 1863. Buyers at sale: John Higgins, M. Griffin, Joel Smith, Dr. B. Manley, M. Sharp, Mrs. M. Crenshaw, W. N. Mundy, M. Irvin, Thomas Crawford, R. P. Shaw, Mrs. E. E. Brownlee, W. M. Griffin, Larkin Mays, W. P. McGee, J.

H. Shaw, Wm. Maddox, Mrs. C. Williamson, Widow, Ben. Smith, Allen Dodson, Robert R. Seawright, John R. Wilson, J. F. McKeown, W. T. Farrar, Mrs. Singletree, Larkin Barmore, George T. Anderson, Eliza Hudgens, Wm. Beeks, B. Charles, James Seawright, Mrs. D. L. Donald, John T. Owen, J. C. Richey, A. M. Agnew, Capt. Venable, Ezekiel Rasor, Enoch M. Sharp, M. G. Hughes, G. M. Mattison, Gideon G. Stone, Michael McGee, W. C. Moseley, J. H. Shaw. 1864 Confederate tax $142.60. 1865 Confederate tax $768.

BOX 166 PACK 4480   JANET ROBERTSON   1861

Will dated Oct 30, 1854. Witnesses: David Robison, Mathew C. Owens, Thomas Robison. Codicil dated Nov 11, 1858. Witnesses to codicil: Thomas Robison, Jesse S. Adams, Leroy J. Wilson. Executors: Wm. S. Robertson annulled in codicl of 1858, Thomas Eakin. Appraisal by Thomas Robison, T. J. Ellis, John H. Mundy. Held notes on David L. Wardlaw, Wm. S. Robertson. 1st Estate Settlement Sep 21, 1863 each legatee received $215. Final Estate Settlement Apr 19, 1869. (4) Legatees. 1. John Robertson 2. Wm. Robertson 3. Eliza Wardlaw 4. Rosa Burnett. Grand Daughter: Elizabeth Burnett married Pinckney G. Bowie and removed to Mississippi. Paid Charles Cox $12.28 for coffin. Paid James D. Chalmers $22.39 for tombstone.

BOX 166 PACK 4481   PETER RICKETTS   1863

Confederate Soldier. Administrator: Wm. Clinkscales. Bond Sep 18, 1863 of $3,000 by Wm. Clinkscales, Hugh Robinson, Bennett McAdams. Wife: Betsy Ricketts. Appraisal Oct 12, 1863 by S. M. Tribble, Bennett McAdams, J. G .E. Branyon. Estate Sale Oct 13, 1863 netted $3,691.48. Buyers at sale: Betsy Ricketts, Robert Martin, F. W. R. Nance, John Pratt, Eliza Sims, J. N. Saylors, Dr. Robert C. Grier, Martha Griffin, James Armstrong, Wm. L. Bannister, H. Laverne, Addison Clinkscales, C. Ellis, Dr. John T. Lyon, J. J. Shirley, R. F. Bryson, Wm. Pruitt, James Davis, Wm. Clinkscales, Missouri Burton, Jane Alewine, Lucinda Williams. Estate Settlement Nov 24, 1865. Widow received $950.42, (2) Children each received $1,918.86. 1864 Confederate tax $168.

BOX 166 PACK 4482   W. Z. RADCLIFFE   1864

Administrator: Wm. B. Bowie. Bond Sep 17, 1862 of $2,000 by Wm. B. Bowie, Andrew J. McKee, Henry B. Bowie. Appraisal Oct 10, 1862 by James C. Stevenson, Ben. H. Eakin, Asa Bowie. Held notes on: H. W. Bowie, Vincent Radcliffe, E. P. Ballard, John H. Mundy, Thomas Stevenson. Estate Sale Oct 10, 1862. Buyers at sale: Widow, James Cunningham, Wm. B. Bowie, Peter Henry, John Mundy, John Pace, Alex. Ellis, Dr. Robert A. Archer, Vincent Radcliffe, Thomas Crawford, Ben. H. Eakin, Samuel Cochran Sr., Robert E. Hill, Thomas Eakin, Wm. G. Gordon, John Simpson, Archibald McCord, James Stevenson, B. A. Bowie, Henry B. Bowie, Robert Hagen, Asa Bowie, J. J. Bonner, Henry Hutchison. Estate Settlement May 26, 1883. (2) Legatees: 1. Mary C. Radcliffe $75 2. Wm. F. Radcliffe $135. 1876 taxes $12.10. State and County tax 1877 $2.76.

BOX 166 PACK 4483   JAMES ROBERTSON   1863

Will dated Apr 11, 1863. Witnesses: S. E. Graydon, Marshall Sharp, Samuel Graham. Wife: Nelly Robertson. Sons: Wilson Robertson, Wade H. Robertson. Daughters: Annie wife of A. M. Graham, Peachey Savage, Pertany Lindsay. Willed I acre of land to son, Wade, to always be kept as a graveyard. 1st Appraisal Jun 17, 1863 by John C. Waters, Larkin Mays, Samuel Graham. 2nd Appraisal Dec 21, 1865 by John C. Waters, John D. Adams, Alex. Turner. 1st Estate Sale: Jun 17, 1863. Buyers at Sale: Larkin Mays, W. H. Robertson, Robert Smith, F. A. Connor, T. H. Speer, J. Killingsworth, S. E. Graydon, James F. Smith, J. J. Golding, Wesley Robertson, J. K. Vance, ----Kilugh, James Rasor. 2nd Estate Sale Dec 21, 1865. Buyers at sale: Wm. Hodges, J. C. Rasor, W. H. Robertson, Marhall Sharp, J. T. Johnson, M. Golding, A. M. Graham, Wm. Riley, J. W. Moore, T. J. Golding, Ben. Owens, A. Dodson, W. Anderson, C. Sharp, F. Arnold, J. Smith, T. Adams. 1st Estate Settlement Feb 13, 1864. (7) Legatees each $61.32, no names. 2nd Estate Settlement Feb 26, 1867. (7) Shares, each share $209.14. 1. Annie Graham 2 shares 2. Wade H. Robertson 2 shares 3. Peachey Savage 1 share 4. Pertany Lindsay 1 share 5. William Robertson 1 share.

BOX 166 PACK 4484   ANDREW RICHEY   1863

Administrators: Ezekiel Rasor, T. Y. Martin. Bond Jan 2, 183 of $8,000 by Ezekiel Rasor, T. Y. Martin, L. J. Rasor, James M. Wright. Apprasial Feb 11, 1864 by Michael B. McGee, Wm. Dunn, David S. Jones, M. C. Henderson. Owned 4 slaves. Estate Sale Jan 12, 1863. Buyers at sale: Nancy Richey, Gabriel W. Hodges, John Williams, Ezekiel Rasor, A. M. Agnew, C. C. Cullins, James Adams, Valentine Young, Micahael B. McGee, J. M. Wright, T. J. Ellis, N. S. Reeves, W. McCombs, G. W. Brooks, Jesse Anderson, M. C. Henderson, J. D. Pace, Larkin Mays, David Hannah, Charles C. Pinckney, W. Marberry, Robert Hagen, P. Hawthorne, J. H. Dean, Wm. C. Anderson, J. C. Clark, Lawrence R. Dantzler, J. Turner, Wm. A. King, J. S. Jones, E. Swancey, J. J. Richey, James Davis, L. J. Rasor, Dr. Newton Sims, Wm. Dunn, T. Y. Martin. Estate Settlement Feb 11, 1864. (6) Children, not named, each $670.51.

BOX 167 PACK 4485   DAVID ROBISON   1864

Will dated Feb 15, 1864. Witnesses: Wm. Hill, James F. mabry, John Darraugh. Executor: Thomas Robison. Daughters: Rachel Leontina Robison, Mary Ann wife of James Gilliam. Son: Wm. Robison. Appraisal Apr 11, 1864 by Wm. B. Roman, Andrew Morrison, Wm. McIlwain, James J. Gilmer. Owned 7 slaves. Held notes on: Wm. Magill, B. M. Winestock, J. Foster Marshall, Wm. Magill & James M. Gilliam, Thomas Robison, Mathew C. Owen. Estate Sale Apr 12, 1864. Buyers at sale: Edward Noble, Thomas Robison, Wm. Hill, Thomas Eakin, Wm. H. Taggart, Jesse Carlisle, Wm. Gordon, Wm. Robison, Dr. Robert A. Archer, John Davis, James Cunningham, D. Pope, John Connor, John R. McCord, James M. Wright, Eliza J. Gordon, Wm. Magill, Samuel H. Irwin, Edward Westfield, J. N. Cochran, Andrew Morrison, Jeptha R. Hamilin, Joseph T. Moore, Alex. Agnew, Leroy J. Wilson, John Darraugh, Charles C. Pinckney, J. T. Gilmer, J. A. McCord, Mrs. Magill, Miss Jane Russell, John T. Owen, James Carlisle, ---Hudgens, James M. Gilliam, John H. Mundy, Hiram T. Tusten, George Syfan, Charles Evans, John Gadsden, Rutledge & Russell, Mary A. Gilliam, Siss Robison, James Gibbs, John A. Norwood, J. J. Adams, Charles Cox, Dr. Isaac Branch, Mrs. Gilliam, James J. Gilmer. 1864 Confederate tax $403.62.

BOX 167 PACK 4486   WARREN RICHEY   1861

Will dated Apr 16, 1861. Witnesses: Isaac Branch, John F. Livingston, James D. Chalmers. Mother: Elizabeth Richey. Executor: J. Albert Richey. Bond Sep 17, 1861 of $2,000 by J. Albert Richey, David J. Jordan, John A.Wier. Appraisal Oct 30, 1861 by John T. Lyon, J. Fraser Livingston, John R. Wilson.

BOX 167 PACK 4487   SARAH ROBERTSON   1864

Will dated May 6, 1856. Witnesses: Abner H. McGee, Hardy Clark, Marshall Sharp. Executor: Wesley Robertson. Widow of Reuben Robertson. Son: Wesley Robertson. Grand Sons: Children of Wesley Robertson 1. Reuben Abner Robertson 2. Wesley Marion Robertson 3. Augustus Lafayette Robertson. Appraisal May 28, 1864 by Wm. T. Jones, Green Berry Riley, Samuel Agnew, Marshall Sharp. Owned 21 slaves.

BOX 167 PACK 4488   PAUL ROGERS   1862

Administrators: P. H. Rogers, W. M. Rogers –both sons. Bond Apr 15, 1862 of $15,000 by W. M. Rogers, P. H. Rogers, Mary A. Rogers, Louis Covin. Wife and (4) Children. Son: D. L. Rogers in Confederate Army and not heard from since the Battle of Fort Donelson. Appraisal Apr 16, 1862 by Samuel R. Morrah, P. S. Guillebeau, P. McCraven, D. M. Rogers. Owned 9 slaves. 1st Return made Apr 1864. 1863 Confederate tax $10. 1864 tax $7.70.

BOX 167 PACK 4489   BENJAMIN ROTHCHILD   1863

Confederate Soldier killed Sep 6, 1862. Administrator: M. Strauss. Bond Oct 6, 1862 of $1,000 by M. Strauss, Franklin F.Gary, John H. Vance, John K. Vance. Father and Brother in Germany. Appraisal: Dec 19, 1862 by. B. Z. Herndon, Franklin F. Gary, Francis A. Connor. Estate Sale Dec 19, 1862 at Cokesbury. Buyers at sale: G. yager, D. Jones, S. B. Jones, S. Valentine, Dr. Jones, L. D. Walker, M. Strauss, Dr. N. Sims, D. S. Beacham, G. M. Hodges, J. M. Cochran. Very little in estate and last entry May 1866.

BOX 167 PACK 4491   JAMES ALBERT RICHEY   1863

Will dated May 14, 1863. Witnesses: David J. Jordan, George Dusenberry, John T. Lyon. Executor: Elisabeth Richey-mother. Appraisal Sep 16, 1863 by John T. Lyon, A. Lewis Gillespie, David J. Jordan, Samuel Gilmer, John W. Lesly. Owned 1 slave. Paid John Enright $30 for coffin.

BOX 167 PACK 4492   GEORGE B. RICHEY   1859

Confederate Soldier. Will dated Jul 17, 1861. Witnesses: J. L. Miller, S. E. Pruitt, James Magill. Executor: Margaret Louisa Richey-wife. Owned 14 slaves, 540 acres of land. Oct 17, 1859 he had purchased 2 acres of land from the other heirs of James B. Richey for $34. Other heirs were namely James F. Donald and wife Mary Ann Donald, James A. Lyon and wife Sarah Jane.

BOX 167 PACK 4493   PETER ROUSE   1862

Free Man of Color. Administrator: James M. Carwile. Bond Jul 17, 1862 of $500 by James M. Carwile, Basil Callaham, J. W. Brooks. Appraisal Jul 26, 1862 by John M.

Bryant, W. L. Going, James S. Barnes. Owned a lot of 4 chairs and a bed. Held note on Basil Callaham. Estate Sale Jul 26, 1862 netted $14.56. Buyer at sale: Basil Callaham. Estate Settlement Oct 15, 1862. (7) Distributees each $3.44: 1. Edmund Rouse, father 2. Dinah Rouse, sister 3. Elizabeth Rouse, sister 4. Rebecca Rouse, sister 5. Jim Rouse, brother 6. Daniel Rouse, brother 7. Polly Rouse, sister.

BOX 167 PACK 4494   NANCY ROBERTSON   1862

Will dated May 18, 1859. Witnesses: James G. Baskin, J. H. Cobb, Robert A. Fair. Executor: Wm. Robertson-son. Bond Oct 3, 1862 of $25,000 by Wm. Robertson, James Seawright, Wm. Donald. Daughter: Matilda Robertson deceased. Appraisal Nov 5, 1862 by James H. Shaw, Ben. Smith, A. M. Dodson. Owned 10 slaves. Held notes on: Moses Winestock, W. L. Hodges, Thomas S. Clatworthy, W. B. Gaines, W. A. Pratt, W. Tollison & Slater Tollison. Estate Sale Nov 4, 1862. Buyers at sale: Wm. Robertson, Ezekiel Rasor, J. W. Richey, W. T. Jones, J. B. Dorr, Mary Pratt, Pleasant Kay, James Taylor, Henry Nixon, B. M. Winestock, Wm. P. McGee, A. M. Dodson, Wm. Barmore, J. I Bonner, J. H. Shaw, Wm. C. Moseley, Sarah Dellinger, Wm. Robinson, Wm. Maddox, Wesley Moseley, Eliza Hudgins, James Killingsworth, Larkin Barmore, James Seawright, J. R. Cllinkscales, Robert Coleman, Reuben Stephens. Estate Settlement Mar 30, 1864. $8,409 distributed. 1. Wm. Robertson 2. E. Carrie Hudgens was the daughter of Emily Klugh 3. Mary Pratt wife of James Pratt 4. Louisa Haynie, (3) Children: Mrs. Tollison, James Pratt, Wm. Pratt. 1862 Confederate tax $36.18. Coffin and funeral cost $18.

BOX 167 PACK 4495   SIMON P. RYKARD   1861

Wife deceased. (4) Children, not named. Administrator: Walter G. Keller. Bond Sep 10, 1861 of $500 by Walter G. Keller, Daniel New, Robert Jones. Appraisal Sep 13, 1861 by Robert M. Lites, Wm. C. Puckett, Henry R. Rykard. Estate Sale Sep 13, 1861. Buyers at sale: Walter G. Keller, Wm. C. Puckett, John C. Chiles, Dr. Neil, H. Eisenmere, Robert Thornton, Thomas Edwards, James M. Reagan, Daniel Carroll, Joseph Keller, Adam Wideman, Wm. M. Cain, B. B. Harveley, R. W. Lites, Peter Rykard, Dr. J. L. Pressly, James Martin, Allen Puckett, S. P. Laird, John Patterson, James Steiffle, Edward O. Reagan. Mar 7, 1865 return of paying debts 50 cents on the dollar. Estate Settlement Apr 3, 1865. Estate Insolvent. Coffin cost $15.

BOX 167 PACK 4496   MARY ROBINSON   1863

Will dated Feb 12, 1861. Witnesses: W. P. Sullivan, Tyra Jay, John W. Hearst. Executor: F. B. Robinson-brother. Sisters: Jane B. wife of Joseph Lindsay, Mattie wife of Wm. Davis. Brothers: 1. F. B. Robinson wife was Peggy and children were: Elizabeth Ann Robinson, Rebecca Jane Robinson, Mary Robinson 2. Henry Robinson deceased had daughter: Elizabeth Jane Harveley. Nephews: Wm. Cowan Robinson, Thomas Alexander Robinson. Appraisal Feb 21, 1862 by Wm. H. Bradley, W. P. Sullivan, Andrew J. Weed, Tyra Jay. Owned 84 acres of land. Estate Sale Feb 21, 1862. Buyers at sale: Owen McDonnell, Thomas V. Creswell, Joseph Lindsay, Thomas Creswell.

BOX 167 PACK 4497   WILLIAM STRAWHORN   1862

101

Will dated Sep 17, 1861. Witnesses: Wm. Buchanan, J. E. Graydon, Wm. N. Mundy, Wm. S. Smith. Executor: Samuel Graham, son-in-law. Son: Robert Strawhorn. Daughter: Frances B. Shirley. Appraisal Mar 3, 1863 by John D. Adams, Daniel S. Beacham, Wm. S. Smith. Owned 1 slave, 116 acres of land. Coffin cost $12.75.

BOX 167 PACK 4498   WILLIAM JOHNSON STEVENSON   1862

Confederate Soldier. Will dated Dec 23, 1861. Witnesses: A. C. Hawthorne, Samuel R. Brownlee, O. P. Hawthorne. Executors: Alex. G. Hagen who married Rebecca Stevenson, sister of Stevenson's wife. After his death John Hagen and John W. J. Simpson became administrators. Mother: Rebecca Stevenson. Sisters: Eliza married John W. J. Simpson, Isabella Aveline, Margaret Hanks lived in Virginia. 1st Appraisal Aug 8, 1862 by Wm. Gordon, Wm. G. Gordon, Peter Henry, J. C. Stevenson. Owned 484 acres of land. 2nd Appraisal Sep 5, 1873 by Peter Henry, J. C. Stevenson, Robert W. Haddon. Estate Sale Jul 1906. Buyers at sale: W. A. Hagen, Dr. Cowan, J. W. J. Simpson, T. L. Uldrick, R. S. Uldrick, Lemuel Strawhorn, J. A. Hagen, Albert Kay, T. S. Ellis, John Smith, James Simpson, Samuel Harris, Wm. B. Going, Doc Bowie, Mr. Greene. Distribution May 4, 1908. (17) Distributees: 1. Estate of John A. Hagen $950 2. W. A. Hagen $950 3. Mary G. Greene $950 4. R. G. Hagen $950 5. Ann A. Jackson $950 6. Margaret Nickles $950 7. Rebecca J. Hanks $950 8. J. W. J. Simpson $131.94 9. Iris A. Whitman $131.94 10. Hattie B. Johnson $131.94 11. J. S. Simpson $131.94 12. Rebecca Ellis $131.94 13. Bettie Killingsworth $131.94 14. Eugene Simpson $131.94 15. Marie Coleman $131.94 16. Mollie Simpson $527.77 17. Carrie L. Baker $316.66. Jun 6, 1908 the following received additional distributions: 1. Fannie Hagen $49.28 2. Wm. A. Hagen $49.28 3. Mary G. Greene $49.28 4. P. G. Hagen $49.28 5. Margaret Wicker $49.28 6. Anna A. Jackson $49.28 7. Carrie Bowen $16.43 8. J. L. Bowen $10.50.

BOX 167 PACK 4499   VINCENT SHAW   1862

Administrator: G. M. Mattison. Bond May 6, 1862 of $1,000 by G. M. Mattison, B. M. Latimer, James H. Shaw. Wife: Elizabeth Shaw. Appraisal May 13, 1862 by James H. Shaw, C. S. Latimer, J. M. Latimer, W. J. Mattison. Held notes on: J. Smith, A. Austin, Wm. Gambrell, Thomas Moore. Estate Sale May 14, 1862 netted $503.39. Buyers at sale: Wm. B. Gaines, Rorbert R. Seawright, W. P. Kay, B. M. Latimer, R. Russell, Wm. Robertson, V. Robertson, D. V. Garrison, J. R. Clinkscales, John G. Grant, L. H. Whitlock, Wm. Davis, Ezekiel Rasor, James Gambrell, Andrew Morrison, Samuel Donald, E. Shaw, James C. Gambrell, P. Shirley, A. Austin, James H. Shaw, James Jones, P. H. Nixon, Turner G. Davis, B. S. Owens, Wm. Stone, Enos Gambrell, John Dunn, W. M. Callaham, P. H. Davis, W.C. Moseley, G. M. Mattison, Malcom Erwin, James Seawright. Estate Settlement Nov 23, 1863. No Information.

BOX 167 PACK 4500   COL. AUGUSTUS M. SMITH   1862

Confederate Soldier. Killed Aug 5, 1862. Will dated Jan 7, 1861. Witnesses: Wm. H. Parker, John A. McDonald, Joseph T. Moore. Executors: James M. Perrin, David L. Wardlaw, W. Joel Smith. Very extensive estate covering many pages of transactions, etc. Wife Sally Smith. Son Lewis Wardlaw Smith an infant. Appraisal Jan 8, 1863 $104,288 (Abbeville holdings only) by George Allen, James S. Cothran, Wm. H. Parker, J. Clark Wardlaw. . Owned 500 acres in Jefferson Co., Ark, owned land in the Northwest

Territory, 2,500 acres in Abbeville, 115 slaves in Arkansas, 135 slaves in Abbeville. Owned Railroad stock and stock in the Graniteville Mfg. Co. Held notes on more than 80 individuals. $50,000 willed to wife & child. 1/10 of estate to be placed in trust for the education of the sons of the poor in Abbeville District.

BOX 167 PACK 4501   ISAAC C. SEAWRIGHT   1864

Administrator: Thomas Hawthorne. Bond Sep 15, 1862 of $7,000 by Thomas Hawthorne, Lanny C. Seawright, H. T. Lyon, John A. Wier. Appraisal Nov 12, 1862 by James Seawright, Robert Brownlee, John Donald, Wm. J. Mattison. Owned 2 slaves. Estate Sale: Nov 13, 1862. Buyers at sale: W. C. Moseley, Widow, P. Kay, Thomas Hawthorne, Ezekiel Rasor, J. P. Seawright, J. L. Robinson, Moses Winestock, Gideon G. Stone, B. Y. Martin, Wm. McGee, J. C. Williams, Ben. F. Moseley, Thomas Bryant, Thomas Pearlstein, Wm. Robison, J. R. Clinkscales. Estate Settlement Feb 12, 1864. 1/3 to widow $985.89, (2) Children, not named, $985.89 each. 1863 Confederate tax $25. 1863 state & district tax $3.65.

BOX 167 PACK 4502   WILLIAM P. SULLIVAN   1863

Confederate Soldier. Administrator: John C. Chiles. Appraisal Mar 23, 1863 by James H. Wideman, John W. Hearst, Samuel Perrin, R. W. Lites, Samuel A. Wilson. Owned 20 slaves, 320 acres of land. Estate Sale Dec 15, 1863 netted $2,887. Buyers at sale: M. Sullivan, James Martin, Ebeneezer Pressly, James H. Morris, W. Williams, J. H. Wideman, Tyra Jay, Samuel Spence, George Patterson, A. H. Watson, John C. Chiles, Wade Cothran, David Ethridge, John Gilchrist, R. W. Lites, Wm. K. Bradley, George W. Pressly, John McDowell, Newton Cochran, Robert A. McCaslan, J. A. Briscoe, Samuel Jordan, John L. Devlin, D. T. Oliver, Wm. S. Harris, Wm. Butler, Jane E. Chiles, Robert T. Bell, Andrew J. Weed. Dec 13, 1870 Ben. F. Sullivan assigned his interests in the estate to James W. Frazier for $950. Estate Setlement Widow and (6) Children. Wdw $10,320.21, each Child $3,440.07. 1. Benjamin Franklin Sullivan 2. Mary E. Sullivan 3. James C. Sullivan 4. Basil M. Sullivan 5. Catherine R. Sullivan 6. Wm. P. Sullivan. 1864 Confederate animal tax $10.50.

BOX 167 PACK 4503   NANCY SHAW (minor)   1863

Guardian: G. M. Mattison. Bond Jan 9, 1864 of $400 by G. M. Mattison, B. M. Latimer, James H. Shaw. Jan 9, 1864 received $188.48 but money not collected until 1870. Jan 1, 1875 amount due Guardian $67.12. 1871 taxes $2.20, 1872 taxes $3.69.

BOX 167 PACK 4504   THOMAS W. SMITH   1864

Confederate Soldier. Administrator: Edny Frances Martin-widow. Bond Nov 2, 1863 of $80,000 by Wm. Smith, Silas Ray, B. P. Hughes. Father: Wm. Smith. (4) Children, not named. 1st Appraisal Feb 6, 1864 by L. H. Rykard, J. J. Adams, John H. Mundy, John Davis, John W. Lomax. 2nd Appraisal Nov 22, 1865 by L. H. Rykard, Wm. McCravey, John Davis, Wm. A. Lomax. Owned 19 slaves. Held notes on: R. H. Davis, Wm. J. Lomax, S. H. Jones, John R. McCord, H. Coleman, John Robertson, James A. Agnew, John C. Pursley. Estate Sale Nov 23, 1865 netted $3,382. Buyers at sale: E. E. Martin, B. M. Martin, John Mundy, Alex. Ellis, Thomas B. McCord, Isaac Keller, Wm. A. Lomax, R. H.

Hughes, A. McCord, David Keller, T. Y. Martin, A. Buchanan, Grant T. Jackson, Wm. L. McCord, Wm. Smith, A. H. Martin, J. F. Greer, John W. Keller, George W. Cromer, B. Buddle. Feb 1879 Thomas W. Smith got his guardianship changed from Wm. S. Marshall to Grant T. Jackson. 1864 taxes $646.56. 1865 taxes $197.19.

BOX 167 PACK 4505   ROBERT SIMPSON   1864

Administrator: David Whitman. Bond Feb 22, 1864 of $12,000 by David Whitman, Elizabeth Simpson, John P. Tucker. Appraisal Mar 9, 1864 by B. D. Kay, George P. Pettigrew, Thomas Morgan. Held notes on: John C. Speer, R. M. Davis, J. O. Evans, J. H. Wiles, Wm. M. Bell, A. Mauldin. Estate Sale Mar 10, 1864 netted $2,605. Buyers at sale: A. A. Mauldin, Elizabeth Simpson, James T. Barnes, David Whitman, John Morgan, J. D. Burkhead, A. Avery, Mrs. Heaton, F. P. Robertson, F. Hall, Mahulda McAdams, Mary McCollum, S. J. Burdette, George Burdette, S. Mauldin, John Craft, Mrs. Evans, David Simpson, H. H. Scudday, J. M. White, J. W. Prince, Mrs. Simpson, Capt. Tucker, J. H. Wiles, Mrs. Waters, Wm. G. Robertson, J. W. Brown, Joseph Burriss, Thomas McAdams, Sarah Simpson, Wm. O'Bryant, Susan Simpson, Samuel Hutchison, P. Tucker, Andrew J. McCurry, Thomas Morgan, Jane Beaty, J. N. Burroughs, John C. Speer, Dr. Cook, T. D. Young, J. T. Burriss, B. C. Kay, Ezekiel White, Wm. M. Bell. Paid A. V. Brooks $81.24 for coffin. 1864 Council fee $10. 1869 Council fee $25. Estate Settlement Oct 8, 1869. Wife, Elizabeth deceased. (8) Children, not named, each received $58.45. One child not included as had not been heard from for 15 years. Final return made Jun 1870.

BOX 168 PACK 4506   EZEKIEL TRIBBLE   1861

Deceased died Sep 1861. Wife: Emily Tribble. Administrator: Wm. H. Parker. Merchant who owned a grocery store in Town of Abbeville. Appraisal Dec 26, 1861 by John A. Wier, John Enright, Mathew McDonald. Owned 3 slaves. Complete listing of store contents. Held Notes on: John Conner, A. B. Cobb, Hugh Wilson, A. Maxwell, J. M. Davis, Wm. M. Hughey, Jacob Loner, Wm. Loner, Thomas J. Hill, Seaborn S. McCurry, Louis H. Russell, Elijah Tribble, G. C. Bowers, James Taggart Sr., John Ruff, Johnson Ramey, John Pryon, J. M. Osborn, J. F. Bell, Clark Hall, Wm. L. McMahan, John Bowen, James Dixon, A. Branyon, Lemuel W. Allen, John A. Hunter, Marshall McCoppin, Lomax & Cobb, Wm. Masters, Abraham Hood, Thomas M. Christian, James Able, G. B. & Sterling Bowen, W. G. Killingsworth. Open and due store accounts from 1855: Ab Allen, J. Allen, Dr. D.S. Benson, J. R. Black, J. A. Black, Joseph Bugen, Wm. Bell, H. Bell, R. F. Bell, W. W. Belcher, J. Augustus Black, Louis Bozeman, G. W. Bunobs, James Brownlee, S. Bowen, G. W. Bowen, Nancy Bowen, H. G. Belcher, Branch & Parker, Young Champlin, James Campbell, J. W. Cann, W. G. Champlin, James D. Chalmers, Wm. Cook, W. Cowan, Wm. Colbert, Jack Champlin, Wm. L. Campbell, David Clellan, Thomas Christian, David Crews, H. Coleman, Norwood Calhoun, James Carlisle, Dick Calen, Joseph Darracott, Old Dick, F. W. Davis, Mrs. Dendy, Dr. W. Davis, Wm. Gallagher, James Going, Wm. Gaines, Power Huckabee, Thomas J. Hearst, Wm. Hackett, A. F. Haddon, Wm. Hughey, Wm. N. Hall, A. W. Haddon, Wm. Hamlin, Wm. Hawkins, John A. Hunter, Frederick Ives, Henry Ives, Wm. Junkin, H. A. Jones, D. F. Jones, C. H. Kingsmore, James Lomax, J. J. Lee, Wm Lyon, A. T. Lipford, Fraser Livingston, R. Lisenbee, Wm. A. Lee, Dr. J. F. Livingston, Thomas Link, Robert L. Martin, George Miller, James Moore, Thomas B. Milford, Luke Martin, J. J. Martin, John Mundy, Robert Martin, Stephen Montgomery, Robert

McBryde, Wm. McCurry, Mathew McDonald, Wm. McGill, Samuel McGowan, Archy McCord, Thomas McBryde, Samuel McGill, Samuel McAleen, Frank McCord, Samuel McClellan, Samuel McKee, Wm. McCord, Wm. G. Neel, Patrick O'Keefe, Dr. Andrew Paul, Wm. C. Power, S. Russell, Louis Russell, Philip S. Rutledge, Hugh Robinson, Grizella Russell, Wm. Robinson, Samuel Robinson, Rutledge & Russell, Henry Russell, Miss Sue Ramey, Edward Roche, George Spine, Dr. J. S. Sanders, D. R. Sondley, David Sloan, Wm. Stevenson, James Taggart Jr., E. J. Taylor, D. M. Tribble, James Verrell, James Wright, Conrad Wakefield, J. G. Wilson, Patrick N. Wilson, Dr. J. J. Wardlaw, Hugh Wilson, Wm. Young. Nov 6, 1861 sale of contents of store as ordered by Court of Equity. Buyers: John A. Wier, John T. Owen, Jeptha R. Hamlin, Samuel Russell, Mathew McDonald, David Jordan, J. W. W. Marshall, James H. Cobb, John McBryde, James F. Livingston, A. L. Gray, Talbert Cheatham, Wm. Hill, John P. Cromer, Wm. Mooney, Philip S. Rutledge, B. M. Winestock, Thomas Christian, Patrick O'Keefe, O. J. Farrington, Frank McCord, Henry S. Cason, F. Robertson, John H. Wilson, James A. Norwood, Robert A. Martin.

BOX 168 PACK 4507   BARTLETT TUCKER   1861

Will dated Feb 22, 1853. Filed Jul 1861. Witnesses: Wm. H. Parker, Robert A. Fair, Thomas Thomson. Wife: Nancy W. Tucker, was his 2nd wife. Children by 2nd wife: 1. Bartley S. Tucker 2. John T. Tucker 3. Thomas M. Tucker 4. Agnes J. Moss 5. Tallulah F. Tucker. Had children by 1st wife that were not in the will nor settlement, no names mentioned. Appraisal Sep 28, 1861 by Alex. Oliver, James M. Latimer, Ezekiel Pickens Speed. 1st Estate Sale: Dec 4, 1861. Buyers at sale: Widow, T. M. Tucker, A. J. Moss, T. F. Bond, J. J. Tucker, W. M. Bell, James T. Barnes, John C. speer, Wm. W. Burton, Bartlett S. Tucker. Feb 15, 1862 widow received 474 acres of land and 5 slaves. She died in 1862. 2nd Estate Sale Dec 18, 1866 netted $2008. Buyers at sale: Thomas M. Tucker, A. J. Wells, F. P. Robertson, Christian V. Barnes, A. J. Bond, Wm. A. Giles, Wm. Moore, Robert L. Hardin, Amanda Johnson, Clement T. Latimer, Robert Hutchison, F. W. Boles, Henry H. Harper, David E. Carlisle, James D. Burton, Bartlett S. Tucker, O. Caldwell, James M. Young, John G. Vanhorn, J. P. Brownlee, Barbara Burton, James Bruce, Wm. F. Clinkscales, Mrs. E. Caldwell, Rignul Groves, H. H. Scudday, Samuel A. Hutchison, George P. Brownlee, Alonzo Z. Bowman, Wm. Burton, Martha Deal. Oct 7, 1867 256 acres sold to Thomas M. Tucker, 90 acres to Thomas M. Tucker, 134 acres to James M. Latimer. Estate Settlement Aug 1870. (5) Distributees each $691.18: 1. B. S. Tucker 2. Thomas M. Tucker 3. Agnes J. Moss 4. Tallulah F. Tucker 5. Heirs of John T. Tucker.

BOX 168 PACK 4508   LEMUEL WILLIAMSON TRIBBLE   1861

Willl dated Dec 15, 1860. Witnesses: Wm. Clinkscales, G. J. McAdams, James H. Haddon. Executors: Stephen M. Tribble, John R. Wilson. Bond Jan 25, 1860 of $0,000 by Stephen M. Tribble, Thomas Crawford, Robert Ellis. Wife: Dicey Tribble. Children: 1. Eliza M. Tribble 2. Ezekiel Tribble 3. John Tribble 4. Lemuel Watson Tribble 5. James R. Tribble 6. Stephen M. Tribble 7. George W. Tribble 8. Pickens A. Tribble 9. Lucinda Brown wife of John Brown. Appraisal Feb 8, 1861 by Wm. Clinkscales, Addison Clinkscales, James H. Haddon. Estate Sale Feb 12, 1861 netted $16,070. Buyers at sale: Lemuel Watson Tribble, P. A. Tribble, Stephen M. Tribble, George W. Tribble, Wm. Allen, Robert C. Sharp, Wm. A. Black, James H. Haddon, J. S. Major, James Armstrong, T. J. Ellis, Alex. G. Hagen, Ben. Shirley, Addison Clinkscales, Col. Clinkscales, James W. Richey,

105

Washington Bowen, W. P. Hay, James Branyon, Edward Hagen, J. I. Bonner, Ezekiel Rasor, Ben. F. Moseley, Bn. H. Eakin, Albert Johnson, M. P. Cochran, J. P. Clinkscales, J. L. Brock, Christopher C. Ellis. 1st Estate Settlement Jan 14, 1864. (11) Distributees each $2014.95: 1. Mary Grubbs 2. R. G. Kay and wife 3. James R. Tribble 4. Stephen M. Tribble 5. John M. Brown and wife 6. George W. Tribble 7. John Tribble 8. Ezekiel Tribble 9. Pickens A. Tribble 10. Eliza Tribble 11. Dicey Tribble. 2nd Estate Settlement Mar 1, 1870. Widow received $49.14 and each child $8.95.

BOX 168 PACK 4509   JOHN J. TUCKER   1863

Will dated Mar 29, 1862. Probated Jan 15, 1863. Witnesses: Robert Hutchison, Wm. Bell, J. P. Burton. Executor: Wm. A. Pressly died in Confederate Army, Amanda C. Tucker-wife. Bond Jun 15, 1868 of $4,000 by Amand C. Tucker, Daniel E. Carlisle, J. F. C. DuPre. Niece: Amanda K. Bond. Father was Bartley S. Tucker deceased. Appraisal Feb 2, 1863 by James T. Barnes, James M. Latimer, Robert Hutchison, Wm. M. Bell. Estate Sale Feb 3, 1863. Buyers at sale: Sterling Bowen, W. P. Bell, James T. Barnes, Wm. Burton, James Boles, Thomas J. Durett, Wm. Ashley, A. J. Morse, Wm. T. Scott, A. P. Stovall, Alex. Oliver, H. H. Scudday, Andrew J. Speer, Thomas Deal, Thomas M. Tucker, Wm. A. Pressly, Lewis Caldwell, Wm. F. Clinkscales, Thomas D. Young, Wm. A. Sutherland, James M. Latimer, Wm. Loftis, Samuel A. Hutchison, J. J. Uldrick, B. D. Kay, John A. Grant, Samuel Hall, Wm. T. Harris, Thomas A. Harris, Nancy Tucker, Clement T. Latimer, James Clark, George W. Kelly, John M. Moseley. Estate Settlement Aug 4, 1870, no details.

BOX 168 PACK 4510   S. R. UNDERWOOD   1860

Administrator: Samuel W. Agnew. Bond Aug 6, 1860 of $4,000 by Samuel W. Agnew, James Donald, Wm. B. Bowie. Appraisal Aug 24, 1860 by John W. Rowland, James Y. Sitton, Wm. Agnew, John M Pruitt. Held notes on: J. P. Gordon, Thomas Pearlstein, F. V. Bell, Richard Duncan, Marion Bell, Frederick Nance, Thomas J. Ellis, Wm. F. Wright, Samuel W. Agnew, W. W. Dove, Lorenzo D. Wright, Jones Doulty, Samuel Robertson, Preston C. Suber, James F. A. Lamond, Hugh Wilson, S. S.. Maroney, Wm. Masters, Edward Smith, Robert E. Gaines, John Webb. Estate Sale Aug 24, 1860. Buyers at sale: Moses Winestock, David O. Hawthorne, Widow, A. C. Hawthorne, P. Y. Silborne, Thomas Soles, James Magill, Samuel W. Agnew, George Richey, J. M. Pruitt, B. C. Sharp, W. B. Huggins, Luke Mathis, A. P. McGee, John Hagen, A. C. Stevenson, P. F. Donald, Robert Hagen, Thomas Hawthorne, James Y. Sitton, P. W. Robin.

BOX 168 PACK 4511   SOPHRONIA VERRELL   1864

Administrator: Robert Jones. Husband: James Verrell. Estate Settlement Apr 20, 1863. Husband and (2) Children, one of whom was deceased. Each received $310.69. Deed share split 50/50 father and sister. Jul 19, 1864 the estate received from the sale of the property of Joshua Davis $65.03 and personal property $933.32.

BOX 168 PACK 4512   ELIZABETH Y. VANDIVER   1864

Executor: Wm. S. McBride. Bond Feb 3, 1864 of $2,000 by Wm. S. McBride, James S. Robinson, Shepard G. Cowan. Appraisal Feb 18, 1864 by Wm. P. Noble, Andrew A.

Noble, George W. Robinson. Estate Sale Feb 18, 1864 Netted $1,264. Buyers at sale: Ezekiel P. Noble, D. G. Paschall, C. L. Pettigrew, Wm. D. Partlow, Thomas Mobley, Miss F. McBride. M. Tennant, Jane Gibert, Charles B. Guffin, Dr. Baker, J. M. Porter, Miss C. Crawford, M. G. Darracott, J. Ingraham, Mrs. McBride, G. M. Robinson, Louis Covin, Peter Hemminger, J. Wilhite, Peter L. Guillebeau, Willis Turman. Estate Settlement Mar 4, 1864. (3) Children, no names, each $328.80.

BOX 168 PACK 4513   JOHN L. WILSON   1864

Administrator: Samuel A. Wilson. Appraisal May 15, 1863 by Patrick H. Bradley, Larkin Reynolds, Lewis Rich. Feb 3, 1863 Elizabeth J. Tittle and Nancy C. Wilson each received $31.44. Estate Settlement Jan 27, 1864. Distributees each received $31.44. Father, brother, sisters. Brother was deceased and his (4) children each received $5.24. No names.

BOX 168 PACK 4514   ROBERT H. WILSON   1863

Administrator: Samuel A. Wilson. Bond Feb 23, 1863 of $8,000 by Samuel A. Wilson, Patrick H. Bradley, Larkin Reynolds. Appraisal Feb 24, 1863 by Wm. C. Cozby, J. Johnson, Wm. M. Smith, F. Miller. Estate Sale Feb 25, 1863 netted $2,075. Buyers at sale: B. Williams, Thomas J. Hill, J. W. Power, John C. Speer, Rev. Buckhead, Robert A. Martin, G. Grant, J. Johnson, B. Williams, Wm. Rampey, F. Wilson, W. C. Drinkard, I. W. Griffin, Irvin Clark, Widow, Wm. Scoggins, J. Clark, Jeff Smith, Samuel A. Wilson, Wm. Bell, Bannister Allen, John McMahan, Robert Stuckey, Wm. Butler, Wm. H. Sutherland, F. A. Wilson, Robert L. Hardin, Wm. Smith, --- Cook, C. Wilson, George Bowen, Alex. Hunter, S. A. Nelson, S. M. White, J. Moseley, Hutson Loftis, Thomas A. Daniel, S. W. Bowen, --- Durham, J. A. Daniel, --- Cunningham. Estate Settlement Feb 25, 1863. Widow $787.74, paid Jan 27, 1864. (4) Children, no names, each $235.20.

BOX 168 PACK 4515   THOMAS COLEMAN WHITE   1863

Confederate Soldier. Will dated Jul 2, 1861. Witnesses: Lewis D. Merriman, Stanley Crews, Charles M. Creswell. Brothers: John Stuart White, John Leonard White. Executor: John Leonard White. Partner in the mercantile firm of Davis & White. Appraisal May 2, 1863 by John A. Stuart, Jefferson Floyd, S. S. Powers. Owned 2 slaves. Held notes on: J. E. Caine, A. P. Riley, A. D. Reynolds, W. E. Venning, R. A. Griffin, J. F. Davis, J. W. & W. A. Harralson.

BOX 168 PACK 4516   SAMUEL J. WILLARD   1869

Administrator: James C. Willard. Bond Jan 5, 1863 of $5,000 by James C. Willard, Wm. Truitt, J. S. Britt. Physician. Appraisal Jan 19, 1863 by Ben. McKittrick, Michael Magrath, J. S. Britt, Wm. Truitt. Held notes on: E. S. Willard, Moses T. Owen, John T. Owen, D. P. Self, Thomas E. Jennings, J. C. Cox, Michael S. Talbert, N. H. Palmer, James A. Wideman, John Elkins, John Agner, S. H. Jones, Michael McGrath, John F. Edmunds, David J. Wardlaw, Nancy W. Cantelon, Thomas E. Jennings, Paul Rogers, Ben. Talbert. Estate Sale Jan 22, 1863 netted $5,079. Buyers at sale: Widow, King Palmer, J. S. Britt, J. C. Willard, S. W. Willis, Ellington Searles, David Morrow, John Tompkins, Moton Pettigrew, John Elkins, C. W. Cowan, John T. Owens, E. S. Willard, Dr. Jennings, W. W. Banks, Dr.

Bradley, S. B. Smith, J. F. Calhoun, Dr. J. S. Sanders, L. Tucker, James Taggart, Ben. McKittrick, Wm. Morris, Ellis Carroll, John Cox, Wm. Truitt, Peter Smith, George Rosenwike, George Patterson, John Wideman, J. P. Caswell. James W. Tompkins married the widow E.Savannah Willard. 1st Estate Settlement Apr 12, 1869. Distributees: Widow and (9) Chldren, no names. 2nd Estate Settlement Feb 22, 1879. Small amount disbursed, no details.

BOX 168 PACK 4517   WADE WALKER   1863

Administrator: Robert W. Lites. Bond Aug 24, 1863 of $8,000 by Robert W. Lites, Edward O. Reagan, Adam Wideman. Wife: Sarah E. Walker. Appraisal Oct 15, 1863 by James Caldwell, Adam Wideman, Andrew J. Weed. Estate Sale Oct 15, 1863 netted $3,897. Buyers at sale: Sarah Walker, David Ethridge, Robert W. Lites, Wm. Jay, Thomas O. Creswell, James E. Gibson, Wm. Butler, Edward O. Reagan, James Martin, Patrick H. Bradley. Estate Settlement Jun 3, 1884. Administrator not to be held responsible for any debts. The Confederate money in his hands, $3,820, was worthless. He had paid the costs of the estate out of his own money since the end of the war. Creditors had been owed about $1,400 but rfused to accept Confederate money. He turned all the Confederate money over to the widow.

BOX 168 PACK   THEODORE WILSON   1863

Adminisstrator: Wm. S. Harris. Bond Oct 19, 1863 of $2,000 by Wm. S. Harris, Larkin Reynolds, Wm. K. Bradley. Appraisal Oct 25, 1863 by Robert Jones, Thomas M. Christian, J. A. Hunter, John McCord. Estate Sale Oct 25, 1863 netted $840. Buyers at sale: Mary Wilson, Robert Jones, Thomas M. Christian, Mathew McDonald, Harvey Wilson, J. T. Douglass, Philip S. Rutledge, Jeptha R. Hamlin, James A. Wilson. Estate Settlement May 29, 1865. Widow, Mary F. Wilson received $232.445. (3) Children each $154.97. 1. John Wilson 2. Anna A. Wilson 3. Adaline E. Wilson.

BOX 168 PACK 4519   JOEL MANLY WALKER   1863

Will dated Oct 24, 1863. Witnesses: T. S. Blake, J. F. Cason, W. F. McMillan. Father: Peter L. Walker. Mother: Mary Walker. Lived Williamston, S.C. Executor: Joseph J. Acker-friend.   Appraisal Jan 20, 1864 by B. F. Mauldin, Joseph Smith, A. B. Campbell. Held notes on: D. J. Barnett, W. H. King, W. H. Acker, Isaac M. Hill. Estate Sale Dec 28, 1863 netted $538. Buyers at sale: B. F. Mauldin, D. J. Barnett, A. B. Campbell, J. B. Lussale, W. O. Derrick, E. Y. Raworth, A. F. Welborn, J. B. Rogers, P. W. Seyle, Major Welborn, W. B. Milliam, Joseph J. Acker. Estate Settlement Feb 16, 1865, no details.

BOX 168 PACK 4520   CADRUS D. WALLER   1864

Will dated Apr 3, 1863. Witnesses: J. A. Bailey, Felix G. Parks, Thomas L. Coleman. Executor: C. A. C. Waller-brother. Brothers: Edward H. Waller, Cadmus G. Waller, Creswell H. Waller, Pelius A. Waller, C. A. C. Waller. Nephews: Richard Waller Funk son of A.W. Funk of Pontotoc, Miss, Wm. Waller Wood son of W. C. Wood of Pontotoc, Miss. Mother: J. Elizabeth Waller. Mrs. Rhoda Kilcrease relic of Wm. E. Kilcrease mentioned in will but relationship not clear. Willed $5,000 to Furman Colllege for funding the "Waller Scholarship". Appraisal Jan 27, 1864 by James Creswell, Allen M. Vance,

Emmanuel J. Wiss, J. A. Bailey. Owned 1 slave. Estate Sale Aug 18, 1866. Buyers at sale: J. E. Waller, John M. McLees, Milton Osborn, F. T. Williams, James Riley, E. A. Calhoun, S. B. Hodges, John R. Tarrant, John Seals. Last return and estte entry Oct 1874.

BOX 168 PACK 4521   ALLEN WEEKS (minors)   1863

Guardian: Wm. Truitt. Bond Jul 6, 1864 of $2,000 by Wm. Truitt, James C. Willard, Joseph S. Britt. (8) Children all minors, no names.

BOX 168 PACK 4522   JOHN J. WIMBISH   1863

Administrator: Alexander F. Wimbish-father. Bond Mar 24, 1863 of $3,000 by Alex. F. Wimbish, Littletoon Yarborough, James W. Guffin. Sister: Antoinette Borne wife of Henry Borne. Father and Sister were only heirs.

BOX 168 PACK 4523   WILLIAM W. WHITE   1863

Will dated Apr 14, 1863. Witnesses: Wm. B. Brooks, J. P. Brooks, Thomas C. Lipscomb. Executor: Lavinia B. White-wife. Appraisal Oct 2, 1863 by Peter McKellar, James C. Ray, Wm. B. Brooks, John T. McKellar. Owned 10 slaves.

BOX 168 PACK 4524   SARAH WIDEMAN   1863

Will dated may 24, 1850. Witnesses: Samuel Perrin, John W. Hearst, John Cothran. Executor: James H. Wideman-son. Very large estate with much activity over many years. Children: 1. James H. Wideman 2. Margaret wife of Thomas J. Lyon 3. Catherine wife of Anthony G. Harmon 4. Mary wife of Pelius A. Waller 5. Martha Wideman 6. Sarah Wideman. Appraisal Jul 23, 1863 by John W. Hearst, Wm. McCain, Robert W. Lites, Adam Wideman, Walter G. Keller. Held notes on: J. B. Adamson, L. N. Traylor, G. S. Patterson, James Evans. Owned 42 slaves. Accounts on: G. S. Patterson, S. G. Furgueron, Thomas Moseley, Mrs. Johnson, L. N. Traylor, Ed Wideman, A. Boyd, S. W. Willis, Jane Lindsay, Moses T. Owen, M. C. Lyon, Anthony Harmon, George Sibert, Patrick H. Bradley. Estate Sale Dec 1, 1863 netted $73,350. 19 pages of sales. Buyers at sale: B. F. Brown, M. A. Owen, J. H. Wideman, Anthony Harmon, R. T. Bell, W. W. Belcher, J. N. Briscoe, Wm. Bosdell, Wilson Watkins, Ben. McKittrick, John C. Chiles, Thomas O. Creswell, Patrick H. Bradley, David Ethridge, Dr. Williams, J. H. Morris, M. C. Lyon, Wm. H. Taggart, S. A. McCaslan, Mary Waller, H. E. Cothran, Wade E. Cothran, J. McDowell, A. Harrell, J. Caldwell, J. C. Smith, W. E. Martin, George S. Patterson, C. W. Cowan, Thomas W. Barksdale, B. D. Barksdale, E. F. Riggs, Moses Winestock, W. M. Williams, W. McCain, George Rosenwike, J. L. Sibert, John Cook, Dr. Manley, J. H. Rush, Robert R. Tolbert, M. A. Owen, John L. Devlin, Wm. Truitt. Accounts owed collected by or at day of sale: J. H. Morrow, Wm. H. Taggart, R. A. McCaslan, James Brown, David Ethridge, Moses Winestock, B. M. Winestock, E. F. Riggs, Thomas O. Creswell, Andrew J. Weed, Robert T. Bell, John H. Rush, Joseph Brown, George Rosenwike, J. S. Horton, D. M. Winestock, Thomas W. Barksdale, Samuel Wilson, Robert R. Tolbert, Ben. Henderson, A. Harr---, J. N. Morris, John H. Chiles, W. K. Bradley, Mrs. M. A. Owens, J. C. Smith, A. T. Wideman. Land sold Nov 1, 1869: 544 acres to L. W. Lyon, 401 acres to C. A. Wideman, 185 acres to Bud Creswell, 271 acres to L. C. Clinkscales, 261 acres to James Creswell. Estate Settlement Nov 8, 1870. (6) Distributees: 1. Margaret C. Lyon

$1,955 2. James H. Wideman $2,195 3. Kitty wife of Anthony Harmon $1,976 4. Mary wife of James W. Reagan $2,577 5. Martha A. Owen $2239 6. Sarah P. wife of B. F. Brown $484. The Browns protested settlement, several pages of complaints. Reagans of Terrell Co., Ga protested settlement. Overall very involved with much information covering many years past introduced.

BOX 168 BOX 4525   WILLIAM WILLIAMS   1864

Deceased died Feb 1863. Administrator: Richard N. Wright. Appraisal Feb 29, 1864 by G. M. Mattison, David Moore, F. W. Branyon, George W. Williams. Estate Sale Mar 1, 1864 netted $745. Buyers at sale: widow bought almost everything, J. S.Carwile, Amanda Williams. Estate Settlement Mar 8, 1864. Distributees: Widow and (8) Children. Each received $312.99. Wife: Lucinda Williams 1. Newton A. Williams 2. George W. Williams in Texas 3. Cloe L. wife of Calvin Graham 4. Ann wife of John Lane 5. Amanda M. wife of Samuel M. Lane 6. Marshall C. Williams 7. Frances C. Williams, infant 8. Mary L. Williams, infant. Petiton activity by Newton Williams against others filed Nov 17, 1869, no details.

BOX 168 PACK 4526   MARY E. WARE   1864

Administrator: Gabriel M. Mattison. Bond Feb 18, 1864 of $3,000 by Gabriel M. Mattison, James H. Shaw, Ben. M. Latimer. Appraisal Mar 4, 1864 by Allen Dodson, Wm. Mundy, James M. Vandiver, Wm. Maddox. Notes held on: James Killingsworth, Richard A. Griffin, Wm. M. Griffin, J. Elledge, J. A. Cooper. Estate Sale Mar 4, 1864. Buyers at sale: J. H. Spoon, James H. Shaw, Larkin Griffin, Wm. Riley, Elizabeth Ware, Gabriel M. Mattison, A. Culbertson, Lewis Taylor, Wesley Robertson, Margaret Crenshaw, Aaron Pitts, J. T. Carter, Thomas Y. Martin, Mary Long, Wm. Maddox, James Killingsworth, Charles C. Pinckney, James C. Rasor, W. B. Gaines, A. Mitchem, J. Elledge, Mattison Hill, Nicholas W. Ware, Allen Dodson, W. T. Jones, Richard A. Griffin.

BOX 169 PACK 4527   WILLIAM H. BUTLER   1864

Will dated Aug 5, 1864. Witnesses H. T. Sloan, John McCreary, T. H. McCreary. Administrator: Wm. H. Butler. Butler clandestinely removed from the state after having sold all the personal property and real estate. He absconded with all the money. Wm. H. Parker, Commissoner in Equity for Abbeville County became administrator in 1865. Bond Jan 26, 1865 of $2,000. Wife: Mary Butler. Sons: Wm. H. Butler, John W. Butler, Thompson S. Butler. Daughters: Mary E. Butler, Susan E. Butler, Sarah A. C. Butler, Margaret M. Butler. Appraisal Jan 26, 1865 by Wm. S. Harris, James Martin, John McCreary, James L. Morrow. Owned 7 slaves. Estate Settlement May 12, 1868. Wm. H. Parker, Administrator had $844.47 to distribute. No details.

BOX 169 PACK 4528   JOHN BICKETT   1865

Confederate Soldier. 14th South Carolina Volunteers. Will dated May 19, 1862 in Confederate service in Virginia. Witnesses: Samuel McGowan, A. W. W. Weed, G. A. Weed. Wife: Sarah Bickett. Sons: Andrew W. Bickett, John H. Bickett. Executor: Andrew Weed. Appraisal Oct 5, 1864 by John C. Lindsay, F. T. White, John L. Devlin, Tyra Jay, Wm. S. Harris. Held notes on: Edward Bowick, Joseph L. Pressly.

BOX 169 PACK 4529   THOMAS BARKSDALE   1864

Confederate Soldier. Killed in Action. Administrator: Andrew J. Ferguson. Bond Jul 23, 1866 of $500 by Andrew J. Ferguson, Champion D. Palmer, Thomas W. McMillan. Wife: Indiana Barksdale. (2) Minor Children: Elizabeth Barksdale, Sarah T. Barksdale. Assets consisted of 2 notes held on: John Martin of $100, Champion D. Palmer of $100. May 22, 1871 wife received $15 and in Nov 1871 $5. Settlement Mar 6, 1873. Wife: Indiana received $90, Children, Elizabeth Barksdale and Sarah T. Barksdale each received $45.

BOX 169 PACK 4530   ANDREW T. BOWIE   1864

Confederate Soldier. Co. K Palmetto Sharpshooters. Died Fredericksburg, Va. Jan 23, 1862. Administrator: Robert E. Bowie-brother. Bond Sep 26, 1864 of $30,000 by Robert E. Bowie, N. J. Bowie, John H. Wilson. Heirs: Mother, no name and Robert E. Bowie.

BOX 169 PACK 4531   FRANCIS M. BROOKS   1866

Administrators: Albert J. Clinkscales, Martha D. Brooks. Bond Jun 16, 1864 of $150,000 by Martha D. Brooks, Albert J. Clinkscales, Wm. H. Brooks. Wife: Martha D. Brooks married James T. Guffin. Had (3) Children at time of is death but James H. Brooks and Wm. T. Brooks both infants died prior to the estate settlement. Appraisal Nov 21, 1865 by David J. Jordan, George M. Miller, J. R. Cunningham, Samuel Gilmer. Held notes on: Thomas L. Boyd, Andrew L. Gillespie, John Evans. Estate Sale Nov 22, 1865 netted $4969. Buyers at sale: James T. Guffin, Philip Rutledge, Joel J. Lipford, Hiram T. Tusten, Thomas J. Mabry, Francis A. Wilson, F. P. Robertson, Albert J. Clinkscales, Talbert Cheatham, Dr. H. T. Lyon, Thomas A. Hill, --- Knox, D. R. Sondley, J. R. Cunningham, Mrs. S. Cheatham, Samuel Link, Wm. Hix, Joel Smith, Wm. H. Brooks, E. Yarborough, F. A. Watson, John J. Gray. Estate Settlement Jan 24, 1866. Widow, now wife of James T. Guffin and only surviving minor child Thomas Jefferson Brooks received a total of $2,362.

BOX 169 PACK 4532   ARCHIBALD B. BOYD   1864

Administrator: Andrew J. Weed. Bond Apr 27, 1865 of $2,000 by Andrew J. Weed, John T. Owen, John L. Drennan. Appraisal Apr 28, 1865 by Edward O. Reagan, Stephen W. Willis, Wm. Bosdell. Estate Sale Apr 28, 1865. Buyers at sale: Wm. T. Sloan, Samuel Roundtree, Peter Harmon, Robert W. Lites, Abraham Martin, James Neeley, Daniel Carroll, Thomas Bosdell, A. S. Weed, Mrs. F. Reynolds, George Patterson, S. F. Smith, Daniel Newby, Samuel W. Willis, Wm. Beasley, Thomas Hardy, Adam Wideman, Peter Carroll, M. Hendrix, Samuel P. Leard, Enoch Sharpton, Peter Henson, Isaac Caldwell, Peter Smith, A. P. Weed, Mrs. A. Traylor, P. H. McCain, Henry Hester, S. B. Smith, John C. Willis, Mrs. E. Beasley, Mrs. Strother, P. Wideman, Thomas Banks, George Rosenwike, Joseph Jay, Clem Corley, Mary Brown. Last estate return and activity Oct 14, 1871

BOX 169 PACK 4533   STERLING BOWEN   1864

Will dated Jan 30, 1864. Witnesses: H. H. Scudday, Wm. Moore, John W. D. Mann. Executor: Wm. M. Bowen. Bond Nov 22, 1864 of $40,000 by Wm. M. Bowen, Thomas J. Hill, Wm B. Martin. Wife: Elizabeth Bowen. Daughters: Susan wife of Wm. B. Martin, Mary wife of Ralph L. Hardin, Elizabeth wife of Fleming Hall, Emily Bowen, Sarah wife of John L. Campbell. Sons: Wm. M. Bowen, George W. Bowen, Josephus Bowen, L. B. Bowen deceased. Grand Daughters: Alice Eugenia Bowen, Frances Bowen. Grand Sons: T. O. Bowen, Logan Bowen illegitimate son of Elizabeth Hall. Appraisal Dec 6, 1864 by J. J. Cunningham, Thomas J. Hill, Wm. Dickson, Wm. Mann, Wm. Campbell. Owned 12 slaves. Estate Sale Dec 7, 1864. Buyers at sale: F. W. Bowen, Wm. Burkhead, Philip Rutledge, Hugh M. Prince, J. M. Martin, H. D. Spauldin, Wm. E. Bowen, Christian V. Barnes, Elizabeth McCurry, H. D. Fleming, Conrad Wakefield, George W. Bowen, John A. Wier, Hiram T. Tusten, W. B. Mauldin, J. M. Moseley, J. H. Miller, Mary Drennan, Wm. M. Harden, J. L. Campbell, Fanny Bowen, J. T. Moore, John C. Speer, Wm. Barnes, J. T. Cunningham, F. P. Robertson, S. S. Baker, Wm. E. Hall, J. S. Smith, Wm. Hicks, Robert A. Pressly, Steward Cann.

BOX 169 PACK 4534   JOHN M. BROWN   1864

Administrator: Margaret L. Brown. Bond Oct 7, 1864 of $10,000 by Margaret L. Brown, Dicey Tribble, Samuel Magill. Appraisal Nov 14, 1864 by Rosemond Wilson, Wm. Clinkscales, Robert Ellis. Held notes on: A. M. Franks, W. T. Brown.

BOX 169 PACK 4535   REV. HENRY BASS   1863

Will dated Sep 9, 1857. Witnesses: Emory Watson, B. Z. Blackmon, James W. Wightman. Wife: Amelia Bass. Daughter: Anna E. Bass. Son: Henry A. Bass. Lived in the Town of Cokesbury. Estate Settlement Aug 17, 1866. (5) Heirs, all mutually agreed. 1. Sidie H. Browne 2. Henry A. Bass 3. W. C. Bass 4. A. M. Browne 5. Anna E. S. Bass.

BOX 169 PACK 4536   GEORGE B. CLINKSCALES   1864

Will dated May 21, 1864. Witnesses: J. J. Cunningham, James W. Black, J. B. Kay. Wife: Eliza A. Clinkscales. Daughters: Martha A. wife of Washington Prince, Barbara A. Clement, Sarah J. Clinkscales. Son: Francis William Clinkscales. Executrix: Eliza A. Clinkscales-wife. Appraisal Oct 29, 1864 by M. B. Latimer, James T. Liddell, Robert C. Harkness, Henry S. Cason. Owned 46 slaves, land in Mississippi. Held notes on: Aaron W. Lynch, James Stone Robert H. Hall, Chesley Hall, George A. Allen, Wm. Moore, John Enright, Wm. A. Black, James R. Black, J. H. Bell, George W. Hall, Wade Ethridge, G. A. Allen, John W. Power, Samuel W. White, J. A. Talmadge, Thomas McAdams, Thomas McClellan, R. G. Caldwell, Samuel C. McClellan, J. R. Jones, Wm. A. Henry. 1864 war tax $1,696. Return Apr 3, 1865 was last estate entry.

BOX 169 PACK 4537   RICHMOND S. COBB   1864

Will dated Jan 29, 1864. Proved Oct 1864. Witnesses: Henry Riley, L. H. Rykard, Vachel Hughey. Wife: Sarah Jane Cobb. Executors: Sarah Jane Cobb, Silas Ray, Willis Smith. Bond Jan 9, 1866 of $3,550 by Sarah Jane Cobb, Silas Ray, L. H. Rykard. Appraisal Feb 20, 1864 by Henry Riley, Vachel Hughey, John Foster. Held notes on: Thomas W. Smith, Wm. Boozer & John J. Boozer, J. Bailey & Burt Riley, A. P. Boozer, Isaac Logan, John A. Morene, G. R. Caldwell, James Irwin, P. W. Goodwyn. Estate Sale Dec 15, 1865. Buyers at sale: Widow, E. Anderson, W. Smith, Thomas Riley, James Anderson, John Foster, G. N. Rush, Thomas Hearst, F. Cobb, Silas Ray. 1864 Confederate tax $547.

BOX 169 PACK 4538   JAMES F. CRAWFORD   1864

Will date not legible. Witnesses: Robert P. Buchanan, J. Bailey, A. T. Bell. Executors: Amarylis E. Crawford-wife, S. A. Crawford-brother. Mother-in-Law: Anna Hawthorne. Appraisal Dec 24, 1864 by G. M. Waddell, John B. Johnson, Thomas Stuart.

BOX 169 PACK 4539   JAMES CROWTHER   1864

Will dated Aug 19, 1863. Witnesses: Michael McGee, Robert Stuckey, Robert Boyd. Exeuctor: Martha Elizabeth Crowther-wife. Appraisal Nov 1, 1864 by Chesley Hall, Wm. Crowther, Sterling Bowen.

BOX 169 PACK 4540   JOHN W. V. CALLAHAM (minor)   1864

Guardian: Sarah G. M. Callaham. Bond Dec 15, 1864 of $1,000 by Sarah G. M. Callaham, James M. Crowther, Martha Pratt. Final entry 1870.

BOX 169 PACK 4541   MINORS of WILLIAM H. COCHRAN   1865

Guardian: Mary Jane Cochran. Bond Feb 5, 1865 of $174 by Mary Jane Cochran, Wm. Mann, Samuel W. Cochran. (4) Minors: 1. Thomas H. Cochran 2. Alpheus B. Cochran 3. Sarah M. Cochran 4. Mary J. Cochran.

BOX 169 PACK 4542   ROBERT D. DRENNAN   1864

Administrator: Andrew J. Weed. Bond Oct 14, 1864 of $4,000 by Andrew J. Weed, W. Watkins, J. C. Lindsay. Wife: Mary Drennan whose father was Andrew J. Weed. Appraisal Oct 26, 1864 by Samuel McClinton, John Devlin, David Atkins, William Fell. Widow took property at appraised value. Held notes on: Puckett & Weed, John L. Drennan, Horace Drennan, John W. Drennan. Esstate Settlement 1875, no details. Andrew J. Weedd cited for failure to file return for 1874. Last estate entry.

BOX 169 PACK 4543   ANDREW DUNN   1864

Will dated Oct 19, 1864. Witnesses: Ben. F. Moseley, M. C. Moseley, John C. Williams, Executors: Samuel Agnew, Mahala Dunn-wife. Son: James Robert Clarence Dunn. Appraisal Nov 17, 1864 by David O. Hawthorne, Andrew Agnew, James W. Blain.

BOX 169 PACK 4544   JOHN H. GARY   1864

Administrator: Franklin F. Gary. Bond Apr 14, 1864 of $5,000 by Franklin F. Gary, M. A. Gary, M. Strauss. Held notes on M. A. Gary, Franklin F. Gary, W. T. Gary.

BOX 169 PACK 4545   WILLIAM M. HUGHEY   1865

Confederate Soldier who died 1864. Will dated Apr 12, 1862. Witnesses: Armistead Burt, A. L. McCaslan, Wm. L. McCord. Executor: Ben. P. Hughes who died before settlement, Elizabeth J. Hughey-wife. Bond Mar 30, 1867 of $2,000 by Elizabeth J. Hughey, Elizabeth Buchanan, James S. Cothran. Appraisal Dec 20, 1864 by Robert Jones, John A. Wier, John A. Hunter, Enoch Nelson, Philip S. Rutledge. Owned 9 slavaes. Owned house and lot in Town of Abbevville. Held notes on: Frederick Ives, Elizabeth Buchanan, David Clay, Walter Thomas, W. R. Tolbert, J. Eldridge, Edmund Cobb, N. J. Davis, Ben. E. Gibert, Wm. Masters, Anthony Greer, Leroy J. Wilson, C. S. McKenzie, John

T. Owen, Andrew P. Paul, James H. Willliams. Estate Sale Jan 18, 1865. Buyers at sale: John T. Owen, F. Robison, John A. Wier, J. A. Allen, Wm. Hicks, Hiram W. Lawson, C. V. Hammond, H. H. Shillito, Wm. R. Mundy, Morris Roche, --- Enslow, Hiram T. Tusten, Edward W. Kelly, Talbert Cheatham, Thomas J. Ellis, J. A. Wilson, --- Holderman, Andrew Simonds, A. R. Venable, Wm. L. McCord, J. J. Wardlaw, John Connor, Jane Russell, Mrs. Burns, Mrs. Beard, Robert Martin, J. Gibbs, John Lyon, Adolphus A. Williams, James Carlisle, --- Inglesby, Ben. P. Hughes, George W. Cromer, Henry Wilkerson, D. R.Sondley, John Turner, Wm. Hill, Nancy Wilson, Mrs. C. McCord, George W. Syfan, Thomas H. Cobb, Josephine Wilson, Quitman Marshall, David J. Jordan, John McBryde, Wm. J. Gray, Jesse Carlisle, Mathew McDonald. Estate Settlement Jan 17, 1865. Wife received $1,642. Jan 12, 1867 petition of Elizabeth Buchanan vs Elizabeth J. Hughey.

BOX 169 PACK 4546   THOMAS HARRIS   1864

Will dated Mar 10, 1864. Witnesses: J. L. Fennel, A.D. Reynolds, Alex. McNeill, J. W. Hutchison. Executor: Henry F. Fuller. Wife: Mahulda Harris. Nephews: Henry F. Fuller, Patrick M. Fuller. Appraisal Nov 21, 1864 by John Sadler, Thomas W. Cooper. Owned 5 slaves. Estate Sale Nov 25, 1864. Buyers at sale: Henry F. Fuller, Mrs. M. A. Harris, Joel Fooshe, Allen Vance, John Day, W. Y. Head, Wm. Carter, B. D. Calhoun, James Fuller, G. H. Braddell, Wm. P. Dukes, Patrick Hefferman, J. R. Bozeman, M. S. Ingram, Daniel Rampey, Y. Pinson, B. Busbee, H. R. Wililams, Wm. Gaines, J. J. Cooper, David W. Aiken.

BOX 169 PACK 4547   ABRAM HADDON   1865

Confederate Soldier. Will dated Feb 23, 1864. Witnesses: R. Jones, Wm. B. Roman, Wm. McIlwain. Executors: Adam J. McKee-bro-in-law, James C. Stevenson. Wife: Hannah Haddon. 1st Appraisal Nov 11, 1865 by Thomas Stevenson, Wm. Gordon, Wm. McIlwain. 2nd Appraisal Dec 8, 1869 by Thomas Stevenson, Wm. P. McIlwain, Andrew Morrison. Estate Sale Dec 9, 1869. Buyers at sale: Adam McKee, J. W. Calvert, James C. Stevenson, Zachariah Haddon, J. L. McCord, Andrew Morrison, Charles McCombs, Chance Clinkscales, James W. Keller, Richard Romans, A. F. McCord, Robert Hagen, J. E. Crawford, Asa Bowie, Reuben Hagen, Peter Miles, Wm. McIlwain, Wm. O. Cromer, Robert H. Cochran, Oliver Cowan, Wm. H. Adamson, Henderson Bowen, James McCombs, Ben. Hagen, James Carlisle, Wm. T. McIlwain, A. Coon, Samuel H. Cochran, J. T. Gordon, Fred. V. Bell, Robert E. Hill, Jim Moton, Hiram Cromer, J. R. Haddon, J. A. Richardson, Jesse Carlisle, Moses Owen, Hugh P. McIlwain, J. L. Simpson, Wm. S. Robertson, Alex. G. Hagen, Samuel T. Eakin, Wm. H. McCombs. Estate Settlement Feb 19, 1873. Wife died May 2, 1869. (5) Distributees each $667. 1. James R. Haddon, 2. D. E. Haddon, 3. Hannah S. wife of Larkin C. Nickles 4. Reuben F. Haddon 5. Lilly Ann Haddon.

BOX 169 PACK 4548   JOHN A. HINTON   1864

Administrator: Samuel S. Fisher. Bond May 23, 1864 of $8,000 by Samuel S. Fisher, Wm. Walker, Amaziah Fisher. Appraisal Jun 8, 1864 by Wm. Duncan, John F. Clinkscales, Wm. Pruitt. Notes Held on: John McDonald, Jesse T. Murdock. 1st Estate Sale Jun 9, 1864 netted $2,493. Buyers at 1st sale: Polly Duncan, Gracy Fisher, Jane Murdock, Betsy Hinton, Joseph Murdock, Bennett McAdams, Cynthia Pruitt, Elizabeth Shirley, John F. Clinkscales, Wm. Callaham, Elias D. Pruitt, Robert Hinton, Samuel S. Fisher, Joshua

Ashley, John H. Saylors, A. J. Shaw, Elizabeth McClain, G. W. L. Mitchell, John W. Shirley, A. S. Armstrong, James M. Carwile, Ben. Pearman, Jeff M. Freeman, Agnes Robinson, Elizabeth Hinton, G. F. Mitchell, Ann Robinson. 2nd Estate Sale Oct 14, 1864 netted $4,157. Buyers at 2nd sale: Robert Hinton, Conrad Wakefield, Wm. Clinkscales, Mandaline Mitchell, Polly Duncan, J. E. Clinkscales, Mary A. Robinson, Samuel S. Fisher, J. T. Murdock, James R. Hinton. Estate Settlement Feb 3, 1865. Distributees: Father, Brother, (3) Sisters each $1,273. Only names were: Mary Duncan, Robert Hinton.

BOX 169 PACK 4549   SARAH J. HILL   1864

Administrator: James H. Cobb. Bond Oct 25, 1864 of $10,000 by James H. Cobb, John Enright, Philip S. Rutledge. Appraisal Nov 18, 1864 by Enoch Nelson, John A. Wier, John A. Hunter. Owned considerable amount of property. Estate Sale Nov 17, 1864. Buyers at sale: C. Golding, Andrew Simonds, W. H. Lawson, D. R. Sondley, John A. Mars, Jane Ramey, Andrew Hill, J. Gibbs, John T. Owen, John A. Wier, Talbert Cheatham, A. L. Gray, F. P. Robertson, Hiram W. Lawson, Edward Westfield, James H. Cobb, John Enright, Elizabeth Hill, Jordan A. Ramey, D. M. Rogers, Thomas Parker, Enoch Nelson. Children: 1. Andrew M. Hill 2. Charity wife of Reuben L. Golding 3. Elizabeth Hill.

BOX 169 PACK 4550   JOHN HUTCHISON   1864

Will dated Mar 29, 1862. Witnesses: Lemuel Bell, Thomas J. OPuzts, J. S. Chipley. Wife: Martha Elizabeth Hutchison. Daughters: Emma Lenore Hutchison, Sarah Ida Hutchison, Mary Hutchison. Son: John Wesley Hutchison. Brother: Irvin Hutchison. Executor: Irvin Hutchison. Appraisal Oct 14, 1864 by Jonathan S. Chipley, Johnson Sale, Richard Davis. Owned 14 slaves. Held notes on: W. T. Hackett, W. M. Chipley, Thomas M. Ross. Estate Sale Nov 28, 1865. Buyers at sale: J. Hutchison, Johnson Sale, R. F. Hutchison, W. S. Chipley, Benny Friedman, Mrs. L. Hutchison, Andrew A. Blythe, Wm. Ellenburg, Mrs. M. Hutchison.

BOX 170 PACK 4551   JAMES J. ADAMS   1865

Administrators: Wm. A. Lomax, Rachel C. Adams. Bond Nov 14, 1865 of $8,000 by Wm. A. Lomax, Andrew Stevenson, John W. Lomax, Rachel C. Adams. Shoemaker. Partner in firm of Roberts & Adams. Appraisal Nov 29, 1865 by Paschall D. Klugh, S. R. Lomax, B. M. Martin. Owned 85 shares of stock in Greenville & Columbia Railroad, $3,500 bonds on Greeville & Columbia Railroad, held warrants against the railroad, owned money for work done for railroad, had $8,000 Confederate money in cash plus $4,000 in Confederate bonds in hand at time of death. Owed quite a number of individuals. Held notes on: John Johnson, J. E. Hodges, J. L. Pratt, James B. Brown, J. W. Medlock, J. D. Adams, J. W. Arnold, Thomas W. Smith, W. C. Norwood, Mattison & Bigham, Larkin Mays, John C. C. Allen & Gabriel Hodges, John H. Connor, Charles Cunningham, Connor & Anderson, S. H. Allen, W. H. Blackburn, W. C. Klugh, Thomas M. Wilson, Valentine Dellinger, W. G. Lomax & J. H. Mundy, J. C. Anderson, Charles C. Pinckney, John C. C. Allen & S. E. Graydon, John C. C. Allen, W. C. Burns, Roberts & Adams, W. G. Lomax, John H. Wilson, J. B. Algary, G. A. Allen, James D. Chalmers, W. J. Lomax, Daniel Malone, J. L. Pratt. Accounts payable to James J. Adams: George W. Conner, Andy Koon, Gabe Williams, Luke Sawyer, Richard Swancey, John L. Clark, James C. Ellis, Wm. G. Lomax, John W. Lomax, Thomas Welch, Sarah Jackson, Francis A. Connor, Leroy J. Wilson, B. H.

Burns, Martin C. Gary, Wm. Waites, J. F. Williams, Wm. Pace, Jubal Watson, Thomas J. Roberts, Abner Mays, F. W. Mooney, John Ivey & Co., Samuel R. Knox, Nancy Keller, Samuel A. Hodges, R. Smith, Lawrence R. Dantzler, Stephen Allen, J. Mat Roach, Robert Strawhorn, B. V. Roberson, E. A. Hodges, Charles C. Pinckney, James M. Eason, Alex. Ellis, W. G. Zeigler. Accounts and notes payable to Roberts & Adams from 1855: Wm. M. Armstrong, Wm. M. Hughey, Hugh M. Wardlaw, Francis Sheppard, James Jones, John D. Keitt, Robert Richey, James H. Caldwell, S. Allen, Wm. McCool, Patrick N. Wilson, H. W. Burgess, L. D. Johnson, Wm. G. Lomax, W. L. Norwood, John Irvin, Oliver Richey, Wm. Magill, W. A. J. Ware, Wm. A. Templeton, W. W. Rochester, G. W. Long, J. Caswell Mundy, Wm. Bridges, James V. Young, Marshall Hodges, Thomas J. Roberts, Hol. Jones, B. N. Roberson, J. D. Pace, John H. Mundy, Wm. C. Burns, S. H. Breazeale, Andrew Brooks, Wm. J. Lomax, Johnson Ramey & James D. Chalmers, John G. Boozer, John C. C. Allen, J. F. Hodges, Robert T. Gordon, Edward Noble, Anne Stokes, Samuel Hodges, John Johnson, Tolbert Johnson, George Franklin, Samuel A. Hodges, David Keller, Edmond Cobb, Cochran-Hodges & Vance. Estate Sale Dec 1, 1865. Buyers at sale: Rachel C. Adams, David Hannah, Paschall D. Klugh, A. B. Hamlin, George W. Hodges, R. C. Adams, Wm. A. Lomax, John D. Adams, Charles Harvey, J. A. Agnew, N. A. Haynes, Ben. White, James M. Calvert, A. W. Moore, Leroy J. Wilson, James N. Cochran, Wm. Smith, John Darraugh, D. Z. Keller, Paul W. Connor, Wm. J. Lomax, Nathaniel Cobb, Michael Hackett, Thomas J. Ellis, W. N. Blake, Wm. Hodges, Andrew Stevenson, Robert Anderson, J. W. Henderson, Joseph T. Moore, A. P. Boozer, J. B. Black, Francis A. Connor, Wm. Sproull, Wm. McIlwain, J. L. Robinson, Gabriel Hodges, Robert Jones, John H. Mundy, J. S. Turner.

BOX 170 PACK 4552   SAMUEL AGNEW   1864

Will dated Dec 27, 1864. Witnesses: G. M. Mattison, Valentine Young, M. C. Henderson. Executors: James A. Agnew did nothing and all fell to A. M. Agnew. Wife: Sarah Agnew. Sons: A. M. Agnew, James A. Agnew. Daughters: Lucy Ann Rasor, Elizabeth A. Agnew, Edney Frances Smith. Appraisal Oct 4, 1865 by Michael B. McGee, J. N. Seawright, M. C. Henderson, S. S. Jones, John W. Blain. Owned 317 acres of land that included the Drummond tract of 200 acres. Estate Sale Oct 5, 1865 netted $5,531. Buyers at sale: W. S. McGee, John C. Rasor, D. J. Tribble, A. M. Agnew, Widow, James A. Agnew, J. N. Alexander, M. Sharp, W. P. McGee, Micahel B. McGee, Silas Jones, Ben. Martin, J. A. Caldwell, Francis A. Connor, J. N. Seawright, Enoch M. Sharp, Ezekiel Rasor, Wm. Mayberry, Wm. Riley, M. C. Henderson, George W. Freeman, Thomas J. Ellis, George Tribble, John B. Vance, H. Boyd, A. F. Greer, W. R. Mundy, Thomas Mayson, Wm. R. Buchanan, Martin G. Zeigler, Gabriel Hodges, Thomas Mahon, Lawrence R. Dantzler, T. N. Seawright, James Cowan, Wm. H. Sharp, James Killingsworth, Ben. Nash, Valentine Young, T. Y. Martin. Estate Settlement Oc 11, 1866. (5) Distributees total $10,853. 1. Lucy Ann Rasor 2. A. M. Agnew 3. Elizabeth A. Agnew 4. Mrs. Edna Smith now Martin 5. James A. Agnew. Tombstone cost $52.

BOX 170 PACK 4553   CHRISTIAN V. BARNES   1866

Pack contains many pages of very detailed information. Deceased died Feb 1866. Will dated Dec 12, 1865. Witnesses: James T. Baskin, James M. Latimer, Wm. A. Giles. Minister and Gristmills Owner. Wife: Susannah Martha Barnes. Executors: James T.

Barnes-son, Christian V. Barnes-son. Grand Son: Henry Barnes. Grand Daughter: Emma J. wife of James A. Brown and daughter of Alpheus Ezekiel Barnes. Prenuptial agreement between Christian Barnes & Susannah Martha Carnes dated Dec 9, 1851. Appraisal Mar 14, 1866 by John M. Moseley, Massalon Bell, Robert Hutchison. Owned House and lot in Lowdnesville, saw mill, Grist Mill on Calhouns Creek, Grist mill at Lowednesville, 150 acres on Calhoun Creek, 160 acres called the "Douglass Tract". Estate Sale Mar 15, 1866. Buyers at sale: George W. Bowen, Josephus Bowen, B. A. Davis, Samuel Sherard, Bannister Allen, Ben. Williams, Wm. T. Mauldin, Samuel Hutchison, E. White, J. M. Craft, Hugh Prince, Thomas A. Daniel, George W. Kelley, F. P. Robertson, Wm. Cook, Pinckney Tucker, Samuel J. Hester, Alonzo Z. Bowman, Alex. Oliver, Lee Cleveland, Thomas A. Cater, John McMahan, Philip Rutledge, James Parnell, John W. Brown, James H. Carlisle, John M. Moseley, James McKee, Joep J. Lipford, Christian V. Barnes, James T. Barnes, John C. Speer, B. D. Kay, Thomas L. Capahen, John L. Scott, Joshua Burriss, Allen V. Brooks, M. Erwin, Massalon Bell, John V. Schroeder, Christian V. Hammond, James Clark, Hugh Wilson, Robert M. Dubose, C. Whitman, A. L. Gray, John Vance, Samuel M. Barnes, R. P. Morrow, Robert Hutchison, James M. Latimer, Samuel S. Baker. Accounts due Christian Barnes, $15,400, at time of his death dating from 1859 Appraised Sep 3, 1875 by B. D. Kay, T. Baker, Theophilus T. Baker. All accounts deemed very doubtful or worthless and sold on that date for pennies on the dollar. Accounts: Andrew Hill, Wm. Penney, Mrs E. M. Ligon, Jordan A. Ramey, Thomas J. Mabry, James T. Allen, J. R. Ashley, Fenton Hall, W. R. White, Wm. J. Lomax, Mrs. F. Tolbert, George W. Daniel, Jane Giles, Allen V. Brooks, Mrs. A. C. Huckabee, Rev. T. A. Harris, James Prince, W. L. Wharton, Samuel S. Baker, Robert Giles, Wm. A. Pressly, John A. Martin, Samuel Speed, R. H. W. Hodges, Wm. A. Campbell, James Jones, B. Allen, Jane Cater, Thomas Link, R. McCord, James Pursley, Mrs. E. Pursley, Talbert Cheatham, David E. Pursley, John Link, Samuel Link, Dr. James Thomas, John W. Griffin, Pinckney Grant, Robert L. Hardin, James W. Huckabee, J. W. Gregory, Rev. J. D. Burkhead, J. P. Tucker, Harrison Tucker, Augustus Smith, J. M. Moseley, L. W. McAllister, J. M. White, Rignul N. Groves, John H. Power, J. W. Beaty, John H. Parker, S. D. Deal, James Grant, Samuel L. Jones, Samuel Lockridge, Andrew Gillespie, Jeff McCracken, Wesley A. Smith, Samuel Williams, Mrs. Hilburn, John M. Campbell, John H. Baughman, James Pressly, Mrs. E. Thomas, Whitfield McCurry, Alex. Oliver, James Bowen, Mrs. C. Tilman, James Clark, John C. Speer, Ansel Swearingen, Nathaniel Cunningham, Campbell McNeill. A number of petitions for and aginst actions were filed. Jun 7, 1875 petition for settlement filed by Ben. J. Cochran & wife Mary E., James M. Barnes of Jameson, Ala., Emma Brown of Jameson, Ala., addressed to Zephaniah Barnes of Louisiana. Sep 7, 1875 Ben. J. Cochran and wife against settlement due to debt owed to the estate by James T. Barnes. James T. Barnes counter sued. W. S. Hammond and wife, Jane received $53. Dec 25, 1877 Zephaniah W. Barnes of Louisiana received $203.81. Estate Setlement May 28, 1881. (7) Legatees each received $334.85. 1. Jane T. Hammond 2. Zepahaniah W. Barnes 3. Albert Barnes and Emma Brown children of Alpheus E. Barnes deceased 4. James T. Barnes 5. Rosannah P. Barnes wife of George Morrow 6. Mary E. Cochran wife of Ben. J. Cochran deceased of Monmount, Ill. 7. Christian V. Barnes.

BOX 170 PACK 4554   WRIGHT H. BLACKMON   1865

Administrator: Mary Jane Blackmon-wife. Bond Dec 18, 1865 of $1,000 by Mary Jane Blackmon, J. B. Black, Sterling E. Graydon. Appraisal Jan 4, 1866 by Joel W. Townsend,

A. C. Watson, Ben. Z. Herndon. Esttae Sale Jan 4, 1866 netted $31.90. Only buyer a sale was the widow, Mary Jane Blackmon. Estate Settlement Jun 10, 1869. A judgement filed against the estate by Lewis D. Merriman greatly exceeded the woroth of the estate.

BOX 170 PACK 4555   JASON T. BROOKS   1865

Confederate Soldier. Administrator: Wm. H. Brooks. Bond May 1, 1865 of $50,000 by Wm. H. Brooks, Andrew Gillespie, M. D. Brooks. Appraisal Nov 8, 1865 by James Pursley, John J. Edwards, David M. Wardlaw. Held notes on: W. A. Allen & James L. Allen, Thomas W. Allen, J. & R. J. White, James M. & J. W. Perrin, Wm. O. Pursley. Estate Sale Nov 9, 1865 netted $2,402. Buyers at sale: Wm. H. Brooks, Francis A. Wilson, J. J. Gray, Lewis Doweler, John Able, Isaac Kennedy, Leroy J. Johnson, John A. Wier, A. Watson, Isaac Kennedy, E. McNeill, John Enright, Jeff McCracken, Thomas McNeill, James W. Perrin, S. E. Cheatham, Campbell McNeill, David Knox, A. B. Hamlin, Dr. J. T. Boyd, Wm. Magill, Johnson Link, Dr. J. W. Thomas, John Walker, John Ligon, David Wardlaw, Jordan A. Ramey, Dr. Thomas J. Mabry, Lewis Drennan, James Gilliam, H. R. Burdette, Joel Smith, Wm. McMillan, J. A. Williams, Samuel Carter, Edward Westfield, J. J. Devlin, James Devlin, John Owen, John Hamilton, Joseph Edwards. Final estte return: Oct 19, 1874.

BOX 170 PACK 4556   J. M. G. BRANYON   1869

Deceased died fall of 1865. Administrators: Richard G. Kay, Rosannah Branyon-wife. Bond Feb 26, 1866 of $3,000 by Rosannah Branyon, Richard G. Kay, Thomas W. Branyon, Stephen M. Tribble. Appraisal Mar 14, 1866 by Wm. Armstrong, Thomas M. Branyon, Lemuel W. Tribble. Held notes on: Wm. Clinkscales, Wm. Allen, A. Branyon, Richard Taylor, George Alewine, Thomas M. Branyon, J. A. Hall, W. T. Walker, W. L. Burton, James Adams, Margaret Alewine, J. S. Robinson, W. C. Hall, Bartholomew Darby. Estate Sale mar 15, 1866. Buyers at sale: Widow, L. W. Kay, Stephen M. Tribble, Robert Seawright, Richard G. Kay, W. N. Wilson, George W. Mitchell, Thomas M. Branyon, J. Smith, A. T. Armstrong, Chistopher C. Ellis, James Bannister, E. Pruitt, Ebeneezer E. Pressly, C. Cox, G. S. Burton, M. Kay. Partial Estate Settlement Mar 1866. Wife, Rosannah Branyon $51.191 (5) Children each $20.76. 1. Reuben O. Branyon 2. Margaret E. wife of E. O. Pruitt 3. John T. Branyon 4. Lemuel J. Branyon 5. Mary T. Branyon. Estate Settlement Mar 15, 1869. (5) Children as in partial settlement each received $302.52.

BOX 170 PACK 4557   CHARLES E. BROOKS   1863

Confederate Soldier died as Prisoner of War at Camp Chase Ohio. Administrator: Wm B. Brooks-father. Bond Oct 25, 1865 of $5,000 by Wm. B. Brooks, Stanmore B. Brooks, Henry H. Creswell. Father: Wm. B. Brooks. Widow and (2) Children. Lived at New Market. Appraisal Nov 8, 1865 by Jonathan S. Chipley, Wm. H. Watson, W. R. Brinkley, A. Anderson Petrer McKellar. Estate Sale Nov 8, 1865 netted $2,857. Buyers at sale: John Butler, H. A. Hollingsworth, Stanmore B. Brooks Jr., Frank Johnson, John R. Moore, Ann Elmore, Larkin Reynolds, Thomas Chipley, Wm. P. McKellar, Alex. McNeill, John R. McKellar, Stanmore B. Brooks, J. Ramsey, John L. Hearst, George W. Caldwell, John T. Parks, Wm. H. Watson, A. F. McCord, James Morrow, W. S. Shadrick, Wm. G. Kennedy, Wm. Hunter, Pickens Brooks, Henry Wilkinson, T. A. Watson, E. Anderson, James Bailey, George R. Caldwell, Robert Jameson, Andrew A. Blythe, Thomas L. Coleman. Estate

Settlement Jan 16, 1866. Estate Insolvent: First Class Creditors paid in full. Second Class Creditors owed $3,237 only received $657. 1st Class Creditors were: H. H. Creswell, E. Andrews, Gilliam & Bailey, John G. Barrett, T. A. Watson. 2nd Class Creditors were: J. R. Moore, H. H. Creswell, Johnson Sale, John Malone, Wm. T. Hackett, W. M. Meriwether, Wm. Boozer, J. R. Tarrant, Allen & Seal, G. R. Caldwell, M. C. Taggart, J. M. Benson, Wm. Ellington, W. S. Shadrick, John Butler, J. A. Jordan, T. A. Watson, Silas Ray.

BOX 170 PACK 4558   ARCHIBALD BRADLEY   1866

Administrators: Mary A. Bradley-wife, Patrick H. Bradley. Bond mar 2, 1866 of $14,000 by Mary A. Bradley, P. H. Bradley, Wilson Watkins, Wm. K. Bradley. Appraisal mar 5, 1866 by Edward O. Reagan, Hezekiah Burnett, A. C. Brown, Speed Ethridge. Estate Sale Mar 6, 1866 netted $3,471. Buyers at sale: Mary A. Bradley, Patrick H. Bradley, Phillip King, Dr. Mitchell, David McLane, Edward O. Reagan, E. A. Searles, Thomas Link, Mary Purdy, J. E. Wilson, Wm. K. Bradley, Wilson Watkins, A. T. Robinson, Tyra Biggles, H. A. Martin, George Rosenwike, Fred Cook, Isaac Caldwell, James M. Gilliam, J. S. Creswell, Thomas C. McBryde, Fuller Lyon, Horace Drennan, Archibald Bradley, Wm. Weed, James Newby, John McLane, Andrew J. Weed, Stephen Willis, Joshua Palmer, J. C. Jennings, John Patterson, George A. Hanvey, W. H. Rush, David Ethridge. Partial Estate Settlement Jul 13, 1866. Widow and (5) Children each received $461.85. Estate Settlement Jan 24, 1870 widow who was now married to Dr. Horace Drennan received $398.28. (5) Children each $111.22. 1. Elizabeth Reid 2. Mary Purdy 3. Patrick H. Bradley 4. G. K. Bradley 5. Children of John Bradley deceased (John Bradley, Ellen Bradley).

BOX 170 PACK 4559   DAVID CLELAND   1864

Administrator: Wm. Dickson, bro-in-law. Bond Mar 26, 1866 by Wm. Dickson, J. J. Cunningham, J. J. Lipford. Appraisal Apr 15, 1866 by Conrad Wakefield, David Callaham, Michael McGee, E. B. Norris, James Young. Estate Sale Apr 13, 1866 netted $599. Buyers at sale: J. W. Cann, Hezeiah Wakefield, M. M. Dickson, Wm. Alewine, Ezekiel Wakefield, J. Alewine, James Tucker Jr., J. P. Milford, T. Alewine, J. Bannister, A. Fisher, J. C. Lipford, Joseph Bowen, Wm. Hall, Wm. Ellison, Wm. Dickson, Mrs. Tribble, John A. Wakefield, Charles Cleland, S. M. Bowen, John S. Cann, Thomas B. Milford, J. L. Clinkscales, James Fisher, J. B. Hall, J. M. Bell, James Carwile, David Milford, Henry S. Cason, Mary Tucker, Archibald M. Pettigrew, Jane Haddon, Thomas J. Lipford, James G. Steifer, J. D. Gaines, Ezekiel B. Norris, W. C. Milford, J. M. Black, W. J. Milford, B. T. Gray, Thomas C. Milford, James Young, M. Crowther, Robert Haddon, John W. Ellison, Conrad Wakefield, Wm. Boyd, Robert Stuckey, David Murdock, Elias D. Pruitt, M. M. McGee, J. J. Shirley, Michael Alewine, Dr. J. W. Milford, J. W. Shirley. Estate Settlement Dec 15, 1870. (6) Distrbutees: Widow, Eliza Cleland, received $299.46 and (5) Children each $41.29. 1. Children of Elizabeth Milford 2. Children of Jane wife of J. C. Milford 3. Nancy Cleland 4. James Cleland 5 Charles Cleland. Nov 16, 1870 W. T. Milford, Ann E. Milford, Talitha R. Milford each received $7.50. Dec 5, 1870 J. W. Ellison $7.50. Dec 3, 1870 W. T. Milford, Wm. Ellison each received $2.50. Jan 23, 1871 F. E. Hampton $5. Feb 21, 1871 Nancy Cleland $41. Apr 29, 1871 Charles Cleland $11. May 4, 1871 Anne E. Milford, Talitha R. Milford $2.50 each. Jan 20, 1872 D. M. Milford $41.20. Mar 8, 1881 W. J. Milford $8, Nov 24, 188- Elaine McMahan $10.75.

BOX 170 PACK 4560   J. WILLIS COBB   1864

Administrator: Mary P. Cobb-wife, Wm. B. Roman. Appraisal Jan 10, 1866 by John S. Turner, James A. Ellis, Simpson Waite, Wm. N. Mundy. Estate Sale Jan 11, 1866 netted $1,320. Buyers at sale: Mary P. Cobb, Miss Emma Cobb, Charles A. Cobb Jr., Andrew J. Buchanan, Dr. Franklin Gary, Francis A. Connor. Estate Settlement Dec 12, 1866. Widow $145.86 and (7) Children $41.67 each. Only Victoria wife of Anrew J. Buchanan and Emma Cobb named.

BOX 170 PACK 4561   SAMUEL G. COTHRAN   1864

Administrator: Wade E. Cothran. Bond Dec 4, 1865 of $3,000 by Wade E. Cothran, John C. Chiles, James S. Cothran. Appraisal Dec 12, 1865 by Samuel Perrin, John C. Chiles, James H. Wideman. Estate Sale Dec 12, 1865 netted $893. Buyers at sale: Wade E. Cothran, John L. Harmon, Robert T. Bell, Robert W. Lites, Samuel B. Cook, E. L. Cothran, Charles Smith.

BOX 170 PACK 4562   SAMUEL CALDWELL   1862

Administrator: Mary F. Calwell-wife. Bond Feb 16, 1866 of $1,000 by Mary F. Caldwell, James K. Vance, John Vance. One minor child, not named. Appraisal Feb 20, 1864 by John Vance, Albert M. Graham, Samuel Graham. Estate Sale Feb 20, 1864. Buyers at sale: Mary F. Caldwell, Casper Sharp, Samuel Graham, A. D. Adams, M. H. Robertson, John Higgins, Wm. Hodge, Albert M.. Graham.

BOX 170 PACK 4563   R. FLETCHER CROMER   1863

Administrator: Dorothy A. Cromer-mother. Never Married. (5) Brothers with one deceased leaving (3) Children. (4) Sister. Brothers and sister not named. Appraisal Nov 29, 1865 by J. F. Keller, Wm. McNary, James Strawhorn. Estate Sale Nov 30, 1865. Buyers at sale: Dr. A. P. Boozer, Dorothy A. Cromer, Louis Rich, Frank Robertson, Olin Watson, Warren Brooks, C. M. Ritchie, J. F. Keller, Wm. McNary, Wm. Mundy, Mrs. R. P. Cromer, A. B. Hamlin, Thomas J. Ellis, Thomas Mahon, James A. Ellis, J. W. Keller, John P. Cromer, Thomas Blake. Estate Insolvent.

BOX 170 PACK 4564   ELIZABETH CLAY   1865

Will dated Jul 30, 1865 Witnesses: Moses O. Talman, James E. Baker, C. J. McAllister. Executor: Wm. A. Clay-son. Grand Daughters: Lucretia Paycos? had (2) Children, Elizabeth Clay, Catherine F. Wells. Owned house and lot in Mt. Carmel. Appraisal Nov 9, 1865 by Philip LeRoy, James McKelvey, John O. Lindsay. Held notes on: John Patterson, Thomas McAllister, Samuel Jordan, Thomas Frith. Last estate return Oct 24, 1879.

BOX 170 PACK 4565   BARNEY CORRIGAN   1863

Administrator: James Wardlaw Perrin. Bond Nov 28, 1865 of $6,000 by James Wardlaw Perrin, Thomas C. Perrin, James S. Cothran. Held notes on: Joshua Dubose, Francis A. Calhoun, Alex. R. Houston.

BOX 170 PACK 4566   THOMAS W. CHILES   1864

120

Deceased died Oct 11, 1865. Administrators: John H. Chiles, George P. Chiles. Bond Nov 6, 1865 of $20,000 by George P. Chiles, lalrkin Reynolds, J. L. Pressly, J. H. Wideman. Widow and (5) Children. Appraisal Nov 21, 1865 by Wm. S. Harris, Wade E. Cothran, John C. Chiles, John L. Devlin. Deceased had $10,290 in gold on hand at his death. Owned 886 acres of land. Held notes on: Robert W. Lites, Israel Bonds, Mary Smith, Adam Wideman, Wm. C. Puckett, J. L. Pressly, Reuben Weed, Francis C. Gray, Wm. S. Harris. Estate Sale Dec 12, 1865 netted $10,919. Buyers at sale: George P. Chiles, Patrick H. Bradley, James Martin, Andrew J. Weed, Thomas C. Perrin, Thomas O. Creswell, James Reagan, John L. Harmon, R. G. Russell, Robert W. Lites, A. Ramsey, Robert F. McCaslan, Wm. H. Butler, J. J. Devlin, Wm. S. Harris, Larkin Reynolds, Samuel B. Cook, E. G. Hinton, Ben. Harveley, Charles Smith, James Bailey, Henry E. White, J. Gibson, John L. Devlin, J. Dendy. Estate Settlement Mar 14, 1867. (6) Legatees: 1. Jane H. Bradley wife of Patrick H. Bradley had been advanced 67 acres plus 647 acres of land 2. Mary Isabella wife of Robert W. Lites 3. Frances wife of Dr. Reuben F. Gray 4. John H. Chiles had been advanced the Hearst tract of 172 acres plus the Royal tract 5. George P. Chiles 6. Mrs. Chiles.

BOX 170 PACK 4567   WILLIAM T. DRENNAN   1864

Deceased died Jan 23, 1866. Administrator: John O. Lindsay, son –in-law. Bond May 3, 1866 of $6,000 by Moses O. Talman, John I. Bonner. Appraisal Nov 26, 1866 by Thomas B. Scott, Gilbert C. Tennant, Samuel R. Morrah, Moses O. Talman. Estate Sale Nov 27, 1866. Buyers at sale: Louis Covin, Samuel R. Morrah, Moses O. Talman, John O. Lindsay, Thomas J. Lanier, Ed. Cowan, Wm. Walker, J. R. Dubose, Andrew Guillebeau, Elijah LeRoy, Thomas B. Scott, Francis A. Calhoun, D. M. Rogers, Wm. Covin, James McCaslan, Thomas Hemminger, Augustus Cowan, --- Albridge, Dr. Edmunds, J. Tennant, Wm. Prather, John I. Bonner, Peter L. Guillebeau, Joseph McComb, Wm. McNair, Wm. Drennan, Wm. Lindsay.

BOX 170 PACK 4568   J. F. H. DAVIS   1864

Administrator: Henry Riley. Appraisal Nov 14, 1865 by James Creswell, Wm. Blake, John G. Boozer. Owned house and lot in Town of Greenwood, store building in Greenwood, livery stables in Greenwood. Held notes and accounts from 1856 on: John Boozer, Wm. Buchanan, James Wesley Buchanan, J. Thomas Buchanan, Stephen Elmore, Wallace Wilson, Stanley Crews, John Fowler, Francis Logan, Robert R. Riley, J. J. Harper, Andrew J. Woodhurst, P. W. Goodwyn, James W. Irwin, Z. Sparks, R. G. Level, James Anderson, John L. Logan, Thomas H. McCurry, Thomas B. Milford, B. D. Worrell, Vachel Hughey, John Vance, J. F. Tolbert, James H. Riley, Wm. McNary, Andrew Riley, James Anderson, John G. Boozer, Jesse C. Ellis, Tapley Anderson, James Bailey, Wm. Boozer, John D. Adams, W. T. L. Burrell, James E. Hughey, Thomas C. Crews, John L. Hearst, Wm. C. Davis, Nathaniel S. McCants, J. W. Irwin, Ben. S. Pulliam, John Selby, John R. Tarrant, John C. Walker, Wm. Harrell, E. G. Tillwell, T. P. Moseley, A. P. LeRoy, J. F. Davis, B. F. Davis, George M. Cromer, James M. Edwards, W. K. Blake, James H. Caldwell, Henry Boozer, Joseph Keller, Wm. Scott, Wm. K. Tolbert, Moses C. Taggart, Perryman & Walker, John Irwin, E. C. Selby, Thomas L. Logan, Wm. Montgomery. Estate Sale Nov 13, 1865. Buyers at sale: Widow, Ben. F. Reynolds, Henry Riley, Levi H. Rykard, W. K. Tolbert, Stanmore Brooks, L. F. Riley, Robert Major, James Creswell, S. J. Cobb, Simeon P. Boozer, Thomas

Hearst, Robert Anderson, John Stockman, Wesley West, John Hinton, Willis Cason, Nathaniel Anderson, Silas Ray, J. A. Bailey, E. Anderson, J. Irwin, A. Anderson, Thomas Jones, B. Black. Final estate return 1874.

BOX 170 PACK 4569   JAMES E. EILIS   1867

Administrators: Dorcas Ellis-wife, James A. Ellis. Appraisal Oct 11, 1865 by Charles Smith, Samuel A. Hodges, Wm. N. Mundy, Charles A. Cobb. Held notes on: A. F. Cromer, R. A. Griffin, J. A. Ellis, Wm. J. Lomax. Estate Sale Oct 11, 1865 netted $1,364. Buyers at sale: Dorcas Ellis, A. B. Hamlin, Thomas J. Ellis, J. A. Ellis, J. W. Richardson, Capt. Irwin, Leonidas D. Connor, Sterling E. Graydon, John C. Allen, Wm. McNary, Wm. R. Mundy, W. M. Ellis, Archibald B. Ellis, John D. McKellar, Wm. Hill, Warren Brooks, Martin G. Zeigler, Francis A. Connor, Charles Smith. 1st Estate Settlement Dec 1867. Each child $695, Widow $2,085. 2nd Estate Settlement Mar 21, 1872. Dorcas Ellis received 1/3. (6) Children each $902.34. 1. James A. Ellis 2. Thomas J. Ellis 3. Archibald B. Ellis 4. Wm. M. Ellis being the only heir of Wm. Ellis deceased 5. Children of Robert Ellis deceased a. Elizabeth Verrell b. Jane Young c. James R. Ellis d. Wm. Ellis e. Benjamin Ellis 6. Children of Jesse C. Ellis deceased a. Celestia Ellis b. Anne Ellis.

BOX 170 PACK 4570   JAMES M. EDWARDS   1866

Administrators: Nancy P. Edwards-wife, Henry Riley. Bond Oct 13, 1865 of $3,000 by Henry Riley, Nancy P. Edwards, Levi H. Rykard, Nathaniel Anderson. Appraisal Nov 20, 1865 by Levi H. Rykard, Robert Riley, John G. Boozer. Estate Sale Nov 21, 1865 netted $799. Buyers at sale: George Cromer, Nancy P. Edwards, Simon P. Boozer, J. A. Bailey, George Anderson, John G. Boozer, Henry Riley, Nathaniel Anderson, Edward Hinton, Edmund Anderson, J. Stockman, Levi H. Rykard, Thomas Jones. Estate Settlement Jun 4, 1874. Wife 1/3 = $163. (6) Children each $54.35. 1. Wm. T. Edwards 2. Margaret Isabella Edwards 3. Elizabeth wife of Robert Hinton 4. Owen Edwards 5. John James Edwards 6. Nancy R. Edwards.

BOX 170 PACK 4571   ROBERT ELLIS   1866

Very large estate covering many pages of various financial related information. Will dated Feb 16, 1866. Witnesses: Robert A. Archer, Robert O. Tribble, John N. Young. Executors: Joseph Ellis, John Cowan. Partner in Blacksmith Firm of Ellis & Latimer. Partner was Benjamin M. Latimer. Brothers: John L. Ellis, Joseph Ellis. Sisters: Elizabeth Tribble, Margaret McAdams, Jane Branyon deceased, Nancy Latimer deceased. Nephew: B. M. Latimer deceased. Niece: Mahala McAdams. Willed 70 acres to Free Man of Color Dave. Appraisal Mar 28, 1866 by Robert Pratt, A. C. Hawthorne, John N. Young. Estate Sale Oct 30, 1866 netted $15,247. Buyers at sale: 100 individuals bought at sale. Open Accounts belonging to the firm of Ellis & Latimer dating from 1855: Chirstian V. Barnes, W. B. Grier, Jacob Clamp, John W. Rowland, Robert Ellis, B. L. Bohanen, H. M. Lynn, Wm. Bell, J. F. Watts, B. B. Belcher, R. B. Geiger, P. R. Pinkerton, Joel Morrison, John Gray, Wm. F. Wright, J. R. Underwood, David Duncan, R. Kumminger, J. W. Calvert, W. B. Story, B. F. Ellis, S. M. Grier, J. M. Reid, R. C. Ross, J. H. Brady, A. S. Reid, Milton Carwile, John Johnson, Wm. H. Thompson, Henry Bratcher, F. M. Bell, Samuel Maroney, Thomas J. Hearst, R. M. Nelson, Marshall Taylor, John Stephens, Jackson Griffin, P. A. Neel, N. C. Jones, Robert A. Boyd, J. C. Lee, W. J. Verdier,

Hugh Wilson, James Magill, J. L. Pratt, Preston McClellan, Wm. Dawkins, John Gaines, John McDonnell, H. F. Anderson, C. P. McAllister, Wm. Stansel, B. F. Wakefield, Miss Joe Pope, James L. Pratt, F. A. Weed, Joseph Smith, A. F. Haddon, A. E. Burgess, W. B. Ware, Sitton & Rowland, J. C. McCloud, Jasper Hawthrone, John Ricketts, A. H. Smith, D. M. Montgomery, Samuel D. Bostick, E. J. McDaniel John Smith, M. T. Hughes, P. R. Stein, J. Y. Reid, Samuel Donald, Robert Patterson, Wm. Hardy, J. A. Wilder, A. E. Hughes, David Junkin, George A. Suddeth, Samuel Robison, S. A. Winestock, Wm. Robertson, W. W. Sharp, J. L. Carwile, David Duncan, R. P.. Allen, Miss Annie Bell, S. A. Daniel, W. R. Luck, Miss Linda Clamp, W. V. Witherspoon, J. L. Hodge, J. F. Donnald, J. W. Brooks, B. F. Brown, James Ware, Marvin Trowbridge, J. M. Hughes, Moses W. Love, James Taylor, Lucinda Thomas, Edward Gaines, L. W. Tribble, Richard Ashley, Warren McCloud, B. A. Arnett, A. J. McQuiston, Amanda Hughes, Wm. Austin, G. W. Hines, W. C. Winn, Bonner & Lindsay, John M. Pruitt, John Hall, J. E. Caldwell, R. A. Boyd, V. H. Lyon, Basil Callaham, Robert A. Archer, John F. Botts, Joohn F. Coker, Haywood Davis, W. L. Gordon, Thomas C. Seal, Frances Gambrell, W. P.. Martin, B. M. Latimer, James Cowan, Arnett Richey, Augustus Ansley, Nancy Robertson, Henry Crawford, H. G. Hughes, E. E. Lindsay, John W. Callaham, S. A. Crawford, James Sitton, R. M. Wilson, W. Chisolm, Samuel Knox, M. J. Doutz, W. A. Stone, John Pitts, W. M. Callaham, W. B. Clinkscales. Notes held by the firm of Ellis & Latimer allowed to Benjamin Latimer: Preston McClelland, John T. Botts, James Magill, Richard Ashley, James Wier, R. Krumminger, Samuel Robertson, Wm. Hardy, James L. Pratt, Robert T. Gordon, S. M. McClain, B. F. Brown, S. A. Gridler, Moses Love, Wm. B. Clinkscales, Wm. A. Storm, J. B. Murphy, Z. R. Jones, Robert Latham, Robert A. Archer, J. R. Underwood, L. W. Tribble, W. F. Wright, Christian V. Barnes, Hugh Wilson, J. Y. Weed, Joseph Smith, David Duncan, M. J. Dowty, Wm. M. Callaham, John Gaines, Wm. Morrison, J. M. Hughes, Haywood Gambrell, George A. Suddeth, Lucinda Thomas, E. J. Hughes, J. F. Coker, Joel Morrison, Marvin Trowbridge, John Pitts, Edmond Gaines, David Junkin. Notes held by the firm Ellis and Latimer allowed to Robert Ellis: John M. Bell, F. M. Bell, James Patterson, James T. Fleming, W. B. Bell, James H. Patterson, Frederick V. Bell, H. W. Shaw, James P. Bowie, Jeptha Murdock, Ben. McClain, Thomas J. Shirley, Wm. McClain, S. T. Bratcher, P. Krumminger, Samuel McClain. Estate Settlement May 31, 1870. (10) Legatees each $391.09. Persons mentioned in settlement: T. J. Burton, Nancy Latimer, Jane Branyon, Joseph Ellis, John Cowan, James Cowan, John L. Ellis, W. T. Latimer, R. W. Burts, M. L. Latimer, S. E. Latimer, A. E. Latimer, G. E. Mattison, Mary J. Callaham, Samuel Callalham, Sarah Lyon, R. H. Branyon, John McAdams, Bennett McAdams, Ann Hawthorne, G. Toney. Estate activity as late as Apr 11, 1882.

BOX 170 PACK 4571   SARAH EDWARDS   1865

Administrator: Henry Riley. Appraisal Jan 6, 1866 by Levi H. Rykard, John G. Boozer, Birt Riley. Estate Sale Jan 6, 1866 netted 425. Buyers at sale: Mrs. N. P. Edwards, Nathaniel Anderson, Henry Riley, Edward hinton, Birt Riley. Estate Settlement Aug 18, 1866. Bailey & Boozer paid $12 for coffin. Estate Insolvent.

PACK 4572   MISSING

BOX 171 PACK 4573   MARTIN C. GARY   1865

Will dated Jul 25, 1863. Witnesses: J. N. Cochran, Newton Sims, Francis A. Connor. Executrix: Louisa K. Gary. Appointed Oct 17, 1865. Nephew: Summerfield M. G. Gary.

BOX 171 Pack 4574   ALBERT CALVIN GRAHAM   1865

Confederate Soldier. Killed in action. Never Married. Father: John Graham. Administrator: Wm. H. Purkerson, brother-in-law. Bond Mar 5, 1866 of $1,000 by Wm. H. Purkerson, Robert C. Gilliam, James M. Graham. Estate Settlement Dec 21, 1869. (6) Distributees each $70.11. 1. Mary Graham deceased 2. James Graham 3. Sarah Graham 4. Martha Purkerson 5. Margaret Graham 6. Eliza Graham. A. A. Blythe paid $10.82 for coffin.

Box 171 PACK 4575   ABRAHAM HADDON   1865

Will dated Dec 25, 1863. Witnesses: Andrew C. Hawthorne, John I. Bonner, Oliver P. Hawthorne. Sons: Robert W. Haddon, Abram Wilson Haddon, John T. Haddon. Executors: Robert W. Haddon - son, John T. Haddon – son. Daughter: Elvira wife of James Magill. Sons: John T. Haddon, Abram Wilson Haddon, Robert W. Haddon. Appraisal Nov 1, 1865 by Thomas C. Ellis, John I. Bonner, Andrew C. Hawthorne, Joseph Ellis. Owned 324 acres of land. Estate Sale Nov 2, 1865 neted $1,933.07. Buyers at sale: Amaziah Rice Ellis, Alex. Hagen, Robert W. Haddon, Wm. Alewine, David O. Hawthorne, James H. Simpson, J. T. Harris, James Cunningham, John P. Pressly, J. L. Walker, John M. Bell, J. T. Norris, Ben. W. Williams, John Cowan, Michael Alewine, John M. Hawthorne, J. H. Johnston, Jacob Alewine, John T. Haddon, Wm. G. Gordon, James Magill, Andrew C. Hawthorne, Albert Johnston, Chalmers Hadon, Marshall Sharp, T. C. Callaham, John T. McClain, James Taylor, Francis V. Pruitt, Robert F. Bryson, Wm. Power, A. B. C. Lindsay, John I. Bonner, John M. Pruitt, John A. Bowie, Wm. Clinkscales, John R. Ellis, Robert McAdams, Samuel Shaw, America Haddon, Wm. Allen, John N. Young, G. S. Tresvant, Wm. J. Phillips. Estate Settlement Feb 28, 1868. (8) Distributees each $99. 1. Talitha C. wife of John Cowan 2. Josephine daughter of James Haddon deceased wife of Robert F. Bryson 3. S. P. Davis in right of wife who was daughter of Abram Wilson Haddon 4. Albert Johnson and wife Rosanna 5. O. F. Haddon 6. Elivra wife of James Magill 7. Robert W. Haddon 8. Not Named. Also receiving inheritance: Indiana wife of John H. Allen, Gus Haddon, Martha Haddon, Chalmers Haddon. Final estate return made Feb 25, 1870.

BOX 171 PACK 4576   ALEXANDER HUNTER   1864

Will dated Jul 20, 1864. Witnesses: J. D. Burkhead, Elvira F. Wood, W. G. Clark. Codicil Jul 25, 1865 which acknowleged that slaves were free. Witnesses J. A. Pressly, Thomas H. Cunningham, Joseph L. Gibert. Executors: James R. Cunningham, Samuel Hunter. Daughter: Sarah T. Cunningham willed 569 acres. Sons: Samuel Hunter, Ben. T. Hunter, Theodore Hunter, Edwin Hunter, Alexander Hunter. Grand Son: James Ramsey son of daughter Sarah. Appraisal Feb 17, 1866 by James M. Martin, Andrew J. Clinkscales, Peter Gibert. Owned 70 slaves and much land. Estate Sale Dec 6, 1866. Buyers at sale: Mrs. S. J. Cunningham, R. L. Williams, Wm. A. Giles, Samuel Hunter, J. R. Cunningham, George W. Daniel, James W. Huckabee, F. P. Robertson, Wm. Taggart, Peter Gibert, Wm. D. Mann, Joseph T. Bowen, James A. McKee, Ephraim F. Power, J. H. Bell, Aaron Boggs, Clement T. Latimer, J. T. Baskin, David S. Benson, Wm. J. Robertson, Maj. Dixon, J. T.

Liddell, Thomas A. Daniel, James M. Martin, Noble Bell, Lovitt G. Johnson, J. E. G. Bell, Mrs. Talbert, George W. Bowen, Gibert G. Dawson, Mc. Cochran, Andrew J. Clinkscales, Craig Milford, Ben. W. Williams, T. D. Young, Edward Cowan, Andrew J. Speer, J. W. Crawford, Martin Campbell, Samuel Gilmer, Christian V. Barnes, George L. Bell, James Clark, Elijah H. Speer, Massalon Bell, W. L. Prince, John W. Power, David Knox, Joel J. Lipford, Rignul Groves, Cassel Loter.

BOX 171 PACK 4577   JONATHAN JOHNSON   1857

Will dated Dec 14, 1855. Proved Dec 16, 1865. Witnesses: James E. G. Bell, James G. Johnson, Robert T. Bell. Appraisal Jan 2, 1866 by James E. G. Bell, Charles P. Allen, James M. Martin. Children: 1. Lovitt Green Johnson 2. Nancy wife of John M. Moseley 3. Huch Mecklin Johnson 4. Rebecca Johnson 5. Martha Bruce. Margaret E. Black.

BOX 171 PACK 4578   WILLIAM JAY   1865

Will dated Aug 27, 1863. Witnesses: W. J. Keller, Andrew J. Feguson, F. Jay. Executors: Hulda Eleanor Jay-wife, Tyra Jay-father. Appraisal Mar 28, 1865 by George W. Pressly, James Drennan, W. B. Keller, Robert W. Lites. Held notes on: J. L. Sibert, G. W. Bland, Thomas Magill, John Douglass.

BOX 171 PACK 4579   ELIZABETH JONES   1864

Administrator: Robert Jones. Bond Dec 15, 1864 of $18,000 by Robert Jones, Willy Ellis, Ben. F. Roberts. Appraisal, no date, by John A. Wier, John A. Hunter, James A. Allen.

BOX 171 PACK 4580   ROBERT P. KNOX   1866

Will dated May 18, 1865. Witnesses: Wm. C. Moore, Thomas G. Herbert, Isaac Branch. Administrator: John Knox-brother. Brothers: David deceased, Nathaniel deceased. Sister: Martha Pennal. Appraisal Sep 1865 by James Gibbes, John A. Hunter, R. A. Martin, John Taggart. Estate Sale Sep 3, 1865 netted $178. Buyers at sale: Campbell McNeill, Robert H. Wardlaw, Wm. H. Taggart, John Knox, Wm. Bonds, Barney O'Connor, Morris Roche, A. Baker, John Aldons, Enoch Nelson, Hiram T. Tusten. Estate Settlement Jul 26, 1875. John Enright paid $75 for funeral. Estate Insolvent. Final estate release Jul 27, 1878.

BOX 171 PACK 4581   DAVID KNOX   1864

Administrator: Nancy Knox-wife. Bond Nov 11, 1865 of $3,000 by Nancy Knox, Leroy J. Johnson, James H. Cobb. Appraisal Dec 13, 1865 of $353 by James Pursley, Robert D. Crawford, Charles Evans.

BOX 171 PACK 4582   MARY KAY   1864

Deceased died in fall of 1864. Will dated Nov 28, 1864. Witensses: John Pratt, Sarah E. Wright, Ed. Johnson. Administrators: Andrew C. Hawthorne-friend, James B. Kay-friend. Individuals participating in the will: Larkin Barmore, Permelia Rasor wife of Ezekiel Rasor, Polly Hawthorne wife of Andrew C. Hawthorne, Nancy Sharp wife of Marshall Sharp, Margaret Donnald wife of Wm. Donnald, Eugenia Brownlee wife of

125

Hugh Brownlee, Lucinda Bell wife of Wm. Bell, Mary Tribble wife of Dr. George Tribble, Valentine Young, John Edward Hodges, Children of Charles Hodges, Nicholas Ware Kay. Appraisal Dec 28, 1864 by Albert Johnson, Thomas Crawford, John L. Ellis. Estate Sale Dec 29, 1864. Buyers at sale: J. B. Kay, John I. Bonner, E. J. Cox, George W. Bowen, Albert Johnson, J. L. Robinson, Wm. Brownlee, Richard Taylor, Wm.. Dawkins, Hester Latimer, Dr. H. Latimer, Ben. W. Williams, Wm. Wickliffe, J. R. Ellis, Wm. Clinkscales, Fred. Bell, George Allen, Ezekiel Rasor, Charles C. Pinckney, Rachel Kerr, Wm. Gaines, Wm. D. Duncan, J. R. Wilson, Andrew C. Hawthorne, Wm. Donald, Marshall Sharp. Estate Settlement Apr 18, 1868. (4) Legatees: 1. L. J. Wright 2. Ezekiel Rasor 3. Larkin Barmore 5. Polly wife of Andrew C. Hawthorne. Tombstone cost $35.

BOX 171 PACK 4583   TERESA LIPFORD   1865

Deceased died Jul 7, 1865. Administrator: James L. White, Lewis Rich. Bond Nov 17, 1865 of $10,000 by James L. White, Lewis Rich, E. C. Lipford, Martha A. O. Lipford. Daughters: Mary Jane wife of Lewis Rich, Miriam Frances wife of James L. White. Sister: Eliza Lipford. Mother: Mrs. Martha A. O. Lipford. Owned 737 acres of land. Appraisal Nov 17, 1865 by Samuel Morrow, John M. Ewing, Wm. Lyon, Larkin Reynolds. Estate Settlement Nov 17, 1865. Sister, Eliza L. Lipford and Mother, Mrs. Martha A. O. Lipford received full claims.

BOX 171 PACK 4584   STEPHEN LEE   1864

Will Sep 11, 1864. Witnesses: D. M. Rogers, James Taggart, M. L. Moragne. Executor: James McCaslan. Wife: Jane Lee. Appraisal Nov 22, 1864 by D. M. Rogers, Moses O. Talman, James Taggart, Wm. H. Taggart. Had $2,759 in gold in posssison at time of death. Estate Sale Dec 19, 1865 netted $2,459. Buyers at sale: James McCaslan, Wm. H. Taggart, Jacob Miller, Caselt Break, Joseph McCombs, James Taggart, Thomas McAllister, Samuel J. Hester, C. W. Cowan, Ben. E. Gibert, Dr. Joseph J. Lee, D. M. Rogers, Wm. Tennant, Moses O. Talman, Archibald B. Kennedy, Rev. Wm. H. Davis, J. W. Fowler, Mrs. S. Forgatee, Samuel Able, Robert A. McCaslan, A. F. Cowan, A. M. Watson, Jane Lee, Dr. James A. Gibert, Samuel Link, Dr. A. W. Lathrop, Pinckney Pitts, T. P. Loner, Moses O. McCaslan. Estate Settlement Jun 15, 1868. (2) Shares: 1. Mrs. Jane Lee $1,713 2. Mrs S. Forgatee $1,713. Caroline Jane Darracott wife of Wm. Darracott and Sarah Jane Gibert wife of Ben. E. Gibert were willed items.

BOX 171 PACK 4585   RANSOM LOVELESS   1864

Administrator: Hezekiah Elgin. Bond Hezekiah Elgin, Joel T. Elgin.

BOX 171 PACK 4586   ISABELLA MILLER   1865

Administrator: George McDuffie Miller. Bond Nov 6, 1865 of $10,000 by George McDuffie Miller, John T. Miller, John A. Wier. Appraisal Dec 4, 1865 by James T. Liddell, James B. Kay, Robert W. Crawford. Estate Sale Dec 6, 1865 netted $2,003. Buyers at sale: George McDuffie Miller, John T. Miller, Thomas A. Cater, Charles A. Botts, Frederick W. Nance, Wm. J. Phillips, H. Coleman, John T. Owen, Robert C. Sharp. Estate Settlement Dec 7, 1870. (5) Distributees: 1. John T. Miller 2. Dr. T. L. Miller, 3. Thomas

A. Cater in right of his wife S. C. Cater 4. George McDuffie Miller 5. Eugenia A. Melton daughter of H. T. Miller. Coffin cost $21. Tombstone cost $135.60.

BOX 171 PACK 4587   ALEXANDER McALLISTER   1868

Administrator: Jesse A. McAllister, S. C. Clinkscales acted as his agent. Bond Nov 16, 1865 of $3,000 by Jesse A. McAllister, Lewis C. Clinkscales, Gilbert G. Dawson. Wife: Mary McAllister. Appraisal Nov 30, 1865 by John Patterson, Wm. S. Baskin, Wm. Mann, Wm. A. Lesly, J. H. Baskin. Estate Sale Dec 1, 1865 netted $1,427. Buyers at sale: Mary McAlister, Rev. John Burkhead, George W. Bowen, Dr. H. H. Scudday, H. D. Fleming, Robert A. Pressly, John A. Crawford, S. A. McCurry. Estate Settlement Mar 20, 1868. Widow 1/3 = $281, (14) Children each $40.27. 1. Dicey E. McAllister 2. Elizabeth McAllister 3. Nancy A. McAllister 4. Martha Wife of John W. Crawford 5. Sarah C. McAllister 6. Jerusha wife of James McMahan 7. S. C. White 8. T. N. McAllister deceased, daughter Mary Alice whose guardian was G. W. Daniel 9. O. B. McAllister deceased, guardian was Ellvira McAallister 10. Rosetta wife of John A. Crawford 11. John A. McAllister deceased, guardian was Nancy E. McAllister 12. F. N. McAllister 13. J. A. McAllister 14. Elizabeth J. McAllister. Annie Taylor received $40.27. Anna McAllister received $13 being 1/3 of a share.

BOX 171 PACK 4588   JOHN T. McCUEN   1865

Confederate Soldier. Killed in 1863. Lived Fork Shoals, S. C. Adminsitrator: Marshall Sharp who died years before settlement, Mijlton Golden. Bond Nov 6, 1874 of $1,000 by Milton Golden, Albert M. Graham, Wm. H. Robinson. Appraisal Nov 8, 1864 by Wade H. Roberts, Newton Sims, Christopher Smith. Owned 168 acres of land. Wife: Mahala McCuen. Estate Sale Nov 8, 1864. Buyers at sale: J. F. Smith, Mahala McCuen, E. R. Ridgeway, M. Shap, N. J. Estes, J. J. Golding. Dec 29, 1875 Sarah Carolline McCuen daughter of deceased who lived in Greenville, appointed her brother-in-law to collect what was due her. Lavinda Ridgeway daughter of the deceased who lived in Greenville and wife of Elijah Ridgeway did the same. Emily Mooredaughter of the deceased and wife of James Moore did the same. 1874 G. M. Mattison was the guardian of the minor children: 1. Martha M. McCuen age 14 2. John McCuen aage 11 3. Wm. S. Owens age 13 who was the daughter of Mary Owens and Wilson Owens. Heirs of 1st Wife were: 1. Lavinda wife of Elijah R. Ridgeway 2. Nancy Jane wife of Wm. Terry Estes Heirs of 2nd Wife were: 1. Sarah Caroline McCuen 2. Emily wife of James Moore 3. Martha McCuen 4. John McCuen 5. Mary wife of Wilson Owens.

BOX 171 PACK 4589   JOHN McBRYDE   1865

Administrator: John M. McBryde. Bond Sep 18, 1865 of $15,000 by John M. McBryde, John Knox, Adolphius A. Williams, John Enright. Appraisal Sep 19, 1865 by Andrew Small, J. W. Kelley, Wm. C. Moore. Merchant. Notes & Accounts due to deceased as of Sep 1865: George Allen, Dr. Robert A. Archer, John D. Ashmore, S. H. Baird, Mrs. A. F. Baker, Rev. Christian V. Barnes, J. M. Baxter, H. C. Belcher, James N. Belcher, John H. Belcher, W. W. Belcher, Washington Black, John A. Bowie, Archibald Bradley, Dr. Issac Branch, Wm. H. Brooks, John Brown, Wm. H. Bruce, C. Bryant, Miss Buchanan, Armistead Burt, Wm. Burton, H. C. & J. N. Belcher, J. N. Belcher, J. T. Boyd, John A. Calhoun, Talbert Cheatham, James H. Cobb, J. S. Cothran, Mrs. John Cunningham, James

E. Calhoun, Joseph Cheatham, Mrs. C. C. Cochran, J. A. Crawford, Steven Cunningham, Miss Campbell, Thomas Christian, James N. Cochran, Thomas Crawford, Clark & Freeland, --- Crompton, F. A. Cheatham, Jessie Chalmers, J. B. Clinkscales, Francis A. Connor, J. H. Cobb, A. P. Connor, Charles Dendy, John Devlin, Isaac Davis, Bart Dill, N. J. Davis, Jeff. Douglass, De La Howe Est., J. C. Dunlop, E. J. Davis, Thomas Eakin, M. L. Edwards, John Enright, John Enright Jr., Jack Ferguson, James W. Fowler, Samuel Fulton, Robert A. Fair, James Gordon, L. B. Guillebeau, George Graves, Sterling E. Graydon, J. W. Griffin & Martin, James Golding, L. L. Guffin, J. C. Gray, A. L. Gray, W. S. Harris, Rev. Thomas Herbert, B. P. Hughes, M. Hackett, T. Hammond, Thomas Hill, W. M. Hughey, Robert W. Haddon, S. Harrison, Gabriel Hodges, Rev. T. Hunter, Jeptha R. Hamlin, Wm. Harrison, R. W. H. Hodges, James A. Hamilton, Charles T. Haskell, Wm. Howland, Halen Ives, Miss Inglesby, Frederick Ives, R. Ives, Thomas Jackson, H. L. Jefferies, S. Henry Jones, Robert L. Jones, Samuel Jordan, Leroy J. Johnson, Isaac Kennedy, Theodore Kennedy, George Kinlock, J. & N. Knox, Walter G. Keller, Robert Keoun, John F. Livingston, Thomas Lanier, Ben. Lanier, Augustus Lee, J. L. Lee, Mrs. Levy, John W. Lesly, W. E. Lipford, Robert Lites, Dr. J. F. Livingston, Dr. Aaron Lynch, Dr. H. T. Lyon, John G. Lyon, D. W. Laughlin & G. T. Jackson, W. P. McClellan, W. L. McCord, J. C. McKee, David McLane, Wm. McWilliams, Samuel B. McClinton, Thomas J. McCracken, Thomas McNeill, Thomas McMahan, Dr. J. F. McCombs, Wm. McDonald, Wm. McCaslan, Bud McCord, A. L. McFarland, George McCaslan, A. W. McCaslan, Miss S. Martin, F. M. Mitchell, A. H. Martin, Wm. R. Maddox, S. S. Martin, Margaret Moore, John Monroe, Robert Mars, W. D. Mars, Samuel Marshall, T. P. Martin, Joseph T. Moore, Dr. Thomas J. Mabry, James M. Martin, W. A. Moore, Lester Martin, M. A. Martin, R. A. Martin, F. Miller, W. C. Moore, John A. Martin, L. P. Martin, N. F. Morrison, Wm. McMeans, James McCaslan, P. C. McCaslan, Miss J. McCaslan, James A. McCord, Samuel McGowan, W. L. McCord, Enoch Nelson, Edward Noble, Pat O'Keefe, John O'Connell, Rosa Pleniman, J. M. Palmer, Robert Palmer, Thomas C. Perrin, Wm. O. Pursley, O. Porcher, John Patterson, F. A. Porcher, James W. Perrin, George Pressly, Samuel Perrin, Wm. Pritchard, Wm. Ruff, John W. Richardson, Wm. S. Roper, J. T. Robertson, Louis H. Russell, Thomas Robertson, Miss M. J. Russell, D. M. Rogers, Philip S. Rutledge, Edward Roche, Thomas Sanders, John Simpkins, Wm. Speer, Dr. L. C. Service, Wm. Smith, Wm. Sproull, James Shillito, W. J. Smith, Harmon Stevenson, Wm. Shillito, Peter Smith, Thomas Stein, B. B. Simmons, D. R. Sondley, James A. Shillito, Sue Taylor, D. W. N. Turner, E. J. Taylor, John Taggart, Thomas Thomson, C. Trenholm, Wm. H. Taggart, Kitty Tillman, D. McNeill Turner, Taggart, McCaslan & Co., G. W. & J. R. Tolbert, L. F. Tolbert, James Taggart, Dr. J. W. Thomas, Moses O. Talman, Capt. Venable, Wm. Venning, J. J. Wardlaw, Robert H. Wardlaw, W. Watkins, John A. Wier, Edward Westfield, John H. Wilson, Leroy J. Wilson, Miss Margaret Wilson, J. & R. J. White, Patrick N. Wilson, Miss S. Wilson, Wm. Wilson, Adam Wideman, D. Wm. Wilson, Wm. H. Wilson, David J. Wardlaw, Adolphus A. Williams, R. H. Winn, Mrs. Witherspoon, Andrew J. Woodhurst, J. J. Wardlaw, John H. Wilson, Dr. Littleton Yarborough. Estate Sale Oct 3, 1865. Buyers at sale: Philip S. Rutledge, Ames Baker, Wm. Hill, Andrew Small, L. D. Adams, John Small, John Conner, Wm. H. Taggart, Joel Smith, Henry S. Kerr, Wm. C. Moore, Wm. Burns, Alex. Bowie, Wm. A. Lomax, Allen Lee, Adolphus A. Willliams, Thomas Seal, Wm. Lanier, James Norwood, Morris Roche, John Knox, Wm. Kennedy, John M. McBryde, Joseph J. Wardlaw, John Enright, Edward Roche, James W. Perrin, John T. Owen, Wm. Robertson, Enoch Nelson, Alex. Wier, John Gibbes, Robert H. McCaslan, Thomas

Christian, John E. Calhoun, Hiram T. Tusten, Robert H. Wardlw, Ben. McKittrick, David McLane, Wm. L. McCord, --- McCrady, J. H. Belcher, Henry Allen, Samuel J. Davis, Wm. Hodges, Wm. B. Kennedy, J. A. Bowie, Dr. Henry Beard, M. W. Bonds, Wm. Hill, Dr. J. W. Marshall, Wm. G. Neil, John Darragh. Funeral expenses $35 paid to John Enright.

BOX 171 PACK 4590   DR. CHARLES R. MOSELEY   1865

Deceased died Mar 1, 1864. Administrators: Lavinia H. Moseley-wife, John M. Moseley. Bond Nov 8, 1865 of $20,000 by Lavinia H. Moseley, John M. Moseley, Ephraim R. Calhoun, James Gilliam. Appraisal Dec 29, 1865 by Wm. Blake, John H. Logan, Franklin R. Calhoun. Owned home tract of 411 acres and Buchanan trat of 262 acres. Notes and Accounts due deceased at time of his death: Wm. Buchanan, R. P. Buchanan, Mary Riley, James Buchanan, Ben. Roberts, Thomas L. Coleman, Mary Black, Bard Factory, Charles A. Cobb, John Partlow, J. S. Tharp, Ben. Robertson, Mary Meriwether, John M. McClellan, Wm. H. Griffin, James Irvin, Wm. Cobb, James Edwards, J. Ray, Stanley Crews, John Thompson, Wm. Thompson, Wm. N. Mundy, David Moore, Lewis D. Merriman, John Sample, John R. Tarrant, Wm. H. Lawson, Thomas Jones, J. Roberts, Pinckney Riley, James Gilliam. Estate still open Oct 1874.

BOX 171 PACK 4591   FRANKLIN MILLER   1866

Administrators: Elizabeth A. Miller-wife, Davis M. Miller. Bond Apr 13, 1866 of $6,000 by Elizabeth A. Miller, Davis M. Miller, John W. Griffin, Jacob Miller. Appraisal May 9, 1866 by Samuel S. Baker, Elijah H. Speer, Edward Calhoun. Estate Sale Nov 9, 1866 netted $2531. Buyers at sale: Elizabeth A. Miller, J. W. Griffin, Wm. J. Robertson, Wm. Moore, David M. Miller, Robert Hutchison, Lemuel O. Shoemaker, Capt. Parker, Ed. Cowan, E. Yarborough. Estate Settlement Jan 16, 1874. Widow 1/3= $85.35. (8) Children each $21.34.

BOX 171 PACK 4592   JOHN McKELLAR   1865

Deceased died Jul 1865. Administrator: W. P. McKellar-son. Bond Sep 29, 1865 of $10,000 by W. P. McKellar, Peter McKellar, John T. McKellar. Wife: Eliza McKellar. Appraisal Oct 31, 1865 by Henry A. Creswell, Stephen Elmore, Jonathan S. Chipley, W. C. Watson, W. T. Hackett. Owned home tract 311 acres, Henderson tract 150 acres. Estate Sale Nov 1, 1865 netted $3,176. Buyers at sale: Stephen Elmore, T. P. Beasley, Wm. P. McKellar, W. R. Brinkley, James Seal, Adam Freeman, E. Anderson, Gaines F. Ross, T. H. Watson, J. Gilliland, Wat. Freeman, Edward Hinton, Dr. F. R. Calhoun, George W. McKellar, John T. McKellar, Bennett Reynolds, S. Chipley, Robert Lites, Wm. S. Shadrack, Stanmore B. Brooks Jr., Harvey J. Reagan, W. H. Rush, J. Hutchinson, M. H. Wilson, Robert Freeman, J. W. Lites, John Butler, John R. Seal, John L. Hearst, Robert H. Mounce, T. Johnson, Adam P. Boozer, Milton W. Coleman, Henry Wilkinson, J. N. Rush, George Caldwell, T. A. Watson, Hugh A. Hollingsworth, Mrs. E. McKellar, John Freeman, J. M. Reagan, Wm. G. Kennedy, Wm. Blake, James H. Ross. Aug 6, 1866 Peter McKellar and his son, John T. McKellar asked to be relieved of security due to their unsatisfaction with the administration of the estate. Estate Settlement Sep 10, 1866. (6) Legatees each $690 except for Agnes Warren who received $90.90. 1. Eliza McKellar, wife 2. Kate wife of Joel W. Lites 3. Wm. P. McKellar 4. George W. McKellar 5. John R. McKellar 6. Agnes wife of R. R. Warren.

BOX 171 PACK 4594   SUSAN E. McCRACKEN   1864

Administrator: John Rosemond Wilson. Bond Nov 1, 1864 of $5,000 by John Rosemond Wilson, Robert Ellis, John Pratt. Appraisal Nov 14, 1864 by Wm. Clinkscales, Robert Ellis, Robert McAdams. Owned 7 slaves. Held notes on: J. T. Boyd, Dr. Thomas J. Mabry, Philip S. Rutledge, F. J. McCracken, Baird-Westfield & Cheatham, Edward Noble, John Pratt, Lavinia Douglass, Mrs. McMillan. Estate Sale Nov 15, 1864 netted $1,828. Buyers at sale: Andrew L. Gillespie, Wm. Clinkscales, John Rosemond Wilson, Thomas Pearlstein, John Kennedy, M. L. Brown, John Pruitt, Mrs. McMillan, Ben. Pearman, Talbert Cheatham. Estate Settlement May 6, 1865. J. F. R. Wilson her son was the only heir. Coffin & hearse cost $133.

BOX 171 PACK 4595   NIDUS MALONE   1873

Will dated Sep 11, 1863. Witnesses: Levi H. Rykard, Rachel Hughes, Edmund Anderson. Executrix: Louisa Malone-wife, Wm. D. Malone acted as her agent. Daughter: Sarah Frances Malone. Appraisal Oct 19, 1865 of $1987 by Levi H. Rykard, Henry Riley, Vachel Hughey, Edmond Anderson, Peter Rykard. Owned 305 acres of land. Estate still active in 1885.

BOX 171 PACK 4596   FERGUS McMAHAN   1865

Deceased died Oct 1866. Will dated Jul 23, 1864. Witnesses: Thomas B. Milford, Pleasant Ferguson, Dr. G. F. Steifer. Executors: Zilphia McMahan died Mar 1877, John McMahan. Wife: Zilphia McMahan. Daughter: Mary McMahan. Sons: 1. Obediah deceased, his children: John McMahan, Elizabeth McMahan, Andrew McMahan 2. Fergus A. deceased, his children: John McMahan, Nancy McMahan, Thomas McMahan. Appraisal Nov 9, 1865 by W. N. Hall, Wm. D. Mann, J. B. Patterson, Thomas B. Milford, Thomas C. Milford. Owned 325 acres of land in (3) tracts. Had owned 7 slaves. Estate Sale Nov 29, 1877 netted $129.70. Buyers at sale: Mary McMahan, W. L. McMahan, J. F. McMahan, T. T. McMahan, J. B. Hampton, R. Taylor, Sarah Fleming, Warren McClellan, Nancy McCurry, Max Below, A. B. Hamlin, Mary Moore, T. H. Cochran, Asa Hall, Wm. D. Mann, Green Fleming, George Martin, John Ferguson, Arthur M. Erwin, John McMahan, Peston C. Suber, Andrew Sutherland, W. N. Hall, Andrew McMahan, Andrew J. McKee, Mrs. Obediah McMahan, Perrin McMahan, W. L. McMahan, James Hampton. Listed as Legatees: W. M. McCurry, Z. E. Jeans, E. P. Burton, Emily Freeman, M. J. McCurry, J. W. McMahan, Sarah Fleming, Nancy McCurry, J. T. McMahan, S. J. McCoppin, Mary McMahan, J. W. McCurry, J. T. McMahan, S. A. McMahan, S. S. McCurry, Elizabeth McMahan, Andrew McMahan, John McMahan, Wm. L. McMahan. Estate Settlement Jan 19, 1878 & Sep 14, 1878. Legatees: 1. John McMahan 2. Wm. L. McMahan 3. Sarah Fleming 4. Nancy McCurry 5. Ibby McCurry deceased, her children were: Wm. McCurry, Z. E. Jeans, Emily T. Burton, Nancy Freeman, M. J. McCurry, J. H. McCurry, S. S. McCurry, S. J. McCoppin 6. Alexander McMahan deceased his children were: John W. McMahan, Thomas F. McMahan, Nancy McMahan 7. Obediah McMahan deceased, his children were: John F. McMahan, Elizabeth McMahan, Andrew McMahan 8. Mary Jane McMahan. Much petitioning and counter petitioning. Final distribution made Mar 10, 1884 to Georgianna McCoppin. Paid L. C. Clinkscales $5 for coffin.

BOX 171 PACK 4597   JOHN MARBUT   1865

130

Will dataed Sep 10, 1863. Witnesses: Gimma A. Carter, M. E. Meriwether, W. B. Meriwether. Executrix: Martha Marbut-wife. (6) Children: 1. John F. Marbut 2. Susan J. Polatty 3. Mary E. Marbut 4. Martha C. Marbut 5. Robert O. Marbut 6. William R. Marbut. Appraisal Dec 3, 1865 by T. S. Blake, George W. Tolbert, Thomas C. Griffin. Accounts due deceased at time of his death: Zachariah W. Carwile, Wm. P. Andrews, W. L. Andrews, Rebecca McCracken, Wm. R. Hilton, Dr. T. S. Blake, Wm. B. Hill Est., Martin Hackett, John Clem, James Fooshe, Dr. Richard C. Griffin, Dr. G. W. Calhoun, Est. of E. Child, J. W. Lipscomb, Thomas E. Jester, T. C. Griffin. Last estate entry 1868.

BOX 171 PACK 4598   HANNAH McCOMB   1864

Will dated Apr 2, 1860 Witnesses: Elizabeth A. Reid, Wm. P. Keaton, John R. Wilson. Executors: Andrew Jackson McKee, Thomas Crawford. Sons: John McComb, James McComb, William McComb. Daughters: Mary Ann Stevenson, Eliza wife of Jackson McKee, Mariah McComb, Nancy McWilliams, Hannah Haddon. Grand Daughters: Hannah Stevenson, Hannah McKee, Hannah Haddon, Hannah McComb. Appraisal Jun 17, 1864. Owned 4 slaves. Owned 497 acres of land including 63 acres in Greenville District. 1st Estate Sale Jun 24, 1864. Buyers at sale: Abraham Haddon, Adam J. McKee, J. R. Wilson, Wm. G. Gordon, Moses McAllister, Robert A. Fair, Wm. McComb, Thomas S. Stevenson, John T. Owen, F. P. Robertson, Thomas Crawford, Dr. Thomas J. Mabry, Miss Tabitha Radcliffe, John Hagen, Edwin Cater, Richard P. Doyle, Wm. Gordon, James Cunningham, Philip Rutledge, Robert H. Wardlaw, J. B. Cochran, Hiram Tusten, A. B. Hamlin, Robert H. Winn, James Cason, John A.Wier, James Bowie. 2nd Estate Sale Dec 1, 1864. Buyers at sale: Adam J. McKee, Dr. H. T. Lyon, Nancy Botts, J. R. Wilson, Nancy McWilliams, Wm. McComb, John A. Wier, Robert A. Archer, John Hagen, John J. McBryde, Thomas Stevenson, John T. Owens, E. McWilliams, Thomas Crawford, John I. Bonner. Final estte return Feb 1869.

BOX 171 PACK 4599   WILLIAM N. MATTISON   1864

Confederate Soldier, 2nd Lt. 19th S. C. Volunteers. Will dated May 6, 1862 at Corinth, Mississippi. Witnesses: Edward Noble, Wm. H. Hammond, Thomas C. Seawright. Executrix: Nancy Elvira Mattison-wife. Appraisal Dec 1, 1864 of $88 by Reuben Latimer, George Roberts, Robert Brownlee, J. W. Kay, G. M. Mattison.

BOX 171 PACK 4600   JANE MATTHEWS   1864

Was a spinster who lived in Charleston, S. C. Will dated May 21, 1852. Witnesses: W. H. Inglesby, P. C. Guerry, W. J. Herriot. Willed to John Branch son of John L. and Margaretta Branch. Nieces: Lavinia wife of Wm. Pettigrew, Margaretta wife of John L. Branch. Executor: John L. Branch. Jan 6, 1864 John L. Branch and Wm. Pettigrew both signed statements that everything to be their wives and free of their control.

BOX 171 PACK 4601   WILLIAM McILWAIN   1864

Confederate Soldier. Will dated Aug 27, 1863. Witnesses: Mathew McDonald, Wm. Taggart, T. R. Owens. Executrix: Margaret Jane McIlwain-wife. Brother–in –law: Henry B. Nickles. Appraisal May 4, 1865 by John Hagen, Andrew Morrison, Wm. B. Roman, Wm. McIlwain. Owned 87 acres of land.

BOX 171 PACK 4602   JAMES H. MORRIS   1866

Will dated Apr 1, 1862. Witnesses: James McCaslan, Robert A. McCaslan, James W. Child. Wife: Elizabeth A. Morris. Father-in law: Moses O. McCaslan. Appraisal Oct 28, 1864 by James Taggart, John Wideman, Wm. K. Bradley, D. M. Rogers. Estate Sale Nov 27, 1865 netted $1,548. Buyers at sale: Elizabeth A. Morris, W. H. Taggart, Samuel J. Hester, A. Ramey, --- Simpson, Ben. McKittrick, James McCaslan, S. P. Hester, Margaret Morris, Robert A. McCaslan, James McLane, James A. Wideman, G. W. Nelson, Samuel Brown, A. B. Hamlin, James Taggart, John Able, J. R. McComb, J. T. Pitts. Estate Settlement May 9, 1866, no details.

PACK 4603 MISSING

BOX 172 PACK 4604   DAVID TERREL OLIVER   1864

Confederate Soldier. Will dated Feb 13, 1864 Desoto County, Miss. Witnesses: Samuel B. McClinton, George K. Pressly, H. T. Sloan. Executrix: Sarah C. Oliver-wife. Daughter: Lizzie Terrel Oliver. Son: James Simmons Oliver. Brother: John T. Oliver. Appraisal Oct 31, 1865 of $2156 by Samuel B. McClinton, Jonathan Jordan, John L. Pressly.

BOX 172 PACK 4605   JAMES H. PURDY   1865

Confederate Soldier. Will dated Nov 14, 1861 as entering Cnfederate Army in Edgefield in company commanded by Capt. Byrd. Proved: Jul 17, 1862. Witnesses: Edwin Parker, James Moore, John A. Wier. Wife Sarah Jane Purdy. Daughter: Mary Jane Purdy. Uncle: James Irwin.

BOX 172 PACK 4606   JAMES PURSLEY   1866

Will dated Aug 7, 1856. Witnesses: Thomas Thomson, Robert A. Fair, Robert J. White. Executor Wm. O. Pursley-son whodied before settlement, Nathan A. Edwards. Bond Feb 24, 1869 of $1,000 by Nathan A. Edwards, Epaminandos Edwards, John G. Edwards. Wife Nancy Pursley. Sons: Ephraim Pursley deceased, Wm. O. Pursley, John C. Pursley deceased, Robert R. Pursley deceased. Daughters: Margaret Pursley wife of Henry H. Penney, Mary J. wife of Jason T. Brooks. Appraisal Mar 20, 1866 by James Thomas Boyd, Wm. H. Brooks, John S. Williams. Owned 347 acres of land in Abbeville and 135 acres in Pickens District. Estate Sale Mar 20, 1866 netted $921. Buyers at sale: Nancy Pursley, Wm. O. Pursley, John S. Williams, Thomas C. Seal, Dr. J. T. Boyd, Dr. J. W. Thomas, Wm. Wilson, Thomas C. Pressly, David E. Penney, Henry Hammond, John H. Penney, John T. Lyon. Final Estate Settlement Return Jun 20, 1879. Nancy Pursley deceased. Wm. H. Kerr and Nancy Jane Kerr each received $121.93 due from Wm. O. Pursley. Notes from Estate of John H. Kerr: Leroy Johnson, Andrew Gillespie, Wm. O. Pursley, J. H. Gray.

BOX 172 PACK 4607   CHARLES COTESWORTH PINCKNEY   1865

Will dated Mar 14, 1865. Witnesses: G. W. Hodges, Stanley M. Crews, M. M. Stansell. Sons: Charles C. Pinckney, Thomas Pinckney. Executor: Charles C. Pinckney. Many details of receipts and spending. 1st Appraisal Aug 7, 1865 in Abbeville by G. W. Hodges, Stanley M. Crews, Lawrence R. Dantzler. 2nd Appraisal May 12, 1866 at El Dorado,

Charleston District by S. D. Doan, James Shoolbreds, Edmund Mazick. Last estate entry 1871.

BOX 172 PACK 4608   JOHN C. PURSLEY   1864

Confederate Soldier. Will dated mar 7, 1862. Witnesses: Joel W. Lites, Wm. M. Newell, Zachariah Haddon. Wife: Frances E. Pursley. Father-in-law: Talbert Cheatham. Executors: Talbert Cheatham, John A. Wier-cousin. 1st Appraisal Jun 14, 1864 by Wm. O. Pursley, Andrew Edwards, Thomas J. McCracken. Owned 4 slaves. 2nd Appraisal Oct 12, 1877 by Leroy J. Johnson, John J. Bass, Epamenandos Edwards. Estate Sale Nov 14, 1877. Buyers at sale: John A. Brooks who purchased the land, James Knox, John H. Penney, Andrew J. Penney, Nathan A. Edwards, Robert Keoun, Nellie E. Hilburn, Epamenandos Edwards, Charlotte Bowie. Sale of the property of Mrs. F. E. Edwards Nov 14, 1877 netted $37.40. Buyers at sale: Nathan A. Edwards, Charlotte Bowie, Allen McCanty, James Knox, Robert Keoun, David R. Penney.

BOX 172 PACK 4609   BENJAMIN S. PULLIAM   1865

Will dated Mar 24, 1862. Witnesses: R. B. Tarrant, A. R. Tarrant, A. M. Tarrant. Executrix: Frances Pulliam-wife. Bond Feb 13, 1867 of $800 by Frances Pulliam, James Strawhorn, Lewis D. Merriman. Daughter: Belinda wife of Charles Cunningham. Appraisal Apr 29, 1865 by Junius Buchanan, James Strawhorn, Wm. Buchanan, Martin Delaney. Estate Sale Mar 2, 1867. Buyers at sale: Frances Pulliam bought almost everything, J. S. Wright.

BOX 172 PACK 4610   LUCY BELL ROGERS & SUSAN F. ROGERS (minors)   1865

Guardian: Caroline T. Rogers. Bond Oct 9, 1865 of $1,000 by Caroline T. Rogers, J. S. Covin, Philip A. Covin. Received money from the Estate of P. Rogers. 1st Return Mar 16, 1866. Last return Dec 31, 1878 with no receipts but costs of $2.65.

BOX 172 PACK 4611   WILLIAM M. ROGERS   1879

Deceased died in 1863. Administrator: Robert McCraven. Bond Jan 21, 1866 of $3,000 by Robert McCraven, Caroline T. Rogers, Lewis Covin, D. M. Rogers. Widow and (2) Children, no names. Appraisal Feb 1, 1864 by Wm. S. McBride, Ben. E. Gibert, Thomas B. Scott, Peter Jennings, George W. Robinson. Final estate entry 1878.

BOX 172 PACK 4612   JABEZ P. ROBINSON   1865

Administrator: Elizabeth Robinson. Bond Aug 5, 1864 of $10,000 by Elizabeth Robinson, Frederick Cook, Edward O. Reagan. Appraisal Nov 3, 1866 by Wm. McCain, John G. Thornton, Walter G. Keller. Estate Sale Nov 3, 1866 netted $226. No Buyers given. Estate Settlement Dec 4, 1866. (4) Shares each $178.22. 1. Mother 2. R. J. Robinson 3. J. E. Robinson 4. John W. Harveley, infant son of mother and husband, B. B. Harveley. Administrator discharged Feb 1877.

BOX 172 PACK 4613   JAMES C. REID   1864

Will dated Apr 26, 1864. Filed Nov 12, 1864. Witnesses: Mary A. Wilson, Mary Wilson, John Rosemond Wilson. Wife: Fannie A. Reid. Had lived in Mississippi and owned land there. Brother: Lemuel Reid.

BOX 172 PACK 4614   N. W. STEWART   1865

Administrators: Rebecca Stewart-wife, J. J. Cooper. Bond Jan 14, 1865 of $60,000 by Rebecca Stewart, J. J. Cooper, John B. Buchanan, John Sadler. Appraisal Jan 27, 1865 by Thomas C. Griffin, Henry Beard, Richard M. White. Owned 325 acres of land. Notes and Accounts due deceased at time of death: H. G. Anderson, Adolphus Anderson, A. L. Anderson, Wm. P. Anderson, W. J. Anderson, A. T. Anderson, Mrs. J. A. Arnold, W. T. Blake, Dudley Byrd, James B. Brown, J. G. Boozer, James Busby, Robert Brown, James Berry, John Busby, Thomas Brooks, W. C. Braddock, Chase Burgess, Ransom Chaney, J. W. Chappell, S. R. Capie, W. O. Connell, C. V. Carrington, B. Chastain, Wm. A. Cheatham, Dr. J. W. Calhoun, S. M. Crawford, James S. Chaney, W. E. Cain, J. B. Chappell, Jonathan Coward, Willis Chaney, Miss Mary Cheatham, Harriet Childs, Miss Gus Cobb, M. W. Casey, Andrew Cobb, Robert Cunningham, Marcus A. Cason, Thomas Cheatham, R. W. Canady, W. A. Douglass, S. J. Donald, Julius Dean, Dr. W. H. Davis, Joel Fooshe, Ben. Fooshe, Fooshe & Carter, J. H. Fooshe, W. W. Griffin, James M. Gilliam, Harris J. Gilliam, Richard Goodwyn, R. G. Golden, Est. of Sumter Griffin, T. Coleman Griffin, W. W. Goodman, D. M. Hill, J. H. Holt, J. W. Hill, J. C. Hill, Willis Hill, A. J. Haslet, Wm. Hickson, F. G. Holloway, J. J. Jester, J. J. Jennings, Caleb Jackson, James Long, John W. Little, Wm. A. Limbecker, W. H. Lassiter, A. J. Leek, J. W. Lipscomb, J. W. Lockhart, G. M. LeRoy, W. B. Meriwether, John Malone, John Mims, W. H. Meriwether, Luany Moorman, Nathaniel Moore, Miss Martha Marbut, Jesse Manning, Cathryn S. Mathews, Abney Mays, Samuel Maxwell, M. J. Meriwether, Daniel Malone, Milton Mitchell, Harrington Mitchell, Nathaniel McCants, W. E. McCaster, John Owens, John Pressly, A. J. Permenter, John Pitts, A. J. Ponder, W. S. Richardson, W. W. Rotten, John Ross, C. A. Smith, Pat Smith, James W. Smith, John Sadler, Miss E. Stewart, J. W. Statrund?, J. B. Sadler, A. M. Smith, James Gilliam Smith, J. Albinus Todd, Robert R. Tolbert, D. T. Teddars, J. R. Tolbert, Thomas Thompson, J. F. Verrell, A. L. Venning, James Vines, Richard Walls, Wm. A. Williams, Samuel Waite, W. A. J. Ware, John White, M. W. Waldrop, W. A. Williams, John M. Walker, S. Walls, W. H. Winn, Ed Wade, W. C. White, Milton White, A. M. Smith Wilson, Mary Whitley. 1st Estate Sale Mar 5, 1865. Buyers at sale: D. T. Colyer, Patrick Hefferman, W. T. Head, J. Creswell, Jones Fuller, James Gilliam, John Moore, John Sadler, Waller B. Meriwether, John Gaulden, Dr. John Ligon, Nathan Ingram, Harriet Fay, John Day, W. H. Lawton, F. G. Martin, Wm. Dukes, J. J. Cooper, J. Richardson, T. L. Griffin, D. Rampey. 2nd Estate Sale Nov 15, 1865 netted $5,630. Buyers at sale: Widow purchased most of sale items, Mrs. R. Stewart, Jones Fuller, Joel Pinson, Thomas Stewart, Harrison Dukes, Joel Fooshe, Charley Creswell, W. T. Head, Thomas L. Griffin, Ben. F. Day, T. J. Pinson, John Gaulden, Rufus Croxton, W. H. Limbecker, W. R. Helton, Henry Beard, George Tolbert, Ben. F. Casley, John Young, Dr. J. H. Stewart, Nathan Ingram, Daniel Rampey, Wm. Mathis, John Vines, Charles W. Fooshe, Richard M. White, J. Parks, J. R. Bozeman, Wiley Dukes, J. J. Cooper, John Sadler, James W. Fooshe, W. R. Burkhalter, J. R. Bullock, James Richardson.

BOX 172 PACK 4615   ANN SMITH   1865

Administrator: Albert Johnson. Bond Jan 13, 1865 of $4,000 by Albert Johnson, John T. Haddon, John T. Lyon. Appraisal Feb 1, 1865 by Henry S. Cason, James W. Black, Joshua Ashley, Thomas Davis. Held notes on: Wm. Bass, John Pratt, Albert Johnson, Thomas J. Cunningham, Joshua Ashley, P. A. Sims, John T. Haddon, E. A. Clinkscales, J. W. Black, E. Cox, J. B. McWhorter, Thomas J. Hill, Dr. Aaron Lynch, Ben. W. Williams, Theresa Ware, R. A. Ware, Martha Ware, Jane Ware, S. E. Phillips, Robert McAdams, John W. Power, W. Alewine. Estate Sale Feb 1, 1865. Buyers at sale: W. Alewine, Miss E. Lynch, J. W. Black, J. B. McWhorter, Joshua Ashley, Albert Johnson, Sarah Ware, S. Ashley, Jane Ware, E. Cox, Ben. W. Williams, E. P. Johnson, Jane Haddon, Thomas J. Hill, John Pratt, W. A. Black, J. N. Mitchell, J. F. Fleming, S. E. Phillips, Henry S. Cason, Miss E. Clinkscales, Fed Bell, John W. Power, Wm. A. Fleming, J. W. Black, John Steward Cann, Dr. H. Latimer, M. S. Ashley, F. P. Robertson, Robert McAdams.

BOX 172 PACK 4616   WILLIAM R. SALE   1864

Will dated Aug 13, 1861. Filed Jul 21, 1864. Witnesses: Wm. P. Andrews, Wm. R. McKinney, Wm. S. Hutchison. Executor: Johnson Sale. Uncle: Johnson Sale. Niece: Elvira Ann McKellar. Cousins: Josephine R. Lake, Ann A. Scott, James Sale who was the brother of Ann A. Scott. Appraisal Aug 11, 1864 by Irvin Hutchison, Richard Davis, Hugh Porter. Owned 190 acres of land. Estate Sale Aug 11, 1864. Buyers at sale: George W. Tolbert, Robert R. Tolbert, Johnson Sale, Jonathan S. Chipley. Last estate return May 1866.

BOX 172 PACK 4617   JANE Z. H. SWILLING   1864

Will dated Jan 25, 1864. Filed Oct 15, 1864. Witnesses: Nathaniel Gaines, Tabitha Hall, Amarizah Rice. Never Married. Owned 735 acres of land. (4) Sisters: 1. Martha Ann wife of Joseph Charles 2. Tabitha wife of Wm. McFall 3. Nancy wife of Lindsay Pratt 4. Harriet Swilling. Executors: Zachariah Hall-uncle, Wm. T. Milford-uncle. Ordered to appear in court Oct 15, 1875 to settle estate: Joseph Charles and Children (Lucinda P. Charles, Mattie Charles), Caroline McFall, John S. McFall, Wm. A. McFall and Children (Caroline McFall, John S. McFall, Wm. McFall), Lindsay Pratt and Child (Leila Lee Pratt). Estate Settlement Oct 15, 1875 (4) Shares of ¼ each: 1. Hattie Swilling 2. Martha Charles 3. Tabitha McFall, 4. Nancy Pratt. The McFalls lived in Anderson District. Land was partitioned and sold in 1876.

BOX 172 PACK 4618   JOHN SPEER   1870

Will dated Nov 1865. Filed Apr 26, 1866. Witnesses: Mathew McDonald, David J. Jordan, Thomas Thomson. Executor: John C. Speer-son. Wife: Mary L. Speer. Daughters: Eliza Speer, Jane C. wife of Madison Weems, Martha daughter of Jonathan Galloway lived Holmes Co. Miss., Sarah Ellington deceased. Sons: John C. Speer, Wm A. Speer deceased, James G. Speer. Appraisal Apr 28, 1866 & Oct 31, 1866 by Thomas T. Cunningham, W. S. Baskin, H. J. Burton. Estate Sale Oct 31, 1866 netted $5,486. Buyers at sale: Joseph Brough, B. D. Kay, Dr. Baskin, John C. Speer, James Clark, John Craft, Joohn F. Craft, J. P. Tucker, Samuel Hutchison, Wm. Moore, A. Z. Bowman, Thomas Cunningham, Allen V. Brooks, Isaac Johnson, Wm. Taggart, James McBride, Ephraim F. Power, James Bowen, J. O. McKee, J. H. Wiley, M. Galloway, F. P. Robertson, Andrew J. Speer, W. M. Bell, N. Cunningham, G. P. Pettigrew, Johnson Hall, Berry Kay,

W. L. Cleveland, W. T. Mauldin, Joseph Burroughs, Thomas C. Milford, Gus Burton. Lands sold Nov 1868. 1. 365 acres to G. F. Burdette 2. 269 acres to Augustus Scudday3. 146 acres to Theodore Kennedy. Owned 1,100 acres. Children of Wm. A. Speer all lived in Troup Co., Ga.: John A. Speer, Daniel Speer, George Speer, Wm. Speer, Sarah Speer. Children of James G. Speer: Virginia wife of David Sadler lived in Anderson Co.; Catherine Wise lived in Orange Co., Fla; Belton Speer and Arthur Speer lived in Orange Co., Fla. Estate Settlement Nov 12, 1874. (7) Distributees each $1,369: 1. Children of James G. Speer 2. Chldren of Wm. A. Speer 3. Martha Galloway 4. Mrs. Ephraim F. Power 5. Jane Weems 6. Eliza Kay 7. Children of John C. Speer.

BOX 172 PACK 4619   W. CLARK SCOTT   1864

Will dated Mar 25, 1864. Witnesses: Samuel R. Morrah, Thomas McAllister, Wm. M. Sutherland. Son Wm. D. Scott. Nephew: Robert Montgomery McCaslan. Sisters: Sarah E. McCaslan, Mary D. Deason, Nancy Y. Dickson. Executor: Wm. H. Davis. Appraisal Sep 27, 1864 by Wm. T. Drennan, James McCelvy, Samuel R. Morrah. Estate Sale Dec 4, 1864. Buyers at sale: Ed Scott, D. M. Rogers, Samuel Truitt, Peter Guillebeau, S. Covin, J. C. Tennant, Wm. D. Mars, Wm. McCameron, Basil Noble, Dr. J. J. Lee, John O. Lindsay, Reuben Scott, Ben. Andrews, G. W. Robinson, J. W. Robertson, H. R. Burdette, Wm. H. Brough, Thomas McAllister, E. Edmounds, Charles Sibert, Sarah Colvard, Robert Boyd. Estate Settlement May 16, 1865. Wm. D. Scott only heir.

BOX 172 PACK   JOHN F. SIMPSON   1865

Confederate Soldier. Will dated Jul 27, 1863   Filed Oct 13, 1865. Witnesses: E. S. Patton, John M. Hawthorne, Perter Henry. Executor: James H. Simpson-son. Wife: Louisa Simpson. Daughter: Carrie Hazeltine Simpson. Son: James H. Simpson. Appraisal Nov 13, 1865 by James C. Stevenson, Wm. B. Bowie, Peter Henry. Estate Sale Nov 14, 1865. Buyers at sale: James H. Simpson, Mrs. A. T. Simpson, E. B. Bowie, Mrs. M. T. Radcliffe, B. A. Bowie, James Cowan, Alex G. Hagen, J. T. Donald, David P. Hawthorne, Thomas B. Means, Wm. B. Bowie, Wm. Cochran, James Magill, James Cunningham, Wm. Gordon, James C. Stevenson, Ben. H. Eakin, Amaziah R. Ellis, F. P. Robertson, Miss E. McWilliams. Last estte return Mar 2, 1884.

BOX 172 PACK 4621   JAMES H. SHAW   1866

Will dated Jan 28, 1866   Filed Feb 9, 1866. Witnesses: B. M. Latimer, J. H. Ware, B. F. Moseley. Blacksmith. Executor: G. M. Mattison. Wife: Mary Shaw. Son: Richard P. Shaw. Nieces and nephew, children of Jane Taylor: 1. Margaret wife of A. M. Dodson 2. R. T. Kirkpatrick 3. Mary Pratt 4. Barbara brock 5. Jane Johnson 6. Elizabeth Kirkpatrick 7. Hannah Kirkpatrick. Owned a large amount of land as Follows: 1. Gaines and Ware tract 750 acres 2. Homes tract 725 acres 3. Gaines place 136 acres 4. Moseley tract ? acres 5. Johnson place 155 acres 6. Owens place 136 acres 7. Saluda tract 752 acres 8. R. P. Shaw place 700 acres. Land appraised Feb 27, 1866 at $18,964. Appraisal Feb 27, 1866 by Stephen Latimer, B. M. Latimer, W. C. Moseley. Blacksmith Shop appraised by M. Erwin, Wm. Maddox. Owned house and lots in Town of Honea Path. Owned 2 houses and lots plus a store lot in Town of Donalds. 200 pages of Accounts due him at time of his death. Accounts Appraised Apr 8, 1867 by Stephen Latimer, Stephen R. Latimer. Accounts totaled $17,090. Estate Sale Mar 8, 1866. Buyers at sale: James

Taylor, Wm. Maddox, Richard W. Burts, Wm. W. Maddox, J. L. Gilkerson, Thomas Carter, James Seawright, H. B. Davenport, Thomas Moore, Gideon G. Stone, R. C. Chamblee, A. C. Magee, M. T. Davenport, M. H. Deal, W. A. Kay, R. P. Shaw, J. L. Brock, Mason Kay, A. T. Armstrong, A. M. Dodson, John Scott, M. Erwin, Silas Jones, J. R. Wilson, C. C. Armstrong, S. M. Agnew, W. T. Latimer, W. H. Sharp, Stephen Latimer, J. B. Dove, M. M. Vandiver, W. S. Vandiver, Wyatt Mattison, Ezekiel Rasor, L. J. Rasor, Wm. Traynham, G. W. Johnson. Estate Settlement Jan 11, 1876. Widow had died leaving Son, R. P. Shaw as only heir.

BOX 172 PACK 4622   SAMUEL D. SPEED   1865

Will dated Apr 1, 1859 Filed Mar 31, 1864. Witnesses: John Cowan, R. G. Beasley, Wm. T. Cowan. Executor: Samuel S. Baker. Bond Dec 5, 1865 of $15,000 by Samuel S. Baker, Joseph T. Baker, Ezekiel P. Speed. Wife: Mary E. speed. Sons: Samuel James Speed, Thomas Wade Speed, Wm. Terrell Speed. Brothers: Wm. G. Speed totally insane for 10 years and living in Coosa C., Ala., Ezekiel Pickens Speed refused to be the executor. Appraisal Dec 9, 1865. Owned 735 acres of land. Jan 4, 1878 Wm. M. Taggart appointed Guardian of Wm. Terrell Speed, Elizabeth J. Speed, Ella M. Speed. He was to represent them in action against Thomas Daniels (alias Thomas Fox) who unlawfully withheld possession of some lands due them. Estate still active in Feb 1879.

BOX 172 PACK 4623   JAMES S. SHIRLEY   1866

Will dated Nov 8, 1862. Filed Feb 14, 1866. Witnesses: Samuel Donald, George McAdams, Robert R. Seawright. Wife: Martha Drucilla Shirley. (5) Children, no names. Executors: Martha Drucilla Shirley-wife, Robert N. Wright. Appraisal Mar 27, 1868 by M. S. Strickland, Lemuel W. Tribble, W. P. Wright. Held notes on: Robert N. Wright, Wm. Ricketts, G. W. Alewine, Thomas Greer, B. F. Keaton, E. M. Kay, J. E. Ellis, George Williams, John Moore, T. Griffin, E. J. Wright, H. E. Hughes, J. T. Kerr, Ben. N. Mitchell, Ben. McClain. Last estate return and entry May 1868.

BOX 172 PACK 4624   MISSING

BOX 172 PACK 4625   HENRY D. SCOTT   1865

Administrator: John D. Adams. Bond Feb 6, 1865 of $8,000 by John D. Adams, George W. Hodges, James J. Adams. Appraisal Feb 21, 1865 by Alex. Turner, Wm. Smith, Samuel Graham. Estate Sale Feb 21, 1865. Buyers at sale: Mary Ann Scott, John Golden, W. M. McClain, W. H. Roberson, Samuel Graham.

BOX 172 PACK 4626   WILLIS SADLER   1866

Administrator: John H. Sadler-son. Bond Feb 5, 1866 of $1,000 by John H. Sadler, John T. Johnson, Harris Y. Gilliam. Widow and (5) Children, no names.

BOX 172 PACK 4627   WAT THOMAS   1862

Administrator: James H. Cobb. Bond Sep 10, 1862 of $200 by James H. Cobb, Joseph T. Moore, John Enright. Appraisal Sep 10, 1862 by John A. Hunter, Philip Rutledge, John A. Wier, John Taggart, J. W. McLaren. Estate Sale Sep 10, 1862.

BX 172 PACK 4628   WILLIAM T. TATOM   1866

Administrator: George Graves. Appraisal Dec 28, 1863 by R. H. W. Hodges, Charles P. Allen, George R. McCalla, Thomas J. Hester. Held notes on: Wm. M. Bell, Thomas McAllister, Wm. Truitt, Wm. Delaney, Alex. R. Houston, E. M. Roberts, Thomas J. Mabry, Wm. H. Taggart, Isaac Branch.

BOX 172 PACK 4629   ALBERT THOMAS TRAYLOR   1864

Administrator: Augustus A. Traylor. Appraisal May 12, 1864 by J. C. Beal, Wm. McCain, Ben. Dale Barksdale.

BOX 172 PACK 4630   SAMUEL TURNER   1865

Deceased died Nov 21, 1863. Administrator: John Turner, Emily Turner-wife. Bond Nov 15, 1865 of $8,000 by Emily Turner, John S.Turner, Wm. McNary, John B. Sample. Appraisal Dec 6, 1865 by A. Milton Blake, Charles A. Cobb, A. J. Bell, Robert P. Buchanan, Wm. Buchanan. Estate Sale Dec 6, 1865 netted $2,345. Buyers at sale: Emily Turner, J. T. Turner, Wm. Turner, Charles A. Cobb, J. B. Bozeman, Wm. C. Caldwell, John Hefferman, John B. Sample, J. S. Turner, Francis A. Buchanan, Charles Smith, Wm. Buchanan, Alex. Ellis, A. Millton Blake, John R. Buchanan, Robert P. Buchanan, John W. Fooshe, James K. Vance, C. B. Adams. Estate Settlement Feb 15, 1866. Widow 1/3=$682, (7) Children each $195: 1. Andrew M. Turner 2. Henry R. Turner 3. Oscar S. Turner 4. Emily C. Turner. Only names given.

BOX 173 PACK 4631   ALLEN VANCE   1865

Will dated Jul 29, 1865   Filed Oct 25, 1865. Witnesses: John T. Parks, W. C. Vance, Emanuel J. Wiss, James Bailey. Codicil, no date. Witnesses: John McLees, J. F. Davis, James Bailey. Executor: John C. Vance. Wife: Mary M. Vance. Son: John C. Vance. Daughters: Mary E. Vance, Laura C. Vance. Brother: James W. Vance lived in Louisiana. Appraisal Nov 16, 1865 by John T. Parks, James Creswell, Sobreski Louis Bond. Owned 20 slaves. 1700 acres of land in Louisiana, house and lot in Greenwood, Wier tract of 485 acres. Notes & Accounts due deceased at his death: John H. Logan, Ephriam R. Calhoun, R. Harris, Francis A. Connor, Ben. Z. Herndon, Wm. Vance, Rebecca Tolbert, Seals & Winston, A. B. Reynolds, Wm. Hill, John Vance, Stephen B. Norrell, J. J. Thompson, John T. Parks, Edward Daly, Jerry Evans, C. A. Waller, T. P. Hearst, J. H. Beard, Dr. Norwood, Henry Rykard, Samuel Shackleford, Henry G. Klugh, Wm. B. Logan, Edmond Harralson, Francis Arnold, Moses Shoemate, Robert Major. Estate Sale Nov 24, 1865. Buyers at sale: James A. Bailey, W. P. McKellar, T. T. Whitlow, James Creswell, G. F. Hearst, W. R. Tolbert, Nathan Ingram, A. C. Collins, James Irwin, T. M. Calhoun, W. M. Blake, Wm. Verrell, James Watt, Thomas Hearst, John Boozer, J. H. Marshall, A. M. Aiken, J. F. Keller, G. B. O'Neil, John Hinton, Wm. Smith, Sobreski Louis Bond, John Vance, Larkin Griffin, T. S. Coleman, Wm. Tolbert, J. D. McKellar, A. Bell, James Strawhorn, G. S. Anderson, John Foster, M. S. Ingram, John H. Logan, J. Anderson, J. Beasley, John B. Sample, T. R. Blake, Wm. Anderson, Wm. Turner, Samuel Bell, R. M. Anderson, Wm. C. Venning, W. T. Farrow, W. T. Turner, Andrew Cobb, Ben. Z. Herndon.

BOX 173 PACK 4632   JOHN ROSEMOND WILLSON   1865

Will dated Oct 12, 1861. Filed Nov 7, 1865. Witnesses: A. C. Hawthorne, Abner H. McGee, Ben. F. Moseley. Executors: Lemuel Reid, Mary Willson-wife. Wife was the daughter of Dr. Reid. Daughter: Eliza Jane Miller. Son: James Willson. Appraisal Nov 13 & 14, 1865 by Wm. Clinkscales, Thomas Crawford, Robert Pratt, Robert McAdams. Held notes on: Thomas B. Milford, Wm G. Killingsworth, John Wakefield, Joseph F. Bell, Wm. Pratt, James Alex. Richey, Ben. McClain, Samuel Mitchell, Robert A. Archer. Estate Sale Nov 15-17, 1865. Buyers at sale: Abner L. Hughes, Ben. H. Eakin, Richard Duncan, Rev. Robert C. Grier, Robert Crawford, Wm. T. Phillips, Pickens A. Tribble, Wm. McDuffie Cochran, John A. Wier, Jacob Clamp, Henry Clamp, J.. H. Bannister, Wm. L. Kay, Samuel Shaw, J. T. Elgin, Wm. Pruitt, James Pratt, Lemuel Reid, G. S. Trevant, Caleb Cullins, John Cowan, James Bell, James E. Anderson, Oliver P. Hawthorne, Ben. Pearman, Wm. H. Burns, James Carlisle, Philip Rutledge, John R. Wilson, James Cowan, A. C. Hawthorne, Wm. C. Pruitt, Thomas Pearlstein, Lafayette Mitchell, Wm. Clinkscales, Amarizah R. Ellis, John I. Bonner, Edmund G. Kennedy, J. McDuffie Miller, Wm. G. Gordon, Alex. Hagen, Rev. D. James, Charles Botts. Last estate entry Sep 16, 1867.

BOX 173 PACK 4633   LETTY WILSON   1865

Administrator: John R. McCord. Bond Sep 29, 1865 of $1,000 by John R. McCord, John McCord, James A. McCord. Husband: Wm. Wilson deceased. Son-in-law: Wm. Moseley. Appraisal Oct 24, 1865 by Ben. Smith, Robert R. Seawight, Gideon G. Stone. Wm. E. Barmore. Owned 200 acres of land. Estate Sale Oct 24, 1865 netted $1,429. Buyers at Sale: John R. McCord, Wm. Maddox, A. M. Agnew, Wm. Moseley, Thomas Christian, Wm. P. Kay, A. S. Hughes, Stephen Latimer, J. N. Drake, Wm. E. Barmore, J. W. Richey, J. L. Miller, Ben. Smith, P. N. Nixon, John Baylos Door, Mrs. Lou Brownlee, Wm. C. Moseley, Jesse S. Magee, Ben. F. Hughes, G. M. Mattison, James P. Nixon, J. M. Rasor, James Cancel, Andrew Morrison, Tomas H. Shaw, Wm. Robinosn, Ezekiel Rasor, Larkin J. Rasor, Joel F. Smith, Robert R. Seawright, John R. Clinkscales, Silas Jones, James Taylor, Wm. Wilson, Daniel Beeks, Edmond Gaines, Allen Dodson. Estate Settlement Nov 9, 1865. Wm. Moseley received in right of his wife $100. His sons, James A. Moseley, Enoch F. Moseley received $50 bequest from Letty contained in her marriage contract. Also receiving $50 from the same contract were: Louisa Brownlee, Emma child of Mary Ann and Elizabeth Luckett Arnold. The remaining $295 was equally dived between Wm. Mosley and John R. McCord. Jan 8, 1867 Wm. F. Arnold & Elizabeth F. Arnold of Coosa Co., Ala. Executed Power of Attorney to Wm. Dunn, she received $51 on Jan 28, 1867. P. H. Nixon paid $25 for her coffin.

BOX 173 PACK 4634   JOSHUA WIDEMAN   1864

Will dated Aug 4, 1864. Witnesses: James McCaslan, Adam Wideman, John C. Hayes. Executor: James T. Horton. Wife: Sarah Wideman. Nephew: James T. Horton. Appraisal Sep 9, 1864 by W. K. Bradley, Wilson Watkins, J. S. Britt. Owned 8 slaves, 400 acres of land known as the McMillan tract. Held notes on: John Paatterson, Wm. E. Link, C. A. Wideman, Adbill Scott, B. C. Napper, J. C. Belcher, Ben. McKittrick, Robert H. Wardlaw. Estae Sale Nov 1865. Buyers at sale: J. S.Britt, L. C. Wideman, James T. Horton, George Sibert, James McLane, Joseph McComb, David J. Wardlaw, F. B. Wideman, James A. Wideman, Wilson Watkins, S. C. Young, M. McGaw, Fred Ives, Edmudn Cowan, James Martin, B. C. Napper, Samuel Spence, Eli C. Thornton, Reuben

Weed, Wm. D. Mars, Thomas Link, David Knox, Thomas O. Creswell, S. C. Wideman. Estate Settlement made in Court of Equity. 1864 Confederate tax $193.04.

BOX 173 PACK 4635   HUGH WALLER WARDLAW   1865

Will dated Jun 8, 1857   Filed Sep 23, 1865. Witnesses: W. W. Perryman, R. M. Perryman, W. L. Appleton. Executors: Thomas C. Perrin, Elizabeth F. Wardlaw-wife, Francis Arnold. Bond Oct 9, 1865 of $25,000 by Elizabeth F. Wardlaw, James H. Wideman, Wm. H. Watson, J. L. Coleman. Bond Dec 24, of 10,000 by Francis Arnold, W. H. Bailey, S. P. Boozer. 1st Appraisal Oct 26, 1865 by Henry A. Creswell, J. B. Brooks, Thomas C. Lipscomb, John R. Tarrant. 2nd Appraisal Jan 20, 1868 by James Creswell, Wm. Blake, W. K. Blake. Owned 1,300 acres of land, 110 hogs. Estate Sale Jan 21, 1868. Buyers at sale: John R. Tarrant, Alex. McNeill, Elizabeth F. Wardlaw, W. J. Eaton, Beverly Bailey, Lewis D. Merriman, Mrs. Bentley, James Anderson, Thomas J. Ellis, Mary Hughes, Thomas McClellan, Adam Byrd, John T. Parks, Thomas J. Hearst, J. S. Eaton, C. M. Creswell, John L. Morgan, Marshall Arnold, Wm. Ellenburg, R. F. Hutchiinson, A. M. Blake, Mrs. S. H. Simmons, Thomas C. Seal, James Creswell, Henry H. Creswell, Mrs. Elmore, Dr. W. L. Anderson, Robert Brooks, J. W. Eaton, J. M. Reagan, C. A. C. Waller, John R. Moore, Joel W. Lites, James Searles, Andrew Blythe, J. Deal, Jonathan S. Chip[ley, A. B. Hamlin, Gaines F. Ross.

BOX 173 PACK 4636   JAMES L. WALLER   1866

Administrator: C. A. C. Waller-brother he failed to make returns for several years. Bond Feb 28, 1866 of $20,000 by C. A. C. Waller, J. E. Waller, R. E. Kilcrease, C. G. Waller. Appraisal Mar 12, 1866 by James Creswell, John T. Parks, Sobreski Bonds. Owned a silver watch, trunk and a sizeable number of books. Estate Sale Mar 12, 1866 netted $46. Buyers at sale: C. G. Waller, E. H. Walker, Rev. John McLees, C. A. C. Waller, Samuel B. Hodges, J. Bailey, A. Watson, G. W. Harrison, James Mounce. Disbrusements Jan 1866-Aug 1866. 1. E. H. Waller a minor heir $40 2. R. E. Kilcrease a minor heir $50 3. C. G. Waller $500 4. J. C. Waller, the widow $500 5. C. A. C. Waller $500 6. C. D. Waller's estte $125.

BOX 173 PACK 4637   SAMUEL A. WILSON   1865

Willl dated Nov 1863.   Filed Feb 6, 1865. Witnesses: John Shillito, John R. Martin, Andrew W. Shillito. Executors: Wm. Wilson-son, Francis A. Wilson-son. Wife: Nancy Wilson. Appraisal Mar 9, 1865 by Talbert Cheatham, James Pursley, Charles Bingley Guffin. Estate Sale Nov 20, 1866 netted $756. Buyers at sale: Dr. Thomas J. Mabry, Francis A. Wilson, Wm. Wilson, John Shillito, Robert Keoun, F. Williams, Rev. J. F. Gibert, Michael S. Talbert, John T. Cheatham, Hiram W. Lawson, E. N. Wilson, Lemuel P. Guffin, Wm. T. McMillan, Wm. Brooks, J. C. Belcher, Henry S. Cason, John Bass. Estate Settlement Feb 12, 1867. Only heirs were the sons.

BOX 137 PACK 4638   JANE WALLACE   1866

Administrator: George Wallace. Bond Jan 10, 1866 of $3,000 by George Wallace, Ben. Smith, Larkin Barmore. Appraisal Jan 29, 1866 by J. M. Seawright, James Seawright, J. W. Blain. Owned 120 acres of land. Estate Sale Jan 30, 1866 netted $1,737. Buyers at sale: George Wallace, Ellen Stone, W. P. Magee, Samuel Donald, Wm. Hagen, Richard Owen, Wm. E. Barmore, Charles Cullins, Nancy Wallace, Mary J. Wallace, A. M. Dodson, Sallie Barmore, Robert C. Sharp, James F. Donald, J. L. Robinson, Robert E. Hughes, Belinda Wallace, Eli B. Bowie, Wm. H. Sharp, James Seawright, John Seawright. Estate Settlement Mar 30, 1869. (9) Distributees each $55.69, no names.

BOX 173 PACK 4639   ALPHEUS TURRENTINE WATSON   1865

Andministrator: Leroy J. Johnson. Bond Oct 2, 1865 of $3,000 by Leroy J. Johnson, John Link, William O. Pursley. Appraisal Nov 1, 1865 by Sterling E. Graydon, Franklin F. Gary, Samuel A. Hodges. Estate Sale Nov 2, 1865. Buyers at sale: James F. Smith, P. W. Watson, A. M. Agnew, George Syfan, J. N. Cochran, Charles Smith, Sterling E. Graydon, F. M. Robertson, Charles Smith, G. M. Hodges, Lawrence R. Dantzler, Wm. Riley, J. E. Watson, Charles Fooshe, Paul W. Connor, A. O. Watson, James T. Center, A. B. Hamlin, James F. Smith, Martin G. Zeigler, Dr. B. C. Hart, John Hefferman, Joseph T. Moore, Francis A. Connor, Leroy J. Johnson, Thomas W. Brooks, John D. Adams, James Rampey, James Herbert, L. H. Moore, James Strawhorn, George Seybt, Augustus M. Aiken, Robert Waite, Mrs. P. W. Watson, George Herbert, T. H. Moore, Isaac Herbert, W. H. Jones, Wm. Hodges, Albert B. Hamlin, John Vance, G. P. O'Neal, Dr. Wm. G. Lomax.

BOX 173 PACK 4640   SAMUEL A. WILSON   1865

Confederate Soldier. Will dated Aug 24, 1863. Witnesses: A. McCaslan, J. H. Cobb, John Taggart. Executors: Willis Smith, Virginia C. Wilson-wife. Father: Robert C. Wilson. 1st Appraisal Apr 20, 1865 by Patrick H. Bradley, Larkin Reynolds, Wm. S. Harris, J. L. White. 2nd Appraisal Dec 8, 1868 by Patrick H. Bradley, larkin Reynolds, J. L. White. Owned 362 acres of land. Estate Sale Dec 9, 1868. Buyers at sale: Larkin Reynolds, Patrick H. Bradley, C. V. Wilson, John T. McKellar, John Butler, Samuel McQuerns, Stanmore Marshall, James Reagan, J. R. Wilkinson, J. F. Smith, George W. Pressly, J. W. Puckett, Harvey J. Reagan, M. McCreary, J. H. McClinton, S. T. Martin, John R. Tarrant, Morris Gracey, Wm. H. Hughes. Estate Insolvent.

BOX 173 PACK 4641   JOHN W., ADELINE E. & ANNA A. WILSON (minors)   1865

Father: Teheodore Wilson deceased. Guardian: Mother, Mary F. Wilson. Bond May 29, 1865 of $1,000 by Mary F. Wilson, Wm. S. Harris, Charles H. Wilson. Each minor due $154.97. 1875 Adeline E. & Anna A. Wilson received from the estate of John W. Wilson.

BOX 173 PACK 4642   WILLIAM YOUNG   1864

Will dated Mar 17, 1853. Field Jan 20, 1864. Witnesses: Thomas Thomson, Mathew McDonald, Robert A. Fair. Administrator: James M. Latimer. Wife: Sarah Young. (6) Children: 1. Mahala wife of James M. Latimer 2. Elizabeth wife of Andrew Pickens Norwood 3. James M. Young 4. Mahulda wife of Clement Latimer 5. Caroline A. Young 6. Joseph P. Young. Appraisal Aug 23, 1864 of $13,114 by Wm. A. Giles, Wm. A. Pressly, John M. Moseley, Wm. C. Cozby. Owned 32 slaves, 1,031 acres of land in (3) tracts. Owned house and lot in the Town of Lowndesville.

BOX 173 PACK 4643   ABNER PERRIN YOUNG   1863

Administrator: Andrew J. Weed. Bond Nov 24, 1862 of $20,000 by Andrew J. Weed, Wm. P. Sullivan, J. C. Lindsay. Wife: Margaret Young. Appraisal Dec 4, 1863 of $397 by Edward O. Reagan, Adam Wideman, Thomas O. Creswell, Archibald Bradley. Held notes on: Andrew J. Weed, A. F. Young, John Bickett, Moses C. Taggart, John H. Young. Estate Settlement Dec 29, 1865. 1/3 to widow, Margaret =$288, she took all the property. (1) Child, A. W. Young, a minor. Last estate return and entry Apr 1876.

BOX 173 PACK 4644   DR. LITTLETON YARBOROUGH   1864

Administrators: Martha Yarborough-wife, Edward T. Yarborough. Appraisal Jun 25, 1864 by R. H. W. Hodges, Thomas Miller, J. Griffin, Sameul S. Baker. Owned 22 slaves, 519 acres of land. Held notes on James F. Livingston, David Jordan, J. Rampey, J. Dubose, David Freeland, John Grant, J. Witherspoon, Samuel Mitchell, James Harper, R. A. Houston, John Carter, R. P. Craven. Estate Sale, no date. Buyers at sale: Martha Yarborough, Robert Wardlaw, Franklin Miller, Edward Yarborough, James Huckabee, Wm. A. Clay, John H. Ligon, James G. Bell, J. W. Griffin, Wm. Taggart, James Clark. Paid John Enright $35 for coffin & hearse. Last return and estate entry Jan 14, 1871.

BOX 174 PACK 3276   ROBERT FOOSHE   1846

Will Dated Dec 21, 1845. Witnesses: Nathaniel McCants, Thomas W. Cooper, Reuben G. Golding. Mentioned in will: Joel Fooshe, John W. Fooshe, Charles W. Fooshe, Louisa Logan. Sister: Martha Jane Davis. Uncle: Charles B. Fooshe. Executors: Charles B. Fooshe –uncle withdrew due to challenge from family members, Charles W. Fooshe. Bond Feb 3, 1846 of $2,000 by Charles B. Fooshe, John W. Fooshe, Wm. Hill. Jan 26, 1846 John W. Fooshe, A. J. Logan, in right of his wife, C. B. Fooshe, Joel Fooshe opposed the will being entered into probate. Jan 31, 1846 will was protested by John H. Wilson, B. Z. Martin, reasoning was that Robert Fooshe in their opinion was of unsound mind when the will was written. Appraisal Feb 17, 1846 by Nathaniel McCants, Reuben G. Golding, Thomas J. Coleman. Estate Sale Feb 18, 1846 netted $1,515. Buyers at sale: John W. Fooshe, Wm. Teaster, Hugh Calhoun, John M. Fooshe, Joel Fooshe, Wm. Douglass, George Holloway, Wm. H. Davis, Ben. F. Davis, John R. Tarrant, Charles F. Fooshe, James W. Pert, Reuben G. Golding, James Johnson, Elihu Riley, Joshua Waites, Thomas J. Calhoun, Andrew J. Logan, Wm. Carter, Coopis Transfird, James W. Richardson, Richard A. Griffin. Coffin cost $10.

BOX 174 PACK 3277   ASA & VALENTINE FRANKLIN (minors)   1845

Nov 18, 1845 petition of Washington Young of Talledega, Ala. Many years previously Valentine Young had willed a legacy to his daughter, Margaret, who married James Franklin. She died leaving the husband and (2) children. They were both under the age of 16 and the family was now about to remove to Talledega, Ala. Washington Young wanted to be appointed the guardian of the Estate due the minors amounting to $250. Bond Nov 18, 1845 of $500 by Washington J. Young, James Franklin, Valentine Young.

BOX 174 PACK 3278   CYNTHIA FISHER & JOHN J. FISHER (minors) 1855

Minors were Cynthia Fisher & Thomas F. Fisher. Thomas F. Fisher another minor had died prior to Jan 1847. Father: Thomas Fisher deceased. Mother: Elizabeth Fisher.

Administrator of Mother's Estate: Samuel C. Fisher who was the brother of their father. Bond Feb 23, 1847 of $600 by Samuel C. Fisher, James A. Gantt, Conrad Wakefiled, John Wakefield. Bond Nov 8, Nov 8, 1847 of $4,000 by Samuel C. Fisher, John F. Clinkscales, Conrad Wakefield. Appraisal of Elizabeth Fisher's Estate Nov 24, 1847 by Wm. Clinkscales, John F. Clinkscales, Basil Callaham. Owned 3 slaves. Estate Sale of Elizabeth Fisher Nov 25, 1847. Buyers at sale: Jacob Alewine, Caleb Burton, Josiah Fowler, John W. Shirley, John Fields, Moses Ashley, James Ware, James Thomson, Robert H. Hall, Robert Haddon, W. C. Fisher, A. W. Hawkins, Wm. Sanders, A. J. Shaw, Wm. Ashley, Stephen M. Fisher, Cynthia C. Fisher, Stephen Fields, Wm. Shaw, James Murdock, Conrad Wakefield, G. W. Hawkins, Henry Branyon, Z. Jones, Thomas F. Branyon, Wm. Clinkscales, Robert Wilson, R. H. Dove, J. W. Wilson, Bennett McAdams, J. F. Clinkscales, J. M. Bolton, Reuben Clinkscales, James Taylor, Ben. McClain, Reuben Branyon, John M. Bryant, Robert B. McAdams, Edward Ashley, Jackson Griffin, John Callaham, John M. Hopkins, Mary A. Fisher, Josua S. Barnes, Thomas Crawford, R. S. Holliman, T. L. Painter, Thomas M. Branyon. Sep 22, 1845 both minors of age. Estate Settlement of Elizabeth Fisher Mar 5, 1849. (10) Distributees: 1. John F. Fisher 2. John M. Bryant 3. Wm. Ashley and wife Jane 4. John W. Shirley and wife Lucinda 5. John Ashley 6. Joshua Barnes and wife Nancy 7. Mary Ann Fisher 8. Cynthia C. Fisher 9. Elizabeth Fisher 10. John J. Fisher.

BOX 174 PACK 3279   THOMAS W. FINLEY (minor)   1855

Administrator: John W. Hearst. Guardian: John Carroll. Bond Jan 12, 1847 by John Carroll, W. E. Anderson, A. H. Brown. Father: James Finley and John W. Hearst was the administrator of his estate. John Carroll married Elizabeth Finley, mother of Thomas W. Finley, in 1844 and became guardian in Sep 1845. Carroll moved to Jackson Co., Fla. 1st Settlement Feb 7, 1851 between Guardian and administrator of $114.62. Final Settlement Mar 15, 1867 based on return of 1852 and interest on the $114.62 from that time. $114.62 ha now become $173.76. Thomas W. Finley died about 1851.

BOX 174 PACK 3280   JOHN G. GIBERT   1846

Administrators: Benjamin E. Gibert-brother, Dionyisious M. Rogers. Bond Jan 5, 1846 of $3,000 by Benjamin E. Gibert, Dionyisious M. Rogers, Benjamin McKittrick, Edward Foster.

BOX 174 PACK 3281   JAMES GRAHAM   1845

Deceased died Aug 1845. Administrator: Wm. Graham. Bond Oct 6, 1845 of $2,000 by Wm. Graham, Wm. Grahm, Jr., James Robertson. Appraisal Oct 28, 1845 by John W. Moore, James Robertson, Samuel Graham. Estate Sale Oct 28, 1845. Buyers at sale: John W. Moore, Patsy Graham, Wm. Graham, John R. Campbell, Lewis D. Merriman, Wade Robertson, Wesley Robertson, Isham George, George Elmore, James Dyson, Zachariah Graham, Meedy Mays, John Sexton, James Moore, Wm. Anderson, Wm. Whitley, Archibald Arnold, Thomas Bozeman, R. Y. Jones. Estate Settlement Dec 30, 1849. Widow, Martha Graham $119.49. (3) Children each $79.66. 1. James M. Graham 2. Polly Ann Graham 3. Thomas J. Graham.

BOX 174 PACK 3282   JOHN GOUDY   1846

Will dated Apr 27, 1846. Witnesses: George W. Cromer, James Irwin, Isaac Branch. Administrators: David Keller, Robert M. Goudy-son. Wife: Amy Goudy. Son: Robert M. Goudy. Daughters: Elizaa Goudy, Jane Goudy, Nancy wife of James Cunningham deceased. 1st Appraisal Jun 4, 1846 by Philip Cromer, George W. Cromer, James Irwin. 1st Settlement Jan 4, 1853. Owned (1) slave. Estate Sale Nov 30, 1858 netted $2,353. 2nd Appraisal Nov 29, 1858 by Wm. McIlwain, J. I. Gilmer, John McCord. 2nd Estate Sale Nov 30, 1858. Buyers at sale: George W. Cromer, Henry Cannon, David Keller, James Irwin, Louis H. Russell, Jane Goudy, W. W. Russell, Thomas B. McCord, John Botts, John W. McCree, D. W. McCord, J. A. McCord, Johnson Ramey, Abraham Lites, Wm. Hill, Thomas Ellis, Andrew J. Lythgoe, James Wilson, E. N. Wilson, John P. Cromer, Theodore Wilson, E. Irwin, John Devlin, W. J. Wilson, Thomas J. Douglass, Wm. B. Roman, James Irwin, Wm. Pace, John F. Keller, John D. Adams, Andrew McIlwain, Dwight Bowie, David S. Benson, Wm. McNary, James McGriffin, Nancy Lathers, John Davis. Estate Settlement Dec 2, 1858. (5) Shares each $258.18. 1. R. M. Goudy now of Tippah Co. Miss. 2. Eliza recently McGriffith 3. Jane Goudy 4. Wm. Goudy 5. Children of James Cunningham.

BOX 174 PACK 3283   MISSING

Box 174 PACK 3284   JAMES A. GRAY (minor)   1846

Aug 9, 1836 James Connor appointed Guardian of James A. Gray. 1839 J. L. Brough paid Connor $65 for James A. Gray's wages. Administrator James Connor who had been his guardian. Bond Jan 23, 1846 of $250 by James Connor, Alex. P. Connor. Appraisal Jan 27, 1846 by John E. Foster, Alex. P. Connor, Robert McComb. Estate Sale Jan 29, 1846 netted $10.31. Estae Settlement, no date. (4) Distributees each $23.06: 1. John G. Gray 2. Randall Townes in right of wife Martha Ann Gray 3. Mary Gray, mother now married to George Cochran 4. Mary F. Gray age 7.

BOX 174 PACK 3285   GEORGE GRAY   1846

Aministrator: James A. Norwood. Bond Feb 2, 1846 of $2,000 by James A. Norwood, Samuel J. Hester, Robert E. Belcher. Appraisal Feb 18, 1846 by Joshua Dubose, Samuel Hester, Alex. F. Wimbish. Estate Sale Feb 19, 1846. Buyers at sale: J. F. Gray, Samuel Hester, J. Mathews, J. Sligh, M. McGehee, Wm. M. Calhoun, J. McKelvey, J. Lyon. Demands 1st Class: Dr. Littleton Yarborough, Dr. Townes, Dr. Gibert. Demands 2nd Class: A. Ammons, John F. Gray, J. Walker, J. A. Norwood, Wm. Bass, Adams & Gray, John Mathews, J. Hill, S. Hill, Dr. Townes, Dr. Gibert. Estate Insolvent paid about 25 cents on the dollar.

BOX 174 PACK 3286   MARY JOHNSON (minor)   1845

Guardian: Robert Hutson. Bond Oct 24, 1845 of $100 by Robert Hutson, Albert Waller, Wm. M. Sale. Placed at Lethe.

BOX 174 PACK 3287   MARY KOLB   1846

Administrator: Thomas Beaty. Bond Mar 5, 1846 of $100 by Thomas Beaty, John Cowan, John Robertson. E. C. Greenlee and Thomas Beaty received through will. Appraisal Mar 6, 1846 by John Cowan, George H. Brownlee, John Robinson. Owned 2 slaves. Estate Sale Mar 6, 1846. Buyers at sale: John Robinson, Robert Ellis, John

Richey, Wm. Oakley, L. J. White, Thomas Beaty, John Cowan, H. Darlington, Bennett Sharp, Robert C. Sharp, Richardson Tribble, George H. Brownlee, John Williams, Ceeda Sharp. Estte Settlement, no date. Creditors paid only. Paid to James Lindsay funeral expenses of 4 yards fine crushed velvet $3, 4 yards homespun 50 cents, paper tacks 12 cents. Paid Thomas Painter $5 for coffin.

BOX 174 PACK 3288   JORDAN MOSELEY   1845

Will dated Apr 2, 1845. Witnesses: Robert Woods, Wm. P. Martin, Noah R. Reeve. Executors: Wm. W. Moseley, James M. Moseley, Benjamin F. Moseley. Wife: Sarah Moseley. Daughter: Dorothy died without issue prior to Feb 1848, Fatina Richey. Sons: Burrell W. Moseley deceased, Wm. W. Moseley, James M. Moseley, Ben. F. Moseley, John L. Moseley. Appraisal Jan 13, 1846 by G. M. Mattison, Noah R. Reeve, R. P. Seawright. Owned 150 acres of land. Held notes on: John Donald, Wm. W. Moseley, Ben. F. Moseley, John Moore, James M. Moseley, Leroy H. Hodges, Wm. Richey, Dr. Andrew Dunn. Estate Sale Jan 13, 1846 netted $4,482. Buyers at sale: James H. Shaw, Wm. C. Moseley, John L. Moseley, Gideon Stone, James Johnson, Wm. Long, W. P. Martin, Reuben Robinson, John Gaines, James M. Moseley, Thomas Carter, Lewis Pyles, Robert R. Seawright, Wm. W. Moseley, James W. Richey, Jackson Robinson, Ben. F. Moseley, Wm. Robinson, John Brownlee, Jesse Scurry, Dorothy Moseley, Jackson Richey, Wm. Richey Jr., John Hughes, M. T. Mattison, Clement T. Latimer, Hugh Calhoun, Sylvanus Adams, Henson Posey, Thomas Robinson, Jesse Ghent. Estate Settlement Feb 23, 1848. (9) Shares each $417.75: 1. Wm. Richey 2. James Moseley 3. J. L. Moseley 4. W. C. Moseley 5. John B. Richey 6. Sarah Richey 7. Through 9. not named.

BOX 174 PACK 3289   AGNES C. McQUERNS   1845

Administrator: Wm. Sanders-brother. Bond Aug 4, 1845 of $8,000 by Wm. Sanders, Bart Jordan, Eli Branson. Appraisal Aug 30, 1845 by Larkin Reynolds, Patrick H. Bradley, George W. Pressly, John Ruff. Owned 7 slaves, 163 acres of land. Held notes on: J. N. Young, L. Branson, Eli Branson, M. Sanders, Wm. C. Puckett, John Sanders. Estate Sale Nov 25, 1845 netted $2,821. Buyers at sale: R. M. Walker, Wm. Sanders, J. C. Martin, Patrick H. Bradley, J. McClinton, G. Stroder, R. H. Wilson, G. P. Crawford, R. C. Wilson, Wilson Watkins, John Gallagher, John Marion, James Wharton, Daniel Holder, Wm. C. Puckett, M. Owens, Thomas H. Bradley, David Wardlaw, Lewis Rich, R. Wilson, E. McQuerns, George Marshall, P. Bluford, John L. Ruff, A. Donald, John Gibson, John Watson, F. Ruff, Samuel B. McClinton, Eli Branson, M. Colvin, J. F. Martin, Wm. Marion, Andrew J. Weed, John McCreary, T. Bluford, Larkin Reynolds, Wiley Harris, Wm. B. Devlin, Wm. Butler.

BOX 174 PACK 3290   THOMAS W. MORTON   1845

Will dated Mar 4, 1845. Witnesses: John Keller, John Davis, James Carson. Wife: Lucinda Morton. Son: Augustus H. Morton. Executors: Lucinda Morton-wife, Augusu H. Morton-son. Owned 1569 acres in Edgefield and 2550 in Abbeville. Appraisal of Edgefield property Jul 31, 1845 of $10,037 by Wm. Tolbert, S. A. Brooks, John W. Rochelle. Appraisal of Abbeville property Aug 30, 1845 of $28,714 by David Keller, John Keller, Philip Cromer. Owned 71 slaves.

BOX 174 PACK 3291   KITTY McCOMB   1846

Deceased died Nov 11, 1845. Will dated Jun 19, 1845. Witnesses: Elizabeth McComb, Thomas K. Sproull, Samuel Marshall. Estate ruled as being Intestate due to Elizabeth McComb, a cousin, being listed as a legatee of $100 in the will. Administrator: John F. McComb. Bond Jan 10, 1846 of $20,000 by John F. McComb, John W. Hearst, James Taggart. Children: John Foster McComb, Margaret Perrin McComb, John Andrew McComb insane. Appraisal Jan 26, 1846 by David McLane, Moses O. McCaslan, Wm. McCaslan. Held notes on: Archibald Bradley, Louis Covin, Peter Smith, John Kennedy, James L. Morrow, Elihu Sproull, Samuel Goff. Estate Sale Jan 27, 1846 netted $6,491. Buyers at sale: J. F. McCombs, John Gray, R. Martin, Wm. J. Hammond, T. Lucas, David McLane, Wm. McCaslan, W. Beardon, P. C. McEwen, Harmon Stevenson, A. Boyd, Andrew McCaslan, J. Robinson, R. O. Wilson, John Charles, Dr. Franklin Branch, Eli Thornton, Thomas P. Dowtin, Dr. Sanders, John Faulkner, Wade Cowan, Wilson Watkins, Adam Wideman, James McLane, J. Lucas, Fred Ives, Wm. C. Bradley, Robert Earnest, Wm. Gillespie. Estate Settlement. Robert A. Martin's wife received $2,669 less her husband's note of $2430 = $239 received.

BOX 174 PACK 3292   WILLIS D. MOUNCE   1845

Deceased was living in Poinsett Co., Ark at time of his death. Administrator: Reuben Griffin Golding--step son. Bond Aug 25, 1845 of $2,000 by Reuben Griffin Golding, Samuel Beard, Joel Fooshe, N. C. Golding. Wife: Susannah Mounce. No Children. Sep 28, 1847 Reuben Griffin Golding was appointed agent of all estate matters. Appraisal Aug 27, 1845 by Samuel Beard, Henry Beard, Simeon Chaney, C. B. Fooshe. Owned 5 slaves. Estate Sale Aug 28, 1845 netted $1,913. Buyers at sale: Susannah Mounce, R. W. Mounce, Robert C. Gilliam, Richard A. Griffin, Samuel Beard, John Day, W. Mounce, John Chaney, Robert Mounce, Nimrod Stewart, Abner Wiseman, Robert Fooshe, John Perdue, Thomas Nichols, Reuben G. Golding, Wm. Thompson. Estate Settlement Jan 21, 1847. Wife received ½ of estate. (6) Distributees each $101.74. Only (3) named: 1. Robert H. Mounce 2. John R. Mounce 3. Michael Lewey in right of his wife, not named.

BOX 175 PACK 4646   JANE BRADLEY   1866

Deceased died in either 1857 or 1858. Administrator: John Patterson. Bond Aug 6, 1866 of $1,000 by John Patterson, Wm. A. Clay, Edward O. Reagan. Husband: Archibald Bradley deceased had died aftrer her death about 1865. John Patterson was her nephew by her sister, Jane Patterson.

BOX 175 PACK 4646 ½   STEPHEN S. ALLEN   1863

Bond Sep 7, 1863 of $150 by John J. Adams, Wm. McNary, Wm. Mundy.

BOX 175 PACK 4647   WILLIAM L. BURTON   1867

Will dated Jan 25, 1867. Filed Mar 4, 1867. Witnesses: James M. Carwile, James Clinkscales, Wm. M. Callaham. Executors: Hugh Robinson, Peter S. Burton Jr. Wife: Amanda Burton. Daughters: Minerva Sophronia, Dora Lavinia. Appraisal mar 22, 1867 by James M. Carwile, F. F. Gray, James Clinkscales, Wm. Clinkscales. 1st Estate Sale Mar 22, 1867 netted $278.80. Buyers at sale: John M. Bryant, J. C. Tucker, Wm. M. Callaham,

Basil Callaham, J. Alewine, Christopher Ellis, M. A. Tucker, Wm. Taylor, A. P. Shirley, Wm. Armstrong. 2nd Estate Sale Oct 22, 1868 netted $2,551. Buyers at sale: Thomas. J. Bowen, John Shirley, P. S. Burton, S. J. Bowen, Wm. Ricketts, Mrs. M. A. Tucker, Andrew J. Shaw. Estate Settlement Nov 23, 1868. Widow Amanda now wife of Thomas J. Bowen $953. Lavinia Burton deceased. Sophronia Minerva $1,143. Widow apparently received an additional $1,143 but not certain.

BOX 175 PACK 4648   WILLIAM W. BELCHER JR.   1866

Will dated Dec 20, 1860   Filed Dec 6, 1866. Witnesses: John G. Edwards, Epaminandos Edwards, George White. Executor: Isaac Branch. Bond Dec 28, 1866 of $1,000 by Isaac Branch, D. R. Sondley, Joseph Moore. Sisters: Sarah A. wife of Robert J. White, Mary F. Belcher. Brother: James C. Belcher. Appraisal Jan 10, 1867 by Hiram T. Tusten, Wm. T. Penney, John T. Owen. Owned 4 slaves at time of will. Estate Sale Jan 10, 1867. Buyers at sale: Wm. J. White, J. N. Belcher.

BOX 175 PACK 4649   AMARINTHA H. & MARY ANN BOWEN (minors)   1866

Father: Alex. C. Bowen deceased. Guardian: Elizabeth Bowen-mother. Bond Nov 27, 1866 of $500 by Elizabeth Bowen, Sterling Bowen, Wm. Wickliffe. Received $66 from the estate of their father. 1st Return Nov 27, 1866. Last return 1871.

BOX 175 PACK 4650   ANDREW H. CALLAHAM   1866

Administrator: Joshua P. Milford. Bond Oct 26, 1866 of $500 by Joshua P. Milford, Thomas Bailey Milford, Thomas Craig Milford. Appraisal Dec 19, 1866 by Conrad Wakefield, Clayton Jones, Joseph R. Black. Estate Sale Dec 19, 1866 netted $300. Buyers at sale: Johua P. Milford, John W. Bowen, Columbus E. Bowen, Michael Alewine, J. S. Campbell, George W. Milford, George Milford, John M. Milford. Estate Settlement Dec 21, 1870. Distributees: Widow and (2) Children. Widow 1/3 = $84. Each child $84 but one child died prior to the payment of the money. No names given.

BOX 175 PACK 4651   JOHN W. CALHOUN   1867

Confederate Soldier killed during war in Maryland. Administrator: Meedy Mays. Bond Feb 8, 1867 of $1,000 by Meedy Mays, Philip S. Rutledge, John A. Mays. Step Father: Meedy Mays. Mother Nancy Mays. Waller B. Meriwether was his Guardian. Did not have any brothers or sisters. Never Married.

BOX 175 PACK 4652   NANCY ANN CALLAHAM (minor)   1867

Guardian Joshua P. Milford. Bond Feb 22, 1867 of $600 by Joshua P. Milford, John M. Milford, Thomas C. Milford. Last entry Oct 3, 1874.

BOX 175 PACK 4653   WILLIAM E. CALDWELL   1866

Will dated Jan 9, 1855. Filed Dec 19, 1866. Witnesses: O. Richardson, H. C. Young, Thomas Byrd. Executors: Nancy A. Caldwell-wife, Edward E. Smith. Bond Dec 1883 by Edward E. Smith, J. E. Caldwell, J. H. Smith, Norris L. Caldwell, J. C. Caldwell. Nancy A. Caldwell died in 1882. Edward E. Smith married Jeanette M. Caldwell. He applied for

147

Letters of Administration Dec 5, 1883. 1st Appraisal Jan 21, 1867 by Newton Sims, Ben. Z. Herndon, J. C. Williams. Appraisal of land Feb 15, 1867 by Joel W. Anderson, Charles W. Smith. Estate Settlement, no date. Heirs: 1. Wm. C. Caldwell lived in Texas 2. Bessie Norris 3. Lillian Caldwell 4. L. R. Caldwell 5. Jeanette M. wife of Edward E. smith 6. Edward Caldwell a minor over age 14.

BOX 175 PACK 4654   JAMES DARBY   1867

Administrator: Wm. Duncan. Bond Feb 7, 1867 of $800 by Wm. Duncan, Robert A. Archer, James Clinkscales. Appraisal Feb 22, 1867 by Hugh Robinson, John F. Clinkscales, James Carwile, Wm. Clinkscales. Estate Sale Feb 22, 1867 netted $560.44. Buyers at sale: James Brock, Rachel Kerr, Caleb M. Shaw, John F. Clinkscales, Bennett McAdams, Wm. Duncan, John T. Strickland, David Loner, Susan Rice, John Bannister, John W. Shirley, F. M. Alewine, Joseph Smith, R. T. Chamblee, John D. Alewine. Estate Settlement Mar 22, 1870. Wm. Duncan received $218 after all debts paid.

BOX 175 PACK 4655   TURNER G. DAVIS   1866

Administrator: Caroline M. Davis-wife, Amaziah Rice Ellis. Bond Oct 19, 1866 of $2,000 by Caroline M. Davis, Amaziah Rice Ellis, J. E. Ellis, Christopher Ellis. Appraisal Nov 7, 1866 by James A. Bigby, George Marshall Bigby George Kay, Thmas Branyon. Estate Sale Nov 7, 1866 netted $745. Buyers at sale: Caroline M. Davis, R. T. Chamblee, A. J. Patterson, George W. Ellis, Amaziah Rice Ellis, Andrew T. Armstrong, Wesley Cromer, John C. Davis, Francis Davis. Estate Settlement Nov 22, 1881. Widow $276. (8) Children each $69.24. 1. C. G. Davis 2. E. S. Whitten 3. A. P. Davis 4. J. A. Davis 5. A. W. Davis 6. Will Davis 7. M. M. Davis 8. M. S. Davis.

BOX 175 PACK 4656   ANDREW GILES   1867

Deceased died Feb 1, 1867. Very large estate with many pages of transactions, petitioning, counter petitioning etc. Will dated Jul 9, 1864. Witnesses: Sarah Cunningham, Eliza F. Wood, Alex. Hunter. Codicil Witnesses: G. S. Bell, J. R. Moseley, W. R. White. Executors: Wm. A. Giles, James T. Baskin. Widow married Thomas A. Cater. Children: 1. John M. Giles died before his father. Children: All lived in Houston Co., Ga. Andrew S. Giles, Mary wife of Solomon Dasher, J. Louisa, Elizabeth. 2. James H. Giles 3. Josiah P. Giles deceased. Children: Eliza wife of Wm. A. Templeton, James M. Giles, Mary Sue wife of George W. Speer. 4. Wm. A. Giles. 5. Mary E. Wife of James T. Baskin. She had (8) children, not named. Appraisal Mar 9, 1867 by Albert J. Clinkscales, James M. Martin, George W. Speer, Wm. V. Clinkscales. Owned 33 shares of Greenville & Columbia Railroad, 28 shares of Savannah & Western Railroad, 49 shares of Bank of Newberry, 267 shares of Farmers Exchange Bank of Charleston. Estate Sale Mar 12, 1867 netted $2,477. Buyers at sale: Wm. A. Giles, Hugh M. Prince, Wm. V. Clinkscales, James T. Baskin, W. S. Baskin, J. D. Welch, Wm. A. Lesly, F. P. Robertson, L. T. Liddell, George W. Bowen, Edward Cowan, J. R. Cunningham, Thomas A. Cater, David Crowell, Andrew J. Clinkscales, Coke D. Mann, Wm. Mann, Samuel J. Hester, Wm. M. Brown, Thomas J. Hill, Andrew B. Wardlaw, Michael B. Latimer, J. W. Griffin, Wm. Cook, E. H. Bingham, Ben. Lee, John McMahan, James Clark, Joseph Ashley, Ephraim F. Power, Samuel S. Baker, George W. Milford, J. M. Martin, Ed Calhoun, J. M. Moseley, Thomas T. Cunningham, Robert Hutchison, J. H. Alewine, W. L. Prince. Estate Settlement (5)

Distributees each $5,626: 1. James H. Giles 2. John Mason Giles 3. Mary E. Baskin 4. Children of Josiah P. Giles 5. Wm. A. Giles. Settlement Oct 28, 1877 Mary E. Baskin received 1/3. She died and her (8) children each received $1,084: 1. Alex. B. 2. Margaret E. 3. Sallie L. 4. James T. 5. Laura 6. Caroline "Carrie" 7. A. G. 8. Mary. Also receiving disbursements: Eliza Templeton $423, James M. Giles $423, Mary Sue Speer $423. Nov 21, 1868 paid Legacies: 1. E. C. Power 2. Lyman W. Martin 3. Laura wife of B. Pooser 4. Due West College.

BOX 175 PACK 4657   BENJAMIN P. HUGHES   1866

Administrator: John T. Lyon, brother –in-law. Bond Jan 5, 1866 of $15,000 by John T. Lyon, Jane C. Hughes, Hiram T. Tusten. Wife: Jane C. Hughes. Appraisal Nov 14, 1866 by J. R. F. Wilson, Andrew L. Gillespie, David J. Jordan. Held notes on: John A. Allen, John T. Owen, Andrew L. Gillespie, L. Graydon, James A. Shillito, Thomas C. Perrin, Wm. A. Richey, James M. Perrin, Harvey T. Lyon, John McCord, J. A. McCord, Wardlaw & Lyon, Hugh Wilson, John T. Lyon, L. S. Pasley, Wm. J. Lomax, Francis A. Connor, Henry A. Jones, Silas Bray, John D. Adams, Isaac Branch, W. E. Buchanan, Thomas D. Douglass, James D. Chalmers, M. P. Latimer, Hiram W. Lawson, Moses T. Owen, Bartlett S. Tucker, Thomas McNeill, A. D. Montgomery, Thomas J. Coumbe, John Baskin, John Patterson, S. Lomax, B. M. Latimer, Martin W. Coleman, Thomas J. Douglass, John A. Hamilton, E. H. Robertson, John A. Wier, Samuel Jordan, G. W. Hodges, John W. Livingston, John Corbett, James A. Richey, Robert M. Palmer, John White, John T. Miller. Estate Sale Nov 15, 1866. Buyers at sale: Jane C. Hughes, John T. Lyon, Samuel Hughes, John Enright, James P. Young, Wm. Hill, John J. Gray, Joseph T. Moore, Thomas McCord, John E. Uldrick, James R. Cunningham, James S. Cothran, Joel J. Lipford, George A. Douglass, Andrew L. Gillespie, Isaac Branch, Philip S. Rutledge. Estate Settlement Aug 12, 1870. Wife was the only heir.

BOX 175 PACK 4658   SAMUEL HAWTHORNE (man of color   1866

Administrator: David O. Hawthorne whohad been his owner as a slave. Bond Aug 11, 1866 of $300 by David O. Hawthorne, Samuel Donald, F. S. Dolan. Blacksmith by trade. 1st Return Jul 6, 1868.

BOX 175 PACK 4659   JOHN HINTON   1875

Deceased died Sep 30, 1866. Administrator: Edna Hinton-wife. Bond Dec 18, 1866 by Edna Hinton, Simeon P. Boozer, S. A. Dike. Appraisal Jan 2, 1867 of $3,001 by Thomas Riley, James Strawhorn, Thomas Jones. Owned about 950 acres of land. Held notes on: C. D. Fisher, Samuell Adams, Ben. F. Roberts, James Davis, S. A. Dike, R. G. Leaval, Mary Boozer, Franklin Beasley, Mounce & Calhoun, Wm. Boozer, Wm. T. Farrow. Estate Sale Jan 3, 1867 netted $2,606. Buyers at sale: Edna Hinton, W. F. Dike, W. K. Tolbert, Andrew Cobb, C. D. Fisher, Ben. Roberts, W. Harrell. W. Harralson, R. H. Mounce, B. Riley, S. Pulliam, J. Turner, A. P. Boozer, J. Beasley, A. Ellis, --- Killingsworth, M. Blake, J. Thomspon, Wm. H. Moore. Estate Settlement, no date. (9) Distributees: 1. Edna Hinton the widow 2. Lavinda M. wife of Thomas Cobb 3. Susan Ann Tolbert who died in Aug 1868. She was the wife of Wm. K. Tolbert but had no children. Tolbert died in Dec 1869 leaving no children or wife but heirs at law: his sisters, Nancy Buchanan and Isabella Rykard wife of Levi Rykard; brother, Joseph Tolbert living in Florida. Edna Hinton believed that Tolbert owed far more to the estate than what was due him. 4. Elizabeth wife of Vachel Hinton 5. Samuel Adams Hinton 6. James Hinton a minor 7. Francis Hinton a minor 8. Margaret Hinton a minor 9. Jennie Hinton a minor. Final return and entry Jan 19, 1877.

BOX 175 PACK 4660   JAMES HUGHEY   1866

Administrator: Joseph L. Hughey. Bond Nov 14, 1866 of $4,000 by Joseph L. Hughey, James A. Ellis, James Strawhorn. Appraisal Dec 11, 1866 by Bert Riley, Wm. McNary, Thomas Jones. Held notes on: John D. Adams, S. A. Dike, J. A. Bailey, C. D. Fisher. Estate Sale Dec 12, 1866 netted $742. Buyers at sale: Widow, Wm. McNary, W. F. Dike, Joseph L. Hughey, Vachel Hughey, James Brown, Wm. Mundy, E. Ellis, Thomas Jones, John Purvis, Willis Smith. Paid W. A. Harralson $35 for coffin. Paid L. P. Boozer $19.65 for funeral expenses.

BOX 175 PACK 4661   JOHN WASHINGTON ISOM   1866

Deceased died Oct 18, 1864. Administrators: Emily Isom –wife who died Jul 15, 1869, James A. Corley Oct 29, 1872. Bond Nov 13, 1866 of $10,000 by Emily Isom, Wm. A.Crozier, James A. Corley. Bond, no date, James A. Corley, Philip A. Covin, Wm. H. Peak. 1st Appraisal Nov 27, 1866 by John Harmon, B. Moragne, Andrew Guillebeau, Joseph Guillebeau. Owned 225 acres of land. 2nd Appraisal Nov 19, 1872 by Wm. C. Ludwick, James C. Jennings, Dr. Sanders. Held notes on as of Nov 19, 1872: Wiley Newby, R. C. Scott, John W. Jones, Sarah B. Jones, J. C. Cox, James Wideman.

BOX 175 PACK 4662   R. MARSHALL KAY   1866

Administrator: John T. Ashley. Bond May 23, 1866 of $500 by John T. Ashley, Rivhard B. Robertson, Isaac H. Robertson. Appraisal May 25, 1866 by John McClain, S. Martin, R. Martin. Estate Insolvent. Debts paid pro-rated.

BOX 175 PACK 4663   ISAAC KENNEDY   1866

Deceased died May 8, 1866. Will dated Jan 18, 1866. Witenesses: George W. Pressly, Wm. R. McKinney, Samuel B. McClinton, Wm. Riley. Executors: Nancy Kennedy-wife, Sarah Drennan in 1869. Daughters: Jane Burnett, Mary Watson, Nancy Kennedy, Sarah wife of J. L. Drennan, Frances wife of Horace Drennan. Grand Sons: Archibald Watson, Samuel Fulton. Appraisal Jul 14, 1866 by Jacob Miller, Wm. Riley, J. C. Drennan, John Devlin. Held notes on: James Taggart, Christian V. Barnes, J. L. Drennan, James M. Yarborough, Wm. G. Neel, Samuel Jordan, P. B. LeRoy, James M. Gilliam, Henry A. Jones, John Sanders, John Patterson, Wm. S. Harris, Joseph McBryde, John Creswell, John McLaren, Richard Kennedy, Edward O. Reagan, Thomas C. McBryde, Adolphus A. Williams, Mary Smith, John Sproull, James E. Calhoun, J. C. Martin, Taggart & McCaslan. Final return 1869. Headstone cost $39.25.

BOX 175 PACK 4664   ELIZABETH LONG   1866

Will dated Jul 13, 1861 Filed Sep 18, 1866. Witnesses: Stephen Latimer, James H. Shaw, Ben. M. Latimer. Executor: James R. Latimer. Sister: Margaret Long. Nieces: ---

Latimer, Sarah F. Callaham, Amelia Long, Emma E. Long. Nehew: James R. Latimer. Appraisal Oct 24, 1866 by G. M. Mattison, Stephen Latimer, Ben. M. Latimer.

BOX 175 PACK 4665   JANE LINDSAY   1869

Deceased died in 1862. Administrator: Joseph C. Lindsay. Bond Nov 23, 1866 of $600 by Joseph C. Lindsay, Tyra Jay, Andrew J. Weed. Appraisal Nov 27, 1866 by Adma Wideman, Robert W. Lites, Edward O. Reagan. Estate Sale Nov 27, 1866 netted $288. Buyers at sale: Andrew C. Brown, J. C. Lindsay, P. Lindsay, D. Nive, Samuel Young, Michael Cuddy, P. M. Young, John P. Kennedy, N. Hanvey, Wm. K. Bradley, James Creswell, Wm. Kennedy, M. Martin, David Ethridge, James O. Spence, Thomas V. Creswell, A. Martin, R. Brown, Hugh Moseley, Andrew J. Weed, Samuel Spence, Mathew Goodwin, James Gibson, Mary Lindsay, Adam Wideman, Thomas Robinson, Thomas O. Creswell, Thomas C. McBryde, Dr. Sanders. Estate Settlement Mar 11, 1869. (7) Distributees each $50.46: 1. Thomas N. Lindsay 2. Patrick Lindsay 3. Susan Hanvey deceased, husband 1/3 (7) children each $4.80 4. Isabella Lindsay lived in Florida 5. Mary Lindsay lived in Florida 6. Jane Lindsay lived in Florida 7. Joseph C. Lindsay.

BOX 175 PACK 4666   DR. JOHN LOGAN   1870

Will dated Jull 17, 1866. Witnesses: J. Dailey, Thomas B. Williams, John T. Parks. Executor: James W. Law. Bond Feb 8, 1868 0f $342.20 by James W. Law, Julius A. Carlisle, George W. Glenn. Daughters: Sue Logan, Ellen Logan. Son: John H. Logan. Grand Son: Wm. Raiford Logan. 1st Appraisal Oct 16, 1866 by Francis Arnold, John B. Johnson, J. A. Bailey, Jones Fuller. 2nd Appraisal Nov 22, 1866 by John B. Johnson, Francis Arnold, J. A. Bailey. Owned 790 acres of land, owned 40 acres in the Town of Greenwood. 1st Estate Sale Oct 30, 1866. Buyers at sale: Frank Fuller, Wm. Bailey, G. P. O'Neil, P. H. Anderson, Jones Fuller, Crawford Hill, R. M. Anderson, W. L. Dukes, James W. Law, Wm. Buchanan, John Cheatham, W. C. Anderson, Wm. K. Blake, J. Bailey, Blackwell K. Murchison, Henry F. Fuller, Pat Anderson, George E. Moore, Joel Pinson, Robert Gilliam, Lewis D. Merriman, Wm. Fooshe, Robert Major, H. R. Williams, George Elmore, James Creswell, Thomas R. Pinson, Allen T. Bell, John McLees, R. E. Chaney, W. B. Meriwether, Ben-a free man, John R. Tarrant. 2nd Estate Sale Dec 4, 1867. Buyers at sale: Wm. H. Bailey, James W. Law, Thomas McClellan, Arthur Leland, Joseph Major, Jesse Meriwether, Samuel H. Benjamin, Wm. P. McKellar, James Creswell, Charles M. Calhoun, Elbert Arnold, Nathan Creswell, Wm. A. Harralson, John Boozer, Mathew Arnold, Thomas McClenon, Mack Nance, Allen Waller, John G. Boozer, Edmond Jacob, Lucian de Jarvis, Wm. C. Young, Samuel Moseley, Ben Brown.

BOX 175 PACK 4667   LOUISA LESLY   1863

Administrator: John W. Lesly. Bond Sep 27, 1866 of $10,000 by John W. Lesly, Alpheus E. Lesly, Wm. A. Lesley. Appraisal Nov 7, 1866 by John T. Lyon, Alpheus E. Lesly, John Fraser Livingston. 1st Estate Sale Aug 1866. Buyers at sale: Phhilip S. Rutledge, Robert Hill, Isaac Branch, James W. Lesly. 2nd Estate Sale Nov 8, 1866. Buyers at sale: Rev. Wm. McWhorter, John H. Wilson, J. R. F. Wilson, Dr. James F. Livingston, James W. Lesly, John T. Lyon, Wm. Hill, Wm. Gordon, Robert H. Wardlaw, Thomas P. McClellan, Rev. John Turner, James D. Chalmers, Alpheus E. Lesly, Hiram W. Lawson, John T. Owen, Miss Eliza Kyle, Isaac Branch, John W. Cochran. Estate Settlement Sep 3, 1873. 1. Heirs of James

Kyle living in Miss. 2. Heirs of Wm. H. Kyle living in Florida 3. Margaret M. wife of Rev. Wm. McWhorter living in Oconee County 4. Eliza N. Kyle living in Abbeville. Final distributees received each $381.36. 1. James Kyle 2. Eliza N. Kyle 3. Wm. H. Kyle.

BOX 175 PACK 4668   MARY McCARTNEY   1863

Will dated Dec 18, 1850. Filed Mar 26, 1863. Witnesses: Mary T. J. Gray, A. L. Gray, Andrew Mantz. Daughter: Jane McCartney. Executor: Isaac Kennedy-friend and neighbor.

BOX 175 PACK 4669   LEWIS & JESSE MILLER (minors)   1865

Both minors died prior to reaching age of consent. Guardian: N. J. Davis. Administrator: James A. Crawford. Bond Feb 25, 1867 of $1,000 by James A. Crawford, John C. Crawford, Robert A. Crawford. Estate Settlement Jan 15, 1870. Jane, wife of John M. Hamilton, of Florida paid $443. She was the minors Mother.

BOX 175 PACK 4670   JAMES McLANE   1865

Administrator: Wm. K. Bradley-creditor. Bond Jan 2, 1867 of $2,000 by Wm. K. Bradley, John Wideman, Asbury T. Wideman. Wife: Milly McLane. (2) Children, not named. Appraisal Jan 17, 1867 by James McCaslan, David Morrah, Archibald Kennedy. Owned 23 acres of land. Estate Sale Jan 18, 1867. Buyers at sale: David Morrah, Milly McLane, Wm. K. Bradley, David Dowtin, Thmas O. Creswell, Jack Furqueron, James McCaslan, Samuel Link Sr., David J. Wardlaw, Wm. McLane, Thomas J. Horton, A. P. Connor, Dr. J. G. Gibert, John McLane, James Mathis, Archibald Kennedy, Samuel Link Jr., Samuel A. Brown, George Hanvey. Estate Insolvent.

BOX 175 PACK 4671   JOHN M. McDONALD   1866

Will dated Aug 9, 1864. Filed Oct 8, 1866. Witnesses: John F. Livingston, Andrew J. Wardlaw, Charles H. Allen. Executor: Thomas Thomson. Wife: Mary McDonald. Father-in-Law: Thomas Thomson. Appraisal Oct 22, 1869 by James D. Chalmers, Robert A. Archer, D. R. Williams. Estate Sale Oct 22, 1869. Buyers at sale: Thomas Thomson, A. J. Lee, James W. McCravey.

BOX 175 PACK 4672   MARY F. McALLISTER   1866

Administrator: Wm. L. Campbell. Bond Aug 24, 1866 of $200 by Wm. L. Campbell, Jesse A. McAllister, George W. Bowen Jr. Appraisal Sep 11, 1866 by S. C. Clinkscales, Joseph Bowen, Wm. D. Mann, Gilbert G. Dawson. Estate Sale Sep 11, 1866 netted $83.55. Buyers at sale: Mrs. D. McAllister, Mrs. S. McAllister, Mrs. A. Taylor, Mrs. M. Crawford, Miss E. Stephens, Ben. M. Campbell, Thomas A. Daniel Wm. D. Mann, Marcus Winn. 1st Return Aug 12, 1869. Coffin cost $3.

BOX 176 PACK 4673   MARY M. PURDY (minor)   1869

Guardian: Mary R. Purdy. Bond Jul 13, 1866 of $500 by Mary R. Purdy, Leroy Purdy, Patrick H. Bradley. Father: James M. Purdy. Mary M. Purdy was the only child.

BOX 176 PACK 4674   CHARLES M. PELOT   1868

Administrator: Lewis D. Merriman. Bond Feb 1, 1867 of $1,000 by Lewis D. Merriman, Wm. H. Parker, Robert A. Fair. 1st Return Feb 3, 1868.

BOX 176 PACK 4675   SUSAN PACE   1864

Administrator: Wm. T. Pace. Bond Aug 24, 1866 of $300 by Wm. T. Pace, Thomas J. Ellis. Daughters: Frances Ann Pace, Sarah Elizabaeth Pace. Last Return Oct 4, 1872.

BOX 176 PACK 4676   DR. ANDREW PAUL   1866

Will dated Aug 7, 1866. Filed Sep 3, 1866. Witnesses: Samuel B. McClinton, John g. Devlin, Samuel F. Edwards. Executor: David M. Wardlaw. Sister: Elizabeth J. Wardlaw. Appraisal Oct 23, 1866 by Samuel F. Edwards, Wm. Magill, Jacob Miller. Estate Sale Oct 23, 1866. Buyers at sale: David M. Wardlaw, Jacob Miller, John McNeill, Wm. Edwards.

BOX 176 PACK 4677   NANCY M. RONEY   1867

Administrator: James M. Wright. Bond Mar 1, 1867 of $100 by James M. Wright, G. W. Hodges, Tyra Y. Martin. Appraisal Mar 16, 1867 by Oshea R. Horton, J. F. Greer, Valentine Young. Estate Sale Mar 16, 1867 netted $62.85. Buyers at sale: Valentine Young, J. F. Greer, George Freeman, Tyra Y. Martin, Wm. Robertson, Oshea R. Horton, James M. Wright, Ezekiel Rasor, Thomas A. Ellis, J. N. Seawright, George Nickles, Michael B. McGee. Final return Jul 13, 1868. Paid Vance & Company burial exenses $10.52. Paid J. F. Greer $13 for coffin.

BOX 176 PACK 4678   ROBERT CLEMENT SHARP   1866

Will dated Jan 8, 1866. Filed Aug 6, 1866. Witenesses: A. C. Hawthorne, J. F. Donald, Thomas Hawthorne. Had (9) Chldren. Executor: Robert C. Sharp-son. Milford Burriss and wife, Vashti and Marshall Sharp challenged probation of the will claiming that that father was nearly 80 in very feeble condition and unduly influenced by others in his will. Appraisal Dec 20, 1866 of $6552 by D. O. Hawthorne, Wm. Agnew, James Cowan, S. W. Agnew, Thomas Hawthorne. 1st Estate Sale Dec 21, 1866 netted $1,751. Buyers at sale: Marshall Sharp, Robert C. Sharp, Wm. H. Sharp, M. J. Bailey, Alex. M. Agnew, Wm. Hagen, Thomas Hawthorne, Robert Hagen, Robert Anderson, Thomas Smith, Andrew Stevenson, Wm. G. Gordon, George Nickles, J. D. Lindley, J. W. Roland, Edward Hagen, John M. Hawthorne, Enoch M. Sharp, David O. Hawthorne, W. L. Magee, Alex. G. Hagen, James N. Drake, George Richey, John Hagen, Hugh R. Barmore. 2nd Estate Sale Nov 30, 1872. Buyers at sale: Silas Jones, Robert C. Sharp, J. F. Singleton, Lawson Albertson, E. Albertson, Robert C. Brownlee, Jack Saxon, Noah Saxon, Wm. Richey, Enoch Gambrell, G. M. Mattison, Larkin Agnew, Wm. Sharp, Wm. Gambrell, J. T. Nabors, John Cowan, Zachariah Haddon. (7) Heirs: 1. Milford Burriss and wife, Vashti of Anderson Co. 2. James W. Sherard and wife Asenath 3. Elizabeth McGee 4. Mary Jane Riggs 5. Wm. M. Sharp 6. Children of Johnson Sharp, Rev. C. B. Betts and wife Aramintha of Winnsboro.

BOX 176 PACK 4679   CORNELIUS M. SHARP   1866

Never Married. Administrator: Marshall Sharp – Brother. Bond Jul 30, 1866 of $2,000 by Marshall Sharp, Wesley Robertson, John T. Johnson.

BOX 176 PACK 4680   JOHN N. & EDWARD C. SELBY (minors)   1867

Guardian: Martha Selby. Bond Feb 18, 1867 of $1,000 by Edmund Anderson, Nathaniel Anderson, Henry Riley. Administrators: James M. Edwards, Edmund Anderson appointed Jul 30, 1862. Return of May 1870 only other entry.

BOX 176 PACK 4681   JAMES F. TOLBERT   1868

Administrator: Wm. H. Parker. Bond Jan 7, 1867 of $4,000 by Wm. H. Parker, Commissioner of Equity. Wife: Mary E. Tolbert. Appraisal Jan 24, 1867 by Peter Gibert, R. J. Williams, Wm. V. Clinkscales, John Wm. Power. Held notes on: Davis Boozer, Isabella M. Tolbert, Thomas Jeffries, Wm. Buchanan, C. A. Huckabee, Thomas Riley, Alex. Hunter, Wm. Boozer, John D. Adams, P. M. Tolbert, Vachel Hughey, Robert Harkness, Sarah J. Cunningham, Robert P. Buchanan, J. Foster Marshall, Silas Ray, Paschal D. Klugh. Estate Sale Jan 24, 1867 netted $581. Buyers at sale: Mary E. Tolbert, Green Johnson, F. P. Robertson, Thomas M. Bell, Lewis Clinkscaless, John M. Martin, Jacob Alewine, John W. Power, S. Cunningham, John McCurry, Henry H. Scuddy. Estate Settlement May 12, 1868. $504 tob e distributed. No details.

BOX 176 PACK 4682   BENJAMIN TALBERT   1866

Deceased died Jun 26, 1866. Administrator: Thomas B. Talbert, Mary Ann Talbert-wife. Bond Aug 10, 1866 of $10,000 by Thomas B. Talbert, Mary Ann Talbert, Wm. Truitt, Samuel B. Cook. Widow married Samuel B. Cook prior to Dec 1869. Appraisal Nov 5, 1866 by Hiram Palmer, James H. Britt, C. P. Holloway. Owned 153 acres of land. Held notes on: George Patterson, Wade Ethridge, Jacob Miller, Wm. Langley, Samuel B. Jones, Wm. M. Rogers, Wm. Truitt, Thomas Collier, Samuel N. Talbert, James S. Talbert, Thomas Thompson, Wm. C. Hunter, Peter Hemminger, John Sanders, Lemuel Robertson, Abram Price, Edmund Cowan, Edward Hinton. Estate Sale Nov 6, 1866 netted $5,526. Buyers at sale: Mary Ann Talbert, Wm. P. Dillashaw, Wm. Truitt, Charles H. Cowan, Reuben Weed, Samuel Jones, J. S. Talbert, Catlett Corley, Dr. Bradley, Wilson Watkins, Thomas Talbert, Mary LeRoy, George W. Mitchell, James Tompkins, G. Covin, J. T. Horton, Edmund Cowan, J. W. Gale, John Sanders, Ben. Hanvey, Ansel Talbert, Joseph Britt, George W. Hanvey, Wm. Mathews, Wm. Bosdell, Abram Martin, Sump Bradshaw, Lemuel P. Guffin, N. E. Brown, G. W. Nelson, Joseph Palmer, Edward Holloway, Thomas Mobley, Ben. McKittrick, David Wardlaw, James Jung, A. C. Brown, W. Martin, Nick Brown, James Truitt, Wm. Weed, C. Waller, Red Brown, John Attaway, George Sibert, Hiram Palmer, Thomas Lubbert, Thomas Horton, J. W. Gailey, James Newby, Andy Crozier, A. F. Gregory, Wm. McKittrick, Gus Traylor, Robert J. McCaslan, J. B. Creswell, John Lyon, L. L. Guffin, Daniel Holder, Wm. Mathis, Thomas C. McBryde, Daniel New, Oscar Shirley, Asa Sturkey, Edward O. Reagan, Fred Edmunds, M. McKinney, R. Price, John Deason, David J. Wardlaw, John Finley. Estate Settlement Dec 10, 1869. Widow and (8) Children: Widow 1/3 $182.36 she had previousl received $652. Children each $36.47. 1. Thomas B. Talbert 2. Michael S. Talbert 3. Samuel Nixon Talbert 4. Mary M. LeRoy wife of James P. LeRoy 5. James S. Talbet 6. Frances A. wife of James W. Gable 7. Ansel G. Talbert a minor 8. John Talbert died Aug 30, 1886, he was by 2nd wife. Supplemental Estate Settlement Dec 10, 1869: 1. James W. Gable and wife 2. J. Simpson Talbert 3. Michael S. Talbert 4. James P. Leroy in right of his wife.

154

BOX 176 PACK 4683   ROBERT R. TOLBERT   1866

Will dated Apr 26, 1866.   Filed Jul 12, 1866.   Witnesses: J. S. Chipley, E. Lake, M. M. Chipley.   Executor: John R. Tolbert.   Appraisal, no date, by J. S. Chipley, Nathaniel Henderson, Irvin Hutchison. Owned 400 acres of land. Wife Elizabeth Tolbert. Children: 1. Thomas N. Tolbert 2. Nancy Ann Tolbert 3. Elias L. Tolbert 4. Walter R. Tolbert 5. John R. Tolbert 6. George W. Tolbert. Paid A. A. Blythe $42 for coffin.

BOX 176 PACK 4684   JOSHUA M. TOWNSEND   1866

Administrator: J. Fletcher Townsend-brother. Bond Jun 1, 1866 of $1,000 by J. Fletcher Townsend, Joel W. Townsend, Robert E. Bowie. Lived in Town of Cokesbury.

BOX 176 PACK 4685   JOHN HENRY WIDEMAN   1867

Will dated Jul 17, 1861. Filed Jan 7, 1867. Witnesses: John I. Bonner, J. F. Kennedy, E. L. Patton. Executor: Adam T. Wideman-brother. Wife: Sarah Catherine Wideman. No Children. Owned 9 slaves at time of will. Estate Settlement Feb 18, 1867. Widow received entire estate.

BOX 176 PACK 4686   ADOLPHUS A. WILLIAMS   1866

Deceased died Aug 1866. Administrator: Margaret G. Williams-mother who lived in Georgia. Bond Oct 1, 1866 of $10,000 by Margaret G. Williams, Robert J. McBryde, Janet McLaren. McBryde & McLaren both moved to Virginia shorlty after signing bond. McBryde's security was dependent on the Estate of his Father, John McBryde which wsas considered to be insolvent. McLaren's security was dependent on the Estate of John McLaren. Jan 28, 1867 Administration Letters of Margaret G. Williams revoked. Petition for Letters by creditors, Joel T. Cunningham & H. Thompson Lyon not granted. Merchant. Appraisal Oct 5, 1866 by John A. Wier, John Enright, John T. Owen. Accounts of over $11,000 due to him at time of his death: Wm. Armstrong, Charles H. Allen, Sarah Allen Mrs. Allison, Wm. A. Allen, Dr. Robert A. Archer, Dr. Robert Bell, John Bass, H. C. Belcher, James A. Belcher, Miss Mary Belcher, Mrs. J. I. Baker, J. C. Belcher, John G. Baskin, W. W. Belcher, Joseph Blackwell, Branch & Allen, Miss Mary Barksdale, John Belcher, David Cleland, Julius Cleary, George W. Cromer, Conner & Anderson, Wm. C. Cook, James S. Cothran, T. J. Cleary, James C. Calhoun, James D. Chalmers, James Cunningham, Estate of John Cothran, A. C. Champlain, John Coumbe, Edward Cobb, John Wesley Cochran, R. L. Chalmers, Thomas B. Crews, James N. Cochran, James Clark, Charles Cox, David Clary, James H. Cobb, James S. Coiner, Wm. B. Davis, Miss Sue DeBruhl, Wm. B. Dorn, Miss Mary Dannelly, Mrs. Charles Dendy, Ben. F. Davis, Epaminenandos Edwards, Stephen C. DeBruhl, Lawrence R. Dantzler, Ben. A. Davis, Dr. Robert Devlin, D. H. Drennan, Robert M. Davis, Thomas Eakin, M. Lewis Edwards, Jane A. Frazier, J. W. Griffin, Mrs. Langdon C. Haskell, Charles T. Haskell, Wm. C. Harris, Wm. Harris, Rev. Green W. Huckabee, Henry S. Hammond, Henry H. Harper, H. L. Hammond, Dr. T. C. Hunter, A. F. Haddon, Miss Alice Hamilton, C. Power Huckabee, J. Turner Gordon, James Ivorie, Samuel Henry Jones, J. T. Johnson, John S. Jeffries, Grant T. Jackson, Dr. David A. Jordan, Allen Lee, Dr. Hiram T. Lyon, A. F. Lipford, Mary A. Ligon, Thomas F. Lanier, C. F. Marshall, Dr. J. W. W. Marshall, Joseph T. Moore, Mrs. B. A. Martin, Dr. Thomas J. Mabry, Dr. Matt Mabry, James Martin, James M. Martin, Dr.

Thomas C. Mabry, Wm. H. McCaw, John McLaren, H. H. McGowan, John McCryde, John McBryde Jr., Miss Julia McCown, Ben. McCreary, Thomas McNest, Ben. McLaughlin, Calvin McClain, Samuel McAter, Milford McWhorter, Enoch Nelson, Wm. G. Neel, Mathew C. Owens, M. T. Owens, James M. Perrin, John C. Pursley, Miss Elizabeth Purdy, Dr. Ed Porter, Wash L. Price, Leroy Purdy, Dr. Ed Parker, Miss Joe Pope, Dr. Andrew Paul, Hugh M. Prince, Wm. H. Perrin, Thomas C. Perrin, Dr. Ebeneezer E. Pressly, James L. Pratt, Philip S. Rutledge, Samuel Reid, Mrs. E. A. Robertson, Mrs. M. V. Richey, Thomas L. Robertson, Roche & Christian, George Richey, Wm. M. Rogers, Ben. Rousey, Beckham Rousey, Augustus M. Smith, George Smith, George W. Syfan, Thomas M. Smith, James T. Sitton, George Stancell, Andrew Small, Hiram T. Tusten, Thomas Thomson, Miss Lou Tribble, James Taggart Sr., Mrs. E. Taggart, M. & C. Winestock, Dr. J. J. Wardlaw, Leroy C. Wilson, John White, Miss Sue E. Wilson, H. S. Wilson, John H. Wilson, J. G. Wilson, John R. Wilson, R. C. White, Wm. H. White, James A. Wideman, Ed Westfield. Notes held on: Tthomas W. Allen, J. C. C. Allen, Dr. Robert A. Archer, J. G. Baskin, Wesley A. Black, James W. Black, John Bass, James A. Brownlee, Wm. Bulloock, W. B. Boyd, Wm. Butler, Elbridge H. Bell, David S. Benson, Wm. P. Belcher, Armistead Burt, George C. Bowen, Wm. R. Buchanan, Samuel H. Beard, J. C. Belcher, J. N. Belcher, B. M. Blease, Charles Cox, James H. Cobb, Wm. E. Champlain, Thomas J. Clary, Willam S. Cochran, David Cleland, J. N. Cochran, James S. Cothran, James E. Cobb, Robert N. Cheatham, Samuel G. Cothran, Leonidas D. Connor, James Clark, James D. Chalmers, Stephen C. DeBruhl, Lawrence R.. Dantzler, J. F. Dannelly, C. Cozzens, J. B. Cartwright, Jesse C. Ellis, Moseley L. Edwards, Robert A. Fair, O. F. Farrington, George Graves, John Gray, W. M. Griffin, Ben. E. Gibert, Ben. McKittrick, Pleasant Searles, J. H. Hester, John A. Hunter, Henry H. Harper, Sarah Hill, Abram F. Haddon, Alex. R. Houston, Andrew M. Hill, Henry S. Hammond, Robert C. Harkness, J. E. Hodges, Wm. Ludlow Hodges, Thomas J. Hearst, A. Harris, Frederick Ives, B. Johnson, Dewitt Jones, Samuel Henry Jones, H. A. Jones, J. W. Jones, D. F. Jones, Grant T. Jackson, Robert Keoun, Wm. E. Link, J. W. Lesly, Alpheus Lesly, Thomas Link, J. S. Link, Harvey T. Lyon, Wm. A. Lesly, T. F. Lanier, James T. Lites, John T. Lyon, L. H. Lomax, J. J. Lipford, George O. Morris, Junius C. Martin, George W. Miller, W. Y. Miller, Thomas J. Mabry, Andrew Morrison, Michael S. Mann, J. F. Marshall, John McNeill, J. M. Martin, T. P. Martin, J. F. McComb, Wm. McCaslan, David McLaughlin, P. C. McCaslan, Wm. M. McCaslan, A. F. McCord, Samuel McGowan, John McBryde, Nimrod McCord, J. McQuerns, J. C. McNab, Wm. G. Neel, Ed Noble, Barney O'Connor, E. L. Parker, T. C. Pressly, Andrew Paul, Hugh M. Prince, Robert M. Palmer, Warren Richey, W. W. Russell, Louis H. Russell, F. P. Robertson, Wm. M. Rogers, J. W. Rousey, Frederick W. Selleck, J. L. Shields, George W. Syfan, George W. Speer, Harmon W. Stevenson, James Shillito, J. R. Seals, Hiram T. Tusten, James Taggart, James Taggart Jr., Walter Thomas, Moses O. Tallman, Willard Walker, Moses Winestock, Andrew Woodhurst, James A. Wideman, Wardlaw & Lyon, John H. Wilson, R. A. Wilson, R. J. White, David M. Wardlaw, Littleton Yarborough.

BOX 176 PACK 4687   WILLIAM Y. WALKER   1866

Administrator: Margaret E. Walker-wife. Bond Nov 6, 1866 of $2,000 by Margaret E. Walker, Benjamin Pearman, R. N. Wright, Wm. Pruitt. Appraisal Nov 20, 1866 by Wilson Ashley, Samuel S. Fisher, Wm. N. Wilson. Held notes and accounts on: Thomas J. Higdon, Caleb Shaw, James Nelson, Thomas J. Kerr, D. O. Hawthorne, Wm. Bannister, Joseph Alewine, Wm. Armstrong, Wm. Burton, Thomas Bannister, John B. Armstrong,

John Shirley, Robert A. Archer, Anna Robinson, John Fields, John Wilson. Estate Sale Nov 27, 1866 netted $1,420. Buyers at sale: Margaret E. Walker, Wm. Pruitt, G. W. L. Mitchell, Christopher Ellis, Robert Pratt, B. F. Driver, E. O. Pruitt, J. F. Strickland, James Adams, James Bannister, Rachel Kerr, John McDonald, L. Jones, Josiah Fowler, John Shirley, W. Washington, Andrew H. Stone, John B. Armstrong, John T. McClain, N. Robinson, W. M. Alewine, Bartlett T. Gray, L. M. Stone, W. J. Shirley, E. Ashley, R. C. Wilson, Wm. A. Fields, Joseph M. Murdock, R. N. Wright, T. H. Stone, Wm. L. Young, James B. McWhorter, Joshua Ashley, John M. Mattison, Ben. Pearman, Wm. Armstrong, James S. Carwile, John D. Alelwine, John F. Clinkscales, S. S. Fisher, Joshua Pruitt. 1st Estate Settlement Feb 13, 1875. Distributees: 1. M. E. Robinson 2. J. R. Walker 3. Jane E. Kay 4. Margaret Walker. 2nd Estate Settlement Nov 6, 1885. Disstributees: Hannah Branyon and Jane E. Kay each $448.85, J. R. Walker.

BOX 176 PACK 4688   JOSIAH WELLS   1867

Will dated Aug 23, 1866. Filed Feb 2, 1867. Witnesses: Thomas B. Scott, E. M. Roberts, Wm. H. Davis. Administrator: John Link. Wife: Frances Wells. Daughter: Lucretia Paschall. Sons: Samuel Wells, Wm. H. Wells. 1st Appraisal Mar 20, 1867. 2nd Appraisal Jan 10, 1868 by Wm. H. Taggart, E. M. Roberts, Thomas B. Scott. Held notes and accounts on: Martha E. Wells, Catherine F. Wells, Wm. H. Wells, Thomas B. Scott, Jane Baker, Mrs. E. Clay, Moore Mitchell, Wm. Sutherland. Estate Sale Jan 10, 1868. Buyers at sale: J. D. Welch, Wm. A. Clay, Frances Wells, Samuel A. Link, Wm. H. Taggart, Lewis Cowan, Wm. D. Mars, Wm. McNair, Dr. E. M. Roberts, B. C. Napier, Samuel C. Link. Estate still active Aug 25, 1875. Coffin cost $8.

BOX 176 PACK 4689   JOHN WEBB   1873

Will dated Oct 6, 1866. Filed Oct 19, 1866. Witnesses: Wm. H. Hammond, Hezekiah Elgin, R. Martin, James Seawright. Executor: James Seawright. Wife: Delilah Webb. Sons: William Webb, John Webb, R. Cowan Webb. Daughters: Milly H. Webb, Martha Webb. Willed $5 tothebastard son of Louisa Templeton. Appraisal Nov 30, 1866 by A. C. Hawthorne, L. F. Donald, Hezekiah Elgin. Estate Sale Nov 30, 1866 netted $217. Buyers at sale: A. C. Hawthorne, N. Drennan, Oliver P. Hawthorne, Samuel Donald, James Seawright, --- Beadell. Estate Settlement Feb 5, 1880. No names.

BOX 176 PACK 4690   MISSING

BOX 177 PACK 4691   WILLIAM ARMSTRONG   1868

Administrator: Ezekiel Harris, Elizabeth Armstrong-wife. Bond Feb 10, 1868 of $4,000 by Elizabeth Armstrong, Ezekiel Harris, Hugh Robinson, John B. Armstrong, John Shirley, John J. Copeland. (12) Children. Appraisal Feb 25, 1868 by Thomas W. Branyon, James A. Cowan, George Shirley. Book account detailing money activities between father and son, John B. Armstrong. Held notes on from 1849: John S. Carwile, Robert A. Archer, Ben. Pearman, J. D. Kay, W. C. Armstrong, Wm. Y. Walker, John G. Gantt, Richard Taylor, John Shirley, A. S. Armstrong, James H. Kay, M. S. Strickland, P. A. Greer, Stephen M. Tribble, Wm. Duncan, Wm. Bell, Roley Bannister, James A. Cowan, Wm. Armstrong, G. W. Alewine, Wiley Mitchell, John B. Armstrong, H. W. Shaw, James Hopkins, Marion H. Kay, John W. Brock, Anna Robinson, John H. Seawright, D. M. Kay, Martha Griffin, Hugh

Gantt, Jesse Robinson, Wm. Bratcher, James Y. Sitton, W. P. Killingsworth, Billy Bannister. Estate Sale Feb 27, 1868 netted $3,871. Buyers at sale: Elizabeth Armstrong, James A. Cowan, J. B. Dorr, Wm. C. Armstrong, M. E. Walker, J. A. Armstrong, Thomas M. Branyon, J. S. Carwile, M. M. Alewine, Wm. Duncan, J. B. Hall, James Wilson, James Adams, James Nabors, J. W. Wilson, Stephen M. Tribble, A.C. Burton, John Shirley, Ezekiel Harris, J. G. E. Branyon, W. W. Rowland, J. L. Robinson, Archibald P. Shirley, Oliver P. Hawthorne, Amarizah R. Ellis, J. M. Drake, Wm. Hood, J. C. Shaw, J. N. Young, Wm. McComb, E. H. Robertson, John Tribble, John Green, R. Chamblee, Richard W. Burts, Hezekiah Eligin, J. J. Wilson, F. P. Robertson, Wm. E. Barmore, Wm. A. Kay, James H. Brock, John J. Copeland, G. W. L. Mitchell, Ben. F. Driver, George Wilson, T. P. Jones. Estate Settlement Mar 15, 1870. (8) Legatees: 1. J. F. Burton and wife $266 2. John Shirley and wife $222 3. Ezekiel Harris and wife $216 4. Richard Robinson and wife, Margaret E. $215 5. John B. Armstrong 195 6. John J. Copeland and wife $216 7. Thomas J. Bowen and wife, Amanda $216 8. Stephen M. Tribble and wife $114. Tombstone cost $51.90.

BOX 177 PACK 4692   JAMES C. CALHOUN   1867

Administrator: Belinda M. Calhoun who moved to sT. Louis. Bond Apr 8, 1867 of $6,000 by Belinda M. Calhoun, John A. Calhoun, James S. Cothran. Estate Sale Mar 8, 1870 netted $157.25. Buyers at sale: Trowbridge & Co., Perrin & Cothran, Robert R. Hemphill, Wm. A. Lee, Lewis W. Perrin. Minor Children were: 1. J. Kirtland Calhoun 2. Treadwell A. Calhoun 3. James C. Calhoun 4. Lucy Calhoun 5. John A. Calhoun. Estate Settlement Oct 3, 1873 1/3 to widow = $97.81. To Children: $195.84.

BOX 177 PACK 4693   URIAH COLVIN   1867

Administrator: Daniel Holder. Bond Oct 5, 1867 of $800 by Daniel Holder, Wm. Reynolds, Daniel Holder Jr. Appraisal Nov 26, 1867 of $10.55 by Daniel Minor, Nathaniel S. Harrison, J. S. Stalnaker.

BOX 177 PACK 4694   JOHN CHARLES   1868

Will dated Mar 12, 1868. Filed Jun 15, 1868. Witnesses: John S. Reid, Francis Wilson, Rebecca Thornton. Daughters: Mary Dixon, Henrietta Dixon. Son-in-law: Robert S. Dixon. Executors: Robert S. Dixon who moved to Stark County, Ga. and for 12 years did not account for the money in his possession that belonged to the estate. He was summoned to appear in court, he failed to appear, on Feb 22, 1893 and his Letters were revoked. Wm. C. McNeill appointed administrator in 1893. Bond Mar 16, 1893 of $250 by Wm. C. McNeill, John O. Brooks, J. H. McNeill. John Charles left (6) Children surviving him: 1. Annie Powell in Alabama 2. Henry Charles in Alabama 3. Peter Charles in Newberry 4. Rebecca McNeill 5. Mary Dixon who had no children and died in 1895 6. Harriet D. Dixon in Georgia, she received $100 in 1895. Estate Settlement Mar 3, 1896. (4) Legatees: 1. W. C. McNeill 2. J. H. McNeill 3. Annie Powell's heirs, not heard from 4. Betsy Breazeal whose whereabouts were not know for many years as she had left South Carolina about 1850. She died prior to John Charles. Anoather list lists (4) Legatees: 1. Harriet Dixon 2. Rebecca McNeill deceased 3. Peter Charles deceased 4. Henry Charles deceased wose wife was Sarah and she received $51.90. Peter Charles heirs each received $38.65: 1. J. D. Charles 2. Ada Caughman 3. A. G.Charles 4. Mary Duncan.

158

Henry Charles heirs each received $21.03: 1. B. F. Charles 2. T. S. Charles 3. Lovenia Price 4. Isabella Busly 5. H. H. Charles.

BOX 177 PACK 4695   KATE CALHOUN   1868

Administrator: James Edward Calhoun. Bond May 16, 1868 of $3,000 by James Edward Calhoun, Edward Noble, James H. Cobb. Estate Settlement Feb 18, 1873 Children now living in Florida.

BOX 177 PACK 4696   NATHANIEL COBB   1867

Administrator: Rosa A. Moore-wife. Bond Nov 18, 1867 of $6,000 by Rosa A. Moore, John Carter, Wm. H. Moore. Apprasial Dec 3, 1867 by Wm. A. Lomax, John H. Mundy, John W. Lomax. Estate Sale: Dec 4, 1867 netted $1,193. Buyers at sale: A. F. McCord, Archibald McCord, A. M. Blake, Wm. R. Mundy, Adam P. Boozer, Allen Cromer, Joseph Davis, Wm. L. McCord, James A. McCord, Wm. H. Moore, G. D. Hurley, John Carter, John Cobb, Abram Cobb, S. A. Dike, Thmas Richardson, R. A. Moore, Louis H. Russell, Charles A. Botts, J. H. Marshall, J. D. Pace, Grant T. Jackson, Charles A. Cobb, James D. Chalmers, John Lomax, Ben. Martin, Samuel Lomax, Franklin E. Bowie, J. E. G. Bell, David Inge. Estate Settlement Jul 22, 1868. Legatees: Rosa A. Moore, widow 1/3. (6) Children each $161.95. 1. James H. Cobb 2. N. S. Cobb 3. Frances wife of John G. Carter 4. James M. Cobb in right of his father, Edmund Cobb 5. Elizabeth wife of J. E. G. Bell 6. Wm. A. Cobb. J. W. Sign $37.50 for coffin. James D. Chalmers $69 for headstone. Thomas Richardson $4 for digging grave.

BOX 177 PACK 4697   ROBERT ALEXANDER CRAWFORD   1868

Administrator: James A. Crawford. Bond Oct 14, 1867 of $2,000 by James A. Crawford, Charles Evans, Jane R. Crawford. Appraisal Dec 9, 1867 by Charles Evans, Wm. J. Hammond, Wm. Magill. Estate Sale Dec 10, 1867 netted $643. Buyers at sale: John J. Edwards, Sallie Armstrong, Edward Westfield, James A. Crawford, Thomas McNeill, Dr. Drennan, John C. Douglass, Lemuel Shoemaker, D. D. Brooks, Wm. Hill, Jeptha R. Hamlin, Jane Crawford, Robert Devlin, Dr. Thomas J. Mabry, Wm. Carter, Thomas Jackson, James Evans, Thomas J. McCracken, H. K. Burdette, John C. Walker, Wm. J. Hammond. Estate Settlement Nov 11, 1869. Widow and (2) Children. Jane Crawford, widow $333.25. Elizabeth wife of John J. Edwards split $333.25 with whom not stated.

BOX 177 PACK 4698   JAMES R. DUBOSE SR.   1867

Administrator: James R. DuBose Jr. Bond Sep 30, 1867 of #0,000 by James R. DuBose, Elizabeth A. DuBose, Robert M. DuBose. Appraisal Nov 25, 1867 by Thomas P. Hester, Francis A. Calhoun, Hugh McCelvey, James McCelvey. Held notes on: E. Perkins, Mary H. Sprouse, V. E. Harper, R. H. Vickers, L. Barber, Robert M. DuBose, James R. DuBose, T. Johnson, J. J. Robertson, T. M. Pinkston, W. S. Pinkston, J. R. Kirkland, J. T. Keough, R. Chappell, W. Ahron, W. Hampton, T. B. Weems, J. F. Nance, G. G. Wingfield.

BOX 177 PACK 4699   WILLIAM A., JASPER N., JAMES R., & JOHN C. DARBY   1867

Minors. Guardian: Wm. Duncan. Bond Dec 23, 1867 of $1,000 by Wm. Duncan, Thomas Crawford, Robert W. Haddon. Jun 18, 1883 Wm. A. Darby, Jasper N. Darby, James R.

Darby all now 21 years of age. Sarah E. Brock of Anderson gave Grand Father, Wm. Duncan rents and profits.

BOX 177 PACK 4700   LENORA EDWARDS   1868

Administrator: George McDuffie Miller. Bond Jul 18, 1868 of $500 by George McDuffie Miller, Joel J. Cunningham, James T. Robertson. Husband: James Harvey Edwards. Feb 9, 1869 estate received money from Thomas J. Mabry who was the administrator of the estate of W. Henderson, balance due from Mabry was $62.18. Estate Settlement Nov 10, 1869. (4) Distributees: Husband, James Harvey Edwards $51.96 and (3) Children each $34.64: 1. James McCanty 2. Allen McCanty 3. Wm. H. Edwards. Joseph McCanty minor settlement made Oct 30, 1873. He had become of age and received $20.91 from his guardian James S. Gibert.

BOX 177 PACK 4701   NANCY McNEES FURMAN   1867

Administrator: James Kincaid Vance. Bond Sep 2, 1867 of $3,000 by James Kincaid Vance, John Vance, Hugh Vance. Lived at Cokesbury at time of death but most of her life lived and owned property in Fairfield District. Had a brother and children of a deceased sister. J. C. Furman administered Fairfield Estate. Appraisal of Cokesbury Estate Sep 18, 1867 by Wm. A. Moore, J. Harp Vance, Gabriel Hodges, John Vance. Sale of Cokesbury Estate Sep 18, 1867. Buyers at sale: Miss E. K. Sims, Newton Sims, Mrs. S. C. Waldrop, James K. Vance, Miss N. M. Sims, J. F. Grier, John Vance, Miss Anna Sims. Estate Sale of Fairfield District property Dec 30, 1867. Buyers at sale: L. V. Sims, J. K. Rabe, James K. Vance, D. B. Kirkland, James Gelston, J. W. Evans.

BOX 177 PACK 4702   GRIZELLA GILLESPIE   1867

Administrator: John Samuel Williams. Bond Dec 20, 1867 of $300 by John Samuel Williams, James C. Pressy, Louis H. Russell. Appraisal Dec 24, 1867 by Samuel Lockridge, John G. Walker, J. F. Williams. Estate Sale Dec 24, 1867. Buyers at sale: James C. Pressly, John Samuel Williams, James Smith, Harvey Edwards, N. Walker, Sarah G. Gillespie, Leroy J. Johnson, H. R. Burdette, Green Ramey. John Bass paid $15 for coffin.

BOX 177 PACK 4703   JOHN GILES   1867

Deceased died in 1865. Administrator: Wm. A. Giles. Bond Dec 16, 1867 of $500 by Wm. A. Giles, James T. Liddell, James R. Cunningham. Appraisal Dec 24, 1867 by James T. Burton, others not listed. Estate Sale Dec 24, 1867 netted $258.13. Buyers at sale: Andrew J. Clinkscales, Wm. Speer, George W. Daniel, Edwin Calhoun, Henry R. Freeman, Wm. Giles, Robert Hutchison, Thomas J. Hill, James T. Baskin, J. M. Martin, George W. Speer, Fannie Giles, J. J. Cunningham, Henry Daniel, George A. Winn, James W. Huckabee. Estate Settlement Aug 30, 1884 (6) Distributees each $55.54: 1. Wm. A. Giles 2. Fannie Scott 3. Joseph Giles 4. Zella Giles 5. James Giles 6. Josephine Giles.

BOX 177 PACK 4704   DENNIS FLETCHER JONES   1867

Will dated Dec 14, 1866. Filed Mar 26, 1867. Witensses: J. H. Wilson, T. E. Roulain, Jake Roulain. Wife: Eliza P. Jones. Executor: Eliza P. Jones-wife. Appraisal Apr 4, 1869 by John H. Watson, Wm. H. Parker, Edward Noble. Owned large law library andother books. Estate Settled in Equity Court.

BOX 177 PACK 4705   JOSEPH F. KELLER   1868

Administrator: Walter G. Keller. Bond Mar 13, 1868 of $6,000 by Walter G. Keller, Thomas J. Edwards, Susanna E. Puckett, Martha J. White, Eliza C. Keller, Saina Ann Keller, Lavinia M. Keller. Never married. Appraisal Apr 17, 18868 by Henry R. Russell, Isaac Caldwell, Tyra Jay, James D. Neel, John C. Chiles. Held notes on: Walter G. Keller, Thomas J. Edwards, John C. Chiles, C. A. Puckett, Thomas McBey, James E. Gibson, Jonah Gibson, James White, James W. Puckett, Isaac Caldwell. Estate Sale Apr 17, 1868 netted $501.85. Buyers at sale: Walter G. Keller, L. A. Keller, C. C. Keller, Thomas J. Edwards, S. E. Peake, James H. Wideman, Shack Moragne, Edward O. Reagan, Dr. J. L. Pressly, James Puckett, James D. Neel, James Reagan, Tyra Jay, Ben. B. Harveley, M. J. White. Estate Settlement Nov 14, 1872. (7) Distributees, father and (6) sisters: 1. Walter G. Keller, father 2. Mary M. Edwards 3. Susan E. Puckett 4. Eliza C. Keller 5. Martha J. M. White 6. L. R. Keller 7. L. Margaret Keller. Seal & Sign paid $110 for funeral expenses. James D. Chalmers paid $79.10 for headstone.

BOX 177 PACK 4706   PASCHAL D. KLUGH   1867

Will dated Nov 25, 1865. Filed Sep 4, 1867. Witnesses: J. J. Wardlaw, Henry Riley, John Taggart. Executor: Henry G. Klugh-son. Daughter: Eliza wife of Wm. C. Norwood living in Georgia. Grand Son: Paschal D. Klugh son of Henry G. Klugh. Appraisal Oct 7, 1867 by Robert Anderson, James Strawhorn, S. A. Dike. Estate Sale Oct 23, 1867 netted $493.42. Buyers at sale: Henry G. Klugh, Henry Nickles, Wm. McNary, W. C. Klugh, R. D. Stanzler, Robert Anderson, Fletcher Hodges, Widow, Louis H. Russell, Wm. Hall, Thomas Ellis. Bailey, Parks & Bailey paid $33.05 for burial expenses. Irvin & Haralson paid $35 for coffin.

BOX 177 PACK 4707   ELIAS KAY   1869

Will dated Oct 7, 1867. Filed Nov 25, 1867. Witnesses: Robert Stuckey, Hugh M. Prince, Edward Davis. Executor: Roger L. Williams. Wife: Ursley Kay. Daughters: Eliza Ann Kay, Mary Catherine Kay. Had other children not named. Willed 3 acres and house to Elizabeth McCurry, not married. Appraisal Dec 11, 1867 by Hugh M. Prince, James Hodge, A. Hodge, J. A. Brownlee. Held notes on: J. W. McAllister, Cowan & Robertson, Joseph Brown, Wm. M. Tate, Robert C. Harkness, T. G. Baker, Wm. R. McAllister, G. F. Steifer. Much detailed information on a note for a land transaction. Estate Sale Dec 11, 1867. Buyers at sale: J. P. Brownlee, Thomas J. Hill, Wesley M. Kay, T. G. Baker, Ben. Lynch, Wm. A. Geanes, George Wilson Bowen, R. F. Bell, J. W. Black, Arsley M. Kay, Samuel J. Davis, Roger L. Williams, R. F. Bell, Elizabeth McCurry, Andrew J. McCurry. Aug 22, 1877 petition for estate accounting filed by Amandeline and E. D. Kay versus Roger Williams. Estate Settlement Aug 1877: 1. Amandaline, widow 2. Elias D. Kay, son deceased 3. Mary C. wife of James Masters 4. Eliza A. wife of Albert Baker 5. Albert W. Kay 6. Marshall Kay age 19 7. Emma P. Kay age 18 8. Ella Kay age 14. Wm. Dixon paid $10 for coffin.

BOX 177 PACK 4708   DR. AARON W. LYNCH   1868

Will dated Jul 7, 1862. Witnesses: J. H. Cobb, James W. Black, W. A. Gainey. Codicil 1864. Witnesses: W. A. Gainey, Ssterling M. Bowen, J. H. Cobb. Executrix: Elizabeth Lynch-wife. Bond Feb 15, 1868 of $155.10 by Elizabeth Lynch, Thomas J. Hill, Henry S. Kerr. Daughters: Eliza Lynch, Martha Lynch, Sarah Jean Lynch. Sons: Wm. Edward Lynch, Addison Watson Lynch. Step-Son: James W. Crawford. Appraisal Jan 20, 1868 by M. B. Latimer, J. T. Haddon, Thomas J. Hill, Sterling Bowen. Estate Sale Jan 21, 1868. Buyers at sale: Elizabeth Lynch, Wm. H. Adamson, George Scott.

BOX 177 PACK 4709   WILLIAM LESLY   1868

Will dated Feb 4, 1860. Filed Dec 28, 1867. Witnesses: Lemuel Reid, Thomas Lesly, John W. Lesly. Executor: Alpheus E. Lesly. Daughter: Virginia E. Montgomery. Sons: Alpheus E. Lesly, John J. Lesly. Grand Son: Wm. A. Montgomery. Grand Daughters: Lucy Rink Norris, Martha L. Norris. Appraisal Feb 4, 1868 by J. Fraser Livingston, Samuel Gilmer, John W. Lesly. Estate Settlement Jun 28, 1869. Alpheus E. Lesly and John J. Lesly received tahe entire estte except for $20 left to the Bible Society.

BOX 177 PACK 4710   DR. JOHN FRASER LIVINGSTON   1867

Will dated Sep 10, 1866. Filed Nov 1, 1867. Witnesses: Wm. Joel Smith, Wm. H. McCaw, Ione Smith. Had (5) Children. Daughters: Sarah Livingston, Eliza L. Wardlaw. Son: John Fraser Livingston, James Wm. Livingston. Executors: John Fraser Livingston, James Wm. Livingston-sons. Appraisal Dec 5, 1867 by John W. Lesly, Alpheus E. Lesly, Samuel Gilmer. Held notes on: John A. Martin, Richard B. Cater, Eliza M. Ligon, James Taggart Sr., Mathis & Sale, John C. Mauldin, C. C. Puckett, J. W. Franks, John Patterson, J. M. Bell, Leroy J. Johnson, J. Foster Marshall, Grant T. Jackson, Donald McLaughlin, Edmond Cobb, F. M. Mitchell, F. A. Baker, Wm. Bullock, Andrew McLane, Charles Cox, Samuel R. Lomax, Harvey T. Lyon, John H. Wilson, M. R. Banner, Wm. R. Buchanan, Dennis F. Jones, James W. Thomas, Charles H. Allen, Edward Noble. ACCOUNTS: John A. Calhoun, James M. Perrin, J. Foster Marshall, Henry Wilson, James Moore, Dr. John S. Reid, Mrs. David Keller, James H. Cobb, Andrew L. Gillespie, Harvey T. Lyon, Williamson Belcher, James T. Liddell, Moses T. Owen, Eliza Ligon, Vincnet Ratcliffe, James A. Norwood, Louisa Lesly, J. J. Wardlaw, Samuel Donaldson, Robert Crawford, James D. Chalmers, Stark Martin, John White, James Carlisle, Edward Westfield, Leroy J. Johnson, Dr. Isaac Branch, Mary Martin, Nathaniel J. Davis, Charity Golding, Alpheus E. Lesly, Andrew J. Woodhurst, John T. Lyon. Estate Sale Dec 19, 1867 netted $1,474. Buyers at sale: John A. Mays, Miss Sallie Livingston, Miss Eliza Wardlaw, John F. Livingston, Turner Gilmer, Wm. McIlwain, James Liddell, John W. Lesly, Mary J. Perrin, John W. Livingston, John A. Wier, James Y. Liddell, Wm. McIlwain, Wesley McIlwain, Mrs. E. L. Wardlaw, John Enright, Harvey T. Lyon, Billy Thomas, Patrick Lee, J. T. Liddell, George A. Douglass, Mary Miller, E. J. Jordan, B. J. Cochran, Jerry Bacon, J. C. Martin, McDuffie Cochran, Thomas Thomson. Apr 1870 paid Mrs. K. C. Perrin $2,500 for house and lot in Town of Abbeville. Estate Settlement Jan 7, 1876 Children of James Wardlaw Perrinand Mary Jane Livingston. 1. Thoas C. Perrin 2. John L. Perrin 3. Sarah A. Perrin 4. Emma C. Perrin 5. Wm. F. Perrin 6. J. Wardlaw Perrin. Eliza L. Wardlaw $4,313.74, Sarah M. Livingston $4,313.74. Legatees each $3533: 1. James Wardlaw Livingston 2. John F. Livingston 3. Sarah M. Livingston 4. Mrs. E. L. Wardlaw 5. Heirs of Mrs. Mary J. Perrin. James D. Chalmers paid $134.70 for tombstone.

BOX 177 PACK 4711   HUGH PORTER   1867

Administrator: Johnson Sale. Bond Oct 25, 1867 by Johnson Sale, Josephine R. Lake, F. W. Andrews, Thomas J. Ouzts. Wife: Elizabeth H. Porter. Appraisal Nov 20, 1867 by Irvin Hutchison, Frank Johnson, John Butler, Stanmore B. Brooks. Estate Sale Nov 20, 1867 netted $465. Buyers at sale: Ben. Porter, Elizabeth Porter, Johnson Sale, M. Devore, John R. Moore, Stanmore B. Brooks, Henry Wilkinson, George R. Caldwell, Dr. Ligon, H. Anderson, Thomas Metts, John Butler, W. Smith, D. J. Witt, J. N. Briscoe, J. W. McDowell, Thomas L. Coleman. Had several children, not named.

BOX 177 PACK 4712   ABRAHAM P. POOL   1867

Will dated Feb 17, 1858   Filed Oct 15, 1867. Witnesses: Wm. Carter, Alex. McNeill, Simeon Chaney. Executors: Nathaniel McCants, James W. Lipscomb-son-in-law. Wife Jemina Pool died in 1895. (4) Daughters: 1. Sarah Eugneia wife of James W. Lipscomb 2. Susan Augustus wife of James M. McBryde 3. Elliott Euphemia wife of Nathaniel T. McCants 4. Emma Ann wife of Thomas L. Moore. Appraisal Nov 25, 1867 by Thomas C. Griffin, Wm. A. Limbecker, Wm. Fooshe, Richard A. Griffin, Thomas S. Blake. Owned large amounts of land including the Meriwether tract, Child tract, Templeton tract, Bell tract and land in Cass County Ga. Owned 38 slaves at time of will. Held notes on: Daniel Holder, Bank of Newberry, Wm. Pool, Elihu G. Sheppard, J. S. Chipley, J. M. Walker, James McBryde, James W. Lipscomb, Joseph S. Tolbert, Wm. Hargrove, Nathaniel McCants, James M. Gilliam, James Pert. Estate Settlement Aug 9, 1899. E. A. Moore and her husband received 1/3 $1,858. (4) Full shares $556: 1. Estate of Eugenia Lipscomb. Her Children were John Lipscomb, Lawto Lipscomb, George Lipscomb, Eugene Lipscomb, Mary Lipscomb 2. Susan McBryde 3. E. E. Moore 4. Estate of E. A. Moore. The (4) full share heirs had previously received $1,890 each.

BOX 177 PACK 4713   JOHN WILLIAM PENNEY   1865

Will dated Feb 17, 1866. Filed Jan 10, 1868. Witnesses: David R. Penney, Talbert Cheatham, Wm. O. Pursley. Executor: Wm. T. Penney-son. Son: John H. Penney. Appraisal Jan 18, 1868 by Charles B. Guffin, James M. Edwards, David R. Penney. Estate Settlement Mar 1881. (8) Legatees: 1. Mary E. Penney 2. John H. Penney 3. L. C. Penney 4. Nancy H. Penney 5. M. A. Walker 6. Margaret H. Penney 7. Alice E. Penney 8. Julia J. Penney. Coffin cost $29.

BOX 177 PACK 4714   THOMAS A. PRESSLY (minor)   1867

Guardian: J. C. Pressly. Bond Dec 23, 1867 of $100 by J. C. Pressly, John S. Williams, John G. Walker. 1st Return Apr 26, 1869.

BOX 177 PACK 4715   WELDON PEARMAN   1868

Will dated Jan 29, 1868. Filed Feb 18, 1868. Witnesses: J. G. E. Branyon, Elias O. Pruitt, H. C. Shirley.   Executor: Benjamin Pearman-son. Wife: Elizabeth Pearman.   Son: Benjamin Pearman.   Appraisal Mar 3, 1868 by J. G. E. Branyon, George Shirley, Stephen M. Tribble, Wm. Pruitt. Held notes on: Caleb Shaw, Wm. Duncan, Richard Robinson, M. F. Freeman, Wm. Shirley, B. F. Driver, James Adams, John Wallace, Hugh Robinson, Jonathan Pearman. !st Estate Sale Mar 5, 1868 netted $479. Buyers at sale: James

Adams, G. L. Mitchell, T. C. Pruitt, S. Pearman, Ben. Pearman, John B. Armstrong Sr., John B. Armstrong Jr., Elias O. Pruitt, James Wilson, Oliver P. Hawthorne, B. F. Driver, Wm. Ricketts, John McClain, James Armstrong, Thomas M. Branyon, M. S. Strickland, Moses Smith, M. E. Walker, A. P. Shirley, J. S. Carwile, Jonathan Pearman, J. H. Bannister, Stephen M. Tribble, Thomas Sampson, J. L. Robinson, Wm. Pruitt, S. N. Pearman, John Carwile, S. M. Fisher, W. M. Saylors, R. N. Wright, R. G. Kay, Mark Latimer, Paschal Kerr. 2nd Estate Sale Dec 1, 1873. Buyers at sale: A. S. Armstrong, W. T. Shaw, J. B. McKee, James Adams, W. L. Burton, W. T. Burton, George Pearman, Ben. Pearman, David Mitchell, A. B. Shirley. Estate Settlement Jan 4, 1879. (8) Legatees each $634.13: 1. Elizabeth Armstrong deceased had (7) Children: A) John B. Armstrong, B) W. R. Armstrong, C) A. S. Armstrong, D) W. C. Armstrong, E) Sarah A. Carwile who had (4) Children: a. Andrew Carwile b. Milton Carwile c. Mary Carwile d. Ebby Carwile F) Isabella Strickland G) Elizabeth Johnson 2. Benjamin Pearman 3. Irene Adams 4. Rhoda Hall deceased with one child, Wm. Calvin Hall 5. Nathaniel Pearman deceased had (5) Children: A) Welldon Pearman B) Sarah Greer C) John B. Pearman D) Isaac Pearman E) Lety Lowden 6. Narisa Armstrong deceased had (2) CChildren: A) Margaret L. Pruitt B) Narisa Branyon 7. Lavinda Wallace 8. Lenora Mitchell. Hawthorne & Agnew paid $24.45 for funeral expenses. Paid widow $10 for morning dress. Paid Clergyman, W. Walters $5.

BOX 178 PACK 4716   SAMUEL REID   1867

Will dated Jan 14, 1867. Filed Oct 7, 1867. Witnesses: W. R. White, J. T. Baskin, Wm. F. Pearson. Executor: James A. Reid-son. Wife: Sopphia W. Reid. Son: James A. Reid. Appraisal Nov 15, 1867 by W. S. Baskin, Alpheus E. Lesly, James M. White. Held notes on: J. W. Lesly, James R. Cunningham, W. M. Cooley, Enright & Starr, S. D. Kay, James H. Kay, J. M. White, Nancy Botts, Ben. F. Mauldin, J. F. Marshall, Thomas P. Moseley, Thomas D. Douglass, James A. Wilson. John T. Lyon, J. White, Thomas J. McCracken, Thomas J. Douglass, R. J. White, George S. Drinkard, Wm. McCravey, W. W. Belcher.

BOX 178 PACK 4717   WILLIAM H. RAMPEY   1867

Deceased died Aug 13, 1867. Will dated May 16, 1867. Filed Aug 31, 1867. Witnesses: Wm. A. Giles, E. W. South, J. J. Scott. Executor: W. T. Townsend. Bond Oct 17, 1892 of $50 by W. T. Townsend, C. H. Bailey, E. Hall. Wife: Margaret Eleanor Rampey. Appraisal Nov 15, 1892 by L. E. Stevenson, Theodore Kennedy, P. M. B. Oliver. Owned Rampey's Mill on Rocky River consisting of 9 acres, owned 206 acres of land. Estate Sale Nov 15, 1892. Buyers at sale: James Scott, J. A. Moore, Richard Bond, Henry Jones, W. H. Livert, John Broadwell, Will Rampey, E. A. Rampey, Eliza Rampey. Estate Settlement Feb 9, 1892. (8) Legatees each $109.71: 1. Elizabeth Turner 2. Dorcas Ann wife of J. H. Cooper 3. Mary E. Townsend 4. Esther Scott 5. James Rampey 6. Eliza Rampey 7. Emily Rampey 8. Samuel Rampey deceased had (9) Children who each received $12.15: A) William Rampey B) Samuel Rampey C) J. Early Rampey D) Calvin Rampey E) Clara Rampey F) Wade Rampey G) Lawton Rampey H) Riley Rampey I) Rebecca Rampey. J. T. Latimer paid $26.50 for burial expenses.

BOX 178 PACK 4718   WASHINGTON W. RUSSELL   1867

Administrator: James A. McCord, Eliza S. Russell-wife. Bond Nov 4, 1867 of $500 by Eliza S. Russell, James A. McCord, D. R. Sondley, John L. McCord. Appraisal Dec 7, 1867 by John McCord, Elijah N. Wilson, Samuel Robinson. Held notes on: Elijah N. Wilson. Estate Sale Dec 7, 1867 netted $13.25. Buyers at sale: Samuel Robinson, S. E. Russell, James A. McCord, Thomas J. Douglass, Jesse Carlisle, S. L. Russell, George A. Douglass, M. A. Russell. Miss S. Eliza Russell received $271 for having taken care of him during the years 1863, 1864, 1865, 1866. Estate Settlement Apar 17, 1868. John Enright owed $30 for coffin & hearse but paid only $8 all the money left in the estate. Estate Insolvent.

BOX 178 PACK 4719   AMANDA RIDGE   1868

Administrator: John H. Ridge. Bond May 4, 1868 of $300 by John H. Ridge, Edmund Cowan, Charles W. Cowan.

BOX 178 PACK 4720   TIMOTHY C. RISLEY   1867

Administrator: James Creswell. Bond Dec 2, 1867 of $1,000 by James Creswell, John T. Parks, James A. Bailey. Appraisal Dec 20, 1867 by James A. Bailey, C. C. Waller, Simeon P. Boozer. Estate Sale Dec 20, 1867 netted $169.05. Buyers at sale: W. G. Farrow, John T. Parks, J. L. Morgan, Simeon P. Boozer, Dr. Kelley, W. P. Anderson, Dr. Milwee, W. P. McKellar, Major Leland, Samuel Hodges, J. W. Greene, Charles Lynch, Ephraim R. Calhoun, Terry Evans, Thomas Creswell, Thomas McCary, Wm. Davis, John R. Tarrant, James Higgins, M. Moseley. Estate Settlement May 21, 1868, no names. Felix G. Parks paid $30 for coffin.

BOX 178 PACK 4721   ISRAEL ROUSE (Man of Color)   1867

Administrator: Alexander P. Connor. Bond Oct 18, 1867 of $800 by Alexander P. Connor, John C. Walker, Wm. S. Shadrack, J. W. Ford. Appraisal Dec 23, 1867 by Samuel Jordan, John Patterson, John Brown. Estate Sale Dec 23, 1867 netted $260. Buyers at sale: Alex. P. Connor, J. W. Ford, John C. Walker, Bob Elmore, Major Jordan, Mary Rouse, Dave Marion, Josh Marion. Nov 22, 1867 and again in Dec 1867 C. J. Allen wrote Wm. Hill, Ordianry saying that nothing had been heard from the administrator.

BOX 178 PACK 4722   JOHN, LULA, EMMA BROWN (minors)   1868

Guardian William McCain. Bond Mar 21, 1868 of $1,000 by Wm. McCain, Wm. J. McCain, John K. McCain. Father: John Brown deceased. Settlement Nov 8, 1882. Emma now Emma Jenkins. John & Lula not mentioned in returns after 1873.

BOX 178 PACK 4723   JAMES P., BARBARA V., MARY J. BROWN (minors)   1869

Guardian: Joshua B. Palmer. Bond Apr 6, 1868 of $800 by Joshua B. Palmer, Wm. Truitt, James M. Truitt. Mother: Frances Brown. Final return of Mary Brown Nov 22, 1883. Final return of Barbara V. Brown Nov 20, 1882. Settlement of James P. Brown Dec 30, 1878.

BOX 178 PACK 4724   JAMES AUGUSTUS BLACK   1869

Will dated Jun 1, 1859 in Richland, S. C. Filed Jan 22, 1869. Witnesses: G. G. Walker, D. P. McDonald, Samuel R. Black. Executor: Wesley A. Black. Sisters: Mary wife of James Young, Matilda E. wife of John M. Shirley living in Choctaw, Miss. Brothers: Joseph F. Black, Wesley Alexander Black. Appraisal Feb 5, 1869 by J. T. Haddon, George W. Bowen, Joshua Shirley, Samuel Shaw, Basil Calllaham. Owned 300 acres of land. Feb 18, 1871 Wesley A. Black released as administrator having paid all claims.

BOX 178 PACK 4725   IRENE, LULA, SAMUEL BOTTS (minors)   1868

Guardian: J. Wm. Robertson. Bond Nov 10, 1868 of $150 by J. Wm. Robertson, Edward Westfield, Thomas C. Seal. Children of Thomas Botts deceased. Grand Mother: Nancy Robertson.

BOX 178 PACK 4726   SOPHRONIA M. BURTON (minor)   1868

Guardian: Thomas J. Burton. Bond Nov 23, 1868 of $2,500 by Thomas J. Bowen, George W. Bowen, Richard Robinson. Father: W. L. Burton deceased. Mother: Lavinia Burton deceased. Settlement: Oct 2, 1883. $959 due Sophronia M. Burton.

BOX 178 PACK 4727   WILLIS BIBBS (Man of Color)   1868

Administrator: James McCaslan. Bond Dec 24, 1868 of $1,000 by James McCaslan, Wm. H. Taggart, Ben. S. Barnwell. Appraisal Dec 26, 1868 by Robert A. McCaslan, Moses O. McCaslan, Ben. S. Barnwell. Estate Sale Dec 26, 1868 netted $788. Buyers at sale: Arthur Covan, Robert Plumer, Robert Patterson, Fred Harris, George Patton, Thomas Fortescue, Wm. Mear, Samuel C. Link, Daniel Conner, Harry Lee, Honis Howlan, Wm. Wear, Lig Davis, Booker McKnight, Wade Patterson, Gus Howlan, Archibald B. Kennedy, Abram Bibbs, Joshua McCaslan, Ben. S. Barnwell, James McCaslan, Shed Boger, Jesse Waller, John Bibbs, Wm. Wary, Gress Howlan, Wm. H. Taggart, Louisa Bily. Estate Settlement Jan 5, 1869. Widow $202.93 and (6) Children each $67.64.

BOX 178 PACK 4728   ALEXANDER BRANYON   1869

Will dated Sep 3, 1868. Filed Sep 14, 1868. Witnesses: G. M. Mattison, Wm. A. Bigby, Thomas S. Mattison. Wife: Anne Branyon, she married Wm. Duncan in 1871. Administrator: Thomas M. Branyon-brother. Bond Aug 14, 1874 of $400 by Thomas M. Branyon, Wm. Duncan, J. F. C. DuPre. 1st Appraisal Sep 29, 1868 by George M. Bigby, John M. Donald, James A. Bigby. 2nd Appraisal Sep 24, 1874 by Robert McAdams, Thomas J. Bowen, Wm. Duncan. Held notes on: J. F. Clinkscales, Henzekiah Hughes, J. M. Hopkins, Nathaniel G. Hughes, R. H. Branyon, Z. B. Jones, James Darby, John Nickles, J. W. Wilson, J. G. Shirley, Thomas M. Branyon. 1st Estate Sale, no date. Buyers at sale Thomas M. Branyon, Rosannah Branyon, J. Tribble, B. O. Branyon, H. Block, James Bigby, B. J. Kay, Dr. Gantt Scales, J. Asbury Bigby, J. R. Duncan, J. H. Brock, T. J. Tribble. 2nd Estate SaleSep 24, 1874 netted $122.74. Buyers at sale: Thomas M. Branyon, Wm. Duncan, J. R. Duncan, J. H. Bannister, J. H. Brock. T. A. Hagen paid $4.72 and J. L. Brock paid $7 for coffin. Last return and last estate entry Feb 5, 1877.

BOX 178 PACK 4729   DAVID L. BOZEMAN   1868.

Deceased died Sep 25, 1868. Administrator: John J. Bozeman-brother. Bond Dec 7, 1868 of $2,000 by John J. Bozeman, John B. Bozeman, J. W. Fooshe. Widow and (4) minor Children. Appraisal Dec 22, 1868 by R. A.Griffin, John C. Young, Wm. B. Meriwether, J. W. Fooshe. Estate Sale Dec 23, 1869 netted $405.67. Buyers at sale: John J. Bozeman, Wm. Ellenburg, E. R. Chaney, Thomas Arnold, Widow, O. D. Goodman, Bob Hackett. Estate Settlement Dec 11, 1871. Widow 1/3= $99.39, (4) Children each $49.69.

BOX 178 PACK 4730   W. BUTLER BROOKS   1869

Will dated Dec 1868.   Filed Jan 19, 1869. Witnesses: Stanmore B. Brooks, Lavinia B. White, Sallie M. Stover. Executors: John R. Moore-son-in-law, Almena Brooks-wife. Sons: Joseph Warren Brooks, Charles Elisha Brooks, Stanmore Butler Brooks, Pierce B. Brooks. Daughters: Mary Ella Brooks, Emma B. Brooks, Elizabeth A. wife of John R. Moore, Carolina Calhoun wife of Samuel Murray Stover of Tenn. Appraisal Mar 11, 1869 of $21,536 by James C. Kay, Peter McKellar, Andrew A. Blythe. Owned 3,115 acres of land. Held notes on: Peter B. Brooks Jr., John R. Moore.

BOX 178 PACK 4731   MAHALA DUNN   1868

Will dated May 27, 1868. Filed Nov 2, 1868. Witnesses: J. W. Blain, John C. Hodgges, D. F. Donald. Executor: Andrew Agnew. Widow of Andrew Dunn. Son: James Robert Clairrence Dunn.   Brother: Enoch Agnew.   Appraisal Nov 24, 1868 by David O. Hawthorne, Wm. Agnew, L. W. Blain, John C. Hodges. Held notes on: T. Y. Martin, John Dunn, Wm A. Richey, Wm. H. Austin, Ben. Owens, David O. Hawthorne, John C. Hodges, Robert R. Seawright, T. A. Hudgens, D. S. Jones, Ben. Joseph, Robert C. Sharp, Wm. Dunn, Nettie Richey, Samuel Agnew, Thomas Hawthorne, Zachariah Haddon, Abner Freeman. Estate Sale Nov 26, 1868. Buyers at sale: Andrew Agnew, John Hodges, George Gaddis, Wm. Vermillion, B. S. Anderson, B. V. Sharp, T. E. Barmore, T. M. Dodson, R. N. Alexander, Wm. Sharp, R. L. Posey, David O. Hawthorne, Wm. Roland, Amaziah R. Ellis, L. S. Magee, Z. Y. Pruitt, T. R. Grier, J. Dunn, E. R. Ellis, George Fuller, Andrew Coon, R. S. Anderson, James Anderson, John N. Seawright, Andrew Moore, Reuben Tribble, L. F. Donald, Wm. H. Moore, W. L. McKay, Will Sharp, John Hagen, Larkin Barmore, John Higgins, Jacob B. Clamp, John Calloway, Henry Clamp, K. M. Thomas, Wm. E. Barmore, Edward Hagen, Robert Dunn, Wm. R. Mundy, Robert Hagen, Fletcher Armala, A. M. Agnew, Wm. L. Robinson, Ben. White, H. A. Bowie, J. T. Smith, G. B. Shirley, John B. Algary, J. S. Magee, James Seawright, James H. Simpson, George Geths, W. P. Magee, S. C. Merriman, M. Golden. Estate Settlement Jul 13, 1874. James Robert Clarence Dunn was only descendant and heir. Nettie Richey given one bed. John C. Hodges given a cow. Left money for a scholarship to Erskine College. James D. Chalmers paid $100 for tombstone.

BOX 178 PACK 4732   ANDREW GILLESPIE   1865

Will dated Jul 5, 1866. Filed Nov 12, 1868. Witnesses: Epaminandos Edwards, E. P. Gray, Nathan A. Edwards. Executor: David Ramsey Penney. Wife: Jenny Gillespie. Daughter: Cynthia Ann Ruff living in Miss. Grand Sons: David Ramsey Penney, John Emory Penney, George Abner Penney. Grand Daughter: Ella Amanda Brooks. Appraisal Jan 5, 1869 by Samuel Lockridge, James C. Pressly, Leroy J. Johnson. Estate Sale Jan 6,

1869 netted $425.05. Buyers at sale: David R. Penney, Wm. H. Brooks, Francis A. Wilson, Wm. H. Penney, Ben Squire, Gabriel Young, Wm. Wilson, John Barnett, Dr. J. W. Thomas, John E. Penney, F. Livingston, Alex. Young, Nathan A. Edwards, James C. Pressly, Leroy J. Johnson, Aaron Johnson, Robert Covin, Samuel McBryde, Joseph R. Cheatham, Samuel Davis. Davied Miers. Estate Settlement Feb 28, 1870. Debts reduced to roughly 50 cents on the dollar. Estate Insolvent. Paid Wm. A. Richey $15 for coffin.

BOX 178 PACK 4733   JAMES I. GILMER   1868

Will dated Jan 25, 1867. Filed Nov 23, 1868. Witnesses: S. A. Breazeale, Robert A. Fair, James S. Cothran. Executor: Robert H. Cochran-son-in-law. Mathew McDonald and Samuel Gilmer both declined to act as Administrator. Appraisal Jan 14, 1869 by J. W. Keller, James Carlisle, Wm. McIlwain, Andrew Morrison, Wm. B. Roman. Estate Sale Jan 15, 1869. Buyers at sale: Wm. Eakin, Samuel Robinson, Hiram T. Tusten, Robert H. Cochran, Thomas Robinson, Wm. McCord, James R. Haddon, J. W. Keller, Wm. McIlwain, Wm. Adamson. Estate Settlement Nov 16, 1877. (2) Legatees: 1. Agnes V. wife of Robert H. Cochran 2. John Gilmer. Paid Sign & Seal $40 for coffin.

BOX 178 PACK 4734   SAMUEL GRAHAM   1869

Will no date. Filed Nov 2, 1868. Witnesses: Wm. Riley, J. M. Thomas, James W. Means. Lived at Cokesbury. Executrix: Sarah Ann Graham-wife. Bond Jan 21, 1869 of $3,000 by Sarah A. Graham, Albert M. Graham, H. H. Hughes, B. C. Graham. Daughter: Lura Correna Graham. Brother: Albert M. Graham. Appraisal Dec 15, 1868 by Wm. Moore, John Graham, John D. Adams. Owned 234 acres of land.   Estate Sale Dec 16, 1868. Buyers at sale: J. F. Smith, Sarah Ann Graham, H. H. Hughes, Wm. H. Robertson, Marshall Sharp, J. N. Alexander, John D. Adams, Daniel Beacham, R. Hughes, J. D. Pace, J. W. Moore, G. P. Hughes, John Moore, B. C. Graham, Albert M. Graham, James Caldwell. Estate Setlement, no date. (8) Legatees each $145.14: 1. C. F. Hughes, 2. Tilda Graham 3. Caroline E. Turner deceased 4. W. L. Graham 5. S. A. Graham 6. T. W. Graham 7. M. A. Graham 8. Lura Graham. Paid Wm. R. Buchanan $10 for coffin.

BOX 178 PACK 4735   MARY SUSAN HUGHEY (minor)   1869

Guardian: Joseph L. Hughey. Bond Jan 4, 1869 of $1,800 by Joseph L. Hughey, James Strawhorn, Wm. F. Dike. 1st Return Jan 4, 1869 received from estate of Frances Duckett, grand mother of Newberry County. Estate Settlement Oct 12, 1876 $1,307.54.

BOX 178 PACK 4736   POLLY ANN LINDSAY   1868

Administrator: John O. Lindsay. Bond Aug 28, 1868 of $1,500 by John O. Lindsay, A. C. Hawthorne, J. P. Kennedy. Appraisal Oct 20, 1868 by J. L. Miller, James Pratt, Robert W. Haddon. Estate Sale Oct 20, 1868 netted $479.35. Buyers at sale: John O. Lindsay, John I. Bonner, Amaziah R. Ellis, John M. Bell, J. P. Kennedy, John Cowan, Wm. Hood, J. J. Bowen, J. L. Miller, J. E. Martin, F. R. Pruitt, James A. Hawthorne, Robert W. Haddon, Edwin Cox, Fred Bell, James Pratt. Estate Settlement Jan 2, 1869. (3) Distributees: 1. John O. Lindsay 2. John I. Bonner and wife 3. A. B. C. Lindsay.

BOX 178 PACK 4737   WILLIAM WHITFIELD McDILL   1869

Will dated Nov 17, 1862. Witnesses: J. N. Young, William R. Hemphill, J. L. Miller. Executor: Robert C. Grier, Wm. M. Grier, took over for his dad, Robert C. Grier when he died. Wife: Jane McDill. Daughters: Elizabeth Law McDill, Margaret Josephine McDill, Emma Jane McDill. Sons: James Taylor McDill, Willis Whitfield McDill, David Chalmers McDill, Jefferson Hayne McDill. 1st Appraisal Mar 27, 1869 by J. N. Young, J. P. Kennedy, Wm. Hood. 2nd Appraisal Feb 10, 1877 by John I. Bonner, James R. Todd, Francis V. Pruitt. Owned 222 acres of landAt time of will owned 6 slaves. Estate Sale Feb 10, 1877 netted $3,332.50. Buyers at sale: Oliver P. Hawthorne, John I. Bonner, Robert R. Seawright, Wm. B. Bonner, Dr. J. L. Miller, J. C. Caldwell, Josephine McDill, Wm. M. Grier, Peter Brownlee, James E. Todd, Joseph F. Lee, Dr. Boyce, M. W. Parker, Rev. Galloway, Oliver Kennedy, Robert Smith, Mrs. E. P. Kennedy, George Scott, Chalmers G. Haddon, Dr. Edwards, Sambo Haddon, Wm. F. Pearson, Rev. Wm. L. Pressly, Frank Smith, Willis Chandler, Hurts Henderson, Wesley Covington, Charlotte Tribble, James T. McDill, Emma McDill. Estate Settlement Apr 28, 1883. (8) Legatees each $320.65: 1. R. A. Bryson & Betty Bryson deceased 2. Emma Jane Hunter 3. Jefferson Hayne McDill 4. Willis Whitfield McDill 5. David Chalmers McDill 6. Josephine McDill 7. James Taylor McDill 8. John C. McDill. Paid James D. Chalmers $30 plus $5 freight for tombstone.

BOX 178 PACK 4738   JAMES MARTIN   1868

Will dated Aug 4, 1863. Filed Dec 7, 1868. Witnesses: Mrs. C. Reid, A. C. Reid, David A. Pressly. Executor: Anna Eliza Martin-wife. Appraisal Dec 29, 1868 by Charles Evans, James S. Gibert, Andrew J. Woodhurst. Held notes on: Ben Hampton, Thomas J. Ruff & Martha Ruff.

BOX 178 PACK 4739   JAMES W. MITCHELL   1868

Will dated Sep 5, 1857. Filed Jul 6, 1868. Witnesses: Wm. P. Martin, J. F. Donald, Alex. E. Kay. Executrix: Chole E. Spruell-niece who was willed the entire estate. Bond Sep 18, 1868 of $200 by Chole E. Spruell, Samuel Donald, Asbury M. Dodson. Brother: Benjamin S. Mitchell lived in DeKalb Co., Ala. Appraisal Oct 2, 1868 by Stephen Latimer, Michael Burts, George A. Kay. Owned 7 acres of land. Benjamin S. Martin had (6) Children: 1. James Martin lived in Tenn. 2. Wm. Martin, 3. Benjamin Newton Martin 4. John Tapson Martin 5. Ephraim Asbury Martin 6. Sarah Rebecca Martin.

BOX 179 PACK 4740   JOHN B. SHADRACK   1868

Deceased died Mr 9, 1868. Administrator: Johnson Sale. Lewis C. Parks declined to be appointed administrator. Bond Apr 17, 1868 of $2,000 by Johnson Sale, Josephine R. Lake, Irvin Hutchinson, Thomas J. Ouzts. Appraisal May 5, 1868 by Peter M. McKellar, Joohn R. Tolbert, Lemuel Bell. Estate Sale May 5, 1868 netted $567.08. Buyers at sale: Wm. A. Creighton, Lewis Parks, Johnson Sale, H. H. Creswell, Stephen B. Elmore, Wm. S. Shadrack, Stanmore B. Brooks, John R. Tolbert, H. M. Sturkes, Jonathan S. Chipley, Dr. John Maxwell.

BOX 179 PACK 4741   WILLIAM C. SMITH   1868

Administrator: John A. Talmadge-son-in-law. Bond Apr 21, 1868 of $500 by John A. Talmadge, Edward Noble, James T. Jordan. Appraisal May 8, 1868 by Joel J. Cuningham,

Hiram M. Lawson, Wm. T. Penney. Estate Sale May 8, 1868 netted $184.30. Buyers at sale: John A. Wier, J. J. Wardlaw, John A. Talmadge, Robert Hill, Capt Perry, Christian V. Hammond, Hiram T. Tusten, O. H. Hart, Thomas Thomson, David Knox. Funeral Expenses $65.

BOX 179 PACK 4742   WILLIAM CLARKE SCOTT   1867

Deceased died Nov 1866. Never Married. Administrator: John O. Lindsay. Bond Nov 28, 1867 of $200 by John O. Lindsay, A. C. Hawthorne, John I. Bonner. Mrs. M. D. Drennan nursed, fed, clothed and boarded him for the lat 19 months of his life. Estate Settlement Sep 1, 1868. Burial expenses $21.88.

BOX 179 PACK 4743   MARY SMITH   1867

Will dated Apr 17, 1862. Filed Nov 26, 1867. Witnesses: James W. Frazier, H. T. sloan, Robert Devlin. Late Husband: G. T. Cannon. Present Husband: W. C. Smith. Sister: Martha Ruff. Brothers: John Glymph, Lemule Glymph. Executor: Thomas Thomson. Appraisal Jun 11, 1868 by John A. Talmadge, B. P. Neel, Enoch Nelson. Owned 3 slaves at time of will. Estate Sale Jan 17, 1868 netted $334.56. Buyers at sale: Dr. Drennan, Thomas Thomson, J. Miller, Lewis Drennan, W. P. Devlin, A. McCord, Albert Frazier, Henry S. Kerr, B. Jordan, S. Jordan, Dr. Joseph Pressly, John A. Talmadge, W. W. Edwards, Wm. Robinson, Dr. H. T. Strong, J. F. Creswell, Ben. B. Harveley, John A. Devlin, Jordan Wideman, Hiram Pressly, John Able, Wm. Devlin, Enoch Nelson, J. Creswell, Thomas S. Edwards. Estate Settlement Mar 19, 1875. Paid John W. Sign $25 for coffin.

BOX 179 PACK 4744   JOHNSON SALE   1868

Will dated May 11, 1866. Witnesses: Thomas J. Ouzts, Hugh Porter, Jonathan S. Chipley. Codicil Oct 16, 1868. Will field Oct 30, 1868. Executrix: Josephine R. Lake-daughter. Grand Children: Joseph Lake, Elizabeth Lake. Partner in the firm of Sale & Ouzts with Thomas J. Ouzts. Appraisal Nov 23, 1868 by Wm. H. Stalllworth, Peter McKellar, Irvin Hutchinson. Owned 297 acres of land. Notes and Accounts due firm of a little over $23,000: J. K. Aiton, Thomas W. Aiken, F. W. Andrews, Wm. Agnew, Elihu Andrews, Patrick Adams, Daniel C. Bulluck, Henry Brooks, E. B. Bell, Hezekiah J. Burnett, Addison Blacksmith, Marshall Brooks, John Butler, Lemuel Bell, S. P. Brooks, J. P. Burnett, Eli Branson, Thomas Branson, Esau Brooks, Elizabeth Child, W. W. Casey, James Callison, John Colbert, Wm. Casey, G. R. Caldwell, Jonathan S. Chipley, Thomas W. Chiles, M. H. Clegg, J. L. Carr, John Q. A. Clark, Abner Clegg, Martin W. Coleman, Holloway Clegg, R. R. Child, Thomas S. Cheatham, Wm. L. Durst, A. Deale, Richard Davis, W. L. Dukes, George W. Durst, G. W. Dooley. John Ethridge, Stephen Elmore, J. H. Ellenburg, Elizabeth Ethridge, Martha Devore, J. R. Faulkner, C. M. Fooshe, Wm. Felknap, Wm. Flinn, J. D. Gilliard, M. Gable, Wm. A. Gaines, Ben. Harling, Jarrett Harris, Wm. Harris, Nannient Henderson, D. W. Holloway, Elizabeth Harris, F. P. Hollingsworth, Abner Hargrave, A. Hollingsworth, John P. Harling, C. Horne, Wm. Horne, Emily Harling, Starling Horne, Samuel Harris, W. C. Hunter, Nathaniel Henderson, Joshua Harris, Joshua Hutchinson, Amp Henderson, Frank Hutchinson, Wash Henderson, Irvin Hutchinson, R. F. Hutchinson, Wm. Johnson, Thomas Jester, Wm. Jester, Esmine Jones, F. Johnson, J. W. Kennedy, W. G. Kennedy, John W. Kemp, W. B. Kemp, Thomas Kissick, L. H. Kemp, J. W. Ligon, H. Luquire, Wm. Langley, Thomas Lake, T. K. Langley, Thomas W. Lipscomb, Wm.

F. Leake, Thomas Maxwell, E. Mounts, B. Manley, John Morine, John Miller, Samuel A. Moore, H. B. Maxwell, John Malone, Mathew Mathis, F. G. Martin, Simpson Mathis, Obed Morris, Samuel Maxwell, W. S. Malone, Martha Marbut, Thomas Metts, Martha McManus, Wm. R. McKinney, Peter McKellar, Ann Ouzts, J. A. Ouzts, E. Pennington, J. W. Philpot, Lewis Parks, John Pressly, Ben Porter, Edward Pressly, John E. Partlow, Wm. Quattlebaum, Eugenia Robinson, Wm. H. Rush, Willis Reynolds, John Ramsay, Wm. Robinson, Sarah Ross, Anna Robinson, Willis Ross, Louanna Robinson, Alfred Rasor, James H. Ross, G. F. Ross, W. S. Richardson, John Rush, Amon Stallworth, W. S. Shadrack, W. H. Stallworth, J. L. Sale, N. S. Shadrack, R. W. Seymour, Martha Sale, John Sentell, J. O. Stewart, Asberry Sale, John Sale, Butler Sale, Wm. Sale, Addison Sale, Albert Sale, Wm. Strand, Charles Sale, Jennie Spann, M. A. Schenck, T. N. Shadrack, Ben. F. Smith, Jacob Smith, Wm. Stalnaker, Hiram Sale, Wm. Strand, Robert R. Tolbert, Lucinda Thornton, John Trapp, David F. Teddards, J. R. Tolbert, George W. Tolbert, Wiley Teddards, Jesse Timmerman, E. L. Tolbert, David Timmerman, Lizzie Townes, Wm. A. Upton, Allen Vance, Mary Vaughn, T.W. Vaughn, J. A. White, Thomas M. Walker, J. W. Wilson, A. T. Watson, L. H. White, James M. Wilson, Wm. S. Williams, Nancy Witt, Boney Williams, Joseph Walker, E. G. Walker, T. A. Watson, E. W. Watson, Butler Worthington. May 15, 1874 paid aid Ella R. McKellar $1,000 in full for all claims against the estate.

BOX 179 PACK 4745   JOHN G. THORNTON   1868

Will dated May 15, 1865. Filed Oct 24, 1868. Witnesses: R. J. Robinson, Wm. McCain, E. R. McCain. Executor: A. W. Reid. Brother: Hasting G. Thornton deceased. Nephews: Henry Reel, Toliver Reel, Albert W. Reel. Niece: Mary Langley whose children were: Mary Emma Langley, Alfred R. Langley, Marshall Langley. Appraisal Nov 17, 1868 by R. J. Robinson, Ben. B. Harveley, Samuel B. Cook. Notes & Accounts due him at death dating from 1852: A. F. Robinson, Francis Wideman, Samuel Wideman, James Boyd, J. H. Rainey, Wm. H. Butler, J. Sturkey, J. L. Robertson, James Henderson, Henry Reel, Wm. Motes, Thomas Coleman, S. P. Leard, W. S. Thornton, S. V. Burdishaw, M. Coleman, Catlett Corley, James Russell, Joel Whitten, Alfred Harrison, W. W. Adams, Theodore Johnson, Nancy Robertson, S. S. Burdishaw, Francis M. Henderson, Samuel B. Wideman, Wm. Truitt, B.Walker, J. Langley, E. W. Thornton, George S. Patterson, George W. Brown, Anthony Harmon, J. L. Ward, H. T. Corley, Ben. B. Harveley, Samuel Beard, Albert W. Reel, John White, Nancy Holloway, Mrs. P. Johnson, Thomas Johnson, Wm. Franklin, John Rush, L. B. Strom, John Creswell, Ben. Blake, Richard Stalnaker, W. Timmerman, F. M. Evans, J. E. Walker, J. C. Beall, John Dickert, E. B. Brooks, Robert S. Minor, Daniel Minor, W. C. Ludwick, Thomas McBryde, George Rosenwike, J. L. Lockridge, J. F. Burriss, E. C. Johnson, W. Brown, Mrs. E. Thornton. Estate Sale, no date. Buyers at sale: A. F. Young, Jacob Langley, Albert W. Reel, J. W. Perrin, Stephen Langley, J. P. Cook, J. C. Dowtin, G. H. Burton, J. W. Ford, J. Caldwell, G. M. Sibert, J. B. Creswell, George Young, W. Caldwell, A. Cushnell, J. A. Link, A. M. Martin, W. C. Robinson, George P. Chiles, S. B. Smith, Henry Reel, B. C. Napper, J. B. Creswell, J. H. Wideman, George W. Broadwaater, Wm. H. Yeldell, A. Bushnell, J. D. Jay, J. C. Mayson, D. W. Sibert, J. E. Hunter, J. Langley, John Baughman, Catlett C. Corley, Ben. F. Brown, H. F. Corley, Philip S. Rutledge, J. M. Miller, W. M. Cain Jr., Ben. B. Harveley, J. S. Harmon, Smuel M. McQuerns, W. M. Cain Sr., W. C. Robinson, J. N. Griffin, Samuel B. Cook, R. T. Bell, Jasper Rush, M. C. Brown, Thomas Robinson, John Price. 1870 Frederick Morris paid $41.65 for his wife's part.

Estate Settlement in 1871. Legatees: 1. F. J. Cook 2. P. S. Thornton 3. --- Varner 4. L. S. Land 5. H. H. Browders.

BOX 179 PACK 4746   JOHN H. WILSON   1869

Deceased died Feb 25, 1868. Administrators: Leroy C. Wilson, Robert E. Bowie. Bond mar 24, 1869 by Robert E. Bowie, Leroy C. Wilson, Nancy J. Bowie, George A. Douglass, George McDuffie Miller. Considerable estate but highly indebted. Appraisal Apr 28, 1869 by John A. Wier, George A. Douglass, John T. Lyon. Held notes on: Jane C. Gray, Donald McLalughlin, W. C. Harris, Samuel Cato, Lewis J. Wilson, Seylla McLalren, L. H. Lomax, Issac Branch, Peter Miles, Joe Smith, Richmond S. Cobb, George M. Madden, Wm. H. Burns, H. W. Hodges. Estate Sale Nov 17, 1869. Buyers at sale: Robert E. Bowie, L. C. Wilson, John C. Douglass, Chance Clinkscales, J. A. Keller, Jeptha R. Hamlin, Callie Ward, Jack Donaldson, Dr. E. Parker, Leroy Wilson, Rebecca Pelot, Charles Pelot, Philip S. Rutledge, E. Stevenson, Lucius B. Ramey, H. Inman, Wm. Evvans, Samuel McGowan, David J. Jordan, Charles A. McClung, George A. Douglass, Ravenna Wilson, Andrew Adams, John T. Miller, James McCravey, E. Moragne, Crockett Donaldson, J. W. W. Marshall, Betsy Valentine, Louisa Douglass, Hiram T. Tusten, Francis A. Baker, Wm. W. Sprouse, J. Carlisle, Mathew McDonald, Cato Hunter, J. W. Keller, D. W. Watson.

BOX 179 PACK 4747   PELIUS AUGUSTUS WALLER   1866

Confederate Soldier killed Feb 20, 1864 at the Battle of Ocean Pond, Florida. At the time of his death he was a resident of Terrell Co.., Ga. Administrator: Joseph B. Watson. Bond Oct 14, 1867 of $10,000 by Joseph B. Watson, Moses C. Taggart, Thomas A. Watson. Wife: Mary L. Waller. Father: Albert Waller. Appraisal Nov 13, 1867 by Robert H. Mounce, Cadmus G. Waller, Lewis D. Merriman. Estate Sale Dec 4, 1867 netted $51.25. Buyers at sale: Cadmus G. Waller, C. A. C. Waller.

BOX 179 PACK 4748   MINORS of R. H. WILSON   1867

Guardian: Patrick H. Bradley. Bond Feb 4, 1867 of $2,000. Minors: 1. Benjamin Wilson 2. John T. Wilson 3. William Wilson 4. George Wilson.

BOX 179 PACK 4749   MARGARET R. WARDLAW   1868

Will dated May 5, 1868. Filed Sep 9, 1868. Witnesses: Leonidas D. Connor, Wm. R. Buchanan, James F. Smith. Executors: David J. Wardlaw, Wm. A. Moore-son-in-law. Sons: Thomas McCollum, David J. Wardlaw. Daughters: Sarah Scott living in Texas, Jane B. Foster, Margaret L. wife of Wm. A. Moore. Appraisal Nov 24, 1868 by J. C. Willard, James H. Britt, Joseph S. Britt. Estate Sale Nov 25, 1868 netted $2095. Buyers at sale: Redmond Brown, Jane Foster, Wm. A. Moore, David J. Wardlaw, Ed. Cowan, Molly Foster, Robert A. McCaslan, Boggs Kennedy, Lucius B. Guillebeau, John McCain, James Truitt, George A. Hanvey, F. M. Hendrix, Joseph S. Britt, David Wiley, Wm. Boswell, John Freeman, Charles W. Cowan, A. M. Martin, James Wideman, Samuel C. Link, John Wideman, J. Mathews, Michael S. Talbert. Estate Settlement Feb 20, 1869. (4) Legatees: 1. Heirs in Texas $500 2. Jane Foster $1,948.42 3. David J. Wardlaw $1,948.42 4. Wm. A. Moore $1948.42. Paid Seal & Sign $50 for coffin and hearse.

BOX 179 PACK 4750   JANE WILSON   1869

Will dated Jul 19, 1860. Witnesses: David Robison, Wm. L. Robertson, Jane A. Carey. Sister: Nancy Wilson. Brother Robert C. Wilson. Nephews: James J. Wilson, John L. Wilson, Samuel A. Wilson, Elijah Wilson, D. A. Wilson, Lewis Wilson. Niece: Elizabeth Tittle. Will of Nancy Wilson dated Jan 16, 1825. Witnesses: Moses Taggart, Robert L. Taggart, Nancy C. Wilson. Sons: Robert C. Wilson, Samuel A. Wilson. Daughters: Grizella Wilson, Nancy Wilson, Elizabeth Wilson, Jane McKinley Wilson. Owned land in Pendleton. Will of Elizabeth Wilson dated Dec 28, 1847. Filed Jan 14, 1867. Witnesses: James S. Wilson, Andrew W. Shillito, Samuel Wilson. Executor: Samuel Allen Wilson. Will of Jane Wilson dated Jul 19, 1859. Will executed Aug 1869. Witnesses: James Carlisle, David Robison, Jesse Carlisle. Executor William Wilson. Brother: Robert C. Wilson. Sisters: Elizabeth Wilson, Nancy Wilson. Nephews: 1. Elijah Wilson who had children, John Francis Wilson and Mary C. Wilson 2. Lewis T. Wilson 3. Samuel Wilson 4. William Wilson. Nieces: Nancy Caroline Richey, Elizabeth Ann Wilson, Nancy Evalina Wilson. Jane Wilson paid Enright & Smith $60 for 2 coffins. Mar 29, 1854 Elizabeth Wilson, Nancy Wilson, Jane Wilson turned 112 acres of land over to their Brother, Samuel Allen Wilson. Apr 6, 1858 the land was returned to them and on Aug 30, 1858 land was given by them to their nieces Jane Evaline Wilson and Eliza Ann Wilson. Witnesses to the above land transactions were: James Carlisle and B. J. Cochran. At the same time the sisters gave a $100 annuity to their brother, Robert C. Wilson for 4 years and the annuity to pass to his children should he die. Estate Settlement 1871. (5) Legatees and their children: I) Robert C. Wilson died Oct 1865 leaving (4) Children and the children of two deceased sons. His children were: 1. Robert Henry Wilson died Dec 1862. His children were: A) Benjamin A. Wilson B) John T. Wilson C) Wm. W. Wilson D) George Lafayette Wilson. 2. Samuel A. Wilson died Dec 1864. His children were: A) Elizabeth J. Wilson B) Samuel Allen Wilson C) Sarah C. Wilson D) John Richmond Wilson. 3. James Wilson 4. Thomas Wilson 5. Nancy Caroline who married 1st a Martin and then Thomas Edwards 6. Elizabeth wife of Archibald Tittle. II) Children of Elijah Wilson: 1. John B. Wilson 2. Priscilla Frances who married a Blackmon 3. Mary C. Wilson. III) Children of Lewis J. Wilson of Madison, Florida: 1. Lillie L. Davis 2. John A. Wilson 3. Edward B. Wilson 4. Robert H. Wilson 5. Luther P. Wilson 6. Ellen G. Wilson 7. Emma R. Wilson 8. Lewis C. Wilson. IV) Children of Nancy Caroline Richey (wife of Joseph Richey) deceased (1862) of Tuscaloosa, Ala. Received ¼ each of $76.35 due their mother. The (4) Children: 1. Franklin E. Richey age 44 of Alabama 2. Jane G. Richey age 38 of Alabama 3. Margaret A. Orril age 36 of Titus Co., Texaas 4. Benjamin L. Richey age 30 of Titus Co., Texas. V) Children of Samuel A. Wilson: 1. William Wilson 2. Francis A. Wilson. 2nd Estate Setttlement Jul 1875. Elizabeth Tittle had not been heard from in 5 years but showed up in 1876. All parties paid the amounts due them from the legacies of their parents. Executor: William Wilson. Appraisal of Jane Wilson's Estate Aug 3, 1869 by James Carlisle, Jesse Carlise, Samuel Robinson. Estate Sale of Jane Wilson Aug 3, 1869 netted $287. Buyers at sale: John B. Wilson, Jesse Carlisle, Wm. L. McCord, Francis A. Wilson, J. A. McCord, Wm. A. Lomax, James L. McCord, James Carlisle, Dr. Keller, A. B. Ellis, John Enright, Wm. Wilson, E. Keller, Edward Roche, E. N. Wilson, Lee Wilson, Wm. H. Adamson, J. L. Keller, R. A. Martin, Sam Burt, John H. Wilson, Robert E. Hill, Bob Smith, James Enright.

BOX 179 PACK 4751   ANDREW EDWARDS   1870

173

Willl dated Oct 22, 1869. Filed Feb 7, 1870. Witnesses: Henry S. Cason, Louis H. Russell, Robert E. Hill. Wife: Hannah W. Edwards. Sons: Mathew Lewis Edwards, Andrew M. Edwards, Nathan A. Edwards, John G. Edwards, Epaminandos Edwards, Amos Whitfield Edwards. Daughters: Jane Elizabeth Mabry, Anna Amanda wife of Robert M. Mann. Appraisal Feb 25, 1870 by James D. Chalmers, John Link, J. R. F. Wilson, Wm. Joel Smith, Francis A. Wilson. Owned Home tract of 461 acres, Camp Ground tract of 155 acres, Mann tract of 126 acres. Estate Sale Dec 20, 1870. Buyers at sale: Nathan Edwards-home tract, Mrs. John Bass-Camp Gound tract, Dr. J. W. Marshall, Dr. Ben Rhett, Bob Covin, Frank Johnson, J. W. Edwards, Samuel A. Link, Charles B. Guffin, Mathew L. Edwards, James M. Edwards, David R. Penney, John S. Williams, Willis Alston, James W. Knox, Isam Speer, George Spencer, Mr. J. J. Bass, David Wier, Wm. H. Penney, Lemuel O. Shoemaker, Osborn Gray, Nellie Hilburn, Francis A. Wilson, J. F. Edwards, Squash Sanders, John Cheatham, Andrew Small, Henry Huey, Dr. Thomas J. Mabry, Dennis Padgett, John G. Edwards, Mrs. H. S. Hammond, Charles Garvey, Willis Cannon, Epaminandos Edwards, Nathan A. Edwards, Wes Gray, Wm. Stuart, Spencer Gillespie, Thomas Williamson, Adam T. Brady, John C. Douglass, Randal Mason, Robert J. White, Squire Davis, Robert Williamson, Leroy J. Johnson, Wm. S. Marshall, Jack Vance, Jacob Pettigrew, Jim Hill, Arthur T. Bass, Frank New. May 19, 1886 John G. Edwards trustee of life estate of his sister, Mrs. A. A. Mann, Amos W. Edwards received $47 from her account. John G. Edwards died and his sister, Margaret J. Bass became the Administrator. Bond $1,400 Oct 8, 1908 Margaret J. Bass, James A. Gilliam, John R. Thornton, Nicholas Schram. Appraisal Nov 8, 1908 by John C. Pursley, James A. Gilliam Arthur F. Bass. Estate Settlement Jul 15, 1909. (3) Legatees: 1. Margaret Bass 2. Whitfield A. Edwards 3. Children of John G. Edwards. Norwood & McDill paid $50 for funeral expenses.

BOX 179 PACK 4752   DANIEL S. BEACHAM   1872

Will dated Nov 12, 1868   Filed Jan 5, 1870   Witnesses: James F. Smith, J. P. Ligon, J. A. Moore. Executor: Mrs. Elliott M. Center-daughter. Son: Jefferson Beacham. Daughters: Elliott M. Center, Mary Frances Higgins living Panola, Texas, Mary Elizabeth wife of Lalrkin Mays living Harrison Co., Texas. Appraisal Jan 7, 1870 by Martin G. Zeigler, Wm. A. Moore, John Vance. Held notes on: Wm. Moore, Green Berry Riley, Sterling E. Graydon, John D. Adams, Samuel Graham, Albert Graham, Wm. Riley. Estate Sale Jan 21, 1870 netted $1,689.49. Buyers at sale: Mrs. M. E. Center, James Thomas, Martin G. Zeigler, Francis M. Godbold, Dr. Paul W. Connor, Wm. Butler, Dr. N. Sims, J. A. Simmons, Samuel A. Hodges, Rev. N. J. Stafford, Oscar B. Simmons, Charlie Simmons, Francis M. Whitlock, Terry Shannon, John Hefferman, Wm. A. Moore, Wm. Anderson, A. O. Watson, J. C. Caldwell, Leonidas D. Connor, Wm. C. Benet, Daniel Tompkins, R. W. Anderson, J. J. Golding, Green Berry Riley, J. A. Moore, James C. Rasor, Issac Richey, Andrew Coon, Washington L. Hodges, J. T. Johnson, A. B. Ellis, Wm. Riley, George W. Rampey, Nelson Cole, Sterling E. Graydon, A. M. Agnew, A. W. Moore, Dock Boyd, Lewis Reeder, John D. Adams, H. H. Hughes, Isabella Bearden, W. Z. McGhee, Henry C. Strauss, Dennis Washington, Addison Washington, Gus Macon, R. W. Anderson, John Stewart, Marcus A. Cason, Humphrey Adams, Thomas Johnson, Burnell Dickson, Nathan Robinson, John Robinson. Estate Settlement May 1, 1872. (4) Legatees: 1. M. F. Higgins 2. Elizabeth H. Mays, 3. Children of Thomas J. Beacham: A) Minneola Beacham B) Nancy Beacham C) Thomas J. Beacham 4. Mrs. M. E. Center.

BOX 179 PACK 4753   JOHN W. BOZEMAN   1869

Deceased died Feb 26, 1868. Administrator: Gilly F. Bozeman who became Gilly F. Holcombe-wife. Bond Mar 24, 1869 of $1,200 by Gilly F. Bopzeman, John C. Young, John J. Bozeman. No Children. Appraisal Apr 8, 1869 by J. W. Brooks, Wm. H. Davis, John Bozeman. Estate Sale Apr 9, 1869 netted 607.39. Buyers at sale: Gilly F. Bozeman, O. D. Goodman, J. W. Fooshe, J. E. Heape, Joel Pinson, W. N. Estes, Thomas Puckett, Taylor Bozeman. 1st Estate Settlement Nov 30, 1869. (5) Legatees: 1. T. N. Bozeman $35.88 2. Z. T. Bozeman $35.88 3. B. T. Bozeman $35.88 4. Children of Winnie Ropp: A) Nannie Ropp B) Carrie Ropp C) Lou Ropp D) George Ropp. Final Settlement Jan 7, 1870. Gilly F. Bozeman ½=$366.26. (2) Half brothers. (1) Half sister. (8) Children either nephews or Nieces of full brother deceased. Mourning apparel for Gilly $24.20. Paid J. M. Richardson $35 for coffin. Paid J. C. Griffin $7.50 for box for coffin.

BOX 179 PACK 4754   MARY BASS   1869

Deceased died Jan 17, 1869. Administrator: Wm. H. Bass. Bond Dec 14, 1869 of $1,200 by Wm. M. H. Bass, J. J. Cunningham, Thomas M. Cheatham. Appraisal: Jan 13, 1870 by Charles B. Guffin, Wm. W. Sprouse, Thomas J. McCracken. Estate Sale Jan 13, 1870 netted $1,031.85. Buyers at sale: Wm. H. Bass, Nancy Mann, Miss Mary Bass, Miss Spicey A. Bass, John Bass, Bob Covin, Leroy J. Johnson, Arthur Bass, Wm. Thomas. Estate Settlement Dec 3, 1881. (6) Legatees each $157.05. 1. Wm. H. Bass 2. John J. Bass 3. Arthur Bass 4. Mary Jane Edwards 5. Spicey Ann Bass never married 6. Nancy Mann.

BOX 179 PACK 4755   ISAAC B. BROWNELL   1868

Deceased died Oct 1868. Administrator: Thomas C. Seal. Bond Dec 12, 1868 of $1,000 by Thomas C. Seal, J. Wm. Robinson, John W. Sign. Had (2) Brothers in Savannah. Seal & Sign paid $110 for funeral services.

BOX 179 PACK 4756   ELIZABETH BLACK   1868

Will Dated Jun 22, 1867. Filed Oct 17, 1868. Witnesses: Wm. F. Pearson, Wm. Ashley, Wesley A. Black. Executor: J. W. Black, John Augustus Black. Daughters: Eliza A. Clinkscales, Mary wife of T. L. Kay, Sarah L. wife of A. Milton Blake. Sons: James W. Black, Joseph Ramsay Black, Wm. Pickens Blackc, John C. Black deceased. Grand Son: Pickens K. Black son of James W. Black. Nephew: George Augustus Black. Appraisal Nov 18, 1868 by Sterling Bowen, Michael McGee, Clayton Jones. Estate Sale Dec 19, 1868. Buyers at sale: Joseph R. Black, Wm. Sutherland, Clara Black, J. H. Bell, Wm. A. Black, H. Kay, Eb Bell, James W. Black, J. A. Armstrong, Francis V. Pruitt.

BOX 179 PACK 4757   ELIZABETH COBB   1863

Deceased died Mar 11, 1869. Administrator: Willis Smith. Bond Apr 14, 1869 of $1,800 by Willis Smith, Uriah M. Mars, Louis H. Russell. Appraisal Apr 17, 1869 by John Foster, Thomas J. Lipscomb, Moses C. Taggart. Held notes on: Richmond S. Cobb, Levi H. Rykard, Wiley Smith, Thomas F. Riley, John G. Boozer. Estate Sale Apr 30, 1869 netted $217.80. Buyers at sale: Stacia Crawford, Willis Smsith, Samuel B. McClinton, Moses C. Taggart, J. T. Smith, Hugh Hollingsworth, Thomas Riley, John Butler, J. F. Ligon. Estate Settlement Feb 6, 1872. (5) Legatees: 1. Stacia Crawford daughter 2. Madison Smith son3. Willis Smith son 4. Wiley Smith son deceased 5. Children of Richmond S. Cobb deceased.

BOX 179 PACK 4758   FRANCIS A. CALHOUN   1869

Deceased died May 30, 1869. Administrator: John F. Calhoun. Bond Oct 13, 1869 of $6,000 by John F. Calhoun, Andrew A. Noble, Peter L. Guillebeau. Wife: Louisa V. Calhoun. Appraisal Oct 28, 1869 by F. E. Smith, Thomas J. Hester, Alex. H. McAllister, James McCelvey. Owned 684 acres of land. Estate Sale Oct 29, 1869. Buyers at sale: J. A. Robinson, Luther Lawton, J. F. Calhoun, Edmund Scott, Wm. Wilson, Troy Calhoun, --- Aldrich, Luke Bugg, Alex. Mitchell, Petrer L. Guillebeau, Moses O. Talman, James McCaslan, Ann Johnson, J. Link, Charles W. Cowan, Alex. H. McAllister, Wm. P. Kennedy, Guilford Cade, Zeke Partlow, W. D. Smith, Mrs. L. V. Calhoun, Wm. D. Mars, San. De Gaffenreid, Thomas Brown, Robert Thornton, Cato Calhoun, Samuel Cade, M. Bell, Stephen Partlow, Samuel J. Hester, Thomas J. Fortescue, Ben. Morrow, B. L. Jones, Ambrose Johnson, Hillary Moore, Wm. A. Lanier, Bedford Calhoun, J. O. Robinson, Ben. A. Calhoun. Estate Settlement, no date. Widow and (9) Children who were all minors except Mary McCaw. 1. Cornelia Calhoun 2. Benjamin A. Calhoun 3. Patrick L. Calhooun 4. Francis A. Calhoun 5. Thomas J. Calhoun 6. Kate Calhoun 7. Louisa Calhoun 8. Emma Calhoun 9. Mary McCaw. Petition between widow and children for dower Dec 9, 1869.

BOX 180   PAPERS of ACTIVITIES, DONORS, ETC. of JOHN de la HOWE

550 pages. Mostly 1821 -1830s   Pack is a great source of information, especially of people involved and donating time and money. Much information about the formative years of this great institution.

BOX 181 PACK 4759   GEORGE DUSENBERRY   1876

Deceased died Aug 11, 1869. Administrator: Margaret E. Dusenberr-wife. Wm. A. Richey, brother-in-law, served as Administrator for a very short period of time. Bond Oct 20, 1869 of $6,000 by Margaret E. Dusenberry, Wm. A. Richey, Robert Dunn, Wm. Dunn. Appraisal Nov 23, 1869 by Thomas J. Mabry, W. R. F. Wilson, J. B. Guffin, Wm. W. Sprouse. Estate Sale Nov 24, 1869 netted $1,062 .61. Buyers at sale: Margaret E. Dusenberry, --- McClung, David J. Jordan, Wm. A. Richey, David Wier, Ben Shavis, Colin Ward, Wm. Sprouse, B. Kennedy, James A. Richey. J. S. Graves was Guardian of Minor Children. Partial Estate Settlement Mar 16, 1870. Widow 1/3 = $901 (5) Children each $360.40. Estate Settlement Feb 7, 1879. (6) Legatees: 1. Margaret E. now wife of J. S. Graves $2,649 2. George C. Dusenberry 3. Elizabeth J. Dusenberry 4. Hannah Dusenberry 5. Nancy C. Dusenberrry 6. Andrew L. Dusenberry The (5) Children each received $10.59. James D. Chalmers paid $51.55 for gravestones.

BOX 181 PACK 4760   DUSENBERRY (minor)   NO YEAR

Nothing in the Pack.

BOX 181 PACK 4761   WILLIAM O. PURSLEY   1868

Will dated Jun 5, 1858. Filed Sep 17, 1868. Witnesses: James Pursley, David Knox, Leroy J. Johnson. Wife: Narcissa Pursley. Executor: Nathan A. Edwards. 1st Bond Oct

21, 1868 of $2,000 by Nathan A. Edwards, David R. Penney, Wm. T. Penney, Epaminandos Edwards. Bond May 21, 1873 of $900 by Nathan A. Edwards, Wm. H. Brooks, Thomas C. Perrin. Brother: David Ephraim Pursley deceased. Appraisal Nov 30, 1868 by Samuel Lockridge, David R. Penney, James C. Pressly. Estate Sale Dec 1, 1868. Netted $439. Buyers at sale: Nathan A. Edwards, Thomas McNeill, Leroy J. Johnson, Louis H. Russell, Mrs. L. C. Kerr, Estther Pennell, James Pressly, David Wier, James Evvans, Wm. H. Penney, Mary Pursley, Ben Gordon, Jack Vance, John Walker, John Barnett, Moseley Edwards, Bob Chamblin, Aaron Johnson, Jack Johnson, James Smith, Samuel Able, John White, Robert J. Cheatham, David R. Penney, James W. Thomas, H. K. Burdette, Francis A. Baker, Thomas J. Mabry, Narcissa Pursley, H. Williams. David Knox bought the blacksmith tools and most of the farm implements. Sale of property proceeds paid to Wm. Hill, Probate Judge. Nathan A. Edwards petitioned that the proceeds of the sale be turned over to him by Hill & Narcissa Pursley, the only heir. Estate Settlement Jun 30, 1873. Distributees were all creditors. Insufficient funds to meet debrts and creditors paid about 8 cents on the dollar. Owed $3,236 Paid $200. Creditors receiving payment: 1. Wm. H. Kerr 2. Nancy J. Kerr 3. Wm. H. Brooks 4. Estate of James Pursley 5. John White 6. Lucretia Ruff 7. Amanda Johnson 8 Isaac Branch. Seal & Sign owed $45 for burial expenses. Estate Insolvent.

BOX 181 PACK 4762 JOHN PATTERSON 1876

Will dated Feb 20, 1869. Filed Jun 17, 1869. Witnesses: Henry H. Scudday, Wm. A. Lesly, Gilbert G. Dawson. Wife: Anna Patterson died prior to estate settlement. Executor: Wm. L. Campbell. Son: John Patterson lived in Attala Co. Miss. in 1879. Grand Son: Jesse Obediah Burt Patterson legacy of $100. 1st Appraisal Jul 30, 1869 by Lewis C. Clinkscales, Wm. Lesly, Wm. Mann, Gilbert G. Dawson. 2nd Appraisal Aug 9, 1876 by Wm. A. Lesly, Wm. Mann, Gilbert G. Dawson. Estate Sale Oct 14, 1876. Buyers at sale: John B. Patterson, Obediah L. Cann, Jane Ferguson, Frances M. McCurry, J. P. Feguson, Wm. L. Campbell, J. B. Hampton, Banister Allen, Pleasant Ferguson, J. J. H. Bannister. Estate Settlement Mar 20, 1877. (9) Distributees: 1. Thomas Patterson lived Choctaw, Miss. 2. Frances Jane Ferguson had son Burt who was deceased 3. Jesse W. Patterson lived in Miss. and had son Jesse Burt Patterson 4. Robert Patterson deceased with Children: Frances M. Patterson, Mary A. Patterson, Jane Patterson, Robert Patterson, Gordon Patterson, Marcus Patterson, Ben. S. Patterson 5. J. Bowman Patterson 6. O. Thompson Patterson deceased with Children: Thomas A. Patterson, Letha A. Patterson, Mary E. Patterson 7. James P. Patterson deceased with Child: Jesse O. Patterson 8. Elizabeth McKee deceased with Children who all lived in Etowah, Ala: Annie C. McKee, Mary McKee, John T. McKee, Wm. Jasper McKee, Jane Frances wife of Wm. Bradley, Tabitha wife of Wm. Catlett, Elizabeth A. McKee 9. Mary E. Cann.

BOX 181 PACK 4763 LARKIN PULLIAM 1870

Will dated Oct 7, 1868. Filed Jan 8, 1869. Witnesses: Robert W. Milford, Robert P. Buchanan, Wm. J. Arnold. Executor: John Pulliam-son. Daughters: Mary A. Milford, Belinda E. Ricks. Appraisal Nov 11, 1869 of $11,783 by Robert P. Buchanan, Robert W. Milford, Wm. Buchanan.

BOX 181 PACK 4764 CHAMPION D. PALMER 1869

Executor: Andrew J. Ferguson. Bond Nov 5, 1868 of $1,200 by Andrew J. Ferguson, Thomas C. Perrin, James S. Cothran. Appraisal Nov 30, 1868 by John T. Lyon, W. R. F. Wilson, Thomas J. McCracken. Owned 9 bee hives. Estate Sale Dec 18, 1868 netted $429.45. Buyers at sale: N. J. Davis, John Lyon, Jackson Edwards, George A. Douglass, Andrew J. Ferguson, George Palmer, John H. Wilson, Thomas W. McWilliams, P. L. McCord, Wesley Edwards, J. A. Wilson, Andy Adams, Widow, Wm. Hall, George Whitlock, J. L. McCord. Estate Settlement: Mar 17, 1870. Estate Insolvent.

BOX 181 PACK 4765   MARY T., JAMES L., REUBEN O., JOHN T. BRANYON (minors) 1869

Father John M. Branyon. Mother: Rosannah Branyon. Guardian: Rosannah Branyon. Bond Aug 3, 1869 of $700 by Rosannah Branyon, Richard G. Kay, Elias O. Pruitt. May 7, 1872 Reuben O. Branyon received legacy. May 17, 1875 John T. Branyon received legacy. Mar 1, 1877 James L. Branyon received legacy. Mar 3, 1882 Mary T. Branyon received legay. She protested that her inheritance had been absorbed except for $92 through board, etc. and that the board charges should not be allowed.

BOX 181 PACK 4766   WILLIS McGEE (minor of color)   1870

Age about 13 and an orphan. Guardian: Morris Wood. Bond Feb 11, 1870 of $400 by Morris Wood, Levi Walker, Reuben Willliams. Uncles: Henry McGee, Robert McGee, James McGee. 1st Return had $15 in his account and paid $6 to Judge of Probate.

BOX 181 PACK 4767   NANCY J. MILFORD (minor)   1869

Guardian: Henry Wilkinson-step father. Bond Apr 5, 1869 of $200 by Henry Wilkinson, Moses C. Taggart, Willis Smith. Fataher: John Milford. Grand Father: Joseph Milford. Final estate entry Sep 25, 1874. Wlikinson was a subponea for failure to file return for 1873.

BOX 181 PACK 4768   ELVIRA R. McKELLAR (minor)   1870

Guardian: Peter M. McKellar-father. Bond Mar 1, 1869 of $1,200 by Peter McKellar, John T. McKellar, Levi H. Rykard. Bond Apr 20, 1870 of $250 by Peter McKellar, John T. McKellar, James Dendy. Due legacy coming from the estate of Wm. A. Sale who ws her uncle. Petioned filed against Josephine Lake as administrator of the estate of Johnson Sale. John McClellan was the guardian of Ellen E. Dendy who had married John T. McKellar one of the securities.

BOX 181 PACK 4769   MARY A. McALLISTER (minor)   1869

Guardian: G. W. Daniel. Bond Jun 18, 1868 of $200 by G. W. Daniel, Gilbert G. Dawson, Massalon Bell. Father: Alex. McAllister. Estte still active Jun 1, 1874.

BOX 181 PACK 4770   JOHN R. & JOSEPH H. MILFORD (minors)   1868

Guardian: Robert W. Milford. Bond Nov 14, 1868 of $100 by Robert W. Milford, James Strawhorn, John H. Mundy. Father: Joseph Milford. Dec 13, 1870 Joseph H. Milford received $20 as his full legacy. Dec 14, 1871 John R. Milford received $20 as his full legacy.

BOX 181 PACK 4771   MARIA McCOMBS   1869

Deceased died Oct 4, 1867. Administrator: Wm. McCombs-brother. Bond Mar 4, 1869 of $2,000 by Wm. McCombs, Andrew J. McKee, John McCombs. 1st Return Feb 5, 1870. Received from the estate of Anna McCombs $441.54, from the estate of Abram Haddon $234.69, from the estate of J. C. Stevenson $16.85. Estate Settlement Oct 1874. (6) Children each $35.48. 1. Wm. Mcombs 2. James McCombs 3. Eliza McKee 4. John McCombs 5. Nancy McWilliams 6. Hannah Haddon deceased, her Children: James R. Haddon, D. E. Haddon, Hannah A. Nickles, Reuben B. Haddon, Lillie Ann Haddon. Funeral expenses $10.

BOX 181 PACK 4772   PINCKNEY MURPHY (man of color)   1869

Administrator: John N. Young. Bond Oct 9, 1870 of $200 by John N. Young, M. Jane Young, C. S. Young. Widow and Children. Appraisal Oct 26, 1869 by D. P. Holloway, Ebeneezer E. Pressly, George Scott. Owned 1 are of land. Estate Sale Oct 26, 1869 netted $122.68. Buyers at sale: Lewis Ellis, D. P. Holloway, Sam Haddon, J. W. Joseph, John M. Bell, Bennet McAdams, George Scott, Gabriel Pearman, W. C. Lemmons, R. T. Taylor, Brice Archer, H. Kennedy. Estate Settlement Jan 7, 1870. Estate Insolvent. Paid Harrison Kennedy $4 for coffin. Paid John M. Bell $1.50 for burial. Paid Dr. J. S. Miller $11.15 for finalmedical services.

BOX 181 PACK 4773   DOCETHEUS C. MOORE   1869

Deceased died Apr 8, 1869. Will dated Dec 29, 1863. Filed Apr 15, 1869. Witnesses: George Franklin, Thomas Stacey, Foster Calvert. Never Married. Executor: Augustus W. Moore-brother. Bond, no date, by Wm. Augustus Moore, Wm. A. Moore, Martin G. Zeigler. Appraisal Jul 3, 1869 by John Carter, J. A. Moore, L. F. Connor. Estate Sale Nov 19, 1869. Buyers at sale: Dr. Pinson, Ed Minor, Ephraim Davis, Frank Lomax, Thornton Foster, Augustus W. Moore, Landon Connor, Willis Makin, J. C. Catowille, Leonidas D. Connor, Jim McCants, Jim Gilbert, John Carter, Thronton Cobb, Moses Clardy, Curtis Brown, Marvin Minion, Dr. Simmons.

BOX 181 PACK 4774   JOSEPH MILFORD   1868

Will dated Aug 16, 1867. Witnesses: Robert P. Buchanan, Wm. Buchanan. Will not accepted due to only two witnesses. Executor: Robert W. Milford-son. Bond Oct 6, 1868 of $200 by Robert W. Milford, John R. Buchanan, Robert P. Buchanan. Sons: Robert W. Milford, Wm, Milford, Thomas B. Milford. Grand Daughters: Nancy J. Milford, Lora Milford, Nancy Milford. Gand Sons: Wm. Milford, Jefferson Davis Milford, Joseph H. Milford, John R. Milford. Appraisal Oct 30, 1868 by Abiah M. Blake, Martin Delaney, Wm. Buchanan. Estate Sale Oct 30, 1868. Buyers at sale: Abiah M. Blake, Robert W. Milford, Thmas B. Milford, Wm. N. Mundy, Francis Pulliam, Charles A. Cobb, Robert P. Buchanan, Wm. Hannah, Martin Delaney, Stephen Pulliam, J. S. Turner. Estate Settlement, no date. (4) Distributees: 1. Rebecca Wilson 2. J. W. Milford 3. T. Butler Milford 4. Nanie J. Milford. W. A. Harralson paid $20.10 for coffin. Dr. W. B. Milwee $3.50 for medical services.

BOX 181 PACK 4775   PHARES MARTIN   1867

Deceased died Sep 12, 1868. Administrator: Phares C. Martin-son. Bond Dec 7, 1868 of $2,000 by Phares C. Martin, G. W. Nelson, A. Crozier. Appraisal Dec 22, 1868 by Peter B. Moragne, Andrew Gulliebeau, Guilford Cade, Joseph L. Bouchillon. Owned 2,100 plus acres of land. Estate Sale, no date, netted $1,169.62. Buyers at sale: Wiley Newby, James C. Jennings, S. Erwin, Phares C. Martin, Wm. A. Crozier, Alex. P. Connor, Frederick H. Edmonds, J. H. Jones, Andrew Gulliebeau, George W. Nelson, James R. Nelson, Mrs. S. Holiday, Asa F. Lipford, Patrick Tennant, A. Baring, J. Martin, James Corley, Guilford Cade, Wm. McCelvey, James Truitt, David Wiley, Thomas Benson, George Hanvey, Thomas Edwards, Burton C. Walker. Big dispute and wrangling over land and money supposed advanced to children. Phares C. Martin became the overseer for his father in 1858 and also acted as his father's agent. He entered into a verbal contract with his father for the Tatom tract of land consisting of 464 acres. The money $2,100 for the purchase was to be paid by his services. He also entered into a contract to purchase the Robert Cheatham tract of land consisting of 80 acres that gave access to Little River. His father died before deeds were drawn up. At the time of the settlement he was claiming ownership of an additional 500 acres. Phares C. Martin also was the center of a land dispute from his Grandmother's Estate. His grandmother, Elizabeth Cofer died in 1863. At her death she owned loand on the Savannah River. She had lived on the land for over 50 years and had been a widow for 30 years. She had (2) sons, Thomas Lawson Cofer who had removed to Missouri in1840 and had not been heard from since 1849 or 1850. He was married at the time but had no children. The other son was Augustus C. Cofer who died Aug 14, 1837 with only (2) children, Martha C. who married Phares C. Martin and California Cofer. Phares C. Martin had long sought that the land be partitioned. James Partlow held a note against Elizabeth Cofer's estte for $8.000 and objected to the divison of the land. Estate Settlement, no date. (10) Distributees: 1. Phares C. Martin 2. Savannah wife of John F. Holliday out of state 3. Wm. A. Creswell and wife who was not a daughter 4. Eveline wife of Wm. Cooper out of state 5. Lula wife of Wm. McCelvey out of state. 6. John Turner who was the son of Wm. Turner and Phoebe Martin, both deceased 7. Susan wife of Wm. A. Corzier 8. Floride wife of Asa F. Lipford 9. Jerusha wife of James Nelson 10. Eusebia wife of Burton Walker. Wm. Perryman paid $30.50 for tow coffins, one for Phares Martin and the other for his daughter, Christiana.

BOX 181 PACK 4776   MARY H. McDONALD   1869

Will dated Apr 2, 1865. Filed Oct 14, 1869. Witnesses: Robert H. Wardlaw, John F. Livingston, John T. Owen. Executor: Thomas Thomson. Spparaisal Oct 22, 1869 by Robert A. Archer, D. R. Williams, James D. Chalmers. Estate Sale Oct 25, 1869 netted $162.58. Buyers at sale: Thomas Thomson, James D. Chalmers, Thomas M. Christian, J. A. Mays, Wm. H. McCaw, J. S. Simpson, Wm. H. Taggart, Dr. Issac Branch.

BOX 182 PACK 4777   JOHN W. BURTON (minor)   1869

Age 14. Father: Joseph Fields Burton. Due legacy from father's estate of about $500. Guardian: John Shirley. Bond Sep 15, 1869 of $1,000 by John Shirley, Ezekiel Harris, George Shirley. Of age Jan 1, 1876 and received $436.74 on Apr 7, 1876.

BOX 182 PACK 4778   WILLIAM LAWRENCE BURTON (minor)   1869

Father: Joseph Fields Burton. Guardian: Ezekiel Harris-uncle. Bond Jul 21, 1869 of $2,000 by Ezekiel Harris, John Shirley, John B. Armstrong. Mar 15, 1873 received from the estate of Wm. Armstrong $5.31 and later from same estate $152. Estate Settlement Aug 11, 1873. Received $471.

BOX 182 PACK 4779   JOSEPH FIELDS & MARY ALCANZA BURTON (minors)   1871

Children of: Joseph Fields Burton. Guardian: Wm. Clinkscales he resigned, Mar 3, 1869 Addison Clinkscales became guardian. Bond Mar 6, 1869 of $3,000 by Addison Carwile, John Pratt, Reuben Clinkscales. James M. Carwile became guardian after the death of Addison Clinkscales because no one was looking out for the minor's interests. Bond Apr 10, 1870 of $3,000 by James M. Carwile, David R. Penney, Addison F. Carwile. Newton McAdams became the final guardian at the death of James Carwile. Mother: Missouri now the wife of John T. McClain. Jun 17, 1872 Joseph Fields Burton received $542.05 from the estate of Addison Clinkscales. Settlement of Joseph Fields Burton Jan 3, 1885. Settlement of Mary A. Burton, now McAdams Oct 20, 1881 $437.12. Elizabeth Burton was also a minor child but died shortly after her father and never became a part of the Guardianship and settlements.

BOX 182 PACK 4780   JANE BURTON (minor)   1879

Father: Joseph Fields Burton. Guardian: Joseph J. Copeland. Bond Mar 15, 1870 of $1,200 by Joseph J. Copeland, Ezekiel Harris, Elizabeth Armstrong. Feb 27, 1871 received from the Armstrong Estate $132.10, from the Burton Estate $398.86. Oct 10, 1879 final return, Jane now Jane Armstrong $347.38.

BOX 182 PACK 4781   ANNIE C. BUCHANAN (minor)   1869

Father: James T. Buchanan. Guardian: Maggie Buchanan-mother who died before any estate activities began. Bond May 17, 1869 of $1,000 by Maggie Buchanan, Sarah Buchanan, Wm. R. Buchanan. William R. Buchanan became guardian upon the death of Maggie Buchanan. Bond Dec 17, 1869 of $1,580 by Wm. R. Buchanan, Joshua Turner, Sarah Buchanan. Annie was entitled to a legacy from the Estate of Robert E. Buchanan. She needed a representative and Wm. R. Buchanan became her representative. Last estate entry Jan 24, 1873.

BOX 182 PACK 4782   MARY E. & MARTHA J. BRADLEY (minors)   1870

Mary E. Bradley age 15. Father: John Bradley deceased. Mother: Mary Bradley. Grand Father: Archibald Bradley deceased. Uncle: John L. Drennan. Guardian: John L. Drennan. Bond Jan 24, 1870 of $1,000 by John L. Drennan, J. H. Drennan, Horace Drennan. Bond Nov 4, 1875 of $600 by John L. Drennan, Wm. P. Devlin, Horace Drennan. Final return Jan 30, 1880, she was now Mary E. Puckett received $262.85. Martha J. Bradley died Oct 10, 1871. Guardian: John L. Drennan. Bond Jan 24, 1870 of $1,000 by John L. Drennan, J. H. Drennan, Horace Drennan. Estate Settlement Dec 5, 1872. (3) Distributees each $43.60. 1. Mary Bradley, mother 2. Sarah F. Bardley, sister 3. Mary E. Bradley, sister.

BOX 182 PACK 4783   HUGH J. & MARY M. ARMSTRONG (minors)   1869

Hugh Armstrong age 18. Father: Wm. Armstrong deceased. Mother: Elizabeth Armstrong. Guardian: Elizabeth Armstrong-motherbecame administrator. Bond Dec 24, 1869 of $1,500 by Elizabeth Armstrong, John Shirley, James A. Armstrong. Final Return Hugh J. Armstrong Mar 15, 1873. Mary M. Armstrong age 14. Guardian: Elizabeth Armstrong-mother. Bond Dec 24, 1869 of $1,500 by Elizabeth Armstrong, John Shirley, James A. Armstrong. Final Return Mary M. Armstrong Nov 12, 1878 she received $34.78.

BOX 182 PACK 4784   JOHN HENRY ASHLEY (minor)   1869

Age 7. Father: Josiah Ashley deceased. Guardian: David P. Hannah-step father. Bond Dec 11, 1869 of $1,500 by David P. Hannah, Benjamin H. Eakin, James H. Nickles. Final Return Apr 26, 1883. Josiah Ashley received $1,014.54.

BOX 182 PACK 4785   SARAH JANE & JAMES EDMOND GRAY (minors)   1869

James Edmond Gray age 4. Sarah Jane Gray age 7. Guardian: John J. Gray. Bond Jan 19, 1870 of $1,000 by John J. Gray, Wm. T. Carter, Sarah E. Cheatham. They were entitled to a legacy from the Estate of Bartlett M. Cheatham of about $300 each. Their mother, Sarah A. F. Gray was a daughter of Bartlett M. Cheatham. Wm. T. Carter was deceased when on Dec 10, 1874 Sarah E. Cheatham requested release from her security obligation. Estate Settlement for Sarah Jane Gray in 1878. Estate Settlement for James Edmond Gray Jan 24, 1888 received $258.79.

BOX 182 PACK 4786   DAVID GREER   1869

Will, no date. Filed Jun 8, 1869. Witnesses: John M. Dunlap, G. M. Mattison, John W. Bigby. Executors: David Moore, G. M. Mattison became administrator in Dec 1876. Bond Jan 3, 1877 of $2,000 by G. M. Mattison, Stephen Latimer, James R. Latimer. Wife Jeanette Greer died Mar 1875 and David Moore settled her estate. Sons: Wm. S. Greer, James L. Greer. Daughters: Mary Phillips, Clarissa Adams. Grand Daughters: Nancy Jane Adams, Clara Ann Adams. 1st Appraisal Jul 31, 1869 by John W. Bigby, George W. Kay, John M. Greer, James A. Bigby. Owned 85 acres of land. Held Notes on: James L. Greer, Mary Phillips, David Moore, H. W. Moore, L. R. Greer, David Greer. 2nd Appraisal Jan 16, 1877 by James R. Latimer, Charles Lanier, Archibald P. Shirley. Estate Sale Jan 19, 1877 netted $938.21. Buyers at sale: Thomas M. Branyon, John Kay, Archibald P. Shirley, John N. Kay, Mary Phillips, M. Erwin, Gabriel Latcher, D. R. Greer, J. Y. Flowers, Lewis F. Kay, G. M. Mattison, Wm. H. Acker, J. L. Brock, Richard W. Burts, George A. Moore, Zack Taylor, George H. Kay, Gabe Pearman, Thomas Robertson, David Arnold, A. J. Trussell, M. J. Austie, Aaron Herrington, John N. Latimer, H. H. Acker, J. B. Kay, Thomas Burts, A. N. Cullins, Lyles Robertson, J. P. Sampson, Daniel B. Armstrong, James R. Latimer, L. M. Branyon, G. M. Greer, C. C. Smith, L. M. Stone, J. W.Wilson, B. H. Greer, Basil Acker, Thomas Robertson, Robert Sampson, C. M. Harris, Thomas Brock, Wesley Sexton, Enoch Gambrell, A. T. Armstrong, Robert Mattison, S. P. Taylor, T. A. Hudgens, Esther Roberts, John H. Ridge, Jesse Kay, Joel Kay, W. S. Fleming, R. E. Moore, R. L. Phillips, J. B. Ashley, Wm. Bagwell, Lewis Gunnells, J. F. Davis, Esther Latimer, John Sullivan, John Yarn, M. E. Gambrell, Austin Magee, W. S. Greer, C. Collins, W. C. Adams, J. H. Woods, Abe Herrington, M. J. Austin, Simpson Holcombe, Wm. Cummins, Thomas Bannister. Estate Settlement Jan 7, 1879. Legatees: 1. Clarissa Adams $65 2. J. J. Greer

$100 3. W. S. Greer $253 4. James L. Greer $253 5. Mary Phillips $433 6. John J. Greer $253 7. Clarissa A. Adams & Nancy J. Cochran split one share.

BOX 182 PACK 4787   WILLIAM GORDON   1877

Administrators: Wm. G. Gordon died Jan 2, 1877, Alex. G. Hagen. Bond Oct 15, 1869 of $1,800 by Wm. G. Gordon, Mary Gordon, Grizella E. Gordon, Thomas S. Gordon, H. W. Gordon. Bond Mar 3, 1877 of $1,200 by Alex. G. Haagen, Thomas S. Gordon, H. W. Gordon. 1st Appraisal Dec 1, 1869 by James Cunningham, Peter Henry, Alex. G. Hagen. Held notes on: Robert J. White, Franklin E. Bowie, Bernard O'Connor, J. M. Bell, Wm. J. Lomax, James Magill, Isaac Gordon. 2nd Appraisal Dec 20, 1877 by James C. Stevenson, Peter Henry, Edward Westfield. Estate Sale Jan 7, 1878 netted $422.97. Buyers at sale: Samuel Pressly, George Scott, J. E. Uldrick, Ben. H. Eakin, James Evans, Andy Wilson, M. J. Gordon, Ed Wilson, Mary Gordon, Newton Nickles, Thomas S. Gordon, Chalmers G. Haddon, George Nickles, Wm. T. Cowan, Harry Gordon, John Hagen, Wm. Hawthorne, Wm. Klugh, Pless Harris, Wm. B. Bowie, Wm. C. Winn, Edward Westfield, Andy Scott, John Devlin, Wm. McComb, Alex. G. Hagen, A. L. Bowie, George Hagen, James Strawhorn, Charley Johnson. Estate Settlement Jul 11, 1879. Widow, Mary Gordon and (5) Children: 1. Thomas S. Gordon 2. Mary Jane Gordon 3. Mrs. G. E. Wilson 4. Harvey W. Gordon 5. Children of Wm. G. Gordon and his wife, Mary E. Gordon. Children were: Mary E. Gordon, Nancy E. Gordon, John R. Gordon, Wm. E. Gordon, Emmett Gordon, Mary Jane Gordon. All of the Children opposed Alex. G. Hagen and his his need to sell the land to pay debtors. Court ordered the land sold. Claims settled 50 cents on the dollar. Estate Insolvent.

BOX 182 PACK 4788   MARGARET GAINES   1856

Will dated Aug 23, 1856. Witnesses: J. W. Livingston, John A. Wier, Wm. M. Haddon. Brother: Andrew Wilson. Nephew: Samuel Wilson son of Brother, John Wilson. Nieces: Sarah Kennedy, Lucinda Morgan, Elizaa Ann Wilson. She owned 3 slaves. Wm. Gaines protested that Margaret Gaines had no right to make a will. Trial to determine the validity of the will scheduled for Jan 16, 1857. Nothing further.

BOX 182 PACK 4789   ELIZABETH A. DUBOSE   1869

Deceased died Jul 24, 1868. Administrator: James R. DuBose-step son. Bond Sep 14, 1868 of $12,000 by James R.DuBose, Robert M. DuBose, Wm. Joel Smith. (4) Children all of whom were minors. Appraisal Dec 15, 1868 by Thomas J. Hester, James McCelvey, Robert N. Boyd, Francis A. Calhoun. Estte Sale Dec 8, 9, 10, 1868 netted $2,503.76. Buyers at sale: Peter Algood, L. C. Lawton, Francis A. Calhoun, Robert McCaslan, John Baughman, Wm. Evans, Thomas Frith, J. D. Welch, W. P. Earnest, John Manning. Wm. Wilson, James A. Norwood, A. B. Johnson, James Clark, Wm. T. Carter, Thomas L. Vance, James Taggart, W. J. Gray, James R. DuBose, Robert W. Hinton, Wm. E. McNair, Sam Erwin, J. T. Latimer, John L. Vance, J. S. Barnett, D. H. Mills, W. T. Tatom, Samuel Hester, Robert Dunlap, Thomas Brough, H. Penney, John Wells, George Ivey, Thomas L. Gray, Wm. D. Mars, Dr. Roberts, A. White, Dr. Gibert, Lucinda Covin, J. M. Burdette, Wm. Carter, Thomas J. Hester, Edmund Scott, Robert McLane, Gus Covin, Lelm Lawton, J. R. Scott, Hiram Cowan, Josh Banks, Wm. Tennant, Frank Anderson, Robert Earnest, Wm. J. Earnest, James Brown, Samuel Morrah, Luther Lawton, Luke Bug, Lewis Covin, S.

183

Noble, Wm. Pinkston, Thomas Mobley, Robert A. McCaslan, John Martin, J. F. Gibert, Samuel Partlow, Thomas Cofer, A. H. McAllister, Cato Calhoun, Elijah Calhoun, C. B. Johnson, John Robinson, John A. Link, Alex. Richey, Ruth Tennant, Hudson Tucker, Wash Calhoun, Samuel Perrin, Mark Bug, Jerry Harrison, Wm. N. McCay, Patrick H. Noble, Wm. H. Pope, Wm. D. Cade, Daniel Hill, George W. Robinson, J. O. Robinson, F. M. Mitchell. Aug 10, 1869 Frank Arnold was erecting a wall around the grave yard. Funerla expences $30. Tombstone $13.65.

BOX 182 PACK 4790   WILLIAM HENDERSON EDWARDS (minor)   1870

Guardian: James Harvey Edwards-father. Bond Mar 9, 1870 of $70 by James Harvey Edwards, James S. Cothran, Samuel B. Knox. Mar 10, 1870 received from the Estate of Mrs. Leona Edwards $35.44. She was his mother who had recently died.

BOX 182 PACK 4791   JOSEPH CRESWELL   1870

Administrator: Samuel O. Young-his mother was a Creswell. Bond Jan 7, 1870 by SDamuel O. Young, James C. Dowtin, F. R. Robinson. Appriasal Jan 24, 1870 by Wm. M. McCaslan, Hezezekiah Burnett, J. M. Smith. Estate Sale Jan 25, 1870 netted $548.57. Buyers at sale: Widow, Samuel O. Young, Miss Hannah Creswell, Samuel McQuerns, A. G. Talbert, J. F. Creswell, L. Lyon, Robert Creswell, Joe Palmer, Wm. Robinson, J. P. Creswell, Hasper Bradley, Hezekiah Burnett, Wm. M. McCaslan, George Hanvey, J. D. Neel, J. C. Dowtin, John McBride, John Gray, James Truitt, Thomas V. Creswell. Estate Settlement Feb 24, 1870. Widow 1/3 = $124.96. Other (7) shares $35.70 each: 1. Joseph McBryde in right of his wife Mary Ann deceased, had (5) children 2. James Creswell 3. Hannah B. Creswell 4. Mary A. Goodwin 5. Jouett Creswell 6. Julie Creswell 7. B. Creswell. Others who received legacies were: 1) T. J. & A. R. Roberts $3.90 2) Dollin Johnson $35.70 3) James Creswell $35.70 4. Thomas McBride $3.90 6. John McBride $3.90 7. George Young & Margaret Young $3.90.

BOX 182 PACK 4792   ELIZA J. CLELAND   1869

Administrator: Wm. Dickson. Bond Dec 31, 1869 of $350 by Wm. Dickson, Wesley A. Black, James R. Cunningham. Husband: David Cleland deceased. She was to have received from his estate. Her estate received amount due to her Dec 15, 1870, $206.46. Estate Settlement Dec 15, 1870. (3) Distributees each $46.09: 1. Mary Ann Dickson, sister 2. Children of John Anderson 3. Wm. Anderson.

BOX 182 PACK 4793   PRESTON A. CHEATHAM (minor)   1869

Guardian: Sarah E. Cheatham-mother. Bond Apr 27, 1869 of $1,200 by Sarah E. Cheatham, James S. Cothran, Thomas C. Perrin. 1871 received from the Estate of Bartlett M. Cheatham $910.90. Estate Settlement Dec 11, 1878. Received from Mother as guardian $1,150.

BOX 182 PACK 4794   JAMES H. CHEATHAM (minor)   1869

Guardian: Sarah E. Cheatham-mother. Bond Apr 27, 1869 of $1,200 by Sarah E. Cheatham, James S. Cothran, Thomas C. Perrin. 1871 received from the Estate of

Bartlett M. Cheatham $910.90. Estate Settlement: Jan 14, 1873. Received from Mother as guardian $770.49.

BOX 182 PACK 4795   PARKER & ELEANOR DANNELLY (minors of color)   1869

Parker age 14, Eleanor age 12. Orphans. Guardian: Alfred Groves-uncle. Bond Nov 12, 1869 of $300 by Alfred Groves, London Hill, Callio Ward.

BOX 182 PACK 4796   HENRY FOSBROOK   1869

Will dated Feb 22, 1869. Filed Apr 8, 1869. Witnesses: Andrew J. Woodhurst, Sarah A. Armstrong, Elizabeth Gibert. Tailor. Executrix: Jane Eliza Fosbrook,-wife. Burial Clothing $12.15. Coffin $15 to James A. Richey. Medical services $20.50 to Dr. Reid.

BOX 182 PACK 4797   JOSEPH J., SUSAN J., FRANCES ISABELLA HANVEY (minors)   1868

GUARDIAN: Edward L. Hanvey-father. Bond Dec 21, 1868 of $150 by Edward L. Hanvey, John H. Jones, James W. Britt. Dec 21, 1868 received from the Estate of Mrs. Jane Lindsay $24. $4.80 each.

BOX 182 PACK 4798   POLLY ANN HOGG (woman of color)   1870

Administrator: John F. Clinkscales. Bond Sep 17, 1869 of $150 by John F. Clinkscales, Joseph W. Trowbridge, Conrad Wakefield. Appraisal Oct 2, 1869 by James M. Carwile, James Clikscales, Stephen Milton Fisher. Estate Sale Oct 2, 1869 netted $62.35. Buyers at sale: J. T. Clinkscales, Edward Ashley, John F. Clinkscales, James Clinkscales. Estate Settlement Jan 12, 1870. Paid H. Robinson & Co. $5.18 for shrouding. Paid Thomas Hogg $25 for care for the final three months of her life. Paid Dr. John A. Robinson $16 for final medical visit. Estate Insolvent.

BOX 182 PACK 4799   JOHN A. HUNTER   1870

Adminisstrator: Hiram W. Lawson. Bond Dec 8, 1868 of $200 by Hiram W. Lawson, James Shillito, Frances J. Lawson. Appraisal Dec 26, 1868 by James H. Cobb, Edward Westfield, James Chalmers. Estate Sale Dec 26, 1868 netted $39. Buyers at sale: Wm. C. Patterson, James C. Lites, James McCord, Hiram W. Lawson, John Enright, Joseph T. Moore, Louis H. Russell, Patrick Hazzard, John C. Douglass, Dr. Isaac Branch. Final return and estate entry Sep 22, 1874.

BOX 182 PACK 4800   JAMES P. HILL (minor)   1870

Age 15. Father: Wm. H. Hill deceased. Guardian: George M. Hanvey-bro-in-law. Bond Dec 7, 1869 of $1,000 by George M. Hanvey, James Redmond Brown, Edward L. Hanvey.

BOX 182 PACK 4801   BUTLER HASKELL (man of color)   1869

Deceased died Sep 23, 1869. Administrator: George A. Palmer-his employer. Bond Oct 12, 1869 of $300 by George A. Palmer, John Enright, T. W. M. Wilson. Appraisal Oct 28, 1869 by James A. Wilson, Charles Wilson, Wm. J. Wilson. Estate Sale Oct 28, 1869 netted $46.92. Buyers at sale: Jackson Edwards, Webster Edwards, George A. Palmer,

Catlett Corley, Johnson Jones. Estate Settlement, no date. Estate had $4.92 left after expenses. Paid Samuel Johnson $8 for coffin.

BOX 182 PACK 4802   MARTIN HACKETT   1870

Will dated May 20, 1869 Filed Jan 14, 1870. Witnesses: James Gilliam, W. W. Rowland, D. R. Greer. Executor: Thomas C. Lipscomb. Wife: Mary T. HACKETT. Daughters: Almena F. Coleman, Emeline S. Rogers, Julia McSwain. Grand Son: Martin Coleman. Grand Daughter: Mary Julia Elizabeth McSwain. 1st Appraisal Feb 3, 1870 by James Gilliam, John T. Parks, J. Biley. Owned a house and lot in Greenwood, over 1,200 acres of land. Appraisal of Land Oct 15, 1886 by C. A. C. Waller, James W. Hill, J. W. Greer. Estate Sale Oct 15, 1886. Buyers at sale: John R. Tarrant, John B. Sample, Thomas Stewart, Wm. Evans, Jack Bacus, Perry Brooks, Math Creswell, Gid Savage, Frank Keller, M. H. Coleman, Moses C. Taggart, L. N. Golding, H. P. Galphin, Joe Williams, C. G. Walker, Dr. B. Cobb, Mrs. A. Watson, Robert Creswell, E. F. Waldrop, John Richter. (20) Parcels of land sold to: John B. Sample, Frank Keller, R. P. Blake, Francis A. Arnold Jr., W. B. Milwee, C. A. C. Waller, Wm. Evans, Thomas Walker, Charlie Foy, Hannah Burton, Robert C. Gilliam, John A. Barksdale. 1,143 acres of land not sold at the sale. Estate Settlement Dec 22, 1886. (3) Shares each $2,642: 1. Mrs. M. J. Galphin 2. Almena F. Coleman and children: Mary Emma Walker, M. H. Coleman, W. M. Coleman Jessie H. Bailey 3. Children of Emeline Rogers deceased: 1. Almena wife of J. J. Clark 2. J. H. Morris, James Alpheus Rogers living in Nevada Co., Ark. Paid A. Blythe $38 for coffin. Paid Leavel & Gage $65 for tombstone.

BOX 183 PACK 4803   Emily Isom   1869

Deceased died Jul 15, 1869. Administrator: James A. Corley-not any kin. Bond Sep 10, 1869 of $1,500 by James A. Corley, Michael McGrath, Frederick H. Edmunds. George W. Cox, Emily's brother, protested against James A. Corley being appointed administrator. Agnes Lane, the mother of Emily Isom, petitioned that D. L. Cox their uncle through marriage be appointed guardian of the children. Appraisal Dec 8, 1869 by Joseph L. Bouchillon, John Harmon, Peter B. Moragne. Held notes on: H. F. Corley, James Taggart, J. C. Cox. Estate Sale Dec 8, 1869 netted $731. Buyers at sale: Phares C. Martin, James Jennings, Wm. H. Peake, George A. Hanvey, W. Newby, H. M. Johnson, John Harmon, M. M. Brown, Ben. Gibert, James A. Corley, N. E. Brown, Peter Guillebeau, Ned Wells, Primus Letny, R. Gregory, Guilford S. Cade, Singleton A. McIntosh, Wm. Jennings, H. Bouchillon, Wade Moragne, Andrew Guillebeau, E. R. Perryman. Estate Settlement Mar 20, 1886. $496.47 to be distribured. Only heirs were 1. John A. Isom 2. Gabriella Isom who married a Dobbins. John A. & Gariella ha to get lien against the property of James A. Corley due to his failure to pay them the $496.47.

BOX 183 PACK 4804   FRIDAY JACKSON (man of color)   1869

Administrator: Edwin Parker. Bond Sep 18, 1869 of $300 by Edwin Parker, Wm. H. Parker, Robert Jones. Blacksmith –Owner of Shop. Appraisal Oct 5, 1869 by John Enright, Philip S. Rutledge, Andrew M. Hill. Estate Sale Nov 1, 1869. Buyers at sale: Widow, J. Wm. Robertson, Archibald Douglass, Samuel Johnson, Lewis Edwards, Aaron Mitchell, John J. Bass, Larkin Reding, Jesse Hill, Jim Patton. ACCOUNTS (buyers of color are maked with an asterisk) due shop at the time of his death: Alec Bush*, Mrs. J. Burns,

J. N. Belcher, B. Z. Blackmon, Henry Lesly*, J. W. W. Marshall, Wm. H. Parker, Andrew Small, Ben Williams*, Joseph Wardlaw, M. Jeff Wilson, David B. Smith, Seal & Sign, Dr. Edwin Parker, Mathew McDonald, John Lesly, Wm. Davis*, Charles Cox, James D. Chalmers, Sam Corzier*, John Davis, John Devlin, Jesse Dendy, B. F. Franks, J. C. Moore, Enoch Nelson, Samuel Robertson, J. F. Simpson, Town Council of Abbeville, J. A. Wilson, Edward Westfield, Eliza Jones, Hiram T. Tusten, Wm. Rutlddge*, Barney O'Connor, James McCravey, Robert Jones, R. A. Hamlin, Charles Fair*, Jones & Hill, Thomas Jackson, Thomas Knox, John Kurz, Wm. McCord, Wm. T. Penney, Philip S. Rutledge, Hugh Wilson, Cully Ward*, Wm. T. Branch, Robert Bowie, Enright & Smith, John Hawthorne, Uriah Mars, Samuel McGowan, Cato Hunter*, Alflred Ellis*, Hiram Cromer*, James S. Cothran, Lem Guffin, Harvey T. Lyon, John T. Owen, N. J. Davis, Frank Hammond, John J. Lesly, Thomas Thomson, Robert J. White, Hutson J. Lomax, J. R. Harralson, John C. Douglass. Estate Settlement Dec 15, 1870. Sale had netted $41.40. Amount received from accounts $31.83.

BOX 183 PACK 4804 ½   DUSENBERRY (minors)   1876

George C. Dusenberry, Hannah Dusenberry, Nancy C. Dusenberry, Anna Lewis Dusenberry. Father: George Dusenberry deceased. Mother Margaret C. Dusenberry. Guardian: Joseph W. Trowbridge. Bond Mar 19, 1870 of $1,000 by Jospeh W. Trowbridge, James S. Cothran, James D. Chalmers. Separate identical bonds for each minor. Trowbridge became unable to fulfill his responsibilities due to near insolvency and agreed to the appointment of Jacob Graves as guardian. Bond Sep 18, 1876 of $1,000 by Jacob S. Graves, M. E. Graves, Wm. A. Richey. Judgements filed against Guardian, Joseph W. Trowbridge and Securities as Hannah owed her legacy $280.72, Nancy Caroline owed her legacy $134.40, Anna Lewis owed her legacy $397.45, George Clarence owed his legacy $1,526.73. Estate Settlement Mar 8, 1880. 1. Elizabeth Jane received $198 2. George Clarence received $454.71. Jan 31, 1882 Hannah received $192.13. Apr 28, 1888 Nancy C. received ---. Sep 10, 1890 anna received ---.

BOX 183 PACK 4805   DR. WILLIAM T. JONES   1869

Deceased died Aug 1869. Will dated Jan 27, 1869. Witnesses: Marshall Sharp, James A. Aagnew, J. R. Smith. Executor: George W. Jones. Daughter: Sarah Ann wife of 1st N. S. Summerfield 2nd George W. Jones. Grand Son: William T. Jones son of daughter Marian Elizabeth Jones deceased. Appraisal Nov 10, 1869 by J. C. Rasor, Wm. Riley, James Killingsworth. Owned 120 acres of land. Estate Sale Dec 8, 1869. Buyers at sale: John Higgins, Joseph Richey, John T. Stevens, J. T. Johnson, J. F. Singleton, A. Room, Archibald Ellis, James M. Thomas, J. R. Owens, A. M. Agnew, J. L. Anderson, Wm. Riley, J. C. Rasor, Wm. Maddox, J. W. Moore, Claiborne Epps, Thomas Bryant, B. H. Smith, Richard Griffin, G. W. Jones, Eli Starks, L. A. L. Jones, Ben. F. Ballentine, Preston Smith, Hannah Arnold, Wm. A. Kay, A. Allen, J. B. Bolt, R. E. Hughes, Enoch M. Sharp, Peter Miller, Lias Owens, Henry Ware, Daniel Beacham, Tyra Y. Martin, G. M. Hodges, James Taylor, Marvin Godbolt, Basil Madox, John Adams, James Seawright. Estate Settlement Jan 30, 1874. Parties did not appear for settlement. Estate Resettlement Jul 12, 1877. Decreed that the original settlement of 1874 was still in force. (2) Heirs: 1. Sarah Ann Summerfield Jones now wife of George W. Jones $427 2. Grand Child, Wm T. Jones $376. Paid Ernright & Smith $45.50 for coffin.

BOX 183 PACK 4806   BOSWELL JOHNSON (minor of color)   1870

Age 16. Orphan. Guardian: Wm. Wilson. Bond Mar 5, 1869 of $500 by Wm. Wilson, Samuel C. Link, J. W. W. Marshall. Final return Aug 3, 1875. Received nothing but of age in 1874.

BOX 183 PACK 4807   ISAAC C. KENNEDY   1869

Confederate Soldier. Died 1865 in Confederate Service. Never Married. Administrator: Lorenzo D. Kennedy, Theodroe Kennedy, J. A. Kennedy. (8) Brothers (1) Sister. Estate Settlement Feb 26, 1872. (11) Distributees each $26.90: 1. Agnes Kennedy, Mother 2. W. T. Kennedy 3. J. J. Kennedy 4. M. B. Kennedy 5. J. A. Kennedy 6. Theodore Kennedy 7. M. L. Kennedy 8. J. T. Kennedy 9. Lorenzo D. Kennedy 10. Martha Kennedy 11. L. E. Stevenson daughter of Jane Kennedy Stevenson deceased.

BOX 183 PACK 4808   PHILIP LeROY   1869

Will dated Mar 18, 1865. Codicil Mar 20, 1865. Witnesses: Peter E. Legrand, John O. Lindsay. Executors: John B. LeRoy, E. J. Belot. Will not vailid due to only two witnesses but was qualified and admitted by the court. New Witnesses: Peter E. Legrand, James McCelvey, John O. Lindsay. Wife: Elizabeth LeRoy. Sons: Thomas Lee LeRoy age 8 weeks, John A. LeRoy, Alexander LeRoy. Appraisal Nov 17, 1869 by Samuel R. Morrah, James McCelvey, Peter E. Legrand. Owned 357 acres of land, 2 slaves at time of will. Estate Sale Nov 17, 1869. Buyers at sale: John B. LeRoy, Jasper Earnest, D. M. Rogers, Lewis Clay, Robert DuBose, Wm. Marion, Samuel Irwin, E. Lawton, C. A. White, Wm. D. Mars, Peter L. Guillebeau, J. L. Covin, G. B. LeRoy, Wm. H. Daniel, J. A. Mars, Alex. H. McAllister, Samuel Link, Jack Ferguson, Wm. Clay.   Estate Settlement Mar 3, 1874. Widow, now wife of F. E. Lawton. Previous advancements to Children: 1. James H. LeRoy $762 2. Elizabeth J. LeRoy $32 3. Susan A. LeRoy $100 4. A. P. LeRoy $19 5. Martha J. Parrish $425.50 6. John B. Leroy $17.50. Estate now paid out the following to them: 1. Elizabeth J. Beltot $442 2. Susan A. Holmes $142 3. A. P. LeRoy $142 4. M. J. Parrish who later married a Langston $142 5. John B. LeRoy $142.

BOX 183 PACK 4809   FANNIE MUNDY (minor)   1870

Age 14. Orphan. Guardian: Allen T. Bell. Bond Mar 11, 1870 by Allen T. Bell, Wm. K. Blake, Wm. A. Blake. Mar 8, 1870 petitioned that Allen T. Bell be appointed Guardian. She was living with this family. She had no close kin and no legacy of any kind coming to her.

BOX 183 PACK 4810   JAMES ROBERT & NANCY E. NICKLES (minors)   1870

Guardian for James Robert: William McCombs. Bond Apr 1, 1868 of $2,000 by Wm. McCombs, John Hagen, Wm. A. Hagen. Guardian for Nancy E.: John L. McCord-bro-in-law. Bond Dec 10, 1870 of $2,000 by John L. McCord, J. A. McCord, J. H. Nickles. Feb 16, 1869 each received $82.02 from the Estate of their father. Oct 21, 1879 Nancy E. received $1,410, she had previously received $672.29. Jan 18, 1883 Nancy E. received the final amount of $1,800.

Mixed in this pack are the following:

THADDEUS GAMBRELL   Guardian: James Gambrell. Apr 22, 1870 received from the Estate of J. C. Gambrell $42.81. Final return Mar 16, 1880

EVELINE GAMBRELL   Guardian: James Gambrell. Apr 22, 1870 received from the Estate of J. C. Gambrell $50. Settlement Feb 23, 1881 $10

M. HALL & SARAH ANN HALL   Guardian: James Gambrell. Apr 22, 1870 received $53.26 from Estate of J. C. Gambrell

MARTHA J. GAMBRELL   Guardian: James Gambrell. Apr 22, 1870 received $39.51 from the Estate of J. C. Gambrell. Final return Mar 14, 1880 received $14.67.

J. P. GAMBRELL   Guardian: James Gambrell. Apr 22, 1870 received $45.26 from the Estate of J. C. Gambrell. 1881 Final Return received $14.38.

BOX 183 PACK 4811   EDWARD H. NICKLES (minor)   1870

Guardian: Andrew Stevenson. Bond Feb 5, 1868 by Andrew Stevenson, George Nickles, Wm. A. Haagen. Settlement Dec 17, 1872 received $11,528.60.

BOX 183 PACK 4812   WILLIAM A. & MARY JANE NICKLES (minors)   1869

Both minors over the age of 12. Father: Thomas Nickles deceased. Guardian of Wm. A.: John L. McCord. Bond Oct 5, 1869 of $2,000 by John L. McCord, Wm. H. Adamson, James A. McCord. Guardian of Mary J.: Bond Feb 5, 1868 of $2,000 by John Hagen George Nickles, Wm. A. Hagen. Guardianship of Mary Jane transferred to John L. McCord, now her husband in 1870. Feb 28, 1870 Mary Jane received $316.92 from Estate of her father, Thomas Nickles. Setllement of Wm. A. Nickles Aug 6, 1875. He received $1,144.60.

BOX 183 PACK 4812 ½   RICHARD M. TODD   1841

Deceased died Jan 15, 1840. Administrator: Wm. Eddins. Bond Feb 17, 1840 of $80,000 by Wm. Eddins, Larkin G. Carter, Nathan Calhoun, JoelSmith. Partner in the firm of R. M. Todd & W. B. Smith in the Town of Greenwood. Very large estate with pages of expenditures, receiptsw transactions, etc. Appraisal Apr 17, 1840 by James Wesley Child, Larkin G. Carter, Richard M. White, Wm. B. Smith, John McLennon. Owned 20 slaves. Notes held by Richard M. Todd: Albert Waller, Wm. Whitley, Solomon Adams, Samuel Goff, James S. Pope, Wm. Waller, James Roman, David Rogers, Isham Harris, Drury Matthews, R. H. Clark, Wm. Wilson, Wm. Eddins, J. Coleman, Thomas Maxwell, Robert Marsh, Daniel Carter, Isaac M. Hill, Burwile Permenter. ACCOUNTS & NOTES of the firm of R. M. Todd and W. B. Smith: Daniel Carter, James McCracken, Miss Mary Vaughn, A. G. Leeks, Permelia Medley, Watson Logwood, Samuel Harris, Thomas W. Pert, Richard Hayle, John Heard, Esau Brooks, Jacob Pall, Ezekiel Purgerson, Uriah Mars, Witchy Forrest, John Kelley, John Logan, Mark Black, Littlebury Barnett, Wm. Cheatham, Catlett Spikes. Estate Sale Mar 5, 1840 netted $12,577. Buyers at sale: Widow, Larkin G. Carter, Lewis Holloway, John Foy, Albert P. Huig, Dr. Holland, Alex. Hood, John D. Adams, Bennett Reynolds, Larkin Griffin, John Chrisley, Stanmore Brooks, James M. Child, Eddins & Carter, Jefferson Coleman, Simpson, Matthews, Jones Coleman, Daniel Carter, Jonathan Johnston, Simpson Mattison, Simeon Chaney, John M. Golding, Ben.

Reams, Stanford May, Thomas Chatham, Nathaniel McCants, Anthony Griffin, Wm. Carter, James McCracken, Edmond Brown, Richard Hagewood, W, N. Moore, Wm. P. Delphs, Horace Ozment, Alfred M. May, John Wilson, Wiley T. Adams, Dr. Sampson V. Caine, Dr. Thomas Dendy, John McClellan, Mastin Rasor, Jackson Chartham, James Matthews, Wm. Butler, Reuben G. Golding, Charles Gabriel, Thomas B. Byrd, Ephraim Drummond, Nathan Calhoun, Henry R. Williams, Wiley D. Mounce, Andrew Logan, Thomas G. Griffin. Estate Settlement Oct 26, 1843. (3) Legatees. 1. Elizabeth Todd, widow $16,661.18 also received $3,279 in 1848 2. Harriet T. Todd, married Patrick H. Eddins $16,661.18 3. Sarah E. wife of Robert Child $16,661.18.

BOX 183 PACK 4813   JOHN HENRY NICKLES (minor)   1868

Guardian: Wm. A. Hagen. Bond Feb 5, 1868 of $1,000 by Wm. A. Hagen, Andrew Stevenson, John Hagen. Settlement Jul 11, 1876 received $866.83.

BOX 183 PACK 4814   GEORGE NICKLES (minor)   1868

Guardian: George Nickles. Bond Feb 5, 1868 of $1,000 by George Nickles, Andrew Stevenson, John Hagen. Father: H. B. Nickles. Settlement Jul 22, 1873 received $1,437.83.

BOX 183 PACK 4815   WILLIAM M. NEWELL   1878

Administrator: Sarah Ann Newell-wife. Bond Jan 6, 1870 of $1,500 by Sarah Ann Newell, Henry M. Winn, Robert H. Winn. Appraisal Jan 24, 1870 by Wm. McCombs, J. E. Uldrick, M. Edward Wilson. Owned 204 acres of land. Land Appraised by Robert T. Gordon, Wm. T. McIlwain, J. E. Uldrick. Land taken by Sarah Ann Newell. Estate Sale Jan 25, 1870 netted $845.42. Buyers at sale: T. Ellis, Sarah Ann Newell, L. W. Cochran, J. A. Stevenson, W. C. Winn, Joe Lyon. Estate Settlement Dec 21, 1870. Wdow $231.46 (8) Children each $57.86: 1. L. A. Wife of M. B. Kay 2. James Milton Newell deceased 3. J. A. Newell 4. Lucinda wife of P. A. McMahan 5. D. E. Newell 6. S. S. Newell. Other two children not named.

BOX 183 PACK 4816 JASPER N, MARY J, ESSIE E, LAWRENCE O. ROBINSON (minors) 1869

All over the age of 14. Guardian: John A. Robinson-brother. Bond for each minor: Aug 4, 1869 of $400 by John A. Robinson, Hugh Robinson, James Clinkscales. All entitled to a legacy froom the Estate of Dr. Frank Clinkscales. Nov 7, 1871 Jasper N. received legacy of $139. Apr 4, 1873 Mary Jane received legacy of $146. Feb 23, 1875 Essie E. received legacy of $160.

BOX 183 PACK 4817   ELIZABETH RICHEY   1869

Administrator: George W. Richey-son. Bond Sep 3, 1869 of $650 by George W. Richey, S. White Agnew, Samuel Smith, Silas Jones. Appraisal Sep 24, 1869 by Wm. Dunn, James A. Seawright, J. W. Blain, Tyra Y. Martin. Estate Sale Nov 29, 1869 netted $605.85. Buyers at sale: L. M. Stone, J. O. Richey, James Nickles, Jane Smith, Basil Maddox, Paul W.Connor, John Beasley, Michael B. McGee, Nimrod Richey, J. N. Seawright, Andrew Stone, R. H. Hughes, Wm. McGee, Alex. M. Agnew, Silas Jones, N. Haynes, J. A. Gilmer, A. Boone, J. C. Hodges, George W. Richey, Mat. Hodges, Ed Maddox, Joel Walker, T.

Smith, George Nickles, G. W. Hodges, S. Martin. Estate Settlement Dec 30, 1870. (11) Distributees each $34.11. Only (2) named: Nancy Richey, Jane wife of Samuel Smith. J. N. Seawright paid $5 for coffin. James D. Chalmers paid $31 for headstone.

BOX 183 PACK 4818   EDWARD RICHEY (minor of color)   1869

Orphan. Guardian: Peter Osborne. Bond Jul 7, 1869 of $300 by Peter Osborne, John Barnett, Samuel Johnson. 1st Return Jun 2, 1870.

BOX 183 PACK 4819   JANE T. BURNS   1870

Deceased died Jul 1869. Administrator: Hugh Wilson. Bond Aug 25, 1870 of $2,000 by Robert A. Fair, Thomas Thomson, Wm. Joel Smith. Husband: Wm. H. Burns deceased.

BOX 183 PACK 4820   FRANCES E. COBB (minor)   1871

Nee: Frances Whitley. Husband: Wm. H. Cobb. Guardian Wm. T. Jones who died, James A. Ellis in 1870. Bond Apr 20, 1870 of $1,600 by James A. Ellis, J. N. Cochran, T. J. Ellis. Estate Settlement Mar 2, 1871. George W. Jones executor of the estate of Wm. T. Jones in Laurens County paid Frances E. Cobb $396.44 & Sampson Whitley $404, minors.

BOX 183 PACK 4821   JAMES CALDWELL   1870

Deceased died Jun 7, 1870. Administrator: Wm. S. Caldwell-brother. Bond Sep 13, 1870 of $6,000 by Wm. S. Caldwell, Thomas R. Wilson, John C. Wilson, David Piester all of Newberry County. Appraisal Nov 30, 1870 by Wm. Agnew, Samuel Donald, Asberry M. Dodson. Held notes on: John Boyle, J. S. Reid, Elias P. Lake, R. P. Holdman, M. G. Booger, Wm. H. Austin, M. B. Chalmers. Estate Sale Dec 1, 1870 netted $2,404.31. Buyers at sale: Dr. James Boyce, C. A. Latimer, Anthony Johnston, Amaziah R. Ellis, Seawright Drake, James Y. Sitton, M. W. Seawright, James Branyon, Malcom Erwin, G. M. Mattison, John Hodges, Samuel Davis, John I. Bonner, J. R.Duncan, Wm. S. Caldwell, R. P. Shaw, John C. McDill, Wm. McGee, Peter Brownlee, Wm. Wilson, Wm. H. Austin, Asberry Dodson, J. W. Wilson, Mat. Lindsay, Dan Pressly, Enoch Gambrell, George A. Moore, W. A. Kay, Bethlehen Latimer, James Hawthorne, W. Ellis Tribble, George Gallman, Jim Wright, Stephen Latimer, Jesse McGee, Wm. Hood, Oliver P. Hawthorne, Thomas J. Burton, James Taylor, Thomas Leake, Len Dodson, Henry Pressly, Thomas R. Wilson, Wm. C. Brock, Joe Robinson, John Pressly, J. W. Mattison, David O. Hawthorne, Samuel Donald, Samuel H. Cochran, Joseph F. Lee, Thomas Crawford, James W. Richey, Samuel Haddon, James Richey, Wm. Robinson, Thomas L. Young, Charles Williams, James Smith, Gideon G. Stone, Dr. G. B. Reid, James Wright, E. B. Rasor, John C. Caldwell. Estate Settlement, no date. Only heir: Son, John C. Caldwell.

BOX 183 PACK 4822   SIMEON CHANEY   1870

Will dated Sep 21, 1868. Filed Oct 12, 1870. Witnesses: Isaac M. Hill, M. B. Lipscomb, E. G. Sheppard. Executor: Ransom Chaney-son. Wife: Susan Chaney. Daughters: Sarah G. whomarried a Sheppard, Emily Cheatham, Mary Jemima Chaney, Eleanor Chaney. Sons: Ransom Chaney, James S. Chaney. Apparaisal Nov 14, 1870 by Wm. S. Richardson, Henry Beard, James Hefferman. Owned 400 acres of land. Estate Sale Nov 14, 1870. Buyers at sale: Susan Chaney, R. E. Chaney, John Day, James Chaney, Ransom

Chaney, W. L. Dukes, B. A. Jones, H. Dukes, W. T. Head. Estate Settlement Jan 1, 1872. All parties received $347. Estate Settlement Nov 7, 1895. (6) Shares each $181.76. !. Eleanor Chaney 2. Ransom Chaney 3. Mary F. wife of H. B. Dukes 4. James S. Chaney deceased 5. Jemina Chaney wife of W. L. Dukes deceased 6. Emily Cheatham. Children of J. S. Chaney: (6) Willis, Carrie wife of R. L. Collins, James S., Robert Chaney, Richard Chaney, Ella Chaney. Children of Jamina Dukes: (10) Jemina, Ben, Artrhur, Ed, Rebecca, Cornelia, Joe, Nannie, Walter. Children of Emily Cheatham (3) Emma, S. E. Cobb, M. A. Sadler.

BOX 183 PACK 4823   NATHAN CALHOUN   1870

Will dated, no date. Filed May 12, 1870. Witnesses Wm. K. Blake, John R. Tarrant, L. C. Parks. Executors: John W. Calhoun, Robert Calhoun. Wife: Amelia Calhoun. Sons: John W. Calhoun, D. P. Calhoun, Robertr C. Calhoun. Daughters: Sarah wife of Thomas M. White deceased, Mary Calhoun. Appraisal Aug 10, 1870 by James M. Richardson, Wm. B. Meriwether, Daniel Rampey. Owned 400 acres of land. Notes and Accounts due him at time of his death: John C. Walker, James L. Hefferman, G. B. Sheppard, Edmund Calhoun, R. A. Griffin, Robert Cochran, Thomas J. Pinson, Robert Calhoun, James W. Smith, Wm. C. Fooshe, Thomas M. Hill, Ben. Fooshe, Gilliam & Bailey, George W. Calhoun, Anderson & Nickles, M. B. Lipford, Clark & White, George C. Johnson, J. W. Lipscomb, J. C. Young, J. T. Carter, J. W. Johnson, Charles Carter, John Boozer, Patrick Hefferman, Lipscomb & Cochran. Estate Sale Dec 6, 1870 netted $2,898. Buyers at sale: Robert C. Calhoun, John W. Calhoun, G. M. Calhoun, Polly Calhoun, James Pinson, Ben. Peterson, Samuel Richardson, Harriet Tagret, John C. Young, Isaac Williams, George W. Rampey, Joel Pinson, Ned Petrerson, Patrick Hefferman, N. Olive Holland, Wash Calhoun, Luke Calhoun, James L. Hefferman, George C. Johnston, Samuel Lowden, Flander McGhee, Thomas C. Pinson, Mary Proffitt, Daniel Rampey, Wiley Williams, Thomas R. White, E. Y. Sheppard, W. G. Rice, J. W. Pinson, Samuel G. Major, Thomas M. Major, Abert McGhee, Henry McGhee. Estate Settlement Nov 15, 1889. Previous settlements in 1870 & 1872, no details. (7) Legatees: 1. Robert C. Calhoun 2. W. B. Calhoun 3. Mary Proffitt deceased, child: G. W. Proffitt 4. Sarah C. White deceased, Children: Alice C. Sloan, W. W. White 5. John W. Calhoun 6. D. P. Calhoun 7. Ben. F. Calhoun. Paid Thomas M. White $34.80 for tombstone

BOX 183 PACK 4824   ADDISON CLINKSCALES   1877

Will dated Dec 25, 1861. Filed May 11, 1870. Witnesses: Andrew C. Hawthorne, Robert C. Sharp, James L. Miller. Executor John Pratt-father-in-law. Wife: Elizabeth Ann Clinkscales. Sons: Milton Melvin Clinkscales, John Calvin Clinkscales to Texas in 1877. Daughters: Mary Frank deceased, Sally Harrison, Laura Cllinkscales. 1st Appraisal Jul 5, 1871 by Bennett McAdams, Robert Pratt, Wm. Clinkscales, Edwin Cox. 2nd Appraisal, no date by Robert Pratt, J. A. Robinson, Wm. Clinksales, J. P. Armstrong, J. O. McClain. 3rd Appraisal Dec 5, 1877 by Robert Pratt, Wm. Clinkscales, R. H. Armstrong, S. O. McClain. ½ Owner with Reuben Clinkscales of house and 4 acre lot in Town of Due West, owned over 600 acres of land. Estate Sale Dec 5, 1877. Buyers at sale: Mrs. E. A. Clinkscales, Wm. A. McWhorter, Dennis Jackson, J. B. McWhorter, J. G. Loner, Miss Lula L. Clinkscales, W. T. Cowan, N. E. Johnson, James Taylor, Wm. L. Young, Addison F. Carwile, Michael McGee, A. C. Pratt, Joseph Ellis, J. H. Clinkscales, J. A. Ricketts, C. Ellis, F. E. Ellis,

John McClain, J. R. Clinkscales, Robert Bratcher, John S. Wilson, G. L. Alewine, John Rouse, Miss Sallie H. Clinkscales, M. M. Clinkscales, John W. Ashley, James M. Carwile, J. O. McClain, George Clinkscales, Beverly Lindsay, Ed Callaham, John A. Robinson, Henry Fair, Wm. Clinkscales, R. P. Callaham, R. H. Armstrong, Wm. M. Allewine, B. C. DuPre, John Pratt, Luther M. Pratt, Henry Clinkscales, Moses S. Ashley, Thomas L. Young, John C. Clinkscales, Jerry Milford, Rich Brownlee, A. W. Erwin, Harvey Clinkscales, Andy Clinkscales. James Pratt guardian of Sallie Harrison Clinkscales and Laura Clinkscales in Nov 1877. John M. Pruitt, Edwin Cox, John A. Robinson commissioners appointed for appraisal and partition of land by the court Jan 8, 1878. Estate Settlement Nov 30, 1883. 1/3 to Elizabeth Ann Clinkscales. $100 to each of (4) Children: 1. Melvin Milton Clinkscales 2. John Calvin Clinkscales 3. Sallie H. Clinkscales 4. L. S. Robinson.

BOX 183 PACK 4825   THADDEUS GAMBRELL, SARAH ANN HALL, MARTHA J. MATTISON EVELINE GAMBRELL (minors) 1870

Father: James C. Gambrell deceased. Grand Father: James Gambrell. Guardian: James Gambrell. Bond Apr 22, 1870 of $500 by James Gambrell, Joel Kay, G. M. Mattison. Estate Settlement Mar 16, 1880. Final Estate Settlement Mar 10, 1881 due to an overpayment.

BOX 183 PACK 4826   BARTHOLOMEW JORDAN   1878

Deceased died Jul 5, 1870. Administrator: David Jordan-son. Bond Jul 30, 1870 of $5,000 by David Jordan, Jonathan Jordan, Samuel Jordan. Appraisal Oct 14, 1870 by Joel W. Lites, Leroy Purdy, Wm. Lyon. Estate Sale Nov 10, 1870 netted $2,275.11. Buyers at sale: David Jordan, Samuel Jordan, H. J. Reagan, Jacob Nelson, J. M. Reagan, Wm. Wharton, Andrew J. Ferguson, Robert Killingsworth, J. A. Keller, P. Letmond, Wm. O. Cromer, Boney Williams, E. W. Watson, W. C. Verrell, Wm. Evans, Edmund Baker, Jackson Burt, John R. Tarrant, D. O. Verrell, John A. Devlin, J. A. Wilson, David J. Wardlaw, S. P. Rutledge, J. R. McKellar, A. Brown, Philip S. Rutledge, Frank Hutchinson, Pedler Watson, W. P. Devlin, Wm. Patrrick, J. C. Lites, Glen Benson. Apr 16, 1873 Appraisal of old notes dating back as far as 1843 by Wm. Lyon, J. W. Lites, Leroy Purdy: Wm. Murphy (1849), P. Alford (1842), W. G. Kennedy (1859), John D. dams (1858), Lewis Ansley (1848), Wm. Reynolds (1842), Daniel Douglass (1848), Elijah McClellan (1855), Mary Smith (1864), W. C. Smith (1864). Had in possession $35,000 in Confederate bonds. Estate Settlement May 15, 1873. (2) Shares: 1. David Jordan 2. Mary Ann, daughter and wife of Lewis Smith.

BOX 183 PACK 4827   NATHANIEL KNOX   1864

Confederate Soldier. Killed in Battle near Richmond in 1862. Administrator: Mary Jane Knox-wife. Bond Mar 4, 1864 of $20,000 by Mary Jane Knox, Wm. Hill. The firm of J. & N. Knox dissolved with his death and firm was insolvent at the end of the war and much in debt. Robert P. Knox was the agent for the firm and he died in the spring of 1865. John Knox paid all the debts of the firm with his own money. This he testified to in 1878.

BOX 183 PACK 4828   ROBERT MARTIN   1874

Will dated Jul 22, 18970. Witnesses: Uriah Jacob Elgin, James W. Richey, Allen J. McAdams. Executors: G. M. Mattison, Jane Martin-wife. Sons: Wm. F. Martin, Allen B. Martin, Calvin Martin, James S. Martin. Appraisal Nov 9, 1870 by James W. Richey, Hezekiah Elgin, Samuel Martin, G. T. Smith. Owned 535 Acres of land. Held notes on: James Cowan, Robert Brownlee, J. L. Walker, John Miller, James Seawright, S. Martin, Francis V. Pruitt, Thomas J. Higdon, Wm. B. Bell, Wm. B. Gaines, D. W. Patton, N. G. Hughes. Estate Sale Nov 13, 1872 netted $4,025.50. Buyers at sale: Jane M. Martin, Alllen B. Martin, Calvin Martin, N. A. Shirley, R. T. Kirkpatrick, Wm. Greer, B. J. Martin, Malcom Erwin, Pinckney Martin, G. B. Reid, Samuel Martin, L. M. Stone, B. L. Morrison, Amaziah Miller, J. B. Dorr, James Hawthorne, Francis V. Pruitt, F. W. R. Nance, Wm. E. Barmore, A. P. Shirley, Mundy Ellis. Estate Settlement, no date. (5) Shares each $791: 1. Jane M. Martin 2. Wm. F. Martin 3. Allen B. Martin, 4. James S. Martin, 5. Calvin Martin.

BOX 183 PACK 4829   NANCY A. McALLISTER   1870

Will dated Jun 12, 1869. Filed Jun 2, 1870. Witnesses: Wm. L. Campbell, Coke D. Mann, Lewis C. Clinkscales. Mother: Mary McAllister. Sisters: Dicey E. McAllister, Elizabeth J. McAllister, Sarah C. McAllister. Owned 190 acres of land.

BOX 184 PACK 4830   MISSING

BOX 184 PACK 4831   JAMES B. SHADRACK   1869

Administrator: Joshua Sale who died, Emma E. Shadrack. Bond Sep 18, 1869 of $2,000 by Emma E. Shadrack, Lewis C. Parks, F. T. Griffin, J. N. Shadrack.

BOX 184 PACK 4832   WILLIAM SUTHERLAND   1866

Will dated may 24, 1866. Witnesses: Lewis Covin, James L. Covin, Marion M. Tarrant. Grand Sons: Wm. Sutherland, James Sutherland. Grand Daughter: Margaret E. Sutherland. Owned 150 acres of land.

BOX 184 PACK 4833   ELIZABETH C. SOUTH   1868

Will dated Jan 31, 1868. Filed Mar 28, 1868. Witnesses: J. M. White, J. M. Rampey, W. C. Cozby. Executor: Elias W. South-son. Grand Daughters: Virgnia M. A. South, Florentine Savannah South, both daughters of Elias South. Appraisal Warrant Sep 13, 1872 by W. C. Cozby, F. L. Rampey, Wm. F. Kennedy.

BOX 184 PACK 4834   ALEXANDER STEVENSON   1870

Deceased died Sep 1868. Administrator: Franklin A. Stevenson-son. Bond Mar 31, 1870 of $800 by Franklin A. Stevenson, Edward E. Stevenson, Charles B. Guffin. Appraisal Apr 25, 1870 of $271.55 by T. B. Wright, Jacob Miller, W. P. Devlin. 1st Reurn Oct 7, 1871. Nothing else.

BOX 184 PACK 4835   ELIZASBETH R. SMITH (minor)   1870

Guardian: Willis Smith-father. Bond Feb 7, 1870 of $1,500 by Willis Smith, Moses C. Taggart, Henry Wilkinson. Settlement Feb 19, 1877 received $6 from the Estate of Thomas Riley.

BOX 184 PACK 4836   WILLIAM C. STEIFLE (minor)   1870

Father: James Steifle. Grand Father: William Chiles. Guardian: James Steifle. Bond Mar 18, 1870 of $1,500 by James Steifle, John C. Chiles, Wade E. Cothran. Settlement Nov 12, 1885 received $614.85.

BOX 184 PACK 4837   THOMAS STACEY   1869

Will dated Nov 17, 1862. Filed Aug 25, 1869. Witnesses: W. C. White, G. P. O'Neal, George M. Smith. Wife: Ann Elizabeth Stacey. (6) Children: 1. David King Stacey 2. Mary Elizabeth Stacey 3. Susan Eliza Stacey 4. Sarah Ann Stacey 5. Thomas Benjamin Stacey 6. Wyatt Aiken Stacey. Appraisal Sep 21, 1869 by R. W. Anderson, G. P. O'Neal, J. F. Coleman, W. W. Franklin, J. R. Jones.

BOX 184 PACK 4838   SAMUEL McELROY   1819

A very long and complicated estate. Will dated Dec 2, 1815. Witnesses: Robert P. Delph, John Swain, Wm. H. Jones. Wife: Peggy McElroy. Daughter: Haley McElroy. Executors: James Hodges who died, Thompson Hodges became administrator in 1831 and he administered estate in 1834. 1st Appraisal Jan 3, 1816 by Valentine Young, John Williams, Wm. H. Jones. 2nd Appraisal Jan 30, 1816 by Joseph A. McKinley, Mathew Wilson. Goods given at that time to the widow. 3rd Appraisal Mar 15, 1831 by Wm. H. Jones, Ben. Rosamond, Wm. Graham. Owned 340 acres of land. 1st Estate Sale Feb 28, 1816 netted $497. Buyers at sale: Joseph McKinney, John Muckerson, John Williams, Mathew Wilson, Wm. Robertson, John Hinton, Alex. Wright, Robert Poole, Henry Wilson, John Youngblood, Isaac Smith, Wm. Graham, Wm. Jones, John Hodges, James Black, Spears, Jones, Vlentine Young, Mathew Williams, Wm. Butler, James Graham, Wm. Sims, Thomas Rosamond, Wm. Henderson, James Henderson, Robert Delph, Ben. Rosamond, Wm. Barmore, John Conner, John Swain, Peggy McElroy, Samuel Wile. 2nd Estate Sale Jan 7, 1829. Buyers at sale: John Hodges, Peter Thackston, Samuel Agnew, James Hodges, Thompson Hodges, James Wilson, Wm. Hodges, James A. Hodges, Dr. James Anderson, James Hutchinson, Wiley Watson, Andrew Anderson. 3rd Estate Sale Mar 29, 1831. Buyers at sale: James Sample, Mathew Sitton, Dr. John Nash, Peggy Phillips, Wesley Conner, Ben. Jones, Thomas Jones, Ben. Rosamond, Wm. T. Jones, Philip Cunnerford, Charles Collins, Ezekiel Hodges, Reuben Hodges.

BOX 184 PACK 4839   JAMES TAGGART SR.   1870

Deceased died Jun 23, 1870. Administrator: Moses C. Taggart-son. Bond Jul 30, 1870 of $2,000 by Moses C. Taggart, Samuel J. Hester, Larkin Reynolds. Appraisal Nov 21, 1870 by Edward F. Parker, James T. Fortescue, Moses O. Talman. Estate Sale Nov 21, 1870. Buyers at sale: James Taggrt Jr., Samuel J. Hester, Moses C. Taggart, Wm. H. Taggart, Hen. Bowen, S. E. Taggart, Geoge Napper, J. R. McComb, Leander Smith, Robert Keoun, Thomas J. Mabry, E. Taggart, R. A. McCaslan, D. Ware, D. M. Rogers, John Link,

Moses O. Talman, W. Marion, Samuel Able, Wm. P. Kennedy. Estate was in considerable debt. Estate Insolvent.

BOX 184 PACK 4840   SAMPSON W. WHITLEY (minor)   1872

Guardian: James Alex. Ellis. Bond Apr 4, 1870 of $1,600 by James Alex. Ellis, Thomas J. Ellis, James N. Cochran. Settlement Sep 26, 1873 received $6.13. Dec 22, 1879 Whiley brought suit against Ellis, Ellis & Cochran alledging mishandling of money due him from Laurens County ($404) by Wm. T. Jones, his late guardian. Jones had been appointed Guardian by the Equity Court of Laurens Co. about 1860. Jones died in 1869 and his estate was administered by his son, George T. Jones. Witley had requested that James Alexander Ellis be made guardian in Mar 1870. The Court ruled against Whitley declaring that the money had been properly used in his behalf and accounted for.

BOX 184 PACK 4801   JAMES H. WALKER   1869

Deceased died Nov 1, 1868. Administrator: Emily E. Walker-wife. Bond Jan 28, 1869 of $1,200 by Emily E. Walker, John G. Walker, Martha J. Walker, Leroy J. Johnson, John S. Williams. (6) Children, no names. Appraisal Feb 5, 1869 by James C. Pressly, David R. Penney, Samuel Lockridge. 1st Reurn Jan 12, 1870. Wm. A. Richey paid $12 for coffin. Dr. Thomas J. Mabry paid $130 for medical services.

BOX 184 PACK 4842   REUBEN WEED   1869

Deceased died in Floorida Oct 22, 1867. Administrator: Andrew J. Weed-son. Bond Jan 29, 1869 of $500 by Andrew J. Weed, Wilson Watkins, John Brown. Had debts owed to him in Abbeville. Nothing further.

BOX 184 PACK 4843   JAMES J. & SUSAN M. WILLARD (minors)   1870

Father: Dr. J. S. Willard died leaving a widow and (5) children only tow of which were now living: James Jefferson Willard & Susan Margaret Willard aho was the oldest at age 12. Sep 30, 1870 James C. Willard, their grand father, and mother requested that Thomas Thomson be appointed their guardian. Bond for each Oct 11, 1870 of $1,500 by Thomas Thomson, Edward Westfield, Wm. H. Parker. Settlement of Susan M. Willard, now Susan M. Stribling May 1879. She received $537.43. Settlement of James J. Willard Jan 1882 with Thomas P. Quarles and H. G. Thomson as administrators due to the death of Thomas Thomson. Willard received $109.08.

BOX 184 PACK 4844   JULENA S. G. YOUNG (minor)   1870

Guardian: Samuel O. Young-father. Bond Dec 13, 1869 of $800 by Samuel O. Young, Andrew C. Brown, Alex. F. Young. 1st Return Sep 30, 1870 received $35.70 from the Estate of Joseph Creswell. Nothing further.

BOX 184 PACK 4845   CATHERINE ZIMMERMAN   1867

Administrator: John H. Zimmerman-son. Bond Mar 27, 1867 of $1,000 by John H. Zimmerman, Henry H. Kinard, John O. Peoples. Nothing further.

BOX 184 PACK 4846   THOMAS R. PUCKETT SR.   1874

Deceased died Sep 15, 1870. Administrator: Thomas R. Puckett Jr.-son. Bond Nov 23, 1870 of $1,000 by Thomas R. Puckett, John H. Pinson, J. G. Turner. Wife: Elizabeth Ann Puckett. Appraisal Dec 12, 1870 by John G. Turner, R. Elmore Chaney, James M. Pinson. Held notes on: Thomas R. Puckett, Dr. J. T. Wilbert, Wm. Baxter, H. L. Hitt, Wm. G. Rice, John H. Pinson, James M. Pinson, M. L. Bullock, W. B. Coleman, Frank Grant, Catherine Owens, Wm. Austin, Catherine Whiteford. Estate Sale Dec 13, 1870. Buyers at sale: John H. Pinson, Thomas R. Puckett, Elizabeth Puckett, B. F. Busby, W. B. Coleman, Cass Collins, Wm. Rice, Thomas Pinson, Henry O'Neal, W. Thompson, Jesse Cunningham, Abron Wells, Mrs. E. A. Puckett, Beaufort Goodman, Robert Patterson, Adolphus Boyel. Estate Settlement Dec 11, 1873. (7) Distributees: 1. John Addison Puckett lived in Atlanta, Ga., killed at 1st Manassas in Jul 1861, his children: Nancy Louise wife of John M. Vance & Henry C. Puckett received $834.75 2. James F. Puckett $573 3. A. C. Puckett lived in Louisiana $672 4. S. Wade A. Puckett deceased $647.25 5. Mary A. Pinson $674.25 6. Thomas R. Puckett $674.50 7. R. M. Puckett deceased $573. Settlement Jun 16, 1874. Final Estate Settlement May 24, 1875.

BOX 184 PACK 4847   IBBY McCURRY   1870

Deceased died Aug 1870. Andmistrator: Thomas J. Hill. Bond Oct 15, 1870 of $150 by Thomas J. Hill, Joshua P. Milford, George Wilson Bowen. Appraisal Oct 29, 1870 by Wm. Wickliffe, Albert B. Hamlin, Samuel S. Sims. Estate Sale Oct 31, 1870 netted $63.99. Buyers at sale: Thornton Moore, Samuel S. Sims, Thomas J. Hill, Wm. McCurry, Elizabeth McCurry, Dr. George F. Steifer, Robert T. Gordon, Nancy McCurry, Albert B. Hamlin, Fields Burton, George W. Bowen.

BOX 184 PACK 4848   JOHN C. CRAWFORD   1870

Will dated Aug 18, 1870. Filed Dec 16, 1870. Witnesses: James T. McCracken, Ann A. Woodhurst, Carrie E. Gibert. Executor: Andrew J. Woodhurst. Wife: Catherine Crawford. Daughters: Jane Crawford, Rebecca Crawford, Nancy Crawford, Lillis Crawford, Lucinda Crawford, Sarah Amanda Crawford, Mary Ann Crawford. 1st Appraisal Dec 21, 1870 of $821.70 by Charles Evans, James T. McCracken, James S. Gibert. 2nd Appraisal Feb 8, 1881 by John R. Woodhurst, Robert Thornton, E. N. Knox. Estate Sale netted $5,901.50. Final Estate Settlement May 15, 1912. (4) Shares: 1. Heirs of Eliza C. wife of M. W. Smith 2. Mrs. J. J. Edwards 3. Heirs of John Crawford 4. Mrs. Mattie Mobley. Individuals receiving funds included: 1) Silas A. Mobley of Stilesboro, Ga. - Thomas M. Mobley of Iva each received $660.30 2) Will Crawford- Mrs. Malissa – Dansby - Mrs. Maggie Turner all of Florida each received $660.30 3) M. W. Smith - J. A. Smith - J. R. Smith - Cassie Simmons - Nannie Drennan each received equal portions of $1,320.60. Children of John C. Crawford Jr. were Eliza Edwards, Wm. Crawford, Malissa Dansby, Maggie Turner, Mrs. A. J. Dempsey, Wm. P. Crawford. John J. Bass paid $25 for two coffins. Dr. Thomas J. Mabry paid $25 for medical services.

BOX 184 PACK 4849   LAWSON ROSS (man of color)   1870

Deceased died Sep 1870. Administrator: Samuel W. Agnew. Bond Nov 28, 1870 of $250 by Samuel W. Agnew, S. E. Agnew, J. H. Bowie. Widow and (4) Children. Appraisal Dec 11, 1870 by John Hagen, Wm. H. Sharpe, J. M. Bailey. Estate Sale Dec 13, 1870 netted

$107.71. Buyers at sale: J. M. McCay, Silas Jones, Samuel W. Agnew, Wm. H. Sharpe, Washington Lomax, John Hagen. Wm. H. Sharpe paid $4 for coffin.

BOX 184 PACK 4850   WILLIAM BOYD   1870

Will dated Aug 8, 1870. Filed Nov 18, 1870. Witnesses: David Murdock, L. D. Murdock, James I. Crowther. Executrix: Sarah Ann Murdock-wife. Appraisal Dec 20, 1870 of $286 by David Murdock, John D. Murdock, Pleasant Ferguson, Clayton Jones. Owned 90 acres of land.

BOX 184 PACK   4850 ½   ISAAC A. KELLER   1929

Will dated Apr 28, 1927. Filed Feb 1, 1929. Witnesses: J. A. Verchot, J. D. Mars, J. M. Nickles. Executor: Farmers Bank of Abbeville. Tombstone to be erected over gfrave in Ebeneezer Cemetery. Brother: W.W. L. Keller. Niece: Lizzie Wilson her son: Issac Wilson. Nephew: David Keller his son: David Keller. Sisters: Julia Pratt, Emma Haddon. To Wofford College & Epworth Orphanage 600 acres of land. To Ebeneezer church to be kept in securities for church & Cemetery upkeep $1,000. To Lander College $200. To the Endowment Fund for Ministers S. C. Conference. Appraisal Feb 1929 by Thomas A. Sherard, P. E. Bell, Wm. A. Stevenson Jr. Disbursements: 1) W. W. L. Keller $300 2) L. W. Keller $195.16 3) I. L. Keller $195.16 4) N. Anna Walker $195.16 5) Julia Ada Johnson $195.16 6) M. Sudie Ligon $195.16 7) H. E. Keller $195.16 8) W. W. Keller $195.16 9) C. W. Keller $195.16 10) Mrs. Lizzie Wilson $489.16 11) Isaac Wilson $488 12) David Keller $489.16 13) David Keller Jr. $488 14) Mrs Julia Pratt $100 15) Mrs. Lena Syfan $323 16) Mrs. Ludie K. Cheatham $323 17) J. E. Keller $323 18) Mrs John R. Lomax 19) Miss Helen Pratt $323 20) David Henry Wilson $323 21) Julia Matilda Perkins $323 22) Hugh Wilson $323 23) Samuel Wilson $323 24) Wm. Horace Wilson $323 25) Pearl E. Schlemmer $323 26) Anna Yancey $323 27) Alpheus K. Wilson $323 28) Wofford College $200 29) Ebeneezer church $1,000 30) Endowment Fund $200 31) Abbeville Memorial Hospital $7, 430.45.

BOX 184 PACK 4851   LEWIS MITCHELL   1820

Much estate activity with many names. Will dated Jan 1, 1820.   Filed Feb 3, 1820. Witnesses: Samuel Anderson, Henry Wilson, Robert Anderson. Aministrator: Lewis Connor. 1st Bond Apr 1, 1820 of $25,000 by Lewis Connor, John Connor, Henry Wilson, Joseph Foster. 2nd Bond Oct 10, 1821 of $25,000 by Lewis Connor, John Conner, HenryWilson, Zachariah Meriwether. Wife: Fanny Mitchell. Son: Steven Mitchell. Daughters: Edna wife of Ellison Posey Fuller, Elizabeth wife of Wm. Hallums, Malinda Mitchell, Martha Mitchell. Appraisal Oct 6, 1820 by Joel Lipscomb, James Arnold, John Cochran, Thomas Wilson, George Connor. Estate Sale Apr 18, 1820. Buyers at sale: Francis Connor, Hart P. Arnold, Juda Mitchell, Wm. Butler, Charles Davenport, Samuel J. Hopper, James Hodges, Morris R. Mitchell, James Martin, Agrippa Cooper, John B. Sample, James Eddins, Isaac Edwards, Mathew Bell, John Reid, Wilkins Holloway, Samuel Benton, Henry Delph, Ellison Posey Fuller, Malinda Mitchell, James Wilson, Robert Young, John Connor, Samuel Arnold, Henry Bishop, James A. Stone, Samuel Banley, Nicholas Meriwether, Alex. Cummings, B. R. Mitchell, Wm. Graham, David Black, Samuel Anderson, Robert Delph, James E. Glenn, John Porter, Reuben Long, Wm. Lummus, Thomas Smith, Daniel Cochran, James Smith, Edward Lipford, Cornelius

Austin, James Sample, Wm. Capps, James Arnold, Robert Smith, John Stephens, Wm. Patterson, Humphrey Klugh, Wm. Hallum, John Hagwood, Wm. Turner, James Leach, Jonas Lawson, Betsy Green, Wm. Loveless, Wm. Holloway, James Graham, John Moore, Alex. Sample, Wm. Henderson, Perter Lomax, John Smith, Dr. Wade Anderson, Nimrod Overba, Henry Wilson.

MIXED in PACK

Estate Sale of STEPHEN MITCHELL Feb 16, 1825 netted $1294. Sale included 3 slaves. Buyers at sale: James Crocker, Archibald Arnold, James E. Glenn, Donald Douglass.

BOX 184 PACK 4852   DANIEL BOYD   1870

Deceased died Sep 27, 1870. Administrator: Lucinda C. Boyd-wife, Wm. Crowther her agent. Bond Dec 3, 1870 of $1,000 by Lucinda C. Boyd, Wm. Crowther, John D. Murdock. Appraisal Dec 19, 1870 by David Murdock, George W. Milford, Wm. Wickliffe, John A. Dickson. Estate Sale Dec 20, 1870 netted $312.12. Buyers at sale: Wm. Crowther, John D. Murdock, James I. Crowther, L. C. Boyd, M. J. Hall, Henry Morrison, John A. Dickson, Robert Boyd, Alonzo Martin, Robert Stuckey, Wm. N. Hall, Wm. Wickliffe, Wm. McCurry, B. Bowen. Estate Settlement May 1, 1875. 1/3 to Lucinda Boyd $107.73. 2/3 to James Robert Boyd only child $215.94. James D. Chalmers paid $23.50 for tombstone.

BOX 184 PACK 4853   BOZEMAN (minors)   1870

David Savannah Bozeman age 2. Telitha Jane Bozeman aage 4. John Lewis Bozeman age 6. Lilla S. Bozeman aage 8. Father: David L. Bozeman died Sep 28, 1868 leaving a widow & (4) Children. Sme type bond for all the minors. Bond Dec 29, 1870 of $500 by John J. Bozeman, John B. Bozeman, J. W. Fouche. Dec 30, 1870 each minor received from their father's estate $126.47. Settlements: 1) 1884 John Lewis Bozeman $70.80. 2) Jan 15, 1885 Lilla F. Bozeman, now Lilla F. Leverett $98. 3) Mar 23, 1888 Talitha Jane Spearman wie of T. N. Spearman $70.85. 4) Feb 1, 1890 David Savannah Bozeman $61.07.

BOX 184 PACK 4854   MARGARET, ELIZABETH F., MARY R. DRENNAN (minors)   1870

Elizabeth Frances Drennan born Feb 7, 1854. Margaret L. Drennan born Oct 15, 1857. Mary R. Drennan born Jan 4, 1861. Father: Robert D. Drennan deceased. Mother Mary Drennan. Guardian: Andrew J. Weed-grand father. Same type 1st Bond for all minors. Bond Dec 30, 1870 of $500 by Andrew J. Weed, John Brown, Horatio Drennan. Settlement of Elizabeth Frances Drennan in 1876 $80.66. Andrew J. Weed died in 1876 and Horace Drennan became the guardian for the two remaining minors. Same type bond for both minors. Bond Jan 8, 1877 of $300 by Horatio Drennan, Henry T. Sloan, Edmund W. Watson. Settlement of Margaret L. Drennan Feb 10, 1877 $161.42. Settlement of Mary R. Drennan Mar 2, 1882 $110.97.

BOX 184 PACK 4855   HUTSON J. LOMAX (man of color)   1870

Deceased died Nov 11, 1870. Administrator: Louis H. Russell. Bond Dec 2, 1870 by Louis H. Russell, Frances Lomax, Mathew McDonald, Jeremiah A. Hollingshead.

Merchant. Wife: Frances Lomax. Appraisal Dec 21, 1870 by John White, Thomas M. Williamson, Jeremiah A. Hollingshead. Estate Sale Dec 22, 1870 netted $177.72. Buyers at sale: Frances Lomax, Louis H. Russell, Hiram W. Lawson, Henry Nash, S. Johnson, M. M. Keller, Mary Small, Thomas M. Williamson, George Adams, Arthur Jefferson, Jesse Robinson. ACCOUNTS open and due him at time of his death: Thomas Absalom, S. J. Anderson, E. Butler, Snowdon Brown, Alex. Bowie, W. H. Burns, J. Berk, Sherard Butler, Wilson Butler, Miles Brown, S. Bents, Lewis Bowie, George Brown, Adam Chandler, Teulon Chiles, Alfred Chapman, Frank Cook, Jack Calhoun, Zack Connors, Sam Crozier, Zack Cannon, Anderson Chiles, George A. Cline, James Chalmers, E. Cane, Lee Davis, Reuben Davis, E. M. Dubose, Elizabeth Dixon, Mrs. Douglass, Hampton Edmonds, George Ellis, Wm. Evans, Charles Fair, Elbert Frazier, Alex. Gordon, Watt Goolsby, L. L. Guffin, Lewis Goolsby, L. P. Guffin, Kit Gordon, Mary Gordon, Jeremiah A. Hollingshead, Londen Hill, Enoch Hodges, Ben Hughes, Robert Hearst, Harriet Henderson, Mrs. Hughes, Maggie Hills, L. Jefferson, Fred Jackson, Sam Jones, Sam Johnston, Arthur Jefferson, Cinthia Kennedy, Manuel Keller, M. E. King, Dennis Livingston, Henry Lomax, James Logan, Petrer Lomax, Annie Lee, T. L. Mitchell, E. W. Moore, Samuel Marshall, Newton Mercer, Verge Maddox, Crecia Miller, L. Moragne, Alfred Mathews, Robert Martin, Aaron Mitchell, Ely Moragne, James L. Murray, George Marshall, A. W. McPherson, Adeline McDonald, Solomon McCaw, Charles McCaslan, James McBride, E. R. Nelson, Henry Nash, Wm. Nedwood, W. G. Neel, Amos Nelson, Edward Patton, George Patterson, Harriet Pope, Robert Plummer, Cornelius Pressly, Louis H. Russell, Citizen Roseman, Coward Rouse, Wm. Richey, Alex. Ramage, Silvia Rapley, Charles Sprouse, Mary H. Sprouse, W. T. Sprouse, T. A. Sullivan, Lewis Spann, Thomas Smith, Wm. Shires, Henry Scott, Emanuel Taggart, Washington Tines, John Tensen, Albert Titus, R. C. Tyler, Francis Venis, Beverly Vance, Sue Wilson, Thomas M. Williamson, John Willis, James Wilson, E. Wideman, Hollings Williams, George Whitlock, Ben Williams, James Williams, Wm. Wharton, Robert Watkins, James Wharton, Sandy Williams, Thomas Winn, Josh Wardlaw, Hugh Wilson.

BOX 184 PACK 4856   JOICEY SAVANNAH NORWOOD (minor)   1880

Guardian: Timothy C. Norwood. Bond Dec 29, 1870 of $200 by Timothy C. Norwood, G. M. Mattison, James A. B. Bigby. Grand Father: Thomas Norwood deceased. Final Return Nov 26, 1880 $80.37.

BOX 184 PACK 4857   ELIZA W. CALDWELL   1869

Will dated Oct 9, 1868. Filed Feb 1, 1869. Witnesses: W. R. White, James Clark, J. N. Burton. Daughters: Adrianna E. Caldwell, Serena L. Caldwell. Sons: Orran J. Caldwell, Edward A. Caldwell lived in Louisana, Edward A. Caldwell, Lemuel J. Caldwell. Owned land in Carroll Parish, Louisiana.

BOX 184 PACK 4858   JOSEPH T. BAKER   1870

Will dated Aug 18, 1870. Filed Nov 3, 1870. Witenesses: Thomas T. Cunningham, Wm. T. Townsend, R. A. Cooper. Executor: Samuel S. Baker. Wife: Laney Baker. Daughter: Elizabeth R. Baker. Sons: John Joseph Baker, Hiram O. Baker, Alert T. Baker, Samuel S. Baker. Appraisal Nov 29, 1870 by R. R. Cooper, Wm. F. Kennedy, Thomas T. Cunnigham. Owned 600 acres of land. Estate Sale Dec 20, 1870. Buyers at sale: Preston C. Suber,

Thomas A. Cann, M. D. Galbreath, Christian V. Barnes, Marshall Cann, George W. Bowen, Albert Baker, Jacob Alewine, J. D. Simpson, Wm. F. Kennedy, John Arnold, J. W. Burroughs, Wm. Giles, Thomas B. Hampton, Henry Daniel, A. Benson, Thomas T. Cunningham, John Young, Clement T. Latimer, Wm. A. Hanks, Wm. A. Simpson, L. C. Brewster, Louis C. Bosler, Wm. D. Mann, John Reid, R. R. Cooper, James W. Burriss, Ben. D. Kay, Roane Baskin, Edward Shaw, James R. Grubbs, John Schroeder, Wm. A. Leslie, B. A. Davis, B. L. Scott.

BOX 184 PACK 4859   JOHN ASHLEY   1870

Administrator: Reuben Clinkscales. Bond Aug 30, 1870 of $150 by Reuben Clinkscales, John F. Clinkscales, Andrew J. Clinkscales. Nothing further.

BOX 184 PACK 4860   JOHN W. CALVERT   1870

Deceased died Mar 6, 1870. Administrator: Sarah E. Calvert-wife. Bond Nov 19, 1870 of $1,000 by Sarah E. Calvert, Robert E. Hill, Augustus F. Calvert. (1) Child: Wm. A. Calvert age 3. Appraisal Dec 6, 1870 by Augustus F. Calvert, Wm. T. McIlwain, James Carlisle. Estate Sale Dec 7, 1870. Buyers at sale: Wm. McIlwain, James H. Nickles, James Richardson, George Davis, Mrs. L. Calvert, N. A. Haynes, Josh Jones, Charles Johnson, S. Richardson, James A. Gilmer, Andrew McIlwain, J. P. Gordon, Mrs. J. W. Calvert, David P. Hannah, James Carlisle, George Nickles, Augustus F. Calvert, Wm. Hill, Fred McIlwain, Andrew Stevenson, John Darraugh, John Hill, John Cason, George Robison, John Hagen, J. R. Haddon, Alpheus F. McCord, Samuel H. Cochran, Robert E. Hill, Mrs. S. E. Calvert, Thomas Eakin, Thomas Robison, Butler Brooks, Wm. R. Mundy, Jacob H. Bowie, John M. Hawthorne, Wm. T. McIlwain. Estate Settlement Jan 31, 1874. Widow $235.36. Son Wm. A. Calvert $470.72. James D. Chalmers paid $20.50 for tombstone.

BOX 184 PACK 4861   JAMES FAIR (minor of color)   1870

Age 15. Guardian: Peter Osborne a cousin who was blind. Bond Sep 6, 1870 of $200 by Peter Osborne, Samuel Johnson, London Kerr. Nothing further.

BOX 184 PACK 4862   ANSEL G. TALBERT   1871

Deceased died Nov 17, 1870. Administrator: Frances A. Talbert. Bond Dec 13, 1870 of $1,500 by Frances A. Talbert, Thomas B. Talbert, Franklin H. Gable. Appraisal Dec 13, 1870 by Wm. McCain, Isaac Caldwell, Henry Gable. Estate Sale Dec 30, 1870 netted $496.30. Buyers at sale: Frances A. Talbert, A. Malone, David W. Dowtin, T. B. Talbert, Samuel Young, Wm. C. Robinson, James McKinney, J. P. Cook, James Quarles, Franklin H. Gable, John B. Creswell, George M. Sibert, Isaac Caldwell, Samuel McQuerns, Tyra Jay, James Gable, James W. Wideman, M. M. Cain, J. R. Creswell.

BOX 184 PACK 4863   CORNELIUS H. PINSON   1872

Will dated Dec 30, 1861. Filed Sep 15, 1870. Witnesses: J. M. Townsend, W. H. Puckett, B. F. Hill. Executor: Aaron A. Pinson-brother. Appraisal Feb 3, 1871 by R. W. Anderson, A. C. Collins, J. D. Fooshe. Estate Sale Feb 3, 1871 netted $18.55. Buyers at sale: J. R. Tarrant, Aaron A. Pinson, John Pinson, A. C. Collins. May 21, 1872 final return and estate entry 45 cents.

BOX 184 PACK 4864   ELIZABETH PHILLIPS   1870

Will dated Oct 23, 1869. Filed Jun 7, 1871. Witnesses: Franklin F. Gary, Frederick T. Hodges, J. B. Arnold. Sister: Jane Phillips, willed everything to her and at her death to avert to Lucinda Hodges wife of Samuel Hodges. Executor: Wade H. Robertson. Bond Feb 1871 of $500 by Wade H. Robertson, Albert M. Graham, J. M. Thomas. Appraisal Jan 21, 1871 by Albert M. Graham, B. C. Graham, Wm. H. Moore. Estate Sale Jan 21, 1871 netted $41.70. Buyers at sale: Jane Phillips, Margaret Freeman, Mary Robertson, M. Golding, F. T. Hodges, Wesley Posey, David Greer, Wm. H. Moore, W. Y. Butler, B. C. Graham, Henry Israel, Moses Norris, Taylor Hodges, Albert M. Graham, J. M. Thomas, Mary Adams. Estate Settlement Jan 1, 1873. $12.73. Funeral expenses $7.35. Coffin $4.

BOX 184 PACK 4865   CARRIE J. CRENSHAW (minor)   1871

Deceased died Nov 8, 1870 in Abbeville County at the home of Allen Dodson. Administrator: Allen Dodson. Bond Jan 23, 1871 of $500 by Allen Dodson, Wm. M. Dodson, John A. Dodson. Minor was due $180, which was received, in the hands of J. T. Dodson of Holmes Co., Miss. Estate Settlement Jul 20, 1872. All money used in expenses. Coffin & Burial expenses $18.

BOX 184 PACK 4866   MARY H. CHILES   1871

Administrator: George P. Chiles-son. Bond Mar 24, 1871 of $8,000 by George P. Chiles, John H. Chiles, Robert W. Lites. Stated that the will was attached but is missing. No other papers in pack.

BOX 184 PACK 4867   JAMES M. RICHARDSON   1871

Very long and involved estate. Will Dated Mar 9, 1871. Filed Mar 17, 1871. Witnesses: John Holland, John A. Stuart, B. A. Jones. Executor: Walter S. Richardson-son. Wife: Mary E. Richardson. Sons: Walter S. Richardson, James A. Richardson, Madison Richardson. Merchant. Appraisal Maar 31, 1871 by Henry Beard, J. N. Hill, Ransom Chaney, B. A. Jones. Owned House & lot in Town of Ninety Six, owned in excess of 1,650 acres of land in Abbeville County, 738 acres of land in Edgefield County. NOTES exceeding $11,000 held on: Henry Adams, Joseph Abney, G. B. Addison, John Adams, Eli Baughman, J. H. Brooks, John J. Bozeman, D. C. Bullock, J. P. Burnett, R. A. Clem, M. Corley, W. E. Clary, F. V. Cooper, White Chappell, M. A. Coleman, Ransom Chaney, J. W. Fooshe, John Fletcher, S. D. Gaines, R. A. Griffin, J. C. Griffin, R. D. Grogan, W. A. Gaines, V. A. Herlong, John C. Hill, Henry Hart, Jacob Haltiwanger, R. Jones, B. A. Jones, D. T. Kinard, W. H. Lawton, W. W. Long, T. Leopard, J. H. Leopard, Ben. Lewis, Goudy Lewis, L. M. Moore, F. Mack, H. H. Mayson, John F. Marbut, J. Morgan, T. L. Moore, R. F. McCaslan, N. S. McCants, John Norman, J. S. Pinson, James H. Rice, Daniel Rampey, John Rushton, John Sheppard, Randall Stewart, Samuel Turner, E. Turner, R. S. Towles, W. L. Turner, John Werton, A. S. Weerts, H. T. Wright, Moses Walton, Rm. White Jr., J. S. White. ACCOUNTS due to him at time of his death: Joel W. Anderson, Henry Adams, John R. Bullock, J. B. Bozeman, Eli Baughman, George Caldwell, R. A. Cain, M. A. Coleman, J. Cason, W. B. Cason, White Chappell, George Caldwell, Mathew Corley, Peter Cockerell, W. C. Clary, Wm. Davenport, Rev. T. S. Daniel, J. W. Fooshe, John Fletcher, Henry Frazier, Madison Frazier, W. A. Gaines, R. D. Grogan, W. H. Holloway, W. T. Head,

F. G. Holloway, W.A. Herling, R. P. Jones, Miss M. King, J. H. Leopard, Goody Lewis, T. N. Leopard, Wm. W. Long, Ben. Lewis, A. R. Meriewether, H. H. Mayson, Ferderick Mack, J. Morgan, W. B. Meriwether, G. S. Meriwether, James Moten, Richard Pinson, James L. Pinson, P. W. Payne, Charlotte Peterson, John Rushton, Jack Ray, W. G. Rice, J. H. Rice, Randall Stewart, Wiley Sample, John Sheppard, R. J. Towles, G. W. Tolbert, Elizabeth Turner, W. S. Turner, J. R. Wright, G. H. Waddell, J. L. White, Dave Williams, Wm. Williams, H. P. Walton, A. J. Werts, H. R. Williams, J. H. White, James Wooten.

BOX 184 PACK 4868   JAMES COWAN   1871

Deceased died Feb 27, 1871. Lived in Town of Due West. Administrator: James B. Cowan-next of kin. Bond Mar 20, 1871 of $1,000 by James B. Cowan, Wm. T. Cowan, Wesley A. Black. Appraisal, no date, by John Cowan, Wesley A. Black, Wm. T. Cowan. Estate Sale Mar 25, 1872 netted $205.76. Buyers at sale: Newton Reid, James B. Cowan, John Cowan, J. W. Brock, John Hagen, John W. Brooks, J. N. Pruitt, Wesley A. Black, C. W. Winbush, Francis V. Pruitt, David O. Hawthorne, J. A. Hawthorne. Estate Settlement Apr 10, 1872. $33.36.

BOX 184 PACK 4869   JOHN M. HAMILTON   1872

Deceased died in 1870. Administrator: Hugh Leaman. Bond Mar 15, 1871 of $7,000 by Hugh Leaman, Wm. Leaman, T. A. Rudd. Wife: Charlotte M. Leaman. Estate Settlement May 27, 1873. Charlotte Hamilton 1/3 =$1,221. Arthur S. Hamilton 2/3 =$2,442.

Mixed in the same pack:

THOMAS STACEY

Administrator: Wyatt Aiken. Appraisal Sep 21, 1869 by G. P. O'Neal, Robert W. Anderson, James F. Coleman, James R. Jones, W. W. Franklin.

BOX 184 PACK 4870   DANIEL NEW   1871

Administrators: Francis New-son, Joshua B. Palmer. Bond Apr 8, 1871 of $10,000 by Francis New, Joshua B. Palmer, Joseph New, Samuel New, Daniel New, Mary Ann Palmer, J. F. Williams, E. F. Williams, Caroline New. Wife Eliza New. Appraisal Apr 17, 1871 by George S. Patterson, L. W. Lyon, C. A. Wideman, John F. Edmunds. Held notes on: Robert W. Lites, George Banks, Jewet Smith. Estatae Sale Apr 20, 1871. Buyers at sale: T. T. Freeman, E. New, Joe New, F. Williams, Jake Brown, Adam Wideman, Herr Palmer, J. Tompkins, Joshua B. Palmer, Catlett Corley, W. R. Puckett, L. W. Lyon, Robert W. Lites, Guy New, Frank New, James Henderson, L. Palmer, John Agner, Dr. T. Jennings, M. Cuddy, Joseph Palmer, Hiram Palmer. Estate Settlement Mar 26, 1872 (9) Distributees: 1. James New 2. Eliza New, Widow 3. Mary Ann wife of Joshua B. Palmer 4. Caroline wife of R. A. Clem 5. John New 6. E. Jane wife of J. F. Williams 7. Francis New 8. Daniel New 9. Samuel New. Funeral expenses $15.

INDEX of ESTATES   (Name of Estate   Year of Estate   Page Found)

Andrew T. Bowie 1864 – 111

Franklin Bowie 1860 – 14

Archibald B. Boyd 1864 – 111

Daniel Boyd 1870 – 199

William Boyd 1870 – 198

Bozeman minors 1870 – 199

David L. Bozeman 1868 – 166

John W. Bozeman 1869 – 175

Bradley minors 1870 – 181

Archibald Bradley 1866 – 119

Jane Bradley 1866 – 146

John Bradley 1862 – 49

John Bradley 1860 – 14

Branyon minors 1869 – 178

Alanson W. Branyon 1864 – 65

Alexander Branyon 1869 – 166

J. M. G. Branyon 1869 – 118

Samuel Branyon 1863 – 66

Jacob B. Britt 1861 – 14

Thomas J. Britt 1862 – 47

Charles E. Brooks 1863 – 118

Francis M. Brooks 1866 -111

Jason T. Brooks 1865 – 118

W. Butler Brooks 1869 – 167

Brown minors 1868 – 165

Brown minors 1869 – 165

John M. Brown 1864 – 112

Isaac B. Brownell 1868 – 175

Hugh M. Brownlee 1863 – 67

John Brownlee 1864 – 65

Samuel R. Brownlee 1861 – 49

Buchanan minors 1864 – 65

Annie C. Buchanan 1869 – 181

James T. Buchanan 1863 – 67

James Wesley Buchanan 1870 – 50

R. W. Bullock 1862 – 50

Jane T. Burns 1870 – 191

W. W. Burriss 1862 – 48

Burton minors 1868 – 166

Burton minors 1871 – 181

Jane Burton 1879 – 181

John A. Burton 1863 – 49

John W. Burton 1869 – 180

Joseph F. Burton 1864 – 64

William L. Burton 1867 – 146

William Lawrence Burton 1861 – 180

William H. Butler 1864 – 110

C

Eliza W. Caldwell 1869 – 200

James Caldwell 1870 – 191

Samuel Caldwell 1862 – 120

William E. Caldwell 1866 – 147

Calhoun minors 1849- 36

Calhoun minors 1850 – 36

Edward Calhoun 1863 – 52

Francis A. Calhoun 1869 – 176

James C. Calhoun 1867 – 158

Kate Calhoun 1868 – 159

John Calhoun 1847 – 34

John W. Calhoun 1867 – 147

Nathan Calhoun 1870 – 192

William P. Calhoun 1849 – 35

Andrew H. Callaham 1866 – 147

James M. Callaham 1863 – 77

John W. Callaham 1864 – 113

Nancy Ann Callaham 1867 – 147

Sherard W. Callaham 1865 – 76

John Calvert 1847 – 34

John W. Calvert 1870 – 201

Lucy E. Calvert 1847 – 38

John M. Campbell 1863 – 71

Obediah Lynch Cann 1862 – 53

Joseph Cantey 1847 – 37

Carlile minors 1855 – 35

John Carlile 1848 – 35

Richard L. Chalmers 1863 – 69

Mariah Chandler 1852 – 77

Simeon Chaney 1870 -191

John Charles 1868 – 158

Cheatham minors 1852 – 36

Cheatham minors 1847 – 36

James H. Cheatham 1869 – 184

John L. Cheatham 1846 – 37

Preston A. Cheatham 1869 – 184

William J. Cheatham 1863 – 77

John Chiles 1850 – 36

Mary H. Chiles 1871 – 202

Thomas M. Chiles 1863 – 76

Thomas W. Chiles 1864 – 120

William Chiles 1872 – 37

H. B. Clarke 1867 – 52

David Clary 1860 – 15

Elizabeth Clay 1865 – 120

David Cleland 1864 – 119

Eliza J. Cleland 1869 – 184

Addison Clinkscales 1877 – 192

Frank Clinkscales 1860 – 57

George B. Clinkscales 1864 – 112

J. Wesley Clinkscales 1866 – 77

Mary Clinkscales 1862 – 53

Edmond Cobb 1849 – 37

Elizabeth Cobb 1863 – 175

Elizabeth Cobb 1864 – 76

Frances E. Cobb 1871 – 191

J. Willis Cobb 1864 – 119

Nathaniel Cobb 1867 – 159

Richmond S. Cobb 1864 – 112

Cochran minors 1865 – 113

John W. Cochran 1861 – 15

Samuel W. Cochran 1863 – 76

Washington S. Cochran 1863 – 68

William H. Cochran 1862 – 51

Uriah Colvin 1867 – 158

George W. Connor 1861 – 53

James Connor 1848 – 35

Barney Corrigan 1863 – 120

John Cothran 1859 – 15

Samuel G. Cothran 1864 – 120

James Cowan 1871 – 203

Luke L. Coyne 1868 – 51

James B. Crawford 1864- 76

James F. Crawford 1864 – 112

John C. Crawford 1870 – 197

Robert Alexander Crawford 1868 – 159

Joseph Creswell 1870 – 184

Cromer minors 1861 – 15

George C. Cromer 1860 – 50

John P. Cromer 1862 – 68

R. Fletcher Cromer 1863 – 120

James Crowther 1864 – 68

James Crowther 1864 – 113

Joseph H. Cunningham 1864 – 52

D

Benjamin F. Daniel 1864 – 71

Dannelly minors 1869 – 185

Darby minors 1867 – 159

James Darby 1867 – 148

E. Lewis Davis 1865 – 73

George A. Davis 1863 – 73

J. F. H. Davis 1864 – 121

Robert M. Davis 1864 – 71

Turner G. Davis 1866 – 148

William C. Davis 1865 -72

Newton Deal 1861 – 53

Aquilla Deason 1864 – 72

Charles Dendy 1859 – 5

Robert Devlin 1863- 71

Thomas D. Douglass 1862 – 72

Drennan minors 1870 – 199

Robert Drennan 1863 – 23

Robert D. Drennan 1864 – 113

William T. Drennan 1864 – 121

Elizabeth A. DuBose 1869 – 183

James R. DuBose 1867 – 159

Joshua DuBose 1848 – 16

David Duncan 1864 – 73

John D. Duncan 1865 – 54

William F. Duncan 1862 – 53

Andrew Dunn 1864 – 113

208

Jesse Ghent 1849 – 44

Jeremiah Gibert 1849 - 45

John G. Gibert 1846 – 143

William Gibson 1859 – 75

Andrew Giles 1867 – 148

John Giles 1867 – 160

Andrew Gillespie 1865 – 167

Grizella Gillespie 1867 – 160

Samuel D. Gillespie 1848 – 42

James Gilliam 1878 – 47

James I. Gilmer 1868 – 168

James Glasgow 1849 – 44

James N. Glasgow 1850 – 39

Sarah Glasgow 1850 – 39

Ann Goff 1853 – 38

Golding minors 1850 – 43

John M. Golding 1849 – 45

Barnett Goolsby 1850 – 39

Harriet Goolsby 1848 – 44

John B. Gordon 1862 – 78

William Gordon 1877 – 183

John Goudy 1846 – 143

Albert Calvin Graham 1865 – 124

Charles Newton Graham 1863 – 78

J. B. Graham 1863 – 78

James Graham 1845 – 143

John Graham 1847 – 45

Margaret Graham 1850 – 38

Samuel Graham 1869 – 168

J. J. Grant 1862 – 55

Gray minors 1869 – 182

George Gray 1846 – 144

James A. Gray 1846 – 144

John H. Gray 1862 – 55

Ann Green 1863 – 78

David Greer 1869 – 182

George W. Griffin 1863 – 78

John L. Griffin 1863 – 78

Vincent Griffin 1855 – 44

Joseph Groves 1850 – 38

H

Martin Hackett 1870 – 186

William C. Hackett 1851- 39

Abraham Haddon 1865 – 124

Abram Haddon 1865 – 114

James H. Haddon 1862 – 55

Orange B. Haley 1863 – 80

Hall minors 1870 – 189

James D. Hall 1863 – 81

John M. Hamilton 1872 – 203

Hanvey minors 1852 – 41

Hanvey minors 1852 – 42

Hanvey minors 1868 – 185

Haarkness minors 1864 -81

William B. Harkness 1863 – 79

Lindsay Harper 1853 – 40

John Harris 1851 – 41

Thomas S. Harris 1852 – 41

Polly Hawkins 1860 – 55

Louisa Haynie 1851 – 41

Francis Henderson 1859 – 6

James P. Hill 1870 – 185

W. P. Hill 1863 – 20

John Hinton 1875 – 149

Nancy Adeline Hinton 1851 – 42

James R. Hodges 1862 – 81

Sarah Hogan 1850 – 40

Horton minors 1852 – 42

Green W. Huckabee 1861 – 17

John Hughes 1859 – 6

Mary Susan Hughey 1869 – 168

Alexander Hunter 1864 – 124

William Hunter 1860 – 17

I

Irwin minors 1863 – 82

John Calhoun Irwin 1863 – 82

John Washington Isom 1866 – 150

J

Friday Jackson 1869 – 186

Francis Jenkins 1862 – 55

Robert H. Harkness 1863- 80

Mary Harmon 1866 – 80

Elizabeth Harris 1860 – 6

Thomas Harris 1864 – 114

Butler Haskell 1869 – 185

Samuel Hawthorne 1866 – 149

Eliza Hearst 1862 – 81

W. W. Higgins 1863 – 79

Sarah J. Hill 1864 – 115

Asbury Hinton 1863 – 79

John A. Hinton 1864 – 114

Thomas Hodge 1861 – 16

W. C. Hodges 1864 – 79

Polly Ann Hogg 1870 – 185

Martha Houston 1849 – 41

Benjamin P. Hughes 1866- 149

James Hughey 1866 – 150

William M. Hughey 1865 – 113

John A. Hunter 1870 – 185

John Hutchison 1865 – 115

James Irwin 1863 – 81

Emily Isom 1869 – 186

William Jay 1865 – 125

Priscella Jessup 1861 – 17

Boswell Johnson 1870 – 188

James Gideon 1861 – 55

L. D. Johnson 1859 – 7

Jonathan Johnson 1857 – 125

Mary Johnson 1845 – 144

Dennis Fletcher Jones 1867 – 160

Dewitt Y. Jones 1862 – 17

Elizabeth Jones 1864 – 125

Jane Jones 1863 – 82

William T. Jones 1869 – 187

Bartholomew Jordan 1878 – 193

David A. Jordan 1864 – 82

Jonathan L. Jordan 1863 – 82

K

Elias Kay 1869 – 161

James H. Kay 1863 – 83

Mary Kay 1864 – 125

R. Marshall Kay 1866 – 150

David Keller 1871 – 56

Isaac A. Keller 1929 – 198

Joseph F. Keller 1868 – 161

Susan Keller 1863 – 82

Isaac Kennedy 1866 – 150

Isaac C. Kennedy 1869 – 188

Kerr minors 1860 – 18

Paschal D. Klugh 1867 – 161

David Knox 1864 – 125

Nathaniel Knox 1864 – 193

Robert P. Knox 1866 – 125

Samuel Knox 1862 – 55

William Knox 1861 – 18

Mary Kolb 1846 - 144

L

John E. Lake 1860 – 57

B. M. Latimer 1860 – 84

Buford Lawson 1863- 56

Joseph F. Lee 1863 – 85

Stephen Lee 1864 – 126

John N. LeRoy 1862 – 56

Philip LeRoy 1869 – 188

Louisa Lesly 1863 – 151

Thomas Lesly 1863 – 84

William Lesly 1868 – 162

Alexander P. Lindsay 1863 – 83

Jane Lindsay 1869 – 151

Polly Ann Lindsay 1868 – 168

W. Winfield Lindsay 1863 – 83

Teresa Lipford 1865 – 126

Lavinia Little 1860 – 19

John Fraser Livingston 1867 – 162

James Yancey Lockhart 1862 – 56

211

Fred B. Logan 1861 – 19

Lewis Logan 1859 – 7

Hutson Lomax 1870 – 199

William Long 1861 – 18

Aaron W. Lynch 1868 – 161

Andrew J. Lythgoe 1863 – 83

M

Nidus Malone 1873 – 130

Christopher Vandel Mantz 1853 – 33

Robert Mars 1861 – 21

J. Foster Marshall 1862 – 58

Samuel Marshall 1861 – 21

James Martin 1868 – 169

Richard A. Martin 1853 – 31

David Mathews 1850 – 31

Margaret Mathews 1860 – 19

Mary Jane Mathis 1861 – 20

William N. Mattison 1864 – 131

Thomas H. Mauldin 1863 – 86

Hugh Maxwell 1850 – 31

Robison B. McAdams 1863 - 86

Mary A. McAllister 1869 – 178

Nancy A. McAllister 1870 – 194

Emma John McCartney 1863 – 33

Patrick McCaslan 1862 – 58

James McCelvey 1863 – 20

Peggy McClain 1859 – 7

John Logan 1870 – 151

George W. Lomax 1863 – 84

Elizabeth Long 1866 – 150

Ransom Loveless 1864 – 126

Robert N. Lyon 1863 – 83

Michael Smith Mann 1863- 85

John Marbut 1865 – 130

Isabella Marshall 1859 – 7

Joseph S. Marshall 1860 – 57

Jacob Martin 1863 – 85

Phares Martin 1867 – 179

Robert Martin 1874 – 193

Jane Mathews 1864 – 131

Mathis minors 1862 – 88

Grace Mattison 1841 – 8

Archibald Mauldin 1862 – 87

George H. Maxwell 1862 – 86

Charlotte McAdams 1861 – 58

Alexander McAllister 1868 – 127

Mary F. McAllister 1866 – 152

John McBryde 1865 – 127

Mary McCartney 1863 – 152

John T. McCaw 1863 – 88

John McClain 1863 87

Simon McClinton 1860 – 21

212

William & Eleanor McClinton 1860 -20

Kitty McComb 1846 – 146

Catherine McCown 1857 – 33

William A. McCracken 1863 – 88

John T. McCuen 1865 – 127

S. S. McCurry 1862 – 88

William Whitfield McDill 1869 – 168

John M. McDonald 1866 – 152

E. H. McDowell 1862 89

Abner H. McGee 1862 – 57

Willis McGee 1870 – 178

William McIlwain 1864 – 131

Rebecca D. McKee 1861 – 20

John McKellar 1865 – 129

James McLane 1865 – 152

John McLaren 1864 – 89

Obediah McMahan 1863 – 88

David McWilliams 1860 – 8

Milford minors 1868 – 178

Nancy J. Milford 1869 – 178

Franklin Miller 1866 – 129

John Julian Miller – 1864 – 88

James W. Mitchell – 1868 – 169

Samuel Mitchell 1863 – 87

Issac Moragne 1860 – 33

J. Thomas Moore 1852 – 31

Mary Moore 1859 – 30

Hannah McComb 1864 – 131

Maria McCombs 1869 – 179

Susan E. McCracken 1864 – 130

Jane McCree 1850 – 34

Ibby McCurry 1870 – 197

William McDill 1850 – 31

James A. Mc Donald 1860 – 19

Mary H. McDonald 1869 -180

Samuel McElroy 1819 – 195

Abner H. McGee 1862 – 86

Andrew McIlwain 1863 – 89

John Thomas McKee 1857 – 32

Elvira R. McKellar 1870 – 178

Virginia McKittrick 1863 – 90

Agnes McLaren 1851 – 31

Fergus McMahan 1865 – 130

Agnes C. McQuerns 1865 – 145

Mary W. McWilliams 1862 – 58

Joseph Milford 1868 – 179

Miller minors 1865 – 152

Isabella Miller 1865 – 126

Nicholas H. Miller 1855 – 42

Lewis Mitchell 1820 – 198

Stephen Mitchell 1825 – 199

Docetheus Moore 1869 – 179

John W. Moore 1861 21

Nancy Agnes Moore 1862 – 58

Oliver J. Moore 1852 – 32

William C. Moore 1850 – 32

James H. Morris 1866 – 132

William Morrison 1852 – 30

Thomas W. Morton 1845 – 145

Charles R. Moseley 1865 – 129

J. H. B. Moseley 1860 – 20

Jordan Moseley 1845 – 145

Mary Moseley 1863 – 86

Tarleton P. Moseley – 1859 – 7

Willis D. Mounce 1845 – 146

Fannie Mundy 1870 – 188

James D. Murdock 1851 – 32

Pinckney Murphy 1869 – 179

N

Daniel New 1871 - 203

William M. Newell 1878 – 190

Nickles minors 1869 – 189

Nickles minors 1870 – 188

Edward H. Nickles 1870 – 189

George Nickles 1868 – 190

John Henry Nickles – 1868 – 190

William C. Nickles 1864 – 90

Jane G. North 1863 – 91

Joicey Savannah Norwood 1880 – 200

O

David Terrel Oliver 1864 – 132

John Belton O'Neall 1864 – 93

Moses T. Owen 1863 – 91

Thomas E. Owen 1861 – 22

P

Susan Pace 1864 – 153

Champion D. Palmer 1869 – 177

Andrew Blum Paslay 1862 – 96

John Patterson 1876 – 177

Josiah Patterson 1860 – 25

Andrew Paul 1866 – 153

William H. Peake 1880 – 46

Weldon Pearman 1868 – 163

Charles M. Pelot 1868 – 152

James A. Pennal 1863 – 94

John William Penney 1865 – 163

James M. Perrin 1863 – 95

Elizabeth Phillips 1870 – 202

Charles Cotesworth Pinckney 1865 – 132

Frances A. Pinkerton 1862 – 96

Cornelius H. Pinson 1872 – 201

Abraham P. Pool 1867 – 163

Hugh Porter 1867 – 163

Jane D. Power 1859 – 8

Elizabeth Pratt 1860 – 24

James L. Pratt 1860 – 8

William A. Pratt 1863 – 97

Thomas A. Pressly 1867 – 163

William Price 1863 – 95

Enoch W. Pruitt 1862 – 93

Allen Puckett 1864 – 96

Thomas R. Puckett 1874 – 196

Benjamin S. Pulliam 1865 – 133

Elizabeth A. Purdy 1863 – 93

James M. Purdy 1866 – 95

Ephraim D. Pursley 1875 -94

John C. Pursley 1864 -133

R

W. Z. Radcliffe 1864 – 98

Allen Reagan 1877 – 69

John S. Reid 1877 – 69

James M. Richardson 1871 – 202

Edward Richey 1869 – 191

George B. Richey 1859 – 100

Warren Richey 1861 – 99

Amanda Ridge 1868 – 165

James Robertson 1863 – 98

Nancy Robertson 1862 – 101

Robinson minors 1869 – 190

Mary Robinson 1863 – 101

Rogers minors 1865 – 133

William M. Rogers 1879 – 138

William Pratt 1863 – 97

Ebeneezer Pressly 1860 – 24

Price minors 1864 – 93

Ally Pruitt 1863 – 94

Samuel E. Pruitt 1864 – 93

Richard M. Puckett 1861 – 95

William C. Puckett 1864 – 97

Larkin Pulliam 1870 – 177

James H. Purdy 1865 – 132

Mary M. Purdy 1869 – 152

James Pursley 1866 – 132

William O. Pursley 1868 – 176

William H. Rampey 1867 – 164

James C. Reid 1864 – 133

Samuel Reid 1867 – 164

Andrew Richey 1863 – 99

Elizabeth Riche 1869 – 190

James Albert Richey 1863 – 100

Peter Ricketts 1863 – 98

Timothy C. Risley 1867 – 165

Janet Robertson 1861 – 98

Sarah Robertson 1864 – 100

Jabez P. Robinson 1865 – 133

David Robison 1864 – 99

Paul Rogers 1862 – 100

Nancy M. Roney 1867 – 133

Lawson Ross 1870 – 197

Israel Rouse 1867 – 165

Wash. W. Russell 1867 – 164

S

Willis Sadler 1866 – 137

William R. Sale 1864 – 135

Johnn Scott 1860 – 10

William Clarke Scott 1867 – 170

Selby minors 1867 – 154

John B. Shadrak 1868 – 169

Robert Clement Sharp 1866 – 153

Nancy Shaw 1863 – 103

James S. Shirley 1866 – 137

Mary G. Shirley 1859 – 10

Robert Simpson 1864 – 104

Ann Smith 1865 – 134

Elizabeth R. Smith 1870 – 194

Mary Smith 1867 – 170

William C. Smith 1868 – 169

Samuel D. Speed 1865 – 137

Ann Spence 1859 – 9

Thomas Stacey 1869 – 203

Ezekiel Stephens 1860 – 25

William Johnson Stevenson 1862-102

William Strawhorn 1862 – 101

William Sutherland 1866 – 194

John Swilling 1860 – 9

Benjamin Rothchild 1863 – 100

Peter Rouse 1862 – 100

Simon P. Rykard 1861 – 101

Johnson Sale 1868 – 170

Henry D. Scott 1865 – 137

William Clark Scott 1864 – 136

Issac C. Seawright 1864 – 103

James B. Shadrack 1869 – 194

Cornelius M. Sharp 1866 – 153

James H. Shaw 1866 – 136

Vincent Shaw 1862 – 102

Jemina Shirley 1860 – 25

John F. Simpson 1865 – 136

Thomas W. Sloan 1859 – 10

Augustus M. Smith 1862 – 102

Lewis Smith 1859 – 10

Thomas W. Smith 1864 – 103

Elizabeth C. South 1868 – 194

John Speer 1870 – 135

Thomas Stacey 1869 – 195

William C. Steifle 1870 -195

Alexander Stevenson 1870 – 194

N. W. Stewart 1865 – 134

William P. Sullivan 1863 – 103

Jane Z. H. Swilling 1864 – 135

T

James Taggart 1870 – 195

Ansel G. Talbert 1871 – 201

Benjamin Talbert 1866 – 154

William T. Tatom 1866 – 138

Thomas Taylor 1859 – 11

Wat Thomas 1862 – 137

John G. Thornton 1868 – 171

James R. Todd 1878 – 46

Richard M. Todd 1841 – 189

James F. Tolbert 1868 – 154

Robert R. Tolbert 1866 – 155

Joshua M. Townsend 1866 – 155

Albert Thomas Traylor 1864 – 138

Ezekiel Tribble 1861 104

Lemuel Williamson Tribble 1861 – 105

Bartlett Tucker 1861 105

John J. Tucker 1863 106

Sabry K. Tullis 1860 – 10

Samuel Turner 1865 -138

U

S. R. Underwood 1860 -106

V

Allen Vance 1865 – 138

Elizabeth Y. Vandiver 1864 - 106

Sophronia Verrell 1864 – 106

W

Waits minors 1845 – 26

James H. Walker 1869 – 196

Joel Manley Walker 1863 – 108

Sanders Walker 1863 – 60

Vincent Walker 1862 – 59

Wade Walker 1863 – 108

William Y. Walker 1866 – 156

Ebeneezer Wallace 1862 – 59

Jane Wallace 1866 – 140

Cadrus D. Waller 1864 – 108

James L. Waller 1866 – 140

Pelius Augustus Waller 1866 – 172

Hugh Waller Wardlaw 1865 – 140

James A. Wardlaw 1863 – 61

Margaret R. Wardlaw 1868 – 172

Cornelia E. Ware 1859 – 12

Mary E. Ware 1864 – 110

A. L. Watkins 1832 – 26

Alpheus Turrentine Watson 1865 – 141

Elihu Watson 1859 – 12

217

George McDuffie Watson 1863 – 60

James F. Watson 1859 – 12

John Webb 1873 – 157

Reuben Weed 1869 – 196

Weeks minors 1863 – 109

Allen Weeks 1863 – 62

Sarah Weeks 1860 – 62

Josiah Wells 1867 – 157

Thomas Coleman White 1863 – 107

William H. White 1863 – 61

William W. White 1863 – 109

Sampson Whitley 1872 – 196

William Whitley 1845 – 25

John Henry Wideman 1867 – 155

Joshua Wideman 1864 – 139

Sarah Wideman 1863 – 109

Willard minors 1870 – 196

Samuel J. Willard 1869 – 107

Adolphus A. Williams 1866 – 155

Arthur Williams 1860 – 11

Eliza Thomas Williams 1861 – 60

John Williams 1856 – 62

Margaret Williams 1861 – 62

William Williams 1864 – 110

John Rosemond Willson 1865 – 138

Wilson minors 1860 – 61

Wilson minors 1865 – 141

Wilson minors 1867 – 172

Jane Wilson 1869 – 172

John Wilson 1847 – 26

John G. Wilson 1862 – 61

John L. Wilson 1864 – 107

Letty Wilson 1865 – 139

Robert H. Wilson 1863 – 107

Samuel A. Wilson 1865 – 140

Samuel A. Wilson 1865 -141

Theodore Wilson 1863 – 108

John J. Wimbish 1863 – 109

Alexander Winn 1862 – 59

Frances E. H. Witherspoon 1860 – 11

R. W. Woods 1832 – 26

Y

Littleton Yarborough 1864 – 142

William Yarborough 1837 – 28

Abner Perrin Young 1863 – 141

Jane Young 1836 – 26

Julena S. G. Young 1870 – 196

Nathaniel Young 1784 – 29

Robert Young 1811- 29

Samuel Young 1817 – 27

Valentine Young 1856 – 27

William Young 1820 – 29

218

William Young 1864 – 141

John F. Youngblood 1823 – 30

John Youngblood 1829 – 29

Z

Catherine Zimmerman 1867 - 196

CPSIA information can be obtained
at www.ICGtesting.com
Printed in the USA
BVHW080931190620
581580BV00001B/24